Global Practices and Training in Applied Sport, Exercise, and Performance Psychology

Global Practices and Training in Applied Sport, Exercise, and Performance Psychology offers case analysis as a vehicle to address issues and experiences in the application of sport, exercise, and performance psychology (SEPP) and the supervision/training of individuals to become professionals in the field. A follow-up to *Becoming a Sport, Exercise, and Performance Psychology Professional* (2014), this book features a discussion of real-world case examples which highlight various aspects of professional practice as well as supervision and training. Professionals from around the world, including the US and Canada, Europe, Asia, Africa, and Australia share diverse experiences, providing a uniquely in-depth, global perspective.

The case studies contained in the book were selected to provide insight into specific elements of applied practice and supervision/training through a global lens as well as demonstrate the value of incorporating case analysis and reflection into one's training and continued professional development. Case analysis is an essential part of learning and instruction. Beyond educating the reader about theories and research on related topics in the field, case analysis allows for more complex levels of learning, including analysis, synthesis, and evaluation of diverse scenarios. In Part I of this book, the cases focus on applied SEPP practice; Part II comprises cases that focus on training and supervision.

This book is essential reading for graduate students and neophyte professionals in the field for whom it is critical to learn how to effectively apply knowledge to real-world SEPP scenarios. In addition, the book is a useful resource for seasoned and expert practitioners and supervisors who can use case analysis as a means of continuing their professional development.

J. Gualberto Cremades, Ed.D., Ph.D., CC-AASP, is a Professor in the Department of Sport and Exercise Sciences at Barry University in Miami, Florida.

Lauren S. Tashman, Ph.D., CC-AASP, is an Assistant Professor of Sport, Exercise, and Performance Psychology in the Department of Sport and Exercise Sciences at Barry University in Miami, Florida.

Performance Enhancement Training Tool

An online learning community for students and professionals in sport, exercise, and performance psychology (SEPP)

Join the global SEPP online learning community where you can post, analyze, reflect on, and discuss cases related to applied practice as well as teaching/supervision. Share real-world or hypothetical cases, post cases to invite feedback or other perspectives/approaches, analyze cases posted by others for professional development and reflective practice, and engage in discussion about cases, perspectives, various approaches, ethical issues and challenges as well as best practices. Cases are organized by category and key words to enable easy access to a large library of diverse cases.

Example case topics:
- Applied practice in youth sport
- Ethical issues and challenges
- Supervision and training
- Clinical sport psychology
- Mental performance coaching
- Biofeedback training approaches
- One-on-one applied practice
- Working with groups/teams
- Exercise psychology
- Working in non-sport performance contexts
- Collegiate sport
- Professional/Olympic sport
- Teaching in sport, exercise, and performance psychology
- Best practices for particular psychological skills (e.g., confidence, motivation, focus)

Memberships (student; professional) available for 1 month, 6 months, and a year. Access the community at http://peinnovate.com.

Enjoy one free month using code: 1free

"Alone we can do so little; together we can do so much." – Helen Keller

Global Practices and Training in Applied Sport, Exercise, and Performance Psychology

A Case Study Approach

Edited by
**J. Gualberto Cremades and
Lauren S. Tashman**

Routledge
Taylor & Francis Group

NEW YORK AND LONDON

First published 2016
by Routledge
711 Third Avenue, New York, NY 10017

and by Routledge
2 Park Square, Milton Park, Abingdon, Oxon, OX14 4RN

Routledge is an imprint of the Taylor & Francis Group, an informa business

Library of Congress Cataloging-in-Publication Data
A catalog record for this book has been requested

ISBN: 978-1-138-80596-5 (hbk)
ISBN: 978-1-138-80597-2 (pbk)
ISBN: 978-1-315-62496-9 (ebk)

Typeset in Galliard
by Wearset Ltd, Boldon, Tyne and Wear

I dedicate this book to my father, Luis Cremades Candela, and to my mother, Maria Luisa Nogués Sanroma, for emphasizing the importance of education in my life.

J. Gualberto Cremades

I dedicate this book to the peers, colleagues, students, athletes, coaches, and teams whom I have had the pleasure of working with over the years. They have and continue to fuel my passion for the field and pursuit of personal and professional growth, and remind me to be thankful that I get to do what I love each and every day.

Lauren S. Tashman

Contents

Editors

J. Gualberto Cremades, Ed.D., Ph.D., is a Professor in the Department of Sport and Exercise Sciences at Barry University in Miami, Florida. Gualberto received his High School Diploma from Escuela Inmaculada Jesuitas and Instituto San Blas in Alicante, Spain. He earned his Ed.D. in Physical Education with a specialization in the Psychological Bases of Movement, and his Ph.D. in Kinesiology with an emphasis on Research Statistics and Measurement. Both degrees were conferred at the University of Houston. He developed his research and consulting skills during his doctoral internship at Manchester Metropolitan University in England, where he was an Erasmus Mundus representative to different European universities. He has taught at the University of Houston, Manchester Metropolitan University, Florida International University, University of North Carolina at Chapel Hill, and Barry University. Dr. Cremades has been an active Association for Applied Sport Psychology (AASP) member during the past 15 years and is currently an AASP Fellow. In addition, Gualberto is an active presenter at conferences, has written nine book chapters, and has published 18 peer-reviewed articles in national and international sport science as well as psychology journals. In the applied setting, he is an AASP Certified Consultant and has worked with exercisers as well as youth, high school, collegiate, professional, and Olympic athletes in a variety of sports since 1994. He has also been providing supervision and mentoring to prospective sport and exercise psychology consultants since 2001 and is the current Master's Program Coordinator of Sport, Exercise, and Performance Psychology at Barry University. Most recently, he has designed and produced with his colleague, Lauren S. Tashman, the Performance Enhancement Training Tool (PETT), a case-based, online learning community for students and professionals in the field (http://peinnovate.com).

Lauren S. Tashman, Ph.D., is an Assistant Professor of Sport, Exercise, and Performance Psychology in the Department of Sport and Exercise Sciences at Barry University in Miami, Florida. She received her Bachelor's degree in Psychology from the College of New Jersey, and her master's and Ph.D. degrees in Educational Psychology with an emphasis in Sport Psychology from Florida State University. At Barry University, she teaches undergraduate and graduate courses, supervises graduate thesis and practicum students, works on various research projects, and is the Coordinator of Sport Psychology Services for the athletic department. Her research interests include, for example, expert performance, psychological factors involved in performance preparation and competition, improving training for sport psychology practitioners and supervisors, and mental performance coaching experiences and interventions. Lauren is a certified consultant with the Association for Applied Sport Psychology (CC-AASP) and has a private practice, Inspire Performance Consulting, LLC, in which she provides mental performance coaching services to athletes, teams, coaches, and other non-sport performers in the south Florida area, as well as supervision and mentoring to individuals pursuing CC-AASP. She has consulted with youth, recreational, collegiate, and professional-level athletes and teams in sports such as golf, softball, tennis, volleyball, soccer, equestrian, basketball, rowing, swimming, diving, track and field, and baseball. She also currently serves as the mental performance coach for a national team. Lauren is an active member of AASP, attending and presenting at the annual conferences since 2003, as well as serving as a member and chair on AASP committees. She has also published articles in peer-reviewed journals on topics such as perfectionism and burnout in coaching, the development and evaluation of an online case-based learning tool for service delivery training, expertise in police work, the experience of competing in an ultraendurance adventure race, and a review on the development of expertise. She also designed and produced with her colleague, J. Gualberto Cremades, the Performance Enhancement Training Tool (PETT), a case-based, online learning community for students and professionals in the field (http://peinnovate.com).

Contributors

Mark B. Andersen, Högskolan i Halmstad/Halmstad University, Halmstad, Sweden

Jamie Barker, Staffordshire University, Staffordshire, UK

Steve T. Barney, South Utah University, Cedar City, Utah, USA

Michala Bednáriková, European Network of Young Specialists in Sport Psychology (ENYSSP) Secretary General, private practice, Bratislava, Slovak Republic

Robyn Braun, University of Texas – Permian Basin, TX, USA

Rebecca Busanich, Plymouth State University, Plymouth, NH, USA

Mark J. Campbell, University of Limerick, Limerick, Ireland

Erika Carlson, private practice, Pleasanton, CA, USA

Sarah L. Castillo, National University, San Diego, CA, USA

Tai-ting Chen, 國立台灣師範大學/National Taiwan Normal University, Taipei, Taiwan

Ashley Coker-Cranney, West Virginia University, Morgantown, WV, USA

Maura Coulter, St Patrick's College, Dublin, Ireland

J. Gualberto Cremades, private practice, Barry University, Miami, FL, USA

Brendan Cropley, Prifysgol Metropolitan Caerdydd/Cardiff Metropolitan University, Cardiff, Wales, UK

Jaume Cruz, Universitat Autònoma de Barcelona/Autonomous University of Barcelona, Barcelona, Spain

Ricardo de la Vega, Universidad Aut ónoma de Madrid/Autonomous University of Madrid, Madrid, Spain

A. P. (Karin) de Bruin, Vrije Universiteit Amsterdam/VU University Amsterdam, Universiteit van Amsterdam/University of Amsterdam, Amsterdam, the Netherlands

Gregory Diment, Team Danmark/Team Denmark, Brøndby, Denmark

Joaquín Dosil, Universidad de Vigo/University of Vigo, Vigo, Spain

Louise Ellis, University of Huddersfield, Huddersfield, UK

Martin R. Eubank, Liverpool John Moores University, Liverpool, UK

Janaina L. Fogaça, West Virginia University, Morgantown, WV, USA

Emma Grindley, University of Idaho, Moscow, ID, USA

Meghan Halbrook, West Virginia University, Morgantown, WV, USA

Madeleine Hallé, private practice, Cirque du Soleil, Montreal, Canada

Stephanie Hanrahan, University of Queensland, Brisbane, Australia

Jakob Hansen, Team Danmark/Team Denmark, Brøndby, Denmark

Chris Harwood, Loughborough University, Loughborough, UK

Kristoffer Henriksen, Team Danmark/Team Denmark, Syddansk Universitet/University of Southern Denmark, Odense, Denmark

Tim Holder, University of Central Lancashire, Lancashire, UK

Chung-ju Huang (Glen), 台北市立大學/University of Taipei, Taipei, Taiwan

Tsung-min Hung, 國立台灣師範大學/National Taiwan Normal University, Taipei, Taiwan

R. I. Vana Hutter, Vrije Universiteit Amsterdam/University Amsterdam, Amsterdam, the Netherlands

Urban Johnson, Högskolan i Halmstad/Halmstad University, Halmstad, Sweden

Richard J. Keegan, University of Canberra, Bruce, Australia

Donald LaGuerre, private practice, Arouca, Trinidad and Tobago

Carsten Hvid Larsen, Team Danmark/Team Denmark, Syddansk Universitet/University of Southern Denmark, Odense, Denmark

Sae-Mi Lee, West Virginia University, Morgantown, WV, USA

Hin-Yue Li, 香港體育學院/Hong Kong Sports Institute, Shatin, Hong Kong

Lukas Linnér, Högskolan i Halmstad/Halmstad University, Halmstad, Sweden

Brittany Loney, Science Applications International Corporation, Washington, DC, USA

Kerry R. McGannon, Université Laurentienne/Laurentian University, Ontario, Canada

Mike McInerney, private practice, Cape Town, South Africa

Aidan P. Moran, University College Dublin, Dublin, Ireland

Taryn Morgan, IMG Academy, Bradenton, FL, USA

Gene M. Moyle, private practice, Brisbane, Australia

Angus Mugford, IMG Academy, Bradenton, FL, USA

Amanda Myhrberg, private practice, Sarasota, FL, USA

Robert S. Neff, private practice, Dallas, TX, USA

Rich Neil, Prifysgol Metropolitan Caerdydd/Cardiff Metropolitan University, Cardiff, Wales, UK

Marissa Norman, William James College, Boston, MA, USA

Odirin Oghene, Université Laurentienne/Laurentian University, Ontario, Canada

Mathew M. Park, Marshall Space and Flight Center, Huntsville, Alabama; John F. Kennedy University, Pleasant Hill, CA, USA

Stuart Pattison, private practice, Cape Town, South Africa

Albert J. Petitpas, Springfield College, Springfield, MA, USA

Maximilian H. Pollack, private practice, Comprehensive Soldier & Family Fitness (CSF2), Fort Carson, Colorado Springs, CO, USA

Yago Ramis, Universitat Autònoma de Barcelona/Autonomous University of Barcelona, Barcelona, Spain

Alison Rhodius, John F. Kennedy University, Pleasant Hill, CA, USA

Santiago Rivera, private practice, Sevilla/Seville, Spain

Julia Rizzo, Springfield College, Springfield, MA, USA

Robert J. Schinke, Université Laurentienne/Laurentian University, Ontario, Canada

Peter Schneider, ENYSSP President, F.C. Carl Zeiss Jena e.V., Universität Leipzig/Leipzig University, Leipzig, Germany

Christian Smith, IMG Academy, Bradenton, FL, USA

Natalia Stambulova, Högskolan i Halmstad/Halmstad University, Halmstad, Sweden

Karl Steptoe, University of Greenwich, London, UK

Lauren S. Tashman, private practice, Barry University, Miami, FL, USA

Melissa Thompson, University of Southern Mississippi, Hattiesburg, MS, USA

David Tod, Liverpool John Moores University, Liverpool, UK

Miquel Torregrosa, Universitat Autònoma de Barcelona/Autonomous University of Barcelona, Barcelona, Spain

Tshepang Tshube, University of Botswana, Gaborone, Botswana

Judy L. Van Raalte, Springfield College, Springfield, MA, USA

Katerina Vejvodova (Kudlackova), private practice, Prague, Czech Republic

Ana Viñolas, private practice, Universidad de Vigo/University of Vigo, Vigo, Spain

Justine Vosloo, Ithaca College, Ithaca, NY, USA

Andrew K. Waterson, High Performance Sport New Zealand, Cambridge, Waikato, NZ

Jack C. Watson II, West Virginia University, Morgantown, WV, USA

Grzegorz Więcław, ENYSSP Coordinator of Applied Department, private practice, Gliwice, Poland

Catherine B. Woods, Dublin City University, Dublin, Ireland

Jodi Yambor, Thomas University, Thomasville, GA, USA

Rebecca Zakrajsek, University of Tennessee, Knoxville, TN, USA

Sam J. Zizzi, West Virginia University, Morgantown, WV, USA

Foreword

Twenty-five years ago, when I first started my career as an applied sport psychology consultant (SPC) in Mainland China I always wished that I could find an applied textbook that would guide me to do my service effectively, rather than having to rely on those "boring" textbooks that simply introduced various classic psychological theories. Eight years ago, after gaining decades of applied experiences, my team began to build a website (see www.mind179.net/; note that content is in Chinese) that aimed to collect, discuss, and spread knowledge and experiences for Chinese researchers and practitioners in the field of sport and performance psychology. The development of this website stemmed from the fact that I often found that we needed more systematic and qualified cases made available for the purpose of training and education. Yet, to me, it still feels that something is missing with regard to how to effectively deliver sport psychology service, as well as how to train graduate students and new professionals. In addition, since I joined the Managing Council of the International Society of Sport Psychology (ISSP) ten years ago and have had more intellectual communication and discussion with worldwide colleagues, I started to realize that there are a lot of similarities among the approaches we adopted that can be integrated or unified. Learning from past experiences and the experiences from worldwide colleagues, sport, exercise, and performance psychology (SEPP) practitioners can yield twice the result with half the effort. Although there is a long history of applying single case studies in this field, I believe the current book *Global Practices and Training in Applied Sport, Exercise, and Performance Psychology: A Case Study Approach* edited by Drs. J. Gualberto Cremades and Lauren S. Tashman, fulfill all of my requirements for a comprehensive and application-based textbook. The book will be helpful to the practitioners in this field who want to learn something useful, something that can truly guide and inspire them in terms of how to do the practice, how to train themselves, and how to train others in an effective manner.

This book is a timely follow-up edition to a book that was also published by Routledge/Psychology Press in 2014, entitled *Becoming a Sport, Exercise, and Performance Psychology Professional: A Global Perspective*, which introduced various topics relating to effective practice and training in the SEPP field, as well as individual experiences of researchers and practitioners from 20 countries and five continents. Building on this previous edition, which has received excellent reviews (e.g., Roberts, 2014), and again drawing the intellectual support from worldwide applied researchers and practitioners, this book presents us with versatile case examples of different perspectives and philosophies on the training and practice of SEPP. For most of the chapters, there will be more than two co-authors from different institutions and even different countries; to my knowledge, such a collaborative approach is quite innovative. Moreover, this book can be viewed as a response to the recently released Position Stand by the ISSP emphasizing the importance of conducting culturally competent SEPP practice (see Ryba, Stambulova, Si, & Schinke, 2013). Through this sharing of case examples of practice and supervision with different populations and cultures around the world and their compilation into a single book, readers can learn a great deal from the globally comprehensive experiences.

This book is quite readable given that it adopts a case-study approach to present some key knowledge and insights of the distinguished authors worldwide, given that there are always a small number of participants in the sport and performance field. Compared to the robust experimental design in a research context, the case study method can provide insightful and unique knowledge with regard to what happens in the real-world, applied context. From a global perspective, it allows in-depth investigation of a variety of problems and issues in various contexts, which might be influenced by different cultures. Notably, authors of each chapter present their cases in a coherent way, in which elements such as background information, philosophy and approach, ethical considerations, needs assessment, preparation, intervention, evaluation, and reflection have been discussed systematically. These thoughtfully presented case studies provide a systematic volume of exemplars that can help direct effective interventions and supervision practices. For readers, the case-study method of presenting this comprehensive applied knowledge can help to visualize a full picture of how to apply the knowledge in their own practice and training. Moreover, the scientific manner of presenting the knowledge can prepare readers to publish their own case studies in related peer-reviewed journals, such as *The Sport Psychologist* (Giges & Van Raalte, 2012) and the *Journal of Applied Sport Psychology* (Barker, Mellalieu, McCarthy, Jones, & Moran, 2013).

Personally, I believe that the philosophy of this book is also in line with the mission of ISSP to promote academic research, applied practice, and professional development in the SEPP discipline throughout the world, and to foster a globally recognized competence in SEPP service. Thus, an important feature of this book is that cutting-edge knowledge and experiences are introduced in a theory-based and readable manner. With such comprehensive coverage on almost every aspect of SEPP training and practice, I firmly believe that it will make a significant contribution to our field. It will benefit readers with different learning goals and purposes, whether neophyte or seasoned practitioner, supervisor or supervisee. In addition, it will be a very helpful textbook, in particular to those colleagues from emerging sport psychology countries, who urgently wish to have a more applied focused textbook that can help them improve their service delivery and training competence. Taken together, this book can serve as a guideline that helps practitioners translate their applied services into publishable applied research, helping them improve their research methodology, avoiding the problems experienced by veterans in the field, and assisting them in learning how to effectively train themselves or supervise others. As such, I highly recommend it to all members of ISSP and worldwide SEPP researchers and practitioners beyond.

Gangyan Si, Ph.D.
Hong Kong Institute of Education
President of the International Society of Sport Psychology

REFERENCES

Barker, J. B., Mellalieu, S. D., McCarthy, P. J., Jones, M. V., & Moran, A. (2013). Special Issue on Single-Case Research in Sport Psychology. *Journal of Applied Sport Psychology, 25*, 1–3.

Giges, B., & Van Raalte, J. (2012). Special issue of *The Sport Psychologist* case studies in sport psychology: Introduction. *The Sport Psychologist, 26*, 483–485.

Roberts, C. M. (2014). Becoming a Sport, Exercise, and Performance Psychology Professional: A Global Perspective by Gualberto Cremades, J., & Tashman, L. S. (2014) book review. *The Sport and Exercise Scientist, 41*, 14.

Ryba, T. V., Stambulova, N. B., Si, G., & Schinke, R. J. (2013). ISSP Position Stand: Culturally competent research and practice in sport and exercise psychology. *International Journal of Sport and Exercise Psychology, 11*, 123–142.

Preface

The primary purpose of this edited book is to use case analysis in order to address relevant issues and experiences in the application of sport, exercise, and/or performance psychology and the supervision/training of individuals to become professionals in the field. It is a follow-up to the previous text titled *Becoming a Sport, Exercise, and Performance Psychology Professional: A Global Perspective*, published in 2014 by Psychology Press, Taylor & Francis Group. Thus, it provides a discussion of case studies which highlight various aspects of professional practice (e.g., models of practice, service delivery with different client populations, ethical issues and challenges, use of technology, development and operation of a private practice, multicultural considerations) as well as supervision and training (e.g., techniques and approaches, ethical issues, peer and meta-supervision, use of technology). Furthermore, professionals from around the world will offer diverse experiences and viewpoints, providing an in-depth, global perspective. In order to facilitate this global understanding of the field, authors from a wide variety of countries have contributed to the book. Specifically, countries represented include Australia, Canada, China, the Czech Republic, Denmark, Finland, Germany, Greece, Hong Kong, Ireland, Italy, the Netherlands, Spain, Sweden, Trinidad and Tobago, the United Kingdom, the United States, and South Africa.

Several factors prompted the development of both edited books. First, sport psychology texts have mainly focused on the "what" of applied practice (e.g., theories, concepts, techniques) rather than the "how" of service delivery (e.g., development of philosophy of practice, approaches for designing and implementing interventions). Second, supervision/mentorship has received little attention in the field, with limited discussion on how to best train individuals to become sport, exercise, and performance psychology (SEPP) professionals. Given the substantial growth in the number of students entering graduate programs in SEPP, the increased awareness about the field and its potential applications, and consequently the increase in the number of individuals seeking certification or licensure (e.g., APS, BPS, CC-AASP), a more prominent focus on supervision and training is needed. In addition, it is important to note that each year new generations of neophyte practitioners become eligible to serve as supervisors and mentors. However, the majority of professionals and academics in the field have not received formal training, and have very limited means to receive informal training regarding how to effectively supervise and/or mentor a neophyte practitioner. Third, the professional organization of the field has evolved to be somewhat fractionized according to region of the world, limiting the ability to gain a global perspective on SEPP practice and training. Therefore, both books were aimed at addressing these flaws in the field and literature. With regards to this specific text, case analyses were used to provide insight into specific elements of applied practice and supervision/training through a global lens, with the additional aim of demonstrating the value of incorporating case analysis and reflection into one's training and continued professional development.

Therefore, this book aims to enhance the knowledge of applied SEPP practice and the training process, as well as the overall quality of future SEPP professionals. The main reason for editing this book is to encourage the development of a community of practice by inviting colleagues in the SEPP field from around the world to share their knowledge, approaches, experiences, and reflections related to applied practice and supervision via the presentation of case analyses. Case analysis is an essential part of learning and instruction. Most texts in sport psychology focus on educating the reader about theories and research on related topics in the field. This allows the reader to accumulate knowledge related to the field, providing an important and necessary foundation for professional development. However, case analysis allows for more complex levels of learning, including application, analysis, synthesis, and evaluation. These higher levels of learning enable the reader to not only amass knowledge related to sport psychology, but also to learn how, when, and why to use that knowledge. Further, case analysis allows learners to apply their knowledge in real-world situations. Consequently, the book is geared toward graduate students and neophyte professionals in the field for whom it is essential to learn how to effectively apply their knowledge to real-world SEPP scenarios. In addition, the book is also useful for more seasoned and expert practitioners and supervisors who can use case analysis as a means of continuing their professional development. Accordingly, this text will aid readers in the development of their professional practice and supervision skills.

The chapters in the book present specific cases demonstrating techniques and models of practice and supervision, as well as different perspectives from around the world. The first chapter introduces the reader to the need for case analysis and reflection in the SEPP field. Following this, the book is divided into two parts: Part I includes cases that focus on applied SEPP practice, and Part II is composed of cases that focus on training and supervision. Finally, the last chapter of the book discusses considerations, strategies, and approaches to incorporating case analysis into SEPP supervision, training, and professional development.

In Part I of the book, neophyte and experienced practitioners from around the world discuss applied SEPP practice cases. Each chapter is structured so that case analyses include the following information: (1) an introduction to the chapter; (2) a discussion of background information on the case (e.g., length of consultation, competition level, context, history with the client); (3) a description of the case (i.e., an introduction to the actual situation or issues); (4) the theoretical framework or philosophy underlying the approach taken in the case; (5) the needs assessment conducted for the case; (6) a discussion of the intervention developed and implemented in the situation; (7) a reflection; (8) suggested readings related to the topic of the chapter and/or particular case outlined; (9) reflective questions which allow readers to analyze the case or related aspects of applied practice; and (10) a reference list of literature used throughout the chapter. In addition, authors' thoughts and insights on the reflective questions included in their chapters are provided in an appendix at the end of the book.

Part II of the book allows readers to get a global perspective on the supervision/mentorship of SEPP trainees. Both the perspectives of supervisees and supervisors are represented. Each chapter is structured so that case analyses include the following information: (1) an introduction to the chapter; (2) a discussion of background information on the case (e.g., information about the supervisor(s) and supervisee(s) in the case and contextual information related to supervision techniques described in the case); (3) a description of the case (i.e., an introduction to the actual situation or issues); (4) a discussion of the approach or philosophy to supervision in the case; (5) a description of the preparation or planning that was done prior to the supervision; (6) a discussion of the supervision process or experience in the particular case; (7) a reflection; (8) suggested readings related to the topic of the chapter and/or particular case discussed; (9) reflective questions which allow readers to analyze the case or related aspects of supervision; and (10) a reference list of literature used throughout the chapter. In addition, authors' thoughts and insights on the reflective questions included in their chapters are provided in an appendix at the end of the book.

The global perspectives on both practice and supervision provided in this book make it distinctive from other texts in the SEPP field. Including cases from authors that practice and supervise in different countries can help to promote a global understanding of the field.

Further, centering the discussion on "how to do it" related to both applied practice and supervision/training in the field is of great benefit to readers as there is minimal literature on cases that explain the process of applied practice and even less on supervision/training methods, techniques, and experiences. In addition, not only have experienced practitioners and supervisors provided cases in the book, but neophyte practitioners' and supervisors', as well as the supervisees', perspectives are also included in this book. Thus, the reader has a rare opportunity to hear the stories of the next generations of practitioners and supervisors as they go through the learning process of becoming a professional in the field.

As noted in the title of the book, one of the objectives of this book is to include cases reflective of a broader "definition" of the field (i.e., sport, exercise, and performance psychology). However, readers will note that there is still a bias toward the field of sport psychology reflected in the book chapters. While exercise psychology and performance psychology are emerging and evolving as disciplines within the field, most practitioners, supervisors, and organizations around the world are still centering practice and training on sport psychology. It was the editors' wish to bring together these three unique but overlapping disciplines in an effort to advance the SEPP field. It is suggested that organizations, university programs, researchers, practitioners, and supervisors continue to advance the SEPP field by incorporating and applying the fundamental principles of psychology to not only sport, but also exercise and performance.

In summary, the intent of this book is to showcase what individuals are doing around the world in terms of applied practice and supervision/training through the use of case analysis. The first half of the book includes cases focused on applied SEPP practice, allowing neophyte as well as more experienced professionals from around the world to discuss their approaches to and experiences with service delivery. The second half of the book discusses cases related to training and supervision, enabling supervisors to discuss their experiences with and approaches to training future SEPP practitioners as well as giving voice to supervisees to discuss their experiences during their training. It is the editors' hope that members of the field across the world read this book and benefit from gaining insight into their peers' and colleagues' thoughts and experiences regarding applied practice and supervision/training. Furthermore, readers can gain an understanding of the advantages of using case analysis and reflection, developing a community of practice within the field, as well as approaches for incorporating case analysis into SEPP training and professional development.

Acknowledgments

As editors, we would like to thank all the contributors who shared their applied practice and supervision insights and experiences with us and the readers in both this book and the previous book. We are grateful to the authors for their efforts and dedication to the global advancement of applied sport, exercise, and performance psychology.

Introduction

1 The Need for Case Analysis and Reflection in Sport, Exercise, and Performance Psychology

Lauren S. Tashman and J. Gualberto Cremades

The practice of sport, exercise, and performance psychology (SEPP) is a dynamic endeavor in which many factors contribute to, as a practitioner, determining how to approach working with clients. Further, it is unlike other helping professions in that a great amount of the work occurs outside of the office in the context of the performance area (Andersen, Van Raalte, & Brewer, 2001). For example, a SEPP practitioner may spend significant amounts of time out on the field at practices, attending competitions, and delivering brief contact interventions in a variety of locations (e.g., locker room, hotel, training room, etc.). In addition, with the current advent of new technologies, practitioners no longer need to be in the physical presence of clients to deliver SEPP interventions (Cheadle, Pfenninger, & Carlson, 2014; Watson & Halbrook, 2014).

Similar to other helping professions and dynamic performance contexts, there is no formula for applied practice. It is not a mathematical equation to be solved, but rather requires the ability to artfully apply research, theory, and literature from SEPP and other related fields. In counseling, for example, Binder (1999) proposed that a gap existed between coursework and supervision experiences. The same gap in training exists in SEPP (Tashman & Tenenbaum, 2013). Thus, neophyte practitioners are challenged with learning how to effectively translate the knowledge they have gained throughout their education into an understanding of how to put that knowledge to use in applied practice. Furthermore, given the unique nature of the work as mentioned above, not only is it a challenge for students and young practitioners to develop professional practice knowledge and experience, but learning how to effectively navigate the myriad ethical considerations and potential issues (e.g., blurring of boundaries, difficulties in managing confidentiality and multiple relationships, misperception about practitioner roles, and potential over identification with clients) is also essential (e.g., Moore, 2003). The dynamic and ill-structured nature of applied practice also poses challenges for more experienced practitioners who often experience isolation (Carlstedt, 2012) and may no longer have anyone to consult with to ensure effective practice (Watson, Lubker, & Van Raalte, 2011).

THE IMPORTANCE OF PHILOSOPHY

A key element underlying SEPP applied practice is the approach or philosophy the practitioner uses to guide and ground his/her work with clients (Henriksen & Diment, 2010). According to Poczwardowski, Sherman, and Ravizza (2004),

> professional philosophy significantly shapes the consultant's approach to the essential elements of the consulting process such as gaining entry, assessment, conceptualization of the issue and the intervention, implementation, evaluation, and bringing closure to the consulting relationship. More specifically, the consultant's philosophy can serve to provide direction when confronted with the unique situations when there is not an established textbook solution.

(p. 446)

At a basic level, Corlett (1996) categorized two types of philosophical approaches to practice: (1) Sophist (i.e., focus on techniques and skills) and (2) Socratic (i.e., focus on self-awareness and critical reflection). Additionally, Keegan (2010, 2014) raised other points about such as a consideration of a continuum from a practitioner-led to a client-led approach, as well as various viewpoints that can underpin one's approach and philosophy. To further clarify and conceptualize philosophy of practice in SEPP, Poczwardowski et al. (2004) proposed a hierarchical structure progressing from stable, internal elements within the practitioner to dynamic, external features of one's practice, including: (1) personal core beliefs and values, (2) theoretical paradigm concerning behavior change, (3) model of practice and consultant role, (4) intervention goals, and (5) intervention techniques/methods. As suggested by Poczwardowski and colleagues' model, SEPP practitioners must clearly understand and communicate their philosophies in order to effectively design and implement interventions with clients. Therefore, exploring and identifying one's philosophy of practice are essential features of professional development in SEPP.

EFFECTIVE SEPP PRACTICE AND TRAINING

It is undeniable that practitioners themselves (i.e., who they are and what they do) significantly determine the effectiveness of the services they provide (Orlick & Partington, 1987). Mugford, Hesse, and Morgan (2014) identified six areas of competency (i.e., characteristics and behaviors) for what they termed the "total consultant," including knowledge, relationships, delivery, organization/management, development, and leadership. In addition, Anderson, Miles, Mahoney, and Robinson (2002) proposed that effective practice should be evaluated based upon the following considerations: (1) goals of intervention; (2) quality of support as evidenced by measures of consultant effectiveness and social validity; (3) assessment of client psychological skills and well-being; (4) client responses to support as evidenced by changes in their knowledge and attitudes toward SEPP and use of mental skills; and (5) objective and subjective measures of client performance. However, what is considered effective? According to Anderson et al., "the definition of effectiveness adopted by each of the stakeholders may differ" (p. 446). Based on this statement, practitioners should be held accountable (i.e., responsible for delivering effective services) to four key stakeholders: clients, those paying for services, themselves, and the profession. Therefore, it is essential that we not only understand what constitutes effective practice, but also provide a means for neophyte practitioners and trainees to amass knowledge and experiences that will help them to develop themselves as effective applied practitioners.

Models of practice have been proposed in order to guide practitioners in their delivery of services. For example, Thomas (1990) outlined a seven-step process including: (1) orientation and initial contact; (2) analysis of the sport (performance); (3) individual or team evaluation and assessment; (4) conceptualization of the needs and clarification of goals for intervention; (5) implementation of the intervention through psychological skills training; (6) post-intervention evaluation and assessment; and (7) follow-up of long-term effectiveness of intervention. Though such models have been proposed and may be used by neophyte practitioners and trainees to guide their initial service delivery experiences, the question still remains as to how they learn to take the SEPP knowledge gained during courses and apply it in this model to achieve the aims of interventions with clients. In order to effectively migrate through the complexity of real-world practice, "practitioners need to move beyond text-book answers and be able to adapt quickly in the real-life scenarios that they find themselves in" (Rhodius & Sugarman, 2014, p. 332). This is an essential consideration because, at best, ineffective trainees/practitioners can be "incompetent" due to various factors (e.g., inadequate education/training, lack of knowledge, resistance to learning, and failure to stay up-to-date with advancements in the field) and, at worst, "impaired" and unable to effectively function professionally due to interference from personal factors (Andersen, Van Raalte, & Brewer, 2000).

Similar to methods of training in other applied practice fields and professions (e.g., counseling, clinical psychology), trainee practitioners engage in supervised practice in order to learn how to synthesize and apply their knowledge. The challenge with this method of training is that they essentially engage in a trial-and-error process at the potential expense of their own learning and professional development, their clients' performance and well-being, and the perceptions of the field (Silva, Conroy, & Zizzi, 1999; Tashman & Tenenbaum, 2013). As Andersen and colleagues (2000) have stated, "the ultimate object of student and peer supervision is the client" (p. 147). Thus, ensuring neophyte practitioners receive high-quality supervision and training is essential. For example, Loganbill, Hardy, and Delworth (1982) proposed that key issues that should be addressed in supervision include competence, emotional awareness, autonomy, theoretical identity, respect for individual differences, purpose and direction, personal motivation, and professional ethics. Further, Hutter, Oldenhof-Veldman, and Oudejans (2015) found that trainees want supervision to provide them with assistance in two key areas: (1) know-how, referring to learning how to effectively proceed with cases; and (2) professional development, referring to being to able to reflect on their experiences, develop their approach, and cope with dilemmas.

In order to appropriately facilitate training and the development of effective applied practice, supervisors must be competent to do so. For example, Hutter (2014) identified a competency profile for supervisors, including elements such as creating a productive working alliance, dealing with diversity, structuring supervision in phases, creating a powerful learning environment, maintaining boundaries of supervision, managing oneself and one's personal life so that it does not impede the supervision process, facilitating transfer of learning from supervision to supervised practice, abiding by relevant codes and one's philosophy of supervision, remaining open to feedback, and striving to professionally develop oneself as a supervisor. However, many SEPP governing bodies around the world (e.g., the Association for Applied Sport Psychology in the United States) have spent more time delineating guidelines for professional practice and little to no time doing the same for supervision. Thus, what has culminated is a haphazard and inconsistent approach to training and supervising of future applied SEPP practitioners. Subsequent, or also often concurrently, to coursework, SEPP trainees utilize real-world clients to practice and hone their service delivery skills. While this is a necessary component to effective training, other methods could be utilized to help bridge the gap between learning and real-world practice (Tashman & Tenenbaum, 2013).

LEARNING AND THE DEVELOPMENT OF EXPERTISE

Learning occurs as a result of the evolution of the accumulation and synthesis of knowledge over time (Rumelhart & Norman, 1978). Various researchers have proposed that learners progress through stages or phases as they become more experienced or expert in a given domain. For example, Fitts and Posner (1967) outlined three phases of learning including: (1) cognitive (i.e., amassing knowledge); (2) associative (i.e., synthesizing, applying, and generalizing one's knowledge); and (3) autonomous (i.e., using one's well-learned knowledge and skills without conscious processing). A few years later, Rumelhart and Norman (1978) outlined three modes of learning: (1) accretion (i.e., the acquiring of knowledge and initial matching of it to information in long-term memory); (2) restructuring (i.e., reorganization of knowledge in long-term memory to facilitate more effective interpretation and accessibility); and (3) tuning (i.e., optimization of the schemas of knowledge to improve its use).

Thus, not only quantitative, but more importantly qualitative changes in knowledge occur during learning that helps learners to advance their skills and abilities (Shuell, 1990). According to Dreyfus and Dreyfus (1986), learners progress through five stages highlighting the qualitative shifts that occur throughout the learning. These are: (1) novice (i.e., learning of facts and characteristics); (2) advanced beginner (i.e., recognition of similarities, development of strategic knowledge, and accumulation of episodic and case knowledge); (3) competent (i.e., distinguishing between relevant and irrelevant information and conscious decision-making processes); (4) proficient (i.e., though still operating in a deliberate and analytic manner, learners are able to use knowledge to intuitively recognize patterns and anticipate and make predictions); and (5) expert (i.e., fluid performance resulting from the ability to intuitively use one's knowledge).

Therefore, as learners gain new knowledge, their ability to use their knowledge becomes more effective. At first they are simply accumulating facts and information (i.e., declarative knowledge; "knowing what to do"), then progress to learning how to apply the facts and information they have learned (i.e., procedural knowledge; "knowing how to do it"), and ultimately, advance to learning in what situations and at what times to utilize their knowledge (i.e., conditional knowledge; "knowing when and why") (West, Farmer, & Wolf, 1991). According to Berliner (1988), individuals in the beginning stages are more rigid in their use of their knowledge, abiding by specific rules, and failing to understand or recognize important information in a given situation. As individuals progress through the phases of learning, they develop the ability to distinguish between relevant and irrelevant information as well as predict and anticipate future events. In the intermediate phases of learning, individuals develop the ability to act somewhat intuitively, but mainly rely on analytical and deliberate decision-making. When an expert level of learning/performance is attained, individuals intuitively and fluidly apply their knowledge. However, even in the final stages of learning, one may revert back to analytical thinking and decision making when novel situations are encountered. Further, Schunk and Zimmerman (2006) identified self-regulatory knowledge as being an essential component to effective learning. This type of knowledge encompasses one's metacognitive knowledge related to the specific domain they are intending to learn about as well as their knowledge about themselves as a learner.

Developing the ability to effectively apply and utilize one's knowledge occurs as the result of engagement in deliberate practice activities specifically aimed at improving one's knowledge and skill (Ericsson, 1998; Ericsson, Krampe, & Tesch-Römer, 1993). Thus, it is not the quantity of time spent learning that is important, but rather the quality of the learning and practice that allows one to develop expertise. Furthermore, quality learning necessitates resources, motivation, and effort (Ericsson et al., 1993). Hence, repetition of performance and continuous opportunities to practice applying one's knowledge are an essential element of effective practice (Guest, Regehr, & Tiberius, 2001).

In dynamic and complex domains where there is no one formula for how to apply one's knowledge across situations, situational awareness must be developed in order to make sense of the situation one is in and effectively determine how to apply one's knowledge. This entails developing the ability to rapidly and effectively perceive and attend to relevant information, integrate that information with one's knowledge and construct meaning from it, and anticipate and make predictions about the future impact of that information (Endsley, 1995). Thus, more experience and expertise enhances one's ability to effectively utilize situational awareness in order to effectively utilize one's knowledge in complex problem-solving situations, whereas individuals with little to no experience lack the knowledge and skill to direct their situational awareness. This results in the overloading of working memory as they need to consciously process all information in a situation in order to determine how to apply their knowledge and what approach to take in a given situation. However, one important point to note is that experts also must resist complete automaticity in dynamic contexts in order to avoid misinterpreting or failing to notice important information due to a bias from their previously accumulated knowledge and experience (Ericsson, 1998).

Therefore, in complex domains (such as SEPP service delivery) one must be able to flexibly and adaptively apply knowledge as each situation brings some novelty in comparison to past situations (Schwartz, Bransford, & Sears, 2005). Developing adaptive rather than routine expertise is then an important focus of training in SEPP. According to Hatano and Inagaki

(1986), routine experts produce the same superior, exceptional, and automatic performance over and over again (e.g., a phone manufacturer who is tasked with ensuring that a product is produced in exactly the same way every time), whereas adaptive experts find innovative, flexible, and creative ways to exhibit superior performance (e.g., a phone designer who is tasked with designing new and better products). Adaptive experts are better at thinking flexibly, handling uncertainty, understanding new situations, and acting flexibly and effectively (Fazey, Fazey, & Fazey, 2005). Thus, effectively performing in complex and dynamic situations requires that individuals learn to diversify their knowledge and skills in order to adapt accordingly to changing environmental conditions (Gentile, 1972). In SEPP applied practice, variables and conditions are constantly changing across clients (i.e., different personalities, backgrounds, sports, levels, etc.) as well as during work with clients (e.g., a client approaches a practitioner during a competition when they are struggling as a result of a weather delay or poor previous performance). Therefore, the ability to diversify one's knowledge and skills and develop adaptive expertise is essential and should be a key feature of neophyte training/supervision, as well as continued professional development.

TURNING KNOWLEDGE INTO SKILL USING CASE STUDIES

The quality of instruction impacts the learning process and one's ability to develop expertise (Bloom, 1976). For example, instruction should be designed to promote reflexive learning in which learning can be reflected upon in order to better integrate one's knowledge and develop deeper understandings of how to put that knowledge into practice (Astleitner, 2005). Further, in order to promote the development of adaptive expertise, learners should be given the opportunity to practice applying their knowledge in a variety of situations (Fazey et al., 2005).

One such method of instruction aimed at allowing learners to practice applying their knowledge in a variety of real-world situations is case-based instruction (Mayo, 2002). Utilizing cases puts learning into context, which is an essential part of the learning process for dynamic, ill-structured domains (Williams, 1992). According to Brown, Collins, and Duguid (1989), individuals will not learn how to effectively apply their knowledge unless it is situated in the context in which it will be used. Case-based, situated learning aims to overcome the inert knowledge problem in which learners can recall the information they have learned, but are unable to effectively utilize their knowledge in real-world situations (Cognition and Technology Group at Vanderbilt (CTGV), 1990). Thus, utilizing case-based instruction methods provides the opportunity to become more flexible and effective in synthesizing and applying one's knowledge in a variety of situations. In addition, providing learners with real-world situations: (1) allows them to engage in authentic practice; (2) enhances their motivation, interest, challenge, and engagement in the learning process; and (3) enables collaborative learning to take place in which they can examine how their understanding of a situation compares to the understanding and views of others (Riedel, Fitzgerald, Leven, & Toenshoff, 2003). Given that students in SEPP initially doubt their abilities and lack confidence in their service delivery skills and effectiveness (Tod, 2007), incorporating case-based instruction into SEPP training not only helps them to more effectively learn how to apply their knowledge, but also aids in alleviating this doubt.

THE IMPORTANCE OF REFLECTION

A final component to maximizing the effectiveness of training and applied practice in SEPP is the use of reflection. Reflection can be described as: (1) thoughtfulness about action; (2) deliberation and choice among competing versions of good practice; and (3) reconstructing experience, the end of which is the identification of a new possibility for action (Grimmett &

Erickson, 1988). To enhance the utility of reflective practice, both reflection in action (i.e., thinking about what you are doing while you are doing it) and reflection on action (i.e., retro-spectively thinking about what you have experienced) should be incorporated into training and applied practice (Schön, 1983). Further, while we naturally reflect on our experiences, struc-tured reflection frameworks should be utilized (Cropley et al., 2010), such as Borton's (1970) what-so what-now what framework, Gibbs' (1988) reflective cycle, Johns (1995) model of structured reflection, and/or Ghaye's (2001) reflective questions.

Several authors in the past few years have promoted the use of reflective practice in SEPP (e.g., Cropley, Miles, Hanton, & Niven, 2007) and highlighted the use of reflection during neophyte practice (e.g., Holt & Strean, 2001). Reflective practice can help practitioners to both develop competence (i.e., the ability to be effective) as well as contribute to effective practice (i.e., the ability to produce the desired effect) (Cropley, Hanton, Miles, & Niven, 2010). For neophyte practitioners, reflection helps them to learn valuable lessons about their professional tools (i.e., psychological skills and strategies), the client–consultant relationship, their learning process and experiences (e.g., strengths and weaknesses, impact of their own sport experiences, emotional reactions), and components of professional philosophy (Stambu-lova & Johnson, 2010). As summarized by Cropley et al. (2010), reflective practice involves learning from one's own and others' experiences so that practitioners can link theory and prac-tice in order to make sense of complex situations. Further, Cropley and colleagues highlighted that reflection benefits applied SEPP practitioners by improving self-awareness, helping to develop procedural and conditional knowledge, and developing one's philosophy of practice.

CONCLUSION

Martindale and Collins (2013) recently discussed the notion of the development of profes-sional judgment and decision-making expertise as it relates to SEPP practice. The authors bring up an important question regarding the idea of whether we allow the development of this type of expertise to occur naturally over time as the result of experience or put processes in place that prompt its development. They mention both the use of case studies and reflective practice as a means for helping "move practitioners up the learning curve at a faster rate by encouraging the formation of a base of experience, and more complete mental models of their domain" (Martindale & Collins, 2013, p. 397). Given the unique nature of applied SEPP practice as well as our responsibility to our key stakeholders, implementing methods such as case analysis and reflective practice for the initial and continual development of professional practice skills is warranted.

REFERENCES

Andersen, M. B., Van Raalte, J. L., & Brewer, B. W. (2000). When sport psychology consultants and graduate students are impaired: Ethical and legal issues in training and supervision. *Journal of Applied Sport Psychology, 12*, 134–150.

Andersen, M. B., Van Raalte, J. L., & Brewer, B. W. (2001). Sport psychology service delivery: Staying ethical while keeping loose. *Professional Psychology: Research and Practice, 32*, 12–18.

Anderson, A. G., Miles, A., Mahoney, C., & Robinson, P. (2002). Evaluating the effectiveness of applied sport psychology practice: Making the case for a case study approach. *The Sport Psychologist, 16*, 432–453.

Astleitner, H. (2005). Principles of effective instruction: General standards for teachers and instructional designers. *Journal of Instructional Psychology, 32*, 3–8.

Berliner, D. C. (1988). The development of expertise in pedagogy. *Charles W. Hunt Memorial Lecture presented at the Annual Meeting of the American Association of Colleges for Teacher Education, New Orleans, LA*, 3–34.

Binder, J. L. (1999). Issues in teaching and learning time-limited psychodynamic psychotherapy. *Clinical Psychology Review, 19*, 705–719.

Bloom, B. S. (1976). *Human characteristics and school learning.* New York, NY: McGraw-Hill.

Borton, T. (1970). *Reach, teach, and touch.* London: McGraw-Hill.

Brown, J. S., Collins, A., & Duguid, P. (1989). Situated cognition and the culture of learning. *Educational Researcher, 18*, 32–41.

Carlstedt, R. A. (2012). *Evidence-based applied sport psychology: A practitioner's manual.* New York, NY: Springer.

Cheadle, C., Pfenninger, G., & Carlson, E. (2014). Infusing technology in sport, exercise, and performance psychology practice. In J. G. Cremades & L. S. Tashman (Eds.), *Becoming a sport, exercise, and performance psychology professional: A global perspective* (pp. 160–167). New York, NY: Routledge.

Cognition and Technology Group at Vanderbilt (CTGV). (1990). Anchored instruction and its relationship to situated cognition. *Educational Researcher, 19*, 2–10.

Corlett, J. (1996). Sophistry, Socrates, and sport psychology. *The Sport Psychologist, 10*, 84–94.

Cropley, B., Hanton, S., Miles, A., & Niven, A. (2010). Exploring the relationship between effective and reflective practice in applied sport psychology. *The Sport Psychologist, 24*, 521–541.

Cropley, B., Miles, A., Hanton, S., & Niven, A. (2007). Improving the delivery of applied sport psychology support through reflective practice. *The Sport Psychologist, 21*, 475–494.

Dreyfus, H. L., & Dreyfus, S. E. (1986). *Mind over machine: The power of human intuition and expertise in the era of the computer.* New York, NY: The Free Press.

Endsley, M. R. (1995). Toward a theory of situation awareness in dynamic systems. *Human Factors, 37*, 32–64.

Ericsson, K. A. (1998). The scientific study of expert levels of performance: General implications for optimal learning and creativity. *High Ability Studies, 9*, 75–100.

Ericsson, K. A., Krampe, R. Th., & Tesch-Römer, C. (1993). The role of deliberate practice in the acquisition of expert performance. *Psychological Review, 100*, 363–406.

Fazey, J., Fazey, J. A., & Fazey, D. M. A. (2005). Learning more effectively from expertise. *Ecology and Society, 10*, 4 [online].

Fitts, P., & Posner, M. I. (1967). *Human performance.* Belmont, CA: Brooks/Cole.

Gentile, A. M. (1972). A working model of skill acquisition with application to teaching. *Quest, 17*(1), 3–23.

Ghaye, T. (2001). Reflective practice. *Faster Higher Stronger, 10*, 9–12.

Gibbs, G. (1988). *Learning by doing: A guide to teaching and learning methods.* Oxford: Further Education Unit.

Grimmett, P. P., & Erickson, G. L. (Eds.). (1988). *Reflection in teacher education.* New York, NY: Teachers College Press.

Guest, C. B., Regehr, G., & Tiberius, R. G. (2001). The life long challenge of expertise. *Medical Education, 35*, 78–81.

Hatano, G., & Inagaki, K. (1986). Two courses of expertise. In H. A. H. Stevenson & K. Hakuta (Eds.), *Child development and education in Japan* (pp. 262–272). New York, NY: Freeman.

Henriksen, K., & Diment, G. (2010). Professional philosophy: Inside the delivery of sport psychology service delivery at Team Denmark. *Sport Science Review, 20*(1–2), 5–21.

Holt, N. L., & Strean, W. B. (2001). Reflecting on initiating sport psychology consultation: A self-narrative of neophyte practice. *The Sport Psychologist, 15*, 188–204.

Hutter, R. I. V. (2014). Sport psychology supervision in the Netherlands. In J. G. Cremades & L. S. Tashman (Eds.), *Becoming a sport, exercise, and performance psychology professional: A global perspective* (pp. 260–267). New York, NY: Routledge.

Hutter, R. I. V., Oldenhof-Veldman, T., & Oudejans, R. R. D. (2015). What trainee sport psychologists want to learn in supervision. *Psychology of Sport and Exercise, 16*, 101–109.

Johns, C. (1995). The value of reflective practice for nursing. *Journal of Clinical Nursing, 4*, 23–30.

Keegan, R. J. (2010). Teaching consulting philosophies to neophyte sport psychologists: Does it help, and how can we do it? *Journal of Sport Psychology in Action, 1*, 42–52.

Keegan, R. J. (2014). Developing a philosophy and theoretical framework: Mapping a rich and complex landscape for the brave explorer. In J. G. Cremades & L. S. Tashman (Eds.), *Becoming a sport, exercise, and performance psychology professional: A global perspective* (pp. 61–68). New York, NY: Routledge.

Loganbill, C., Hardy, E., & Delworth, U. (1982). Supervision: A conceptual model. *The Counseling Psychologist, 10*, 3–42.

Martindale, A., & Collins, D. (2013). The development of professional judgment and decision making expertise in applied sport psychology. *The Sport Psychologist, 27*, 390–399.

Mayo, J. A. (2002). Case-based instruction: A technique for increasing conceptual application in introductory psychology. *Journal of Constructivist Psychology, 15*, 65–74.

Moore, Z. E. (2003). Ethical dilemmas in sport psychology: Discussion and recommendations for practice. *Professional Psychology: Research and Practice, 34*, 601–610.

Mugford, A., Hesse, D., & Morgan, T. (2014). Developing the "total" consultant: Nurturing the art and science. In J. G. Cremades & L. S. Tashman (Eds.), *Becoming a sport, exercise, and performance psychology professional: A global perspective* (pp. 268–275). New York, NY: Routledge.

Orlick, T., & Partington, J. (1987). The sport psychology consultant: Analysis of critical components as viewed by Canadian Olympic athletes. *The Sport Psychologist, 1*, 4–17.

Poczwardowski, A., Sherman, C. P., & Ravizza, K. (2004). Professional philosophy in the sport psychology service delivery: Building on theory and practice. *The Sport Psychologist, 18*, 445–463.

Rhodius, A., & Sugarman, K. (2014). Peer consultations with colleagues: The significance of gaining support and avoiding the "lone ranger trap." In J. G. Cremades & L. S. Tashman (Eds.), *Becoming a sport, exercise, and performance psychology professional: A global perspective* (pp. 331–338). New York, NY: Routledge.

Riedel, J., Fitzgerald, G., Leven, F., & Toenshoff, B. (2003). The design of computerized practice fields for problem solving and contextualized transfer. *Journal of Educational Multimedia and Hypermedia, 12*, 377–398.

Rumelhart, D. E., & Norman, D. A. (1978). Accretion, tuning, and restructuring: Three modes of learning. In J. W. Cotton & R. L. Klatzky (Eds.), *Semantic factors in cognition* (pp. 37–53). Hillsdale, NJ: Lawrence Erlbaum Associates.

Schön, D. (1983). *The reflective practitioner*. New York, NY: Basic Books.

Schunk, D. H., & Zimmerman, B. J. (2006). Competence and control beliefs: Distinguishing the means and the ends. In P. Alexander & P. Winne (Eds.), *Handbook of educational psychology* (2nd ed., pp. 349–367). San Diego, CA: Academic Press.

Schwartz, D. L., Bransford, J. D., & Sears, D. (2005). Efficiency and innovation in transfer. In J. Mestre (Eds.), *Transfer of learning from a modern multidisciplinary perspective* (pp. 1–51). Charlotte, NC: Information Age Publishing Inc.

Shuell, T. J. (1990). Phases of meaningful learning. *Review of Educational Research, 60*, 531–547.

Silva, J. M., Conroy, D. E., & Zizzi, S. J. (1999). Critical issues confronting the advancement of applied sport psychology. *Journal of Applied Sport Psychology, 11*, 298–320.

Stambulova, N., & Johnson, U. (2010). Novice consultants' experiences: Lessons learned by applied sport psychology students. *Psychology of Sport and Exercise, 11*, 295–303.

Tashman, L. S., & Tenenbaum, G. (2013). Sport psychology service delivery training: The value of an interactive, case-based approach to practitioner development. *Journal of Sport Psychology in Action, 4*, 71–85. DOI: 10.1080/21520704.2012.744375.

Thomas, P. (1990). An overview of the performance enhancement process in applied psychology. Unpublished manuscript, United States Olympic Training Center at Colorado Springs.

Tod, D. (2007). The long and winding road: Professional development in sport psychology. *The Sport Psychologist, 21*, 94–108.

Watson II, J. C., & Halbrook, M. (2014). Incorporating technology into practice: A service delivery approach. In J. G. Cremades & L. S. Tashman (Eds.), *Becoming a sport, exercise, and performance psychology: A global perspective* (pp. 152–159). New York, NY: Routledge/Psychology Press.

Watson, J. C., Lubker, J. R., & Van Raalte, J. (2011). Problems in reflective practice: Self-bootstrapping versus therapeutic supervision. In D. Gilbourne & M. B. Andersen (Eds.), *Critical essays in applied sport psychology* (pp. 157–172). Champaign, IL: Human Kinetics.

West, C. K., Farmer, J. A., & Wolf, P. M. (1991). *Instructional design: Implications for cognitive science*. Upper Saddle River, NJ: Prentice Hall.

Williams, S. M. (1992). Putting case-based instruction into context: Examples from legal and medical education. *The Journal of the Learning Sciences, 2*, 367–427.

Part I

The Practice of Service Delivery

2   We All Start Somewhere

The Experience of Consulting for the First Time

Maximilian H. Pollack and Marissa Norman

In this chapter, two second-year master's students will discuss their first encounter implementing mental skills training techniques with an athletic team. The progress that was made throughout the experience will be discussed. Throughout this chapter, the reader will gain a better understanding of the experience of working with a team as a first-time consultant. Among the many points that will be presented, some include: how to approach a session; what to expect when working with a team; some of the challenges a first-time consultant may experience; and the key lessons learned by the consultants in this particular case study. Do keep in mind that this was the first experience for both consultants in training. This case study represents how each of these consultants approached their work with the team. While reading the chapter, the reader is encouraged to think about alternatives to approaching the sessions, structuring lessons, incorporating different methods of teaching, and working effectively in a group-based approach.

BACKGROUND INFORMATION

The experience of providing sport psychology interventions on a regular basis as students in a master's-level program is presented within this chapter. The sport psychology consultants, Maximilian H. Pollack and Marissa Norman, provide a firsthand account of their experience working with a collegiate tennis team. All consultations were under supervision from a certified consultant with the Association for Applied Sport Psychology (CC-AASP), who worked with the team prior to this experience. The graduate student consultants completed one year of relevant education prior to working with the team. This chapter describes the first-time consultants' experience with their initial client. Over a seven-month period, Max and Marissa worked with the tennis team weekly. Each week a new topic was covered based on the needs of the team and suggestions from the coaching staff. The supervisor communicated with the coaches of the tennis team every week in order to ensure effective planning of meetings. These meetings were based on proper understanding of the situations the team was experiencing on the court.

Marissa Norman obtained her Bachelors of Science in Psychology at the University of Rhode Island (URI), as well as two minors in Kinesiology and Sociology. Being a former Division I track and field athlete, Marissa has practiced mental skills firsthand, but this was her first opportunity to use her knowledge of mental skills with other athletes.

Maximilian H. Pollack obtained his Bachelors of Science in Psychology at the University of Central Florida (UCF), where he played collegiate rugby as well as many other sports. His passion for helping individuals achieve their peak performance is powered by his most important goal: achieving ultimate happiness and enjoyment in life. Max uses his experiences and education with the purpose of helping others overcome any obstacle while also pursuing their ultimate goals.

DESCRIPTION OF THE CASE

The tennis team consisted of about ten female tennis players, in which a majority were international student athletes. The team played at a very high level of competition; however, the coach believed that working on the mental aspect of performance would help increase their potential. The team's goal coming into the season was to win the women's tennis national championship. Based on discussions with both the head coach and supervisor, the sport psychology consultants focused their early sessions on building strong relationships within the team. Helping them get to know each other was essential, knowing that team cohesion facilitates performance and productivity (Gammage, Carron, & Estabrooks, 2001). The sessions were designed to be fun and educational. All sessions were hands-on and often took place after practice, when energy levels of the athletes were usually low.

THEORETICAL FRAMEWORK/PHILOSOPHY

Each consultant and the supervisor incorporated his/her own theoretical framework and philosophical approach into the work with the team. However, it was also important for us to approach the sessions with common ground in order to work effectively as a unit in our work with the athletic team. Therefore, we worked together to mold their different frameworks and philosophies and build an approach that would suit the team best. This approach consisted of a primary focus in cognitive behavioral therapy (CBT), but also included ideas and approaches related to mindfulness (being present in the here and now). CBT focuses on one's thinking and how it is interrelated to one's emotions and behavior. Consistent with this focus, a CBT framework emphasizes that the problem is essentially in one's faulty thinking (Claspell, 2010). With a focus on self-awareness and attention, mindfulness is a mental state in which an individual voluntarily focuses on present involvements in a nonjudgmental way (Cottraux, 2007).

In terms of the delivery of the sessions, our teaching philosophy was very hands-on, with an emphasis on education and techniques that could be transferred from the classroom to the court with ease. In addition to education and transferability, accountability was a primary focus in the sessions. We felt that it was important to strengthen autonomy and overall focus through individual responsibilities that would be upheld by the team. Each session was approached based on the current and most relevant needs of the team at that point in time. There was constant communication between supervisor, coach, and consultants to structure the sessions effectively.

NEEDS ASSESSMENT

For this particular case, the coach identified the needs of the team and what he wanted his athletes to develop. The coach and the supervisor were in constant communication, allowing the supervisor to relay messages to the consultants in training. This was a consistent cycle. Further, a performance profile (Butler & Hardy, 1992) was also used during the work with the team to have each athlete rate where she believed her mental skills were at the time. Based on the information from the coach and the performance profiles, we reviewed the data in order to find overarching themes that appeared to be strengths and weaknesses not only for individual athletes, but also for the team as a whole. From this information, we determined what the focus would be for their upcoming sessions with the team. Team strengths and weaknesses were determined and discussed as well. The sessions were structured to strengthen the weaknesses and take advantage of the strengths the team possessed.

INTERVENTION

Preparation

Each session was planned days in advance through the collaboration of the two consultants and their supervisor. The entire process of researching literature, creating a session that would best fit the athletes' needs, and agreeing on the session took an average of two to three hours. An hour before each session, we would meet to make sure that we had all of the necessary materials for the session and a mutual understanding of the key comments they wanted to address. The process was perfect in its imperfection. The experience involved stress, anxiety, and an unconditional commitment, while also including excitement, enjoyment, and great experiences. Creation of the activities and lesson plans were among the most difficult tasks in the process because they took a lot of planning and extra time. As full-time students in a demanding sport psychology graduate program, time was hard to come by. The delivery of the activities came easy on some days and more difficult on others. There were a lot of extraneous variables including mood of the team, recent situations the team had experienced, relationships between the coach and team, schedules of both consultants-in-training and the supervisor, along with the confidence and preparation of the consultants-in-training. The process was truly helpful for both the consultants-in-training and the supervisor as we supported and received feedback from each other.

Sessions

Altogether, there were a total of 11 sessions that took place while working with this female collegiate team. Each session generally lasted 45–90 minutes. Most of the sessions took place in the classroom with each consultant and the supervisor present, while others took place in an outside space or on the tennis court. Keeping the sessions interesting was crucial since the athletes would meet after their vigorous practices. Their energy levels were typically low at the onset of the sessions; therefore, we placed emphasis on creating fun, interesting, and educational sessions.

Based on the needs assessment and research done by the consultants, the primary emphases of the sessions were on enhancing self-talk and building team cohesion, accountability, and effective communication. Throughout working with the team, we would observe the athletes in their practices and competitions to determine their ability to incorporate what they learned in each session out on the court. We would then discuss the transferability of the mental skills with the athletes along with discussing ways in which they could be more successful when applying their mental skills on the tennis court. The coach of the team provided our supervisor with a primary focus for what he wanted his athletes to work on throughout that week based on their performances in practice and matches. It was evident that there was continual improvement in the skills discussed throughout the sessions based on feedback from the coach, actions of the athletes, and their perception of themselves. The greatest improvements were in team cohesion and accountability based on these sources.

Example Sessions

In order to illustrate the approach we utilized, a brief description of a few of the sessions with the team is provided. For example, in one of the early sessions we used an activity called "Create a Monster" in which the athletes had to work together to form a single monster that moves five feet and creates a sound. This activity was intended to illustrate the team's current dynamic with regards to cohesion, communication, and leadership. It was intended to highlight the team's strengths and weaknesses in these areas. The chosen activity was also designed to create an engaging and fun atmosphere, which we believed would be important for an introductory session. It was a useful approach for this session because it involved working together in groups, trusting one another, communicating, and becoming closer as a unit through collaboration. Thus, it helped us to identify how well the athletes got along, who the leaders were, and which areas of their team dynamic and individual performance might need improvement. In addition, this was an amusing activity that had the team laughing and enjoying their first session together. With the use of this simple activity, the team built a better understanding of each of their teammates and had fun in the process.

In another session we wanted to focus on the communication among the athletes. Based on varying cultural backgrounds and observations from the previous year where the team seemed to misinterpret each other, we wanted to do a session that would help the athletes understand the role perception plays in communication. Further, we wanted to highlight the impact of the nature of communication (i.e., how something is said) versus the content of communication (i.e., what is said) as well as the role of emotions. To facilitate the session on this topic we used an activity in which the athletes had to communicate while expressing various emotions. There was a box containing pieces of paper with specific emotions written on them and the box was passed around to each athlete. Each athlete would read a sentence written on the whiteboard at the front of the classroom while expressing the emotion picked from the box. The emphasis for this activity was on helping the athletes understand how to communicate effectively and increase self-awareness when communication was ineffective.

Self-talk was a primary focus in many sessions due to the team's weakness in this area, as identified by the performance profile. Thus, a couple of activities were used specifically for increasing the athletes' self-awareness of their self-talk and finding ways of improving it. For example, the focus of one session was to give the team a chance to practice their positive, motivational, and instructional self-talk, as well as get them to further understand the effects that negative self-talk can have on their performance. The goal of the session was to have the athletes use short and specific self-talk as well as understand what type of self-talk they were using. The consultants set up the session by having the athletes split into two groups and hold a backpack (one backpack was weighted while the other was not) while turning negative comments that we gave them into either positive or instructional statements. The weighted backpack was used as a distraction to represent any negative thought or distraction that may take place on the court.

Additionally, an activity conducted out on the tennis court consisted of the athletes playing their sport while incorporating more effective instructional self-talk rather than ineffective self-talk. The athletes were split into two equal teams and each team had to play four points on the court. After each point, the athletes on each team had to speak to each consultant either with positive, instructional, or motivational self-talk about their past point. In addition, each teammate had to give their fellow teammates constructive feedback about their play on the court to improve team support and facilitate taking and giving constructive criticism. During this activity the consultants were also able to observe many other related aspects of the individual athletes' and team's process and performance (e.g., body language, use of self-talk, motivation, buy-in, team cohesion, etc.).

As a final example, there was also a session dedicated to incorporating deep-breathing techniques to enhance their recovery in practice and in match situations. The athletes first measured a baseline of heart rate during one minute of natural breathing. Then, they participated in vigorous exercise for about three minutes to increase their heart rate. Subsequently, they then utilized deep breathing with a five-by-five count to see how quickly they could get their heart rate down to a more stable rate. Self-talk along with imagery were also incorporated to help with this process.

For each of the sessions with the team, a debrief was conducted at the end of the meeting. The key debrief points were focused on how the athletes already incorporate the skill or lesson into their life/performance, how they could improve upon their use of mental skills, and what they learned from each activity. The debrief ultimately culminated in a discussion of what they could do to incorporate what they learned in their future practices and performances.

REFLECTION

Working with this group of amazing athletes was an enormous privilege and learning experience for both consultants. After every session, we would complete a written reflection on our experiences, thoughts, and feelings to improve our self-awareness and professional knowledge (Anderson, Knowles, & Gilbourne, 2004). We both can agree that textbooks did not fully prepare us for this experience, but rather the application portion of our education was where we learned the most. A few valuable lessons we learned throughout this process are highlighted below.

Flexibility

Flexibility is crucial. As a consultant it is important to be able to work in a variety of settings (e.g., classroom, tennis court, outside, etc.) and in different conditions. There were times when we planned an hour session and were only able to meet with the team for 20 minutes, while there were other days where no sessions were planned but the coach wanted us to meet with the athletes at the last minute. For example, there was one situation where a session was planned with a lot of material to cover but due to an extended practice the team arrived late to the session. When this occurred, the session had to be modified and in many ways simplified to accommodate the change in overall time of the session. Although this was frustrating, we did not take it personally since we understood that it was part of the experience of working with a team that had high aspirations to succeed. Since we both had already developed a plan for the session, it just required some tweaking to accommodate the change in time. Having previously developed a goal of what we both wanted to accomplish in the session made the process of determining what information would be addressed and what activities would be used more fluid.

We also found it necessary to be flexible during sessions. For example, we had planned a match role-play session with the intent of demonstrating how the athletes could help coach and support each other and even themselves in challenging moments. Though we thought we had developed a strong plan for the session, we quickly realized that the athletes felt uncomfortable doing the activity (i.e., there were signs of shyness, confusion, and embarrassment). We needed to adapt quickly and change the activity, getting the same lessons across but in a different way. Thus, a key lesson learned from this experience was that it's important to have a backup plan and be able to think quickly on your feet because things don't always turn out as planned.

Another component of flexibility is being able to endure challenging situations and get better from each and every one of them. As new consultants, it took us longer to prepare and develop sessions. At times, these sessions would take hours to create and then our supervisor or the coach would express that they didn't feel like the session would be sufficient for the team, leading to last-minute changes that completely changed the activity and lesson plan. We had to keep in mind that this constructive feedback was necessary to our professional growth as consultants. Thus, we learned that even when you think your plan is a game winner, having someone from the outside with a greater understanding of the game or applied practice can help you understand how to make your approach and session plan more effective. Though getting constructive feedback is often difficult and frustrating, it can be a blessing in disguise.

Control the Controllables

As consultants, we have either experienced or will experience ourselves talking to athletes about controlling what we can control and not focusing on what we can't control. We must take the uncontrollables into account but not put too much emphasis on them because that takes away from our ability to cope with the situation effectively. As new consultants, we experienced the controllables and uncontrollables just as any athlete would in his or her sport. Through these experiences we realized the only thing that changes is the context and one's perspective. For example, we both felt comfortable and more confident working as a consulting team, having each other to fall back on. Consulting for the first time, it was reassuring to face the challenge with a peer by one's side. While working with this team, most sessions were planned to have both consultants as well as the supervisor present and ready to participate in the sessions. However, there were times when one of us or our supervisor would not be able to make a session, which left the other consultant feeling concerned or overloaded. We both admit that in this situation we at first felt more nervous and feared making a mistake; however, we eventually were able to practice mental skills for ourselves and switch our focus to things within our control. For example, we realized that all of this concern was taking place due to ineffective thoughts that were racing through our minds. Thereafter, we took a few minutes to incorporate deep-breathing techniques while gearing our thoughts to the upcoming presentation and the excitement of being able to lead a session on our own. Thus we realized that the reinterpretation of this experience was key; one's perception of an uncontrollable situation is all in the eyes of the beholder, and it is therefore, just like we tell our athletes, in our control no matter how scary it may seem at first.

Another uncontrollable that was experienced during this initial applied practice was the interest or mindset of the athletes. There were days that the athletes were not in the right mindset or they lacked the interest necessary to get the most out of the sessions. As consultants, this can be upsetting and can trigger some unfavorable emotional responses from within, but we realized we had to keep in mind the nature of the situation and our roles. We had to do the best we could with the cards we were dealt and expect that there would be days that some of the athletes might talk while we were talking, stare at their phones during a session, or not participate in activities. Although not an easy task, we geared our focus on facilitating a great session, getting the most out of the athletes that were present, and generating a better understanding of how to perform in adverse situations. For example, we adopted the mindset of winning over the crowd throughout the sessions. We knew what to expect but kept our focus on the presented material and our engagement with the athletes, and used teamwork to try our best to get everyone involved. The moment that one of us became frustrated with the lack of participation from several of the athletes was the moment that the presentation suffered. Therefore, we realized the importance of keeping our cool and staying focused on what we could control.

A final lesson related to managing the uncontrollables was our experience with the inevitability of making mistakes as neophyte consultants. We both went into our first session hoping to perform at our best. To our surprise this was far from the case and we both made mistakes throughout the sessions. At first this was a difficult realization because we felt we were fully prepared. However, we realized that we still had a lot to learn and that, just like any athlete, we too would improve with practice and more experience. Therefore, we learned that it is important to realize that you do not have to be perfect right off the bat. Rather, doing your best to prepare for every encounter and reflecting on what you did well in your sessions will help you set the standard for high-level performances. It is also important to take into account what could have been better and if you focus on changing one thing from a previous session to the next it will bring you closer to being the best professional you can be on a consistent basis.

Building Effective Relationships

Our world is built around relationships. Consulting is an art and comes with practice, but it makes all the difference when relationships are created successfully. Early on in the sessions with the team, there were several barriers that we faced with the athletes. One barrier in particular was the age difference between the athletes and us (about 2–3 years), which felt slightly awkward at first. This made it more difficult to challenge the athletes toward the beginning of the working relationship due to lack of comfort. At the start of the work with the team we introduced ourselves in a professional way, but we both admit that we were not being ourselves. Reflecting on this, we realized that the athletes did not appear comfortable with us and were very quiet at the beginning of the sessions. It wasn't until we became more comfortable being ourselves in sessions and in turn allowed ourselves to be more genuine that the athletes started engaging in discussion and asking questions. Over time, laughter erupted, humorous examples were presented, and emotional encounters among the athletes took place, which facilitated stronger relationships between the athletes and us. Therefore, we learned that rapport grew with each new experience that we had with the athletes and the more face time we had while the athletes were at matches or practices the better the relationship became. It was evident that the team put forth increased effort and contributed more when they became more comfortable with us. Thus, we realized that building these relationships takes time but is important and certainly attainable.

Growth Mindset

A final point of reflection from our experience relates to the importance of adopting a growth mindset. Based on Carol Dweck's (2006) research on the impact of mindsets, one's drive to learn and challenge oneself as well as the attitude brought to the situations you experience are important considerations. Dweck (2006) stated, "The mindsets change what people strive for and what they see as success ... they change the definition, significance, and impact of failure ... they change the deepest meaning of effort" (p. 46). With this sentiment in mind, through our experiences with this team, we realized that we must grow substantially each and every opportunity that we get not only as consultants but also as people. Consistent education is crucial to growth in any domain and becoming more knowledgeable about different theories as well as sport psychology techniques is important for professional development.

We both implemented a growth mindset throughout each new experience and encounter with the athletes. We were always in search for what we did well and what we could do better during the next opportunity. We noticed that when we felt that our presentations were going to be "scary" we refocused on viewing it as just another opportunity for us to test our applied practice skills and prove to ourselves that we had what it took to help these athletes improve. The program at Barry University certainly provided ample opportunity to grow each and every day by constantly reading up on the latest research, shadowing our professors and peers in sessions with other individuals and teams, communicating about recent or upcoming challenges, discussing approaches and theories, and always keeping an open mind about each new opportunity. Most of all, one of the greatest takeaways from this experience as new consultants and while attending Barry University was always knowing that no matter how good you think you are, there is always room for improvement.

Looking back on the experience of consulting for the first time, it was evident that we both enjoyed the experience as well as learned a lot during the process. However, it would be unjust not to mention the other side of the experience, which consisted of stress, anxiety, and frustration. One of the biggest lessons learned through these times was when consulting gets hard it's always helpful to reflect back on why you chose to be a part of this field of work. Although we entered into this field for different reasons, remembering why we started helped to change perceiving our negative emotions as stressors to embracing challenges that are just part of the job. The challenges help motivate them to pull through and do our very best throughout the process. Even though this is a "job," we learned that it is important to have fun with what you do. Not many careers can compare to consulting with athletes and helping them reach consistently high levels of performance. Although consulting consists of continuing education, creativity, and a lot of hard work, it is important to enjoy the process.

Final Reflections

This chapter discussed two consultants' experiences working with athletes in a collegiate setting for the very first time. During the process, the consultants experienced a wide range of emotions varying from excitement to frustration. Although we both had a full year of master's-level classes that had helped us to prepare for this experience, we learned the most through the opportunity to apply what we had learned in class in the real world. Reflecting on each session about our individual strengths and weaknesses allowed us to grow as consultants. Although this was an imperfect process, it helped us to begin to strengthen our applied practice skills that will continue to develop throughout the course of our professional careers. We learned that our minds are always ready for more, even if at times more seems like way too much. Having the opportunity to work in a demanding environment helped us to learn how to handle ourselves the best way possible even when the task seemed daunting. It made us more prepared for the next stage of our professional development, and looking back we are happy that we accepted the challenge.

SUGGESTED READINGS

Brown, C. H. (2009). The consultant as a performer. In K. Hays (Ed.), *Performance psychology in action: A casebook for working with athletes, performing artists, business leaders, and professionals in high-risk occupations* (pp. 309–327). Washington, DC: American Psychological Association.

Dweck, C. S. (2006). *Mindset: The new psychology of success.* New York, NY: Random House.

Hanrahan, S. J., & Andersen, M. B. (2010). *Routledge handbook of applied sport psychology: A comprehensive guide for students and practitioners.* London: Routledge.

Tammen, V. V. (2000). First internship experiences: or, what I did on holiday. In M. B. Andersen (Ed.), *Doing sport psychology* (pp. 181–192). Champaign, IL: Human Kinetics.

Tonn, E., & Harmison, R. J. (2004). Thrown to the wolves: A student's account of her practicum experience. *Sport Psychologist, 18*(3), 324–340.

Weinberg, R. S., & Gould, D. (2014). *Foundations of sport and exercise psychology* (2nd ed.). Champaign, IL: Human Kinetics.

REFLECTIVE QUESTIONS

1. What should consultants consider in order to effectively prepare for working with a team?
2. How can you build your confidence as a first-time consultant?
3. What should one consider in order to determine the best style/approach to use as a sport psychology consultant?
4. What are the pros and cons to working with multiple consultants in the field?
5. What are some of the ethical considerations when working with a client or team of similar age?

REFERENCES

Anderson, A., Knowles, Z., & Gilbourne, D. (2004). Reflective practice for applied sport psychologists: A review of concepts, models, practical implications, and thoughts on dissemination. *The Sport Psychologist, 18,* 188–203.

Barbazette, J. (2008). Facilitation skills for E-trainers: the training clinic. www.tk08.astd.org/PDF/Handouts%20for%20Web%202-11/TH106.pdf.

Butler, R. J., & Hardy, L. (1992). The performance profile: Theory and application. *The Sport Psychologist, 6,* 253–264.

Claspell, E. (2010). Cognitive-behavioral therapies. *Routledge handbook of applied sport psychology: A comprehensive guide for students and practitioners* (p. 131). London: Routledge.

Cottraux, J. (2007). *Thérapie cognitive et emotions: La troisième vague* [Cognitive therapy and emotions: The third wave]. Paris: Elsevier Masson.

Dweck, C. S. (2006). *Mindset: The new psychology of success.* New York, NY: Ballantine Books.

Gammage, K. L., Carrón, A. V., & Estabrooks, P. A. (2001). Team cohesion and individual productivity: The influence of the norm for productivity and the identifiability of individual effort. *Small Group Research, 52*(1), 3–18. DOI: 10.1177/10464964010320010.

3 Mental Transformation of a Professional Tennis Player in Four Months

Katerina Vejvodova (Kudlackova)

The mental game is a crucial aspect of every great tennis performance. Tennis is a dynamic sport, where lots of things happen every minute. Points may be long or short, but in fact the longest part of every match consists of "between points preparation." The rules allow players 20 seconds between every point in Grand Slams and 25 seconds in ATP tournaments to prepare for the next point. That is a lot of time to think – a lot of time to use your mind for perfect, average, or poor preparation. It all depends on a player's ability to take advantage of his/her own psychological skills.

I played tennis in college and later worked as a coach. Today I help athletes to become better by using their mind. I feel like knowing the three positions related to tennis – being a player, coach, and performance enhancement consultant – helps me to better understand the issues that may occur. On the other hand, it is sometimes challenging to stay objective and ignore personal experiences that may negatively affect my work with clients. Below is a case in which I believe things worked out well and mental training was helpful.

BACKGROUND INFORMATION

I have worked as a performance enhancement professional since October 2011. I started in a sports psychological consulting company in Prague, but soon became independent and started my own business that I still have today. I have spent hundreds of hours working with athletes from different sports in an office, but also spend time working with them in the field. The thing that keeps me motivated is the fact that I can influence others and be useful for them on their transformational journey of becoming more mentally tough and happy with their sports performance and life.

In June 2013, a professional tennis player (around 400 ATP at that time) approached me asking for help with his mental game, after having found out about me and my work via the internet. His main concerns at the time were loss of motivation and joy from playing, struggle to move up in ATP ranking, fear of failure and making mistakes, and low confidence. We had never met before nor had I heard about him prior to him contacting me. He was 25 at that time, having no prior experience with performance enhancement professionals (neither a sport psychologist nor mental coach). I have my own website, where I introduce my work and describe how sport psychology can be helpful. He was experiencing similar things that I was describing on my website and thus decided to contact me via telephone. During the conversation, he wanted to know what to expect. He asked questions about the length of the sessions, their content, and price. He also wanted to know whether I have sufficient experience working in the field and whether I know anything about tennis. I have played tennis competitively since I was 8 years old and he was quite happy to hear that. I have found that athletes are happy speaking to someone who knows their sport even though it can actually disturb the whole process, especially if the consultant brings in her/his own biases. However, the clients do not realize that and thus welcome professionals who are competent in their sport. We spoke for about ten minutes and set up the first in-person meeting for the upcoming week. Unfortunately, at that time I did not yet have my own office. Thus, we agreed to meet at a local café.

My goal during the first session was to collect information and get to know my new client as much as possible. In addition, I wanted to explain some basic mental processes going on in his head during his performance and explain the rules of our cooperation. I have a basic outline for every first interview I have with clients and in this case we followed that format. Questions about family, school or work, sports history, past injuries, crisis during performance, present and past coaches, training schedule, etc. were covered. The athlete also had an opportunity to talk about whatever he felt was relevant and important for me to know in order to help him better. According to what he was telling me, I explained several mental processes going on during his performance (e.g., his body was getting tense due to impaired breathing and he was having negative thoughts related to the end of the match). I knew that being at the top level, he needed complex care and thus decided to propose a long-term cooperation with the purpose of teaching him more about mental skills (e.g., deep breathing, thought and emotional control, imagery, etc.) and helping him to incorporate them into practice and competition. He was interested in knowing more and thus we set up the next session.

At the end of the first session we discussed the logistics of our work together. I told him the price and handed him a short contract detailing the rules underlying our relationship (e.g., privacy of information, price, cancellation of planned sessions, etc.). Clients are required to sign and date the document, indicating that he/she has been informed about the type of work I do to protect myself from any potential misunderstandings. We agreed that a good frequency for our sessions would be once per week. I prefer this period between sessions since I feel that one week gives clients enough time to work on new mental skills and reflect on their personal transformation.

DESCRIPTION OF THE CASE

The athlete (James for the purpose of this text) comes from a sporting family and has two older sisters. As a little kid, he was engaged in many other sports such as gymnastics or basketball, but he fell in love with tennis and thus it became number one for him. His dad helped him a lot throughout his career (especially in juniors) but was also the one putting a lot of pressure on him later. Due to his financial situation, James did not have a personal coach at the time he approached me, which is very difficult at this level of sport. He described his own mental condition as unstable, sometimes fine but sometimes struggling. He was having problems winning important points (e.g., break balls or set points). Negative thoughts would often catch up with him and thus it impaired his motor performance, and the chances to make mistakes during crucial moments increased. He did not have any mental preparation routine and basically practiced like many others – technique, tactics, and physical conditioning. Mental training was something he needed the most; which is why he found me and wanted to work on it systematically. He felt that it was the missing piece of his game. Our cooperation consisted of three stages. The first part of it focused on education (mental training) and lasted about four months (ten sessions). The second part was aimed at his relationship with his dad, because it affected his performance quite a lot. This work took us about a month and is still something that he needs to be reminded about every now and then. The third and final part of our cooperation was incorporation of all that was learned into every day preparation. We used our final sessions to reflect upon past tournaments and to prepare James for the upcoming matches.

THEORETICAL FRAMEWORK/PHILOSOPHY

Since the client agreed to a long cooperation, I decided to set up a complete mental training plan according to what I had been taught during my master's program at Florida State

University. I used various resources in designing the intervention, such as both applied and theoretical sport psychology books (e.g., Orlick, 2007; Tenenbaum, 2008; Williams, 2009) and internet sources such as sport psychology articles (e.g., mindful.org), forums (e.g., LinkedIn sport psychology groups), and psychology-related TedX videos. I wanted to educate James first so that he understood the connection of body and mind during his performance. Thus, we included psychological skills trainings (PST) (Kudlackova et al., 2013; Taylor et al., 2008; Thomas et al., 1999). After the educational phase of our cooperation, it was much easier to make him engage in regular exercises for concentration, relaxation, activation, self-talk, etc. before, during, and after playing. When I work, I often use written materials. I like the fact that athletes can take them home and review them whenever they need to. It helps them to remember what we have worked on. We write a good amount during our sessions, which gives me additional time to think of what is important and needs to be discussed. In addition, some athletes have good visual memory and thus remember information better after they write it down. We incorporated cognitive behavioral theory (CBT) while working on self-talk and body language.

I also decided to include sessions using a Gestalt approach. I learned this technique in a certified coaching course here in the Czech Republic. Gestalt is very useful when dealing with distorted relationships, dilemmas, or emotional blocks as it helps clients to get a new perspective of the whole situation. In this particular case, I used it specifically with regards to James' relationship with his dad. According to what I knew from James and his father (I never met him but we had several long phone conversations and exchanged some emails as well), it seemed that this was a big obstacle in James' journey. He felt obligated to play well and prove to his dad that he is a great player since his dad often told him that he didn't believe this was possible. His dad always analyzed lost matches and emphasized what went wrong. James did not even want to talk to him anymore, as he knew that the main topic of the conversation would be the mistakes he had made during his performance. Thus, the Gestalt approach allowed us to explore and work through the impact of this relationship on James' performance.

NEEDS ASSESSMENT

In order to follow the progress of our cooperation and James' improvements, we engaged in performance profiling. For that I followed guidelines from Butler and Hardy (1992). I use this tool regularly as I consider it "client-friendly." It is easy, takes only a while and makes sense to clients. We started simply by discussing good performance and great players. After that I asked James to write down characteristics of great players, such as being confident, being able to focus, being positive, etc. His list was quite long and all the characteristics can be found in Table 3.1. Once we had the list, I asked him to tell me how important these things are for the great players. We used a rating scale from 1 (not being important at all) to 10 (being extremely important) and slowly assigned numbers for every characteristic. Finally, I asked James to go through the list again and rate himself for each characteristic, thinking of the last month. Once again, a rating scale from 1 (not being good at all) to 10 (being extremely good) was used. After that, I had a clear idea of things we needed to work on. Characteristics with perceived highest importance (in this case there were several of with the value of 10) and lowest self-evaluation (in this case the value of 2 for focus and mental preparation) were the priorities for mental training.

We used performance profiling twice during our cooperation. First in June (during the second session) and then again in September once we were done with the basic educational part of mental training (after ten sessions). This assessment is subjective and gives us an idea about how an athlete perceives the importance of mental skills for his performance, as well as his own ability to engage in them and use them in real settings. My client enjoyed evaluating himself since he has never thought about himself this way. It was interesting for him to think

Table 3.1 Performance Profiles from June and September 2013

| | June 2013 | | September 2013 | |
	Importance of the Item	Self-evaluation	Importance of the Item	Self-evaluation
Confidence	10	3	10	7
Focus	10	2	10	8
Goal-setting	10	7	10	9
Self-talk	10	4	10	8
Relaxation	8	1	9	5
Mental toughness	10	4	10	7
Communication	10	9	10	9
Body-language	8	3	10	7
Motivation	10	3	10	9
Imagery	7	1	9	7
Activation – energy regulation	9	3	9	7
Dealing with injury	10	9	9	9
Emotional control	7	7	10	8
Determination	10	5	10	9
Mental preparation	10	2	10	8
Technique	10	8	9	7
Tactics	8	3	9	7
Physical condition	9	8	9	8

Note
Scale ranges from 1 (not important at all, not good at all) to 10 (very important, very good).

of different things that may be important in order to be a great player. Based on this informa-tion, I created a special individualized mental training program for him. We decided to meet once each week and work on techniques that would help him to improve his self-regulation and overall confidence, and increase joy from playing. Table 3.1 provides a list of the identified key aspects of his performance, as well as his pre and post ratings.

INTERVENTION

As mentioned previously, the whole cooperation with James was divided into three stages. The first part of the intervention lasted for about four months (about ten sessions from June to September). First, we were meeting at different places – mostly at his club but sometimes even in a café or restaurant, because I did not yet have my own office. Later, we moved to my office and I am happy that the first sessions did not disrupt our relationship and that we still continue working together. During the first stage of our cooperation I taught him how to use various psychological skills such as goal-setting, concentration, deep breathing, imagery, and self-talk. We also had several sessions emphasizing his confidence, mental prep-aration before every match, energy regulation, emotional control, and body language. In addition, I observed him in practice and in two different tournaments. I collected some material and presented it to him later. I recorded him and we observed the between-points routines together. I asked him questions related to his behavior, thoughts, and emotions. We would pause the video whenever needed and talked about how he felt at the moment, what he was thinking, how his behavior looked, and how he can make it all more effective, enjoyable, and beneficial for his performance. It was sometimes hard for him to recall certain moments. If so, we tried to visualize them or think of what could have been going on in his head. I recorded both practice and competitive events once each month and it seemed like a reasonable period for changes to occur.

After the first stage of the intervention we stopped working together as the athlete changed his coach, who convinced him that our sessions were not useful. However, after three months James stopped working with the coach because of his negative attitude. At this time, James came back to me and wanted to keep working on his mental game. He seemed quite negative after that. His confidence was lower again and he felt a bit lost. It was unfortunate that we had to go over some things again, but every experience can be helpful if one takes the proper lesson from it. He kept the positive things from working with the former coach in his mind and remembered all the important things related to his performance that could help him become a better player.

The second stage of the intervention aimed at the father–son relationship. The Gestalt approach was very effective here. I introduced James to the new technique as the type of work we have done before (mental training) was very different. I told him, we could "imitate" his dad being present with us and continue on according to where it takes us. At the time, James started to understand how the relationship disrupts his performance and that led him to agree on the new approach. He was informed that we could stop the process at any time, so he felt quite confident trying it. I asked him to pick one chair that would represent his dad in the room and place it wherever he felt appropriate. He picked one and put it next to his seat – not very close, but not far either. Both chairs were facing me at the beginning. Gestalt approach emphasizes current feelings, thoughts, and behavior and thus I asked questions such as: "How are you feeling at this moment? What would you like to tell your father now? What are you thinking now? What would you like to do now?" (Crkalova & Riethof, 2012). Once we explored his current state having his dad by his side, I offered him the opportunity to experience his dad's feelings, thoughts, and attitudes by changing the seat.

He accepted my challenge and sat down in his dad's seat. All of a sudden he was able to experience his "dad's shoes" – his feelings, thoughts, behavior. It enabled James to understand his dad better and forgive him for some of the things that were not pleasant (e.g., ongoing blame for mistakes he had made). At the end of the whole process James felt calm, free, and happy for what he had realized. Thanks to these calm and happy feelings, his relationship with his dad no longer disrupted his game. I also discussed the whole situation with his dad via a long email and telephone conversation, and he agreed that he would try to work on himself as well and stop overanalyzing past matches with James. He realized that James was an adult now and that he needed to give him space for his own growth. It was a crucial transformational step for both father and son.

The last stage of our cooperation (in progress at the time of writing this chapter) aimed at James' current needs, helping him to implement the skills and strategies we had previously discussed and worked on. I helped him to take advantage of all the techniques he learned (e.g., imagery, deep breathing, thought control) and apply them before, during, and after competition. The frequency of our sessions decreased, as he now knows better what to do and how to regulate his own mental as well as physical state. Every now and then we exchange some messages or set up a meeting to analyze what has been done and discuss what still needs to be done. Due to his financial situation, I do not travel with him, but we are in touch via Skype, email, or other form of electronic communication even during tournaments. We have an agreement that whenever he feels he needs to discuss any issues, he lets me know. Most of the time, when he approaches me from abroad, he needs support or help applying specific mental skills into practice and competition. For example, he was traveling to Russia to play a tournament on a hard court. He was not used to the fast surface and was a little insecure before his match, having only been able to practice twice there. We discussed the situation and decided to incorporate specific imagery emphasizing the feeling he has on the court while playing. His goal was to see himself hitting the ball nicely in front of his body, feeling the ball, energy and satisfaction from what he was doing. He did that twice the day before his match for about five minutes and once in the morning during the competitive day. James felt these exercises were helpful and his game was more consistent at the times he needed it to be. Similarly, in other instances we would work on other issues using not only imagery, but also other skills such as deep breathing, goal-setting, thought regulation, etc.

REFLECTION

As I reflect on the case, I would do several things differently. First, I would have tried to sort out the working space so we could have had privacy every time we met from the beginning. I believe it was unprofessional to meet at public places and I could have put James in awkward and uncomfortable situations. However, I figured that during the first educational stage of our cooperation, it was not such a big deal to be in a public place. We did not discuss any person-ally challenging topics, but rather focused on education and performance enhancement. Second, I would pay more attention to his relationship with his dad early on. However, not too early as I felt the "training" and educational part of my work helped the whole process and built James' trust. He probably would not have been so open with me right at the beginning and it could have made the Gestalt approach more complicated and inefficient. Finally, I would and still am planning on making him understand that the more I see him, the better I can help him, which of course means more sessions and more money on his side. That is always a sens-itive issue and I hope that once he progresses and gets into the top 200 this will be possible.

On the other hand, I believe I did some things quite well. First, I never pushed him into anything and always paid attention to what he wanted to talk about. I was always there for him and never refused to help him. Second, I was always able to explain to him what happens to his body and mind in different situations. That helped him to build his own self-awareness and develop the ability to reflect upon his own actions. That is also obvious from pre and post per-formance profiles (see Table 3.1). Changes occurred for almost every psychological item. We did not record remarkable improvement for the item of communication and dealing with injury. However, that may be due to his high rating both before and after. In addition, we included items such as tennis technique, tactics, and physical conditioning in order to see how important these things were for James and how much he still needed to work on them. Phys-ical conditioning and technique did not change much; however, tactics changed quite a lot. We discussed the tactical part of his game several times and I feel like I had an advantage here, being able to discuss this aspect of the game since I had a strong background in tennis.

Third, throughout the process I was regularly getting feedback from him, which helped me to adjust my approach and communicate in a way he could understand. I believe that this is one of the most important considerations as it really determines whether the process goes well, has a positive impact on the client, and whether the consulting relationship continues for a long time or ends after several sessions.

SUGGESTED READINGS

Cremades, J. G., & Tashman, L. S. (2014). *Becoming a sport, exercise, and performance psychology profes-sional*. New York, NY: Psychology Press.
Gallwey, W. T. (1997). *The inner game of tennis: The classic guide to the mental side of peak performance*. New York, NY: Random House.
Mack, G., & Casstevens, D. (2001). *Mind gym*. New York, NY: McGraw-Hill.
Nadal, R., & Carlin, J. (2012). *Rafa*. New York, NY: Hyperion.
Orlick, T. (2007). *In pursuit of excellence*. Champaign, IL: Human Kinetics.
Tenenbaum, G. (2008). *The practice of sport psychology*. Morgantown, WV: Fitness Information Technology.
Williams, J. M. (2009). *Applied sport psychology: Personal growth to peak performance*. New York, NY: McGraw-Hill Higher Education.

REFLECTIVE QUESTIONS

1. How would you approach working with a client who is losing his confidence?
2. Based on what criteria would you set up a mental training plan for a new athlete who has approached you?

3. How would you conduct and utilize the performance profiling approach?
4. How would you approach your first meeting with an athlete?
5. How would you engage other individuals directly affecting your client into communicating or even working with you in order to help the client?

REFERENCES

Butler, R. J., & Hardy, L. (1992). The performance profile: Theory and application. *The Sport Psychologist, 6,* 253–264.

Crkalova, A., & Riethof, N. (2012). *Pruvodce svetem koucovani a osobnostni typologie.* Prague: Management Press.

Kudlackova, K., Eccles, D. W., & Dieffenbach, K. (2013). Use of relaxation skills in differentially skilled athletes. *Psychology of Sport and Exercise, 14,* 468–475.

Orlick, T. (2007). *In pursuit of excellence.* Champaign, IL: Human Kinetics.

Taylor, M. K., Gould, D., & Rolo, C. (2008). Performance strategies of US Olympians in practice and competition. *High Ability Studies, 19*(1), 19–36.

Tenenbaum, G. (2008). *The practice of sport psychology.* Morgantown, WV: Fitness Information Technology.

Thomas, P. R., Murphy, S. M., & Hardy, L. (1999). Test of performance strategies: Development and preliminary validation of a comprehensive measure of athletes' psychological skills. *Journal of Sports Sciences, 17*(9), 697–711.

Williams, J. M. (2009). *Applied sport psychology: Personal growth to peak performance.* New York, NY: McGraw-Hill Higher Education.

4 Helping an Elite Athlete Move from 0 to 100 Post-Injury

Donald LaGuerre

This chapter is based on my experiences over a three-year period, working with an elite athlete in Trinidad and Tobago. The athlete competed in an individual sport with his sights set on the 2016 Olympics. However, during a training session in 2013 he suffered an injury that ruled him out of training. This happened at a critical point in his training program as he was preparing for a host of international competitions prior to the 2014 Commonwealth Games.

The purpose of this case study is to discuss some of the challenges faced by the athlete in regaining his confidence. Further, challenges faced by the consultant in providing mental training support to the athlete will also be discussed. In particular, the indirect objection from the assistant coach the sport psychology consultant (SPC) encountered in the lead-up to full recovery and personal best performance of the athlete was a significant feature of the work in this case.

BACKGROUND INFORMATION

In 2012, a former coach of mine recommended me and the services I provide to the athlete. After he made contact with me through social media we set up our first meeting. We decided to meet for the first time at a national sporting event we had both planned on attending. This introduction was very informal and set the tone for future sessions.

To date, having sessions in a structured office-type environment has never been done in the work with this athlete. Two of the main locations where we meet are his training facilities and the living room of his home. Our sessions normally begin with very general topics such as local news and activities we did during that particular day.

As a consultant, I not only listen to personal stories from the client but also, where applicable and beneficial, I share some of my life experiences. For instance, I remember an occasion where the athlete was telling me about a tactical error during a race. This mistake caused him to suffer a tragic loss. Immediately, I was able to reflect on my past experiences as an athlete. Similar to this experience I have made mistakes in the past when playing football. At the high-school level one mistake cost us to suffer a semifinal loss and create school history. Sharing this along with an understanding that things can be improved and that one mistake does not define someone had a major impact. Situations like these are ideal in helping athletes understand that they are not alone. I always try to keep things very simple as well. This is essential so that the client not only understands me but also ensures he/she is engaged.

When we first began our sessions we would meet frequently. On average, sessions were held weekly or biweekly. There was a great need for these sessions since the client was injured and experienced some of the psychosocial challenges commonly experienced by an injured athlete (Clement, Arvinen-Barrow, & Fetty, 2014). It took about four months before he was fully recovered.

DESCRIPTION OF THE CASE

Generally speaking, this athlete was normally very intrinsically motivated to train and perform optimally. His passion for the sport was undeniable and clearly visible with the effort and level of focus illustrated during training. His approach made the transition from the junior level to senior and elite level a smooth one. However, he suffered a shoulder injury during a sporting event and was unable to train for a while. Eventually, he went through physical therapy, after which he was cleared to begin training. Being in practice after not being able to train for a while had a major effect on his level of motivation and confidence. There was a particular instance during his training program that illustrated a clear example of his lack of motivation. Usually, he would go to the gym promptly at five o'clock in the morning. Eventually, this shifted to later times and in some instances no training at all. The challenge here was to help a previously naturally motivated athlete find that internal drive once more. Obviously, this impacted his level of confidence and understandably so. Therefore, key features of the work done with this athlete were goal-setting (Vidic & Burton, 2010) and relaxation (Martens, Vealey, & Burton, 1990).

THEORETICAL FRAMEWORK/PHILOSOPHY

The approach used in this case was cognitive behavioral (Dobson & Dozois, 2001) in nature. The athlete was given specific examples of how his thoughts were having a negative impact on his behavior and vice versa. This was essential as he was unaware and confused as to the underlying causes of his dramatic change in behavior and attitude to training.

To illustrate the importance of making small changes and the impact this could have on performance and motivation, we performed various exercises. For example, one of the exercises that illustrates my approach and worked well with the client entailed creating a handout listing the things he did well. In order to do this we first spoke about the things that he believed he had control over as well as those that he could not control. This particular exercise was done so that he would become more task oriented or, in other words, greater efforts by him would increase his chances of success during competition (Newton & Duda, 1993). After our discussion he would be given enough time to write down all the things that he believed he had control over. It was important not to give him a time limit for this activity because he generally does not like to be rushed. Understanding a client's personality is key here. Another reason for not rushing him was to ensure that he was comfortable and could think clearly. It is for this reason that there were no set times for our sessions. The next step was for him to write down the things he has no control over. Through this exercise, he noticed that a pattern of behavior had been formed. During his injury and underperformance, his mind had often been on the things he has no control over. It was explained that both were written down on the handout for two particular reasons. The "controllables" were listed because that is where his mind needs to be since these were his strengths. The "uncontrollables" were listed to build awareness of the things that can limit the amount of attention he is giving to his strengths. Some examples of what he could control were his technique, breathing, and pre-competition routine. The things he had no control over included factors such as his opponents' actions, the venue, and weather conditions. This might seem simple, but thinking about how hot the sun is and how good the opponent is can limit how much attention is given to the pre-competition routines or starts.

NEEDS ASSESSMENT

Because I had been working with this athlete over a two-year period, we were able to build a strong professional yet informal relationship (Andersen, Van Raalte, & Brewer, 2001). After the first year, we would meet occasionally. Structured sessions were planned when either of us decided that the time was right. To determine what his needs were, we simply met one-on-one at his house for an informal conversation. After this meeting, it was decided that a cognitive behavioral framework was the best approach to work on the underlying issues that were eventually discovered. This meeting set the trend for our professional relationship. Our correspondences, sessions, meeting locations and conversations were very relaxed. As our sessions progressed, I observed his behaviors and actions in training and local competitions so that I could form a complete view based on what he described to me and what I noticed.

As a consultant, it is important to have a holistic perspective on what the client's needs are. To do this I spoke with him, his coach, and his mother. Before talking with anyone else, I ensured that he was aware of what I was doing in order to maintain the openness and trust that we had. During this initial meeting with the athlete, I explained the need for my holistic understanding of what his needs were so that I could best tailor his performance-enhancement program. I then had the buy-in from him to meet and talk with these different stakeholders, offering me a holistic point of view on what his needs really were. We use our eyes to see the world and this determines the viewpoint we have on our experiences. Therefore, in order to fully understand him, I needed to see through his eyes, his coach's eyes, and his mother's eyes.

The end result was a list of areas for improvement that sometimes overlapped across the different viewpoints. From the athlete's perspective the anxiety he felt was twofold. It comprised both a cognitive aspect (i.e., negative thoughts due to the pressures of competition) as well as physical responses such as trembling and tightening of muscles (Martens et al., 1990). In most instances, the end result of the anxiety he experienced was subpar performances (Hanin, 2000). His mother spoke about some of the communication and personal issues he had with a coach. The head coach highlighted the importance for him to be focused on his goals. Finally, spending time in the training environment helped me understand and observe the athlete in his natural environment and this proved to be a key element. What was uncovered was the importance of goal setting, effective communication with the coach, and prayer.

INTERVENTION

Despite the different psychological challenges faced as a result of the injury the athlete obtained, training had to continue. The goals of qualifying for the XX Commonwealth Games and the 2016 Olympic Games were still very much alive. In the lead-up to these global events, there are a host of other international competitions used to help athletes maintain their fitness and compete against the world's best athletes. At one of these international events the athlete had a spell of anxiety (Martens et al., 1990). I was not present on this trip, but my services were subsequently required to assist him in refocusing on his ability (Gray, 2004) and relaxing (Martens et al., 1990).

In working on helping him to resolve his anxiety, the first challenge faced was overcoming injury with the use of psychological intervention (Cupal & Brewer, 2001). In other words, we worked on helping him become mentally tough so that he could fully recover from the psychological effects of the injury (i.e., being less motivated to attend gym sessions; feeling that his performance has diminished; anxiety, etc.). My role and function was to help him understand that this was a fixable challenge. It was essential to focus on some of the positive aspects of his training and development since he was mostly thinking about the negative implications of the injury. Specifically, I spoke to him and did the following:

- highlighted past successful experiences;
- discussed previous strategies that helped him recover from injury;
- helped him recognize that post-therapy his training would have been less intense and gradually he would improve his level of performance and intensity;

- reminded him that he had a very strong and competent coaching staff;
- asked leading questions so that he himself would come up with the answers;
- on one occasion I asked: "What helped you to recover mentally, after your previous injury?" This question caused him to really think back and analyze the things that previously helped him have a successful return to competition.

The main approach I utilized in helping him in dealing with his return from injury and anxiety was effectively setting both long-term and short-term goals. The long-term goals were used to give the athlete a sense of direction and purpose; the short-term goals outlined the necessary steps to achieving his overall objectives (Vidic & Burton, 2010).

The following goals were determined and written down during one of our sessions:

- Long-term goal:
  - qualify for the 2016 Summer Olympics in Rio de Janiero, Brazil.

- Short-term goals:
  - attend physical therapy sessions;
  - compete in several local and international tournaments to gain UCI points;
  - execute a training program to be at his peak for tournaments;
  - deep breathing and muscle relaxation exercises to cope with anxiety and nervousness prior to competition;
  - cue word: "execute" game plan at the start of races.

During the first couple of months of work with the athlete, all sessions were free of charge. This continued until he eventually got a major sponsor and offered to pay for the services. As sponsorship grew, the team also grew. The ambience of the training environment changed and so did the mood of the athlete. He became unhappy in training but was not sure why. He would go out and give 100 percent effort as always, but something was amiss. This issue came up in one of our sessions. What was uncovered helped him understand the dynamics of the team and reflect on himself. Initially, there were four athletes on the team, but over the course of our work together the size of the team had more than doubled. Increasing the size of the team meant that there were more people around during training. This posed a challenge for the athlete because he enjoys his space; he is extremely focused during training and this helps him perform optimally. His old teammates and coaches understood this about him. New team members did not quite understand that he wanted his personal space during training. Eventually everything worked out because after discovering the root cause of his unhappiness he shared his feelings with his teammates.

The athlete's assistant coach also played a role in the work with this athlete. I was told in confidence that the assistant coach stated that he felt the athlete was dependent on the consultant and that this could only hurt his performance when I was not around. This is a valid point, but my aim is to empower athletes and encourage them to solve problems independently. Thus, I did not agree with what was said about my practice. This situation proved to be a very sensitive one. As a consultant, it is important to have good rapport with the athlete as well as the coaching staff. In responding to the claims that the athlete was dependent on me I had to ensure that I was as objective as possible and also consider the personality (i.e., in this case outspoken and passionate) of the coach. Eventually, I decided that it would be best to wait for him to approach me to discuss the potential issue. Because I am approachable and have a very good relationship with the coaching staff, my decision proved to be the best one. A potentially problematic situation was resolved without saying a word. There was never any tension, doors were still open to be around the team, and I was encouraged to continue working with the athlete.

In addition to this, the assistant coach had a very controlling style of leadership (Conroy & Coatsworth, 2007). As an individual athlete he worked best with a coach who had a democratic style (Hollembeak & Amorose, 2005). With this new issue forming, it was obvious that communication had to be addressed. Effective communication is what sometimes separates an expert coach from a mediocre one (Bloom, 1996). Although the intention of the assistant coach was good, there were some negative implications (Fraser-Thomas & Côté, 2009).

Another issue that came up was my lack of presence at international events. At times it was important for me to be present prior to international meets. This was necessary because it would have had a positive impact on the athlete. The added support in coping with the pressures of competition and helping him to relax was lacking. A solution to this came in the form of televideo, which helped improve service delivery (Nelson & Velasquez, 2011). Some applications, such as Whatsapp, Viber, and Skype, were used to conduct sessions when he was away. However, there are pros (Heaney, 2013) and cons (Cotterill, 2012) to using technology and social media, and these needed to be taken into consideration when using them with the client.

For our sessions, Whatsapp (a popular free app that can be used to send and receive text messages and voice recordings within seconds) worked well. What I particularly like about this app was the fact that we were both able to see two things. It showed us when a message was delivered as well as when it had been read. This avoided the confusion of whether a message was delivered or not. Viber also has these features. Additionally, calls can be made, although the quality is sometimes poor and connections can be lost. Skype proved to be the best application for us as it is the only one of the three that offers real-time audiovisual features. The use of communication apps worked well in limiting the negative impact my lack of presence had on his performance.

However, as mentioned above, there are some ethical and confidentiality implications in using technology and any type of online consultations (APA, 1996). To limit some of the possible negative consequences in using these apps, the following steps were taken:

1. We both found a very quiet and private place to be during these interactions so that we were away from crowds and other individuals.
2. Headphones were used as opposed to speakers (phones and laptops).
3. Sessions were not recorded and no screenshots were taken.
4. During sessions both parties made sure to be comfortable with the surroundings prior to and during online sessions.

It has been three years since our first meeting. The work done with this athlete has had a positive impact on his performance. These positive results have helped us maintain our informal yet professional relationship (Andersen et al., 2001). Additionally, I believe that working with him free of charge initially and having discussions about other areas such as personal development helped illustrate my commitment to helping him perform optimally (Bond, 2002). This obviously had a positive impact on our relationship by showing that I was committed to him and his overall development versus being driven by a desire to make money.

REFLECTION

The experiences working with this athlete were very positive and educational. An athlete's true strength was tested, challenges were faced that offered opportunities to grow, and relationships were strengthened. Thinking back on the strides he made provides many lessons about the human spirit. As an athlete, injuries are a daunting experience. Transitioning from being injured to regaining full fitness calls for hard work, discipline, commitment, and faith. Some of these qualities were lacking in this athlete, thus creating low confidence and a confused and unmotivated individual. Helping him understand the negative impact the injury was having on him called for ongoing sessions. In meeting with him over a few months, we were able to analyze the effect of the injury on his training. Working on the target areas (i.e., anxiety, goals, communication) allowed him to use practical strategies in order to improve his performance.

One of the greatest challenges faced by this athlete was not only the fear of re-injuring himself, but actually doing so after making a full recovery. He believed that all the hard work had been done in vain. It was a daunting experience for him to have to start over again. These were the reasons he began losing interest in training and lost that intrinsic motivation he once had. There was no easy solution to this problem. To ensure that he understood this I first suggested that we meet at a location of his choice. His home was the best location and this was very important since I needed him to be as comfortable as possible so he would really open up in order for me to understand him fully. I kept our session very informal by beginning with general questions such as: "What did you do today?" I left the decision of talking about the injury up to him. As the session continued I took it upon myself to ask some leading questions versus directly telling him what I thought he should do. Some of those questions included:

- What helped you recover from your last injury?
- Did you have any of these negative thoughts before?
- How long did it take you to regain your confidence after the last injury?

The purpose of asking these questions was to ensure that he did some in-depth thinking about strategies used in recovering from past injuries. Using this approach allowed him to take ownership of making the best decisions and taking the most effective actions toward a full recovery.

Besides the challenge of helping an elite athlete recover from injury, the other major issue I faced involved the athlete's assistant coach, who felt sessions between the athlete and I would have a negative impact on the athlete's psychological state. His belief was that the athlete should be able to prepare himself mentally to cope with the challenges of training and competition. It was the assistant coach's view that the athlete would develop a dependency on our sessions versus being independent and empowered to perform optimally. This made the athlete very uncomfortable, to the point where there was a need for us to address the issue of communication.

In dealing with this potential issue I suggested that the decision to continue or terminate our sessions rested solely in his hands. I took this approach to avoid pressuring the athlete as well as to avoid confrontation or conflict with the assistant coach. In going forward, the athlete decided he would continue our sessions. Some of our sessions were unknown to the assistant coach. He was later made aware of the sessions after it was clear that the athlete was not dependent on them. It should be noted that this occurred in the lead-up to a personal best performance.

SUGGESTED READINGS

Crossman, J. (2001). *Coping with sports injuries: Psychological strategies for rehabilitation.* Oxford: Oxford University Press.

Watson, N. J., & Czech, D. (2005). The use of prayer in sport: Implications for sport psychology consulting. *Athletic Insight, 7*(4), 26–35.

REFLECTIVE QUESTIONS

1. How should a practitioner's approach differ when working with an elite athlete versus an athlete at a lower level? Why?
2. How should you approach working with an athlete that has lost his or her motivation after an injury?
3. What do you do when an athlete is interested in seeing you for individual sessions but the coach is against it?

4. How can you help an athlete increase his or her level of confidence?
5. How would you approach working with an elite athlete who no longer wants to train?
6. What may be one of the biggest hurdles faced by athletes after an injury?
7. How could the approach utilized in this case study be tailored to work with athletes within a team environment?

REFERENCES

Andersen, M. B., Van Raalte, J. L., & Brewer, B. W. (2001). Sport psychology service delivery: Staying ethical while keeping it loose. *Professional Psychology: Research and Practice, 32*, 12–18.

APA (1996). Report of the ethics committee, 1995. *American Psychologist, 51*, 1279–1286.

Bloom, G. A. (1996). Life at the top. In J. H. Salmela (Ed.), *Great job coach!* (pp. 139–178). Ottawa: Potentium.

Bond, J. (2002). Applied sport psychology: Philosophy, reflections and experience. *International Journal of Sport Psychology, 33*, 19–37.

Clement, D., Arvinen-Barrow, M., & Fetty, T. (2014). Psychosocial responses during different phases of sport injury rehabilitation: A qualitative study. *Journal of Athletic Training, 50*(1), 95–104.

Conroy, D. E., & Coatsworth, J. D. (2007). Assessing autonomy-supportive coaching strategies in youth sport. *Psychology of Sport and Exercise, 8*, 671–684.

Cupal, D. D., & Brewer, B. W. (2001). Effects of relaxation and guided imagery on knee strength, reinjury anxiety, and pain following anterior cruciate ligament reconstruction. *Rehabilitation Psychology, 46*(1), 28–43.

Dobson, K. S., & Dozois, D. J. A. (2001). Historical and philosophical bases of the cognitive-behavioral therapies. In K. S. Dobson (Ed.), *Handbook of cognitive-behavioral therapies* (2nd ed., pp. 3–39). New York, NY: Guilford Press.

Fraser-Thomas, J., & Côté, J. (2009). Understanding adolescents' positive and negative developmental experiences in sport. *The Sport Psychologist, 23*, 3–23.

Gray, R. (2004). Attending to the execution of a complex sensorimotor skill: Expertise differences, choking and slumps. *Journal of Experimental Psychology: Applied, 10*, 42–54.

Hanin, Y. L. (Ed.) (2000). *Emotions in sport*. Champaign; IL: Human Kinetics.

Heaney, C. (2013). Keeping sport and exercise scientists 'appy': online and mobile technologies in sport and exercise science. *The Sport & Exercise Scientist, 37*, 14–15.

Hollembeak, J., & Amorose, A. J. (2005). Perceived coaching behaviors and college athletes' intrinsic motivation: A test of self-determination theory. *Journal of Applied Sport Psychology, 17*, 20–36.

Martens, R., Vealey, R. S., & Burton, D. (1990). *Competitive anxiety in sport*. Champaign, IL: Human Kinetics.

Nelson, E. L., & Velasquez, S. E. (2011). Implementing psychological services over televideo. *Professional Psychology: Research and Practice 42*(6), 535–542.

Newton, M., & Duda, J. (1993). Elite adolescent athletes' achievement goals and beliefs concerning success in tennis. *Journal of Sport & Exercise Psychology, 15*, 437–448.

Vidic, Z., & Burton, D. (2010). The roadmap: Examining the impact of a systematic goal-setting program for collegiate women's tennis. *The Sport Psychologist, 24*(4), 427–447.

5 The Challenges of Providing Performance Psychology Services in Taiwan

A Case Study

Chung-Ju Huang (Glen), Tsung-Min Hung, and Tai-Ting Chen

In Taiwan, the certification system for sport psychology consultants (SPCs) has been established since 2008. Typically, our certified SPCs endeavor to improve athletes' performance at the national and international levels and provide quality services for athletes and coaches. Given that sport psychology services gradually become the norm at all levels of competitive sport, there are some challenges to advance sport psychology service delivery and increase the credibility of SPCs working with athletes. The focus of this chapter is to describe the experience of providing sport psychology services to an elite boxer, highlight our working approach, and discuss several reflections on our services. Hopefully, the reader can learn some useful strategies that have worked in Taiwan and make the necessary alterations to apply this approach to one's own culture.

BACKGROUND INFORMATION

The opportunity to provide sport psychology consultation for a boxing team was largely credited to the persistent requests of a high-school coach. This coach holds a doctorate degree in sports science, is a licensed fitness trainer, and formerly coached the national women's boxing team in Taiwan. He not only teaches boxing techniques, but also places considerable emphasis on physical conditioning training. However, the coach observed that his boxers often failed to reach their target goals despite exhibiting favorable advantages due to physical conditioning and technique. He inferred that this might be due to a lack of good psychological qualities. After accepting the coach's request, the SPC was assigned to collaborate with the boxing team. The SPC provided three hours of consultation services per week over a span of two years. In order to establish a trusting relationship, the SPC observed the interactions between the coach and the athletes as well as the team management philosophy, and developed a better understanding of boxing techniques and physical training. The SPC also researched boxing knowledge and regulations in order to better communicate with the coach and athletes. The sport psychology services provided by the SPC included psychological skills education and training, team management, individual consultations, small group consultations, and competition observations. Psychological skills training focused on recognizing demanding situations and coping with pressure as well as building self-confidence; individual consultations focused on resolving individual challenges; and group consultations focused on reinforcing athlete–athlete and coach–athlete interactions. Additionally, the SPC accompanied the team to competitions to assess the stability of athletic performance and the application of psychological skills during training and competitions.

DESCRIPTION OF THE CASE

Tina is an 18-year-old female boxer who had won a Youth World Championship gold medal. The SPC spent more than a year working with her. Coincidentally, she was actively preparing for the Asian Games during the year in which psychological services were provided. It was highly anticipated by the public and media that she would win a medal at the Asian Games, which imposed considerable pressure on her. Her coach requested the SPC assist her in improving her performance in order to reach her goals.

Based on a conversation with the coach and Tina, the SPC discovered that she was experiencing increasing stress from internal and external sources because of the approaching Asian Games. In terms of external stress, Tina was considered an athlete of value by relevant government units and gained considerable media attention because she had won a gold medal in an international tournament. Additionally, her coach had high expectations of her, requesting that she should comply with a challenging training regime. Her coach also arranged for her to train with heavyweight boxers to foster her persistence and fighting spirit, which caused her to feel fear and stress. In terms of internal stress, Tina was constantly physically and mentally fatigued due to excessive and intensive daily training. She felt she could never meet her coach's expectations. These emotions negatively influenced her motivation, and even led to withdrawal. She also demonstrated communication challenges with her coach, revealing an emotional suppression that inhibited her from expressing her needs and opinions. Moreover, she felt frustrated that she was unable to gain a competitive advantage even though she demonstrated superior physical conditioning over her peers.

The effects of internal and external pressures negatively affected Tina. The coach attempted to resolve Tina's issues once they became apparent to him. Following her physical conditioning assessments, Tina and several other athletes traveled to the United States under the coach's supervision to attend a six-week conditioning enhancement program at a professional training center. The SPC continued to provide individual consultations to help with her stress management challenges. Tina felt extremely depressed during her stay in the United States because of the intensity of the program. The SPC sent her emails of encouragement, and provided social support to help her conquer her challenges. Later, the SPC accompanied Tina to an invitational competition in China. Unfortunately, she was defeated by a Chinese contestant during the second round. After the competition, the SPC attended a debriefing between Tina and her coach, in which the reasons for Tina's defeat were highlighted, including the inability to identify opportunities and land effective attacks, over-thinking, worrying about the outcome, throwing too few punches, and inability to focus on the match. These issues implied that the stress Tina experienced was disrupting her concentration. The SPC and the coach collaboratively pitched a number of constructive suggestions to Tina, urging her to boldly experiment with new techniques to accentuate her superior qualities of speed, punching power, and coordination. During the course of the invitational competition, athletes at the same level would privately arrange friendly matches against one another. After accepting the suggestions proposed by the SPC and her coach, Tina set aside her burden of winning, overcame her flaws, and endeavored to try new tactics, consequently transforming into a confident athlete toward the end of the competition. Both Tina and her coach believed that enhancing stress management and concentration were key training objectives.

THEORETICAL FRAMEWORK/PHILOSOPHY

Tina's major issue was that her commitment to her goals began to waver under the influence of internal and external pressures, causing her to withdraw. Consequently, she was unable to exert her full potential during competitions. In order to help the boxer enhance her athletic performance, sport psychology consultations based on the model of cognitive behavioral therapy (CBT) were implemented. The process of enhancing positive behaviors and reducing negative behaviors in the pursuit of a specific goal is the focus of this approach, which has proven appealing to SPCs working on performance enhancement in athletes (Smith, 2006).

Using this approach, clients are generally asked to learn to adapt according to their cognitive experiences, to view challenges positively, and to propose solutions to issues. Then, the clients can obtain favorable emotional regulation and establish reasonable beliefs through cognitive change, ultimately gaining self-recognition and achieving behavioral change (Kurpius & Morran, 1988). Therefore, the SPC utilized strategies to encourage cognitive restructuring and self-instruction to facilitate the growth of Tina's awareness of psychological weakness and her application of appropriate mental skills. Following a cognitive behavioral approach, cognitive restructuring was used to set task-oriented goals focusing on self-improvement in an attempt to modify Tina's maladaptive thoughts regarding achievement and to strengthen her intrinsic motivation. In addition, mental imagery was used to familiarize Tina with game strategies and to help her scrutinize her modified skills. Further, positive self-talk was utilized to activate mental processes to change negative thought patterns in an effort to increase self-confidence, effort, and cognitive and emotional control (Williams, Zinsser, & Bunker, 2010).

NEEDS ASSESSMENT

To effectively resolve Tina's challenges, her coach and the SPC engaged in extensive discussions to determine which sport psychology services were applicable to her. Her coach remained in close contact with the SPC. He believed that this was the first time he had trained such an outstanding, world-class athlete, and that she stood a chance of winning a medal in the Asian Games and potentially advancing to the Olympic Games. The coach also aspired to develop a training model that could foster Olympic-level athletes, which is unprecedented in Taiwan. To achieve this goal, he had spent countless hours in learning and contemplation, and desperately needed the SPC's assistance. After engaging in extensive discussions with the coach, and observing the training and competitions of Tina, the SPC and coach decided to begin with strengthening her mental toughness. Mental toughness refers to a collection of values, attitudes, behaviors, and emotions that enable individuals to persevere and cope with adversity while also promoting and maintaining their adaptation to positive situations (Gucciardi, Godon, & Dimmock, 2008). The characteristics of a mentally tough athlete cover self-belief, desire, motivation, concentration, the ability to cope with stress and anxiety, as well as the ability to manage physical and mental suffering (Jones, Hanton, & Connaughton, 2002). Therefore, the level of Tina's mental toughness was evaluated in order to develop effective interventions via several channels. First, communication with her coach and the observation of practices and competitions were undertaken to understand the mental toughness issues for the boxer. Second, the SPC utilized a measure of mental toughness (Huang, 2004) that includes three subscales (self-discipline/being positive, coping with pressure, and endurance in the face of pain) to evaluate Tina's level of mental toughness using a five-point Likert scale. The average scores on the mental toughness subscales were 4.0 for self-discipline, 3.5 for coping with pressure, and 4.0 for endurance in the face of pain. The lowest score of all was the ability to cope with stress. Third, based on the results of the inventory evaluation, a follow-up interview was conducted to identify the client's mental toughness issues. Tina was interviewed to discover the extent to which she: (a) could autonomously participate in daily practice; (b) was confident in her ability to attain her goals; (c) could cope with the adversities happening at practice and competition; and (d) could quickly recover from physical exhaustion after practice. Following these procedures, it would be helpful to the SPC to undertake a more objective assessment of Tina's needs. However, taking into consideration the time left for the intervention, the SPC focused on developing strategies to enhance the boxer's mental toughness, including her self-belief, desire and motivation, and self-control ability, in the hopes of helping her to achieve her goal of winning a medal in the Asian Games.

INTERVENTION

As a result of the needs assessment, several aspects of mental toughness that the boxer needed to develop and strengthen were identified. To facilitate the development of these aspects of mental toughness, the boxer was taught various psychological skills, including goal-setting and self-talk, and her coach was asked to use specific strategies to change his coaching behavior. First, with regard to cognitive restructuring, and in order to enhance her training motivation, the issue of over-training needed to be addressed. When the body sent out fatigue or pain signals, Tina actively communicated with her coach to avoid possible injuries. The SPC also instructed the coach to value the responses of his athletes and to establish mutual trust with them.

Second, the SPC instructed the coach to explain the training regime to Tina, pointing out how each aspect of her program benefited her abilities, and how these abilities could be utilized to gain a competitive advantage during competitions. This enabled her to understand the importance of her training routine. For example, physical conditioning training often consists of numerous core exercises at varying intensities, such as deep squats, half squats, and leg lifts. The reason for these exercises is to elevate punching power, which originates from the lower body. Once Tina better understood that these exercises could help her overpower her opponents, she felt less burdened and more joyful when doing them. Similarly, different training sets translate into different power training effects. Once she began to discuss training sets with her coach, she became more enthusiastic about the training. She even trained during the weekends.

Third, the boxer must surmount the strategies and tactics used by her opponents by fully utilizing her strengths. Once the problems of physical conditioning and power were effectively resolved, the next problem to take into account was competition tactics. In the past, Tina employed a conservative style of boxing, which could neither highlight her physical conditioning and power superiority nor reflect the aggressive boxing styles popular in international competitions. And yet Tina's advantages in boxing originated from her speed, power, coordination, and control. The coach and the SPC jointly provided her with constructive suggestions so that she would more willingly experiment with open boxing styles during practice matches and actively create opportunities to land effective attacks. Tina practiced aggressive boxing strategies during daily training in order to flexibly apply these strategies to competitions. At present, boxing competitions are extremely aggressive. If boxers are unable to actively utilize their strengths, it is hard to subdue opponents in an even match. In a number of later regional competitions, Tina was able to adopt a more aggressive boxing style, for which she received considerable praise from other coaches. The recognition of other coaches elevated Tina's confidence, and reassured her that her changed approach was for the better.

Fourth, the boxer's pressure management during competitions had to be improved. During competitions, Tina's strong desire to win might cause her to lose concentration. In particular, when she was at a slight disadvantage, her body and mind might begin to stiffen, and she would start to exhibit dampened coordination and adopt increasingly conservative strategies, eventually losing the match. The SPC believed that favorable outcomes came from a smooth process, and therefore recommended the use of situational simulations to enhance Tina's concentration during competition. Tina and her coach first predetermined several scenarios that she needed to overcome and identified counter strategies, and then they engaged in repeated drills and corrections. This taught Tina how to think and respond in different circumstances, and taught her to focus on resolving problems rather than winning. Gradually, Tina felt that she could more easily cope with difficult situations. Her perceived stress lowered and she could more naturally exert herself, thereby fueling her self-confidence.

Fifth, the SPC encouraged Tina to set short- and mid-term goals. She was advised to set more rational processing goals and record these goals into her training log rather than focusing on the goal of winning a medal at the Asian Games. Additionally, a brief log was required to monitor the progress of every strategy and practice reflection, even during periods of travel abroad.

The SPC continued to counsel Tina in changing her negative thoughts toward herself in instances of failure. He reminded her of her dream of becoming a great boxer, explaining that each match expanded her views and enriched her life, and that she could learn from both success and failure. The SPC suggested Tina learn to digest the frustration generated from failure, and explained that her daily training would ready her for change and assist her in gradually realizing her dreams. After an eight-month intervention, Tina's level of mental toughness was evaluated again through a face-to-face interview. The result of the evaluation was satisfying, indicating that she felt a significant improvement in terms of being positive and confident, and in terms of controlling her own emotions under pressure. Regarding positivity and confidence, Tina said:

> Recently, I feel like I am in peak form. I feel better during weight loss, competition, and training than I did before. My competition performance, physical conditioning, and technique have all been above par recently, and I feel that I am performing better than before. Regarding technique, I stand more firmly during competitions and jump around less. My goal is to do well at the Asian Games, hopefully receiving a medal or even winning the championship.

Regarding coping with stress, she asserted:

> I am better at managing pressure. In the United States, training was so exhausting that I almost collapsed, but I managed to pull through. I didn't cope well with pressure during the competition in China. However, my adaptation to competitions has improved. I am less worried and more focused on exerting the techniques that we practiced.

Regarding pain endurance, she stated:

> I was in agony during training then. I almost broke down and cried. Now, I am more positive. The persistence and hard work I put into training are all worthwhile for my future.

REFLECTION

One of the most critical missions for a competent SPC is to help resolve the challenges encountered by coaches and athletes. Therefore, through the applied experience, the SPC developed more mature and flexible consulting skills, and learned how to provide an efficient sport psychology service. The consultation with the boxer provided opportunities for the SPC to integrate theory and practice, gradually increasing the ability to self-reflect. These improvements contributed to the establishment of a more professionalized SPC role (Wylleman, Harwood, Elbe, Reints, & de Caluwe, 2009).

In Taiwan, SPCs are typically worried about undermining coaches. However, this problem was non-existent in the context of this boxing team because the coach placed complete faith in the SPC. The coach understood that the cooperation with the SPC was intended to help the boxer achieve her goals and make history. Moreover, during the consultation, the SPC also encountered the issues of mental toughness himself. The SPC was required to actively and immediately identify ways to help the client surpass her own limits within difficult situations, and perform better than her rivals. Therefore, Tina's response and performance always stimulated and challenged the SPC. After the completion of the service, the SPC felt a qualitative improvement in his ability to rapidly rebound from pressure and negative emotions, and became more competent. Below are some general reflections about the work done with the client.

Establishing relationships is a key aspect of being a successful SPC. Therefore, throughout the SP service, time was spent on developing relationships with the coach and athlete.

This was done through strategies such as staying at residential training camps, attending dinner and breakfast meetings, walking to the field with the coaches and athletes, attending training, email and telephone contact with coaches, and attending coaching staff meetings. Further, a quality SP service should include collaborating with other professionals from different fields of sports science. In practice, SPCs are able to formulate better solutions to athletes' issues if relevant referential information is available to them. For example, if information relating to physiological indicators and injury prognosis are available during consultations, SPCs can immediately deduce the presence of injury or fatigue caused by overtraining. Then, SPCs can combine these diagnostics with psychological assessments to develop better interventions and provide more effective services. Therefore, the training center or the team should try to establish a platform that offers relevant test results for specific items to sport science practitioners, assisting the athletes and coaches in formulating optimal strategic decisions.

The SPC in Taiwan is not a permanent member of a team. Relevant services are typically incorporated six months to a year prior to each competition. Thus, SPCs are faced with understanding athletes' new problems, acquainting themselves to new team members, and familiarizing themselves with new training items. As sport psychology consultation services do not include long-term monitoring, psychological assessments have to be re-administered to reflect extant conditions of athletes. This process is extremely time- and labor-intensive. Moreover, the majority of SPCs are members of university faculties who are only able to provide limited services once or twice per week. In this regard, job opportunities for SPCs are indeed necessary for the provision of long-term services that can offer immediate and quality SP consultations.

SUGGESTED READINGS

Barker, J. B., McCarthy, P. J., & Harwood, C. G. (2011). Reflections on consulting in elite youth male English cricket and soccer academies. *Sport and Exercise Psychology Review, 7*, 58–72.

Brown, J. L. (2011). Cognitive-behavioral strategies. In J. K. Luiselli & D. D. Reed (Eds.), *Behavioral sport psychology: Evidence-based approaches to performance enhancement* (pp. 113–126). New York, NY: Springer.

Cotterill, S. T., & Symes, R. (2014). Integrating social media and new technologies into your practice as a sport psychology consultant. *Sport and Exercise Psychology Review, 10*, 55–64.

Huang, C. J., Hung, T. M., & Chen, T. T. (2014). The process of providing sport psychology services in Taiwan. In J. G. Cremades & L. S. Tashman (Eds.), *Becoming a sport, exercise, and performance psychology professional: A global perspective* (pp. 39–44). New York, NY: Routledge.

Sharp, L., & Hodge, K. (2011). Sport psychology consulting effectiveness: The sport psychology consultant's perspective. *Journal of Applied Sport Psychology, 23*, 360–376.

REFLECTIVE QUESTIONS

1. How might an SPC work with an athlete who is referred by a coach?
2. What are your considerations for choosing an appropriate measure to evaluate an athlete's psychological characteristics?
3. What kind of theoretical framework would you use when working with an athlete similar to the one described in this chapter?
4. What kind of psychological skills would you utilize to enhance an athlete's mental toughness?
5. What challenges might an SPC face when the athlete is a busy traveler? How could the SPC and athlete deal with these challenges?

REFERENCES

Gucciardi, D. F., Godon, S., & Dimmock, J. A. (2008). Towards an understanding of mental toughness in Australian Football. *Journal of Applied Sport Psychology, 20,* 261–281.

Huang, C. J. (2004). Establishing the construct of mental toughness for sport: Preliminary investigation and instrument development. Unpublished doctoral dissertation, National Taiwan Normal University, Taipei, Taiwan.

Jones, G., Hanton, S., & Connaughton, D. (2002). What is this thing called mental toughness? An investigation of elite sports performers. *Journal of Applied Sport Psychology, 14,* 205–218.

Kurpius, D. J., & Morran, D. K. (1988). Cognitive-behavioral techniques and interventions for application in counselor supervision. *Counselor Education and Supervision, 27,* 368–376.

Smith, R. E. (2006). Understanding sport behavior: A cognitive-affective processing systems approach. *Journal of Applied Sport Psychology, 18,* 1–27.

Williams, J. M., Zinsser, N., & Bunker, L. (2010). Cognitive techniques for building confidence and enhancing performance. In J. M. Williams (Ed.), *Applied sport psychology: Personal growth to peak performance* (6th ed.; pp. 305–335). Boston, MA: McGraw-Hill.

Wylleman, P., Harwood, C., Elbe, A. M., Reints, A., & de Caluwe, D. (2009). A perspective on education and professional development in applied sport psychology. *Psychology of Sport and Exercise, 10,* 435–446.

6 The Ethical Intricacies of Injury Rehabilitation Within a Dance Training Context

Gene M. Moyle

When working within physically based career pursuits such as dance, dealing with the challenges of injuries and injury rehabilitation has been observed to be a regular occurrence. As a result, dance training institutions have a responsibility to assist students in accessing the multidisciplinary healthcare services required to effectively treat injuries, in addition to increasing their knowledge of injury prevention, safe dance practice, and injury rehabilitation processes. Best-practice models in dance science, medicine, and healthcare typically follow those observed in elite sport, where multidisciplinary health teams are embedded within the organization and work closely with artistic staff to support students' recovery.

As a psychologist employed by a dance training institution, a key component of such a role typically focuses upon supporting students in dealing with both the physical and psychological impacts of injury, whether past, current, or in the future in light of potential career-ending injuries. When working within a team of health professionals and alongside artistic teaching staff, a range of ethical issues can often arise on a daily basis, with multiple stakeholders invested in the individual dance student. The following case study explores the ethical intricacies of working within such a context.

BACKGROUND INFORMATION

"Lucy" was a 15-year-old student who had been accepted into an elite vocational dance training institution. She entered the new full-time training environment with a known 12-month history of stress fracture pathology in both feet, including a chronic second metatarsal fracture, chronic bilateral hip pathology, and pain when walking, standing, and dancing. Despite her existing injury status and history, she was considered to be very talented and had been observed to be the "star pupil" of her previous dance school. From the age of 11, Lucy had reportedly undertaken an exceptionally high dance training and performance workload through participation in competitions, examinations, and performances; with her level of involvement and consequent workload escalating dramatically from 13–14 years of age onwards due to encouragement from her then dance teacher, despite her reported injuries. She stated that she had taken time off from dancing for three months (July–September) during the previous year to try to address her injuries, which had contributed to the timeframe regarding her inability to engage in pointe work for approximately seven months.

Lucy's acceptance into the training institution was on the proviso of entering directly into an intensive three-month rehabilitation program with the focus on returning her to full-time training load as soon as possible. As a result, her case was managed by the psychologist (i.e., this author) in collaboration with a team of internal and external multidisciplinary health professionals who were collectively responsible for managing the health and welfare of all enrolled students. Furthermore, as part of standard processes, Lucy's rehabilitation plan (i.e., timetable for her psychology, physiotherapy, coaching, medical, myotherapy sessions, etc.) was shared with her respective dance teachers. This approach was standard practice and was in place to ensure all stakeholders were kept informed about what dance-related activities Lucy was allowed to engage in, including confirmation of when she could be officially excused from dance classes to attend her other rehabilitation-related appointments.

Lucy stated that it was only confirmed that she had been accepted into the training institution a few days before the commencement of the training year, and as a result her mother traveled with her to move interstate and stay for a couple of weeks into the new term to oversee her transitioning into an independent living situation. At 15 years of age, Lucy reported that this was the first time she had lived independently of her family; she stated that she had strong relationships with her parents and sibling.

The psychologist undertook regular weekly brief sessions with the student (between 30–60 minutes in duration), amounting to a total of 22 sessions within the first three months of Lucy's dance training and rehabilitation program. Selected weekly sessions were delivered in combination with the kinetic educator, with a focus on dance technique execution with targeted performance psychology input, and were informed by current research into the neuroscience and conceptualization of pain (Karin & Moyle, 2011; see Moseley, 2012). These individual sessions were in addition to the standard performance psychology curriculum, which included targeted classes and workshops with Lucy's year group on a range of topics identified as helpful for this type of student dance population (Moyle, 2007, 2008, 2010, 2012; Nordin-Bates, 2010). Furthermore, three phone discussions regarding Lucy's progress were also undertaken with her mother during this same timeframe, with Lucy's full knowledge and consent.

No previous existing history existed between the student and health practitioners (including the author) prior to her commencement at the training institution. Lucy reported that she had previously experienced anxiety and had accessed counseling support for a couple of sessions at that time, but had not engaged any further with other psychological support services. Lucy's understanding of meditation, relaxation, and breathing exercises was explored within one of the first sessions with the psychologist, where she stated that she had undertaken meditation previously, but did not like it.

DESCRIPTION OF THE CASE

Lucy presented as a focused and intelligent adolescent dance student who was navigating a significant personal transition involving moving states, changing schools (both dance and academic), general adolescent physical and mental growth/development, in addition to navigating living independently from her family of origin for the first time. Parallel to this transition was the critical adjustment she was undertaking in terms of her new full-time dance training, in addition to the recognition that she was accepted into the program despite being injured; therefore a primary focus was centered firmly upon her successful rehabilitation.

As outlined previously, Lucy was entering an elite training program with chronic physical injuries that included significant pain when walking, standing, and dancing. Despite it being confirmed to the health team that she was talented and had previously demonstrated high levels of potential, Lucy was also adapting to the new dance training workload that usually incurs both physical and emotional stressors even for non-injured dancers. As a result, Lucy presented with a range of psychological issues, including feeling inadequate in being able to undertake the training activities she was required to do, as well as any challenges that were placed on her as part of her rehabilitation process, such as guilt about letting other people down (i.e., disappointing teachers, health professionals, and her family if her rehabilitation was not successful and she did not end up meeting the original expectations set for her regarding her potential) and a strong fear of injury/re-injury.

THEORETICAL FRAMEWORK/PHILOSOPHY

The primary theoretical models utilized within this case study included cognitive behavior therapy (CBT), solution-focused therapy, acceptance-commitment therapy (ACT) as applied to sport (see Gardner & Moore, 2004, 2007, 2010; Moore & Gardner, 2014), mindfulness as applied to dance (Moyle, 2016; Moyle & Jackson, 2013; Moyle, Jackson, & McCloughan, 2014), and psychological skills training (PST). More specifically, aspects typically covered within the framework of PST, as outlined by Andersen (2009) and Taylor and Taylor (1995) based upon a CBT approach, were additionally explored and applied (i.e., relaxation, self-talk, imagery, goal-setting, concentration).

A primary consideration in the philosophical approach to Lucy's treatment, which was a belief strongly shared by both the kinetic educator and psychologist, included a strong focus on the mind–body connection and ensuring Lucy's injury rehabilitation process assisted in reinforcing this perspective for her. Somatics combined with science in dance education has been extensively researched, discussed, and identified as a critical component within effective dance training and education (Batson & Schwartz, 2007; Caldwell, Adams, Quin, Harrison, & Greeson, 2013; Eddy, 2009; Fortin, Vieira, & Tremblay, 2009; Gerber & Wilson, 2010; Huddy, & Roche, 2014; Kearns, 2010; Sze, Gyurak, Yuan, & Levenson, 2010), in addition to injury prevention in dance (see Hutt, 2010).

NEEDS ASSESSMENT

Assimilation of information from a range of sources assisted in the needs assessment conducted for Lucy, determining her proposed and ongoing treatment during her initial three-month intensive rehabilitation program. These sources included: initial psychology intake consultations; physiotherapy reports; medical screenings (i.e., MRIs); ongoing observations, reflections, and discussions between the treating health practitioners and her respective dance teachers; in addition to the firsthand reflections captured in a rehabilitation journal kept by Lucy (who consented to sharing this information with the kinetic educator and psychologist only).

These varied sources of information indicated that Lucy was experiencing: increased levels of performance anxiety related to her "performance" in dance classes and rehabilitation sessions; a lack of confidence; a fear of failure; an inability to deal effectively with pressure; anxiety related to consideration of career transition issues (i.e., exploring whether to stop dancing and/or return home to her family); adjustment issues related to moving away from home and living independently for the first time at 15 years of age; managing her academic progress regarding completion of her Higher School Certificate alongside her full-time dance training; and adjustment issues related to general adolescent mental and physical transitions (e.g., physical growth and female maturation processes).

INTERVENTION

While Lucy undertook a range of activities as part of her rehabilitation program (e.g., physiotherapy, strength and conditioning, myotherapy, dance technique coaching, medical consultations), the current discussion focuses on the key approach in Lucy's treatment – the kinetic education (i.e., somatic) and psychology combined sessions. This approach was discussed and developed in collaboration between the kinetic educator and psychologist, and included a highly integrated approach between these two areas.

On top of the regularly scheduled individual somatic and psychology consultations, on a weekly basis Lucy would undertake a combined session with both practitioners. The aim of these sessions was to support the development of Lucy's respect for her body's signals (i.e., pain), including the awareness that these signals were not always accurate, in addition to helping her to take "back" control of her body. The format of these combined sessions included:

1. a 30-minute relaxation and imagery session with the psychologist;
2. brief discussion between kinetic educator and psychologist regarding Lucy's responses to the relaxation and imagery session (i.e., what worked, what did not), including her reported current experience of pain and status of her psychological state; and
3. a 30-minute combined somatic practice session delivered by the kinetic educator and the psychologist which focused upon tactile feedback related to alignment and re-training of dance technique, reinforcement of imagery used in the relaxation session with the psychologist, and the introduction and/or reinforcement of performance cues to tie all mind–body aspects together.

The psychology sessions, both individual and combined, were focused on addressing Lucy's identified needs, and included hypnosis-based relaxation sessions, imagery, CBT, ACT, mindfulness, and PST. Individual sessions followed a more traditional approach in looking to support Lucy in developing the mental skills to effectively cope with the various adjustments and transitional issues she was facing. Furthermore, the sessions assisted in checking in on the psychological progress of her injury rehabilitation, particularly within the context of being accepted into full-time dance training not being at full capacity (i.e., injury-free) and the pressure that was reportedly, and observably, being experienced by her.

As Lucy had identified that she had previously tried meditation and it did not work for her, the approach to her relaxation and imagery sessions centered on utilization of hypnosis suggestibility techniques (i.e., induction stage) to assist her in reaching a comfortable state in which to then introduce further relaxation techniques. These techniques included: progressive muscle relaxation (PMR), body scans, diaphragmatic breathing, and mindfulness. Once a relaxed mental state was achieved, it was then paired with guided imagery focusing upon the parts of her body she reported as particularly painful at the start of the session.

REFLECTION

The provision of health services within a performing arts training institution is not dissimilar to those models encountered when working within a sporting institute or organization. The integrated nature of such service delivery is of benefit to the "end-user" (i.e., athlete, dance student) when managed effectively; however, the complexities regarding ethical concerns in such a context become paramount for the practitioner to understand. These ethical issues tend to center around the challenges presented by managing multiple relationships and boundaries, confidentiality, informed consent, and conflicting demands related to the psychologist's organizational role(s).

As outlined by Moyle (2014), there are a range of ethical issues that surface when working within unique sport, exercise, and performance settings, such as a dance training institution. In the current case study, ethical issues included:

1. Management of student information and confidentiality among a team of multidisciplinary health practitioners and numerous artistic teaching staff, including the management of direct contact and communication with the student.

   a. For example, certain artistic staff responsible for Lucy's year level would be observed to interrogate her directly with regards to her rehabilitation progress; often trying to find out what was specifically discussed within her individual psychology sessions. As an adolescent, and with the power differential of being questioned by one of the institution's staff members (who would also be one of her examiners), this would often place Lucy in a position of coercion and stress. It was the responsibility of the psychologist to address this with the staff member directly, outlining the potential negative impacts upon Lucy (both mentally and physically), in addition to continuing to highlight the ethical responsibility of the psychologist in maintaining confidentiality as a requirement of the Australian Psychological Society's (APS) Code of Ethics (2007). Furthermore, assertiveness training was undertaken with Lucy that focused upon effective and respectful communication, should such circumstances arise in the future.

2. Management of potential multiple relationships of the practitioner.

   a. For example, in addition to the specific service provided to Lucy via the individual psychology and combined sessions with the kinetic educator, the psychologist was also required to fulfill the role of rehabilitation case manager and performance psychology teacher to her year level. These multiple roles necessitated a conscious awareness of the multiple relationships occurring with Lucy, and involved the careful management of potential ethical conflicts before they arose.

3. Management of an adolescent (i.e., under legal age) client including such issues as the level of parental consultation with regards to their level of involvement, the limits of confidentiality, and associated boundaries.

4. Management of the expectations of artistic teaching staff and administration regarding the student's rehabilitation progress and dance technique re-training. In addition, aiding in their understanding of how Lucy's progress in these areas impacted upon her ability to complete practical examinations resulting in course progression considerations (i.e., whether Lucy would have to repeat the same year level again because her injury rehabilitation progress was too slow).

The consideration of confidentiality concerns was paramount to the establishment of the effectiveness of psychological (and other) rehabilitation interventions with Lucy. The boundaries of confidentiality were clarified directly with her within the initial session, including outlining explicitly how her general health and rehabilitation information would be utilized. This was very important in light of the integrated case management model and the standard protocols of sharing information related to Lucy's training progress with the health and artistic teams collectively. Additionally, it was critical to building and maintaining the therapeutic relationship, that the general information shared as part of her rehabilitation program (including the combined intervention sessions with the kinetic educator) was clearly distinguished from the information she shared with the psychologist during sessions. Further, given her status as a minor, discussions with Lucy were undertaken that explored the requirements of confidentiality and reporting with respect to her parents. A process was agreed to with regards to interactions and what explicitly would be shared with either of her parents should they make contact, outside of the legal requirements of breaking confidentiality should Lucy be at risk of harming herself or others.

Another key ethical consideration related to this case included the question of "Who is the client?" The psychologist was employed by the training institution with a focus on delivery of psychological services to all enrolled students, through individual sessions and group performance psychology training lectures and workshops. These psychological services additionally included addressing the psychological aspects of injury experienced by injured students via supporting effective rehabilitation processes. In such situations the practitioner has to balance the institution's (and typically the student's) desire to return to full-time training load as soon as possible, which could be at odds with the student's actual health and well-being needs.

Ultimately, a duty of care needs to be prioritized toward what could be argued to be the primary client (i.e., the dance student) and his/her immediate and long-term health and well-being needs. When dealing with an adolescent population, firm consideration needs to be given to any long-term hindering impacts upon both their physical and/or mental development.

Ultimately, the author has observed that management of injury rehabilitation of dancers and athletes by a multidisciplinary team is highly beneficial and more effective than independent treatment approaches. Furthermore, joint intervention processes have been observed to provide a rich context through which mind–body connections can be explored in depth, as long as the ethical issues of confidentiality, boundaries, and multiple relationships are clearly discussed and understood.

ACKNOWLEDGMENTS

The author would like to acknowledge Janet Karin OAM, who was a co-collaborator on this case and contributed significantly to the establishment of the identified approach and co-servicing model that was undertaken.

SUGGESTED READINGS

Buckroyd, J. (2000). *The student dancer: Emotional aspects of the teaching and learning of dance*. London: Dance Books Ltd.

Hamilton, L. H. (1997). *The person behind the mask: A guide to performing arts psychology*. Greenwich, CT: Ablex Publishing Corporation.

Hamilton, L. H. (1998). *Advice for dancers: Emotional counsel and practical strategies*. San Francisco, CA: Jossey-Bass Publishers.

Hamilton, L. H. (2008). *The dancer's way: The New York City Ballet guide to mind, body, and nutrition*. New York, NY: St. Martin's Griffin.

Hays, K. F. (2009). *Performance psychology in action: A casebook for working with athletes, performing artists, business leaders, and professionals in high-risk occupations*. Washington, DC: American Psychological Association.

Hays, K. F. (2012). The psychology of performance in sport and other domains. In S. Murphy (Ed.), *The Oxford handbook of sport and performance psychology* (pp. 24–45). Oxford: Oxford University Press.

Hays, K. F., & Brown Jnr., C. H. (2004). *You're on: Consulting for peak performance*. New York, NY: American Psychological Association.

Kogan, N. (2002). Careers in the performing arts: A psychological perspective. *Creativity Research Journal, 14*, 1–16.

Nordin-Bates, S. M. (2012). Performance psychology in the performing arts. In S. Murphy (Ed.), *The Oxford handbook of sport and performance psychology* (pp. 81–114). Oxford: Oxford University Press.

Moyle, G. M. (2014). Dr. Seuss and the "Great Balancing Act": exploring the ethical places you'll go within Australian sport, exercise, and performance psychology. In G. Cremades & L. S. Tashman (Eds.), *Becoming a sport, exercise, and performance psychology professional: A global perspective* (pp. 45–52). New York, NY: Routledge.

REFLECTIVE QUESTIONS

1. If you were the psychologist in this case study, how would you approach managing the various confidentiality issues related to working with Lucy?
2. Who is "the client" in this case study? Is there more than one? If so, which client takes priority – ethically or legally?
3. What type of case management and treatment approach(es) could be applied in this situation?

4.   What ethical considerations are additionally required when dealing with a client who is a minor? As the psychologist, how would you manage these considerations?
5.   What is the primary outcome that needs to be achieved?

    a.   For Lucy?
    b.   For Lucy's parents?
    c.   For the health team?
    d.   For the artistic teaching team?
    e.   For the training institution?
    f.   Are any of these at odds with each other? If so, how could they be managed?

REFERENCES

Andersen, M. B. (2009). The "canon" of psychological skills training for enhancing performance. In K. F. Hays (Ed.), *Performance psychology in action: A casebook for working with athletes, performing artists, business leaders, and professionals in high-risk occupations* (pp. 11–34). Washington, DC: American Psychological Association.

Australian Psychological Society. (2007). *Code of ethics*. Melbourne, Victoria: Author.

Batson, G., & Schwartz, R. E. (2007). Revisiting the value of somatic education in dance training through an inquiry into practice schedules. *Journal of Dance Education, 7*(2), 47–56.

Caldwell, K., Adams, M., Quin, R. H., Harrison, M., & Greeson, J. (2013). Pilates, mindfulness and somatic education. *Journal of Dance & Somatic Practices, 5*(2), 141–154. DOI: 10.1386/jdsp. 5.2.141_1.

Eddy, M. (2009). A brief history of somatic practices and dance: Historical development of the field of somatic education and its relationship to dance. *Journal of Dance & Somatic Practices, 1*(1), 5–27. DOI: 10.1386/jdsp. 1.1.5/1.

Fortin, S., Vieira, A., & Tremblay, M. (2009). The experience of discourses in dance and somatics. *Journal of Dance and Somatic Practices, 1*(1), 47–64. DOI: 10.1386/jdsp. 1.1.47/1.

Gardner, F. L., & Moore, Z. E. (2004). A mindfulness–acceptance–commitment based approach to performance enhancement: Theoretical considerations. *Behavior Therapy, 35*, 707–723.

Gardner, F. L., & Moore, Z. E. (2007). *The psychology of enhancing human performance: The mindfulness–acceptance–commitment (MAC) approach.* New York, NY: Springer.

Gardner, F. L., & Moore, Z. E. (2010). Acceptance-based behavioural therapies and sport. In S. J. Hanrahan & M. B. Andersen (Eds.), *Routledge handbook of applied sport psychology: A comprehensive guide for students and practitioners* (pp. 186–193). New York, NY: Routledge.

Gerber, P., & Wilson, M. (2010). Teaching at the interface of dance science and somatics. *Journal of Dance Medicine & Science, 14*(2), 50–57.

Huddy, A., & Roche, J. (2014, July). Identity and the dance student: Implementing somatic approaches in the transition into tertiary dance education. Paper presented at *Contemporising the past: Envisaging the future*, World Dance Alliance Global Summit, July 6–11, 2014, Angers, France.

Hutt, K. (2010). Corrective alignment and injury prevention strategies: Science, somatics or both? *Journal of Dance & Somatic Practices, 2*(2), 251–263. DOI: 10.1386/jdsp. 2.2.251_7.

Karin, J., & Moyle, G. M. (2011). Carabosse's curse: The dangers of giftedness. Paper presented at *International Association of Dance Medicine & Science*, 21st Annual Meeting, Washington, DC, USA.

Kearns, L. W. (2010). Somatics in action: How "I feel three-dimensional and real" improves dance education and training. *Journal of Dance Education, 10*(2), 35–40. DOI: 10.1080/15290824.2010.10387158.

Moore, Z. E., & Gardner, F. L. (2014). Mindfulness and performance. In A. Ie, C. T. Ngnoumen and E. J. Langer (Eds.), *The Wiley Blackwell handbook of mindfulness: Vol. 1.* (pp. 986–1003). Hoboken, NJ: Wiley-Blackwell.

Moseley, L. G. (2012). Teaching people about pain: Why do we keep beating around the bush? *Pain Management, 2*(1), 1–3. DOI: 10.2217/pmt.11.73.

Moyle, G. M. (2007). Learnings from the implementation of performance psychology as a subject within a University dance program. *Proceedings of the 17th Annual Meeting of the International Association of Dance Medicine & Science, Canberra, Australia.*

Moyle, G. M. (2008). Performance psychology applied to dance. *Australian Journal of Psychology, 60*(1), 172. DOI: 10.1080/00049530802385558.

Moyle, G. M. (2010). The art of the positive pas de deux: Putting positive psychology into dance! In Mrowinksi, V., Kyrios, M., & Voudouris, N. (Eds.), *Abstracts of the 27th International Congress of Applied Psychology* (pp. 451–454).

Moyle, G. M. (2012). Performance in the spotlight: Exploring psychology in the performing arts. *InPsych*, *34*(6), 11–13.

Moyle, G. M. (2014). Dr. Seuss and the "Great Balancing Act": Exploring the ethical places you'll go within Australian sport, exercise, and performance psychology. In J. Gualberto Cremades & L. S. Tashman (Eds.), *Becoming a sport, exercise, and performance psychology professional: A global perspective* (pp. 45–52). New York, NY: Routledge.

Moyle, G. M. (2016). Mindfulness and dancers. In Amy Baltzell (Ed.), *The Cambridge companion to mindfulness and performance* (pp. 367–388). New York, NY: Cambridge University Press.

Moyle, G. M., & Jackson, S. A. (2013, November). Mindfulness-meditation on the move: Implementation of an ACT-based mindfulness practice intervention and training within a University Dance program. Paper presented at the Australian Society for Performing Arts Healthcare Conference, 22–24 November 2013, QLD Conservatorium, Brisbane, QLD Australia.

Moyle, G. M., Jackson, S. A., & McCloughan, L. J. (2014). *Mindfulness on the move: The impact of mindfulness training within a university dance program.* Manuscript in preparation.

Nordin-Bates, S. M. (2012). Performance psychology in the performing arts. In S. Murphy (Ed.), *The Oxford handbook of sport and performance psychology* (pp. 81–114). Oxford: Oxford University Press.

Sze, J. A., Gyurak, A., Yuan, J. W., & Levenson, R. W. (2010). Coherence between emotional experience and physiology: Does body awareness training have an impact? *Emotion, 10*(6), 803–814.

Taylor, J., & Taylor, C. (1995). *Psychology of dance.* Champaign, IL: Human Kinetics.

7 Barcelona's Campaign to Promote Parents' Sportspersonship in Youth Sports

Jaume Cruz, Yago Ramis, and Miquel Torregrosa

BACKGROUND INFORMATION

During the last decade of the twentieth century, Spain in general and Barcelona in particular experienced a sporting boom. Following the nomination of Barcelona to host the XXV Summer Olympic Games, sport became a priority in all its dimensions. New infrastructures were built for the Olympics, the different institutions invested both in elite and youth sport, and sport was also a priority in the research domain. Within this context youth sport was a center of interest. Researchers were interested in investigating the nature of the competitions, the quality of the experience through which young people passed during their participation in sport, and the degree of preparation and the quality of participation of coaches, parents, referees, and organizers (Boixadós, Valiente, Mimbrero, Torregrosa, & Cruz, 1998; Cruz, Boixadós, Torregrosa, & Mimbrero, 1996; Petrus, 1998).

The Barcelona Sport Council, having assessed coaches' and players' suggestions on fair play and sportspersonship in youth sport, realized that the main problems associated with sporting competitions were related not to on-field situations but rather had occurred off the field. While athletes' attitudes and behaviors were considered acceptable, spectators' behaviors, especially those directed toward referees and officials, were inadequate.

DESCRIPTION OF THE CASE

Despite the great success of Spanish athletes in the 1992 Barcelona Summer Olympics, and the fact that numerous new sports facilities were built in the city, the status of sport in school-age children had not significantly improved. Indeed, six years after the conclusion of the XXV Olympic Games, a study conducted by the Barcelona Sport Council, which organizes 76.6 percent of the sports activities of school-age children, found in a survey of 600 football and basketball coaches that 52.2 percent of respondents had no sports qualification (Petrus, 1998). Thus, the Barcelona Sport Council organized a Congress: "Physical education and sport in school age in the city of Barcelona," with the slogan *we want not only a more sporting city, but also a more educational sport.* One of the consequences of this Congress was that the Barcelona Sports Council requested the *Grup d' Estudis de Psicologia de l'Esport* (Research Group in Sport Psychology; GEPE) of the Universitat Autònoma of Barcelona to design a campaign on the psychological aspects of parents' positive participation in sport (Cruz, Boixadós, Torregrosa & Valiente, 2000).

THEORETICAL FRAMEWORK/PHILOSOPHY

Arnold (1999) highlighted the importance of sports in providing particularly rich contexts for personal growth. On one hand, there is a shared belief that sport contributes to the moral development of young athletes because the foundations of sport reflect concern for fairness and well-being. On the other hand, it is argued that sportspersonship is worsening in youth sports due to parents' and coaches' emphasis on winning at all cost and overemphasis on success, as it happens in professional sport (Cruz, 1998; Cruz, Boixadós, Valiente, & Torregrosa, 2001; Gutierrez, Jerez, & Cremades, 2014; Pilz, 1995). However, the main results of a systematic review based on empirical studies assessing morality in sport (Shields & Bredemeier, 2007) revealed mixed effects from multiple sampling variables, such as the age of the participants, the type of sport (i.e., contact vs. non-contact sports), whether sport was competitive or merely recreational, as well as other contextual features. Our position, from a cognitive-behavioral point of view, is that the effects of sport participation on young athletes depend basically on the influences of the different socialization agents: parents, coaches, peers, referees, and officials (Boixadós et al., 1998; Cruz, Boixadós, Valiente, & Capdevila, 1995).

NEEDS ASSESSMENT

In 1998, the Congress "Physical Education and Sport in School Age" was held in the city of Barcelona. During the Congress, the Barcelona City Hall organized a public hearing about the youth sport situation, in which 200 teenagers concluded that three out of the five main concerns related to sport competitions were the parents' behaviors as spectators. Specifically, they reported: (a) their wish for less hostility and more respect for athletes; (b) the need for families to generate a good environment of friendship and respect; and (c) the need to create behavioral rules for spectators. The Barcelona Sports Council accepted the challenge to have "not only a more sporting city, but also a more educational sport." According to this challenge, the Barcelona Sports Council ordered various professionals to work together to create an attractive campaign theoretically based on sportspersonship in sport. Thus, a group of psychologists worked together with sport scientists, publicists, and politicians in the design of the campaign to promote fair play, positive participation, and sportspersonship of parents in youth sport. The publicists and an artist took the lead in the design of the materials, the psychologists were in charge of the scientific-based messages included in all the materials, the sports scientists contributed their knowledge of youth sport and the specific competitions, and the politicians funded and promoted the initiative.

We decided to produce various materials in different formats with a shared message (the slogan) always included in all the materials. This multiplicity of materials and messages was intended to impact the different populations (i.e., children, parents, coaches, and sport coordinators). The visual aid of the campaign was the image of three fingers (see Figure 7.1) and the slogan "*Quan els teus fills estan en joc, compta fins a tres*" (the Catalan equivalent to "when your kids are playing, count to three," which means think of what you will do before you do it) was at the same time the title of the whole campaign. Following the slogan, three points were emphasized in the campaign: (1) cheer for effort as much as for success; (2) respect decisions from coaches and officials; and (3) show sportspersonship.

INTERVENTION

As the campaign was conceived to be as widespread as possible, not being focused on specific sports or social groups, multiple resources were produced in order to reach diverse sport participants. Six different products were designed in order to highlight the principles of Barcelona's campaign: a booklet, leaflets, posters, a video, a webpage, and workshops. The booklet was the main element of the campaign, explaining: (a) the philosophy and objectives of youth sports; (b) the family functions related to sport; (c) a Decalogue (i.e., set of commandments) outlining recommendations for families; and (d) a short explanation of the socialization process through sport.

Figure 7.1 Image of the Barcelona Campaign

The Philosophy of Barcelona's Campaign

Acting upon the conclusions that were established at the City Hall public hearing, Barcelona's campaign was focused on the promotion of parents' pro-fair-play behaviors as well as self-control to avoid anti-fair-play behavior. Accordingly, the slogan of the campaign was the afore-mentioned *"Quan els teus fills estan en joc, compta fins a tres..."* (Catalan equivalent to "When your kids are playing count to three"). This slogan was intended to make parents think twice about their children's sport participation when playing, as well as about the implications of their actions as youth sport spectators.

The philosophy of the campaign was summarized in a Decalogue of recommendations that was included in the multiple media products:

1. Discuss with your children and get them involved when choosing a sport, trying to allow them to decide on which sport to participate in.
2. Practice sport or physical activity, modeling a healthy lifestyle.
3. Value the physical development and health outcomes of sport programs more than performance.
4. Cheer and applaud both the skilled play and effort demonstrated during competitions.
5. Applaud the good performances of the opposing team, regardless of the score.
6. Give support to the coaches and do not give technical instruction that may contradict them.
7. Respect the rules of the sport as well as the referee calls, even if you believe they are wrong.
8. Promote respect and good relationships with the supporters of the opposing team.
9. Teach your children to take care of the facilities and sport equipment.
10. Collaborate on the tasks of support and organization of the team and club.

The Campaign Media

Once the campaign had the approval from the Council of Barcelona, a panel of experts gathered to design the content and resources of the campaign. This panel was composed of four sport psychologists with expertise in educational values in youth sport and two technicians from the Directorate of Sport and the Directorate of Education of the Barcelona City Hall. The campaign was intended to include clear and direct messages to raise parents' awareness of the values, goals, and dangers associated with youth sport participation. Once the general content was decided, the proposal was assessed by 15 professionals from educational and sport institutions. These professionals suggested modifications on the contents in order to disseminate the campaign to as many participants as possible.

Booklet. In order to present an in-depth description of the campaign, a 24-page booklet was designed. The booklet was the main product of the campaign and was structured based on four subjects:

1. Objectives and philosophy of youth sport: This section described the physical, sportive, psychological, and social objectives of youth sport in terms of the potential benefits that a healthy participation could bring to youngsters.
2. Family functions: In this section, some general advice was given to parents and families. Functions such as favoring sport participation, ensuring the quality of participation, showing an adequate degree of interest (i.e., neither uninterested nor overprotective), acting as a role model showing respect to referees and opponents, and collaborating on logistical duties with the club were included.
3. Recommendations for families: Based on these functions, the recommendations for families were structured and developed on the aforementioned Decalogue. In this section, specific behaviors were included.
4. Socialization through sport participation: The final section was a general reflection about the importance of promoting an active and healthy lifestyle during childhood and adolescence, not only in terms of the positive implications at the physical level, but also in terms of developing social relationships and learning constructive values such as cooperation, respect, or creativity.

The booklet was disseminated with help from a high-circulation newspaper in Barcelona, which included 100,000 booklets as a supplement in its weekend copies.

Leaflets and posters. Leaflets and posters were mailed to the sport clubs of the Barcelona area. In the clubs, each child was given a leaflet, which had to be delivered to their parents. These media included the slogan as well as the Decalogue for parents. The main theme of these elements included the image of the campaign, a sketch designed by Forges, a famous Spanish cartoonist (see Figure 7.1).

Workshops. The members of the campaign designed a one-hour workshop that was presented in multiple local sport councils, clubs, and sport organizations in general. The contents of the workshop were oriented toward parents and sport coordinators to define the objectives of youth sports, as well as to define the functions and obligations of the different sporting agents.

TV and radio interviews. The campaign was also publicized through interviews to the program promoters. The interviews explained the general philosophy of the campaign as well as the specific actions taken regarding its implementation. These interviews were broadcasted on a local TV channel, as well as on the local radio.

Webpage. The webpage for the campaign was intended to allow individuals and organizations to publicly show their support for the values of the campaign and to adhere themselves as promoters of the philosophical principles of the "Count to Three" Campaign. Although at the time the Barcelona Campaign was launched the internet was not as accessible as it is today, the website is still active and hosted on Barcelona's City Hall webpage. This adherence program is still active and once every year the most outstanding organizations and programs in favor of fair play in youth sports are awarded the "Count to Three" prizes (www.comptafinsatres.com).

Assessment of the Campaign

The success of the campaign was assessed in two ways: (1) the level of awareness of the campaign by users; and (2) the level of pro-fair-play and anti-fair-play behaviors of spectators in youth soccer and basketball matches. These two sports were selected as the main target not just because they were the most popular in the population, but also because higher levels of anti-fair-play behaviors had been detected in these sports prior to the campaign.

Level of awareness. The intention of this assessment was to clarify the levels of penetration of the Barcelona Campaign in its multiple approaches. A general survey conducted four months after the launch of the campaign indicated that more than one-quarter of the respondents knew about the campaign. The most successful ways to increase awareness, as we could draw from the results, were the leaflets and posters. Specifically, 33 percent and 24 percent, respectively, of the people who had heard about the campaign had been reached through these two types of media. These outcomes suggest that the more effective way to get through to people about the campaign was directly via the clubs, and specifically the children (Figure 7.2).

The dissemination based on global mass media (i.e., TV, radio, and newspapers), was not as efficient, with 10, 7, and 5 percent, respectively, of respondents having heard of the campaign via these media. This can be explained because the campaign was only broadcasted via local channels and newspapers; thus only the regular consumers of these media could be reached by them.

The least successful media in terms of dissemination were the workshops and the webpage, with 4 and 1 percent, respectively, of the respondents having known about the campaign via these media. However, these results are misleading, because people attending a workshop or visiting the website would have had previous knowledge of the campaign by other means.

Spectators' level of pro- and anti-fair-play behaviors. As previously noted, a more detailed assessment of the campaign was the direct observation of the behaviors of parents during youth football and basketball games (age 9–10 years old). Behaviors were grouped into three dimensions: (1) *encouragement* referred to those communications aimed to applaud or give support to the actions of the game; (2) *instruction* included all communications aimed at giving technical assessment or evaluation, telling the people what to do in a specific situation; and (3) *punishment* referred to those providing reproachful communication in response to any specific action.

A total of 41 football and basketball games (19 and 22, respectively) were observed, including both male and female youth sport games (26 and 15, respectively). In terms of to whom the communications were addressed, we found that 96 percent were directed to players, 4 percent to referees, and none to the coaches. However, the distribution of behaviors was different depending on the target of the communication. On the one hand, players received mostly encouragement from their parents (68 percent), a moderate quantity of technical instruction (27 percent), and only 5 percent of punishment (see Figure 7.3). On the other hand, referees received only 4 percent of encouragement (in some cases in an ironic tone), a similar amount of instructions as players (28 percent), but mostly criticism (68 percent).

An interesting additional result was the comparison of regular season games ($n = 34$) with final games ($n = 7$). In these final games, the players received more instruction (from 25 to 31

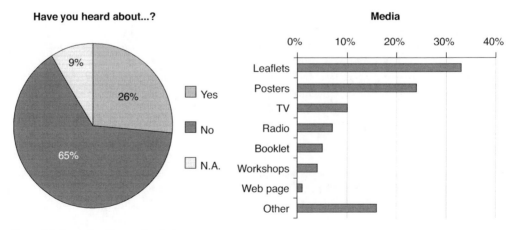

Figure 7.2 Campaign Penetration Index

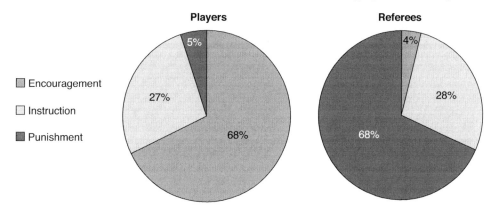

Figure 7.3 Distribution of Parents' Communication to Players and Referees in all the Games of the Season

percent) and less punishment (from 6 to 2 percent), and referees received also more instructions (from 26 to 32 percent) and less encouragement (from 6 to 0 percent). These results suggest that by the end of the season, when games are perceived as more crucial, spectators tended to be more focused on the game and be more directive to both the players and referees.

REFLECTION

The results of Barcelona's Campaign to promote parents' sportspersonship in youth sport were promising in terms of the level of awareness by spectators of youth sport and the level of positive communication messages given to the players. Similar results were found in the study of Walley, Graham, and Forehand (1982) using self-instructional leaflets that were distributed to adult observers in an attempt to increase their positive verbalizations in a youth baseball league. However, in our study, referees of football and basketball games received only 4 percent of encouragement and 68 percent of criticism, reflecting that some parents place too much emphasis on winning. In this sense, we have to assume that the elements of the campaign were insufficient by themselves to change the spectators' behaviors toward referees.

In general, the campaign attempted to influence spectators' behaviors, but the ones that behave in an appropriate way did not receive any positive reinforcement. If we want to modify parents/spectators behaviors in youth sport, we need to praise them for the positive and supportive behaviors they exhibit toward players, coaches, and referees and not for the verbalizations that reflect a win-at-all-cost attitude. In this sense, it is interesting to follow new developments on parents' positive participation in sport, such as the "Juga verd" ("play green campaign" – Alastrué & González, 2013), which proposed giving extra points based on parents' and spectators' behaviors so they are taken into account in the outcome of the matches.

This system gives a maximum score of ten points: (a) three points depend on the competitive score (i.e., scoreboard); (b) the coaches can give two extra points to the opposing team valuing the behaviors of their players and coach; (c) one parent, known as the "spectator tutor" assesses the behavior of the audience of their own team, giving one extra point; (d) the audience can also assess the behavior of the opposing players and give another extra point; and (e) the referee called the "game facilitator" is responsible for three points, one assessing the spectators' behavior of each team, another assessing the coaches', and one extra point (using the green card) in remarkable fair-play behaviors of the players, such as helping the referee in conflict situations, encouraging peers frequently during the match, or helping an opposing player in a difficult situation.

In sport, everybody has to do their best to win, but if we want to educate children through sport in order to win a game, we have to take into account that not only do they need to score more than the opposing team, but the fair-play behaviors and verbalizations of players and spectators also matter. Our final reflection, from a cognitive-behavioral perspective, is that if we want to change the values in youth sport, we have to change the contingencies of the sport context as well, especially the ones related to parents and spectators, such as rewarding parents for their supportive behavior toward referees and applauding the players' fair-play behaviors toward their opponents.

SUGGESTED READINGS

Gonçalves, C., Silva M. J., Cruz, J., Torregrosa, M., & Cumming, S. P. (2010). The effect of achievement goals on moral attitudes in young athletes. *Journal of Sports Science and Medicine, 9*(4), 605–611.

Harwood, C. G., & Knight, C. J. (2015). Parenting in youth sport: A position paper on parenting expertise. *Psychology of Sport and Exercise, 16*, 24–35. DOI: 10.1016/j.psychsport.2014.03.001.

Kavussanu, M., Stamp, R., Slade, G., & Ring, C. (2009). Observed prosocial and antisocial behaviours in male and female soccer players. *Journal of Applied Sport Psychology, 21*, 62–76.

Lee, M. J., Whitehead, J., & Balchin, N. (2000). The measurement of values in youth sport: Development of the youth sport values questionnaire. *Journal of Sport and Exercise Psychology, 22*, 307–326.

REFLECTIVE QUESTIONS

1.   Explain the role of parents and spectators in the socialization process of young athletes.
2.   What kind of values are transmitted through sport?
3.   What are the strengths and limitations of Barcelona's Campaign to promote parents' sportspersonship in youth sport?
4.   Explain the most inadequate spectators' behaviors that were observed in basketball and soccer games and what effects could produce these behaviors in children.
5.   What does the "Juga verd" (play green) campaign add to previous values campaigns and which psychological principles are the basis for this campaign?

REFERENCES

Alastrué, P. & González, C. (2013). Juga verd play. Nou model d'esport escolar [Play green. A new model of youth sport]. Retrieved from www.cebllob.cat/data/informaciones/2950.pdf.

Arnold, P. (1999). The virtues, moral education, and the practice of sport. *Quest, 51*, 39–54.

Boixadós, M., Valiente, L., Mimbrero, J., Torregrosa, M., & y Cruz, J. (1998). Papel de los agentes de socialización en deportistas en edad escolar [The role of socialization agents on youth sport athletes]. *Revista de Psicología del Deporte, 14*, 295–310.

Cruz, J. (1998). Do the rules protect fairplay in professional sport. In *Proceedings III European Seminaron Fairplay* (pp. 235–249). Lisboa: Horizonte.

Cruz, J., Boixadós, M., Torregrosa, M., & y Mimbrero, J. (1996). ¿Existe un deporte educativo?: papel de las competiciones deportivas en el proceso de socializacion del niño [Is there an educational sport? The role of sport competitions on the children socialization process]. *Revista de Psicología del Deporte, 9–10*, 111–132.

Cruz, J., Boixadós, M., Torregrosa, M., & y Valiente, L. (2000). *Participa amb ells!: Assessorament a famílies que participen en competicions escolars [Participate with them! Assessment for families participating in youth sport competitions].* Barcelona: Ayuntamiento de Barcelona.

Cruz, J., Boixadós, M., Valiente, L., & Capdevila, L. (1995). Prevalent values in young Spanish soccer players. *International Review for the Sociology of Sport, 30*, 353–373.

Cruz, J., Boixadós, M., Valiente, L., & Torregrosa, M. (2001). Se pierde el fairplay y la deportividad en el deporte en edad escolar [Is the fair-play missed in youth sport?]. *Apunts D'Educació Física i Esport* 64, 6–16.

Gutiérrez, D., Jerez, P., & Cremades, G. (2014). Passing on values of fair play and sportsmanship through the practice of sport psychology. In J. G. Cremades & L. S. Tashman (Eds.), *Becoming a sport, exercise, and performance psychology professional* (pp. 53–60). New York, NY: Psychology Press.

Lee, M. J., Whitehead, J., & Balchin, N. (2000). The measurement of values in youth sport: Development of the youth sport values questionnaire. *Journal of Sport and Exercise Psychology, 22*, 307–326.

Petrus, A. (1998). Esport, educació i diversitat [Sport, education and diversity]. *Keynote address at the Congrés de l'Educació Física i l'Esport en Edat Escolar a la Ciutat de Barcelona.* Barcelona, May 21–23.

Pilz, G. A. (1995). Performance sport: Education in fair play? Some empirical and theoretical remarks. *International Review for the Sociology of Sport, 30*(3–4), 391–418.

Shields, D. L., & Bredemeier, B. L. (2007). Advances in sport morality research. In G. Tenenbaum & R. C. Eklund (Eds.), *Handbook of sport psychology* (3rd ed.; pp. 662–684). Hoboken, NJ: Wiley.

Walley, P. B., Graham, G. M., & Forehand, R. (1982). Assessment and treatment of adult observer verbalizations at youth league baseball games. *Journal of Sport Psychology, 4*, 254–266.

8 Developing a Philosophy and Theoretical Framework

Two Cases that Changed my Approach to Consulting Style

Richard J. Keegan

There are many instances in life where we might claim a particular skill or attribute cannot be taught: Instances of exquisite sporting skill, for example, or in this case the philosophical and theoretical underpinnings of applied psychological practice. More realistically, however, when people claim a skill cannot be taught, it may simply be because we do not have the language or understanding to effectively teach it (yet). Examples include the eventual successful studies of germs, electricity, planetary orbits, and evolution. While it can be much easier, and sometimes even quite pleasing, to invoke some kind of mystery or magic in explaining complex phenomena, it is usually possible to observe, analyze, theorize, and test our ideas – scientifically – until the underlying mechanisms are understood. In 2010, I developed a simple framework for analyzing consulting styles and summarized "I wish someone had told me about this" (Keegan, 2010, p. 48). That article and the reflections it stimulated were triggered by events several years earlier, at a time when relatively little had been written about philosophical and theoretical frameworks in applied sport, exercise, and performance psychology (SEPP).

I have subsequently gone on to write a book detailing the principles and practices involved in delivering applied SEPP (Keegan, 2015), as well as outlining the "landscape" of philosophical and theoretical frameworks in SEPP (Keegan, 2014). Likewise, Poczwardowski and colleagues (2004, 2014) have continued to write on the subject, proposing a framework with very similar core concepts. Given that the following case studies are grounded in my own experience and, indeed, helped to stimulate the reflections and models that followed, I will analyze them in relation to the framework they helped to inspire (Keegan, 2014, 2015).

Fundamentally, this approach to philosophical and theoretical underpinnings identifies three core types of assumptions: (1) *the aims of SEPP practice* (performance enhancement, well-being, athlete development, etc.); (2) *the nature of the phenomena* we are working with, or more technically, the ontological and epistemological assumptions that are made (positivism, interpretivism, and others); and (3) *the consulting style* one chooses (simplified, as many different "schools" exist). Keegan (2015) illustrates likely alignments between choices made at each level, such that certain ontological assumptions should be paired with particular consulting styles and practices (outlined below). The two case studies presented will demonstrate the importance of understanding and developing one's philosophy and theoretical framework in order to support one's professional practice. It needs to be emphasized that the following examples are presented as illustrations of what I consider a key mistake in my career – naively offering a successful approach from one client (Belle) to another, seemingly similar, client (Lynn). As such, the examples are not presented as an example of "best practice" as they took place in my very first year of supervised practice.

BACKGROUND INFORMATION

During the first year of my supervised practice, I was very privileged to be offered a voluntary role with a talent development academy for female field hockey players. As part of this role,

I was assigned a group of ten players to mentor, while the lead psychologist provided services to the majority of the squad. While it was not compulsory to provide focused psychological support to each of these players, I was required to meet each player, introduce myself, and offer psychological services (including coverage of ethics/confidentiality and the scope of the service we were to provide). I met with a total of ten players, six of whom sought to establish a program of individualized support. Two of those players, here given the pseudonyms "Belle" (age 19) and "Lynn" (age 20), presented with strikingly similar issues and experiences. Both players had recently transitioned into the "development academy," as well as making the move to university, and both were experiencing issues with fragile confidence. Clients' names, ages, team/club names, the sport, and any identifiable information have been changed to protect confidentiality, but the records of events are drawn directly from my consulting notes at the time.

DESCRIPTION OF THE CASES

Both Belle and Lynn were defensive players, meaning that mistakes were often costly (i.e., if they made a mistake, the team would be highly likely to concede points). Both described having extremely fragile confidence, such that if a mistake were made confidence would be lost, leading to self-doubt, hesitation, and diminished performance. This issue was being exacerbated following selection for a new specialist training academy, designed to identify and support future international players. Both players felt they were not the "number one" selection in their position (for club or country), and felt insecure about future selections (several national "camps" were arranged each year preceding national representative competitions, for which squads were revised each time). Upon making mistakes, both players reported strong increases in self-awareness and negative self-talk, including *catastrophizing* (i.e., inferring more serious consequences to their mistakes than were ever really likely) (cf. Beck, 1978). Likewise, both players reported the type of "black-and-white" thinking that often leads to reduced self-esteem (and worse) – for example: "*Either* I made zero errors *or* I must have played badly, and I will miss selection as a result."

THEORETICAL FRAMEWORK/PHILOSOPHY

At the beginning of my supervised practice, like many neophyte practitioners (cf. Tod & Bond, 2010), I tended to deploy a "mental skills training" (MST) approach. Predicated on the educational assumptions described by Ravizza (2001), MST has also been closely linked to the tradition of cognitive-behavioral therapy (CBT; e.g., Andersen, 2000; Behncke, 2004; Greenspan & Feltz, 1989; Meyers, Whelan, & Murphy, 1995). Both MST and CBT frequently assume, for example, that the core mental skills will be beneficial to most athletes; either the skill is already possessed but not deployed properly, or it can be learned and then deployed to enhance performance. As such, I operated on the assumption that, in principle, MST should work for anybody (see "generalizability" below).

The philosophical and theoretical underpinnings of the approach I was using can be classified using the framework from Keegan (2014, 2015). The *aims of service* focused on performance; either enhancement or "fixing" performance problems. With the support service taking place within an elite development academy, this was implicitly the main emphasis. *The ontology and epistemology* of the MST work I performed at this time was adopting the "hard science" tradition (cf. Keegan, 2014), claiming that its theories are "true" and strengthened/enhanced by each supportive study/paper (aka "certaintism" in Keegan, 2015). Further, a hard science approach asserts that what works for one athlete will work for another athlete in similar circumstances (i.e., the theories are "generalizable"). In contrast, for example, a soft science tradition would reject the idea of generalizable theories/models and treat each person (or group) as completely unique (aka "construalism" in Keegan, 2015) because each athlete's psychological reality/experience is *construed*. This "construction" of reality can occur at the individual level (i.e., phenomenology or existentialism) or among the social group, including friends, partners, family, coaches, etc. (i.e., constructivism, interpretivism). Hence, a practitioner adopting construalist assumptions would be unlikely to apply common techniques such as MST in the way described here. Further still, the approach termed "Be Careful" (cf. Keegan, 2014) would assume that such theories, techniques, and even measurement approaches are all deeply fallible and likely flawed (aka "fallibilism" in Keegan, 2015). As such, a fallibilist approach would proceed with extreme caution, adopting the "least bad" options on a case-by-case basis and monitoring them carefully. A fourth option exists, termed "Just Do It" (aka "pragmatism"), which involves doing whatever seems to work in the circumstances. Philosophically, this implies that whatever "worked" must have been true, but it can be a problematic approach as a result (see Keegan, 2014, 2015). For example, a lot of mistakes can be made using trial and error to find out what works, and that can leave a bad impression with the client. Regarding *consulting styles*, I had generally been trained to have confidence in the published literature I had studied at the time, and I had only experienced sport psychology delivered by "experts" in an educational manner. I had also just completed fours years of formal training in psychology and so, naively, I felt like an "expert." As a result, I tended to adopt a more "practitioner-led" consulting style, rather than allowing the client to lead by setting priorities, topics, etc. (e.g., Keegan, 2010). A practitioner-led style is a good fit for "hard science" ontological assumptions and performance-focused aims, whereas a client-led approach is arguably more suitable to a focus on well-being and the assumptions of soft science or construalism (cf. Keegan, 2015).

NEEDS ASSESSMENT

Both athletes completed an intake questionnaire indicating reasons for seeking support, identifying any current injuries or medications, and screening for any issues requiring referral to a clinical psychologist. No clinical issues were reported, but Lynn was currently recovering from a knee ligament injury that had required a lengthy lay-off, albeit without requiring surgery. Both athletes indicated they had previously received sport psychology workshops, but not one-to-one support. As noted above, both athletes attended a structured intake interview, during which they decided that sport psychology could be a worthwhile service while attending the academy. Following these intake processes, both athletes participated in biweekly (i.e. every other week), unstructured, face-to-face meetings (detailed in Tables 8.1 and 8.2). Performance profiles were completed between the second and third meetings by both athletes (cf. Butler & Hardy, 1992; Doyle & Parfitt, 1996). Each subsequent meeting constituted an opportunity to review progress and modify strategies as needed. The second meeting with both athletes was observed by my supervisor, in person.

In both cases, I reconciled the data collected with the confidence models of Bandura (1977) and Vealey (1986). According to self-efficacy theory, both athletes were dependent on "performance accomplishments" as a source of self-efficacy, and the recent step-up in level had reduced the amount of success they experienced. Further, the new coaching team they were dealing with had identified numerous areas to improve and develop *for selection purposes*. As such, both athletes seemed to be using a relatively narrow range of extrinsically identified outcome measures for self-evaluation, as opposed to a wide array of intrinsically valued process and performance measures. Under Vealey's model, all three core factors were unfavorable: (1) a distinct change in the objective sporting situation, from "high-potential" to "time to perform"; combined with (2) low trait self-confidence; and (3) an assumed focus on normative and outcome-focused definitions of success. This would leave both athletes with very few options for generating positive self-evaluations. I believed that both theories would suggest each athlete would be well-advised to identify her own, intrinsically determined evaluation strategy, using multiple measures of performance, and focusing on process or performance, not normative comparisons. Performance profiling and goal-setting appeared to be highly compatible with this strategy. Within Bandura's model, using self-talk as a form of "verbal persuasion" also seemed highly suitable.

INTERVENTION

Both athletes were happy to set goals based on their performance profiles, including long-term and short-term goals, subjective and objective evaluations, and with an increased emphasis on process and performance goals rather than outcomes such as selections or team results (cf. Burton & Weiss, 2008; Hemmings & Holder, 2013). With goals for psychological support focusing on subjective perceptions of confidence, both athletes also agreed to participate in a cognitive behavioral intervention involving capturing and challenging negative thoughts concerning performance (daily, as well as with a particular emphasis on the time before, during, and after competitive performances). In each case, this was to be supported using a self-talk diary and, subsequently, the physical cueing of more positive/adaptive thoughts. At the time that this support was delivered, I used Burton's (1983) cognitive theory of goal-setting, as well as the argument that goals provide multiple self-selected and highly influenceable measures of success (as noted above). I used the metaphor of hanging a weight off multiple pegs versus only one peg – the former being more resilient and thus creating more robust confidence. Regarding self-talk, I drew from the theory that thoughts determine behavior (cf. Johnson, Hrycaiko, Johnson, & Hallas, 2004), as well as the argument that self-talk may influence performance through improving confidence and self-esteem (e.g., Zinnser, Bunker, & Willams, 2006). In both core intervention strands, or mental skills, the evidence at the time was equivocal in the analysis of Gardner and Moore (2006), although there was arguably a stronger body of evidence supporting goal-setting (e.g., Burton & Weiss, 2008). The evidence supporting these two strategies could be described as "supportive" rather than "conclusive," and from the certaintist philosophical perspective, there was sufficient evidence to proceed.

Lynn took a very different approach to the performance-profiling task, having recently been shocked by the comprehensive evaluations offered by coaches and performance analysts. Despite face-to-face guidance, she focused only on the "improvables" identified in these meetings, and was extremely reluctant to include attributes that she considered strengths. She insisted that she could not draw confidence from scoring well on such attributes. This undermined the performance-profiling process and the ensuing goal-setting process, as all her goals were effectively dictated by the recent evaluation (i.e., they were extrinsic). Likewise, while she expressed genuine willingness to attempt the self-talk diary and to learn the skill of deploying productive self-talk, she never actually took any action (despite receiving the same template as Belle). Lynn was continually frustrated by her failure to recover from a knee injury, which was preventing her from training and thus from pursuing the technical skill improvements she desired. It appeared, however, that this slow recovery may also have been caused by non-adherence to the prescribed rehabilitation. Over time, Lynn chose to focus on university work and social life, and gradually disengaged from the activities offered by the academy.

In contrast, Belle completed a thorough performance profile in between sessions, following the instructions I had provided very well. This performance profile formed a strong framework for supporting both immediate confidence (i.e., in strengths) and goal-setting. Belle also demonstrated excellent adherence to the self-talk diary, and quickly transitioned to the use of physical cueing (orange stickers placed on the phone, TV, steering wheel, bathroom mirror, etc.) to prompt more adaptive self-talk. Like Lynn, Belle also experienced a minor injury – at an inopportune time close to a key selection – but she persisted with rehabilitation and recovered quickly. In the end, Belle was successful in both regaining her place in the current team as well as in gaining the attention of another national-level team, who subsequently signed Belle. The relocation that followed led to the ending of the psychological support.

Table 8.1 Abbreviated Case Notes of Psychological Support Provided to Belle

Session Details	Session Summary
Meeting 1 Time: 10:00 Client: Belle Location: Consulting room Duration: 30 mins	Had very productive chat with Belle who quickly identified confidence as her main issue. She plays at Borewood, who have just brought in a batch of new (and elite) players. Thus Belle feels some pressure from these players PLUS the weight of expectancy from having such a strong squad. Borewood have got off to a bad start this season and now every team-talk points out that "one more defeat would lose us the league". This really bothers Belle who plays in defense, causing her to "catastrophize" a single, normal error into losing a goal into losing a match into losing the league.
Meeting 2 Time: 14:00 Client: Belle Location: Consulting room Duration: 1 hour	Observed by supervisor. Session went very well, rapport with Belle is good. Had to change original session plan as Supervisor didn't want to watch us complete a performance profile. PP done as homework by email instead. We explored issues from first meeting and both agreed that a focus on staying positive and playing freely (without worry) would be beneficial.
Meeting 3 Time: 14:00 Client: Belle Location: Consulting room Duration: 1 hour	Had good chat with Belle about recent performances and appearance from subs bench at weekend. Apparently coming on from bench was a lot easier and we discussed this in terms of fear-of-failure and having nothing to lose when appearing as a sub compared to being first pick. We reviewed the performance profile, edited, and finalised. Belle's homework for next meeting was to set herself a few goals on the basis of this.
Meeting 4 Time: 11:45 Client: Belle Location: Phone consult Duration: 30 mins	Belle rang unexpectedly. She was quite distressed after being dropped from the first team at Borewood, we discussed how her manager asks for a positive reaction and looked at ways Belle could be seen to react positively, and also ways she could get back into the team without simply waiting for another player to play badly or get injured. We explored the way it had affected her and there was a clear theme of a very negative inner monologue. This led to a discussion around changing her self-talk. Belle was a little skeptical but agreed to complete a daily self-talk diary at least seven times (i.e., until the next meeting).
Meeting 5 Time: 13:00 Client: Belle Location: Consulting room Duration: 1 hour	It was good to hear Belle had already been working hard on her self-talk and had taken to this with great vigor. Likewise her performance profile had come together well and she had even (independently) agreed with her coach that the most improvement will come from working on her confidence. We explored options for transforming the negative self-talk she was recording into more helpful thoughts – i.e., more proactive not simply descriptive. Decided to use "orange dots" to act as eye-catching reminders to be deliberately positive and begin developing this new habit.

Meeting 6
Time: 13:00
Client: Belle
Location: Consulting room
Duration: 1 hour

Excellent session. Reviewed recent performances and difference between appearing from bench versus starting the match. This progressed to a discussion of the different kinds of thinking relating to good performances versus troubled performances and we started to suggest that good performances are often preceded by "free-flow picture thinking" while negativity and worry, especially verbal, were often related to poor performances. We then related this back to Belle's homework on positive self-talk. Having highlighted a difference between verbal versus "picture thinking," I guided Belle through a few imagery scenarios (a first for me!) with a view to including imagery in Belle's match-day preparations. She reported that the scenarios we went through made her feel confident and happy.

Meeting 7
Time: 13:00
Client: Belle
Location: Consulting room
Duration: 1 hour

Belle delighted with recent performances and attributed some of this to psychological support. Noted lack of worry/nerves recently. Reported being in a "zone" before and during matches. Progressed ideas by exploring whether new skills could be used to her advantage rather than as "solutions" to a "problem" (nerves). This seemed a good way to move forwards.

Meeting 8
Time: 13:00
Client: Belle
Location: Consulting room
Duration: 1 hour

After some very good recent performances, Belle had injured her foot in training (metatarsal), very disappointed, quite upset. Given recent emphasis on "finding the positives" we set off down this route. Most productive line of questioning came from "would you still have worked this hard and played so well if you knew in advance that you wouldn't play?" … answer yes, but why? To play in next match … probed … to impress coaches and selectors … probed … for intrinsic reward and enjoyment … (aha!). From here we were able to re-introduce the positives (e.g., it will help me be stronger, it's only one match). We also rehearsed the difficult conversation she would have with her coach about missing the next game.

Meeting 9
Time: 10:00
Client: Belle
Location: Consulting room
Duration: 1 hour

Belle felt on top of her confidence and was recovering well from the foot injury. When we looked for "next steps" she immediately stated that the next step would be to become a tougher player and not be so "nice." We reviewed the performance profile to find where this would fit in, and set new goals. We also developed a plan to help her develop these attributes, by rehearsing key scenarios in imagery and justifying being "not herself" (i.e., nasty) using self-talk.

Shortly after this session Belle was signed by another team and moved away from the academy – ending our time together. She was content not to be referred to another psychologist in the new location.

Table 8.2 Abbreviated Case Notes of Psychological Support Provided to Lynn

Session Details	Session Summary
Meeting 1 Time: 10:30 Client: Lynn Location: Consulting room Duration: 30 mins	Lynn came across as very quiet and reserved, and was quite conscious that she was new to the academy. She was concerned about fitting in studies and a "normal" life work plus the demands of the academy. Lynn identified a lack of confidence permeating most of her performances, particularly the higher levels such as internationals or training camps. Seemed to be weighed down by expectations, and/or a little surprised or upset about the higher standard she was now facing, leading to less praise and more "room for improvement."
Meeting 2 Time: 13:00 Client: Lynn Location: Consulting room Duration: 1 hour	Observed by Supervisor. Lynn was feeling a little fragile and threatened, having received lots of constructive feedback upon arriving at the academy – lots of quite technical details from coaches and analysts. Also seemed to be self-defeating to the point of learned helplessness or "self-handicapping," unwilling to consider "taking responsibility for her own improvement." Same issue with performance profile: shifted to homework instead – specifically tried to emphasize that PP would highlight current strengths as well as areas to improve – as a beginning of rebuilding confidence.
Meeting 3 Time: 10:00 Client: Lynn Location: Consulting room Duration: 1 hour	We talked about Lynn's discontentment with a "slow start" as a result of her (nearly healed) knee injury. I took the approach of removing barriers and went through things one-by-one. What Lynn really wants is technical improvement as this is why she believes she is attending the center. As a result we completed a performance profile focusing on technical aspects, which emerged to be a list of "improvables" rather than a full technical PP. We agreed that this reflects a level of perfectionism in Lynn, but at this time she explained that she could not draw confidence from "doing what she's already good at."
Meeting 4 Time: 11:00 Client: Lynn Location: Consulting room Duration: 1 hour	Tone of session was more positive today, Lynn explained that she appreciated having someone (me) "actually on her side." Lynn had still not completed her recovery to full training, so all the technical/skill-based attributes in her performance profile were not able to be assessed/reviewed. We discussed alternative ways of making progress with her confidence, and explored the idea of self-talk. We developed a recording sheet for her to complete each evening to review her negative thoughts during the day and explore their impact and alternatives.
Meeting 5 Time: 10:00 Client: Lynn Location: Consulting room Duration: 1 hour	Decent session, the rapport is good but I'm starting to doubt whether I've got to the bottom of things with Lynn. Having created and postponed a list of improvables, Lynn is also not completing her self-talk diary. In this session Lynn complained that basic lack of sleep was causing the majority of her problems and had done so on many recent occasions (especially National camps). We discussed sleep hygiene and how different activities and thought patterns might be contributing. I asked Lynn to note down a few observations about what factors seemed to influence her sleep to see if we can identify a clear pattern.
Meeting 6 Time: 11:00 Client: Lynn Location: Consulting room Duration: 1 hour	I instigated this session after not hearing from Lynn – despite seeing her around the academy quite frequently. We talked through various issues, particularly her experiences since arriving at the academy/university. We reviewed the "case formulation" we had reached – new standards damaging confidence leading to decreased performance – as well as the strategies we had deployed to overcome this situation (PP to highlight strengths, positive self-talk, sleep hygiene). Lynn had no particular issue with any of these, but had not done them and would not commit to trying them or anything new. Instead, Lynn talked through various concerns, from her hockey to her wider social life. She was also not completing her knee rehab properly, and so was not able to train and improve as desired. We explored whether it would be best to focus on the psychology of rehab or pick up once she had recovered, she chose the latter.
Follow-up	Several months later I met Lynn in one of the cafés nearby. She had decided to leave the academy and focus on studies and her social life. She insisted she was happy with the support she had received (including from me), and that simply hockey was not her passion.

In retrospect, Lynn did not adhere to the recommendations we agreed upon in our meetings, nor the rehabilitation prescribed by her physiotherapist, and thus she was never able to train and pursue the technical improvements she sought. Lynn requested that we delay working on her confidence until she had recovered from her knee injury sufficiently to train, but this recovery did not occur and the psychological support was terminated.

REFLECTION

What worked wonderfully for Belle never progressed beyond initial agreement with Lynn, and she decided to stop attending meetings, ending the support process. On reflection, I began to realize that Lynn's goals and ambitions were different from Belle's. Hence, despite describing very similar experiences, she had been affected by both recent negative/constructive feedback from academy coaches as well as the knee injury. One option would have been to pause our pursuit of performance and provide emotional support to help cope with these "setbacks." If, however, she truly believed she was unable to improve to the levels required by coaches at the academy, then our support should have focused on managing this transition out of the talent pathway. However, when I assumed Lynn's aim/goal was to pursue performance and selection, and therefore sought a solution to the problem of underperforming, I was ultimately incorrect: even if she was keen to portray this image. The two athletes experienced a very similar problem in very different ways. For one, assuming performance aims, hard-science assumptions and a practitioner-led consulting style was the perfect fit. For the other, the aims should have been to pursue well-being and emotional support, the assumptions should have been "soft-science" (personal and unique experiences), and the consulting style should arguably have been much more client-led. Failing to adopt a different, more suitable, theoretical/philosophical approach with Lynn led, in my view, to the failure of the psychological support. In contrast, Belle thrived over both the short (selection) and long (ongoing performance) term.

Looking back, I was disappointed that I allowed Lynn to postpone all further participation until her knee rehabilitation was completed. When I review the session notes now, I can see a clear pattern of self-handicapping and learned helplessness. She insisted on profiling and setting goals related to technical and performance improvements, in the full knowledge that her injury would prevent progress over the short to medium term. Lynn was also relatively poor at following her injury rehabilitation program, either believing that the injury was not serious enough to warrant such effort, or that the physiotherapist's work within sessions (and/or "natural healing") should be sufficient. Having declined to complete the goal-setting task meaningfully (by setting inappropriate, unachievable goals) and after failing to complete the self-talk diary for no clear reason (having agreed to it face-to-face), I was hoping to offer Lynn more autonomy by allowing her to determine when we should meet in future. I was concerned she may have felt obliged to speak to me as a new arrival at the academy, and she had recently been bombarded with extrinsic demands from coaches, performance analysts, physiotherapists, and possibly academic staff too. In the end, offering autonomy around when-or-whether to meet next was misguided. I would have been much better advised to focus on autonomy *within* the sessions rather than promoting or recommending particular mental skills. To be clear, I should have been more "client-led," but regarding content, questioning style, and aims/goals; not regarding if/when to meet!

The literature regarding learned helplessness and self-handicapping generally refers to deep-seated beliefs and unconscious patterns, which the client is neither aware of nor able to explicate (e.g., Abramson, Seligman, & Teasdale, 1978; Dweck, 1999). Spending time listening to Lynn in a nonjudgmental and supportive manner may have allowed her (or us) to identify and examine such habits and patterns, and perhaps explore how and why they developed (e.g., Rogers, 1957, 1961). Such an approach would involve taking an extremely personal approach to exploring Lynn's unique "lived experiences" (i.e., "soft science" or "construalist" ontology). Such an approach would arguably involve adopting a "client-led" consulting style, encouraging

Lynn to both identify and prioritize topics of discussion, as well as gently encouraging the exploration, evaluation, and analysis of these stories in order to build self-awareness and empowerment. It would be a long journey, but the changes that might ensue would be much more likely to "stick," as they would have been based entirely on Lynn's experiences and her own evaluation of it (i.e., no prescription or direction).

In contrast to Lynn, Belle was happy for me to work within a mental skills framework, underpinned by a "hard-science" philosophy, which is arguably implicit with MST (as described by Keegan, 2014). There was a clear alignment between my own philosophical and theoretical assumptions and Belle's requirements/expectations. Where these assumptions were not compatible with Lynn's real needs and beliefs, the support was ineffective. The problem, to be clear, is that my assumptions at the time were completely unconscious, and had been passively inherited from the environment in which I had trained/developed. When I naively applied the same assumptions in working with Lynn, the support was unsuccessful. Reflecting back, these relationships were an extremely important and valuable formative experience for me. They led me to the conclusion that a SEPP practitioner's philosophical and theoretical assumptions need to be aligned with the client's needs and expectations; the quality of the outcomes depends on it. This leads to a new problem, because I have never met a client who was able to eloquently express their beliefs or needs regarding ontological assumptions or consulting style. While expressing aims and objectives for support should be much easier, it is possible that Lynn specified aims that "she felt she ought to" rather than her real support needs.

I would accept (at least in part) the criticism that deliberately seeking to identify the correct philosophical approach places a huge burden on the SEPP practitioner. If we accept the conclusions of this case study, then the practitioner must carefully infer the client's real aims, goals, and needs, and then carefully adopt a particular ontological and epistemological stance, as well as a compatible consulting style (with the possible exception of "pragmatism" where we learn from "just doing it"). The alternative, however, is to either adopt a single overall style/framework – which may not be suitable for all clients – or to carry out psychological support with no clear self-awareness of these issues. Given the importance of philosophy and theories in the above case studies, such a naive approach could be ineffective or even detrimental. I would also be sympathetic to the criticism that learning about philosophical and theoretical assumptions is difficult; nobody teaches it explicitly, and very few applied practitioners would want to read the deep philosophical writings that underpin some of these issues. To address these concerns, I developed a basic, introductory framework for engaging with these issues (outlined in Keegan, 2014, 2015). The models are unashamedly simplified to allow practitioners to engage with a topic that is dense, and often uses impenetrable terminology (even more so than that used here!). As a result, however, the magic and mystery surrounding these issues should be gradually evaporating. This chapter started by challenging the notion that: "You just can't teach philosophical and theoretical frameworks." Having read these case studies and the supporting materials, would you agree? The assumption underlying this chapter is that we can teach philosophy if we understand it sufficiently. Learning about philosophical and theoretical frameworks is difficult, and may still involve making mistakes. However, if we are able to reflect on practice in an educated and informed way, then we can at least learn from them, and continue to improve our practice.

SUGGESTED READINGS

Keegan, R. J. (2010). Teaching consulting philosophies to neophyte sport psychologists: Does it work, and how can we do it? *Journal of Sport Psychology in Action, 1*, 42–52.

Keegan, R. J. (2014). Developing a philosophy and theoretical framework. In J. G. Cremades & L. S. Tashman (eds.). *Becoming a sport, exercise, and performance psychology professional: A global perspective.* New York, NY: Routledge.

Keegan, R. J. (2015). *Being a sport psychologist.* London. Palgrave MacMillan.

REFLECTIVE QUESTIONS

1. What were the similarities and differences between these two athletes?
2. What signs and symptoms are presented in this case study that could have been used to inform the selection of a philosophy and consulting style:

    a. for Belle?
    b. for Lynn?

3. What might be the pros and cons of being able to adopt different theoretical and philosophical frameworks with different athletes?
4. What were the warning signs that Lynn's needs and expectations were not well suited to the assumptions being used, and what could have been done about it?
5. How could you incorporate an awareness of philosophy and theoretical frameworks into your own practice?

REFERENCES

Abramson, L. Y., Seligman, M. E. P., & Teasdale, J. D. (1978). Learned helplessness in humans: Critique and reformulation. *Journal of Abnormal Psychology, 87*, 49–74.

Andersen, M. B. (2000). *Doing sport psychology*. Champaign, IL: Human Kinetics.

Bandura, A. (1997). Self-efficacy: Toward a unifying theory of behavioral change. *Psychological Review, 84*(2), 191–215.

Beck, A. T. (1972). *Depression: Causes and treatment*. Philadelphia, PA: University of Pennsylvania Press.

Behncke, L. (2004). Mental skills training for sports: A brief review. *Athletic Insight: The Online Journal of Sport Psychology, 6*(1), 1–24.

Burton, D. (1983). Evaluation of goal-setting training on selected cognitions and performance of collegiate swimmers. Unpublished doctoral dissertation, University of Illinois, Urbana-Champaign.

Burton, D., & Weiss, C. (2008). The fundamental goal concept: The path to process and performance success. In T. S. Horn (Ed.), *Advances in sport psychology* (pp. 339–376). Champaign, IL: Human Kinetics.

Butler, R. J., & Hardy, L. (1992). The performance profile: Theory and application. *Journal of Applied Sport Psychology, 5*(1), 253–264.

Doyle, J., & Parfitt, G. (1996). Performance profiling and predictive validity. *Journal of Applied Sport Psychology, 8*(2), 160–170.

Dweck, C. S. (1999). *Self-theories: Their role in motivation, personality, and development*. Philadelphia, PA: Psychology Press.

Gardner, F. L., & Moore, Z. E. (2006). *Clinical sport psychology*. Champaign, IL: Human Kinetics.

Greenspan, M. J., & Feltz, D. F. (1989). Psychological interventions with athletes in competitive situations: A review. *The Sport Psychologist, 3*, 219–236.

Hemmings, B., & Holder, T. (2013). *Applied sport psychology: A case-based approach*. London: Wiley & Sons.

Johnson, J. J. M., Hrycaiko, D. W., Johnson, G. V., & Hallas, J. M. (2004). Self-talk and female youth soccer performance. *The Sport Psychologist, 18*, 44–59.

Keegan, R. J. (2010). Teaching consulting philosophies to neophyte sport psychologists: Does it work, and how can we do it? *Journal of Sport Psychology in Action, 1*, 42–52.

Keegan, R. J. (2014). Developing a philosophy and theoretical framework. In. J. G. Cremades & L. S. Tashman (eds.). *Becoming a sport, exercise, and performance psychology professional: A global perspective*. New York, NY: Routledge.

Keegan, R. J. (2015). *Being a sport psychologist*. London. Palgrave MacMillan.

Meyers, A. W., Whelan, J. P., & Murphy, S. M. (1995). Cognitive behavioural strategies in athletic performance enhancement. In M. Hersen, R. M. Eisler, & P. M. Miller (Eds.), *Progress in behaviour modification*, Vol. 30 (pp. 137–164). Pacific Grove, CA: Brooks/Cole.

Poczwardowski, A., Sherman, C., & Ravizza, K. (2004). Professional philosophy in the sport psychology service delivery: Building on theory and practice. *The Sport Psychologist, 18*, 415–429.

Poczwardowski, A., Aoyagi, M. W., Shapiro, J. L., & Van Raalte, J. L. (2014). Developing professional philosophy for sport psychology consulting practice. In A. G. Papaioannou & D. Hackfort (Eds.), *Routledge companion to sport and exercise psychology: Global perspectives and fundamental concepts* (pp. 895–907). London: Routledge.

Ravizza, K. (2001). Reflections and insights from the field on performance enhancement consultation. In G. Tenenbaum (Ed.), *The Practice of Sport Psychology* (pp. 197–216). Morgantown, WV: Fitness Information Technology.

Rogers, C. (1957). The necessary and sufficient conditions of therapeutic personality change. *Journal of Consulting Psychology, 21*(2), 95–103.

Rogers, C. (1961). *On becoming a person: A therapist's view of psychotherapy.* London: Constable.

Tod, D. & Bond, K. (2010). A longitudinal examination of a British neophyte sport psychologist's development. *The Sport Psychologist, 24*, 35–51.

Vealey, V. S. (1986). Conceptualization of sport-confidence and competitive orientation: Preliminary investigation and instrument development. *Journal of Sport Psychology, 8*, 221–246.

Zinnser, N., Bunker, L., & Williams, J. M. (2006). Cognitive techniques for building confidence and enhancing performance. In J. M. Williams (Ed.), *Applied sport psychology: Personal growth to peak performance* (5th ed.; pp. 349–381). New York, NY: McGraw-Hill Higher Education.

9 Using Acceptance Commitment Training in a Team Sport Leading Up To, During, and Following the 2014 Winter Olympic Games

Kristoffer Henriksen, Gregory Diment, Jakob Hansen, and Carsten Hvid Larsen

Working as a sport psychology consultant (SPC) is exciting and has great variation in the tasks and skills required. Some days you are in the office, other days on the "playing field"; some days in training other days in competition; in some cases you work with individual athletes and in others with teams and even sport coaches and managers; in some periods you aim to improve basic psychological skills and in others you focus on peak performance. Undoubtedly, preparing athletes for the Olympic Games and helping them perform during this pinnacle event is a challenging but also meaningful key task for SPCs, and one in which they are expected and want to perform at their best. The present chapter describes an intervention aimed at helping a curling team perform their very best at the Olympic Games.

BACKGROUND INFORMATION

Team Denmark sport psychology works from a coherent professional philosophy (Henriksen, Diment, & Hansen, 2011). Such a philosophy is a dynamic entity and the team has on several occasions discussed and revised parts of it. A recent addition is an increased focus on third-wave cognitive therapy methods such as mindfulness and acceptance commitment therapy (ACT).

The present chapter describes a sport psychology intervention in Olympic-level curling coming from an ACT perspective. The purpose of the intervention was to prepare the national Danish curling teams for the 2014 Olympic Games. The teams' cooperation with the sport psychology consultant (SPC) started two years prior to the 2014 winter Olympics and lasted through the Olympic Games (in which the consultant took part) and ended approximately one month after the end of the games. The intervention targeted both the male and female teams.[1] The SPC has been associated with curling as a consultant since 2009 and he supported the Danish curling teams during the 2010 Olympic Games. Thus, he knew the sport and key people in it (sporting directors, national coach, medical staff, and players) very well before the onset of the intervention.

DESCRIPTION OF THE CASE

For a majority of elite-level athletes, success at the Olympics is the dream goal, and being a part of an Olympic team is often described as the highlight of an athlete's career. Winning an Olympic medal even has the potential to change an athlete's life (McCann, 2008). Just as the Olympic Games are often emphasized by athletes as a unique and peak experience, it is also described by athletes as a very stressful event (Pensgaard, 2008). Denmark has traditionally had very few participants and very little success at the Winter Olympic Games. In 2014, the Danish curling teams represented the only potential Danish medals. It was therefore expected that the majority of Danish media attention during the Games would center on these athletes. The overall focus of the intervention was thus to strengthen the athletes' ability to perform under a level of pressure and attention that would expectedly exceed anything in their prior experience.

Curling is a precision sport played in teams, and it challenges athletes mentally on several levels. On the individual level, all the players have to be able to make a curling shot with the right speed and direction under pressure. On a team level, the four players need to have ongoing communication to make optimal decisions during the sweeping. On a leadership level, the skip has to lead the team and make good tactical decisions in collaboration with the rest of the team.

THEORETICAL FRAMEWORK/PHILOSOPHY

Following a national evaluation of the sport performance system in 2008, Team Denmark (the Danish elite sports institute) decided to strengthen the sport psychology service delivery in Danish elite sport by establishing a permanent staff of sport psychologists. An initial task of the team was to develop a systematic and coherent professional philosophy. The aim of this philosophy was to create an overall framework for the sport psychology work in Team Denmark and, by extension, to ensure effective sport psychological interventions based on a coherent service delivery model that integrates the entire efforts of the consultant's work (Poczwardowski, Sherman, & Ravizza, 2004). During the past six years, Team Denmark's sports psychology team has continued to work closely with Danish elite athletes, gaining more experience, and has regularly participated in ongoing professional and personal development activities such as supervision, international conferences, and study trips to other national elite sports institutions. These experiences have led to the continual evolution and development of our professional philosophy. Today, the professional philosophy is structured in five levels: (1) basic beliefs and values; (2) theories of intervention and behavior change; (3) objectives of the sport psychology intervention; (4) the content and focus of the intervention structured in "the Team Denmark sport psychology model"; and (5) sport psychological services and methods.

Beliefs and values represent the consultant's or team of consultants' fundamental beliefs and values about the athletes, coaches, and the nature of elite sport. Consistent with the case presented in this chapter, two examples of basic beliefs from the philosophy are: (1) Doubt and worry are natural and inevitable parts of elite sport. Therefore, we define mental strength as the ability to act in accordance with motives and values, even when facing difficult thoughts and feelings. (2) Championships are like a magnifying glass that amplifies both positive and negative thoughts and feelings, and even give rise to new ones. Therefore, the SPC should strive to support athletes not only before, but also during and after important events. *Theories of intervention* describe the theories on which the practical work is based. The Team Denmark sport psychology team primarily works from a cognitive psychology tradition (including third-wave cognitive methods), systems theory, and the holistic ecological approach. These beliefs and intervention theories are connected to the *overall objective* of ensuring that Danish elite athletes obtain the right mental skills to perform at the highest international level while experiencing meaning and value in life as elite athletes. In terms of *content and focus*, Team Denmark's sport psychology model highlights awareness of personal values and motives alongside focus and emotional coping as key focus areas of the sport psychology intervention. Finally, *services offered* include individual and team sessions as well as championship support. The idea of the model is that a good intervention requires consistency between all five levels.

Based on applied experiences, we have recently included into the philosophy an increased focus on third-wave cognitive therapy methods such as ACT and mindfulness-based interventions (Gardner & Moore, 2007). Third-wave cognitive therapy is different from a classical cognitive behavioral therapy (CBT) approach. A central idea of a classic CBT approach in sport psychology is to change dysfunctional patterns of thought–emotion–behavior interactions into more functional ones (Beck, 1995). Classic CBT approaches aim to teach athletes to control their internal states, for example to regulate arousal or performance anxiety and to deliberately enter their individual ideal performance state. A classic CBT approach for treating performance anxiety in sports could involve, for example, mapping negative automatic thoughts and reframing to formulate more rational ones. However, our experiences from delivering sport psychology service at the Olympics (Henriksen, 2015) is that the athletes are rarely able to foresee and map all problematic thoughts in advance or to find their ideal performance state during the unique pressure of the event. The Olympic Games are simply unlike anything that the athletes have ever tried before (and therefore are difficult to prepare for in specific detail), and often evoke new and difficult feelings and thoughts.

Unlike CBT, third-wave (ACT) approaches assert that thought suppression and control techniques can trigger a metacognitive scanning process (Purdon, 1999), and that excessive cognitive activity and task-irrelevant focus disrupts performance. Success on a particular task is related to the degree to which an athlete can accept the presence of negative thoughts, physiological arousal, emotions such as anxiety or anger, and remain attentionally engaged in the task, while behaving in accordance with his or her values. Values describe how the athlete wants to behave or "what kind of athlete he wants to be" (e.g., "I want to be a constructive leader and teammate, to work hard and to motivate the team during adversity"). In an ACT perspective, practitioners should therefore not help the athletes engage in the futile task of managing and controlling internal states, but rather introduce an agenda of willingness to accept negative thoughts and emotions in pursuit of valued ends (Hayes, Strosahl, Bunting, Twohig, & Wilson, 2004). The aim of the ACT practitioner, therefore, is to provide three key aspects: (1) teaching athletes to open up, to accept, and to be willing to experience the full range of thoughts and emotions that are a natural part of pursuing an elite sports career; (2) teaching athletes to mindfully engage in the present moment, including task-focused attention; and (3) helping athletes formulate personal values that describe how they would like to be as an athlete and help them engage in actions that display these values.

NEEDS ASSESSMENT

The focus of the interventions was based on interviews with individual athletes and the coach, interviews with the teams, a literature review, and observations. First, the consultant conducted individual interviews with the athletes and the coach, followed by team meetings in which the coach was present. The focus of the interviews was the team's strengths, weaknesses, and challenges in the context of high-pressure championships in periods of performing well and in periods of adversity. The teams had several experiences of championship performance from European and World Championships to draw upon. Second, the consultant made observations of the teams during the national qualification for the European Championship, where the athletes experienced pressure to perform. The consultant observed team dynamics, communication, and how the team coped with pressure and adversity. In this phase, the consultant drew upon his/her own experiences of delivering sport psychology during a Summer and a Winter Olympic Games and on typical challenges mentioned in the literature (e.g., Blumenstein & Lidor, 2008; Gould, Guinan, & Chung, 2002; Gould & Maynard, 2009; Greenleaf, Gould, & Dieffenbach, 2001). The consultant's starting point was that the Olympics are different from a European or a World Championship. The consultant used the image of the Olympics as a magnifying glass and described how he had witnessed athletes ending up in endless battles trying to control uncontrollable thoughts and feelings. Half of the players had been to the games before, and the other half was debutants. The interviews became a co-creating inquiry based on the experiences of the athletes and the consultant to uncover the specific needs of the teams and of the individual athletes.

The team formulated as the goal of the intervention to prepare both the individual athletes and team to perform under pressure, cope with adversity, and deal with the unexpected. The plan took its starting point in the ACT approach. The athletes and coach should not learn how to manage specific thoughts and emotions, but rather acquire metacognitive strategies to deal with what comes up in a flexible, accepting, and values-connected way.

INTERVENTION

The intervention focused on the individual player's development in parallel with that of the team. The work took place in designated team workshops, individual consultations, and through the SPC taking part in training sessions and in the European Championship.

Leading Up To the Olympics: May 2012–February 2014

In the preparation period, the team intervention focused on developing the team's structure, values, and communication skills. This was done through a series of team meetings. The main question that structured the process was: "What kind of team do you want to be?" To support this process, the consultant asked reflective questions such as: "How do you want to communicate when you are in adversity and in success?"; and "What are good ways for you to recover together after a mistake or a loss?" The inquiry initiated important in-depth conversations in the team, which led to the formulation of initial team values.

The consultant also asked the team to discuss the players' individual roles and mutual expectations. This took place through team conversations where the consultant asked each individual "What do you want to contribute to the team?"; "What can the others expect from you?"; and "What do you need from your teammates to be the best athlete you can be?" The other players could then describe their expectations toward the player, and the team agreed on mutual expectations. The team formulated specific actions to carry out the values and roles, and the actions were implemented and trained in training sessions and games. These strategies were supplemented by psycho-education sessions about stress, identity, and recovery. In parallel, the development of the individual players focused on concentration skills and the handling of stress and emotions. Building the athletes' individual skills took place through a combination of individual sessions and team sessions to allow the team to gain insight into each other's typical reaction patterns.

As the Olympic Games approached, the work was intensified, as was the consultant's presence in the training environment. In the last half of the year before the Olympics, focus was increasingly directed toward handling the media and publicity, and coping with stress and pressure. This phase of the intervention focused on three key components: (1) a final clarification of values and committed actions; (2) functional analysis to increase awareness about dysfunctional versus functional behavior; and (3) learning to defuse from dysfunctional thoughts and emotions, and to reconnect to values, the present, and the task.

Values clarification and committed action. The SPC worked in-depth helping every athlete clarify his/her final values. The consultant asked questions such as: "What have you learned about yourself through the last one-and-a-half years?"; "What are important values to you as an athlete?"; and "how do you want to act when you experience pressure and adversity?" The individual values were shared in a team meeting, during which the team was asked to revisit and (re)formulate the team values from the question "How do you want to act as a team when you get to the Olympics, on and off the ice, during success and adversity?" Central team values were written down and the team discussed what actions would show commitment to these values in different kinds of situations, including adversity, pressure, and success. Examples of values were: "never give up," "constructive and supportive communication," "go for it – be brave and dare to make the bold decisions," and "dedication and focus on and off the ice." These where all described in terms of specific actions in different situations.

Awareness about reactive and dysfunctional behavior versus functional behavior. A central idea in the ACT literature is that behavior always has a function. Often, when athletes behave in ways that are non-consistent with their values and with how they wish to behave, these behaviors alleviate pressure, reduce anxiety, or have other secondary benefits. Acting to reduce unpleasant feelings rather than committing to values is called "reactive responses." A key for an athlete to learn to act more consistently with his/her values and be less reactive is to understand his/her typical reactive patterns and the rewards involved. Therefore, the SPC spent a great deal of time helping the athletes clarify their reactive patterns in order to help them move more toward valued ends. Playing safe in certain defining moments is an example of a reactive pattern that was an issue for the teams (and likely for most teams). This happened when the team entered a game-deciding moment. The aggressive but difficult shot can change momentum and set the team up for a win, whereas a miss can cost the entire game. In these situations, feelings of nervousness, anxiety, and tension would be accompanied by thoughts about the consequences of a miss. The reactive response would be to play the safe shot. In the moment, this would ease the uncomfortable feelings. Unfortunately, the team would also miss a game-changing opportunity and even miss out on living their value to "go for it – be brave and dare to make the bold decisions." Through inquiry the SPC and the team mapped such dysfunctional and reactive behaviors, and the team became more aware of typical challenging situations and reactive responses.

Defusing from dysfunctional thoughts and feelings to reconnect to values, the present, and the task. A third intervention focus was to educate and train the athletes to defuse from dysfunctional thoughts and feelings, and reconnect to their values and focus on the present and the task. This included a range of defusion exercises and techniques, as well as mindfulness training. In the exercises the athletes were trained to observe their own thinking as thinking without reacting to it, and also to label it. As examples of labeling we introduced "Ms. Critic" and "Mr. Perfectionism." The players would often get very judgmental after a mistake. Frustrating feelings and thoughts about not being good enough would come up, followed up by doubt before the next shot. In other words, the players would be stuck in the past or the future. As the athletes learned to observe such thoughts and became familiar with them, they were able to label them, for example: "Here comes Mr. Perfectionism. He is telling his usual 'You are not good enough story.' It's okay and only natural for him to turn up after a mistake. I do not have to listen to him." This created distance from the thought and the athlete was able to reconnect to and behave consistently with the team values.

According to the coach's observations and the athletes' own reflections, the athletes became more aware of their team and individual values, and they all improved their ability to commit to these values and behave in a values-consistent way even in the face of unpleasant emotions and thoughts that would often come up in situations of pressure and adversity. In other words, the reactive and dysfunctional behavior decreased.

Intervention During the Olympic Games: February 2014

The curling tournament started on day one of the Games. The team had to play a round robin against the nine other teams in the tournament. The four best teams qualified for the playoffs.

The SPC participated in the team's pre-game meetings. The coach covered the tactical aspects in collaboration with the team. The consultant followed this up by asking for the mental focus points for the game, rehearsing the mental game plan, reminding the athletes how to deal with adversity and pressure situations, and by repeating the trained ACT skills. Central questions during pre-game meetings were: "What behaviors and actions are important out there today?" and "What kinds of adversity or mental challenges will you possibly face today – and how will you behave in these situations?" Sometimes the consultant asked more specific questions such as: "How do we handle a bad start?"; "How do we communicate in a period of adversity?"; and "How do we want to behave in game-deciding moments?"

After each game, the SPC participated in a post-game meeting, where the coach went over tactical issues. Here, the consultant engaged the athletes in an evaluation process by, for example, asking how they evaluated the frequency of balance between value-based and committed behaviors versus reactive responses, and by selecting specific challenging situations during the game and scrutinizing how the team acted in the situation and what they learned for the next game.

An example of a situation with reactive behavior was in the first game of the tournament, where the team was in a tough decision-making situation under pressure. A key team value was to be "bold and brave" and dare to go for the openings and game-changing opportunities when they showed up. However, in the situation they felt a strong anxiety and had many "what-if thoughts." One athlete thought: "If I miss we will lose and it will be my fault and the media will be very critical." The increased tension and presence of negative thoughts in the situation were very unpleasant, and the athlete made a safe and defensive play. The values-consistent decision would have been to make an aggressive but more difficult and risky play and be willing to be with the anxiety associated with this decision. In the following debriefing, the SPC helped the team see such patterns and understand that the play had been an expression of a reactive path. The athletes described their perceptions of the situation, the thoughts and feelings present in the moment, the secondary reward of the action (the defensive play), and how the athlete would have liked to act in the situation. The SPC validated and normalized their experience, repeating that anxiety is natural in pressured situations, and the goal is not to make it disappear but to accept it and make room for it, in a way that it becomes more like a radio in the background. The team revisited planned strategies designed to recognize these thoughts and feelings, and to then engage in values-consistent plays even in the face of such feelings. In the next game, the team was more aggressive and bold.

One strategy for the athletes to behave in accordance with values was to stop, step back, and notice that anxiety had entered the field. Instead of trying to control the anxiety, they should accept the feelings and thoughts as natural occurrences in situations of threat, and recognize their desire to play safe as a misguided attempt to control the uncontrollable. By greeting the thoughts and feelings as natural, it becomes possible to let go of their smothering effect. This is then followed by an effort to reestablish a true connection with their team values.

Individual consultations supplemented the team meetings when an athlete wanted to talk more in-depth. The athletes could initiate this by asking the SPC for a talk, but the consultant also took part in many informal situations such as walking from the apartment to the dining tent, sitting and eating in the tent, and hanging out in a relaxing area. These informal activities are crucial during championships. Even athletes who are familiar with their consultant sometimes have difficulties initiating an in-depth dialogue. Our experience is that athletes think their wishes are irrelevant, that they do not know how to initiate, or that they are afraid that talking about problems will only make them worse. In the present case, most in-depth personal talk grew out of an informal chat.

Even though the athletes felt well prepared before the Olympic Games, thoughts and feelings of an unexpected character or intensity still came up in pressure situations. One unaccustomed challenge in curling at the Olympics that has a magnifying emotional effect is that all the players have to wear microphones during the matches, and there are more people watching the matches on TV than normal. The communication and coping process takes place with the media present on the "shoulder of the players." The television coverage is very intense, and the players easily get the feeling that "big brother" or the nation is watching very closely. This led some players to become aware in a judgmental way of their own behavior. In accordance with the overall approach, the athletes learned to cope with this by staying present and focusing on the values and the task.

Over the course of the tournament, the SPC worked to repeat, support, and reinforce when the athletes made value-based committed actions, and debriefed when they became reactive and emotional in their behaviors. The coach and athletes experienced a decrease in reactive behavior and an increase in commitment to value-based actions in adversity and pressured situations. As one of the players expressed after a loss:

> I am happy that I am so aware of my own values as a person and as a player. That makes it much easier to stay focused on who I want to be, and what it is all about (i.e., staying focused on the task) when I stand there and feel like my body and feelings are taking me for a roller-coaster ride.

Both teams got sixth place – one win away from making it to the playoffs. Not everything turned out how they hoped (such is the nature of sport and no one can be non-reactive to emotions), but the team was generally satisfied that they did their best and really worked among themselves and the challenges they faced.

The SPC in turmoil. The Olympics are also a busy, stressful, and challenging period for the SPC. Without clear values it is easy to fall into dysfunctional and reactive behavior. After a couple of losses, the media asked the SPC if he wanted to join them for a studio broadcast to discuss how he works with the teams to recover after a loss. The media had at that point been critical of the team's performance. On the one hand, the SPC saw it as an opportunity to tell the nation that the team worked very hard and professionally and that struggling to perform at the Olympics is not unusual. On the other hand, the SPC did not wish to risk compromising his confidentiality with the players, which is an important value for him. He ended up turning the request down, but the media continued putting pressure on the consultant to take part, saying that he did not have to be very specific. The consultant now experienced doubt. Maybe he could help the team by attending the media show. In addition, he did not like to say no. The doubt created tension and discomfort. The consultant knew that in order to perform at his best – much like the athletes – he had to stay present and re-establish contact with his values. Thus, the consultant called a colleague who asked: "Which of your values do you want to serve as your compass?" They discussed the situation and agreed that the reactive response would be to say "Sure, I can come on your program." This would alleviate tension since he would not have to say no to the media and would end the pressure and the critique coming from their request. The value-based response, on the other hand, would be to say no and keep the integrity and confidentiality of the team, to focus on the next task with the team, and to remain part of the team and not an outside commentator. To do this, he had to be willing to accept the discomfort of turning down the media request and to let the criticism go unanswered. In this case, clarification of values and analysis of reactive responses through collegial sparring helped the consultant stay focused.

Back Home after the Olympic Games: March 2014

Approximately a month after the team returned to Denmark, the consultant had a debriefing team meeting as well as individual debriefing sessions. In these meetings, the SPC interviewed the athletes about their experience and what they learned. The teams described a hard but also thrilling experience, where the acquired ACT skills helped them stay focused and to "be the kind of athletes they wanted to be." They also described that they had gotten to know themselves in a new and more nuanced way, which they would benefit from in the future as athletes and individuals. A couple of players retired, but the others made a values-based decision to commit to another four-year period heading for the next Winter Olympic Games, with the willingness to face new challenging and stressful situations in the pursuit of a meaningful and rich career as an Olympian.

REFLECTION

Many athletes only ever take part in one Olympic Games, and if they take part in more than one it will often be in different roles (e.g., debutant, experienced, underdog, favorite). This means the athletes are basically always unprepared for the emotional turmoil of the Games and how it will affect them. It is our experience that not knowing what emotions will show up in addition to the unaccustomed strength of such emotions makes it difficult to teach athletes to prepare for, manage, and control inner states. Therefore, we argue that acceptance and commitment-based interventions are well suited in the preparation of athletes to compete in the Olympics. We suggest that such interventions can preferably focus on helping athletes: (1) learn to notice and be open, accepting, and non-judgmental of the multitude of thoughts and emotions that naturally arise in high-pressure competitions; (2) develop their ability to be in the present moment and refocus to the task when they are distracted; and (3) become more aware of their values, valued behaviors, and game plan. With the athletes we often refer to these core skills as: opening up, being present, and doing what matters. To guarantee a coherent support to the athletes, the ACT perspective must not be seen as simply a number of methods, but rather they must be a part of a coherent professional philosophy that integrates the whole sport psychology framework, including basic beliefs, theories of intervention, objectives, and specific services and methods (Henriksen et al., 2011).

In the present intervention, we found that a precise and formulated professional philosophy accounts for part of the success because it provided consistency in messages and methods over the course of a two-year period. The central focus on ACT skills turned out to be helpful for the athletes. It gave them the strength to respond in a flexible and values-based way to many of the challenges they faced. However, even though the ACT-based skills are trained and learned beforehand, it can be difficult for the athletes to keep an open mind and connect to their values once they are at the Games and the pressure builds to a maximum. One point for improvement would therefore be to practice the skills further in high-pressure situations. This would require that the governing body invest the time and money to send the SPC to European and World Championships with the teams even earlier in the years leading up the Games. Such championships are the only opportunities for the SPC to really engage with the teams when they are exposed to high-pressure situations, and the time between competitions provides valuable opportunities for the teams to reflect and learn. However, keep in mind that the Games are still like a magnifying glass and different from any other championship. We therefore still advocate that the SPC should support teams during the event. To develop effective strategies for sport psychological support during championships (e.g., test and decide on the role of the SPC during pre-game meetings, matches, and evaluations), the decision to send the SPC to the Olympic Games should be taken as early as possible.

It is equally important that the SPC is aware of his/her own values and able to notice and counteract emotional and reactive responses to stressful situations. Therefore, we recommend that SPCs undergo mindfulness training and engage in supervision regarding their own role and behavior (Williams & Andersen, 2012). We further recommend that the consultant have a collegial support set up. In the present case, the consultant found himself in a number of situations where he had to make difficult decisions and found it hard to distinguish between the values-based and the emotional-reactive path. The setup for the collegial supervision could have been more planned before the SPC for the Games. Such a support setup can be on-site or via regular Skype sessions, but it is important that there is a clear plan and strategy for the provision of supervision (planned and acute), particularly when colleagues are in different time zones. This is something that the Danish sport psychological team will prioritize and improve for the future.

NOTE

1. As agreed with the teams and in order to anonymize individual athletes, the chapter describes the intervention in both teams. The overall focus and process within each team was in reality almost identical, whereas each team's values and particular episodes and experiences differed. When we describe specifics of the intervention we will not specify which team was involved.

SUGGESTED READINGS

Gardner, F., & Moore, Z. (2007). *The psychology of enhancing human performance: The mindfulness–acceptance–commitment (MAC) approach*. New York, NY: Springer.

Hayes, S. C., Strosahl, K. D., Bunting, K., Twohig, M., & Wilson, K. G. (2004). What is acceptance and commitment therapy? In S. C. Hayes & K. D. Strosahl (Eds.), *A practical guide to acceptance and commitment therapy* (pp. 3–29). New York, NY: Springer.

Henriksen, K. (2015). Sport psychology at the Olympics: The case of a Danish sailing crew in a head wind. *International Journal of Sport and Exercise Psychology, 13*, 43–55.

Henriksen, K., Diment, G., & Hansen, J. (2011). Professional philosophy: Inside the delivery of sport psychology service at Team Denmark. *Sport Science Review, 20*, 5–21.

REFLECTIVE QUESTIONS

1. What difference would it make to you as an SPC to formulate and work from a coherent professional philosophy (if this is not already the case)?
2. How would you use the ACT perspective versus more traditional cognitive interventions to work with an athlete/team on performance anxiety?
3. How would you, through a focus on team and personal values, assist athletes in handling high-stress situations and adversity during and between matches?
4. What are particularly relevant issues for you as an SPC to consider when preparing athletes for a championship during which expectations, media attention, and pressure are expected to exceed anything the athletes experienced before (e.g., at the Olympics)?
5. How can an SPC prepare for delivering service in high-pressure contexts, for example through colleague support systems and clarification of his or her own values?

REFERENCES

Beck, J. (1995). *Cognitive therapy: Basics and beyond*. New York, NY: Guilford Press.

Blumenstein, B., & Lidor, R. (2008). Psychological preparation in the Olympic village: A four-phase approach. *International Journal of Sport and Exercise Psychology, 6*, 287–300. DOI: 10.1080/1612197X.2008.9671873.

Gardner, F., & Moore, Z. (2007). *The psychology of enhancing human performance: The mindfulness–acceptance–commitment (MAC) approach*. New York, NY: Springer.

Gould, D., Greenleaf, C., Guinan, D., & Chung, Y. (2002). A survey of US Olympic coaches: Variables perceived to have influenced athlete performance and coach effectiveness. *The Sport Psychologist, 16*, 175–186.

Gould, D., & Maynard, I. (2009). Psychological preparation for the Olympic Games. *Journal of Sports Sciences, 27*, 1393–1408. DOI: 10.1080/02640410903081845.

Greenleaf, C., Gould, D., & Dieffenbach, K. (2001). Factor influencing Olympic performance: Interviews with Atlanta and Nagano US Olympians. *Journal of Applied Sport Psychology, 13*, 254–184. DOI: 10.1080/104132001753149874.

Hayes, S. C., Strosahl, K. D., Bunting, K., Twohig, M., & Wilson, K. G. (2004). What is acceptance and commitment therapy? In S. C. Hayes & K. D. Strosahl (Eds.), *A practical guide to acceptance and commitment therapy* (pp. 3–29). New York, NY: Springer.

Henriksen, K. (2015). Sport psychology at the Olympics: The case of a Danish sailing crew in a head wind. *International Journal of Sport and Exercise Psychology, 13*(1), 43–55. DOI: http://dx.doi.org/1 0.1080/1612197X.2014.944554.

Henriksen, K., Diment, G., & Hansen, J. (2011). Professional philosophy: Inside the delivery of sport psychology service at Team Denmark. *Sport Science Review, 20*(1–2), 5–21. DOI: 10.2478/v10237-011-0043-6.

McCann, S. (2008). At the Olympics, everything is a performance issue. *International Journal of Sport and Exercise Psychology, 6*, 267–276. DOI: 10.1080/1612197X.2008.9671871.

Pensgaard, A. M. (2008). Consulting under pressure: How to help an athlete deal with unexpected distractors during Olympic Games 2006. *International Journal of Sport and Exercise Psychology, 6*, 301–307. DOI: 10.1080/1612197X.2008.9671874.

Purdon, C. (1999). Thought suppression and psychopathology. *Behaviour research and therapy, 37*(11), 1029–1054.

Poczwardowski, A., Sherman, C. P., & Ravizza, K. (2004). Professional philosophy in the sport psychology service delivery: Building on theory and practice. *Sport Psychologist, 18*(4), 445–463.

Williams, D. E., & Andersen, M. B. (2012). Identity, wearing many hats, and boundary blurring: The mindful psychologist on the way to the Olympic and Paralympic Games. *Sport Psychology in Action, 3*, 139–152. DOI: 10.1080/21520704.2012.683090.

10 Psychological Service Provision to the Elite Football Performance Network

Supporting Coaches, Players, Parents, and Teams

Karl Steptoe, Jamie Barker, and Chris Harwood

Previous work in professional football has highlighted many of the barriers that have been experienced by practitioners (e.g., Barker, McCarthy, & Harwood, 2011; Gamble, Hill, & Parker, 2013; Pain & Harwood, 2004), particularly regarding the misconceptions of sport psychology and its value in performance enhancement. The common, primary perceived role of sport psychology in football is to assist in performance enhancement across the development pathway (Gamble et al., 2013). This was the case in the example discussed in this chapter in which an intervention was developed and provided for a British football (soccer) academy. An initial meeting with the academy director outlined the specific needs, the role of the sport psychologist (SP) and the resources that would be available, and created a strong foundation from which to develop an effective program. The expectation was that the program would be compatible with the 5Cs model (commitment, communication, concentration, control, and confidence) of sport psychology that club coaches were familiar with (Harwood, 2005, 2008).

BACKGROUND INFORMATION

The opportunities for sport and exercise psychology practitioners to work in British football were enhanced in October 2011 with an agreement between the Premier League, its clubs, representatives of the Football League, The Football Association, and other key football stakeholders to develop the Elite Player Performance Plan (EPPP). The EPPP represented commitment to a long-term strategy for youth development, with football clubs receiving greater levels of funding determined by the award of a category status between 1 (highest award) and 4 (lowest award). Such status levels are determined by an independent audit that considers factors including: productivity rates, training facilities, coaching, and education and welfare provisions when determining the academy status. Although there is a financial benefit to the club and academy, the EPPP has been developed with six principle objectives: (1) increasing the number and quality of home-grown players gaining professional football contracts and playing first-team football at the highest level; (2) creating more time for players to play and be coached; (3) improving coaching provision; (4) implementing a system of effective measurement and quality assurance; (5) positively influencing strategic investment into the Academy system, demonstrating value for money; and (6) seeking to implement significant gains in every aspect of player development.

As part of the EPPP audit, academies are required to demonstrate investment and commitment to the technical, tactical, physical, and psychological development of their young players to satisfy the criteria of category 1 status. Category 1 status requires the appointment of an accredited SP or practitioner in training with the British Psychological Society (BPS), which is regulated by the Health and Care Professions Council (HCPC). This regulation has consequently enhanced the opportunities for individuals on this training route and altered how psychology support is delivered within professional football. The following case study predominantly details consultancy carried out by the first author under the supervision of the third author, within a professional football academy who sought the services of an SP to assist in their objectives of gaining category 1 status on the EPPP. In this case study, we outline our work across a foundation phase (FP), youth development phase (YDP), and professional development phase (PDP) consisting of male footballers from the ages of 9–21 years. This work includes comparative and complementary examples of consultancy in football carried out by all the authors.

DESCRIPTION OF THE CASE

The initial objectives for the SP were to help the academy meet the criteria required for an EPPP audit that had been scheduled for three months and comprised work with players at the individual and team levels, coaches across the development phases, and parents of the FP players. In this "football case" the following issues are discussed: (a) individual player support on match days; (b) meeting the demands presented by key transitions and stages of development (e.g., player reviews, scholarships, professional contracts, being released from the academy, and education demands); (c) group delivery of the 5Cs coach and parent education; (d) assessment of team factors influencing belief and cohesion; and (e) the development of coaching behaviors to impact individual and team confidence. In addition, it is important to reinforce that such consultancy work took place in the context of an interdisciplinary performance, coaching, and welfare-oriented environment. Specifically, close working relationships were required with the first-team SP, the sport science team, house parents at players' accommodation, the academy's social welfare officer, head of education, and head of recruitment to establish ethical communication channels to reinforce key training factors and to determine player referral protocols. Rapport building at the outset of the intervention was central to creating a positive foundation for future interventions.

THEORETICAL FRAMEWORK/PHILOSOPHY

This case is built on humanistic, cognitive, and cognitive behavioral principles. Training and personal development in areas including cognitive behavioral therapy (CBT), acceptance commitment therapy (ACT), and mindfulness have enhanced what has always been a strong humanistic "core" (by the first author) and have in turn influenced a modification to theoretical allegiances. This growth has been driven by a reflective process that has continually sought more effective ways of providing appropriate support to clients and to meet the "real life" demands of working in the applied field that include infrequent contact with clients, inconsistent session duration, and managing multiple client needs of performance and well-being. While examples within this case do not represent specific examples of CBT or ACT, much of the consultancy work with players, parents, and coaches was closely aligned to specific CBT and ACT principles. These included collaborative work, use of guided discovery, integration of behavioral and cognitive strategies, a focus on work in the present that is problem- and goal-oriented, the use of independent work, active engagement in cognitive/behavioral experiments to test underlying assumptions/core beliefs, and altering the client's relationship with internal processes (i.e., thoughts and feelings) toward enhanced self-regulation. To maintain a humanistic foundation, within a sport portrayed as being abrasive, irrational, emotional, and unpredictable (Gilbourne & Richardson, 2006), consultancy focused on raising players' awareness of how they could simultaneously satisfy the goals of the academy while ensuring that they were on target to realize personal objectives.

Previous experience (from all authors) has highlighted the importance of being accepted as a member of the coaching team. This immersion facilitates practitioner confidence that services are welcomed and demonstrates that sport psychology is an acceptable part of football culture. To assist in this aim, a club training kit was provided to the SP and close work with coaching staff was encouraged. Experienced practitioners have cautioned that being so closely identified with the academy and coaching staff may lead to increased intervention efficacy and adherence, however, on the other hand, this could lead to negative perceptions from players; for example, the belief that work with the SP would have a negative impact on team selection and assessment (e.g., Barker et al., 2011).

NEEDS ASSESSMENT

A program of individual player profiling was set out across the phases that identified the following: (a) players that would most benefit from SP support and those that may present clinical issues requiring referral (Performance Classification Questionnaire; Gardner & Moore, 2006); (b) desired behaviors associated with the 5Cs (Harwood, 2008); (c) the demonstration of psychological characteristics associated with elite performance (PCDEQ; Macnamara & Collins, 2011), and mental toughness (SMTQ; Sheard, Golby, & van Wersch, 2009). In addition, meetings with coaching staff, introductory group presentations to teams across the development pathway, training and match observation, and semi-structured interviews with individual players and coaches comprised an intake assessment and promoted discussion around the salient psychological demands faced by players at each stage of development.

Key issues in youth development have been identified as including fear of failure and stressors associated with making errors, opponents, team performance, family, selection, contracts, social evaluation, and making transitions to playing at higher levels (e.g., Reeves, Nicholls, & McKenna, 2009). Young players in academies are considered to be under great pressure to produce consistent elite performance and be selected for the Premier League, and as a result experience numerous personal and interpersonal challenges that affect development (Richardson, Gilbourne, & Littlewood, 2004). The profiling process highlighted key issues that are shown in Table 10.1.

Table 10.1 Key Issues Faced by Players According to Developmental Phase

Phase	Key Issues
Foundation Phase	Frustration at playing out of position
	Low confidence
	Relationship issues with other players
	Distress at being released from the academy
	Inappropriate influence/pressure from parents
	Perfectionism and fear of making mistakes
Youth Development Phase	Anxiety over contracts and concerns over transition to scholar
	Low self-confidence and perceived lack of control over career
	Concentration in training/matches/school
	Comparison with others
	Belief that working on psychology will be seen by coaches as weakness
	Living away from home
	Issues relating to injury rehabilitation (frustration/motivation)
	School demands
	Perfectionism and fear of making mistakes
	Few success measures beyond outcome and external reward
Professional Development Phase	Unhelpful beliefs about what coaches think of them
	Belief that working on psychology will be seen by coaches as weakness
	Dealing with disappointment and setbacks (e.g., dropped/released)
	New players challenging position
	Issues relating to injury rehabilitation (frustration/motivation)
	Perfectionism and fear of making mistakes
	Lack of control over career
	Few success measures beyond outcome and external reward

Although services were required through all phases along the development pathway, it was made clear that specific older players (PDP) represented a priority as they were perceived to be experiencing various behavioral, emotional, and cognitive maladaptive reactions to the demands of training, competition, transition, and education. Assessment of the academy's requirements highlighted a need to manage the limited contact time available with players, plan multiple methods for disseminating support, and prioritize age groups for individual work. Having considered the physical, cognitive, emotional, and social characteristics synonymous with youth development as well as the priorities of the academy, a program was proposed to maximize the academy's resources for sport psychology support.

Models of practice were employed to meet the disparate and changing goals of consultancy. For work with players identified as needing support by the coaches, a medical model was adopted as it could not be assumed that they had the coping resources to deal with their presenting issues; for work with all other players at an individual and team level, a psychological skills training (PST) model was used (Poczwardowski, Sherman, & Ravizza, 2004). Weekly meetings and regular communications with support staff working with individual players (e.g., nutritionist, physiotherapist, strength and conditioning coach) led to the development of an interdisciplinary sport science model and collaboration to meet psychological goals. Parent education was highlighted as an appropriate focus at the FP, coach education and individual player support at the YDP, and at the PDP coaches requested that psychological training should emphasize the development of team cohesion and belief, in addition to providing individual player support.

INTERVENTION

A "fixture list" of psycho-education sessions was advertised to players, coaches, and parents. In addition to providing workshops and individual sessions to players, coaches attended workshops that introduced each of the 5Cs and encouraged the design of training sessions that would reinforce key psychological behaviors that demonstrated positive psychology in training and in matches. Further, parent sessions also served as a focus group enabling discussion and communication of the psychological aims and intentions of the academy.

Player Workshops

Introductory presentations were first made to players across all phases outlining the role of sport psychology, the 5Cs framework, and the various ways that they could access sport psychology services (e.g., one-to-one consultation, telephone, email, text, Skype). In line with previous research (Harwood, 2008), these sessions were interactive, with discussions around key behaviors associated with each of the 5Cs and how they could be reinforced in training and match situations. Time had to be negotiated with each coach to release the players, which they were many times reluctant to do because of their own targets for training time, and as a result, service delivery was often provided to smaller available groups (e.g., goalkeepers or injured players).

Individual Consultancy

One-on-one consultations followed either referral from academy staff, conversations with players in between visits, or drop-in sessions and player requests during the day. There was no specific consultation room allocated to these sessions, but player meeting rooms, classrooms, and coach offices were utilized when free; on occasion home visits were also made. Confidentiality was assured throughout, with player meeting records taken and agreement over the action points each player wanted coaches to be aware of. It was explained that this was important to enable reinforcement of the work that we were doing; however, this was always guided by what the players were comfortable with sharing. Time with players was limited and therefore a brief intervention was often provided based on Anshel's COPE model (1990). This model enabled us to work on controlling emotions, organizing information, planning an appropriate response, and executing the response by "acting it out."

For scheduled sessions (where more time was allocated), it was possible to work toward empowering players to be in greater control of their response to thought processes and to modify any maladaptive thinking patterns. For example, work was undertaken with an under-16 player who was referred by his coach, as he believed the player to be low in confidence following recent errors in games. In addition, a decision was imminent on whether this player would be offered a scholarship and it was felt that this might also be contributing to a dip in performance. Through Socratic questioning, the player became aware of perfectionist thoughts that revealed beliefs associated with not being allowed to make errors if he were to receive a scholarship. Exploration of how this belief and other patterns of thinking contributed to performance and well-being became a priority of work. The player was first asked to keep a record of thoughts during the week to include training and match-day experiences so that these could be discussed. Instead of completing record sheets, which can often appear to a young player as "school work," the player sent key thoughts by text message as and when he became aware of them; this also increased communication and enhanced rapport. The player was encouraged to look for evidence that supported an alternative perception of making errors, and examples from the real world were also provided as and when they arose. One such example that served to normalize the player's personal experience was a professional footballer's response to his high-profile errors in a Premiership match, when interviewed after the game: "You want to go into a hole where no one can see you. Football is about coming back from things like that and it has happened to great players."

Cognitive-behavioral intervention(s) that included the practice of thought management strategies and pre- and post-performance routines provided the player with alternative goals for match days beyond outcome. He became able to see each performance as an opportunity to "research" the skills that would enable him to perform optimally, which promoted learning as a valuable measure of success. Assessment of this work was sought from two perspectives: (1) the player's feedback on decreased attention to negative thoughts and a reduction in the strength of belief he had in maladaptive assumptions (e.g., I am not allowed to make mistakes if I want to become a professional); and (2) discussions with the coaches revealed target behaviors that they considered as signatures of poor psychology and mental state (e.g., negative body language, failure to regain position, and a withdrawal of effort). Thus, changes in these responses to errors were considered a sign of improved psychological performance.

Remote support (i.e., telephone, text, email, and Skype) played a vital role in maintaining communication with players and coaches in between visits and following up on work set. It also acted as a more relaxed "first contact" after referral in which a scheduled session could be arranged for the next visit. This flexible access enabled players to discuss key issues as they were experienced, and feedback suggested they felt more comfortable communicating away from the academy as it increased feelings of confidentiality.

Coach Education

The Academy staff met every Friday for one hour as part of a continuing professional development (CPD) program. This provided the opportunity to highlight ongoing work at a team and individual level, educate the coaches on the 5C topics, and offer feedback on player profiling. These were always lively discussions that often revealed core beliefs about the role of sport psychology. There appeared to exist a knowledge of the "correct thing to say" with regard to sport psychology topics; however, coach behaviors and comments often contradicted these statements. An example of this was discussion that sought to understand the extent to which coaches held a fixed versus growth mindset relating to a player's mental performance. While all coaches supported the idea that a player could develop in that area when asked in a group setting, they would go on to say that a certain player "has not got what it takes" or that they are a "confidence player" using their experience in the game as justification. Although these sessions were compulsory, conversations with coaches continued after the workshops, suggesting their increasing value.

Parent Focus Groups and Workshops

Research has associated parent behaviors with child-athlete beliefs, values, motivated behaviors, and performances (Fredricks & Eccles, 2004). In addition, parental social support has been related to progression from academy to professional football (Holt & Dunn, 2004). Parents are considered to have a great influence on player learning and participation, and they have the power to shape responses and pre-performance behaviors (e.g., Keegan, Spray, Harwood, & Lavallee, 2010). Therefore, workshops and focus groups with parents of players at the FP were prioritized as they were considered to be best positioned to reinforce the academy ideals. This work also provided secondary gains by increasing communication between the academy and parents. These consisted of five sessions that provided education around each of the 5Cs, discussion of the key behaviors associated with each, and finally outlining the positive role that the parent could play in shaping and reinforcing these positive psychological behaviors (see Table 10.2). Session notes were sent to all parents after each session that outlined key points and offered suggestions on how they could support their child in each C.

To assess the efficacy of this psycho-educational intervention, data were collected from 56 football parents. Parents completed pre- and post-intervention measurements that assessed parental confidence in influencing psychological skills, parents' perceived available social support, and parental perceptions of their sons' motivation, competence, response to pressure, and training and match performance (5Cs, Harwood, 2008; PASS-Q, Freeman, Coffee, & Rees, 2011; IMI, Ryan, 1982). Of the 56 parents that took part in the assessment, 29 attended the biweekly 5Cs focus groups, which meant that the 27 non-attending parents acted as a natural control group. Post-intervention assessment revealed that parents in the intervention

Table 10.2 Examples of 5C Parent Education and Strategies

5Cs	Example Behavior	Example Strategy
Commitment	Consistently gives high effort in training sessions and games.	To keep players' commitment high, praise your child's effort levels and progress rather than results.
Communication	Shows respectful body language to coach, teammates, and officials.	Show respect for coaches, referees, and opposition in order to role model good communication to your child. Being a composed communicator to others will help your child to control their emotions too.
Concentration	Refocuses with their "head up" after mistakes, goals, and setbacks.	Reassure your child that it is okay to make mistakes. Explain that mistakes are a part of learning new skills and that everyone makes them.
Control	Recovers quickly from mistakes or setbacks in a game by putting energy into the next important task.	Talk to your child to understand what support they would like from you before and after games.
Confidence	Displays inventive or creative play, rather than playing cautiously.	Avoid overanalyzing your child's performances. Players will learn more and stay confident if they can reflect on their own strengths and weaknesses and decide what to focus on next time.

group were more confident at using control and communication strategies and they also increased their socially supportive behaviors. They also reported an increase in their son's motivation in training and in matches, together with improvement in match-day performance.

Enhancing Team Belief

Discussion with coaches in post-match debriefs at the PDP increasingly centered on the perceived need to enhance team belief and cohesion if they were to achieve team objectives of finishing in the top three places of the league. Specifically, coaches wanted to address decrements in performance standards that were evident in the closing stages of matches (e.g., attention, tactical intention, and decision making). Individual sessions were arranged with all players to gain an understanding of the factors influencing belief and team confidence, as well as their perceptions of their own ability, current psychological demands of performance, qualities of teammates, motivational climate, and team cohesion.

To encourage honest and accurate accounts, it was important to engage players in a task that they would find enjoyable in addition to the requisite questionnaires. Thus, a sociometric approach was also included. With this in mind, players were presented individually with a picture of a team bus and a bus-seating plan with seats numbered 1 to 28, and given the following scenario:

> Place all players (including yourself) on the bus in order of who has the qualities necessary to be in the starting line up on match days and to achieve the team goals for the season. Do not give any consideration to playing position; you do not have to have players represented in all positions in the first eleven seats on the bus.

Finally, there were three positions at the front of the seating plan, one of which represented the driver of the bus, and players were asked to seat the coaching staff in order of who they perceived to have the greatest control over taking the team toward their season's objectives.

Four key themes were identified from the sociometric and psychometric data that enabled the development of interventions to influence team belief through (1) providing leadership clarity, (2) addressing current inappropriate measures of success, (3) combating the "negativity disease," and (4) raising awareness of how individuals impact team momentum. Players suggested there were differences between coaches in terms of how they influenced training and match environments. This enabled coaches to understand why players responded in different ways to the coaching team and how the presence of some members could negatively impact psychological performance. Overall, their perceptions of the motivational climate were above average for supporting cooperative learning, the importance of the players' roles, and acknowledgment of effort and improvement. In addition, the team reported above-average perceptions of punishment for mistakes, unequal recognition, and intra-team-member rivalry. Cooperative learning and unequal recognition were the strongest team perceptions.

An absence of specific goals and appropriate measures of success were apparent particularly for players who were frequently not involved as part of the starting 11 and who consequently felt undervalued by the coaches. These perceptions in turn influenced "the negativity disease" which highlighted the impact that player discussions and behavior had on team belief and momentum, particularly on match days, and so effort was made to clarify their important role within the squad. Specific work involved coaches working more closely with the substitute's bench during games toward a more positive contribution; raising awareness of how their behavior is interpreted by the rest of the team; and setting clear objectives so that they would perceive this time as a learning opportunity and an integral part of their development.

Finally, the impact of verbal and nonverbal communication skills on team momentum was highlighted at a group level. Based on the data gained from the bus seating plans, players were given responsibility for maintaining and increasing belief in a designated teammate through their responses to game situations and player actions. We termed this charging the "belief battery" and players became aware of how they could support and encourage each other when it was needed most, and understand the impact of their own emotional/behavioral responses during games and how this influenced perceptions of momentum.

REFLECTION

Player development programs within UK professional football academies continue to integrate expertise across sport science disciplines, providing exciting opportunities for the SP to assist in the training of adaptive psychological behaviors and maintenance of positive well-being. Our experiences have highlighted members of the players' support network (e.g., coaches, parents, team members) as influential in shaping player thoughts, feelings, and behaviors. These individuals are often best positioned to deliver and reinforce key psychological messages as a result of the time they are afforded and the credibility and respect that they have built with each group of individuals. It is, therefore, of paramount importance that the SP builds strong working relationships in this area, providing education, support and accessibility to services to all those involved in player development. Despite a positive advancement in perceptions of psychology and the SP within football, there remains a reluctance by some players to engage. As a result the SP must continue to find creative ways of disseminating messages for performance enhancement, while being flexible in response to requests for support as well as skilled in intervening appropriately during short and infrequent contact times. Finally, football presents both the challenge and opportunity to provide services at the individual level, through one-to-one consultation and at the group level through workshops and team training sessions, to multiple clients that can include the football club, coaches, players, and parents. Such an environment requires considerable intervention in order to highlight and develop mental strategies that work toward the attainment of specific player aspirations compatible with team and academy objectives.

SUGGESTED READINGS

Evans, A. E., Turner, M. J., Slater, M. S., & Barker, J. B. (2013). Using personal-disclosure mutual-sharing to enhance group functioning in a professional soccer academy. *The Sport Psychologist, 27*(3), 233–243.

Harwood, C. G. (2008). Developmental consulting in a professional football academy: The 5C's Coaching Efficacy Program. *The Sport Psychologist, 22*(1), 109–133.

Harwood, C. G., & Steptoe, K. (2013). The integration of single case designs in coaching contexts: A commentary for applied sport psychologists. *Journal of Applied Sport Psychology, 25*, 167–174.

REFLECTIVE QUESTIONS

1. How can an SP work toward reducing or managing the barriers that exist in seeking sport psychology support?
2. What key skills can the SP develop in coaches to enable them to positively affect team belief?
3. What skills could an SP focus on to positively affect momentum during a game?
4. What strategies can the SP develop with individual players to help maintain belief post-match after a team loss?
5. What are the key messages that an SP could disseminate to parents to shape a young player's perception of achievement and success in training?

REFERENCES

Anshel, M. H. (1990). Toward validation of the COPE model: Strategies for acute stress inoculation in sport. *International Journal of Sport Psychology, 21*, 24–39.

Barker, J. B., McCarthy, P. J., & Harwood, C. G. (2011). Reflections on consulting in elite youth male English cricket and soccer academies. *Sport & Exercise Psychology Review, 7*(2), 58–72.

Fredricks, J. A., & Eccles, J. S. (2004). Parental influences on youth involvement in sport. *Developmental Sport and Exercise Psychology: A Lifespan Perspective, 204*, 145–164.

Freeman, P., Coffee, P., & Rees, T. (2011). The PASS-Q: The perceived available support in sport questionnaire. *Journal of Sport and Exercise Psychology, 33*(1), 54–74.

Gamble, R., Hill, D. M., & Parker, A. (2013). Revs and psychos: Role, impact and interaction of sport chaplains and sport psychologists within English Premiership soccer. *Journal of Applied Sport Psychology, 25*, 249–264.

Gardner, F. L., & Moore, Z. E. (2006). *Clinical sport psychology.* Champaign, IL: Human Kinetics.

Gilbourne, D., & Richardson, D. (2006). Tales from the field: Personal reflections on the provision of psychological support in professional soccer. *Psychology of Sport and Exercise, 7*, 325–337.

Harwood, C. G. (2005). Goals: More than just the score. In S. Murphy (Ed.), *The sport psych handbook* (pp. 19–36). Champaign, IL: Human Kinetics.

Harwood, C. G. (2008). Developmental consulting in a professional football academy: The 5C's Coaching Efficacy Program. *The Sport Psychologist, 22*(1), 109–133.

Holt, N. L., & Dunn, J. G. H. (2004). The psychosocial competencies and environmental conditions associated with soccer success. *Journal of Applied Sport Psychology, 16*, 199–219.

Keegan, R. J., Spray, C. M., Harwood, C. G., & Lavallee, D. E. (2010). The motivational atmosphere in youth sport: Coach, parent, and peer influences on motivation in specializing sport participants. *Journal of Applied Sport Psychology, 22*(1), 87–105.

Macnamara, A., & Collins, D. (2011). Development and initial validation of the psychological characteristics of developing excellence questionnaire. *Journal of Sport Sciences, 29*(12), 1273–1286.

Pain, M. A., & Harwood, C. G. (2004). Knowledge and perceptions of sport psychology within English soccer. *Journal of Sport Sciences, 22*, 813–826.

Poczwardowski, A., Sherman, C. P., & Ravizza, K. (2004). Professional philosophy in the sport psychology service delivery: Building on theory and practice. *The Sport Psychologist, 18*, 445–463.

Reeves, C. W., Nicholls, A. R., & McKenna, J. (2009). Stressors and coping responses among early and middle adolescent premier league academy soccer players. *Journal of Applied Sport Psychology, 21*, 31–48.

Richardson, D., Gilbourne, D., & Littlewood, M. (2004). Developing sport mechanisms for elite young players in a professional soccer academy: Creative reflections in action research. *European Sport Management Quarterly, 4*, 195–214.

Ryan, R. M. (1982). Control and information in the intrapersonal sphere: An extension of cognitive evaluation theory. *Journal of Personality and Social Psychology, 43*, 450–461.

Sheard, M., Golby, J., & van Wersch, A. (2009). Progress toward construct validation of the Sport Mental Toughness Questionnaire (SMTQ). *European Journal of Psychological Assessment, 25*(3), 186–193.

11 The Use of Biofeedback in the Remission of Pre-Competition Sickness in Athletes

Breathing your Way to Success

Louise Ellis

Pre-competition sickness, nausea, and gastrointestinal problems are somatic symptoms experienced by a number of elite athletes and performance artists (Lederman, 1999). While there are some very famous and indeed successful athletes who experience heightened anxiety and pre-competition sickness, there are others who find the consequences of pre-competition sickness disruptive and overbearing. Causes of pre-competition sickness have been attributed to changes in psychophysiological states, such as changes in cognitive thought processes, breathing patterns, and increased adrenaline.

One technology gaining increasing momentum in sport psychology is the application of biofeedback training. Biofeedback modalities have, for example, been effective in applied psychophysiology to improve breathing (Gilbert, 2005) and reduce panic attacks (Meuret, Wilhem, & Roth, 2001), and in sport psychology to improve imagery (Oishi, Kasai, & Maeshima, 2000) and manage competitive stress (Lagos, Vaschillo, Vaschillo, Lehrer, Bates, & Pandina, 2008). Biofeedback is a process of monitoring physiological responses, such as muscle tension, galvanic skin response, heart rate, respiration rate, body temperature, and electrical activity of the brain – known as neurofeedback. Biofeedback is an effective, objective, and evidence-based approach and can facilitate athlete understanding and self-regulation of psychophysiological responses.

The following case study presents a five-phase biofeedback protocol utilizing a pursed lip breathing technique (PLB) to assist in the remission of pre-competition sickness. A combination of biofeedback training, cognitive behavioral therapy, and specific transfer of techniques to training and performance were associated with a remission of symptoms, in particular pre-competition sickness.

BACKGROUND INFORMATION

The client presented is a 14-year-old female lacrosse player in the England Lacrosse Centre of Excellence Academy (Centex). The Centex program was formed in January 2004 as a talent identification pathway to benefit players who aspired and had the potential to represent England on the under-19 women's lacrosse team. Initially, the client and her parents consulted a doctor (general practitioner – GP) regarding anxiety and sickness before competition. Upon ruling out medical issues, the GP suggested they seek advice from a sport psychologist, which led to the client contacting the author. A conversation was conducted with the client and her parent over the telephone to obtain demographic information and to establish the main reason(s) for initial contact. Consistent with many athletes the performer had superficial knowledge of sport psychology, yet expressed a keen interest in the area. In the initial telephone consultation and subsequent needs analysis, the client presented with a recent (one-year) history of cognitive worry, somatic symptoms of shallow breathing, and pre-competition sickness.

The symptoms had manifested further since selection for the Centex Squad, and consequently had now transferred into her pre-competitive state in school matches. The Centex squad training sessions included physical, mental, tactical, fitness, match play, and individual and group feedback. As a consequence of perceiving such evaluations with lack of control and heightened concern, the client struggled to regulate her anxiety. She reported that her cognitive worry increased the night before, and she endured unmanageable symptoms of nausea and sickness in the morning of squad training; consequently, she was unable to eat breakfast. The client had also previously consulted a nutritionist to assist. She felt these symptoms were affecting her performance, energy levels, and enjoyment in the build-up to squad training. She also reported not being entirely comfortable with her breathing, especially during match play conditions, and would particularly struggle in the early part of a match.

I drew the client's attention to the fact that I had worked with international lacrosse players at senior level and athletes with pre-competition sickness associated with anxiety before. However, in order to maintain the utmost integrity toward the client and my own service provision, I also informed the client that should I feel she would be best served by another sport psychologist after the first meeting then I would point her in the right direction and recommend her to an appropriate colleague.

The client expressed a keen interest to meet, thus a formal face-to-face meeting was arranged to conduct a "needs analysis" and assess the client's psychological strengths and areas for development. After discussion, she advised her parents she would feel more comfortable having the consultations at her home; this way, her mother could be present should she require any further support or clarification. In total, the client engaged in six weekly sessions of biofeedback and cognitive training.

DESCRIPTION OF THE CASE

The case study presents a five-phase biofeedback protocol utilizing PLB to assist in the remission of pre-competition sickness. The PLB technique has predominantly been utilized in advanced psychophysiology with patients with "advanced COPD (Chronic Obtrusive Pulmonary Disease) who hyperinflate their lungs during attack of bronchospasm, panic, or exercise, and as an adjunctive measure in patients undergoing exercise rehabilitation or of respiratory muscle training" (Berkow & Fletcher, 1992, p. 632). Less attention has been paid to the technique in the sport psychology literature, although a wealth of breathing and stress management strategies have been widely used. Gevirtz and Schwartz (2003) called for the PLB technique to be utilized with other conditions, and suggested the use of oxygen or feedback instruments. In their comprehensive review, they could find no research on the use of PLB with patients other than those with COPD.

The biofeedback protocol presented in this case study consisted of five main phases: (1) pre-intervention baseline assessment; (2) introduction to the PLB technique; (3) PLB – non-visual biofeedback; (4) PLB – visual biofeedback; and (5) post-intervention baseline assessment. A respiration sensor, which measures the relative expansion of the abdomen or thorax during inhalation and exhalation, was utilized. In this protocol, it was worn over a cotton-based top to reduce static and artifacts, and placed over the client's abdomen. While some biofeedback and neurofeedback technologies are suited to lab-based settings only, the biofeedback training technology utilized in this study is suited to transportation and use in mobile settings, providing basic protocols and good practice are followed to reduce artifacts.

Five-Phase Biofeedback Protocol Utilizing PLB

The *first phase* of the biofeedback protocol involved obtaining a two-minute baseline respiration rate assessment to determine the client's average respiration rate. Obtaining an accurate baseline assessment was essential in order to compare the baseline assessment to phases three and four using the PLB technique. In *phase two*, the practice phase of the protocol was conducted for one minute. It is important to note that breathing incorrectly, in particular over-breathing for more than one minute, can cause cutaneous and peripheral blood circulation to be reduced, and can have other undesirable physiological symptoms, such as tingling in the fingers and lips, reduced sensory perception, balance, dizziness, and vision (Gilbert, 2005). Therefore, one-minute practice phases were introduced initially to reduce the potential side-effects of incorrect breathing.

Two-minute PLB measurement and training protocols were carefully selected in phases three and four in order to provide the client sufficient time to obtain a rhythm of using the PLB technique in each phase. This *third phase* required the athlete to practice the PLB technique with no visual feedback from the biofeedback screen. Non-visual biofeedback training was utilized initially to avoid potentially distracting the client away from performing and feeling the correct PLB technique. In *phase four*, the client was required to conduct a further two minutes of PLB using visual biofeedback. The final stage, *phase five*, consisted of a two-minute post-intervention baseline assessment. The program for this client consisted of six biofeedback sessions using varied "time use" of PLB. To elaborate, the use of two-minute breathing blocks may not always be appropriate for an athlete in the actual build-up to competition, therefore a discussion on appropriate and intuitive "time use" by the athlete was conducted. Furthermore, practice and transfer from sitting, standing, and walking conditions were varied from sessions one to six, the aim being to facilitate greater adherence and smoother transference into performance and training. The client also kept a daily breathing log over the six weeks.

THEORETICAL FRAMEWORK/PHILOSOPHY

Over the course of my career, I have continued to develop my knowledge on therapeutic approaches to move overall service provision to an eclectic-integrative approach where I am able to draw upon specific skills from a number of different approaches in order to maximize benefit for the client. The American Psychological Association-approved biofeedback training course I undertook in the United States in 2009 has proved a very welcome addition to my service delivery. It is a clear, evidenced, and objectively based method and has facilitated further understanding of the relationship between physiological and cognitive processes. Recognizing boundaries and competence in this area are essential; therefore, acting with integrity and honesty are central to my service provision.

Historically, and since supervised experience in 1998, my service delivery has emanated from: (1) extensive consultancy experience with professional and non-professional athletes; (2) peer mentoring; (3) attendance at conferences and workshops; (4) previous successful sport psychology programs reported in the literature from a variety of sport disciplines; (5) prominent frameworks; and (6) a humanistic athlete-centered approach based on counseling rather than just on mental skills. While some of these therapeutic approaches are more clinically based, I feel it is important to gain a holistic understanding of such approaches in order to make confident referrals as and when required.

Over the last ten years I have integrated the spiritual and transcendent aspects of the human experience within my framework. A number of applied sport psychologists have also emphasized the importance of including the spiritual dimensions in their consultancy (e.g., Watson & Nesti, 2005). Professionals in the field of spiritual psychology acknowledge that the mind, body, and the spirit all work together; therefore, they must be studied together. Transpersonal psychology encourages a spiritual, holistic perspective of physical and mental health that is not necessarily integrated by humanistic psychology alone, it can address spiritual development, altered states of consciousness, and peak performance experiences, for example. While I have employed both client-centered and consultant-led approaches combined with cognitive-behavioral theory in this case, the use of biofeedback has enabled further understanding of the interaction of the mind and body. In other cases, however, where spiritual dimensions and practices have been explored (e.g., meditation), sensitivity is required around this topic, and thus I ensure this is predominantly athlete-driven.

NEEDS ASSESSMENT

During the time lapse of two weeks from initial telephone contact to the first formal meeting, I: (1) engaged in peer-reviewed and scientific reading on applied psychophysiology and biofeedback case studies relating to anxiety (e.g., Faager, Stahle, & Larsen, 2008; Gevirtz & Schwartz, 2003); (2) reflected on and reviewed previous successful consultancy and protocols I had conducted with athletes with pre-competitive sickness and anxiety in professional football, gymnastics, and swimming; and (3) drew upon knowledge obtained during biofeedback courses. Personal aims, procedures, and objectives for the first meeting were to: (1) outline my service philosophy and what the client and her parents could expect; (2) dispel any myths about sport psychology and clarify the role of biofeedback – in particular the use of biofeedback in my practice would assist the client with performance-related issues, and would not be used as a form of medical diagnosis; (3) establish a trusting, positive relationship and learn about the individual's current performances; and (4) assess and obtain further understanding of the client's psychological strengths and areas for development.

Drawing upon successful procedures with other client groups and previous consultancies, a multimodal assessment of needs was used, applying a combination of interviewing techniques, biofeedback assessment/training, and behavioral analysis. The first meeting was conducted at the client's home. A semi-structured interview approach (Patton, 2002) was employed which would establish whether the program would also focus on performance enhancement, mental skills, or counseling in addition to biofeedback training. Open-ended questions focused on previous successful performances, experiences, and thought processes the client was having at the present time, and client self-reflection and description of her breathing patterns in the build-up to competition. Indirect behavioral analysis and observation of the client's breathing patterns in the session proved very useful, in particular viewing the client's breathing while she was describing and demonstrating her breathing patterns. I also used a combination of empathetic and reflective responses; this enabled the client to elaborate and also kept conversation open and flexible rather than rigid. I was also aware that being unconditional, friendly, knowledgeable, and flexible are all important assets (Partington & Orlick, 1987). These methods were adhered to in subsequent meetings.

INTERVENTION

Based on the information obtained in the multimodal assessments, it was agreed that the overall objectives of the support were to: (1) improve the client's anxiety management, in particular to manage cognitive worry which manifested the night before and in the morning; (2) alleviate and reduce pre-competition somatic anxiety symptoms, such as sickness; (3) improve the client's attentional focus – specifically the client was experiencing heightened "internal negative focus," focusing upon the symptoms and feelings in the body upon awakening in the morning, thus also further eliciting anxiety of the mind. Therefore, during the course of the six-week program, five steps were taken to implement the intervention: (1) education (verbal and written) to assist with adherence – in order for adherence to take place with any intervention the conscious mind must understand and be convinced that change can take place; (2) individualization (e.g., client and consultant led); (3) practice; (4) implementation (i.e., integration into lifestyle, training, performance); and (5) follow-up monitoring and reflection during each phase of the biofeedback intervention. The typical protocols for each session included written documents, scripts, and tangible evidence in the form of biofeedback data.

Following the needs analysis and adhering to the stages above, the client was provided with a PLB technique more commonly used in applied psychophysiology. The five-phase biofeedback protocol I had developed and utilized successfully with other athletes formed part of the first session and the subsequent five sessions. The PLB technique in this case study emphasized diaphragmatic breathing. It has been well documented that elite performers have found performance routines, thought-control strategies, and emotional-control strategies (e.g., imagery, physical relaxation, breathing control) beneficial in controlling anxiety. Research has also shown that breathing techniques can reduce muscular tension in the chest, shoulders, and jaw area (Cox, 1998), and create a general feeling of calmness and relaxation. Therefore, it was felt that the use of the PLB technique via the five-phase biofeedback protocol, combined with cognitive behavioral therapy, would: (1) assist with her anxiety management, and thus would also provide her with an additional internal focus rather than focusing on thoughts and situations beyond her control; and (2) assist with the remission of excessive shallow breathing to a more productive diaphragmatic breathing pattern. In summary, this PLB breathing technique was psychophysiological, in that it would help to regulate the mind and body by decreasing the client's somatic response and improve internal focus.

To address the client's cognitive anxiety, the client was also provided with an Automatic Thought Monitoring Form (which I adapted) (Greenberger & Padesky, 1995) to monitor thoughts over the forthcoming week (during and outside normal training). The client was informed that the benefits of this approach were to identify how she was communicating with herself and establish the type of situations that evoked these thoughts. Therefore, providing the client with this initial task would enable me to help the client operate deeper, at cause level, not just effect. The client was also told that in the short term this was a "catch 22," because over the course of the week she was actually being asked to pay attention to the type of thoughts and situations; however, in the longer term this would help to find out the causes and would enable further and timely cognitive interventions to be provided.

Ongoing informal and formal feedback was collated during each phase of consultation and helped to develop an effective and trusting relationship with the client. Obtaining feedback on a regular basis enabled monitoring of adherence strategies to be assessed and, where applicable, enabled refinement and adjustments to be made. This was achieved through monitoring and re-monitoring questioning and behavioral observation. Formal feedback was obtained using an adapted version of the Consultant Evaluation Form (Partington & Orlick, 1987) and has been well documented as a useful tool for evaluation. Vealey (1988) has identified the importance of multiple criterion measures in addition to performance, specifically other behaviors and cognitions are also important for evaluation, such as persistence, satisfaction, effort, and enjoyment. Thus, informal feedback was obtained through discussions with the client and her parents and answering client questions.

The performer received the PLB technique very well; in the first session the client's respiration rate decreased in the two PLB biofeedback training conditions when compared with the pre-intervention baseline assessment. Moreover, the client's post-intervention respiration rate was lower than in the pre-intervention baseline assessment. This was a result of the effectiveness of PLB emphasizing diaphragmatic breathing. The first real test of this was toward the end of the second week, when the client attended a Centex squad. The client was very diligent and followed the PLB technique the night before, upon awakening, and in smaller cycles in the build-up to competition. This was the first time the client was free from pre-competition sickness in over a year. While the client at this phase still had some cognitive worry, she attributed the PLB technique to assisting with the remission of the pre-competition sickness. In subsequent sessions, combined with cognitive interventions, we worked on the client improving her thought process and gradually introducing breakfast to help with energy levels.

REFLECTION

The importance of "reflective practice" for future "effective practice" and professional development has been well documented (e.g., Anderson, Knowles, & Gilbourne, 2004; Cropley, Hanton, Miles, & Niven, 2010). Being self-critical and analytical is an essential part of my practice, and while general evaluations can obtain rich information, they cannot replace the importance of "in-action" (i.e., while doing something) and "on-action" (i.e., after having done something) reflective practice (Schön, 1983).

The multi-modal approach which I adopted in the first consultancy session in this case study produced valuable results and thus enabled me to provide the client with an initial intervention in the later part of the first session. Specifically, the client was taken through the five-phase biofeedback protocol and a plan was devised for the application of PLB. I am a supporter of Cox's (1998) notion that on completion of the first consultancy session, it is important, where possible, to give the performer some form of action. Cox (1998) has argued that this is similar to patients visiting their GP's surgery, "who will expect some tangible form of remedy for their concerns" (p. 132). It is important to note that while I support Cox's philosophy above, I am also greatly aware of Hardy, Jones, and Gould's (1996) seven valuable points, one of which postulates that "being able to recognize that at the time doing nothing is also the best intervention" (p. 293). During *in-action* reflection I felt confident in my decision to provide the client with the five-phase protocol. Obtaining rich information from the client in advance of the first meeting in part facilitated this.

Engaging in *on-action* reflective practice in previous consultations with other athletes also enabled phase two to be firmly embedded into the five-phase biofeedback protocol used in this case study. To expand on this, while chatting to a rather inquisitive professional footballer with pre-competition sickness I answered one of his questions while attaching the biofeedback modality to him. In my haste, I inadvertently discussed the PLB technique before taking his basal respiration rate. Having observed the client's breathing style throughout the session, I quickly noticed he was manipulating his breathing pattern in the PLB format. In-action, I quickly had to interrupt the basal assessment and "hold my hands up" that it was remiss of me to discuss the technique first as I could see he was beginning to breathe in that manner. This would impact upon his baseline assessment. We then restarted the baseline assessment with further clarification on my part. *On-action* reflection subsequently enabled phases one and two to be more clearly defined, and thus assisted in similar education and training phases with the client in this case study.

After every meeting with the client, I continued to make regular notes. Personal reflection on the whole process of service delivery has allowed my personal practices and perceptions to be challenged. Thus, it has empowered me to make specific changes to future programs to increase their effectiveness. Reflective practice for effective future practice is an essential ingredient for professional development, and sharing good practice in our field.

SUGGESTED READINGS

Gevirtz, R. N., & Schwartz, M. S. (2003). The respiratory system in applied psychophysiology. In M. S. Schwartz & F. Andrasik (Eds.), *Biofeedback: A practitioner's guide* (pp. 212–244). New York, NY: Guilford Press.
Schwartz, M. S., & Andrasik, F. (2003). *Biofeedback: A practitioner's guide.* New York, NY: Guilford Press.

REFLECTIVE QUESTIONS

1. When conducting a baseline assessment, what information would you provide and what information might you withhold from the client at this stage and why?

2. When introducing breathing techniques to an athlete for the first time, how long should you spend in the practice phase and why?
3. What changes might you expect to see from pre-baseline to the practice phase that you may also see in the intervention phase?
4. What are artifacts in biofeedback, and what steps would you take to prevent the risk of artifacts?
5. What are biofeedback modalities? What modality might you use for a client you have been working with, and why?

REFERENCES

Anderson, A. G., Knowles, Z., & Gilbourne, D. (2004). Reflective practice for sport psychologists: Concepts, models, practical implications, and thoughts on dissemination. *The Sport Psychologist, 18*, 188–203.

Berkow, R., & Fletcher, A. J. (1992). *The Merck manual of diagnosis and therapy* (16th ed.). Rahway, NJ: Merck.

Cox, R. (1998). The individual consultation: The fall and rise of a professional golfer. In R. J. Butler (Ed.), *Sport psychology in performance* (pp. 129–146). Oxford: Butterworth-Heinemann.

Cropley, B., Hanton, S., Miles, M., & Niven, A. (2010). Exploring the relationship between effective and reflective practice in applied sport psychology. *The Sport Psychologist, 24*, 521–541.

Faager, G., Stahle, A., & Larsen, F. F. (2008). Influence of spontaneous pursed lips breathing on walking endurance and oxygen saturation in patients with moderate to severe chronic obstructive pulmonary disease. *Clinical Rehabilitation, 22*(8), 675–683.

Gevirtz, R. N., & Schwartz, M. S. (2003). The respiratory system in applied psychophysiology. In M. S. Schwartz & F. Andrasik (Eds.), *Biofeedback: A practitioner's guide* (pp. 212–244). New York, NY: Guilford Press.

Gilbert, C. (2005). Better chemistry through breathing: The story of carbon dioxide and how it can go wrong. *Biofeedback, 33*(3), 100–104.

Greenberger, D., & Padesky, C. (1995). *Mind over mood: Change how you feel by the way you think.* New York, NY: Guilford Press.

Hardy, L., Jones, G., & Gould, D. (1996). *Understanding psychological preparation for sport: Theory & practice in elite performers.* Chichester: Wiley.

Lagos, L., Vaschillo, E., Vaschillo, B., Lehrer, P., Bates, M., & Pandina, P. (2008). Heart rate variability biofeedback as a strategy for dealing with competitive anxiety: A case study. *Biofeedback, 36*(3), 109–115.

Lederman, R. (1999, June). Medical treatment of performance anxiety: A statement in favour. *Paper presented at the seventeenth Annual Symposium of Medical Problems of Musicians and Dancers*, Aspen, CO.

Meuret, A. E., Wilhem, F. H., & Roth, W. T. (2001). Respiratory biofeedback-assisted therapy in panic disorder. *Behaviour Modification, 25*(4), 584–605.

Oishi, K., Kasai, T., & Maeshima, T. (2000). Autonomic response specificity during motor imagery. *Journal of Physiological and Anthropological Applied Human Science, 19*(6), 255–261.

Partington, J., & Orlick, T. (1987). The sport psychology consultant evaluation form. *The Sport Psychologist, 1*, 309–317.

Patton, M. Q. (2002). Qualitative evaluation and research methods (3rd ed.). Newbury Park, CA: Sage.

Schön, D. A. (1983). *The reflective practitioner: how professionals think in action.* London: Temple Smith.

Vealey, R. S. (1998). Future directions in psychological skills training. *The Sport Psychologist, 2*, 318–336.

Watson, N., & Nesti, M. (2005). The role of spirituality in sports psychology consulting: an analysis and integrative review of literature. *Journal of Applied Sports Psychology, 17*; 228–239.

12 Sport Psychology and the Performance Environment

Reflections on a Season-Long Intervention with an Amateur Rugby Club

Stuart Pattison and Mike McInerney

Working with teams in a performance environment is a common task for sport psychology professionals. It presents a unique challenge, addressing multiple factors in the search for enhanced performance. Combining the development of individuals' mental skills with the refinement of the broader environment in order to facilitate consistent high levels of performance requires a sensitivity and flexibility that makes the job of a sport psychologist inherently fascinating. This chapter will use a case study of a season-long intervention with a club rugby side as a canvas on which to examine the framework for the work of sport psychologists with teams.

Our approach to sport psychology interventions with teams is centered on the influence of environmental and contextual factors. Although there is agreement among coaches regarding the importance of creating suitable environments for athletes, there is very little attention paid to this concept in the sport team literature (Cotterill, 2012). Having said this, our experience, along with the work of various practitioners and researchers, has supported an increasingly holistic approach to understanding the sports performance environment (Fletcher & Hanton, 2003). Certain studies justify this shift in thought indicating links between psychological and organizational climate with significant individual-level outcomes such as satisfaction, commitment, performance, involvement, reduced performance errors, and stress (Cotterill, 2012; Ostroff, Kinicki, & Tamkins, 2003). As Cotterill (2012) states, "building a positive and supportive team environment is crucial to the successful development and performance of most teams, and in particular those that are successful over a long period of time" (p. 22).

BACKGROUND INFORMATION

Understanding the broader cultural and historical context of the team we were working with is paramount in intervening from an ecological perspective (Henriksen, Stambulova, & Roessler, 2010; Larsen, Henriksen, Alfermann, & Christensen, 2013). Villager F.C., officially established in the year 1876, makes it the second oldest rugby club in South Africa. Throughout its history, Villager has experienced a number of successes, winning trophies and entrenching itself as a permanent fixture at the top levels of club rugby. In 1996 the club turned professional, resulting in a movement toward the remuneration of players. With limited restrictions from the Western Province Rugby Football Union, the local clubs began remunerating players. The vast amount of financial input needed to keep the club competitive slowly became insurmountable, and coupled with loss of memberships and diminishing sponsorship, Villager F.C. simply struggled to survive. The quality of player performance deteriorated and in 2013 the club, for the first time in its history, was relegated to the second tier of competition, Super League B.

In 2013 the newly elected committee decided to return the club to amateur status, thus removing player remuneration. Having been exposed to this "professional status," many of the players rebelled against this new system and moved to alternative clubs. The exodus resulted in the club finishing last in the Super League B. At this point, a dedicated Villager committee decided (despite discussions around closing the club down) that closing the door on the 136 years of rugby heritage was not an option. They brought in a new coaching staff and pushed for an increased player base. Villager's stance concerning the payment of players meant it was uniquely positioned in the landscape of club rugby. While not an uncontested policy, it gave the club a clear sense of identity and a clear vision – something we would look to use as a lever throughout the course of our intervention with the club. Our responsibility was to assist in creating an environment through which the athletes could successfully develop, grow, and learn as individuals and as performers, thus improving the club's overall performance. The following account outlines the process we embarked on.

DESCRIPTION OF THE CASE

We have taken a critically reflexive approach to this chapter, examining a particular case through the subjective lens of our own experience as practitioners. The foundation of this approach is an understanding of our world as socially constructed and that there is an inherent subjectivity in how we make sense of our experience. As both authors and subjects of this chapter, we deliberately use this approach as a way of foregrounding ourselves and our role in the construction of a coherent narrative of this case.

Through previous collaboration with the coaching staff, the first author of this chapter (Stuart) developed strong rapport with the coaches, especially the head coach. The trust and honesty that had been built between the two of them facilitated our entry into this particular team. Having seen success working together on a similar case in the past, we were invited to join the coaching staff to provide sport psychology services for the 2014 Villager F.C. season. Coupled with these responsibilities, Stuart also assumed the role of a full-time active player within the first team. Stuart's role in the club was therefore two-pronged and created an interesting dynamic in the facilitation of our intervention.

As a 27-year-old white male at a South African rugby club with a traditionally white player base, Mike had the cultural background to easily assimilate into the club. However, sport psychology in South African sport is far from a core service and is rarely used. Although the "mental game" is very much part of the discourse of players, supporters, and coaches alike, a full-time consultant at a rugby club is an unusual sight. Thus, being positioned as the "sport psychologist" placed Mike outside the realm of the players and created a little uncertainty within the coaching staff, in a role that was simultaneously novel and unfamiliar for both coaches and players.

THEORETICAL FRAMEWORK/PHILOSOPHY

Recent research efforts have revealed the performance environment experienced by athletes to be unique, complex, and dynamic, with high performance largely dependent on a variety of different factors (e.g., Douglas & Carless, 2006; Pain & Harwood, 2008). In addition, multiple studies indicate the strong effect of organizational environment structures on the competing athletes (e.g., Fletcher & Hanton, 2003; Fletcher & Wagstaff, 2009). In line with this development in the literature, our approach with this particular case drew on a holistic ecological approach with a focus on the broader developmental context or environment in which athletes perform rather than on the individual athlete in isolation (Henriksen et al., 2010). Greater emphasis was therefore placed on the interaction between the athlete and his/her environment (e.g., Bengoechea, 2002; Krebs, 2009). Consequently, the six fundamental principles of the holistic ecological approach (Larsen et al., 2013) were used as a framework underlying our intervention in the current case (see Table 12.1).

Table 12.1 Six Principles Underlying a Holistic Ecological Approach to Intervention

Principle	Description and Impact on Intervention
1	Athletes are intricately connected to their environments. Aim to involve significant contributors (e.g., coaches, parents, teammates). Situate intervention in context of training and competition to facilitate application of skills.
2	Design intervention after thorough analysis of environment. Consider all strengths and weaknesses in organizational structure and culture.
3	Act in a way that optimizes the entire surrounding environment (i.e., integrated rather than fragmented or in opposition). Create positive dialogue with and among various agents in the environment.
4	All sporting contexts inevitably sit within a larger cultural setting. Design intervention to take into account cultural and historical context.
5	Aim to create a strong, sustainable, and coherent organizational culture in order to position team for success.
6	Help create an environment that sees athletes as whole human beings. Develop a holistic package of psychological skills that athletes can use in sport and other life spheres.

While these principles present clear guidance for intervention design, it is important to consider that all sporting contexts will differ in nature and therefore occupy a unique set of circumstances. After understanding the flexibility of this guidance, it is suggested that practitioners use the principles as a foundation from which assessment, delivery, and evaluation stem (Larsen et al., 2013).

NEEDS ASSESSMENT

Fifer, Henschen, Gould, and Ravizza (2008) stated:

> when beginning any mental skills program with a team or individual athlete, the sport psychology consultant must assess the needs of that specific team or individual, and since each sport, team, and athlete are unique, each mental skills program must be tailored specifically for the needs of that group.
>
> (p. 363)

Keeping this in mind, assessment is not only something required prior to intervening, but rather continues throughout the entire intervention, promoting a responsive and iterative process. It is important to note that the distinction between intervention and assessment is not completely clear and that the process of assessment is itself an intervention. We had a number of conversations with key stakeholders to gather data and develop rapport, utilizing an approach in which interviews, informal meetings, and observations were prioritized over psychometric testing (Fifer et al., 2008).

Meetings with Coaching Staff and Head Coach

After establishing and obtaining commitment from the head coach, it was important for us to iron out our role and responsibility as sport psychologists moving forward. This process also allowed us to establish buy-in from the coaching staff, manage expectations, and build a sound relationship for the future maintenance and sustainability of the program. We agreed that our responsibility as sports psychologists would involve individuals' mental skills training and counseling, factors concerning team dynamics (e.g., cohesion, motivation, communication, goal setting), and intervening in the systems of the broader environment (e.g., club policy, functions, personnel). We would fulfill these responsibilities through attendance at practices/matches, social functions, and team/club meetings.

Pre-Season Player Interviews

As part of our assessment process, we created the opportunity to interview individual players during the pre-season fitness testing. This facilitated the development of rapport and trust with the players, encouraging them to utilize our expertise to enhance their overall performance. In addition, we served as a liaison between players and coaches, as well as a source to confide in (explaining the scope and limits of confidentiality). We used interviews to learn more about the athletes (e.g., motivation, strengths, weaknesses) as well as their current situations and performance (Fifer et al., 2008). With the club's current player base in jeopardy and new faces in both playing and coaching groups, we also asked about the motivation behind players' decisions to either stay or join the club. This information provided some access to the value the players saw in the club, and also provided us with a number of broader cultural factors to mobilize during the intervention.

Observation

A further aspect of the assessment process was observation. Although this took place informally throughout the pre-season training sessions, there were also opportunities for formal observation during pre-season matches. During these games, we looked specifically for examples of the club's norms, norm setters, types of communication, body language, strengths, and moments that might define the identity of a "Villager" player. We gathered and fed back this information to coaches, who could build on key areas during training.

In-Season Support Forms

An ecological approach to performance enhancement requires working with both individuals and the group as a whole. One of the ways in which we gathered information from (and intervened with) individuals was through electronic communication (online forms and chat). We used a form to assess the individuals' psychological and coaching needs before, during, and after matches. We asked questions such as: *What kind of attention do you respond to pre-game? What nature of warm-up do you respond to pre-game? What sort of communication do you respond to from the coaches pre-game? What does your pre-game routine ideally look like? What kind of instruction do you respond to during the game? What support do you ultimately need from our coaching staff.* This was invaluable information for the coaching staff, who could focus in on specific individual needs, as well as structure feedback, motivation, and instruction accordingly. In addition, feedback from players suggested they felt looked after and responded positively to someone addressing their personal needs within a team setting.

Challenges

At the early stage of assessment, without a strong core of first-team players, we spent a significant amount of time developing relationships with players from all club levels. While this had value in establishing us as recognizable members of the coaching staff, many of these players were not part of the group we ended up working with. Many players who ended up becoming a prominent feature in the first team only arrived after our assessment had concluded. This highlights the difficulties of thoroughly assessing an organization, given the fluctuating pool of players typical in a sporting setting.

INTERVENTION

The major premise of an ecological approach is the emphasis placed on the environment in which the athletes are situated. Our intervention aimed to strengthen the foundation of the club by developing the strong cultural heritage of Villager F.C. Our assessment process had indicated the importance of the club's history and the motives for many of the new arrivals at the club. Mobilizing those factors and making them a concrete part of the club's functioning was a priority. We combined individual work and group sessions (consulting with players and coaches, together and separately) with formal and informal interventions designed to strengthen existing aspects of the environment or introduce new systems. The intervention was flexible and adjusted to meet the shifting demands of the club throughout the season.

Team Culture and Pre-Season Preparation

Culture and vision. Given the priority of establishing a strong and coherent organizational culture (Cato & Gordon, 2009; Kotter, 1996) when working within an ecological approach, we understood the importance of instituting a collective vision accepted by the club, the coaches, and all the players involved. The purpose of establishing a coherent vision was simple: to enhance cohesion as a club, create clear direction for every individual; establish "buy-in" from all parties involved in the set up; develop the environment for consistency; and set up indicators for evaluating our progress along the way (West & Unsworth, 1998). It was important to involve all parties in the construction of this vision (Cato & Gordon, 2009), and we gathered input from both new and "old" players and coaches, as well as the club committee, and the newly formed players committee.

Using an online form we asked the following questions: *What is your vision for 2014? What do you believe the goals should be for 2014? What does the "ideal club" look like for you? What does a "Villager player" look like for you? What does a "Villager coach" look like for you? What values do you think need to be prioritized for 2014?* All responses were consolidated into one final working document, providing the basis for the club's vision. Looking for themes, we collated the data and compiled a table of on-field and off-field visions and values. This table reflected the vision of a club that wanted to grow in numbers as well as in the quality of players and people. They wanted to be respected for their skill, success, the club's status and its history, as well as be a welcoming club with a family atmosphere and a healthy "vibe." Their vision was to achieve all of this with unity and transparency across all teams and club members.

Norms and values. We knew that the club's norms (i.e., ways of thinking, feeling, or behaving that are deemed appropriate by the team and its associated organization; MacPherson & Howard, 2011) would form a significant part of the culture and could provide the basis for a successful and consistent team performance. Following the guidelines of Stevens (2002), we made the formal identification and promotion of norms a core component of our intervention. The answers to the questionnaire, together with the data we collected from the assessment process, provided us with the foundational club norms and values that its members strive to embody. We summarized these values as: pride in club and heritage; clear communication and understanding; dedication; loyalty and commitment; honor and respect; passion; and honesty.

Motto, slogan, and identity. In order to establish the values and norms as part of the club's language, we involved the players in a process of creating a motto or slogan that would crystallize what the team stood for and capture the essence of the club's vision. We hoped that this slogan would be used as a verbal cue for players to use when wanting to return to the norms or values they had committed to enacting. The players were given the opportunity to present their team motto and vote to decide the motto for the season. Two phrases were chosen. The first, "Sometimes good things have to fall apart so better things can fall together," stood as a representation and acknowledgment of where the club had come from, and where the club was heading. The second was simply "Feed the wolf." Its origin lay in a tale about a wise man who explains to a young boy the idea that within each and every one of us there is a constant and fierce battle between two wolves, one evil and one good. The boy questions the wise man as to which wolf wins the battle and the man proudly answers with "whichever wolf you feed." Both phrases were used consistently throughout the season, but it was the second phrase which became the most prolific in the language of the team and club.

With Villager FC reverting to "amateur status" and deciding to move away from the model of remunerating players, the priority was now placed on building long-lasting, healthy relationships among good people who were involved simply for the "right reasons" (another mantra that soon became a part of the club's internal language). This was a defining feature of the club and a significant component of its identity. In order to foreground this principle throughout the season, we initiated a brief exercise at the start of each practice. A player was nominated in advance to share a story about his journey and why he was playing for Villager F.C. This was based on guidelines for personal disclosure and mutual sharing interventions (Holt & Dunn, 2006).

Goal-setting. At the end of February 2014, a summary of the overall vision and values were presented to the potential first-team squad who, in a workshop setting, unpacked these findings. The purpose of this was to identify the means by which the squad could achieve and embody the aforementioned visions, values, and norms. During this session, a number of specific, measurable, and time-based goals were set to support the underpinning values for the season ahead. It was decided that specific goals would be set and reviewed in two-week blocks with an ultimate season goal of being promoted to Super League A. In addition to a clear and concise goal-setting process, the players generated a set of protocols requiring strict adherence to successfully and efficiently working together for the season ahead.

The processes we have described above all took place prior to the start of the season. In many respects, these provided a foundation for the work that followed as we often drew on the discussions and decisions the team made during this process. Overall, this was probably where we played our most active role throughout the season. These exercises were especially important considering how fragmented the club had been when we arrived. Uniting the players and coaches behind a common cause was a crucial task for us.

Communication and Dialogue

Effective systems rely on clear communication, something the holistic ecological approach recognizes in its mandate to promote dialogue between the various parties in the athlete's environment. In association with the head coach, we assisted in developing the following interventions to prioritize the communication and dialogue between players, management, coaches, and support staff.

Weekly online forms. We developed a small questionnaire to be completed online by all players on a weekly basis. This form captured responses on aspects such as: the need to see the team doctor; minutes played in the previous game; injury status; players' performance ratings; personal target areas for the week ahead; mental or emotional concerns; and availability for training days and the upcoming game. The responses were used, in conjunction with the head coach, to plan the schedule and structure for the week ahead as well as provide us, as sport psychologists, insight into players' concerns needing private consultation through the week ahead.

WhatsApp communication groups. We incorporated technology that would make communication more efficient, increase levels of participation, and facilitate both formal and informal channels of communication. We used the WhatsApp application as a vehicle for efficient communication on a regular day-to-day basis. There were four main WhatsApp groups: (1) a first-team group for the purpose of communicating the information applicable to the players and maintaining a high level of camaraderie; (2) a coaching staff group to discuss player management, logistics, and necessary information pertaining to specific portfolios; (3) a medical/support staff group to discuss player injuries, rehabilitation, and the management thereof; and (4) a senior players group to discuss team concerns, leadership influences, and strategic decision making for upcoming games and practices. We found that this further enhanced accountability and fostered commitment among the players. As sport psychologists, we monitored and interacted in all of these groups as a way of keeping a finger on the pulse of the team's mood, language, and level of interaction.

Group Sessions

Considering the magnitude of the goal that Villager F.C. had set itself, it was crucial to ensure that a professional and consistent level of focus and commitment was upheld by all players and coaching staff. Through a season, which generally lasts seven months, it is inevitable that both the players and the coaching staff will lose sight of the goal at some point in time. There were a variety of interventions, by means of group sessions, that were specifically implemented in an attempt to promote consistent focus and high levels of commitment.

Performance reflection and analysis. Throughout the intervention, we conducted group sessions with players and coaches. One goal of this process was to provide an opportunity for players to communicate with coaches, and each other, about concerns relating to the performance of the team. In order to reduce any stigma associated with calling these sessions "sport psychology sessions," we integrated these discussions into video and statistical analysis. These sessions provided further opportunities for us (as sport psychologists) to complement the observational data from match day with the players' reflections on what was happening during crucial moments of the match.

The players were not only encouraged to take ownership of this process but also to participate in the discussion, promoting accountability and autonomy as well as enhancing their motivation, refining team focus, and keeping standards and expectations high. This approach was consistent with Horn and Harris' (1996) suggestion that coaches involve the athletes in a self-monitoring process of evaluating their individual and team performance. A combination of reviewing the stats, video clips, and considering selected psychological aspects enabled the players to evaluate their performance, tweak the coming week's preparation plans, learn from previous mistakes, gain motivation from their strengths, and set appropriate goals for the next opponent. In addition to discussing the weekly goals, the players would use this time to reflect on the values developed as a group, as well as the protocols established to ensure we were on the right track as a club.

Informal roles. On certain occasions, our group sessions had objectives beyond performance and goal-setting reviews. For example, one such session highlighted the informal roles taken on by players within a team in order to foster role clarity and emphasize player contributions beyond their execution of position-related tasks (Stevens, 2002). We presented a list of informal roles and responsibilities present within a rugby setting such as: enforcer, motivator, non-verbal leader, star player, team player, verbal leader, mentor, spark plug, comedian, each with its own definition and description (Beauchamp, Schinke, & Bosselut, 2011). The players were then offered the opportunity to select the informal roles that they believe they occupied. Subsequently, the group was offered the opportunity to nominate players for certain categories. On game days, we would place the informal role categories above each player's locker space as a reminder of the value they bring to the team and the areas they can lead in on the field. Player reflection indicated that this exercise assisted in developing and enhancing self-confidence, enriching the levels of motivation, and further creating a greater sense of belonging, identity, and purpose within the group.

Challenges. There were a number of challenges associated with conducting these group sessions. Scheduling was difficult due to the scarcity of time available and reluctance to prioritize mental skills training over physical and technical skills training. One major challenge was ensuring buy-in from the entire players group. Considering the status of sport psychology within South Africa and given its lack of prominence, a number of players failed to see the benefit of these sessions. While there was clear buy-in from the majority of the group, there were a few individuals who consistently indicated their lack of investment. Whether these individuals sabotaged or impeded the value of the sessions is unclear; however, they definitely had an impact on how we, as practitioners, experienced these sessions and thus felt about the value we were adding to the greater group.

A holistic ecological model to performance enhancement requires the intervention take place within the performers' training and competitive environment. This was difficult to achieve, given the scarcity of evidence-based mental skills training exercises that take place on the training field and not in a classroom. There is a clear need for future research to investigate this form of intervention.

Coach Mental Training Sessions

On a variety of occasions the sport psychologists took the opportunity to conduct small workshops aimed at educating the coaching staff in areas that we believed would improve player management and coaching skills. Multiple objectives were set, such as: (a) providing theory around a coach's influence on a team or individual player; (b) presenting ways to enhance player–coach communication; (c) ensuring coherence in club values; and (d) providing a platform to establish, monitor, and evaluate team and club goals.

One-on-One Consulting

A large part of what we do as sport psychologists includes individual mental skills training. Although our involvement in this case focused primarily on the group as a whole, there were opportunities for us to work in a one-on-one capacity. As mentioned earlier, we had the opportunity to meet with any players struggling with or requiring support other than what the coaches could provide. In addition, we interacted with injured players, using their time off training and playing to expose them to theory related to the impact of injury on their confidence and motivation, as well as what steps they could take to improve positive recovery.

The value of one-on-one interaction is contingent upon a strong relationship, trust, and rapport. When working in a group setting, with a large number of players and coaches, it can be challenging to develop the kind of relationship that will facilitate a successful one-on-one interaction. This is perhaps why intervening on a systemic level is beneficial; however, finding more time to emphasize the one-on-one relationship could have had a significant impact on the success of the intervention.

REFLECTION

The team itself was successful throughout the season. They did not always perform at the upper limits of their potential, but showed the kind of character and bravery that were often spoken about as important parts of the Villager culture. This kind of culture helped the team to the top of the league, winning 11 consecutive games and thereby resulting in promotion to the premier league. Overall, this was an exceptionally successful season for the club, who exceeded expectations by managing to return to the upper levels of club rugby.

In the current case, we were tasked with working at an individual, interpersonal, and systemic level to develop a psychological climate and psychological skills that would improve the level and consistency of performance. We managed to make effective changes across the board, establishing a strong, high-performance environment. In many ways, the fragile state of the club meant that its members and the coaching staff were very receptive to implementing new ideas. Backed by the head coach, with whom we had developed a sound collaborative relationship, we were given the scope to intervene in a way we deemed fit. As a playing group with a mix of new and old faces who had not yet had the opportunity to cement a particular culture, they were amenable to developing the type of psychological climate we believed would be most successful.

As practitioners, we believe that working from a holistic ecological model provides a foundation from which to successfully intervene within a team context. However, there are a number of areas in which further development is required. For example, the view of sport psychology as supplementary to the process of performance development implies that sport psychology exists independently from the training and performance of skills. In order for performance development to take advantage of the cognitive processes at work within performance, there needs to be a commitment to fully integrating the principles of sport psychology into training and competition. Although much of what we did had significant value, there were difficulties in ensuring the consistent application, of the processes we initiated, on the training field. Much of the work we did was well received by players and coaches alike, but translating that into real-life behavior was inconsistent.

This chapter is not meant to provide any kind of definitive evaluation of our intervention. We do not mean to imply that the teams' on-field success was the result of our involvement. The intervention was well received by the participants and a process we were proud to have been involved in. However, as practitioners, we still believe that there are a number of obstacles facing the application of sport psychology, some of which we have highlighted throughout this chapter. We hope we have provided insight into the framework, reasoning, and experience of delivering a sport psychology intervention within a team setting.

SUGGESTED READINGS

Andersen, M. B. (2005). *Sport psychology in practice*. Champaign, IL: Human Kinetics.

Henriksen, K., Stambulova, N., & Roessler, K. K. (2010). Successful talent development in track and field: Considering the role of environment. *Scandinavian Journal of Medicine & Science in Sports*, *20*(2), 122–132.

Heyman, S. R. (1984). The development of models for sport psychology: Examining the USOC guidelines. *Journal of Sport Psychology*, *6*(2), 125–132.

Ravizza, K. (1987). The integration of psychological skills training into practice sessions. In J. Salmela, B. Petoit, & T. Blaine (Eds.), *Psychological nurturing and guidance of gymnastic talent* (pp. 5–12). Montreal: Sport Psyche Editors.

Ravizza, K. (1988). Gaining entry with athletic personnel for season-long consulting. *The Sport Psychologist*, *2*(3), 243–254.

Sullivan, J., & Hodge, K. P. (1991). A survey of coaches and athletes about sport psychology in New Zealand. *The Sport Psychologist*, *5*(2), 140–151.

United States Olympic Committee. (1983). USOC establishes guidelines for sport psychology services. *Journal of Sport Psychology*, *5*, 4–7.

REFLECTIVE QUESTIONS

1. What other psychology principles/concepts/models/frameworks could be applicable in this particular case?
2. What were some of the limitations of this case? How did, or could, we have handled these limitations?
3. What could we do differently in the future in this type of case?
4. What factors could have been damaging to our intended approach? What could we have done differently to take these into consideration when designing and implementing our intervention?

5.   What psychological advice can we give coaches when considering developing high-performance environments for athletes?

REFERENCES

Beauchamp, M. R., Schinke, R. J., & Bosselut, G. (2011). Informal roles in sport teams. *International Journal of Sport and Exercise Psychology*, 9, 19–30.

Bengoechea, E. G. (2002). Integrating knowledge and expanding horizons in developmental sport psychology: A bioecological perspective. *Quest*, 54(1), 1–20.

Cato, S. T., & Gordon, J. (2009). Relationship of the strategic vision alignment to employee productivity and student enrollment. *Research in Higher Education Journal*, 15, 1–20.

Cotterill, S. (2012). *Team psychology in sports: Theory and practice*. New York, NY: Routledge.

Douglas, K., & Carless, D. (2006). *The performance environment: A study of the personal, lifestyle and environmental factors that affect sporting performance*. London: UK Sport.

Fifer, A., Henschen, K., Gould, D., & Ravizza, K. (2008). What works when working with athletes? *The Sport Psychologist*, 22(3), 356–377.

Fletcher, D., & Hanton, S. (2003). Sources of organizational stress in elite sports performers. *Sport psychologist*, 17(2), 175–195.

Fletcher, D., & Wagstaff, C. R. (2009). Organizational psychology in elite sport: Its emergence, application and future. *Psychology of Sport and Exercise*, 10(4), 427–434.

Henriksen, K., Stambulova, N., & Roessler, K. K. (2010). Holistic approach to athletic talent development environments: A successful sailing milieu. *Psychology of Sport and Exercise*, 11(3), 212–222.

Holt, N. L., & Dunn, J. G. (2006). Guidelines for delivering personal-disclosure mutual-sharing team building interventions. *Sport Psychologist*, 20(3), 348–367.

Horn, T. S., & Harris, A. (1996). Perceived competence in young athletes: Research findings and recommendations for coaches and parents. In F. L. Smoll & R. E. Smith (Eds.), *Children and youth in sport: A biopsychosocial perspective* (2nd ed; pp. 435–464). Dubuque, IW: Kendall-Hunt.

Kotter, J. P. (1996). *Leading change*. Boston, MA: Harvard Business Press.

Krebs, R. J. (2009). Bronfenbrenner's Bioecological Theory of Human Development and the process of development of sports talent. *International Journal of Sport Psychology*, 40(1), 108–135.

Larsen, C. H., Alfermann, D., Henriksen, K., & Christensen, M. K. (2013). Successful talent development in soccer: The characteristics of the environment. *Sport, Exercise, and Performance Psychology*, 2(3), 190–206.

MacPherson, A. C., & Howard, P. W. (2011). The team perspective: Promoting excellence in performance teams. In D. Collins, A. Button, & H. Richards (Eds.), *Performance psychology: A practitioner's guide* (pp. 139–160). London: Elsevier.

Ostroff, C., Kinicki, A. J., & Tamkins, M. M. (2003). *Organizational culture and climate*. Hoboken, NJ: John Wiley & Sons, Inc.

Pain, M. A., & Harwood, C. G. (2008). The performance environment of the England youth soccer teams: A quantitative investigation. *Journal of Sports Sciences*, 26(11), 1157–1169.

Stevens, D. E. (2002). Building an effective team. In J. M. Silva & D. E. Stevens (Eds.), *Psychological foundations of sport* (pp. 306–327). Boston, MA: Allyn and Bacon.

West, M. A., & Unsworth, K. L. (1998). Developing team vision. In G. M. Parker (Ed.), *Handbook for best practice for teams*, Vol. 2 (pp. 295–310). Amherst, MA: HRD Press.

13 Mental Training of a Boccia Athlete Participating in the London 2012 Paralympic Games

Ricardo de la Vega

During the last decades, there has been an increasing interest in different aspects related to the quality of life of disabled individuals (de la Vega & Rubio, 2014; Gaskin, Andersen, & Morris, 2010). Simultaneously, a considerable increase in sport and physical activity has also influenced the development of sports for disabled individuals with representation at the highest international level, as is the case of the Paralympic Games. Regarding athletes with cerebral palsy, the development of high levels of competitive excellence in different sports, such as boccia, have required the support of sports science professionals. Therefore, sports psychology and sport psychologists attained a relevant place in the high-performance and adapted sports context.

In this chapter, a case study focused on the work performed with an athlete on the Spanish Nacional Boccia Team is presented. The assessment and intervention process performed with the athlete, allowing a critical approach to the sport psychologist's role into the disability sport context, is presented in this innovative work.

BACKGROUND INFORMATION

In preparation for the 2008 Paralympic Games in Beijing, a study was conducted with the Spanish National Boccia team that demonstrated the impact of mood control on performance in the individual and collective competitions the team participated in (de la Vega, Galan, Ruiz, & Tejero, 2013). The results showed a stable pattern of non-emotional disturbance, although the degree of depression was statistically higher in collective competition as opposed to individual competition, and fatigue was associated with perceived athletic performance in individual competition. We discussed the results and outlined the importance of deepening the relationship between mood and perceived performance in highly competitive environments for athletes with disabilities.

One of the authors of the study was the national coach himself (who holds a degree in sport psychology) and the current Vice President of the Spanish Sports Federation for People with Cerebral Palsy and Brain Injury (Federacion Española de deportes de personas con paralisis cerebral y lesion cerebral, or FEDPC for its acronym in Spanish; www.fedpc.org). With his support, the psychological training of the athletes interested in joining a new training program ahead of the 2012 Paralympics in London was considered relevant.

The sport of boccia is related to bowls and pétanque, and is contested at local, national, and international levels. It was originally designed to be played by people with cerebral palsy, but now includes athletes with other severe disabilities affecting motor skills. In 1984, it became a Paralympic sport, and in 2008 was being practiced in over 50 countries worldwide. Boccia is governed by the Boccia International Sports Federation (BISFed; www.bisfed.com) and is one of only three Paralympic sports that have no counterpart in the Olympic program. The objective of the game is to throw leather balls as close as possible to a white target ball called the jack. The balls can be moved with hands, feet, or, if the competitor's disability is severe, with an assistive device such as a ramp.

Boccia players are assigned to one of four sport classes depending on their functional ability: (a) BC1 – players in this class throw the ball with the hand or foot. They may compete with an assistant who stays outside of the competitor's playing box, to stabilize or adjust their playing chair and give the ball to the player when requested; (b) BC2 – players in this class throw the ball with the hand. They are not eligible for assistance; (c) BC3 – players in this class have very severe locomotor dysfunction in all extremities. They have no sustained grasp or release action and although they may have arm movement, they have insufficient range of movement to propel a boccia ball onto the court. They may use an assistive device such as a ramp to deliver the ball. They may compete with an assistant; assistants must keep their back to the court and their eyes averted from play; and (d) BC4 – players in this class have severe locomotor dysfunction of all four extremities as well as poor trunk control. They can demonstrate sufficient dexterity to throw the ball onto the court.

DESCRIPTION OF THE CASE

The case presented in this chapter focuses on an athlete named "J," a 33-year-old male with eight years of experience on the national team who had won three Olympic medals and third place in the 2010 Boccia World Championship BC1 category. Eight months ahead of the competition, J requested specific psychological training to prepare for the 2012 Paralympics in London. He made this decision after speaking to both his club and national team coaches, who believed he should know how to handle the pressure of his leadership role in the upcoming London Paralympics. Before carrying out this program of psychological training, J had not done any psychological work beyond his participation in the previous investigation conducted prior to the 2008 Beijing Paralympic Games (de la Vega et al., 2013).

In regards to brain impairment, J was diagnosed with athetoid cerebral palsy (Harris, 1989) with localized damage to the basal ganglia, characterized by severe, sudden alterations in muscle tone (i.e., the individual is unable to control changes in muscle tone). These uncontrolled movements increase during periods when the diagnosed individual feels a higher level of emotional stress, such as major international competitions, whereas they decrease during sleep. Despite this damage to the brain, the intellectual capacity of the athlete is intact.

The most relevant case information is presented below in the following sections: coach request, assistant perspective, and teammate perspectives.

Coach Request

A request from the athlete's coach began the psychological training process with J. As the coach mentioned, "although he has extensive international experience, he plays a central role on the national team and should know how to handle pressure well." J plays a major role among players on the national team since he is considered to be a model for all athletes. However, he stated that the first pitch strongly influences J, who can "collapse" if the pitch is not as good as he had hoped.

Assistant Perspective

The assistant was interviewed and pointed out that very high expectations were placed on J. He appeared confident but actually had doubts about his current level and whether he will reach his performance goals. The assistant indicated one of J's problems is that he thinks too much about the outcome of competitions, which causes him to get tired even the night before the event, presenting somatic disorders such as diarrhea and digestion problems that make him feel uncomfortable.

Teammate Perspectives

A sociogram was first used to determine the relationships among the athletes on the team (Carron, 1982). Subsequently, interviews were conducted with the teammates J had a better relationship with. The interviews revealed that he was a very competitive person, talented and pleasant, but getting a bad result could dramatically decrease his performance. His teammates considered him a nervous, responsible, and trustworthy person.

THEORETICAL FRAMEWORK/PHILOSOPHY

The basis of the intervention focused on framing the athlete's psychological responses in five basic dimensions: cognitive, emotional, psychophysiological, behavioral, and social. These dimensions are conditioned by two other essential factors: the athlete's personality and motivational processes (de la Vega & Ruiz, 2014). Human beings in general, and this athlete in particular, always seek the proper levels of behavioral adaptation toward the environment, in such a way that J will mobilize his available resources (technical, tactical, physical, and psychological) to achieve that adaptation (Araujo & Davids, 2009).

The aim was to perform a thorough functional analysis of these dimensions through the assessment and intervention process, adapting the intervention to the findings. The easiest way to perform the assessment was based on a cognitive perspective, so that the modulation and adaptation of the athlete's thought processes was sought, which influenced the rest of the dimensions. At the same time a behavioral approach was taken which aimed to decrease the practice of certain inappropriate behaviors and allow for the implementation of new behaviors better adapted to the specific context of high-performance sport.

In addition, a humanistic approach was used to mobilize motivational resources, which attempts to direct the athlete's internal energy toward achieving his process and performance objectives. A crucial aspect was the orientation of his emotions, which deepened the intrinsic motivations that mobilized J's resources and conduct. Specifically, logotherapy (Frank, 1959) was used to help and shape finding the "whys" that mobilized J for all the work he must do to prepare for the Paralympics in London.

NEEDS ASSESSMENT

The initial assessment process was conducted at a training camp for the National Team at the Peak Performance Centre (Centro de Alto Rendimiento; CAR for its acronym in Spanish) in San Cugat (Barcelona/Spain). Specifically, two types of tools to assess basic psychological dimensions were used: (1) those focused on identifying the athlete's personality traits, and (2) those focused on examining his response to specific and meaningful contexts. In order to identify the athlete's personality traits, a combination of interviews and self-report measures was used. Self-report measures included: personality assessment (Costa & McCrae, 2008) and the Sports Performance Psychological Questionnaire (Gimeno, Buceta, & Llantanda, 2001).

Three situations were designed to analyze the athlete's psychological response. In the first one, images of meaningful situations from the athlete were shown on a large screen (i.e., his entrance into the Beijing Olympic Stadium for the 2008 Paralympics and his performances at past Paralympics). In the second one, the athlete was asked to visualize different situations experienced in the past Paralympics. In the third one, a competition was simulated in which a number of variables were manipulated: the presence of stressors (e.g., coaches and teammates), pressure of the result (e.g., possibility of being called up for the next competition), and the uncertainty of the outcome of the other competitions. The following assessment protocol was used in the first two situations: structured interview about responses in each of the basic psychological dimensions, assessing J's perceived ability (on a scale of 0 to 10) to control a number of variables (e.g., attention, anxiety) and physiological monitoring (e.g., heart rate, breathing rate, skin conductance level) through Biofeedback 2000© (www.schuhfried.com). The simulated competition was continually monitored with Biofeedback 2000© and was followed by a semi-structured interview.

In addition to the psychological assessment mentioned above, the main attentional processes involved in boccia were also assessed: the capacity to direct attention (Stroop Effect for ten minutes with target stimulus); selective attention (Visual Pursuit Test, Vienna Test System©); and space–time perception (Time/Movement Anticipation, Vienna Test System© (ZBA) (www.schuhfried.com/viennatestsystem10/vienna-test-system-vts/)). These were assessed both with and without sound distraction (words such as loss, disaster, error, etc., read aloud every ten seconds). Due to J's limited mobility, a particular signal was established that directed the evaluator to push the system's button.

Once the results of the needs assessment were analyzed, the following objectives for improving J's performance were established:

1. Improve selective attention when distracted and the ability to maintain attentional focus (before, during, and in between competitions).
2. Increase the control of psychophysiological responses (e.g., electromyography, galvanic skin response) in order to increase the perception of emotion and anxiety control through biofeedback relaxation training.
3. Establish a competition plan by incorporating appropriate behaviors (e.g., attentional focus, emotional regulation) and precise goals (e.g., long-term maintenance of appropriate behaviors, achieving optimal motivation).
4. Optimize the cognitive processes of coping with the competition, regulating his expectation of the result and focusing on the tasks (e.g., focusing on the jack, visualizing prior to performance) that lead to achieving his goals.
5. Design a systematic desensitization and virtual reality exposure to help J learn how to cope effectively when faced with a specific anxiety-provoking situation (i.e., the first throw).

INTERVENTION

The intervention took place in Madrid, Spain between September 2011 and the 2012 Paralympics in London. Weekly psychological training sessions were held during two National Team training camps. Support for the intervention with J was provided by the invaluable collaboration of the Vice President of the FEDPC and former coach, the coach from J's club, the coach for the National Team, and J's assistant.

Psychological training sessions were conducted at the rate of one or two weekly sessions lasting up to 40 minutes in order to not fatigue the athlete. In the month of April we changed our schedule from meeting one day a week to meeting once or twice depending on the athlete's schedule. The following describes the work that was conducted to achieve each of the objectives outlined above.

Improve Attention

The intervention process for the improvement of selective attention was developed in a total of three phases. In the first phase, the intervention was based on the principles of Posner and Raichle (1994) and Fernandez-Duque and Posner (1997), which have shown to be valid for boccia. These authors distinguished three types of attention networks: orienting (corresponds to the direction of one's attention), vigilance (corresponds to the intensity of one's attention), and executive attention (corresponds roughly to the selectivity dimension). The training was based on the use of the computerized system multimedia Vienna Test System© (www.schuhfried.com), designed to improve each of these attentional components.

For the second phase, virtual reality was implemented in which a series of more than 100 situational possibilities of play were performed, presenting the images for increasingly shorter periods of time. In each situation, J had to decide in what direction he should throw the ball and with what intensity. At this stage, distractions were added (mainly acoustic and visual) so he was practicing staying focused on the relevant stimuli.

Finally, in the third phase, training situations were created in which the player was to apply the skills trained to improve attentional focus in competition. At this stage, visual and auditory distractors were also incorporated (e.g., deciding when to make the release while listening through headphones to negative messages about himself and what he would do).

Increasing Emotion and Anxiety Control

Stress, tension, and anxiety play a fundamental role in mental balance. Initially, the characteristics of the autonomic nervous system were explained as well as the operation of its sympathetic and parasympathetic branches, in order to provide J with an understanding of the body's response to stress. Jacobson's progressive muscle relaxation (Cautela & Groden, 1978) was used to increase the differential control of certain muscles and their activation level, allowing J to loosen up in specific situations through the relaxation of the agonist and antagonist muscles (essentially from the upper half of the body).

To complement this, a program for regulating the level of physiological arousal was performed using the Biofeedback 2000© program. Specifically, the following functions were monitored: respiratory rate, heart rate, and sweating. The program involved three stages: (1) educational program about the importance of these parameters and its applications in boccia; (2) learning self-regulation of each of the physiological functions trained in quiet conditions; and (3) application of self-regulation behaviors learned in the competitive context.

Establishing a Competition Plan

In line with the classic model of Lazarus and Folkman (1984), if the athlete perceives that he has the resources to address potentially stressful situations that may occur in competition, and does not divert his attention to irrelevant stimuli or variables, he will perceive the situation as manageable and will be likely to perform commensurate to his potential. The idea of introducing competition plans or routines has been widespread in sport psychology (Cohm, 1990; Orlick, 1986), so that personal resources and coping strategies for various situations are pre-planned, thus increasing the athlete's perceived control and perceived effectiveness.

A structured competition plan is intended to achieve the following key objectives: (1) know one's resources (e.g., strengths, weaknesses, mechanical, tactical, and psychological knowledge); (2) identify alternative resources available if other resources fail or if the situation is not as expected; and (3) use the plans to keep attention focused on relevant performance factors (e.g., ball, intensity, direction).

Optimize the Cognitive Processes of Coping with Competition

In conjunction with the implementation of competition plans, a very important part of the intervention done with J was to address the perceived importance of the Paralympics and his interpretation of this situation as uncontrollable (i.e., overestimating the dreaded competition and underestimating his resources and coping skills, resulting in catastrophic anticipations of the result). In this regard, it was considered important to incorporate rational emotive therapy (RET; Ellis, 1980), explaining the ABC triad (i.e., situation, thinking, and behavior).

RET training consisted of analyzing thoughts emanating between stimuli prior to execution (e.g., moments before the first throws), and the consequences (e.g., poor throw). In the case of J, specific thoughts such as "I can't do it" or "I will disappoint my teammates" were detected and analyzed with him. This way, we could modify and structure each thought in a positive way with efficacy: "I have trained hard and I am prepared. I can do this," "If I focus on the jack, my throw will be smooth." As a side note, practitioners need to be aware that communication processes are especially important with cerebral palsy athletes. One must be patient in this type of training in which the athlete must be in a comfortable environment, with enough time to finish practice and without feeling any kind of pressure.

In order to help J cope with this anticipatory anxiety, we introduced a process of coping by exposing the athlete gradually to the stressful situation, so that a perception of self-efficacy and increasing control was obtained. To do this, integrating both imagery training in practice and gradual exposure to training situations as similar as possible to the context of the Paralympic Games was introduced.

Systematic Desensitization for Coping with Anxiety

To carry out the process of counter-conditioning, it is assumed that the response of anxiety and fear can be generalized to similar stimulus configurations (Rogerson, 1997; Wolpe & Plaud, 1997), which undoubtedly can be a serious problem for J facing Olympic performance. For this specific case, a list of situations that generated anxiety in J was established and a scale from 0 (low anxiety) to 100 (high anxiety) points was used to determine the strength of his anxiety response for each situation.

Of the situations that J described, two were chosen for the intervention due to the strong anxiety response he indicated having in each of these situations. The situations were: (1) before the first throw in individual competition (this situation was scored with 90 points); and (2) the last throw when the athlete has to be very precise (this was rated as 80 points). In order to evoke an adaptive response, J visualized the situation utilizing the self-regulation techniques he had learned until he was able to reach an acceptable level of self-regulation in his anxiety levels. This acceptable level was established with a score lower than 40 on the 0 to 100 scale. Once J reached each objective, two positive reinforcements were used: J's favorite soda along with a gesture that was previously agreed upon, such as placing a hand on the athlete's shoulder to show empathy and support. J practiced this imagery process during several sessions and then moved on to performing the imagery in situations with a simulated context that would bring about his anxiety levels. This enabled him to work on self-regulating his anxiety in more competition-like situations.

REFLECTION

At the London Paralympics the athlete won the individual silver medal, the gold medal in the doubles competition, and the Olympic diploma (i.e., certificate awarded to the top eight finishers in competitions at the Olympic Games) in the team competition. Despite the apparent effectiveness of the intervention, it is useful to discuss elements that could have optimized the work with the athlete.

Focusing on the most positive aspects of the intervention, one must realize that the established objectives were accomplished. The idiosyncrasies of cerebral palsy imply that a practitioner must adjust the athlete's psychological training accordingly. For example, the spasticity and high muscle tension that individuals with cerebral palsy experience are factors that need to be considered in order to effectively assess, design, teach, and implement relaxation and activation control (e.g., baseline levels of activation may be higher than expected). In the attentional focus training, each phase was adjusted, helping J in his performance with the computer attentional test by establishing cues that indicated he had perceived the stimulus (i.e., the sport psychology practitioner was the one pushing the proper corresponding device key). The benefits in J's case were evident in regards to the psychological objective demanded from the start. In addition, the support from the national team coach was essential to reach a positive working alliance with the athlete and technical staff.

In regards to limitations, there were inaccurate expectations regarding the difficulty of the intervention. Among these expectations, the more evident were the biases that the practitioner himself had to break down in regards to the logical limitations of working with cerebral palsy athletes. Thus, the following were needed for an optimal relationship between the practitioner and J: patience when communicating with the athlete; collaboration with the technical staff; and using facilities that were adequate for a wheelchair during practice. After discussing my work with several colleagues, I consider that in future interventions the educational work with technical staff and disabled athletes is desirable and essential for an optimal working alliance. Thus, we must educate our future generations through Departments of Psychology and Sport Science so that more practitioners develop their skills and applied service in a context that is enriching at the personal and professional level.

In a general reflection on the limitations and future interventions with disabled athletes, one must consider four essential aspects: (1) the need to integrate psychological training in the athlete's annual planning; (2) the importance of simulated practice in which the athlete has to adapt his/her abilities and coping mechanisms to each situation; (3) the relevance of studying each specific case due to the specificity of the etiology that can be present in the context of incapacity; and (4) the creation of an international network of professionals who can share information in regards to applied work within the context of sport and disabled athletes.

SUGGESTED READINGS

Hanrahan, S. J. (2005). Able athletes with disabilities: Issues and group work. In M. B. Anderson (Ed.), *Sport psychology in practice* (pp. 223–248). Champaign, IL: Human Kinetics.
Hanrahan, S. J. (2007). Athletes with disabilities. In G. Tenenbaum & R. C. Eklund (Eds.), *Handbook of sport psychology* (3rd ed.; pp. 845–858). Hoboken, NJ: Wiley.
Martin, J. J. (2005). Sport psychology consulting with athletes with disabilities. *Sport and Exercise Psychology Review, 1*(2), 32–39.

REFLECTIVE QUESTIONS

1. How do emotion and anxiety regulation play a role in helping an athlete to regulate his/her arousal?
2. How would you design a psychological competition plan for an athlete in preparation for a competition?
3. Think of a fear an athlete might have related to his/her performance. Describe how you would use systematic desensitization to help him/her overcome that fear.
4. What things do you need to consider in order to effectively implement psychological skills training for athletes with disabilities?
5. How would you design and implement cognitive strategies, such as rational emotive therapy, when working with athletes with disabilities to improve their coping strategies?

REFERENCES

Araujo, D., & Davids, K. (2009). Ecological approaches to cognition and action in sport and exercise: Ask not only what you do, but where you do it. *International Journal of Sport Psychology, 40*, 5–37.
Carron, A. V. (1982). Cohesiveness in sport groups: Interpretations and considerations. *Journal of Sport Psychology, 4*, 123–138.
Cautela, J. R., & Groden, J. (1978). *Relaxation: A comprehensive manual for adults, children, and children with special needs.* Champaign, IL: Research Press.
Cohn, P. (1990). Preperformance routines in sport: Theoretical support and practical applications. *The Sport Psychologist, 4*, 301–312.

Costa, P., & McCrae, R. (2008). The revised NEO personality inventory (NEO-PI-R). In G. Boyle, G. Matthews, & D. Saklofske (Eds.), *The SAGE handbook of personality theory and assessment: Volume 2 – Personality measurement and testing* (pp. 179–199). London: SAGE.

de la Vega, R., Galán, Á., Ruiz, R., & Tejero, C. M. (2013). Precompetitive mood and perceived performance in Paralympic boccia. *Revista de Psicología del Deporte, 22*(1), 39–45.

de la Vega, R., & Rubio, V. (2014). Promoting physical activity and performance excellence among individuals with disabilities. In J. G. Cremades & L. S. Tashman (Eds.), *Becoming a sport, exercise, and performance psychology professional: A global perspective* (pp. 92–100). New York, NY: Psychology Press.

de la Vega, R., & Ruiz, R. (2014). Evaluación psicológica: saber lo que cada uno necesita. In M. Roffé, & S. Rivera (Eds.), *Entrenamiento mental en el fútbol moderno* (pp. 121–135). Sevilla: FutbolDLibro.

Ellis, A. (1980). Rational-emotive therapy and cognitive behavior therapy: Similarities and differences. *Cognitive Therapy and Research, 4*, 325–340.

Fernandez-Duque, D., & Posner, M. I. (1997). Relating the mechanisms of orienting and alerting. *Neuropsychologia, 35*, 477–486.

Frank, V. (1959). *Man's search for meaning: An introduction to logo therapy.* Boston, MA: Beacon Press.

Gaskin, C. J., Andersen, M. B., & Morris, T. (2010). Sport and physical activity in the life of a man with cerebral palsy: Compensation for disability with psychosocial benefits and costs. *Psychology of Sport and Exercise, 11*, 197–205.

Gimeno, F., Buceta, J. M., & Llantada, M. (2001). El cuestionario "Características Psicológicas Relacionadas con el Rendimiento Deportivo" (C. P. R. D.): Características psicométricas. *Análise Psicológica, 1*, 93–133.

Harris, S. R. (1989). Early diagnosis of spastic diplegia, spastic hemiplegia, and quadriplegia. *American Journal of Diseases of Children, 143*, 1356–1360.

Lazarus, R. S., & Folkman, S. (1984). *Stress, appraisal and coping.* New York, NY: Springer.

Orlick, T. (1986). *Psyching for sport: Mental training for athletes.* Champaign, IL: Human Kinetics.

Posner, M. I., & Raichle, M. E. (1994). *Images of mind.* Scientific American Books.

Rogerson, J. (1997). Canine fears and phobias: A regime for treatment without recourse to drugs. *Applied Animal Behavior Science, 52*, 291–297.

Wolpe, J., & Plaud, J. J. (1997). Pavlov's contributions to behavior therapy: The obvious and the not so obvious. *American Psychologist, 52*(9), 966–972.

14 Helping a Helper Get Healthy

The Case of Eleanor's Eating and Exercise Behaviors

Sam J. Zizzi

The case of "Eleanor" presented in this chapter is an amalgam of several clients with similar presented issues within a community-based, insurance-sponsored weight management program. As the consultant and faculty member, I have contracted with an insurance agency to provide behavioral services to participants at high risk for dropout of the program. The focus of these services is to help clients develop a sustainable approach to healthy living built around eating well and regular physical activity. Phone-based behavioral coaching is provided to participants approximately every six weeks during the course of the first year of their weight management program. Email or text contact is used between the phone sessions. The core of the program is delivered to the client at a local fitness facility by trained fitness and dietary professionals. The first coaching session occurs approximately 3–4 weeks into the program, after their fitness assessment and attendance at the gym, but usually before the consultation with a registered dietician. The consultants function within a collaborative environment working alongside exercise physiologists, personal trainers, and registered dieticians. Fitness facility staff enter objective data on participant visits and body measurements monthly into a secure web-based database, and all participants complete required self-reported behavioral surveys prior to program entry. Additional details on this program are available in the published literature (Abildso, Zizzi, & Reger-Nash, 2010; Zizzi, Abildso, Henderson, & Shaffer, 2014) or by visiting the program's companion site at healthperformance.wordpress.com.

BACKGROUND INFORMATION

Eleanor is a 43-year-old participant in the weight management program. She heard about the program from a colleague and was excited she could attend a local gym for $20 each month, and receive some additional help. She is Caucasian, and lives in a small, rural area of West Virginia. She has a husband who is a construction worker and has two teenage children. She also helps to care for several older members of her family in the surrounding area, including grandparents and aunts/uncles. She is employed as a school cook in a small school district, with a working schedule of approximately 6:30 a.m.–2:30 p.m. Eleanor stands 5'7" and weighs 280 pounds (BMI = 42). She currently reports no other chronic disease co-morbidities.

DESCRIPTION OF THE CASE

Eleanor reports a sporadic history of healthy eating and regular exercise. She has been sedentary for her entire adult life with the exception of a few periods of walking regularly. About five years ago, she lost 50 pounds on Weight Watchers, but has since gained it all back. She joined the program because she found out that if she completes one year, she will be eligible for bariatric surgery (i.e., the insurance agency will subsidize the surgery). When asked about her experience in the fitness facility, she says exercise "hurt" at first and she is averaging two days a week in the first month (which is the minimum required attendance to stay in the program). With this level of activity and controlling some of her portions, she managed to lose 16 pounds in the first month of the program. In the second month, she gained one pound back, and attributed this to the additional stress related to the illness of a family member. She presents as an extreme "pleaser" or accommodator, who derives most of her good feelings from helping others. Within the sessions, it is clear she has difficulty managing the emotions related to eating well and maintaining assertive communication with her family regarding her health. Overall, in addition to her stated goal of earning bariatric surgery, her goals are to lower her blood pressure, prevent diabetes, and be more comfortable physically.

THEORETICAL FRAMEWORK/PHILOSOPHY

The overarching philosophy for the behavioral services that are provided in the program is to create self-determined and self-regulated clients. Thus, all services are designed to help clients explore the most effective forms of motivation, as well as to develop the most needed self-regulatory skills in order to sustain their efforts on behavior change. These services focus specifically on eating and exercise behaviors, unless counseling issues emerge that require intervention or referral. In terms of the therapeutic process, the consultant's work is built on training in counseling, health behavior change, and motivational interviewing. The work draws from several cognitive behavioral approaches, including rational emotive therapy (Ellis, 1994), mindfulness principles, and motivational interviewing techniques (Rollnick, Miller, & Butler, 2008).

The cognitive themes that stand out with unhealthy clients often center around dysfunctional perceptions of themselves (e.g., "I am a failure because I can't eat a healthy diet") or the behavior change process (e.g., "It is just overwhelming to do all of this right"). When these themes emerge, the consultation focuses on bringing awareness to, and inspection of, one's thought patterns. Mindfulness principles of awareness and nonjudgment of thoughts can be quite helpful in these moments as the patterns take time and patience to change. These same principles may also be applied to eating or exercise behaviors as well. I like to frame the process of behavior change as an experiment, and therefore it is useful to understand successes and failures from an objective, informational standpoint. A sense of humor often helps clients poke fun at themselves, and their neurotic thoughts and behaviors, in these moments. Finally, with resistant or ambivalent clients, I have found motivational interviewing techniques quite useful. The simplicity of the neutral stance and empowering style allows consultants to be still while clients make their own arguments for change. The primary ideas are to explore the client's motivation toward specific components of the eating or exercise prescription, to avoid the idea that we know what they should be doing to improve their health, and to empower them toward their path for change.

NEEDS ASSESSMENT

For assessing her strengths and weaknesses, the social ecological (Stokols, 1996) and transtheoretical models (Prochaska & DiClemente, 1992) were used to structure surveys and intake protocols. These models, when used in combination, provide a nice balance of information related to a client's readiness to change, as well as the facilitators and barriers to change across multiple levels, ranging from intrapersonal, interpersonal, to micro-environmental. A pre-intake health information survey includes medication usage, exercise and eating self-efficacy, social support, barriers, a screening for clinical depression, and several variables related to environmental supports (or lack of) for exercise. These supports include travel time to/from the exercise facility, access to exercise equipment in their home, and access to safe locations for walking outdoors near their home.

The intake session protocol includes sections on adult exercise history, weight loss history, weekly social and work schedules, enablers and barriers, and behavioral goals. Subsequent sessions build on these categories, and use process data from their progress in the program to continue the work. A detailed description of this model of consultation is available in the companion textbook from this series (see Zizzi & Gilchrist, 2014).

Eleanor's Needs

Based on the self-reported and objective data available, along with the subjective report of the client in sessions 1 and 2, several strengths and weaknesses were identified for Eleanor. Some facilitating factors that support her change efforts include a predictable work schedule, reasonably good access to the fitness center, and a growing sense of health risk (though she is not currently experiencing many negative health effects of her weight). She is around food all the time, and does report this as a barrier to healthy eating along with "not being motivated," "healthy foods are not filling," "family/spouse doesn't want to eat them," and "cost of healthy foods." She likes how she feels after exercise, but is not confident of her ability to stay consistent at the gym and seems particularly negative toward eating on the weekends and at family events. Her poor initial fitness and physical size (BMI = 42) are also barriers, causing her experience of exercise to include some pain and discomfort.

Additionally, she was suffering from mild clinical depression and self-esteem issues related to her body image and weight. She is taking Zoloft for her depression, and has been on this medication for over a year. However, if she is consistent with her exercise, she may experience mood-related benefits. She has been told by her doctor that her blood pressure is getting high and she is at high risk for developing diabetes. Almost everyone else in her family (who is older) has been diagnosed with at least one chronic disease.

INTERVENTION

Following the client's lead and preference, I spent much of the first two sessions on eating behaviors. Her exercise behavior had been moderately (1–3 times per week) consistent, including some evidence of walking outside of the exercise facility. Her eating behavior appeared inconsistent, and she reported difficulty managing her choices under stress, and within some family contexts.

The transtheoretical model processes of change were of particular use in this case. It was clear that though she reported being in the action stage on the surveys (and had obviously started the program), her readiness was in the contemplation or preparation stage for both healthy eating and exercise. Thus, the matching interventions of self- and social-liberation seemed appropriate to help challenge her identity as a sedentary, unhealthy eater and to help build self-efficacy for her new habits. An example discussion is provided below:

CONSULTANT: Could you tell me about how your family has reacted to your participation in the program?

ELEANOR: Well, they are kind of supportive. I mean, my husband says he is excited. I'm trying to be healthy but he doesn't really want to eat the new recipes I have been trying out for dinner. Sometimes I have to fix a second dinner for him and my boys. He will walk with me sometimes in the evenings though.

CONSULTANT: Have you talked with them about why you are doing it, and your goals?

ELEANOR: We talked about it at dinner last week. The boys are super supportive, and their attitude is rubbing off on their father fortunately. It's the rest of the family that worries me. They just see me as the cook, and someone who always brings something tasty to parties or cookouts. And of course the one who will eat what the others will fix. (Laughs a bit uncomfortably at herself.)

CONSULTANT: Would you consider letting everyone else in the family know about your goals?

ELEANOR: Yeah, maybe I should.

CONSULTANT: Well that is up to you, I trust your judgment. But it does sound like talking with your husband and kids worked out OK. Is it something you might be willing to try before our next session?

This conversation also included a discussion about her co-workers, and also some people she had met at the gym. The idea with this piece of intervention was to help the client explore all of the social and environmental supports available and to access them proactively to make this experience last longer than previous attempts. I function under the assumption that if the client doesn't learn some new skills and do some things differently, then they will repeat previous mistakes and eventually be unsuccessful. I like to get them to identify and plan for the top 1–2 barriers in the way of their success to reduce the likelihood of relapse.

The elements of stress management and emotional eating were not so easily addressed within the bounds of the transtheoretical model. To approach these topics, I used motivational interviewing techniques to explore the specific self-regulation skills that needed work. Because she presented as an extreme people pleaser (i.e., high in the personality trait accommodation), I felt that a traditional self-efficacy building process through goal-setting would be ineffective. In my experience, clients with these characteristics often lack a strong ego, and are instead "filled up" when they help others (as opposed to accomplishing their own goals). Accommodators avoid interpersonal conflict and often lack assertive communication skills, so navigating family dynamics can be challenging. So, you can approach the idea of self-regulation and behavior change to become a better helper. For Eleanor, this meant being a healthier mom to model that behavior for her boys and to be around for many years in a healthy state to see their lives play out. It also meant being a healthier family member so she could: (1) continue to care for less healthy people in her family and (2) not depend on others to take care of her later.

During this family-centered discussion, Eleanor expressed anxiety about confronting her family with the news that "she was going to be healthy." The discussion, an excerpt of which is shown below, revealed additional barriers related to dysfunctional thinking patterns and lack of emotional regulation skills in certain circumstances.

CONSULTANT: Eleanor, let's think through one of these upcoming family events to see how it might go if you decide to try something new. Can you think of a specific event coming up soon?

ELEANOR: Yes, at my aunt's house. They will expect that I'll bring one of my cakes, and maybe some of the cookies that I always fix. Plus, if I'm on this new diet, there probably won't be anything there I can eat. I'll probably just not eat. But they will expect me to eat … hmmm.

CONSULTANT: What are some options to approach this situation differently?

ELEANOR: I'm not sure … a few of them have heard I am in the program and I'm sure they are not going to be supportive. If I bring a salad or something like that, they will suspect I'm up to something. If I don't eat the food they fix, they might be offended. They know I like it, so it will just be weird.

CONSULTANT: Is there a middle path, where you could still bring something they expect but also bring yourself something healthier to eat? Or maybe eat something before you go? I imagine you could also have small portions of the dishes they prepare too.

ELEANOR: Yeah, I guess I could. I would feel better if I made a plate and showed them I was eating something they fixed. I don't want them to be offended.

CONSULTANT: I want you to find a solution that works for you, so whatever approach you are comfortable with, let's try that. Maybe we can role play to see how it will go.

This conversation shows my efforts to position myself in a neutral stance recommended by motivational interviewing advocates. The approach highlights a guiding style designed to increase the autonomy of the client while holding them accountable to changes they have indicated in the session. The benefits of this approach in health behavior change are that clients who are resistant or less ready to change may respond better, and are allowed "permission" to choose their direction and their pace of change. Later on in this conversation, the session went deeper into some of the dysfunctional thinking patterns. These underlying messages included "All of my family must support this or it just won't work," "I should be so much better at healthy eating," and "It's really my aunt's fault because she made me this way." We spent some time disputing these beliefs in our second and third sessions together, and the work clearly challenged Eleanor's core beliefs. It is my opinion that our work was meaningful to her, but that it did cause her some anxiety because we uncovered some emotional issues linked to her role in the family and her self-identity. Several times within the sessions, she was either crying or close to tears.

REFLECTION

Ultimately, it is not known if this consultation was maximally effective. After the third session, and a few follow-up contacts via email, the client was non-responsive. This pattern is not atypical for clients in the weight management program – approximately 55 percent of participants drop out of the program before reaching the one-year mark, but some of these participants become successful on their own. As with many clients in our work, they eventually stop coming in for services and you can only hope the lessons learned will carry over from intentions into behavior change. I often think of planting seeds with clients. If you can cultivate some soil to grow something in the future, and get some seeds in that soil, the client may reap the benefits at a later time. In this situation, even if Eleanor was not successful in the program in meeting her goals, maybe the next attempt will be her shining moment of change.

Tele-Therapy With Obese Participants

Many of the students and young professionals who are trained to do this work in our program express initial reluctance to use the phone as the primary medium for service delivery. There are certainly limitations with respect to picking up non-verbal cues and affect from in-person sessions that are not available on the phone. However, experience has taught the team of consultants that many obese participants appear more comfortable discussing health behaviors on the phone because they feel less judged about their body. There is an anonymity to the phone that appears to facilitate rapport building and trust between typically unhealthy clients and healthy consultants. There is also evidence that in rural settings, phone-based approaches are appropriate and can be equally effective as in-person sessions (Perri et al., 2008).

Difficulties When Working With High Accommodators

One large difference consultants may face if they make the transition to working with less healthy clients (compared to sport participants) is that many clients are not particularly goal-oriented, conscientious, or confident. Clients with the trait of high accommodation present several challenges, and require a higher degree of clinical skill compared to many other clients. First, I have found them highly emotionally intelligent and tuned-in to the dynamics of the consulting session. They are innately better than some clients at sensing any sort of conflict or disapproval in the session (from the consultant) and altering their behavior to minimize that feeling. I have been "tricked" many times into believing I'm doing a great job by one of these clients when later I realized that they were just trying to make me feel like I'm doing a good job! I urge any consultants who intend to do this work to work on your counseling skills and get trained in motivational interviewing.

Health Incongruence and Limited Access

It can be a challenge working with clients who are less healthy than you, and who live in areas with limited access to healthy foods and places to be active. I do think it takes some time to get used to working with this population, especially for those of us who initially approach sport and exercise psychology from the sport angle. The athletes I have worked with usually need to change or improve <10 percent to make a big difference in their sport performance. They also usually have a history of setting and achieving goals through hard work. Athletes have support staff built to make them successful (e.g., physical trainers, coaches, dieticians) and they have access to structured practice environments. The clients in the weight management program often need to change >50 percent of their habits and often lack many of the key self-regulatory skills necessary to sustain change. Their environment is also not often facilitative either. So, there is much work to be done with these clients, and they can definitely use our help. While the pace of work is often slow and can be frustrating, it can also be highly rewarding.

SUGGESTED READINGS

Rollnick, S., Miller, W. R., & Butler, C. C. (2008). *Motivational interviewing in health care: Helping patients change health behavior.* New York, NY: Guildford Press.
Walen, S. R., DiGiuseppe, R., & Dryden, W. (1992). *A practitioner's guide to rational-emotive therapy.* Oxford: Oxford University Press.
Wansink, B. (2007). *Mindless eating: Why we eat more than we think.* New York, NY: Bantam.
Zizzi, S., & Shannon, V. (2013). The ethical practice of exercise psychology. In J. Watson & E. Etzel (Eds.), *Ethics in sport and exercise psychology* (pp. 77–87). Morgantown, WV: FIT Information Technology.

REFLECTIVE QUESTIONS

1. How can you use the social ecological model to inform your needs assessment approach?
2. What are the major challenges that Eleanor is facing in sustaining a healthy lifestyle?
3. What dysfunctional thoughts might be challenged in this case?
4. What are the benefits of taking a motivational interviewing approach to health performance consultations?
5. What are some ethical considerations in this case?

REFERENCES

Abildso, C., Zizzi, S., & Reger-Nash, B. (2010). Evaluating an insurance-sponsored weight management program with the RE-AIM model, West Virginia, 2004–2008. *Preventing Chronic Disease 7*(3), 1–12.
Ellis, A. (1994). The sport of avoiding sports and exercise: A rational emotive behavior therapy perspective. *Sport Psychologist, 8,* 248–261.
Perri, M. G., Limacher, M. C., Durning, P. E., Janicke, D. M., Lutes, L. D., Bobroff, L. B.,... & Martin, A. D. (2008). Extended-care programs for weight management in rural communities: the treatment of obesity in underserved rural settings (TOURS) randomized trial. *Archives of Internal Medicine, 168*(21), 2347–2354.
Prochaska, J. O., & DiClemente, C. C. (1992). The transtheoretical approach. In J. C. Norcross & M. R. Goldfried (Eds.), *Handbook of psychotherapy integration* (pp. 300–334). New York, NY: Basic Books.
Rollnick, S., Miller, W. R., & Butler, C. C. (2008). *Motivational interviewing in health care: Helping patients change health behavior.* New York, NY: Guildford Press.
Stokols, D. (1996). Translating social ecological theory into guidelines for community health promotion. *American Journal of Health Promotion, 10*(4), 282–298.

Zizzi, S., Abildso, C., Henderson, N., & Shaffer, K. (2014). The West Virginia PEIA weight management program: An innovative approach to obesity prevention and treatment in Appalachian communities. In V. M. Brennan, S. K. Kumanyika, & R. E. Zambrana (Eds.), *Obesity interventions in underserved communities: Evidence and directions* (pp. 282–289). Baltimore, MD: Johns Hopkins Press.

Zizzi, S., & Gilchrist, K. (2014). A theory-based model for health performance consultations. In G. Cremedes & L. Tashman (Eds.), *Becoming a sport, exercise, and performance psychology professional: International perspectives* (pp. 102–110). New York, NY: Taylor & Francis.

15 Modeling

An Effective Method for Enhancing the Teaching of Physical Education by Primary School Generalist Teachers

Maura Coulter and Catherine B. Woods

Opportunities for children to be active should be facilitated through the school and in the community setting (Woods, 2014). *Whole-school* interventions are identified as one of the seven investments that work for the promotion of physical activity by the Global Advocacy for Physical Activity (GAPA, 2011). These interventions have the potential to reach the majority of children, as in many countries physical education is mandatory. This provides an opportunity to increase participation even among the least active children, who are otherwise difficult to target through other programmatic efforts. The role of the teacher in physical education is to help the child develop the knowledge and skills necessary to maintain lifetime activity and fitness, and to become independent in his or her physical activity and fitness pursuits. However, physical education has a range of objectives and represents only 2 percent of a young person's waking time (Fox & Harris, 2003), at least half of which involves only light physical activity. While physical education plays an important role in children's learning about health and physical activity, it should only be considered as part of a whole-school approach.

BACKGROUND INFORMATION

Many countries have witnessed a decrease in the time given to physical education in schools (Hardman & Marshall, 2009). Current guidelines in Ireland for primary school physical education recommend, but do not require, a minimum of 60 minutes of physical education per week (Government of Ireland, 1999). Recent research (Woods, Moyna, Quinlan, Tannehill, & Walsh, 2010) shows that on average Irish primary school children receive 46 minutes of physical education weekly.

A lack of training, almost non-existent in-service training, and lack of facilities are given as the main reasons for the lack of enthusiasm about teaching physical education among primary school teachers (Coulter & Woods, 2012). Barriers, such as physical education being perceived as a low-priority subject, lack of financial resources, insufficient equipment and facilities, and low level of principal support exist not only in Ireland but in other countries as well (Hardman & Marshall, 2009). Given that schools and physical education have a statutory responsibility to deliver learning about health and physical activity within a broad and balanced curriculum, it might be assumed that teachers have the knowledge, commitment, and expertise to do this effectively – but evidence shows us that this is not the case. Therefore, the intervention discussed in this chapter was implemented as a year-long continuing professional development program designed primarily to support teachers in their teaching of physical education to ensure children's learning. The intervention also aimed to broaden the children's experiences of physical education beyond team games, and to motivate them to participate in these activities both in and out of school.

DESCRIPTION OF THE CASE

The case-study school was a large, suburban, mixed primary school with a number of classes at each of the eight primary school levels (from junior infants – level 1 – to sixth class – level 8). The school was situated in an affluent area, though a number of children (1 percent) came from the Traveling Community (i.e., Irish ethnic minority nomadic people). Social classes 1 (professional workers) and 2 (managerial and technical) accounted for 59 percent of the population in the school area in contrast to 32.9 percent for the national population (Ryan, 2009). There were 28 class teachers and 815 pupils (aged 4 to 13 years) in the school. Each class had approximately 29 children and was timetabled for 45 minutes of physical education each week.

THEORETICAL FRAMEWORK/PHILOSOPHY

Correlates of Physical Activity

In order to change school-children's behavior we must understand its influences. Understanding why and how young people engage in physical activity will provide more leverage for intervention efforts designed to encourage health-promoting lifestyles. Aligned to the social ecological model (Sallis, Owen, & Fisher, 2008), correlates (i.e., factors associated with behavior) and determinants (i.e., factors with a causal relationship) can generally be classified into five groups: (1) demographic and biological variables (e.g., gender, age); (2) psychological, cognitive, and emotional variables (e.g., depression, perceived ability); (3) behavioral attributes and skills (e.g., previous physical activity and sedentary time); (4) social and cultural variables (e.g., parental encouragement); and (5) physical environment variables (e.g., access to facilities). A distinction can be made between modifiable and non-modifiable (e.g., age, gender, genetics, and, to an extent, social class) correlates and determinants of behavior. Those that can be modified or controlled are the ones we need to understand and prioritize in the design of evidence-based interventions (Sallis, Owen, & Fotheringham, 2000). Modifiable determinants may include individual factors (e.g., motivation toward physical activity or perceived competence in motor skills), or environmental factors such as social influence (e.g., social climate created by adult leaders) and the physical environment (e.g., access to leisure and sports facilities, transport infrastructure within one's locality).

Review studies summarizing the existing literature on correlates of physical activity in children (e.g., van der Horst, Paw, Twisk, & van Mechelen, 2007; Sallis, Prochaska, & Taylor, 2000) consistently show that boys are more physically active than girls and that physical activity levels decrease with increasing age. Examining the social and physical environmental correlates (Ferreira, van der Horst, Wendel-Vos, Kremers, van Lenthe, & Brug, 2007), physically active and inactive groups of young people systematically differ from each other with regard to perceived social support from significant others (e.g., peers, family, teachers) and perceived family norms toward physical activity (e.g., parental physical activity habits) (Ferreira et al., 2007). These data suggest that a complex set of social variables in the social climate of everyday life of children will determine the development of a physically active or inactive lifestyle. The behavioral correlates suggest that community sports participation is significantly related to adolescent physical activity, whereas participation in school sports is not (Drake et al., 2012; Sallis, Prochaska, & Taylor, 2000). Longitudinal observations in Finland have shown that regular and persistent participation in youth sport strongly increases the probability of being physically active in adulthood (Telama, Yang, Hirvensalo, & Raitakari, 2006). Individuals participating in youth sport are usually motivated, their participation is regular and often persists over many years, and through training they learn many new skills, which can have high health benefits (Drake et al., 2012). Within the school setting, the social environmental factors impacting the relationship between youth sport participation and adult physical activity include the teacher–child relationship, the provision of physical education in the school, the relationship of the school with the community, and educational policy such as physical education curricula. The focus of the teacher needs to be on the theoretical elements of fitness such as: (a) increasing participation rates and improving fitness literacy; (b) focusing on lifetime physical activity rather than traditional games and sports; (c) commitment to teaching children how to be physically active and to understand why this is important; and (d) helping the child become self-motivated and skilled in activities (McConnell, 2015). In summary, physical education can provide opportunities for children to be, and to acquire and develop the skills to be, physically active.

The Youth Physical Activity Promotion Model

There is no single theory or model that thoroughly explains physical activity behavior or confirms how best to intervene with specific populations, particularly from a public health or population perspective. The Youth Physical Activity Promotion (YPAP) model was developed to better understand and promote youth physical activity behavior (Welk, 1999) and was used to guide this intervention. The reader can refer to this model and how we applied it to our intervention in our previous chapter, published in Cremades and Tashman (2014). In the YPAP model, reinforcing factors influence a child's physical activity behavior directly and indirectly. The direct effect is when teachers actively help a child, for example, by teaching the child skills during their physical education lesson. The indirect effect is seen when significant others influence the child's evaluation of the activity, their ability, and whether the opportunity is worth it (through the predisposing factors). Therefore, reinforcing factors were developed in this program by teachers, parents, and peers working together and combining their efforts to encourage active participation.

The enabling factors are those that permit a child to be active; these are classified as biological or from the physical environment (Welk, 1999). A child's fitness level, skill level, or percentage body fat are biological factors that influence activity. In addition, the physical environment the child is exposed to, the presence or absence of parks, equipment, and structured exercise or sport programs are also known to influence physical activity. Both direct and indirect effects of enabling factors are noted in this model. Essentially, YPAP suggests that youth who have positive self-perceptions (am I able?) and feel that participating has valued benefits (is it worth it?) are more likely to regularly participate in physical activity (Welk, 1999).

NEEDS ASSESSMENT

Questions and interviews were used to understand the case teacher's perspectives on the teaching of physical education (see Coulter & Woods, 2012 for further information). Results showed that a limited range of physical education strands with no aquatics and little to no outdoor and adventure activities was being taught in the case-study school. Teachers cited reasons such as a lack of subject content knowledge and also a lack of confidence in teaching physical education (pedagogical content knowledge). Thus, the teachers were willing and positive about the opportunity to be a part of an intervention that would increase their physical education knowledge and pedagogical knowledge, ensure they taught the recommended amount of quality physical education, compile resources to assist teachers in teaching physical education, and establish how best to provide them with support during the intervention.

Simultaneously, the children's perspectives on physical education and physical activity were examined using a self-report questionnaire (see Coulter & Woods, 2011 for further information) and focus group interviews. In order for children and youth to develop a lifestyle of regular physical activity to maximize the long-term health benefits, they need to be "turned on" to physical activity by making it enjoyable. This will keep children coming back because of an intrinsic desire to be physically active. Getting children to enjoy physical activity is not a hard sell (Coulter & Woods, 2011). Children are built to move, they want to move; however, it is not something that should be left to chance. Therefore, schools should provide opportunities for physical activity during the school day. Results indicated that the majority of children (93.8 percent) indicated a high level of enjoyment of physical activity. However, even at this young age, boys indicated significantly higher levels of enjoyment of physical activity compared to girls. The key, then, is to understand what promotes this enjoyment, harness it, and build it into the school experience for all children. It was decided along with the teachers and the children that the intervention would center on the teaching of outdoor and adventure activities (O&AA), as this was an area in which the teachers had never taught and that the children had not experienced as part of their physical education program.

INTERVENTION

The intervention was designed to enable the teachers, a very diverse group across all eight primary school levels, to develop an understanding of the content of the O&AA strand of the curriculum and the teaching methodologies recommended for its implementation. O&AA could consist of a broad range of activities and learning experiences, but some of these experiences can be costly (e.g., water-based activities such as canoeing) or may require going off-site. Therefore, the focus of the program was on curriculum content suitable for teaching on-site. To achieve the O&AA aims and objectives effectively for the case-study school, the teachers were engaged in the intervention design process itself. This process was flexible and allowed for negotiation and encouraged collective participation through discussion and reflection on all aspects of the intervention, such as suitability of lesson content. Concrete resources and materials were provided (a folder which contained a scheme of work, six lesson plans, and tips for teachers about to teach O&AA) relevant to each class for each teacher ($n=28$), ensuring content emphasized skill development in a continuous and progressive way. The resources were designed to make the process of teaching the lessons as easy as possible and the lessons were detailed in terms of content and pedagogical approaches to be used. The key feature of the lesson plans were as follows:

- Each lesson included a warm up, a specific skill to be taught, as well as time for the children to practice the skills and engage in other activities.
- The main activity was based around orienteering activities, with activities on walking and/or outdoor challenges and/or understanding and appreciation of O&AA.
- Teaching points were highlighted in each lesson.
- Continuity and progression from junior infants (year 1) to sixth class (year 8) was evident.

The following is a brief list of the type of resources that were constructed to assist the teachers with their class management; the equipment was divided into boxes containing the relevant equipment for each class level:

- Maps for activities (e.g., point-to-point orienteering, star and photo orienteering) were drawn and laminated along with controls and control cards.
- Photographs were taken of various places and objects around the school for photo orienteering.
- Scavenger and treasure hunt clues/worksheets.

In facilitating the intervention it was important to recognize the diversity of the teachers, acknowledge their learning preferences within their individual contexts, and be flexible in the type of support provision each required. During the implementation of the intervention, a facilitator (an expert in physical education teacher education) was available in the school all day (5.5 hours) each week for six weeks to offer a continuum of support (from high to low as deemed necessary by the teacher), as well as through modeling and other techniques for all teachers. Each teacher received personalized support upon request during their scheduled hour-long physical education lesson, which included: 66 complete lessons modeled by the facilitator, 45 partial lessons modeled or team taught, and 19 lessons explained to the teacher prior to the lesson being taught by the class teacher. Modeling the lessons for the teachers worked on a number of levels. It produced practical experiences that teachers could see, copy, try out, and alter in a safe environment. Thus, it provided concrete examples of how to deliver the lessons in the school context, with all its limitations and challenges. The modeling of the lessons by the facilitator would also provide teachers with the opportunity to observe and question pedagogical content knowledge. Teachers would observe the facilitator teaching his/her own class and would be able to see not only "what" (content) to teach but also "how" (pedagogy) to teach it.

The lessons included learning opportunities for the children to be physically active and learning objectives focused on the cognitive, psychomotor, and affective domains. Cognitively, children developed new vocabulary and skills associated with O&AA. For example, skill development included map reading while moving and how to orientate their position. Affectively they learned to work as part of small groups in order to collaborate and cooperate with each other to achieve a common goal. In order to ensure that the intervention was meeting the intended objectives, the process was evaluated regularly to ensure the aims of the intervention were meeting the needs of the teachers and children. This was done by speaking informally with each teacher during the intervention facilitation, engaging in formal group interviews with teachers and children, and observing and evaluating teaching.

REFLECTION

Learning is a social activity that can enhance the "ability of children to act, interact, and react effectively with other people as well as with themselves" (Gallahue & Cleland-Donnelly, 2003, p. 20). O&AA lessons offer a wealth of opportunities for affective growth, including personal and social development in physical education. In these lessons children should be able to achieve "I can…" moments in order for their self-esteem to be nurtured and for them to progress through enhancement of predisposing factors as per the YPAP model. O&AA requires children to work as a team, helping, sharing, and engaging in decision making together. Thus, positive physical education experiences can contribute to social inclusion by equipping children with the skills, motivation, and confidence to belong to a group, team, or club. It also provides opportunities for the children to learn to develop trust and to have group success all leading to confidence and independence.

Throughout the intervention in the school, teachers noticed a change in children's attitude toward physical education during the O&AA lessons. Children showed enthusiasm for the variety of activities in the lessons. Overall they enjoyed the O&AA program, with some being sick with excitement. The children enjoyed the responsibility, and respected the freedom they were given by their teachers when they were allowed to move freely around the school when orienteering. They commented on not being under the teacher's nose all the time. The children wanted to be active and were achieving the recommended amount of moderate to vigorous activity (50 percent) in their lessons.

The children's concept of enjoyment and fun being inherent in physical education was evident from the beginning of this intervention. Throughout the intervention, fun and enjoyment remained important to the children and the teachers. Other teachers in fifth grade and below felt their classes loved O&AA: "I had one little one say the other day when she was coming in through the hall with her Mum, to the Mum said, this is where we have fun, Mum."

The teachers also recognized that the children enjoyed working in teams and being challenged in the activities. Teachers also noted the social dynamic in physical education was changing as the O&AA program continued: "The way they were talking and encouraging and there was no arguing which I often find I have problems with in teams or maybe it was just the dynamic of it and they go off." This observation was supported by other teachers and the principal, who recognized the impact that the intervention had on the children: "I see a significant change in that where you had girls who would stand to the side ... and they didn't want to be there. Whereas now it's cool to be involved in PE and to be there."

The children who may have been on the periphery of groups during games according to teachers were now coming into their own and they were growing in self-confidence. Others wanted to be in their groups, maybe because they now felt that this person had something to offer in the O&AA physical education lesson: "the kids really loved it and every single one of them was involved compared ... if you were doing games on the pitch." The intervention had a motivating effect on the children through enjoyment of the lessons and the teachers demonstrated a positive response to the support they were receiving from the intervention facilitator. Physical activity was also an important feature throughout the intervention, and although teachers recognized that certain "less active" activities were necessary for progression and continuity of the lessons, they felt the children didn't like these activities as they were inactive. Children were motivated by active lessons and complained when lessons were inactive and began to complain that "this wasn't PE."

The comments here show that the new teaching styles and the subject content were acceptable to the children. They were learning, having fun, being active, were able to be responsible for their own learning, and were given problems to solve, all of which were motivating factors in the intervention. Through the intervention, children's self-esteem was being nurtured and they had positive, physically active experiences. Children were able to recount what they had learned and the fact that the physical education lessons they experienced as part of the intervention were different, compared to other physical education lessons, where they took part for competition and recreational purposes.

As a result of the intervention, there was a change in children's attitudes toward physical education, with children enjoying O&AA lessons and the new teaching styles being employed by the teachers. The children's physical education experiences throughout the intervention were positively impacted and this could in turn lead to increased learning. Other benefits of the teacher's professional development program, highlighted by both teachers and children, were inclusion, whereby all children were involved in O&AA lessons compared to limited participation by girls and some boys in physical education prior to the intervention. It was beyond the scope of the intervention to evaluate its effect on other aspects of children's learning, although research suggests that participation in physical activity may improve academic performance (Sallis, McKenzie, Kolody, Lewis, Marshall, & Rosengard, 1999; van der Mars, 2006), and may contribute to children's alertness and concentration, with benefits for learning (Bailey, Armour, Kirk, Pickup, & Sandford, 2009).

Future Effective Implementation

Six conclusions were reached following implementation of the intervention to ensure efficacy. These are: (1) understand the school context and what teachers have been exposed to previously, and know what their current practices are. From this knowledge, develop a realistic program; (2) the importance of resource provision as a starting point for teacher's learning, as without resources the likelihood of teachers considering teaching specific physical education strands will be reduced, but also sharing and storage of these resources by the whole school is necessary. This will not only ensure that resources are used, but it will help foster collaboration in the teaching of these new areas; (3) the importance of the individualized nature of support required by teachers and the funding to provide teachers with ongoing learning opportunities in physical education; (4) subject knowledge should be given as a precursor to pedagogical content knowledge so that small steps in teacher change are seen initially by beginning with improving content knowledge which is vital. However, this must be supported by showing how this new knowledge is applied in a relevant teaching context; (5) collaborative learning should be included as a component of effective professional development in the design of the intervention; and (6) the value of physical education in schools, the teachers' and children's understanding of physical education, the school's overall physical education program and physical education ethos.

The goal of helping children become physically active for a lifetime is a difficult one – should we concentrate on giving children more of what they enjoy while moving or should we focus on teaching them the acquired skills to help them enjoy activity in the future (Locke & Lambdin, 2003)? Teachers have the potential to inspire a passion for physical activity in children. They need to develop programs that are meaningful, worthwhile, and relevant for children. They need to design learning experiences to help children achieve success as success can inspire and encourage children.

SUGGESTED READINGS

Cale, L., & Harris, J. (Eds.) (2005). *Exercise and young people: Issues, implications and initiatives.* Hampshire: Palgrave.

Cale, L., & Harris, J. (2006). School-based physical activity interventions: effectiveness, trends, issues, implications and recommendations for practice. *Sport, Education and Society, 11*(4), 401–420.

Lavin, J. (2008) *Creative Approaches to physical education: Helping children achieve their true potential.* London, Routledge.

Liukkonen, Jarmo (2007). *Psychology for physical educators: Student in focus.* Champaign, IL: Human Kinetics.

The Elementary School Journal (2008) *108*(3) – (special edition).

REFLECTIVE QUESTIONS

1. Who are the key stakeholders in this intervention? Why is this an important consideration?
2. What are some key psychological correlates for physical activity in children? Why is this an important consideration when designing an intervention?
3. What is the difference between modifiable and non-modifiable correlates of physical activity? Why should modifiable correlates be targets for intervention?
4. Outline an example of how the Youth Physical Activity Promotion Model could be used to promote physical activity in a youth population.
5. How can modeling be used as an effective intervention strategy for increasing teacher confidence when teaching a new subject?

REFERENCES

Bailey, R., Armour, K., Kirk, D., Pickup, I., & Sandford, R. (2009). The educational benefits claimed for physical education and school sport: An academic review. *Research Papers in Education, 24*, 1–27.

Coulter, M., & Woods, C. B. (2011). An exploration of children's perceptions and enjoyment of school-based physical activity and physical education. *Journal of Physical Activity and Health, 8*, 645–654.

Coulter, M., & Woods, C. (2012). Primary teachers' experience of a physical education professional development programme. *Irish Educational Studies Journal, 31*(3), 329–343.

Drake, K. M., Beach, M. L., Longacre, M. R., MacKenzie, T., Titus L. J., Rundle A. G., Dalton, M. A. (2012). Influence of sports, physical education and active commuting to school on adolescent weight status. *Pediatrics, 130*(2), e296–304.

Ferreira, I., van der Horst, K., Wendel-Vos, W., Kremers, S., van Lenthe, F. J., & Brug, J. (2007). Environmental correlates of physical activity in youth: a review and update. *Obesity Reviews, 8,* 129–154.

Fox, K., & Harris, J. (2003). Promoting physical activity through schools. In J. McKenna & C. Riddoch (Eds.), *Perspectives on health and exercise* (pp. 181–201). Basingstoke: Palgrave Macmillan.

Gallahue, D., & Cleland-Donnelly, F. (2003). *Development of physical education for all children.* Champaign, IL: Human Kinetics.

GAPA (2011). Non-communicable disease prevention: Investments that work for physical activity. Retrieved from http://ncdalliance.org/sites/default/files/rfiles/GAPA%20Investments%20that%20work%20for%20Physical%20Activity.pdf.

Government of Ireland (1999). *Primary school curriculum physical education.* Dublin: The Stationery Office.

Hardman, K., & Marshall, J. (2009). *Second world-wide survey of school physical education.* Berlin: ICSSPE.

Locke, L. F., & Lambdin, D. (2003). *Putting research to work in elementary physical education: Conversations in the gym.* Champaign, IL: Human Kinetics.

McConnell, K. (2015). Fitness and wellness education. In J. Lund & D. Tannehill (Eds.), *Standards-based physical education curriculum development* (pp. 365–383; 3rd ed.). Burlington, MA: Jones & Bartlett Learning.

Ryan, S. (2009). Socio-Economic Profile of Dublin 15, Blanchardstown Area Partnership, Dublin, Ireland.

Sallis, J. F., McKenzie, T. L., Kolody, B., Lewis, M., Marshall, S., & Rosengard, P. (1999). Effects of health-related physical education on academic achievement: Project SPARK. *Research Quarterly for Exercise and Sport, 70,* 127–135.

Sallis, J. F., Owen, N., & Fisher, E. B. (2008). Ecological models of health behavior. *Health Behavior and Health Education: Theory, Research, and Practice, 4,* 465–486.

Sallis, J. F., Owen, N., & Fotheringham, M. J. (2000). Behavioral epidemiology: A systematic framework to classify phases of research on health promotion and disease prevention. *Annals of Behavioral Medicine, 22,* 294–298.

Sallis, J. F., Prochaska, J. J., & Taylor, W. C. (2000). A review of correlates of physical activity of children and adolescents. *Medicine and Science in Sports and Exercise, 32,* 963–975.

Telama, R., Yang, X. L., Hirvensalo, M., & Raitakari, O. (2006). Participation in organized youth sport as a predictor of adult physical activity: A 21-year longitudinal study. *International Journal of Behavioural Medicine, 18,* 76–88.

Van Der Horst, K., Paw, M. J. C. A., Twisk, J. W. R., & van Mechelen, W. (2007). A brief review on correlates of physical activity and sedentariness in youth. *Medicine and Science in Sports and Exercise, 39,* 1241–1250.

van der Mars, H. (2006). Time and learning in physical education. In D. Kirk, D. Macdonald, & M. O'Sullivan (Eds.), *The handbook of physical education* (pp. 191–204). London: Sage Publications.

Welk, G. J. (1999). The Youth Physical Activity Promotion model: A conceptual bridge between theory and practice. *QUEST, 51*(1), 5–23.

Woods, C. B., (2014). The role of theory in designing physical activity interventions for school aged children. In J. G. Cremades & L. S. Tashman (Eds.), *Becoming a sport and exercise and performance psychology professional: A global perspective* (pp. 111–118). New York, NY: Routledge/Psychology Press.

Woods, C. B., Moyna, N., Quinlan, A., Tannehill, D., & Walsh, J. (2010). *The children's sport participation and physical activity study: Research report no. 1.* Dublin: School of Health and Human Performance, Dublin City University and the Irish Sports Council.

16 Initiating Mental Performance Programming with United States Army Special Forces Operators

Brittany Loney

The first truth of Special Operations Forces (SOF) is: "Humans are more important than hardware." To reflect adherence to this truth, in 2009 U.S. Army Special Operations Command (USASOC) received funds to establish the Tactical Human Optimization, Rapid Rehabilitation and Reconditioning (THOR3) program investing in the human warrior. THOR3's objectives are to increase the Special Forces (SF) Operator's physical and mental performance, aid in rapid recovery from injuries sustained in combat or training, and help them stay healthy, enhancing the Operator's career longevity. At the time of its inception, the components of the THOR3 program were strength and conditioning, performance nutrition, physical therapy, and sport psychology. However, the sport psychology pillar remained unfilled within SF Groups until January 2012.

The 3rd Special Forces Group (Airborne; 3SFG(A); 3rd Group) was the first of five active-duty SF groups to implement the sport psychology component of THOR3. This chapter will explore the challenges, highlights, and lessons learned from the pilot program of sport psychology within THOR3. However, the history and culture of 3SFG(A) will be described first in order to provide context for the intervention.

BACKGROUND INFORMATION

A Culture of Courage

SF Operators are renowned for their ability to deploy in small teams, operate independently, and conduct their mission in volatile, uncertain, chaotic, and austere (VUCA) environments. In order to wear the Green Beret, Operators must complete a very difficult assessment and selection process requiring mental, physical, and interpersonal abilities. Once the Green Beret is earned, SF Operators train to the highest of military standards in order to meet the requirements of some of the military's most critical missions.

The creed of SF is De Oppresso Liber or Free the Oppressed. In order to meet this objective, SF units perform seven doctrinal missions: unconventional warfare, foreign internal defense, special reconnaissance, direct action, combating terrorism, counter-proliferation, and information operations (USASOC, n.d.). These missions make SF unique in the U.S. military because they are employed throughout peacetime, conflict, and war. The continuous use of SF creates a demanding operational tempo (OPTEMPO), which can be very stressful for the SF Operator and his family.

DESCRIPTION OF THE CASE

The intervention outlined in this chapter was conducted with 3SFG(A), stationed at Fort Bragg, NC. Since 9/11, the 3rd Group has been heavily involved in Afghanistan and Central

Asia and played a critical role in building the Afghan National Security Forces (USASOC, n.d.). This has created a very high OPTEMPO for 3SFG(A) over the last decade plus.

The 3rd Group has a history of serving beyond the call of duty in combat. During the multiple lengthy deployments in support of the War on Terror, 3rd Group Operators have served with distinction. At the time of this writing, some of the honors included: the Medal of Honor, two Distinguished Service Crosses, 56 Silver Stars, 183 Bronze Stars with Valor Device, and 239 Army Commendations with Valor Device (USASOC, n.d.). For example, ten members of Operational Detachment – Alpha (ODA) 3336 were awarded Silver Stars for their actions during the Battle of Shok Valley. This is the largest set of citations for a single battle since the Vietnam War. As cited in Jennings (2010), the then-Commander of the U.S. Army Special Operations Command (SOCOM), Lieutenant General John F. Mulholland, Jr. said:

> As we have listened to these incredible tales, I am truly at a loss for words to do justice to what we have heard here, where do we get such men? ... There is no finer fighting man on the face of the earth than the American Soldier. And there is no finer American Soldier than our Green Berets. If you saw what you heard today in a movie, you would shake your head and say, "That didn't happen." But it does, every day. The valor shown by 3rd Group has not come without a sacrifice; 36 of the finest warriors have given their life for their country.

The heroics associated with 3SFG(A) were also exemplified by Staff Sergeant Robert James Miller, who was posthumously awarded the Medal of Honor in 2010 for his actions on January 25, 2008 (USASOC, n.d.). Miller's team was on a combat reconnaissance patrol in the Kunar Province when they were ambushed, seriously wounding the Commander. Holding his ground wounded and under intense enemy fire, Miller provided suppressive fire on multiple insurgent positions allowing for his teammates to retrieve the wounded Commander from the line of fire. Single-handedly, Miller eliminated several insurgents before succumbing to his wounds, sacrificing his life for the United States. This is just one of the dozens of examples of the ultimate sacrifice 3rd Group Operators have made for their country.

THEORETICAL FRAMEWORK/PHILOSOPHY

Breaking in the Ranks

SF Operators have to perform within high-stress situations in VUCA environments where wrongfully placed trust can get you or your team killed. Therefore, the community tends to be tight-knit and contains a high degree of skepticism of "outsiders." Further, because these Operators are selected for and have proven their ability to perform well in the highest-stress situations conceivable, approaching the concept of performing under pressure as a female civilian who has never seen combat was difficult. Lastly, traditionally military careers are thought to be severely degraded and/or a strong stigma was attached to an Operator who sought mental health services. Services related to the mind or psychology are initially disregarded or further denounced. Therefore, the first objective was gaining credibility, relevance, and the trust of the 3rd Group Operator. Breaking into the ranks required three essential elements: genuinely care, be the quiet professional, and maintain a "white belt mentality."

Genuine care. During my first month working with 3rd Group, the group Chaplain told me the greatest key to success with SF Operators is "they need to know you care before they care what you know." Once they know that, he said, you better be relevant and competent. Contractors within the military setting also tend to have a relatively negative stereotype within the population, which made it increasingly critical to show my true intent and passion. This translated into putting in time and effort without compensation. It was not uncommon to be out with a team all night in the cold rain and then going right into a regular "shift" of work. It also meant exceeding expectations by providing them with much more than what they expected, and this population already had high expectations. Genuinely showing care in the military often times interferes with personal time, so a degree of self-sacrifice is expected. No matter the time or day, I was available. Some practitioners may disagree, citing a need for boundaries; however, from my experience with this population this was necessary to initiate a successful program. The sacrifice an Operator makes to his/her country put my personal time sacrifice into perspective.

The quiet professional. The SF population places great value on being a quiet professional. Essentially, this meant being confident and competent in what I did, yet allowing my work to speak for itself. Humility is a delicate balance and in its truest form I believe it to be perceived through words and demeanor. In a population trained to detect insincerity, it was critical to truly have my ego in check, maintaining a confidence in my expertise and the value of sport psychology within the military context. At times this was difficult. With a group of skeptics who have seen more stress than I have read about, I questioned the value and relevance of myself within this environment. Their skepticism was contagious, leading me to research more, make more applicable connections, and reach outside performance psychology to enhance my value. There have also been times when I had to reflect on my ego as successes began to accumulate. In the end, an Operator's success was theirs, not mine. This helped keep me grounded in a healthy confidence. I had to allow the skepticism to drive my motivation to learn and adapt, while the Operator's successes reinforced the relevance and value of my chosen profession. Too much confidence and they lose respect for you, too little confidence and you lose respect for yourself.

White belt mentality. The last approach that facilitated breaking in the ranks was approaching all situations with what my mentors called a "white belt mentality." Wearing my white belt involved continuously learning my environment, perfecting my craft, having a genuine curiosity about the Operator's experience and expertise, and having a healthy dose of skepticism with regards to performance psychology techniques and concepts. As one is trying to be relevant and gain credibility it can be counterintuitive to take a step back to learn and listen first. While at times this made me feel relatively worthless, the Operators appreciated the time I spent learning versus speaking. My initial rule was no unsolicited advice; however, when asked I had to be ready with a well-thought-out applicable response. Therefore, I could not get complacent simply "hanging out" watching training or getting to know the Operators. It was critical that I was always engaged, ready, and confident, with a practical application of performance psychology to the SF environment. It was as if I was always waiting for a pitch I never knew was coming with the game on the line. As with any performance, my preparation and mindset for the moment the critical pitch came was essential. My mental preparation involved becoming skeptical of some of the performance psychology concepts and techniques I learned previously. I listened to what I was teaching then challenged it from an Operator's perspective. Often times this led me to research areas outside the direct realm of sport and performance psychology and brought me into uncharted territory to find other answers to the same questions.

NEEDS ASSESSMENT

At Any Given Moment

There is a certain level of responsibility that comes when working with any population; *provide the best service possible to the best of your ability at any given moment*. First, what is *the best service possible*? In order to answer this question we need to know what the population needs and wants. In order to derive this assessment, some of the main methods I used were observations, informal conversations with current and former SF Operators, formal interviews with leadership, peer mentorship from professionals within all human performance domains, and review of recommended SF resources. Once I developed a good working idea of the needs and wants, I had to candidly assess my current abilities to meet this demand. This often involved learning concepts outside the realm of traditional performance psychology. For example, I began to expand my repertoire of current expertise after realizing the Operator needed to remember large amounts of critical information, struggled with chronic stress, had difficulty sleeping, and had to effectively teach foreign security forces military tactics. While some of the performance psychology skills can help with each of these areas, I did not think it would have been *the best service possible*. From my perspective, if the identified need was related to the brain and performance and was not being fulfilled, then it was my job to develop the competence required to fulfill the need. This led me to embrace a strong multidisciplinary approach.

The last component of the initial statement is "*at any given moment*." This relates to standing at the home plate ready, not knowing when the pitch would be thrown. This required me to ensure personal self-care and mental training, which included a commitment to physical fitness, sleep quality, personal purpose, continuous self-development, and the use of mental preparation and self-regulatory techniques. Despite the circumstance and life events of the moment, I had to ensure consistent high-quality performance. Not only would this impact my performance, but also my credibility in teaching others how to have consistent high performance.

Optimizing Elite Warriors

The major underpinnings of the interventions designed to facilitate high-level performance among SF Operators are multidisciplinary, integrative, and adaptive. Keeping sport and performance psychology at the heart of the intervention, I integrated research from various domains pending the Operator's needs. I found that neurophysiological approaches (e.g., biofeedback training, neuroscience explanations) facilitated client buy-in and adherence to mental tactics (Lagos et al., 2008). Further, cognitive psychology and sport psychology provided insights into perception, anticipation, and decision-making (Tenenbaum & Razon, 2008). Educational psychology, specifically andragogy (i.e., adult learning methods), supplemented my approach to training adults and helping SF Operators more effectively teach foreign forces (Merriam & Leahy, 2005). Further, motor learning, educational psychology, and neuroscience concepts and techniques helped improve skill acquisition curriculum (Schmidt & Wrisberg, 2004). Realizing Operators relied heavily upon working memory and long-term memory, applied neuroscience drove the development of cognitive capacities (Takeuchi et al., 2010). Further, the OPTEMPO of the military population can lead to chronic stress (Juster, McEwen, & Lupien, 2010), sleep deprivation (Durmer & Dinges, 2005), and jet lag (Waterhouse, Reilly, Atkinson, & Edwards, 2007), which initiated the exploration of the most cutting-edge stress mitigation (Thayer, Åhs, Fredrikson, Sollers, & Wager, 2012), sleep optimization, and chronobiology literature (Carrier & Monk, 2000).

INTERVENTION

Based on the needs assessment and review of all the outlined areas of research, three intervention objectives were identified: (1) increase mental and physical performance; (2) aid in rapid recovery; and (3) extend career longevity. The model presented in Figure 16.1, while not exhaustive, provides insights into the methodology used to meet the aforementioned goals. Objectives 1 and 2 will be discussed in greater detail below. Objective 3 was met by continuous application of the model's components and monitoring of the Operator's lifestyle of a high-performance brain (HP brain).

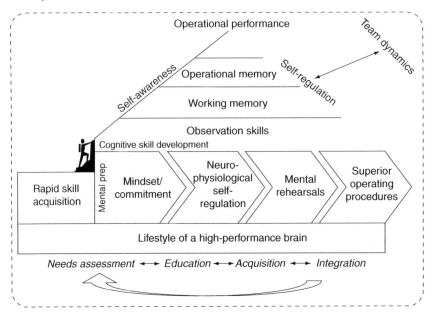

Figure 16.1 Model Depicting THOR3 Intervention Goals and Approach

Objective 1: Increase Physical and Mental Performance

The primary goal of THOR3 is to increase performance; however, ambiguity exists in defining performance within the variety of missions SF Operators must successfully conduct. As previously mentioned, learning one's environment is critical prior to developing an intervention. However, this environment is extremely complex and mostly unobservable, thus fully understanding their performance was relatively unattainable. My main observations involved isolated aspects of what makes up the complete SF Operator (e.g., shooting, teaching). It was like piecemealing the isolated observations of blocking drills and passing drills during a football practice into an accurate reflection of how the game must be played and won. This is incredibly difficult, so it was critical to educate the Operator about the capabilities, concepts, and techniques so they could employ the mental training appropriately for their desired outcome. An effective mental training plan required a large degree of Operator responsibility.

Through a high degree of Operator input and learning the environment, the primary mental performance pillars included in the 3SFG(A) intervention were HP brain, mental preparation (MP), cognitive skill development (CSD), and rapid skill acquisition (RSA). The foundation of all training was the HP brain, which focused on the seven most critical aspects of one's lifestyle that impact one's brain function (i.e., move, eat smart, perceive, learn, socialize, recover, live purposefully). Once the Operator's foundation was solidified, further layering of the components occurred. The MP section refers to performance psychology concepts and skills. This includes, but is not limited to, growth versus fixed mindsets (Dweck, 2006), goal-setting/commitment strategies (Locke & Latham, 2002), neurophysiological self-regulation (Thayer et al., 2012), imagery/mental rehearsals (Morris, Spittle, & Watt, 2005), and performance routines/superior operating procedures (SOPs; Cotterill, 2010). These techniques, as indicated in the aforementioned model, help propel the Operator forward with regards to performance and also build the foundation for CSD. The primary cognitive skills that underlie operational requirements were observation skills, working memory enhancement (Takeuchi et al., 2010), and short- and long-term memory (McDaniel & Bugg, 2012). Lastly, in order to better prepare the Operator for advanced military schools and accelerate his progression along the learning curve, RSA techniques (e.g., learning style integration, optimal review sessions, and motor skill acquisition) were important aspects of specific mental training regimens (Silver, Strong, & Perini, 2000). It is important to note that neurophysiological underpinnings for each area and technique used were discussed with the Operator. This was a critical aspect associated with buy-in and enhanced their understanding of how and why the techniques were effective.

The MP techniques closely resembled performance psychology interventions. Speaking with the Operator or team about goals, commitment, one's deep-rooted reason "why?," and values were generally a natural starting point. Because one's underlying growth or fixed mindset (Dweck, 2006) impacts their overall approach to training and performance, it was commonplace to provide the Operator with education about the topic and the impact of one's mindset on goal attainment. This usually progressed into a discussion involving how thoughts impact performance through emotional and physiological means (Ellis, 1995). Therefore, the subsequent component in the model is neurophysiological self-regulation. Most Operators had a tendency of being most receptive to physiology-based self-regulation as they perceived this to be more concrete due to the use of biofeedback-assisted training. Heart rate variability (HRV) was the primary parameter assessed during biofeedback-assisted mental training (Berntson et al., 1997). The Operators were trained to regulate their HRV in a controlled, minimal-distraction environment progressing into environments with greater distractions and difficulty (e.g., quiet room, gym environment, operational training environments, pre-mission exercises). Conversations regarding thought control naturally emerged, allowing for greater receptivity and the adoption of self-talk strategies. Cognitive appraisals regarding threat versus challenge (Tomaka, Blascovich, Kelsey, & Leitten, 1993), controllability (Nicholls, Polman, & Levy, 2012), and predictability (Anshel, 2000) were specifically addressed. Generally, once the Operator was proficient in self-regulatory skills, the use and value of mental rehearsals (i.e., imagery) was discussed (Morris et al., 2005). SOPs (i.e., performance routines; Cotterill, 2010) were usually the last mental enhancement technique introduced because it was important for the Operator to understand the mental skills that would be incorporated into an SOP. Backwards planning with regards to the thought–performance relationship (i.e., thoughts → emotions → physiology → performance) was used to help the Operator determine the SOP components. The Operator created and revised his routine until a high degree of efficacy was achieved.

In the ideal mental performance training regimen, the HP brain and MP components composed the foundation for CSD, which focused on training the cognitive skills underlying operational performance. At the start of this intervention, CSD was the least established aspect and required the most development with regards to applicable training methods. I also firmly believe that CSD, in conjunction with HP brain, greatly contributed to the perceived relevance of the mental performance program among the Operator population. In the interest of brevity, observation skills, working memory, and memory are highlighted. Generally, progression of the aforementioned cognitive skills followed the order provided, as memory was strongly influenced by one's working memory capacity and observation skills.

One cannot accurately recall what one did not initially perceive and process more deeply. Therefore, the most critical cognitive skill with this population was observation, as this tended to underlie situational awareness, subsequent decision making, personal safety, and the accurate reporting of situations (Endsley, 2000). The components of observation training were developing/refining observational filters and cues (Desimone & Duncan, 1995), sensory processing speed, sensory scanning and integration, and attentional shifting (Posner, 2011). Working memory training was also an important component associated with CSD. Because controversy exists with regards to the transfer of general working memory training (Morrison & Chein, 2011), drills were adapted to fit the requirements associated with the Operator's performance context. Working memory underlies other higher-level cognitive functions, such as fluid intelligence, long-term memory, attention control, and problem solving (Conway, Kane, & Engle, 2003). The final cognitive skill addressed is memory. This skill is pertinent because information must be remembered with minimal use of memory aids in order to maintain operational security and retain information for later reporting potentially advising national security. It is important to note that if an Operator wanted to enhance their memory, we first addressed foundational areas (e.g., HP brain, MP, and other CSD elements). Once these aspects were progressing, the Operator received specific memory training. Techniques included, but were not limited to, the method of loci, strategies for names and faces, methods for numbers, creative visualization techniques, memory retrieval cues, and mind mapping (McDaniel & Bugg, 2012). Acquisition of memory techniques involved progressing from benign information to operationally relevant information in increasingly complex environments. Due to the synchronous benefits, CSD was combined with physical training (Curlik & Shors, 2013).

Although this mental performance training intervention appears distinct in the progression, skills often overlapped and at times were taught in a different order, depending on the flow of the consultation and Operator needs. The timeline and overall time of consultation also varied with the Operator's needs and goals, OPTEMPO, and speed of skill acquisition/progression rate. At times, a "band-aid" approach was needed to help an Operator through an event, whereas in other instances an Operator had a year to train prior to deploying. Therefore, this was not a one-size-fits-all intervention and much of the consultation was fluid; however, this model outlines a general progression that appeared effective with this population.

Objective 2: Aid in Rapid Recovery

The second objective of the THOR3 program was to increase the rate of recovery facilitating the progress of an Operator getting back onto the "battlefield." The same model, specifically the HP brain, MP, and CSD components, were applied to accelerate recovery. During the initial phases of the rehabilitation process, the focus was on ensuring the Operator was engaging in lifestyle habits that would increase their ability to recover. Stress and sleep were the first priorities as they have a great impact on the body's state of healing. If the injury was sustained in combat, sleep quality and quantity tended to decrease and a neurophysiological sustained stress response was probable. In order to enhance healing, elements of the HP brain and MP techniques were combined. Specifically, neurophysiological regulation techniques (e.g., HRV training, mindfulness) and SOPs via sleep and distress routines were developed.

Once the Operator's neurophysiological state of healing was maximized, goal-setting tended to be the next step. This helped the Operator focus his attention toward controllable goals and motivated him to engage in physical therapy and make the right choices with regards to activity. In the process of goal setting, other aspects of MP and CSD were integrated. This helped the Operator feel like he was still engaging in military-related training and progressing as a team member. Leadership development tended to be well-received during rehabilitation. Mental rehearsals were another area the Operator used daily to minimize degradation of skills (e.g., shooting, medical tasks, communication) that could result.

As return to duty approached, goals were refined and mental rehearsals became increasingly critical. Many of the same strategies used throughout the rehabilitation process were now being used to ensure greater trust in the injured area and tactical skill mastery. CSD techniques were further integrated into rehabilitation and early training environments in order to facilitate the Operator's ability to effectively observe his environment, recognize patterns, remember critical information, and make good tactical decisions. This tended to facilitate the "mental rust" that may exist when an Operator is returning to his tactical environment.

REFLECTION

This chapter explored the challenges and lessons learned of program initiation, the underpinnings of intervention design, and the topics and techniques used to meet the THOR3 objectives. Program initiation required breaking in the ranks with a tight-knit, experienced, and skeptical Operator population. Three elements were described as being essential to building rapport and credibility: genuinely care, be the quiet professional, and maintain a white belt mentality. I have carried these principals with me to any work I have done since. While I may have experienced some success without them, I do not believe I would have earned the same degree of trust and respect of my clients. Each principal is a journey; while they become more ingrained they take continuous monitoring and self-regulation. The most difficult principal has been becoming the quiet professional, delicately balancing humility with a healthy confidence. Working within this setting can be difficult, demanding, and incredibly direct, shaking my confidence at times. Conversely, when I interacted with other professionals in performance psychology I had to reflect on my pride to engage my humility. I ascribe to the mantra "Impact over Ego." This mantra has further informed my outlook on professional sharing and what I truly entered this field to do … help people make themselves better.

Providing *the best service possible to the best of my ability at any given moment* has been the driving source of my consulting philosophy. *The best service possible* entails knowledge of the needs and wants of the population and the most effective way to meet these requirements. *To the best of my ability* means that if the most effective method is not within my capabilities, I must reflect and answer: "Should it be?" If the answer was yes, I developed the competence to become a subject matter expert in the identified area to best serve the Operator. Some example topics included: chronic stress/adrenal fatigue, sleep optimization, circadian rhythms, and CSD. Lastly, I had to practice what I preach, putting into practice performance psychology principles so that I could be ready to perform *at any given moment*. This belief led to the adoption of a multidisciplinary approach to the service delivery discussed. The interventions developed to meet the objectives of the THOR3 program were designed with this motto keenly in mind.

SUGGESTED READINGS

Asken, M. J., Grossman, D., & Christensen, L. W. (2010). *Warrior mindset: Mental toughness skills for a nation's peacekeepers.* Millstadt, IL: Warrior Science Group.

Dweck, C. (2006). *Mindset: The new psychology of success.* New York, NY: Random House.

Grant, A. (2013). *Give and take: A revolutionary approach to success.* London: Hachette UK.

Medina, J. (2008). *Brain rules: 12 principles for surviving and thriving at work, home, and school.* Seattle, WA: Pear Press.

Ruiz, D. M., & Mills, J. (2010). *The four agreements: A practical guide to personal freedom.* San Rafael, CA: Amber-Allen Publishing.

REFLECTIVE QUESTIONS

1. What was the greatest takeaway you learned from the chapter? Describe how you can immediately begin applying this takeaway to your consulting work.
2. What were some of the challenges the author faced when initiating work within this environment? What challenges do you face when working with your clients? What is a new approach you could try to overcome one of the greatest challenges you face?
3. What is your consulting model and/or philosophy? Describe how you would apply your model and/or philosophy with this population.
4. What other concepts or techniques would you have considered integrating within the interventions?
5. What components of CSD did the author highlight in this chapter? How would you go about developing these or other cognitive skills with your population?

REFERENCES

Anshel, M. H. (2000). A conceptual model and implications for coping with stressful events in police work. *Criminal Justice and Behavior, 27*(3), 375–400.

Berntson, G. G., Bigger, J. T., Eckberg, D. L., Grossman, P., Kaufmann, P. G., Malik, M.,... & Van Der Molen, M. W. (1997). Heart rate variability: origins, methods, and interpretive caveats. *Psychophysiology, 34*, 623–648.

Carrier, J., & Monk, T. H. (2000). Circadian rhythms of performance: New trends. *Chronobiology International, 17*(6), 719–732.

Conway, A. R., Kane, M. J., & Engle, R. W. (2003). Working memory capacity and its relation to general intelligence. *Trends in Cognitive Sciences, 7*(12), 547–552.

Cotterill, S. (2010). Pre-performance routines in sport: Current understanding and future directions. *International Review of Sport and Exercise Psychology, 3*(2), 132–153.

Curlik, D. M., & Shors, T. J. (2013). Training your brain: Do mental and physical (MAP) training enhance cognition through the process of neurogenesis in the hippocampus? *Neuropharmacology, 64*, 506–514.

Desimone, R., & Duncan, J. (1995). Neural mechanisms of selective visual attention. *Annual review of neuroscience, 18*(1), 193–222.

Durmer, J. S., & Dinges, D. F. (2005). Neurocognitive consequences of sleep deprivation. *Seminars in Neurology, 25*(1), 117–129.

Dweck, C. (2006). *Mindset: The new psychology of success*. New York: NY: Random House.

Ellis, A. (1995). Changing rational-emotive therapy (RET) to rational emotive behavior therapy (REBT). *Journal of Rational-Emotive & Cognitive-Behavior Therapy, 13*(2), 85–89.

Endsley, M. R. (2000). Theoretical underpinnings of situation awareness: A critical review. In Mica R. Endsley & Daniel J. Garland (Eds.), *Situation Awareness Analysis and Measurement* (pp. 3–32). Boca Raton: CRC Press.

Jennings, P. (2010, May 20). Danger close: ODA 3336 in the Shock Valley. *Defense Media Network*.

Juster, R. P., McEwen, B. S., & Lupien, S. J. (2010). Allostatic load biomarkers of chronic stress and impact on health and cognition. *Neuroscience & Biobehavioral Reviews, 35*(1), 2–16.

Lagos, L., Vaschillo, E., Vaschillo, B., Lehrer, P., Bates, M., & Pandina, R. (2008). Heart rate variability biofeedback as a strategy for dealing with competitive anxiety: A case study. *Biofeedback, 36*(3), 109–115.

Locke, E. A., & Latham, G. P. (2002). Building a practically useful theory of goal setting and task motivation: A 35-year odyssey. *American Psychologist, 57*(9), 705.

McDaniel, M. A., & Bugg, J. M. (2012). Memory training interventions: What has been forgotten? *Journal of Applied Research in Memory and Cognition, 1*(1), 45–50.

Merriam, S. B., & Leahy, B. (2005). Learning transfer: A review of the research in adult education and training. *PAACE Journal of Lifelong Learning, 14*, 1–24.

Morris, T., Spittle, M., & Watt, A. P. (2005). *Imagery in sport*. Champaign, IL: Human Kinetics.

Morrison, A. B., & Chein, J. M. (2011). Does working memory training work? The promise and challenges of enhancing cognition by training working memory. *Psychonomic Bulletin & Review, 18*(1), 46–60.

Nicholls, A. R., Polman, R. C., & Levy, A. R. (2012). A path analysis of stress appraisals, emotions, coping, and performance satisfaction among athletes. *Psychology of Sport and Exercise, 13*(3), 263–270.

Posner, M. I. (Ed.) (2011). *Cognitive neuroscience of attention*. New York, NY: Guilford Press.

Schmidt, R. A., & Wrisberg, C. A. (2004). *Motor learning and performance*. Champaign, IL: Human Kinetics

Silver, H. F., Strong, R. W., & Perini, M. J. (2000). *So each may learn: Integrating learning styles and multiple intelligences*. Alexandria, VA: Association for Supervision and Curriculum Development.

Takeuchi, H., Sekiguchi, A., Taki, Y., Yokoyama, S., Yomogida, Y., Komuro, N.,... & Kawashima, R. (2010). Training of working memory impacts structural connectivity. *Journal of Neuroscience, 30*(9), 3297–3303.

Tenenbaum, G., & Razon S. (2008). Integrating emotions, perceptions, cognitions, and motion under perceived pressure conditions. *Interservice/Industry Training, Simulation, and Education Conference (I/ITSEC)*, Paper No. 8066.

Thayer, J. F., Åhs, F., Fredrikson, M., Sollers, J. J., & Wager, T. D. (2012). A meta-analysis of heart rate variability and neuroimaging studies: Implications for heart rate variability as a marker of stress and health. *Neuroscience & Biobehavioral Reviews, 36*(2), 747–756.

Tomaka, J., Blascovich, J., Kelsey, R. M., & Leitten, C. L. (1993). Subjective, physiological, and behavioral effects of threat and challenge appraisal. *Journal of Personality and Social Psychology, 65*(2), 248.

United States Army Special Operations Command. (n.d.). 3rd Special Forces Group (Airborne). Retrieved from www.soc.mil/USASFC/Groups/3rd/3rdSFGHomepage.html.

Waterhouse, J., Reilly, T., Atkinson, G., & Edwards, B. (2007). Jet lag: trends and coping strategies. *The Lancet, 369*(9567), 1117–1129.

17 Learning to Fly

Ups and Downs

Madeleine Hallé

Cirque du Soleil is one of the most recognized entertainment companies in the world, with 21 different circus shows and more than 1,500 artists. Created in 1984, Cirque du Soleil imposed a completely new style of circus show integrating theatre, live singers and musicians, dancers, clowns, and among the best acrobats in the world. All these aspects are organized around a story and each detail contributes to the "wow" effect.

In order to get this high level of performance, Cirque du Soleil has developed a unique training program for selected athletes and artists in Montreal. This program, offered over a 20-week period, covers artistic, acrobatic and physical training, second-language learning, performance nutritional and psychological support, and medical care. A very extensive team of specialists, including interpreters as a main resource, works on a daily basis with artists in training in a group or individual manner.

BACKGROUND INFORMATION

John was cast by Cirque du Soleil as a potential candidate to replace an artist on one of our strongest aerial acts, the High-Bar from the show *Alegría*. This apparatus, suspended 60 feet in the air, consists of three fixed bars standing at different levels, which allow the eight artists involved to spin around the bars and "fly" from one to another. Flyers either catch the bar directly or a catcher picks them up in the air. Being an Olympic medalist and World Champion on High Bar, John had the proper profile to integrate such a type of acrobatic and artistic performance.

Alongside many of his fellow teammates, John was invited to join the General Training Program at the Montreal International Headquarters. This program is intended to train artists who will eventually become replacements on existing shows. Therefore, potential candidates must be able to recreate the exact same acrobatic and artistic performances as the artist being replaced, which also includes doing secondary cues. These secondary cues are, most of the time, short acrobatic, artistic or acro-artistic passages. They are not part of the main number, but they contribute to the esthetic of the scene or to the comprehension of the story underlying the show. All the artists have a certain number of cues to do as part of their workload.

This 20-week program gathers over 50 artists and includes about ten different circus numbers. Specialized coaches are assigned to each act. The artists are hosted at the residence and get a salary for their training period. However, they are not guaranteed to score a contract immediately at the end of the training program. Contracts are granted to the best performers and are offered according to the openings on the show.

The team of performers on the High Bar act is made up of eight artists from seven different countries, including: the United States, Japan, Ukraine, China, England, Brazil, and Canada. Seven out of eight have a high-level gymnastics background, but no circus experience. At that time, only one candidate had been performing in the circus industry for over five years. The team of specialists supporting the High Bar group included: two acrobatic coaches, one artistic coach, and four interpreters (English, Japanese, Chinese, and Portuguese). One of the coaches spoke Russian and French, while the other one spoke French and English. Also, the artists could get support from a team including a performance psychology advisor, a sport psychologist, a sport nutritionist, a conditioning coach, approximately six acting coaches, and a whole dedicated team of interpreters and technicians overseeing the communication and security aspect of the equipment. The weekly workload represented approximately 50 hours and broke down as follows: (1) 20 hours of acrobatic training; (2) three hours of artistic sessions directly on the apparatus; (3) five hours of physical preparation; (4) 12 hours of artistic training with classes such as dance, percussion, singing, and acting; (5) three hours of pilates and yoga; and (6) three hours of performance psychology and nutrition, either in group or individual sessions. Furthermore, some artists had three hours of English and French classes during the evening. Physiotherapy treatments occurred outside of the regular training schedule.

DESCRIPTION OF THE CASE

Once at Cirque, John was quickly faced with a brand-new reality. His gymnastic references were now being altered in order to fit a complex environment, which included partners, music, and lighting, and where acting and demonstrating emotions goes hand in hand with the art of performing. John was exposed to a new learning process, namely on the artistic level, where he was truly a beginner. Under the supervision of some very demanding specialists, he had to progress quickly in order to successfully complete the 20-week program that would allow him to perform the whole act and respective cues from the show. The complexity of the acrobatic and artistic requirements, the amount of people involved in the process, the workload, and the daily risks related to acrobatic performances are only some of the challenges the new artist had to face.

From the beginning, John was impressed with the height of the apparatus and intimidated by the fact that he needed to fall into the net, despite hanging from a safety belt. He admitted he was scared. Although unintentional, he felt peer pressure, since none of his colleagues seemed to be scared. He was afraid he would not get a contract. After the first few tries at jumping without a security belt, John fell twice on the net since he was not able to land into the catcher's hands properly. He injured one hand and ended up on medical leave for two days. He disagreed with the decision of the physiotherapist and already foresaw himself being rated negatively and falling behind in the program. Once back to training he was impatient and wanted to skip through the educational basics, without taking the time to feel comfortable again, build his self-confidence, and gain his colleagues' trust. This situation only increased his anxiety level.

Furthermore, he claimed he was having a hard time meeting the expectations since he only had access to the acrobatic coach's instructions through the words of an interpreter. He felt he was lacking important pieces of information. The sequence where he must land in the hands of the catcher caused him great stress because he needed to fully rely on somebody else. All he could do was make sure he was in the right place at the right time; otherwise he would end up 60 feet lower! Finally, the moment he used to take to concentrate before executing each movement was now being replaced by some artistic acting. Hence, he didn't know how and when to focus anymore.

Following a performance psychology session on trusting others while performing, John felt his partners were questioning him, which only increased his doubts and influenced his level of self-confidence. This specific moment led him to ask for an individual performance psychology meeting.

THEORETICAL FRAMEWORK/PHILOSOPHY

Usually, the first few performance psychology sessions at Cirque du Soleil are based on an educational perspective. In order to do so, we use an interactionism model (Reynolds, Turner, Branscombe, Mavor, Bizumic, & Subasic, 2010). As a matter of fact, we need to take into consideration the performer's characteristics, the tasks to be achieved, and the environment where it happens, in order to fully understand the needs as far as psychological skills are concerned. Therefore, significant attention is given to self-knowledge, capacities, and existing psychological skills. Among important factors, there is self-confidence, but also the sense of responsibility, commitment, courage, and autonomy. The second aspect we need to consider is the task to be performed. Circus acts at Cirque du Soleil distinguish themselves by the way they intertwine art and acrobatics within a given movement or sequence. Such combinations significantly increase and alter the initial task and require a level of concentration and emotional management different from previous experiences. Lastly, but just as essential, comes the analysis of the impact of the environment. The circus environment is so complex that it turns out to be an enormous challenge on its own. For instance, the height at which the acts are performed, the amount of partners that need to be synchronized, the rhythm imposed by the music, the change of lighting, the need to adapt a sequence after falling into the net, the reaction of the audience, and the amount of performances on a weekly and annual basis contribute to the complexity of the performances. All these factors may influence the performance and cause a great deal of stress.

The second perspective we give to performance psychology at Cirque is the corrective approach, which aims to mitigate the problems linked to performance. In this respect, we use the cognitive-behavioral (Ladouceur, Fontaine, & Cottraux, 1995) and systemic (Blanchette, 1999) approaches. For this specific case, there needed to be a behavior change in order to manage the fear factor related to a specific task like falling down. Further, lack of self-confidence and trust in others could lead the artist to try to modify his technique and consequently the way he accomplishes a movement. Therefore, we needed to go beyond the educational approach of integrating psychological skills to performance, diminishing the level of fear and increasing the level of confidence before eventually returning to psychological skills.

NEEDS ASSESSMENT

During the first individual meeting, after analyzing that fear was the main issue of concern, the artist did a self-evaluation on various elements (see below) using a scale from 0 to 10, the highest grade being 10. Self-ratings on these areas were done during the first and last individual meetings. However, the same evaluations were also discussed verbally during each meeting. These items included in the evaluation were derived from ten years of previous work done with experienced artists, new artists in training, and interpreters as they are frequently the main confidant of the foreigner artists. Other measures such as self-evaluation of competencies have been used, but these few elements have been more useful. John's evaluation at the first meeting was:

- General stress level according to the training program: 6
- Comfort level during artistic performance: 4
- Confidence level during acro-artistic performance of the act: 5
- Confidence level on risk-management skills: 3
- Fear level for the High Bar act: 8
- Fear of not getting a contract: 9

INTERVENTION

In addition to the weekly group meetings, which utilized an educational approach, John had ten individual meetings of approximately 40 minutes each. He had homework to do in between meetings and was supervised on a daily basis, which altogether allowed him to solve his performance-related issue while evolving toward his final presentation.

Meeting #1

The first meeting with John consisted of identifying and distinguishing the different sources of fear as well as assessing his level of fear in these areas. For example, fear of falling on the net without a security belt as opposed to the fear of not being caught by the catcher or not getting a contract, which are different types of fears, but need to be treated just as adequately, were discussed. The artist brought forward a few cognitive and behavioral solutions, including: (1) working thoroughly on the stressful elements; (2) getting more feedback from the coach and the sport psychologist; (3) analyzing the training videos as well as his colleagues' performances on the show; (4) and discussing with the catcher the visual, temporal, and kinesthetic key elements to land in his hands successfully. Introducing breathing in the preparation routine and desensitization to the height of the apparatus by increasing the length of time spent on the bar were also other solutions brought forward. Further, the systematic desensitization approach (Ladouceur et al., 1995) was added to the anxiety-inducing elements related to the act.

Meeting #2

In such context of fear, analyzing peer pressure was necessary in order to adapt it to the circus reality at the learning phase. In the current situation, fear of heights and falling on a net was unacceptable for John, even embarrassing, according to the cultural background and previous disciplines of his fellow artists. As a matter of fact, admitting to being scared in certain countries is equal to being a loser, enough to be rejected by fellow colleagues and coaches. Furthermore, falling down in gymnastics inevitably has a consequence for the results, where falling at Cirque instead sparks a certain level of sympathy from the audience. The artist had to change such irrational perceptions, which were causing him a considerable amount of stress. The work John had to do that week included: (1) discussing with the interpreter the reaction of the catcher if he were to fall into the net; (2) opening discussion with colleagues about being scared when learning an aerial act; and (3) checking with the coach if he was normal for being scared of not being caught and falling into the net.

Meeting #3

This third meeting focused on developing a greater understanding and acceptance of the coaches' expectations as far as the steps to achieve the basics that needed to be repeated at every training session, and the evolution pace. Recognizing the coaches' level of expertise allowed the artist to establish personal goals and work alongside them instead of imposing his own ideas. The discussion consisted of comparing the coaching in gymnastics, the trust John had for his previous coach, and his attitude toward the actual acrobatic coach of the High Bar act. The work he had to do was to ask for an individual meeting with the coach during the week in order to receive explanation on the progressions planned for the act.

Meeting #4

The goal of this meeting was to develop greater communication with his colleagues and team of specialists, despite the language barrier, based on functional communication focusing on the task to be achieved. The homework John had to do was to learn technical words and instructions in various languages (especially Russian) and practice them as much as possible during training. The subject of communication also brought up the importance of speaking about ourselves and expressing certain emotions, like trusting others. This was done during the weekly group sessions. Lastly, the subject of communication also came up as far as interacting with other artists during downtime, like at the residence or during outings.

Meeting #5

The goal of this meeting was to understand and accept cultural differences along with his colleagues' behavior. The fact of working with artists from seven different countries only heightened the manner in which cultural differences could play a significant role. John had to pay attention to his colleagues' behaviors in various contexts and asked the interpreters some questions in order to understand them better. For example, how does someone from Russia, Japan, or China deal with fatigue? What is acceptable or not acceptable behavior?

Also, each circus discipline brings its own culture; aerial work, for example, needs specific details that other acts will not need. In that sense, experienced artists will be less ready to forgive mistakes coming from a lack of respect of these rules. These implicit rules are not written and can be learned only by discussion with peers and paying attention to them. Coming from a gymnastic background, John had to reconstruct his own references to fit with them, namely on safety, trust, respect, and courage.

Meeting #6

The goal of this meeting was to identify the necessary elements toward gaining self-confidence and trusting others. Such exercise had to be done in a very concrete manner and directly applied during training. For instance, the artist determined that shouting at the catcher right before executing a movement gave him confidence. Since that's not a familiar practice in gymnastics, it took some time before the artist accepted to do so. He also had to evaluate himself regarding his confidence during artistic classes and on his trust for his colleagues during group exercises or short presentations.

Meeting #7

This meeting allowed John to identify the feelings of shame and embarrassment, and his perception of ridiculousness emerging from the artistic classes. We worked around this feeling of embarrassment by focusing on the notions of work in progress and self-improvement. Mainly, John watched videos of some artistic classes of the second and the sixth week and compared his evaluation of himself to the ones he would give to colleagues. He also had to identify some of his improvements in choreography or improvisation, for example. Finally, he had to watch video of the presentations to the public and pay attention to his own work and the applause of the spectators.

Meeting #8

This meeting contributed to integrating recuperation techniques in order to sustain a heavy workload. That specific week, John had to integrate more relaxation sessions he already knew into his training. Among other methods, pilates, yoga, and daily meditation sessions were adopted.

Meeting #9

This meeting served to discuss types of attitudes John could adopt as well as ways in which he could enjoy the training program despite feeling homesick. John had to talk about how much he was missing his family and his old friends at home and how this would affect his attitude during training. When asked if he had at the moment of the training found some good friends and about his feeling close to them, he realized that for a while these new friends would be his closest family and his parents would be the further ones. He also realized that he had more to share with these new friends than with his old friends who could not even imagine his new life. Finally, he decided, as many other colleagues have, to use Skype and send SMS more often and it turned out to be the most practical and efficient methods to cope with this feeling of home-sickness. Finally, we worked on his pride, of being part of this training and hopefully of this beautiful show *Alegría* and its family.

Meeting #10

During this meeting we went over the different types of fears that had been identified in the first meeting. We spoke about the initiatives that were taken to overcome those fears, the con-sequent improvements, and finished with a self-evaluation. He felt a lot better, he was more confident, and his desire to get a contract was stronger. Also, because of his new friends, he was emotionally stronger and could consider being away from home for many months, even years. His final evaluation showed clear improvement:

- General stress level according to the training program: 2
- Comfort level during artistic performance: 8
- Confidence level during acro-artistic performance of the act: 8
- Confidence level on risk-management skills: 8
- Fear level for the High Bar act: 5
- Fear of not getting a contract: 2

Extra Work

Having interdisciplinary sessions with the nutritionist, physical trainer, interpreter, and dance teacher supporting John enriched the individual counseling experience. Thus, following many conversations with the coach in order to identify John's technical weaknesses, we were able to introduce more effective movements through visualization. This intervention also helped the coach adapt his instructions in order to increase the level of confidence John needed to have in himself and his partners. A meeting was also scheduled between John and the artistic coach in order to establish the necessity of introducing, as quickly as possible, this intrinsic component of the circus into his performances, although perceived as a risk enhancer from John's stand-point. Observation sessions during John's artistic and acrobatic classes allowed us to pinpoint certain specific habits he needed to change and others he needed to introduce in his routine. Last but not least, the nutritionist considerably helped John attain the required weight for a flyer, as well as helped him to efficiently recover from fatigue.

REFLECTION

Several elements can be highlighted in this case study:

1. The first element is certainly the importance of taking into consideration how the environment could have an impact on the artist's performance. At Cirque du Soleil,

adaptability is a must if we consider not only that the environment is very complex, but also often very unpredictable. Self-confidence does not only apply at the primary level of the conviction to accomplish something, but mostly at the second level, adapting to unexpected situations.

2. Trusting others often results from past personal experiences and cultural values. In artistic gymnastics, both the performance and security rely solely on the athlete, while at the circus you must rely on all your partners, a team of technicians, riggers, lighting specialists, and musicians to name only a few. This interdependency implies that the artist must learn how to work with others and become responsible for communal space.
3. Cultural differences have a big impact on numerous performance elements. For example, the notion of security comes out differently according to cultural backgrounds.
4. Identifying the source of fear related to performing needs to be done as precisely as possible: How and when is it triggered? Precise feedback will allow the artist to adapt the technical work, develop the appropriate mindset and relevant imaging, and even use other techniques such as systematic desensitization.
5. Interdisciplinary intervention is a considerable asset considering the artist is surrounded by consultants, while still being at center stage of the performance.
6. On-site observation sessions are a vital source of information since they allow us to always be on top of our game by seizing different attitudes, verbalizations, and interactions done by the artists.
7. Regarding professional reflections, adaptability is certainly the main competency in this specific case, as well as in any complex environment like Cirque. In this particular case, being able to judge the impact of the various fears on John's capacity to perform, to work with specialists in order to get the best of everyone in their capacity to support John in his daily work, to work not in a purely clinical or in a purely sport psychology framework but rather referring to both as needed, were some of the very strong qualities that contributed to successful intervention with this client.

SUGGESTED READINGS

Jacobs, P. (2010). *The circus artist today: Analysis of the key competencies.* Brussels: FEDEC.
Décamps, G. (2012). *Psychologie du sport et de la performance.* France: De Boeck.
Hays, K. F., & Brown, C. H. (2004). *You're on! Consulting for peak performance.* Washington, DC: APA.
Ménard, J. F., & Hallé. M. (2014). Circus also needs performance psychology: Facts and realities of consulting at Cirque du Soleil. In J. G. Cremades & L. S. Tashman (Eds.), *Becoming a sport, exercise, and performance psychology professional: A global perspective* (pp. 127–135). New York, NY: Routledge.
Psychologie-Québec. (2002). *Dossier spécial, Psychologie de la performance.*

REFLECTIVE QUESTIONS

1. How did the models implemented help the psychologist understand the problem in its full context?
2. How do cultural differences impact performance? How might a psychologist need to take into consideration cultural differences when working with performers?
3. If you were the psychologist in this case, how would you assess/analyze John's fear of performance?
4. How would you implement the fear–trust–responsibility continuum into working with John?
5. What are the benefits to the client of working in an interdisciplinary team of specialists?

REFERENCES

Blanchette, L. (1999). *Application Systémique en Santé Mentale.* Montréal: Presses Université de Montréal.

Ladouceur, R., Fontaine, O., & Cottraux, J. (1995). *Thérapie Comportementale et Cognitive.* St-Hyacinthe, Québec: Edisem.

Reynolds, K. J., Turner, J., Branscombe, N. R., Mavor, K. I., Bizumic, B., & Subasic, E. (2010). Interactionism in personality and social psychology: An integrated approach to understand the mind and behaviour. *European Journal of Personality, 24,* 458–482.

18 Multicultural Performance Psychology

The Acculturation Struggles of a Successful International Amateur Combative Sport Athlete Emerging onto the World Scene

Robert J. Schinke, Kerry R. McGannon, Rebecca Busanich, and Odirin Oghene

The first author has been involved in the world of international combative sports for nearly 20 years. Over the span of his career, this consultant has worked with many international amateur and professional athletes who have relocated to his home country of Canada from Europe, Asia, Central America, South America, and Africa (Schinke, 2007). It was observed that many of these relocated athletes underwent a one-sided acculturation process when navigating life in a new and different country and cultural context, whereby little to no formal support was provided and athletes were expected to adjust on their own to the cultural norms and practices of the host country (Schinke & McGannon, 2014). Since 2004, the consultant has embarked on a trajectory of evidence-based practices concerning high-performance acculturation, with funded projects relating to research and practice with Canadian Indigenous athletes at the elite and youth sport levels (e.g., Schinke et al., 2006), immigrant elite athletes (e.g., Schinke, McGannon, Battochio, & Wells, 2013), and coaches (e.g., Schinke, McGannon, Yukelson, Cummings, & Parro, in press). Through these research endeavors, it has been found that the training and competition experiences of these athletes are complex, with acculturation processes often compounding the barriers that impede performance enhancement. In keeping with the focus area of multiculturalism requested by the co-editors, and culturally inclusive applied practice (see Ryba, Stambulova, Si, & Schinke, 2013; Ryba & Wright, 2005, 2010), the athlete case study presented here focuses on the acculturation of an immigrant high-performance combative sport athlete, whose evolving performance experiences are situated as part of his acculturation experience.

BACKGROUND INFORMATION

The present case study unfolded in the period 2013–2014, while the first author, referred to from this point onward as the consultant, worked with a national combative sport team. The consultant began his work with this national team nearly 20 years ago, when he helped prepare the Men's Junior National Team for that year's world championships. During this initial sojourn into the first of several combative sports, one of the athletes achieved a silver medal and several others also performed above expectations. From 2002 to 2012, he transitioned exclusively to professional combative athletes, assisting more than 20 professionals in world title matches featured on major television networks. Early in 2013 he was asked to return to the combative sport context focused upon assisting with quadrennial planning in preparation for a major international tournament.

The current case study is situated within this broader context, where athletes were developed within a team context with high levels of performance anxiety, low levels of financial support from the federal government, and a disconnect between personal effort and the likelihood of international success. Within this context, the athlete to be discussed has been known to struggle with pre-performance nerves. Though his anxiety was readily apparent to the coaching staff, there was no understanding of its origin and also whether there was a means to alleviate it after many years of maladaptive responses to competition (e.g., withdrawing from tournaments and under-achievement). The initial suggestion to the consultant was that he should focus his efforts on the athlete candidates who were more likely to succeed as they sought to achieve podium finishes at smaller tournaments at the beginning of the 2013–2016 quadrennial (i.e., a quadrennial is a successive four-year plan with each year's training plan built upon the previous year's, with the ultimate objective of technical, tactical, and psychological competencies to achieve excellence during year four).

DESCRIPTION OF THE CASE

The athlete is a national team member originally from an Islamic country who practices his religion, Islam, devoutly, which is a central part of how he prepares for each performance. With the athlete's daily life and his specific performance strategies, he seeks to focus and find himself through prayer, prayer beads, speaking Farsi, and referring to his faith in relation to his hopes and dreams as an athlete and as a person outside of sport. Until recently, this athlete was inconsistent in his performances at the international level; yet to have success during a large international tournament. On several occasions, he unexpectedly won small international tournaments against world ranked top 20 opponents, suggesting that his ability exceeded his performance record. On other occasions his performance has been far less than he and his national team coaching staff expected. The athlete would often lose his first fight to an opponent well below his ability and experience levels. Broadly speaking, this athlete has been labeled and known as an "anxious performer"; at times he has become withdrawn and has even avoided tournaments altogether as a result of his nervousness to perform and fail as an athlete and as a man. This unpredictability caused by pre-performance anxiety positioned the athlete as a liability to the team, especially at important major games tournaments.

Consequently, the athlete has proved to be an interesting case, with his challenges, as we will explore, often rooted in his identities as Islamic, Middle Eastern, and strong, stoic male, and how these identities contrast with the cultural norms of his host nation, where sport psychology is an integrated resource. Precisely, the athlete seemed to be conflicted between an identity conforming to a particular form of masculinity and what it means to be a male athlete – a physically and emotionally strong, independent and self-sufficient Islamic athlete who is expected to exhibit courage, mental toughness, pride, and dominance within his performance and what is revealed in the forthcoming case as fear, vulnerability, and to some degree, an initial reliance on support staff – characteristics sometimes laughed at by others within his team, and likely also within his family of origin. This conflict in two competing identities reveals an athlete who is confused and experiencing psychological distress and wishing for help, but at the same time reluctant to appear more vulnerable by asking for help from a mental training consultant, which would reinforce an identity as mentally fragile, weak, and lacking in autonomy, thus putting his masculinity as an athlete and man into question.

THEORETICAL FRAMEWORK/PHILOSOPHY

There has been growing recognition that high-performance athletes, amateur and professional, are frequently transnational (Kontos, 2009; Magee & Sugden, 2002; Meisterjahn & Wrisberg, 2013; Weedon, 2011). These athletes tend to relocate across national borders in order to seek better living conditions for themselves and their families along with better sport opportunities (Lidor & Blumenstein, 2009; Schinke et al., 2013; Stambulova & Ryba, 2014). Relocated individuals are known to begin their acculturation immediately upon landing in their new country (Berry, 1997). In relation to sport, scholars have found that even when athletes travel to unfamiliar countries for short amounts of time, they experience acute cultural adaptation, whereby they undergo culture shock and its manifestation of psychological overload due to the many differences they encounter as compared with practices they are accustomed to (Ryba, Haapanen, Mosek, & Ng, 2012). For athletes who seek to relocate for more extensive periods of time, or permanently, acculturation is a complex and fluid process that recently has been clarified as without end (Schinke & McGannon, 2014; see also Chirkov, 2009). For the athlete who relocates, challenges might include linguistic barriers, unfamiliar diet, clothing that is more or less modest than they are accustomed to, training conditions that might be more or less stringent, coaching communication that misaligns as a result of being more or less directive, and unfamiliar and even conflicting teammate norms and expectations (Schinke, Yukelson, Bartolacci, Battochio, & Johnstone, 2011; Yukelson, 2010). Though the reader might regard these complexities simply as barriers that can eventually be resolved and acclimated to by the athlete, research has shown challenges tend to arise within daily training and competition several years post-relocation (Schinke et al., 2013). Each new episode where the athlete is challenged to reconcile norms incongruent with personal values catalyzes an internal struggle that necessitates positive resolution, where the athlete is able to continue in collaboration with teammates and coaching staff (Schinke & McGannon, 2014). Alternately, unresolved acculturation challenges can move the athlete for a period of time, and/or indefinitely, toward maladaptive behaviors, such as alienation, and even self-imposed de-selection (Schinke & McGannon, 2014; see also Berry, 1997). Thus, acculturation is best thought of as fluid and ever-present throughout an athlete's sporting experiences.

Added to the complexity of acculturation, it might be misconstrued within sport contexts that relocated athletes should resolve such challenges on their own and without the support from coaches, teammates, and peers (Yukelson, 2010). Thus, acculturation is often not addressed and, as such, may be ultimately navigated by the athlete in isolation, perhaps due to naive coaches and teammates, a lack of clear understanding regarding how to support positive acculturation practices within the sport context, or perhaps due to a deliberate lack of engagement (Schinke et al., 2013). Indeed, more often than not, this is the underlying expectation of transnational athletes within sport contexts. Alternately, there are more inclusive (and adaptive) sport contexts where teammates and coaches support relocated athletes throughout their membership within the sport team in the form of emotional support or by engaging with the relocated athlete in a shared acculturation process, where the norms and practices of several cultures within the sport context are encouraged and co-exist instead of adhering only to the predominant cultural system (Battochio et al., 2013). Examples of a more inclusive multicultural sport context can be found within Major League Baseball and National Hockey League teams, where activities include celebrating several festivities relevant to team members, eating foods that are national dishes of team members, learning one another's languages, and understanding aspects of the various religions practiced within the team's composition (see Battochio et al., 2013). The ideal format of acculturation is foreseeably a shared process, whereby the sport team context becomes a welcoming environment for all athletes and coaches to reveal themselves and their various identities (Schinke & McGannon, 2014; see also Chirkov, 2009). The openness of the sport context permits better acceptance and communication among team members and perhaps even a more expressive athlete within training and competition environments, due to the habitual tendency to have aspects of one's identity embraced, and with that express oneself in a supportive environment (Schinke et al., 2013; Schinke et al., in press). Conversely, the stress of not having one's cultural background and identity acknowledged or subverted creates psychological distress and/or the adoption of behaviors that are not healthful or facilitative to performance (Blodgett et al., 2014; Schinke et al., 2013; Tibbert, Andersen, & Morris, in press).

NEEDS ASSESSMENT

The consultant's first exposure to the athlete was at a world tournament where he suffered a panic episode in advance of his first and only performance, which was a close loss to a lesser opponent. Prior to the performance, the athlete sequestered himself to his room for the final 24 hours, during which time he was non-communicative to the coaching staff and unable to eat or sleep. This was known to be a consistent behavior for the athlete, so much so that the head coach warned the consultant that his positive mood several days in advance of his fight would begin to shift in the final 48 hours, to the point where he would become unrecognizable and unapproachable in his final 24 hours. This warning then came to fruition during the aforementioned major games event. The athlete sequestered himself to his room in the final 24 hours prior to the event, despite discussions in advance of this time period where he had agreed to collaborate. This athlete's anxiety reached a crescendo within the final six hours. Once he had consumed his pre-bout meal, the athlete began to complain of an upset stomach during his bus ride to the venue. These complaints then became more audible and escalated on-site within the final three hours pre-competition. He began to dry heave until his staff-imposed warm-up began, with only a few bouts to go before he entered the ring. This athlete was clearly experiencing a panic episode, and this was confirmed when after the fight the athlete returned to sound health and his general disposition shifted back to a positive team member almost immediately. There appeared to be little to be done with the athlete from the vantage point of coaching and also sport psychology provisions. The athlete was not heard from by the mental training consultant until early the following year, a few months before the next major games tournament, where the athlete aspired to compete once more as a member of the team.

The staff were aware of his high level of anxiety, but no one was willing to consider the backdrop of his cultural identity and how this identity contributed to his barriers to perform. The athlete truly felt conflicted. He was nearing the end of his amateur career and had yet to achieve his objectives. He was also not being taken seriously by the coaching staff in relation to the team's yearly training plan. On the other hand, there was also some recognition by the athlete that he was unable to regulate his emotions without support. The support of a mental training consultant, though available, proved to be a source of embarrassment to the athlete. This suspicion on the part of the first author was confirmed when the national team staff and board of directors chose to permit the athlete last-minute entry into one final major games tournament. The consultant was in the process of meeting with each athlete, and went out with the athlete one evening early on, two weeks in advance of the major games tournament, while at a staging training camp. By this point, the athlete already had one success working with the mental training consultant against a world ranked opponent, where in advance of the bout his warm-up was restructured to include a slower and steadier progression to heightened arousal through breathing techniques and a careful monitoring of his progress in the hours leading up to the performance. However, after the win, the athlete withdrew before his second fight two days later by opting not to fight. The athlete then confided that he did not believe there was a problem with his performance pattern of avoidance, but on the other hand he was willing to try anything that might make a difference and augment his performance to the next level. The athlete later confided during a walk that he was aware of his limitations and had linked his impeded performance to diminished self-regulation and the stigma of working with someone to garner mental strength, both of which should have been evident from the beginning as a source of humiliation for him.

INTERVENTION

From the walk discussed above, the athlete entered skeptically into dialogue with the mental training consultant in order to find "magical solutions" to the anxiety that had plagued his athletic career. As this process began, the consultant struggled as he attempted to reveal his work as creditable and also nimble enough to work with the athlete as a culturally saturated athlete. Concurrently, the consultant also sought to acknowledge his own identity as someone who also practices his faith, values family, and prioritizes the various parts of cultural identities in his practice – his and the client's. The discussions began with an agreement to remain in regular contact with the consultant once they entered into the athlete village. The athlete and consultant would then go on daily walks around the village and discuss aspects of the athlete's personal life, so that the two could begin to forge a friendship, where trust could become the baseline to further work. Much of the dialogue underpinning these walks was about sharing customs and practices. For example, some of these discussions entered into the topic area of the athlete's and consultant's religions, where they shared how they practiced their respective faith at home and how this might extend into major games village life through the shared visiting of a multi-faith service each week. Concurrently, these walks served as an opportunity to monitor the arousal level of the athlete as he waited to begin his tournament early in the second week in the major games village. As the days drew nearer to performance, he would seek out the consultant to walk with him before sleeping at night. In the darkness, the athlete slowly began to share when he was feeling anxious. The more he shared these thoughts, albeit in darkness, the more he began to explore his anxiety, what his triggers were, and how he was managing these to some degree.

As the work progressed, 72 hours before the athlete's first performance, he entered into an autogenic training exercise that was taught to the consultant by a highly successful sport scientist from another country, as a strategy to address an anxious professional client. This training began in the athlete's room, and revealed more of a shift toward engaging with the consultant as opposed to the other possibility of self-imposed alienation. Though he would have been reluctant to enter into this exercise earlier, by this point in the collaboration the athlete and consultant worked well together, often went to meals together, and enjoyed each other's company. Indeed, much of the bridging of customs unfolded over walks and meals, opening up the additional possibility of mental skills implementation on-site. Two days before the athlete's first performance, the two people went to the competition arena and used a Team Canada athlete dressing room to conduct the training on-site. The training technique was timed to fall in the day when there was audience noise as other athletes were competing. The relaxation was then paired with the audience noise to develop a new self-regulation skill in-situ. Once the technique was completed, the two immediately departed the performance context and returned to the comfort of the village for a late evening snack and debrief.

For the entire duration of the tournament, the athlete became the very best version of himself. The results were surprising to many as the athlete continued to progress through the tournament, into the medal rounds, and finally into the finals. The finals concluded with the athlete winning his first major games gold medal. Once the result was achieved, the athlete was debriefed by his coaching staff and the mental training consultant. Presently, this athlete is looked at in a different manner than he was originally. Carefully surrounded and managed, he has engaged more deeply within his sport context and become a strong tournament competitor. The athlete's tendencies continue to be present, but he has also become more receptive to working in a team environment where he is able to resource whatever help he needs in order to be a mentally tough athlete. There continues to be some struggle on the part of the athlete to remain vulnerable with his support staff, but he deliberately seeks to overcome his challenges by remaining in regular contact with the mental training consultant, as he now is beginning to consider the possibility of Olympic qualification and medal success.

REFLECTION

The case study delineated above reveals a success story, whereby an athlete was able to achieve his potential at a major games tournament, and exceed staff expectations. Though this success reveals promise for the athlete's future, it is viewed with caution as he approaches year three of the quadrennial. When consultants work with athletes whose cultural values run counter to sport psychology integration, there are likely to be relapses and/or issues that occur, since an athlete simply does not give up all aspects of his or her cultural identity upon relocation, nor should he or she be expected to do so. Values and/or behaviors of the athlete that run counter to effective service provision will likely impede his contribution toward the deepest possible integration of skills. Consequently, the consultant needs to be mindful of where internal conflicts might exist for each client and become proactive in ensuring that the athlete's growth continues throughout each year, well in advance of the next major international tournament. Earlier international success is a helpful evaluation criteria of athletes such as the one discussed within this case study, and so too is the athlete's sustained commitment to applied sport psychology services. When monitoring athlete engagement, as the present case study shows, the consultant must also be mindful of who the athlete is in terms of her/his various cultural identities, and how these identities intersect within the training and competition contexts to foster and sometimes impede development and performance. At the same time, cultural identities are not one-sided, and thus the consultant must also be reflexive and mindful of his or her own identities and how these frame what is valued and how this might align or misalign with an athlete (McGannon & Johnson, 2009; Schinke, McGannon, Parham, & Lane, 2012). Moreover, in light of the foregoing, the acculturation process is known to be fluid and ongoing, with athletes at times engaging in the cultural practices of the host sport context, and at times when there is a value conflict with aspects of the athlete's cultural identity, also resisting support. Moreover, complicating this fluidity is again the point that various social agents within the sport context also have their own taken-for-granted cultural identities and cultural practices, which when not acknowledged or considered in conjunction with the athletes', can result in conflict and/or performance issues (Schinke et al., 2013; in press). These athletes ought not to be classified as having some personal deficit that results in resistance nor lack of acceptance, but rather moving within and between these complex dichotomies in relation to each experience and interaction with various others within the sport context.

SUGGESTED READINGS

Chirkov, V. (2009). Critical psychology of acculturation: What do we study and how do we study it, when we investigate acculturation. *International Journal of Intercultural Relations, 33*, 94–105. DOI: 10.1016/j.ijintrel.2008.12.004.

McGannon, K. R., Schinke, R. J., & Busanich, R. (2014). Cultural sport psychology: Considerations for enhancing cultural competence of practitioners. In L. S. Tashman & G. Cremades (Eds.), *Becoming a sport, exercise, and performance psychology professional: International perspectives* (pp. 135–142). London: Routledge.

Ryba, T. V., Haapanen, S., Mosek, S., & Ng, K. (2012). Towards a conceptual understanding of acute cultural adaptation: A preliminary examination of ACA in female swimming. *Qualitative Research in Sport, Exercise and Health, 4*, 80–97. DOI: 10.1080/2159676X.2011.653498.

Ryba T. V., Stambulova N., Si, G., & Schinke R. J. (2013). ISSP position stand: Culturally competent research and practice in sport and exercise psychology. *International Journal of Sport and Exercise Psychology, 11*, 123–142. DOI: 10.1080/1612197X.2013.779812.

Schinke, R. J., & McGannon, K. R. (2014). The acculturation experiences of (and with) immigrant athletes. *International Journal of Sport and Exercise Psychology, 12*, 64–75. DOI: 10.1080/1612197X.2013.785093.

REFLECTIVE QUESTIONS

1. What strategies might a consultant use to overcome resistance toward mental training when these services have been regarded through an athlete's lens as a sign of personal weakness?

2.   What strategies can be used to better frame stress in an immigrant athlete, when stress is experienced as embarrassing?
3.   What strategies might be used to overcome a coach's negative label of an athlete?
4.   What aspects of the boxer's identity contributed to his pre-competition anxiety?
5.   How might the case study above be framed as part of a critical acculturation process?
6.   When working with an immigrant athlete, why is recognizing one's own identity an important aspect of the acculturation process?

REFERENCES

Battochio, R. C., Schinke, R. J., McGannon, K. R., Tenenbaum, G., Yukelson, D., & Crowder, T. (2013). Understanding immigrated professional athletes' support networks during post-relocation adaptation through media data. *International Journal of Sport and Exercise Psychology, 11*, 101–116. DOI: 10.1080/1612197X.2013.785093.

Berry, J. W. (1997). Immigration, acculturation, and adaptation. *Applied Psychology: An International Review, 46*, 5–68. DOI: 10.1111/j.1464-0597.1997.tb01087.x.

Blodgett, A. T., Schinke, R. J., McGannon, K. R., Coholic, D. A., Enosse, L., Peltier, D., & Pheasant, C. (2014). Navigating the insider–outsider hyphen: A qualitative exploration of the acculturation challenges of Aboriginal athletes pursuing sport in Euro-Canadian contexts. *Psychology of Sport and Exercise, 15*, 345–355. DOI: 10.1016/j.psychsport.2014.02.009.

Chirkov, V. (2009). Critical psychology of acculturation: What do we study and how do we study it, when we investigate acculturation. *International Journal of Intercultural Relations, 33*, 94–105. DOI: 10.1016/j.ijintrel.2008.12.004.

Kontos, A. P. (2009). Multicultural sport psychology in the United States. In R. J. Schinke & S. J. Hanrahan (Eds.), *Cultural sport psychology* (pp. 103–116). Champaign, IL: Human Kinetics.

Kontos, A. P., & Arguello, E. (2005). Sport psychology consulting with Latin American athletes. *Athletic Insight*. Retrieved December 20, 2014, from www.athleticinsight.com/Vol. 7Iss3/LatinAmerican.htm.

Lidor, R., & Blumenstein, B. (2009). From one Olympics to the next: A four-year psychological preparation program. In R. J. Schinke (Ed.), *Contemporary sport psychology* (pp. 71–88). New York, NY: Nova Science.

Magee, J., & Sugden, J. (2002). "The world at their feet": Professional football and international labor migration. *Journal of Sport and Social Issues, 26*, 421–437. DOI: 10.1177/019373250223825.

McGannon, K. R., & Johnson, C. R. (2009). Strategies for reflective cultural sport psychology research. In R. J. Schinke & S. J. Hanrahan (Eds.), *Cultural sport psychology* (pp. 57–75). Champaign, IL: Human Kinetics.

Meisterjahn, R. J., & Wrisberg, C. A. (2013). "Everything was different": An existential phenomenological investigation of US professional basketball players' experiences overseas. *Athletic Insight, 15*(3). Retrieved from www.athleticinsight.com/Vol. 15Iss3/Diff.htm.

Ryba, T. V., Haapanen, S., Mosek, S., & Ng, K. (2012). Towards a conceptual understanding of acute cultural adaptation: A preliminary examination of ACA in female swimming. *Qualitative Research in Sport, Exercise and Health, 4*, 80–97. DOI: 10.1080/2159676X.2011.653498.

Ryba T. V., Stambulova N., Si, G., & Schinke R. J. (2013). ISSP position stand: Culturally competent research and practice in sport and exercise psychology. *International Journal of Sport and Exercise Psychology, 11*, 123–142. DOI: 10.1080/1612197X.2013.779812.

Ryba, T. V., & Wright, H. K. (2005). From mental game to cultural praxis: A cultural studies model's implications for the future of sport psychology. *Quest, 57*, 192–212. DOI: 10.1080/00336297.2005.10491853.

Ryba, T. V., & Wright, H. K. (2010). Sport psychology and the cultural turn: Notes toward cultural praxis. In T. V. Ryba, R. J. Schinke & G. Tenenbaum (Eds.), *The cultural turn in sport psychology* (pp. 1–28). Morgantown, WV: Fitness Information Technology.

Schinke, R. J. (2007). A four-year chronology with national team boxing in Canada. *Journal of Sport Science and Medicine, 6* (Combat Sport Special Issue 2), 1–5.

Schinke, R. J., & McGannon, K. R. (2014). The acculturation experiences of (and with) immigrant athletes. *International Journal of Sport and Exercise Psychology, 12*, 64–75. DOI: 10.1080/1612197X.2013.785093.

Schinke, R. J., & McGannon, K. R. (2015). Cultural sport psychology and intersecting identities: An introduction to the special section. *Psychology of Sport and Exercise, 17*, 45–47. DOI: 10.1016/j. psychsport.2014.10.010.

Schinke, R. J., McGannon, K. R., Battochio, R. C., & Wells, G. (2013). Acculturation in elite sport: A thematic analysis of immigrant athletes and coaches. *Journal of Sport Sciences, 31*, 1676–1686. DOI: 10.1080/02640414.2013.794949.

Schinke, R. J., McGannon, K. R., Parham, W. D., & Lane, A. (2012). Toward cultural praxis: Strategies for self-reflexive sport psychology practice. *Quest, 64*, 34–46. DOI: 10.1080/00336297.2012.653264.

Schinke, R. J., McGannon, K., Yukelson, D., Cummings, J., & Parro, W. (In press). Sport acculturation of immigrant coaches relocating to Canada. *Journal of Sport Psychology in Action*.

Schinke, R. J., Michel, G., Gauthier, A. P., Pickard, P., Danielson, R., Peltier, D.,... Peltier, M. R. (2006). The adaptation to elite sport: A Canadian Aboriginal perspective. *The Sport Psychologist, 20*, 435–448.

Schinke, R. J., Peterson, C., & Couture, R. (2004). A protocol for teaching resilience to national team athletes. *Journal of Excellence, 8*(4), 9–18.

Schinke, R. J., Yukelson, D., Bartolacci, G., Battochio, R. C., & Johnstone, K. (2011). The challenges encountered by immigrated elite athletes. *Journal of Sport Psychology in Action, 2*, 1–11. DOI: 10.1080/21520704.2011.556179.

Stambulova, N. B., & Ryba, T. V. (2014). A critical review of career research and assistance through the cultural lens: Towards cultural praxis of athletes' careers. *International Review of Sport and Exercise Psychology, 7*, 1–17. DOI: 10.1080/1750984X.1 2013.851727.

Tibbert, S. J., Andersen, M. B., & Morris, T. (in press). What a difference a "mentally toughening" year makes: The acculturation of a rookie. *Psychology of Sport and Exercise, 16*. DOI: 10.1016/j.psychsport. 2014.10.007.

Weedon, G. (2011). "Glocal boys": Exploring experiences of acculturation of migrant youth footballers in Premiere League academies. *International Review for the Sociology of Sport, 47*, 200–216. DOI: 10.1177/1012690211399221.

Yukelson, D. (2010, October). Adaptation and developmental transitions of intercollegiate student-athletes. Paper presented at the annual conference of the Association for Applied Sport Psychology, Providence, RI.

19 Training the Trainers in Botswana

The LifeMatters Program Tailored to Community Youth Coaches

Stephanie J. Hanrahan and Tshepang Tshube

Botswana is a landlocked country in Southern Africa with roughly 2.1 million inhabitants. The most popular sports in the country are football (soccer; mostly played by males), netball (mostly played by females), and volleyball (played by both genders). Botswana won its first Olympic medal in the 2012 London Games (a silver medal in the men's 800 m). There are only two people in the country with a PhD in sport psychology (Tshepang Tshube and Leapetswe Malete).

BACKGROUND INFORMATION

This project came about when Tshube was a PhD student at Michigan State. His advisor, Deborah Feltz, was a keynote speaker with Stephanie Hanrahan at the XV Brazilian Conference of Sport and Exercise Psychology. Stephanie had presented in Brazil on LifeMatters, a program of games and mental skills shown to enhance the life satisfaction, self-worth, happiness, and resilience of disadvantaged youth. When Deborah returned to Michigan she described the content of the conference keynote presentations to Tshube. He immediately thought that such a program could play a useful role in Botswana and proceeded to contact Stephanie. Stephanie, who for years had wanted to see the Okavango delta in Botswana, jumped at the offer. So, with the support of a community outreach grant from the Association for Applied Sport Psychology, Stephanie arranged to spend two months in Botswana. So, an Australian ended up running a program in Botswana and the Hanrahan–Tshube partnership was formed – it all started in Brazil!

DESCRIPTION OF THE CASE

Re Ba Bona Ha (through the Botswana National Sports Council) targets youth across towns and villages in Botswana with a primary goal of keeping them meaningfully engaged, but also in developing and identifying talented athletes to compete for Botswana at an elite level. Although Re Ba Bona Ha wants to use a holistic approach for athlete development, they have always lacked mental skills training instructors. The organization also has the objective of capacity building teachers, community member volunteers, and coaches. Hanrahan had an established program (LifeMatters) that combines games and mental skills that has been shown to enhance life satisfaction, self-worth, and happiness of disadvantaged youth (Hanrahan, 2005, 2012, 2013). The aim was to tailor LifeMatters, which had previously predominantly been used in Latin America, to suit the objectives of Re Ba Bona Ha, and to start the program with teachers and coaches, who could then pass on the program to students and athletes.

THEORETICAL FRAMEWORK/PHILOSOPHY

Historically there has been a deficit approach to young people – trying to reduce or prevent problems. The focus is shifting to one of positive development, working to develop the capabilities of youth so they can make positive contributions to society (Lerner et al., 2011). The Lerner and Lerner Five Cs model of positive youth development (Lerner et al., 2005) suggests that positive youth development requires healthy development in the following areas: *competence* (i.e., positive view of one's actions in domain-specific areas including social, academic, cognitive, and vocational), *confidence* (i.e., an internal sense of overall positive self-worth and self-efficacy), *connection* (i.e., positive bonds with people and institutions), *character* (i.e., respect for societal and cultural rules), and *caring* (i.e., a sense of empathy for others). Hanrahan (2005) developed a program that addresses these five Cs by combining games and mental skills training, and found that participation in the program enhances the self-worth and life satisfaction of orphaned teenagers (Hanrahan, 2005) and teenagers living in poverty (Hanrahan, 2012), and has also been used effectively with former gang members (Hanrahan, 2013). The program is based on self-determination theory (Deci & Ryan, 2008), with components specifically included to enhance the basic psychological needs of autonomy (e.g., through peer-led activities), relatedness (e.g., through team building), and competence (e.g., through success achieved in challenges, homework, and structured activities). Hanrahan has run the program with orphans, teenagers living in poverty, and former gang members in Mexico, adolescents in the slums of Buenos Aires, and inner-city youth in Cleveland, Ohio.

NEEDS ASSESSMENT

No formal needs assessment took place. The Botswana Sports Commission, the Botswana National Olympic Committee, and their affiliates have repeatedly indicated the need to introduce psychological skills to coaches and athletes. Newspaper coverage of previous sporting performances of top Botswana athletes and teams have stressed that psychological support would enhance the quality and consistency of performances. For example, Amantle Montsho, a former world champion 400 m runner, commented that the lack of psychological support contributed to her relatively poor performance at the 2009 World Championships. Even a book that has nothing to do with sport (*The Paroled Pastor*, written by a local history professor) mentions the need for sport psychology services in Botswana (Makgala, 2014). Nevertheless, the content of questionnaires and handouts were checked by Tshube to ensure cultural relevance. Minor changes were made to the wording of some items (e.g., changing "athletic" to "sport," "races" to "ethnicities," and modifying the use of some prepositions).

INTERVENTION

LifeMatters is a ten-session program that combines games, mental skills, discussions, and thoughts-for-the-day. See Table 19.1 for an overview of the program, and Hanrahan (2012) for a detailed description of the program. To be able to reach as many youth as possible, the plan was to deliver the program in Gaborone (the capital of Botswana) to 20 coaches/teachers representing 16 different schools. Then, the coaches would be divided into pairs and deliver the program to groups of 20 youth each, with Stephanie and Tshube available to answer questions during program delivery (i.e., the coaches would be running ten separate programs in ten rooms within the same building). The Botswana Integrated Sports Association (BISA) arranged for the coaches (the majority of whom were also teachers) to be absent from their schools during the 3.5 days of the workshop. Through the teachers, BISA also arranged for school students to attend workshops over an entire weekend. We ended up

Table 19.1 Outline of the Ten-Session Program

#	Games[a]	Discussion/Activity	Handout	Thought for the Day	Homework
1	Ice breakers Link tag Help me tag Chain tag	Why I am here Object that best represents you – now and in six months		Control the controllable	Six things you can control and six things you can't control
2	Have you ever… Knee tag Speed ball	What have you controlled? Optimal activation Abdominal breathing and cue words Progressive muscular relaxation	Factors that affect performance Self-reflection homework	Nobody can make you feel inferior without your consent. (Eleanor Roosevelt)	Self-reflection (e.g., what brings you joy, what would you really like to do)
3	Human knot (with and without blindfolds) Fake n' push	Self-reflection homework Things you controlled in the past couple of days Goal-setting	Goal-setting	Obstacles don't have to stop you. If you run into a wall, don't turn around and give up. Figure out how to climb it, go through it, or work around it. (Michael Jordan)	Progress toward personal goal or working on controlling something
4	Pendulum Blowing in the breeze Four-way thumb wrestling Toe tapper (pairs and group)	Share progress/obstacles in achieving goals Attention/concentration Breath and count Past, present, future Number grid	Number grids (for concentration exercise)	Always look for the positive	Write three positives that you experienced (big or small) 20 questions prep
5	Autumn leaves Balance activity Mirror Three-four coordination challenge	Positive experiences Progress toward goals Counting out loud backwards by sevens 20 questions	List of participants	There is no success without failure	Write a positive (warm fuzzy) about each participant

6 Four-way suspension Triangle tag Imagery games	Collect homework Situations in which you were able to refocus attention Imaging with five senses	Imagery	I can accept failure. Everyone fails at something. What is important is to always try. (Michael Jordan)	Goals/controllables/refocusing attention
7 Keep it up (balloons) Ball and chain Push to stand (twos, threes)	Personal progress Write and share imagery scripts Personal declaration of short-term goal	Envelopes with warm fuzzies (provide each participant with the positive statements from co-participants)	If you don't live every instant in your life, you lose it; live every moment	Work toward goal Practice coordination challenge
8 Mine field Nose and toes Target tag Group push-up	Self-talk Create slogans	Self-talk	One of the slogans created by the group	Ten affirmations
9 Electric fence Push to stand (fours, fives)	Check affirmations are positive Practice saying affirmations out loud Possible uses of affirmations Examples of thought stoppage in past 24 hours Self-confidence	Self-confidence	One of the slogans created by the group	
10 Move person from A to B (if time)	Progress made during program Pairs – review main points of program and present	Evaluation		

Note

a Descriptions of many of the games can be found in Hanrahan and Carlson (2000).

with 21 coaches for the 3.5-day workshop, but only ten were available to attend both days on the weekend (although another nine helped run the program with the students on either Saturday or Sunday). Some of the coaches were concerned about feeding the students, thinking that the two meat pies per student that had been allocated from the funds provided by AASP would not be enough. Because they could not acquire food from all of their schools for the kids on the weekend, the decision was made to invite fewer than the originally planned 200 students to attend the program over the weekend. More than one teacher paid out of their own pocket for the transport and food for their students. Interestingly, one of the students commented in the evaluation of the program that the thing they liked least about the program was that there was too much food! We ended up with 109 students for the weekend program, who were then divided into six groups. The evaluations from the coaches and the students were overwhelmingly positive, with many stating that the LifeMatters program should become part of the school curriculum, or at least made available to all athletes in the country.

The program was perceived to be of such benefit that BISA provided accommodation, food, and transport costs for the LifeMatters program to be delivered to 20 coaches each in Francistown and Kasane (cities/towns 435 and 935 kilometers from Gaborone). Twenty coaches and the president of BISA attended the program in Francistown, followed by 12 of them working together to run the program over a weekend with four groups of 20 students. Three coaches did not attend the weekend activities due to: a relative's home being broken into; babysitting obligations; and attending a teachers' union meeting, none of which had been foreshadowed the day before. On the second full day of the workshops for the coaches in Francistown, two newspaper journalists arrived to report on LifeMatters. They both ended up participating in the workshop activities and staying for most of the day. Stephanie was surprised that BISA automatically paid for the lunches of the journalists (it is culturally appropriate in Botswana to provide food to any media who cover an event).

REFLECTION

On many occasions, Stephanie and Tshube discussed cultural differences they noticed. Reflections on the popularity of the program, issues that influenced the running of the LifeMatters program, participant feedback, and future directions are discussed below. It is important to note that although many of the cultural factors were things that Stephanie noted as being different to her experiences in other countries, some of them were Tshube's observations of Stephanie's behaviors that were not culturally relevant or appropriate.

Popularity of the Program

The program in each city began with a formal speech by the president of BISA or the head of the Department of Physical Education, Health, and Recreation at the University of Botswana emphasizing the importance of this opportunity to learn psychological skills. Speakers concluded by stating the need to transfer the psychological skills acquired in these workshops to their own lives and to teach the skills to students as well as other coaches. Teachers/coaches could not hide their excitement in expressing joy in being the first group enrolled in the Life-Matters program. On more than one occasion, Tshube was approached by coaches and students from the university who inquired why they had not been told about the program. Culturally, there was the expectation that they would be able to attend. Tshube was put in the uncomfortable position of stating that the program targeted community coaches and that we only had supplies for a specified number of participants. It was exciting to see, however, the strong desire many people had to learn about sport psychology.

Issues Influencing the Program

Time. In Botswana people deliberately schedule things (e.g., funerals and weddings) to start two hours earlier than they really do, knowing that generally people will be late. Most days the sessions began about 30 minutes later than scheduled. In a program that was already limited in time, losing time in this manner was frustrating (particularly for Stephanie). When coaches arrived late (sometimes four hours late), there was no sense of urgency and little or no attempt to apologize or explain.

Aside from the starting hour, time was also an issue when it came to participant presentations. Generally, Stephanie found that participant presentations during sessions in Botswana took longer than when the program had been run in Mexico, Argentina, Australia, or the United States. There are two places in the LifeMatters program when participants make presentations to the entire group: during the session discussing multiple methods to enhance confidence and in a review during the final session. Stephanie noticed that even when it had been noted time was limited, most people would begin with a greeting of some sort and a short pause before beginning. During the presentations participants frequently tended to cover material broadly and speak of other components they had learned in the program that were not directly on point. No one ever went off on tangents that were entirely unrelated to the topic at hand, but few of the presentations could be considered succinct.

Lion and impala analogy. Within the LifeMatters program are seven different tag games. "Tag" is not a commonly used term in Botswana. When explaining one of the tag games to the students, one of the coaches used the analogy of the lion (the person who needs to do the tagging ("it" in the United States and "up" in some states in Australia) and the impalas (the people trying not to be touched or tagged). It was then always easy to ask, "Who is the lion?" anytime it became unclear who was supposed to be trying to tag others. We think this analogy can be useful anywhere, not just in Africa!

Program content. Tshube and Stephanie discussed whether or not any of the program content needed to be modified to fit Botswanan culture. It was readily agreed that no changes needed to be made to any of the games, and that generally the handouts were fine (although the self-talk handout could benefit from some minor editing). One cultural change (that may relate more to the culture of age than nationality) relates to the three favorite Cs icebreaker activity, where participants think of their favorite color, cuisine, and cartoon character, and then try to find other people with similar favorites. Culturally, men do not talk about cartoon characters. The coaches (particularly the men) seemed to be uncomfortable with the task, although there was no such feedback from the youth participants. For the third coaches' program, which was held in Kasane, we switched "cartoon character" to "car" to keep within the theme of three Cs. We did comment, however, that when they work with youth, they may want to replace "car" with "cartoon character."

We also realized that some of the youth were not aware of the meaning of the word "least." In the program evaluation is a question asking "What did you like least about this program?" Although some students provided answers such as "Nothing, I liked everything," "Not having breakfast provided," or "Running too much"; a significant number had replies that suggested the word "least" had not been read or understood. Examples are: "knowing many thing that will make me to perform well," "teachers teachs nicely [sic] about performance and how to relax after exercising," and "it make the changes in our life to be the best one's in the future." Generally, the respondents who may have misunderstood the question were those who demonstrated poorer levels of literacy (as shown in their written responses).

Feed the young children first. It is culturally inappropriate to deny a child food when they ask for it, even if the food is meant for someone else. When we had ordered pies for the students' lunches in Gaborone, Stephanie did not know when Tshube's eight-year-old daughter (who attended half a day when the nanny was not available) requested a pie, that one should be given to her even if it meant that later in the day we would need to find additional food if there were not enough pies for the students attending the workshops.

Balloons don't talk. One of the activities in the program involves balloons. Some of the balloons had writing on them. At one point Stephanie asked: "What does the balloon say?" She was greeted by confusion and silence. The balloon is not saying anything. Stephanie needed to have asked: "What is written on the balloon?"

Speak slowly. Even though teachers/coaches had a reasonable understanding of written and spoken English, some teachers requested that Stephanie speak slowly and also repeat important components of each session for them to understand and follow her presentations in a foreign accent.

Excellent behavior. Stephanie noted that compared to groups of youth from many other countries with whom she had worked, the students in Botswana were extremely well-behaved. When an adult (who was not a teacher of any of the kids present) addressed a group of roughly 80 kids who were milling around a hall waiting for the program to begin, he obtained instant attention with just a greeting of "Good morning," with a polite mass reply of "Good morning sir" followed by complete silence. It should also be noted that although not all students were on time at the beginning of the day, they were very good about returning to their assigned rooms on time after a one-hour break for lunch.

Power/water outages. On more than one occasion the power went out (once for about six hours, the majority of the day's workshop). Unfortunately, interruptions in the power supply have become a somewhat regular occurrence in Botswana. Generally no one comments. Curtains are opened to allow in light, and doors are opened to circulate air (in locations that have fans or air-conditioning), and work continues without interruption. It is a good thing that the LifeMatters program does not rely on (or use) PowerPoint presentations in the educational process. Water only tends to be cut on weekends. With water not always being guaranteed to be on tap, people fill urns with water at the beginning of the day (or when water becomes available).

No Staples, OfficeMax, or Office Depot. To prepare for the workshops we needed to organize folders, pencils, and other equipment (e.g., balloons, balls, string, decks of cards) for activities. We spent an entire day driving in and around Gaborone trying to obtain folders for the 200 expected student participants. After visiting at least nine stores and buying every folder in stock, we were still 20 folders short! Thankfully the University of Botswana donated some folders to cover the shortfall.

Participant Feedback

The workshops concluded with an evaluation on the last day. A total of 60 teachers/coaches (Francistown – 19, Gaborone – 20, and Kasane – 21) had the opportunity to anonymously evaluate the workshop by responding to six questions. Questions asked for three things that they learned from the program, and what they particularly liked and disliked about the program. The last three questions examined what participants will remember in a year, what they will use in their lives, and any other comments they had about the program. It is important to note that most of these participants had never been in a sport psychology session before. Participants indicated that, even though they learned something from all the mental skills covered during the training program, four broad themes/categories emerged from their feedback. These categories are managing anxiety and emotional control, developing and managing self-confidence, temper and anger management, and lastly general knowledge acquired from the workshop including factors that affect performance and the power of the mind. Even though there were no major differences across the three towns, coaches from Kasane indicated that the workshop played a crucial role to arm them with skills to manage their anger. Seven of the eight data units on anger and emotional management were derived from coaches in Kasane. We both observed on the first day in Kasane that coaches consistently mentioned that they would like to learn anger and temper management skills in the workshop. It was not clear whether this anger was directed at athletes or environments outside sport (e.g., family and teaching). Two major categories emerged in what coaches liked most about the program. The first category was fun and interactive activities (games) used in the program; the second category was the simplicity of the games and activities that enabled participants to transfer acquired skills into life experiences outside sport. It is atypical in Setswana culture for adults to play games, and it was great to see positive feedback about these adults engaging in these games. One of the participants, who was Tshube's former high-school teacher, mentioned to Tshube that the activities were great for her personal development and are easily transferable to life.

The only negative feedback from the program was related to workshop logistics (e.g., time accorded to the program and when and who should have attended the workshop). Even though all teachers/coaches were provided with a folder with a program outline and all handouts used in the program, some coaches requested that they be provided with a detailed description of all the games and activities performed during the program. They argued that the detailed description would be a good referral document for when they deliver the program. Only four teachers/coaches suggested that a video be provided in future sessions.

Two major categories that emerged on what teachers/coaches will remember in a year and what they will use in life are the mental skills taught in the program (e.g., goal-setting and imagery) and quotes (i.e., thoughts for the day) used in different sessions of the program. A total of 17 data units specifically indicated that teachers/coaches would remember and use imagery, while 14 indicated that they would remember and use goal-setting. In some cases, teachers/coaches used phrases such as "stay focused," which could be interpreted as staying focused on set goals and/or controlling emotions in a stressful situation (e.g., in a game situation). In some cases, teachers/coaches indicated that they would remember and use all the mental skills taught in the program. Teachers/coaches had favorite quotes and lines used during the program, which were profound in the evaluation. For example, "controlling the controllable" and "no one makes you feel inferior without your consent" were the two lines and quotes that had the highest number of data units, in what teachers/coaches would remember and also use in their lives.

The last question sought their general views on the program. Two general categories emerged of the importance and role of the program in their teaching profession, coaching, and in their lives outside sport; and the need to have lengthened the duration of the program. Teachers/coaches used statements such as "it was an eye opener" and "it should be taught at foundational level in primary schools" and "it should be taught to all teachers and coaches across Botswana" to express their appreciation of the program. A total of five teachers/coaches specifically indicated in the evaluation forms that the time allocated to the program should have been lengthened. On a general note, evaluations indicated that teachers/coaches were thankful of such a development in their careers as teachers and coaches.

Where to from Here?

With television and radio coverage of the LifeMatters program, representatives from many sporting federations and organizations expressed interest in attending the training program. Although Stephanie has returned to Australia (at least for the moment), Tshube will continue to run workshops around Botswana. In addition, we expect that the majority of the 60 coaches who attended one of the three workshops will run the LifeMatters program within their own schools (and perhaps with other groups of coaches as well). BISA is considering having the LifeMatters program delivered during the training camps of various sports.

SUGGESTED READINGS

Hanrahan, S. J. (2012). Developing adolescents' self-worth and life satisfaction through physically active games: Interventions with orphans and teenagers living in poverty. In R. Schinke & S. J. Hanrahan (Eds.), *Sport for development, peace, and social justice* (pp. 135–148). Morgantown, WV: Fitness Information Technology.

Main, M. (2007). *The essential guide to customs & culture: Botswana.* London: Kuperard.

Schinke, R., & Hanrahan, S. J. (Eds.) (2009). *Cultural sport psychology.* Champaign, IL: Human Kinetics.

Tlou, T. (1984). *History of Botswana.* Gaborone: Macmillan Botswana.

Vanqa, T. P., (1998). *The development of education in Botswana: The role of teachers' organisations.* Gaborone: Lightbooks.

REFLECTIVE QUESTIONS

1. How would you use Lerner and Lerner's Five Cs model to design an intervention to positively influence youth development?
2. Discuss the similarities and differences of race and ethnicity. How would these influence your intervention development?
3. Name and describe three factors that you might need to keep in mind if you were to deliver a pre-existing mental skills training program from your country in a country with different values, norms, and beliefs.
4. What are three things in your life that you take for granted that may not be readily available in other parts of the world?
5. What are two biases you may have that could potentially get in the way of effectively working individually with an athlete from a different culture?

REFERENCES

Deci, E. L., & Ryan, R. M. (2008). Self-determination theory: A macrotheory of human motivation, development, and health. *Canadian Psychology, 49*(3), 182–185.

Hanrahan, S. J. (2005). Using psychological skills training from sport psychology to enhance the life satisfaction of adolescent Mexican orphans. *Athletic Insight, 7*(3). Retrieved September 6, 2005, from www.athleticinsight.com.

Hanrahan, S. J. (2012). Developing adolescents' self-worth and life satisfaction through physically active games: Interventions with orphans and teenagers living in poverty. In R. Schinke & S. J. Hanrahan (Eds.), *Sport for development, peace, and social justice* (pp. 135–148). Morgantown, WV: Fitness Information Technology.

Hanrahan, S. J. (2013). Using games to enhance life satisfaction and self worth of orphans, teenagers living in poverty, and ex-gang members in Latin America. In R. Schinke & R. Lidor (Eds.), *Case studies in sport development: Contemporary stories promoting health, peace, and social justice* (pp. 91–103). Morgantown, WV: Fitness Information Technology.

Hanrahan, S. J., & Carlson, T. B. (2000). *GameSkills: A fun approach to learning sport skills.* Champaign, IL: Human Kinetics.

Lerner, R. M., Lerner, J. V., Almerigi, J., ... von Eye, A. (2005). Positive youth development, participation in community youth development programs, and community contributions of fifth grade adolescents: Findings from the first wave of the 4-H Study of Positive Youth Development. *Journal of Early Adolescence, 25*(1), 17–71.

Lerner, R. M., Lerner, J. V., Lewin-Bizan, S., Bowers, E. P., Boyd, M., ... Napolitano, C. (2011). Positive youth development: Processes, programs, and problematics. *Journal of Youth Development, 6*(3), 40–64.

Makgala, C. J. (2014). *The paroled pastor.* Maun, Botswana: Black Crake Books.

20 The App(lication) of Technology into Sport, Exercise, and Performance Consulting

The Case of Phil

Jack C. Watson II, Ashley Coker-Cranney, and Meghan Halbrook

We live in an increasingly technology-driven world. Individuals under the age of 25 have grown up with technology readily available to them. They have consistently had technology integrated into their schools as well as their personal and social lives. As such, they are very comfortable with the use of technology and even expect the use of technology in most areas of their lives.

Practitioners in psychology/counseling and sport psychology have seen the benefits associated with the use of technology in practice. They have added technology to their practices to better serve individuals who have difficulty meeting with practitioners for various reasons, such as location, travel, and transportation issues. Practitioners have also used technology for some time to schedule appointments, keep notes, collect information, and many other purposes. Thus, this chapter provides an overview of a case that identifies how a sport psychology practitioner has integrated various forms of technology into her work with a university athlete. As will be discussed in the chapter, the process of integrating technology into practice brings up many practical, ethical, and legal implications for practitioners to consider.

BACKGROUND INFORMATION

Phil, a 21-year-old Caucasian male, is a Division I Collegiate baseball player at BTU, a large public university located in the Mid-Atlantic region of the United States. BTU recently changed conferences (four years ago), and now competes in one of the five power conferences. Phil is in his junior year of school, and is majoring in Sport Management. He currently has a 3.0 cumulative GPA and is on track to graduate on time. Phil was born and raised in Florida, but chose to attend BTU, almost 1,000 miles from home, because he wanted to play for Coach Smith, who has been very successful over the years, having advanced to the College World Series on two occasions. Coach Smith has strong recruiting ties in Florida, and likes to recruit from the state.

Phil became a starter on the team in the middle of his sophomore season, and has been a consistent starter and contributor since that time. As a right fielder, Phil is considered by his teammates to have a very strong arm, and has traditionally been a better than average hitter, with a batting average right around 0.300, and generally hitting in the second position on the team.

In one particularly memorable game at the end of last season, Phil made a play on a ball and missed his cut-off, throwing the ball over his teammate's head and all the way to home plate in an important situation at the end of the game. This was a crucial mistake because it allowed the player who hit the ball (i.e., the winning run) to take second base on the overthrow, putting him in scoring position. The next batter hit a single, scoring the runner from second to win the game. At the time, Coach Smith yelled at Phil about the importance of hitting the cutoff. However, no changes were noticed in Phil's performance after that play.

After the end of the BTU season, Phil started to experience some performance problems while playing in his summer league. During this summer league, Phil developed some anxiety related to hitting cutoffs. This problem primarily occurred during games, not practice. Since these problems began, Phil's interactions with his teammates seemed to have changed. He was secluding himself in the dugout more than normal, and was not as upbeat and supportive of others as he used to be. Phil also started slumping at the plate. While batting, he began swinging at pitches outside the strike zone, and seemed to be trying to hit every ball with power. This resulted in Phil striking out more often and not hitting the ball where it should be hit. As a result, he was moved to the seventh spot in the team's batting order. These changes in performance were concerning to Phil, his coach, and the team because he had always been a strong contributor to the team, and his performance problems were worsening.

Phil had been working off and on with Dr. Jones, a sport psychology consultant who has been employed by the university athletic department and counseling center for five years. Dr. Jones has a Ph.D. in sport psychology, and a master's degree in counseling. She is a licensed professional counselor (LPC), trained to work with both performance and clinical issues. Dr. Jones has been working with the entire baseball team for many years, but she also works with individual athletes upon request. While not on a regular basis, Phil has met with Dr Jones several times since starting at BTU. He always felt that working with her would improve his chances of playing professional baseball.

Phil has traditionally worked more with Dr. Jones during the fall and winter months because of the many in-season demands of playing baseball during the spring. As a member of the baseball team, Phil travels a great deal, and misses a lot of class. The baseball team currently has a 53-game regular season schedule that spans from February to May. Because of his travel schedule, Phil often leaves campus for 3–4 days a week when the team travels. This means that he misses at least 1–2 days of class in a week when the team plays away games.

Because of his recent performance problems, Phil and his coach talked, and they both felt that it would be a good idea for Phil to meet with Dr. Jones. He started meeting with Dr. Jones regularly in the fall and these sessions carried over into the spring and the start of the regular season.

DESCRIPTION OF THE CASE

During the course of their consultation, Dr. Jones developed a deep understanding of Phil's presenting concerns. Foremost in Phil's mind were his performance issues related to hitting his cutoffs and batting. Specifically, he discussed symptoms of over-arousal, including racing heart and shallow breathing, as well as increased muscle tension, feeling rushed to execute plays, and negative self-talk focused on previous failures and the consequences of his underperformance. Phil reported that these symptoms were overwhelming at times and that he was unsure how to handle them, feeling hopeless that he would get back on track.

However, perhaps more concerning to Dr. Jones was Phil's increased isolation from teammates. Phil's anxiety about his performance issues, evidenced by his uncharacteristic batting patterns, negatively influenced his relationships with his teammates. Moreover, his withdrawal from teammates was indicative of his lapse in confidence, which was not improved by his batting and fielding problems. Dr. Jones was particularly concerned that this isolation may also indicate depressive symptomology, and thought it wise to monitor Phil for changes in mood that may signal a need for clinical intervention.

As a result of his performance anxiety and decreased social interaction, and combined with his busy training and competition schedule, Phil experienced difficulty with focus and attention. While he had always been a "B" student, set to graduate on time, his grades slipped a bit during the fall semester, and Phil had reported that they were down a bit again this semester. Dr. Jones was concerned about these changes in his academic performance and how they may have been influenced by his performance problems and interactions with teammates.

THEORETICAL FRAMEWORK/PHILOSOPHY

Dr. Jones was trained, originally, from a cognitive-behavioral perspective. Over the past three years, she has incorporated mindfulness techniques into her consultations. Specifically, although not formally trained in acceptance and commitment therapy (ACT), she educated herself about its basic principles and began using concepts from ACT in some of her consultations with various clients. During her previous work with Phil, Dr. Jones helped him learn deep breathing and imagery to enhance his performance. She regularly discussed with him what it looked like to be in the present moment and began building self-talk awareness into their work together. During that time, they explored his values related to sport and developed action plans to help him lead a more value-guided athletic career; they often considered how his sport values connected with his life values and how to make the two more congruent. Doing so helped Phil stay focused, dedicate more energy toward those things that would help him attain his long-term goals, and improved his performance experience.

During their current consultations, Dr. Jones thought it would be important to build upon the skills Phil had previously learned and explore ways in which he could be less judgmental of his performance. She hoped that by helping him to diffuse his thoughts, he would feel less of a need to control them, which would afford him the ability to allocate precious attentional resources to his performance. She also asked him to resume his use of imagery for relaxation to address his anxiety concerns and introduced him to meditation, which he was able to do via the guidance of an app on his phone. He had previously found guided imagery helpful, so the introduction of meditation would both reduce his heightened arousal and facilitate a present-minded, nonjudgmental awareness of his experience. Although she believed these methods would address Phil's cognitive and somatic anxiety and negative self-talk, his confidence would be more difficult to address. Therefore, she thought it appropriate to begin addressing his anxiety and self-talk, laying the groundwork for addressing his confidence.

NEEDS ASSESSMENT

To more accurately assess for Phil's presenting concerns and triage each concern appropriately when formulating her intervention, Dr. Jones utilized several different means to help her conduct an effective needs assessment. For the first week, she asked him to utilize his journal, which she had acquainted him with in earlier consultations, to track his thought process and points of concern. In that journal, she asked him to write down at least three successes and three areas for improvement for each journal entry. In doing so, she was able to identify areas of confidence, as well as self-talk patterns and anxiety-provoking occurrences. Since he was traveling a lot, Dr. Jones asked Phil to complete his journal electronically using his smartphone note-taking app. This allowed him to jot down "the important stuff" in the moment and then expand on it later. Doing so allowed him to develop perspective about those things he worried about before a game, which he often forgot about after the game. By increasing his awareness of these thoughts and reactions, he was able to use arousal regulation skills he learned previously and track his progress. His journals were then easy to send to Dr. Jones.

Dr. Jones also asked Phil to fill out an online questionnaire before each consultation. Dr. Jones utilized the online survey technology after she extensively researched its security, ease of use, and privacy policies. After choosing her application, available to clients on a computer, tablet, or smartphone, she asked her clients to spend approximately five minutes prior to their sessions to complete the surveys. Doing so allowed Dr. Jones to better prepare for sessions and streamline her clients' concerns each session, keeping them focused on the tasks at hand. Phil appreciated how it allowed him and Dr. Jones to track his progress and setbacks and notice patterns in his experiences that they could collaborate on to develop management skills. Dr. Jones also used the online survey technology to administer the Beck Anxiety Inventory (BAI) (Beck, Epstein, Brown, & Steer, 1988) and the Beck Depression Inventory II (BDI-II) (Beck, Steer, Brown, 1996) to assess and track Phil's anxiety and depressive symptomology.

Dr. Jones also attended practices and games when possible to better observe Phil and his teammates. These observation periods helped her to better understand his ability to deal with adversity and success, and to observe communications with his teammates.

Following her initial consultations with Phil, Dr. Jones felt as if Phil's performance problems were cyclically affecting his isolation and academic issues. Because Phil sought Dr. Jones' consult for his performance problems, she deemed that they were the most appropriate starting point for intervention. That said, Dr. Jones remained vigilant of additional areas of concern related to decreased social contact and/or depression as well as academic-related concerns.

INTERVENTION

Technology for Logistics

Throughout the course of her consultation with Phil, Dr. Jones used several forms of technology for varying purposes. For instance, Phil made initial contact with Dr. Jones via text message. They had used text messaging as a primary mode of communication in the past. Phil felt most comfortable speaking briefly with Dr. Jones via text-based interactions such as Hipaa-Chat or Whatsapp. Dr. Jones preferred using HipaaChat because it allowed her to protect her clients' personal information, given its encryption and focus on HIPAA compliance.

Dr. Jones also used SignUpGenius (www.signupgenius.com) to relay appointment information to her phone's calendar function and send automatic reminders to Phil regarding their upcoming appointments. The link to her scheduling page was available in her email and text message signatures, as well as on her social media and webpage, making access to sign up for appointments easy for her clients. This technology allowed clients to cancel, swap, or reschedule appointments as needed, without contacting Dr. Jones directly. Clients were asked to use an alias name on the site to protect their confidentiality.

Given Phil's travel schedule, Dr. Jones' use of technology was particularly beneficial. For instance, if she chose to send him handouts or worksheets, she could easily send those to him using file share sites, such as Google Drive or Microsoft Cloud. He could then retrieve the worksheets on his computer or mobile device. Although she did not utilize file sharing often, she found it helpful to sometimes give brief readings between sessions when athletes' travel schedules made in-person meetings difficult. This required Phil to sign into the file-share site in order to see the content.

During those times when Phil was on the road, he and Dr. Jones sometimes video-conferenced, using software such as Google Hangouts, FaceTime, or Skype to catch up. These communications were sometimes challenging because of issues with connectivity (e.g., dropped calls) and privacy (e.g., teammates walking into the room). However, it was a useful resource when the opportunity to meet in person was not available.

Additionally, using online survey applications, such as LimeSurvey (www.limesurvey.org/en), that could be completed in a matter of minutes, allowed Dr. Jones to assess Phil's progress while he was away and monitor his symptomology for any changes that needed immediate attention. She could send the surveys to him at a designated date or time frame and receive the results instantly, which made the technology highly accessible without burdening either of them.

Dr. Jones also followed the university baseball team on social media. She did so to help her stay abreast of the team's performance, but it also allowed her to follow less obtrusively the play of the athletes with whom she was working. Early in her career, Dr. Jones had identified the difficulties of having a strong social media presence as a young female working with athletes on a university campus. Several of her athlete clients had tried to "friend" her, at which point she took down her social media presence. However, she started her accounts up again later, but used these only for professional purposes, and did not post any personal information on them. Further, she kept her privacy settings at the maximum level. This allowed her to follow the teams and individuals with whom she worked, but not to be followed by others whom she did not approve of.

Technology as Intervention

Dr. Jones utilized bio/neurofeedback technology (e.g., J&J C2+ 6 Channel Computerized Biofeedback System) during sessions to help Phil build awareness of his internal states and encourage effective self-regulation. By using bio- and neurofeedback, Phil was able to see when he was physiologically aroused or unfocused and pay special attention to his physical sensations in those moments. Bio- and neurofeedback, themselves, do not help athletes control internal states; instead, they act to show the user current activity, reactions to changes in activity, and, in the case of neurofeedback, encourage the body to heal itself by restoring more well-functioning patters (EEGInfo, 2015; Stoler, 2014). Therefore, Dr. Jones used bio- and neurofeedback with Phil to help him recognize symptoms of his internal states and use traditional sport psychology interventions (e.g., diaphragmatic breathing, guided imagery, thought diffusion) to better manage his arousal and anxiety. Through the practice of traditional skills, using bio- and neurofeedback to monitor internal states, Phil learned how to control his anxiety, focus his thoughts, and control his reactions to different situations.

While Phil was on the road, he was able to use different popular apps (e.g., Breathe2Relax, GPS for the Soul) that he had downloaded onto his phone to help him continue to practice breathing and awareness of his thoughts and sensations. These practice sessions while traveling helped Phil keep his sport psychology skills at the forefront of his mind. In fact, he would often text Dr. Jones after practice a few times each week to let her know how it had gone.

Other technology utilized by Dr. Jones included multimedia creation software that could be readily available on Phil's computer or mobile device. Specifically, she used video-editing software to help create a highlight reel for Phil and other players on the team to watch their successful attempts at hitting and fielding. Each ten-minute video was paired with music of each player's choosing and created with the help of the team videographer. Phil downloaded his film to his smartphone so he could watch it at any time. Phil found it particularly useful to watch his film as part of his pre-competition routine to help him focus on his successes. Doing so improved his self-talk throughout the early innings of his games and reminded him to hunt for the good instead of ruminating on the bad. Further, Dr. Jones created various imagery scripts for Phil. Several scripts were related to hitting and fielding, whereas others were related to encouraging a relaxed state; Dr. Jones recorded her voice for each of them. Each script lasted approximately five minutes. Each script was also added to Phil's phone and he made them part of his pre-game playlist to help him prepare for practices and games. Having short scripts, accessible on his smartphone at any time, helped Phil practice his skills more frequently. Phil appreciated that he could practice his skills anywhere without others knowing what he was listening to.

REFLECTION

Ethical/Legal Considerations

Dr. Jones was concerned about several ethical and legal issues related to her consultations with athletes on campus and on the road. She made sure to discuss these legal and ethical issues with a psychologist in the student counseling center, as she wanted to practice in a professional manner. However, the individual with whom she consulted about these legal and ethical issues was always quick to mention that the ethical practice of sport psychology seemed a bit different from the practice of traditional psychology, and often seemed to push the boundaries of ethical practice in traditional psychology. While not discussed in this chapter, Dr. Jones was well versed in the seven-step ethical decision-making model developed by Hadjistavrolpoulos and Malloy (2000), and would use it to help make all ethical decisions. The legal and ethical issues of most concern to Dr. Jones were competence, confidentiality, informed consent, use of social media, boundaries, and liability issues.

With regard to competence, Dr. Jones realized that there were two areas of competence that she needed to be concerned with (Mallen et al., 2005) when utilizing new technology in practice. Dr. Jones first needed to ensure that she was competent with the use of this technology in terms of how to troubleshoot problems and help clients utilize the technology as needed. Further, Dr. Jones had never been trained to provide services from a distance using synchronous (e.g., Google Hangouts, FaceTime or Skype) or asynchronous (e.g., text messaging, online surveys, use of social media) communication. Therefore, she had to ensure that she was competent in her use of this technology for treatment. After extensive research on the types of technology she intended to use, both as a consumer and a facilitator, Dr. Jones needed to take steps to ensure that her therapeutic style was valid and reliable when used via distance technology, given that neither CBT nor ACT were developed and validated using technology to consult from a distance. Finally, Dr. Jones had not received any formal training in ACT, but had taken steps to learn about its use. She has also consulted with a psychologist about its use, and received supervision in her application of the framework. As a result, she felt as if she was competent to use these skills.

Dr. Jones also had legitimate concerns about the confidentiality associated with consulting from a distance. Dr. Jones was able to develop a good relationship with Phil prior to consulting with him from a distance, and was therefore able to gain informed consent from him in person. However, it was still essential that Dr. Jones talked with Phil about the possible limitations, risks to confidentiality, and possible misunderstandings that could occur when consulting from a distance (APA Ethics Code 4.02). It is not possible to guarantee confidentiality when using such technology, so it was recommended to Dr. Jones that she have Phil sign a teletherapy/distance-consulting waiver, which outlines the potential risks to confidentiality related to this form of work.

The use of social media by sport psychology practitioners has been discussed by many practitioners. In 2010, it was reported that 77 percent of psychology doctoral students and psychologists had a presence on social media (Taylor, McMinn, Bufford, & Chang, 2010). This percentage is higher for younger individuals, especially those in college. Further, social media has become an almost default way for younger generations to communicate with each other, and they do so oftentimes without concern for confidentiality issues. The mere presence of a practitioner on social media allows for clients to locate information and form opinions about them (Behnke, 2008). Therefore, it is important to limit the amount and type of information located on these sites and to carefully consider who will have access to this information. Further, using such technology with clients does bring confidentiality issues into question, and clients should be informed about this.

From a legal perspective, it is also important for Dr. Jones to consider the liability issues and cross-boundary certification/licensure issues. With regard to liability issues, it is important for Dr. Jones to find out if her liability insurance covers her practice across state lines via distance technology or for the use of other forms of technology in her practice. Most liability insurance carriers only cover clients for services that are within the scope of their licenses (Ohio Psychological Association, 2010). Therefore, if the use of technology for the provision of services is not considered to be part of Dr. Jones' license, then her malpractice insurance would not cover any problems that may occur as a result of such services. With regard to cross-boundary certification/licensure, it is important for Dr. Jones to check jurisdictional laws to determine if she is able to practice with Phil while he is traveling with his team out of state. If not, Dr. Jones may be practicing illegally and would not be covered by her insurance for any problems that occurred as a result of such services.

Concerns and Lessons Learned

Sport, exercise, and performance psychology consultants and counselors should consistently be evaluating their cases for ways to improve their approach in future consultations. If given the opportunity to address a case similar to Phil's in the future, Dr. Jones may consider targeting her initial intervention at Phil's depressive symptomology or social isolation as opposed to his performance concerns.

Dr. Jones is encouraged to take a self-reflective approach to her consulting. She should take steps to assess her skills, approach to consulting, use of technology, and other aspects of her consultation with Phil. Additionally, it is important to assess Phil's experience with technology and psychological skills training. Was Phil happy with the suggested applications, time commitment, and perceived progress toward his goals? What would he change? Were there times Phil was uncomfortable with using the technology, possibly due to fear of confidentiality or privacy? What types of clients are most likely to embrace the use of technology? Are there presenting issues or concerns that would rule out the use of some forms of technology for treatment? Each client and his/her needs are unique and should be addressed as such. Technology is perpetually evolving, making the opportunities to expand consultant and client knowledge, growth, and reach more prevalent than ever before. However, the use of technology does not answer all of the questions and should only be used when appropriate for the practitioner, client, and presenting concerns. Further, the ethical and legal issues surrounding the use of technology in the practice of sport, exercise, and performance psychology should be considered closely in all situations.

SUGGESTED READINGS

American Psychological Association. (2012, July). Guidelines for the Practice of Telepsychology, draft for public comment.

Behnke, S. (2008, July/August). Ethics in the age of the Internet. Retrieved from www.apa.org/monitor/2008/07-08/ethics.html.

Hadjistavrolpoulos, T., & Malloy, D. (2000). Making ethical choices: A comparative decision-making model for Canadian psychologists. *Canadian Psychologist, 41*(2), 104–115.

Hersen, M. H., & Thomas, J. C. (Eds.). (2007). *Handbook of clinical interviewing with adults.* Thousand Oaks, CA: Sage Publications.

Kanani, K., & Regehr, C. (2003). Clinical, ethical, and legal issues in e-therapy. *Families in Society: The Journal of Contemporary Human Services, 84,* 155–162.

Mallen, M. J., Vogel, D. L., & Rochlen, A. B. (2005). The practical aspects of online counseling: Ethics, training, technology, and competency. *The Counseling Psychologist, 33,* 776–818.

Ohio Psychological Association. (2010). Telepsychology guidelines. Retrieved from www.ohpsych.org/psychologists/files/2011/06/OPATelepsychologyGuidelines41710.pdf.

Taylor, L., McMinn, M. R., Bufford, R. K., & Chang, K. B. T. (2010). Psychologists' attitudes and ethical concerns regarding the use of social networking web sites. *Professional Psychology: Research and Practice, 4*(2), 153–159.

Watson II, J. C., & Halbrook, M (2014). Incorporating technology into practice: A service delivery approach. In G. Cremedes & L. Tashman (Eds.). *Becoming a sport, exercise, and performance psychology professional: A global perspective* (pp. 152–159). New York, NY: Routledge.

Watson II, J. C., Schinke, R., & Sampson, J. (2013). Ethical issues affecting sport and exercise psychology in the tele-health era. In E. Etzel & J. Watson II (Eds.). *Ethical issues in sport, exercise and performance psychology* (pp. 139–150). Morgantown, WV: Fitness Information Technology.

REFLECTIVE QUESTIONS

1. What are the major challenges Phil is facing? How would you prioritize those concerns?
2. What client/team factors should be considered when deciding whether a client/team is a good candidate for the specific types of technologies listed in the case study? Consultant factors?
3. How might your approach to using technology in consultation change if Phil were a youth athlete on a travel team? A high school athlete with no interest in playing in college? In an adult recreational league?
4. What are the ethical/legal concerns of using technology in sport, exercise, and perform-ance psychology consultations? When is technology not appropriate for utilization? How might you, as the consultant, navigate those concerns?
5. What disadvantages might each of the types of technology used in this case present in a real-world situation?

REFERENCES

Beck, A. T., Epstein, N., Brown, G., & Steer, R. A. (1988) An inventory for measuring clinical anxiety: Psychometric properties. *Journal of Consulting and Clinical Psychology, 56*(6), 893–897.

Beck, A. T., Steer, R. A., & Brown, O. K. (1996). *Beck Depression Inventory manual* (2nd ed.). San Antonio, TX: Psychological Corporation.

Behnke, S. (2008, July/August). Ethics in the age of the Internet. Retrieved from www.apa.org/monitor/2008/07-08/ethics.html.

EEGInfo (2015). What is neurofeedback? Retrieved from www.eeginfo.com/what-is-neurofeedback.jsp.

Hadjistavrolpoulos, T., & Malloy, D. (2000). Making ethical choices: A comparative decision-making model for Canadian psychologists. *Canadian Psychologist, 41*(2), 104–115.

Hersen, M. H., & Thomas, J. C. (Eds.). (2007). *Handbook of clinical interviewing with adults*. Thousand Oaks, CA: Sage Publications.

Mallen, M. J., Vogel, D. L., & Rochlen, A. B. (2005). The practical aspects of online counseling: Ethics, training, technology, and competency. *The Counseling Psychologist, 33*, 776–818.

Ohio Psychological Association. (2010). Telepsychology guidelines. Retrieved from www.ohpsych.org/psychologists/files/2011/06/OPATelepsychologyGuidelines41710.pdf.

Stoler, D. R. (2014). Neurofeedback: How does it work? Exploring how neurofeedback works to treat your injury, diagnosis, or symptom. *Psychology Today*. Retrieved from www.psychologytoday.com/blog/the-resilient-brain/201410/neurofeedback-how-does-it-work.

Taylor, L., McMinn, M. R., Bufford, R. K., & Chang, K. B. T. (2010). Psychologists' attitudes and ethical concerns regarding the use of social networking web sites. *Professional Psychology: Research and Practice, 41*, 153–159.

Watson II, J. C., Schinke, R., & Sampson, J. (2013). Ethical issues affecting sport and exercise psychology in the tele-health era. In E. Etzel & J. Watson II (Eds.), *Ethical issues in sport, exercise and perform-ance psychology* (pp. 139–150). Morgantown, WV: Fitness Information Technology.

21 Technology in Practice
A Case Study

Robert S. Neff and Erika Carlson

Rapid advancements in today's technology have revolutionized the way people communicate and learn. The field of sport psychology could benefit enormously if it harnessed some of these new technologies to teach, motivate, and track client progress. The current chapter will start by listing several of the biggest reasons why it makes sense to incorporate technology into mental skills training (MST) practice, followed by a case study to demonstrate how it can address the biggest challenges associated with delivering mental training programs. In so doing, a new mobile app will be highlighted, called MentalApp®, that simplifies mental training into an understandable and convenient path toward peak performance. It gives coaches and sport psychology consultants (SPCs) the enhanced ability to deliver content, track client progress, effectively work with long-distance clients, as well as service large groups.

BACKGROUND INFORMATION

Despite the growth and effectiveness of SPCs working with athletes, there remain a number of issues that limit access to mental training. In addition, another challenge is that the mental training may be designed or implemented in such a way that it loses its effectiveness (especially with younger athletes – in their teens, twenties, and even thirties).

Limited Access to MST

Unfortunately, most performers do not have regular access to mental training for a few different reasons (Neff, Weinberg, & Jurica, 2010; 2011). First, it is generally advocated that MST be conducted over an extended period of time and this is rarely feasible except perhaps at the highest level of competition – and even at that level it is still a rarity (Weinberg & Williams, 2011). School, work, travel, family commitments, and health concerns can all get in the way of attending regular meetings and training sessions. Combine this with the relatively few individuals who are certified in the field (by the Association for Applied Sport Psychology or other certifying body), and there are few people who can offer services to the many performers who need and want it.

The Cost of MST

Another limiting factor is the cost of MST. Of course, there is wide variation in terms of the cost (depending on the experience/knowledge/marketing of the consultant, as well as the athletes'/teams' ability to pay), but it would not be out-of-bounds to say that MST costs approximately $100 to $150.00 per hour or more. The cost, either as an individual or as a team, is a definite issue for athletes and athletic departments. For example, in a survey of athletic directors, sport psychology experts were seen as nice to have but not essential (versus strength and conditioning coaches), given the cost (Wilson, Gilbert, Gilbert, & Sailor, 2009). They would like their athletes and coaches to have the advantage of working with SPCs, but with budgets the way they are, it is almost seen as a luxury rather than a necessity. Thus, until recently mostly high-level athletes with sufficient resources are the ones who can generally take advantage of MST through consultants. In fact, these barriers to "sport psychology for all" (i.e., cost and availability) have been discussed for over 20 years in the literature and continue to be a challenge (Weinberg & Gould, 2011; Weinberg & Williams, 2011).

Web-Based Programs

Several of the problems noted above can be solved by an individualized internet-based program (Weinberg, Neff, & Jurica, 2012). Specifically, a web-based MST program would have the advantages of reaching a much broader audience than the current one-on-one training model, while at the same time greatly reducing the cost. Furthermore, the web can provide users with convenient access to a wide range of educational resources, which might not ordinarily be available to athletes. In essence, the internet could provide the opportunity to interact with the learning environment to create more meaningful learning experiences. For example, athletes have different learning styles and they could have the option of listening to an audio clip, watching a video clip, simply reading about a technique, or possibly talking with someone virtually through web-video technology.

Smartphone Technology

Although web-based programs appeared to deal with the critical issues of cost and access, recently the rise in smartphone use has presented an even better alternative for the delivery of mental training. Specifically, smartphone sales have now surpassed computers, with over a billion users in the world today (*Business Insider*, 2013). With the ease of being able to carry smartphones everywhere, athletes of all ages are turning off their computers and using their mobile devices to learn, work, and play (Sung & Mayer, 2013). In addition, researchers are reporting that attention spans are getting smaller, there are more distractions in the learning environment, and it is harder to get tasks done (Rosen, Carrier, & Cheever, 2013). These shorter attention spans and greater distractibility also carries over to athletes, who require more efficient ways to organize themselves and track their goals (Duckworth, Grant, Loew, Oettingen, & Gollwitzer, 2011).

Development of MentalApp®

In order to capitalize on the changing technological landscape, MentalApp® was developed to specifically address the aforementioned challenges as well as the key elements needed for a successful mental skills intervention (Neff & Frey, 2013; Weinberg, Neff, & Jurica, 2012). These elements include the following: (1) affordable, (2) mobile-based, (3) automated, (4) customizable, (5) prioritizes information for athletes, (6) content taught by SPCs, (7) follows best practices in mental training, (8) uses short videos to hold attention, (9) uses goal setting and tracks client progress seamlessly, (10) efficiently works with long-distance clients and large groups, and (11) provides useful tools and support to enhance individual program success. Even when convenient and affordable, mental training is still not easy as performers must be able to satisfy three "mastery steps" in order to perform consistently well in competition: (1) understanding the key mental skills; (2) memorizing the skills into habits; and; (3) applying the skills appropriately when needed. When used by a trained SPC, MentalApp® can enable all three to occur effectively and efficiently.

In order to make MentalApp® available to potential clients, there was a significant amount of marketing preparation necessary. First, the Dallas company had to "optimize" its website so it could be found by the search engines (i.e., search engine optimization or SEO). The essence of SEO is that the website has a page ranking based on its relevance to the keyword phrase used in the search. A more relevant site will have the keyword phrase in its titles and content, and it will also have many other third-party sites linking to it with "anchor text" similar to the keyword phrase.

Other ways companies can draw attention to themselves using technology include banner ads, social media, blog posts, autoresponders, and digital downloads. Banner ads are hyperlinked images or videos that are positioned in the most visible areas of websites. The most popular online ads are Google's Adwords. These advertisements show up on the sides and top of search engine results. The more you pay, the more visible the ad is when someone searches for the keyword phrase connected to the ad. Social media is used to increase website traffic by getting people's attention with a catchy phrase or video clip and then providing a link to the company's site. Blog posts are popular ways to get people's attention and trust prior to providing website information or an offer. Last, autoresponders enable companies to automatically provide content in response to a completed form requesting name and email. Marketing campaigns can then go out, promoting other products and services. Digital downloads enable consumers to get content immediately.

DESCRIPTION OF THE CASE

To demonstrate the use and applicability of MentalApp®, a case involving a 13-year-old male golfer named "Tucker" who has received mental training 2–3 times a month for nine months will be outlined. Tucker competes on the 11–14-year-old Oklahoma Junior Golf Tour. Tucker's parents and coach were concerned with how angry and frustrated he was during and after competitions. They also wanted him to have more self-discipline and motivation during practice.

Tucker is highly talented so he has aspirations of not only playing professional golf but also becoming the greatest of all time. His work ethic is generally poor and he is not very focused or disciplined when at practice. He has a golf coach and his father manages Tucker's practice and tournament schedule. His father is very driven and outcome-oriented. As a result, during competition Tucker also tends to focus on the outcome and what others will think of him if he underperforms. Tucker is one of the best junior golfers in the country for his age, and everyone in Tucker's family knows what his national rankings are and how each tournament will affect those ranking. Companies are offering Tucker sponsorships for equipment, and several college coaches have already expressed interest in recruiting Tucker, but he has told them he will be going pro and skipping college.

THEORETICAL FRAMEWORK/PHILOSOPHY

A cognitive emotional behavioral framework (Corstorphine, 2006) is the primary approach underlying the MentalApp®. However, since the focus is on performance enhancement, no psychological disorders are diagnosed or treated. In this particular case, the client was taught skills to improve awareness of thoughts and emotions so he could become more self-reliant in the control of his performances. Awareness training has been at the core of cognitive-based models for over a century, since changing a thought requires the prior awareness of that thought. Then, as the thought is changed to a more adaptive one, emotions are affected, and with practice, controlled (Ellis, 2008). More recently, mindfulness meditation has emerged as a popular form of awareness training. Large participant studies have demonstrated how mindfulness is associated with emotional well-being (Branstrom, Duncan, & Moskowitz, 2011). A mastery model of training was also employed so key information could be understood, retained, and applied during competition and other adverse conditions. Originally proposed by

Benjamin Bloom in the late 1960s, mastery learning programs have generally been shown to lead to higher achievement in all students as compared to other more traditional approaches to learning (Guskey & Gates, 1986).

NEEDS ASSESSMENT

The online Emotional Intelligence Test (PsychTests, 2011) was used to provide a baseline score for comparative purposes as the intervention progressed. Tucker scored a 92 (25th percentile). An online needs assessment was also done where the athlete and parent rated on a ten-point Likert scale mental-related issues that affect athlete performance. The scale runs from 1 (immediate need) to 10 (ideal/no need to improve). Tucker did indeed score very low (below five out of ten) in the areas originally discussed with his parents (i.e., anger, frustration, motivation, discipline, and work ethic), as well as a few other areas (i.e., confidence, negativity, self-criticism, and organization). His initial score was 60 (out of a possible 140 points). Last (after Tucker registered for MentalApp®), Tucker completed the integrated "Mental Toughness Test" that calculates a score based on a list of actions that help in the development of mental toughness (e.g., journaling, charting, goal-setting, use of routines, imagery, relaxation, self-talk, etc.). Tucker scored 21 out of a possible 72 points. There were 18 items and scoring for each item was on a four-point Likert scale (1 = not yet, 2 = sometimes, 3 = often, or 4 = daily).

After the issues were identified and rated in the initial online meeting, Tucker's father expressed gratitude for how clearly the issues were documented and the quality of the PowerPoint presentation that introduced the mental training program. He then commented that he was happy he decided to do a broader internet search for "mental training" outside of just his local city. He had asked Tucker's coach and several parents for a referral but no one had any suggestions. There were no local businesses that provided mental training and he was initially uncertain about working long-distance. When he found a mental training business in Dallas he thought he was going to have to drive five hours to meet the consultant. However, through the use of MentalApp®, face-to-face consultation was not needed, but rather a GoToMeeting link was provided that enabled a video-conference. If it were not for technology, Tucker's father would not have been able to find or initiate MST for his son.

After Tucker and his father completed the initial online video meeting, a link was provided to make payment fast and convenient. PayPal, Google Checkout, and Amazon Payments are among a few popular services. The agreement and informed consent was then attached to an email so Tucker's father could sign. Once payment was made, an ebook was immediately sent, along with instructions for some preliminary reading.

INTERVENTION

Tucker was excited to begin work with MentalApp® and stated: "I love that I can do part of this mental training on my iPhone and iPad!" A registration code was emailed to Tucker along with the website (www.MentalApp.org). The code automatically connected Tucker to his consultant so his progress could be easily monitored. The MentalApp® registration process included some introductory screens that oriented Tucker, explained the main features, and finished with a welcome video from the Learn area.

When Tucker opens the app, a homepage (see Figure 21.1) provides him with options. When he opens the Learn area (see Figure 21.2), short videos are available that are organized into five levels, starting with goal setting. Once the first-level videos were completed, a customizable monitoring chart (mChart) was unlocked, along with the next level of videos. By the time the second level was completed, Tucker had made significant modifications and the program began addressing his individual needs. In this way, Tucker was guided down the most common MST pathway

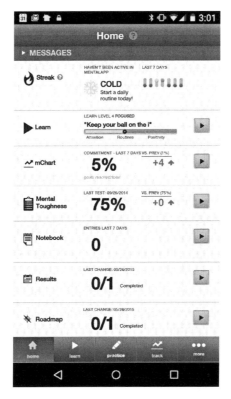

Figure 21.1 MentalApp Home Page

Figure 21.2 MentalApp Learn Area

(goal-setting–imagery–self-talk–emotion control). Tucker also was given an ebook that was designed to supplement MentalApp® and provide some printable worksheets as well. Because all of the mental skill content was delivered digitally, the consultant was able to focus on making sure Tucker understood how to practice and apply the skills. MentalApp® also enabled the consultant to know if Tucker had watched the videos and used the training tools.

The mChart is the primary training tool and is designed to help Tucker remember and track his weekly actions. It's divided into three sections – Health, Mental, and Physical – and comes pre-loaded with the most common training goals. Tucker was shown how to customize each section so only his goals remained. Then, each day when his alarm went off, Tucker opened MentalApp® and completed his mChart by answering yes or no as to whether he completed the goal for the day. Tucker and his SPC could easily look at the "7-Day Trend" page to see whether his goals were being met for the previous seven days. Those that were not met became a topic of discussion during his next consultant session. For the first time, Tucker was consistently completing his goals on a weekly basis. Tucker's father commented that he had never seen Tucker be so disciplined. Tucker's confidence grew enormously, as did his independence from his parents. Most exciting, though, was Tucker's comment after four weeks of using MentalApp®: "I'm now remembering to do all the actions in my mChart without being reminded by MentalApp® or my parents!" Monthly assessments were taken and Tucker loved to see evidence of his improvement: (1) Emotional Intelligence Test – 98 (up from a pre-test of 92); (2) Needs Assessment – 94 (up from a pre-test of 60); and (3) the MentalApp® Mental Toughness Test – 43 (up from a pre-test of 21). All of these scores confirmed that Tucker's hard work was paying off, which further improved Tucker's confidence and sent a message to his parents that the money was well spent. However, the ultimate goal of the intervention was to produce mastery, so post-tests were again completed after two, three, and six months. Tucker continued to show improvement through the third month and maintained his scores after the sixth month, with strong evidence of self-sufficiency being demonstrated.

As stated earlier, one of the biggest benefits of using technology is the increased ability to remember and master skills. When athletes compete, they know how important muscle memory is to high performance. There simply is not enough time to think about how to execute a skill. It has to come automatically. This is equally true for the mental side of performance. MentalApp® is the primary tool that Tucker and his consultant used to build mental habits (that lead to mental toughness). To assist Tucker with the necessary repetition of the new mental skills he was learning, MentalApp® also includes a Practice area (see Figure 21.3) and a Track area (see Figure 21.4). The Practice area has tools to help with relaxation, imagery, and mindfulness.

The Track area has tools to help Tucker get feedback about how his training and performance is changing across time. The tracking tools include the mChart, the Mental Toughness Assessment, a digital Notebook to record training and performance thoughts, a Results area to track his golf performance, and a Roadmap area where he can see his outcome goals that serve as motivation.

While Tucker was going through the videos and using the associated tools, his coach and parents were also training mentally using mental skills programs created specifically for them (see CertifiedMentalCoach.com and ParentMentalTrainer.com, respectively). Both are online courses that teach mental skills and other role-specific essential content using automated voice-over PowerPoint videos and short quizzes. Because Tucker's coach and parents learned this essential mental training information, they were all much better at supporting him as he went through the adversity associated with becoming an elite athlete.

There are many biofeedback and neurofeedback devices on the market for athletes to learn how to recognize and control their physiological states and emotions. The general design involves a device that collects data from the athlete and displays it on-screen for the purpose of feedback. Because Tucker is a young teen, his consultant chose a system that involved games (flying planes and driving cars). In order to control the video images, Tucker had to properly change his

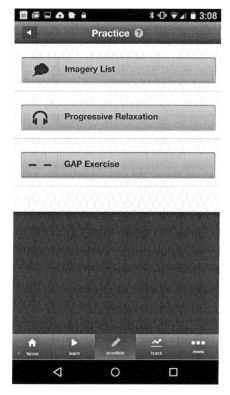

Figure 21.3 MentalApp Practice Area

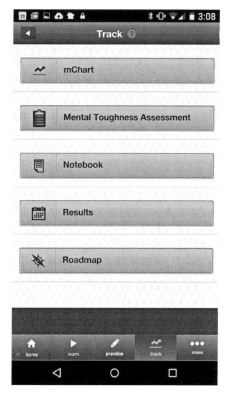

Figure 21.4 MentalApp Track Area

brainwaves between high beta (problem solving) and alpha/theta (relaxation/meditation). MentalApp® and Tucker's consultant taught him several methods to control thoughts and hence brainwaves, so this neurofeedback game was an ideal one for him to use for practice.

After each session, an email would be sent from the consultant to Tucker, his coach, and his parents to keep them all in the loop regarding assignments, progress, and any areas of concern. Consistent emails ensured an open line of communication so all parts of Tucker's "support triad" could stay on the same page. After a breakthrough performance, Tucker sent an emotional email to his consultant expressing his thanks for their work together. Tucker was in such a negative place when he started the mental training process that his coach and parents could hardly believe his improvement. With permission from Tucker and his parents, his consultant posted parts of his testimonial online. Because Tucker's work was performance enhancement-related and not disorder-related, Tucker felt comfortable with his success story going public. Over the following months, dozens of parents of young golfers would read Tucker's words and become interested in mental training for their children as well.

REFLECTION

Reflection on the Case and Use of Technology

For Tucker in particular, technology was an essential part of MST. Being a teen, it's not likely he will be excited about interacting only through email, he doesn't like to read more than a few pages at a time, and weekly long-distance travel is out of the question. With the distance between client and consultant being so large, the task for the SPC to market, sell, build rapport, deliver content, track progress, and refine the process would otherwise be next to impossible. Even for local clients, it can be a challenge to provide effective oversight. One of the most challenging parts of working with teens is providing a good source of confidential accountability. Do they follow through between sessions? If so, what do they do and how often? How can you be sure mental skills practice is being completed? Additionally, what objective evidence can the SPC provide to the client, coach, and parents that mental training is having a positive effect? Besides technology being "cool" to teens, it also provides a solution to all these issues.

As beneficial as technology is and will continue to be, MST is still far more effective when an SPC is involved. Besides the obvious benefits of a human relationship and consistent accountability, SPCs are trained to modify initially automated core MST programs to improve effectiveness. Google and other leading technology companies are working hard on artificial intelligence (AI), but even the most optimistic advocates of AI don't see SPCs becoming obsolete within the next decade.

As we continue to have more types of technology available to more people around the world, it will be essential for us to continue improving the user experience related to MST. That means more convenience and more intuitive apps and programs. For clients to look forward to their MST time each day (and actually do it daily!), there will need to be more fun and enjoyable activities that deliver a measurable effect on thoughts, emotions, and performance. Clients, coaches, and parents will need to see (and trust) that these improvements are happening and are being caused by mental training. Last, we'll want to better integrate "on-field" feedback into apps so clients know more precisely what actions they need to take to enhance their mental toughness and performance.

Incorporating Reflection into Work with Clients

There are several key times in the learning process when clients can be given the opportunity to reflect on the content taught and what it might mean for their future performance and well-being. Here are five such times:

1. Immediately after teaching: The client can talk in their own words about specific topics taught, exposing areas of strength and weakness. This would make it clear for the consultant what items could be added to future sessions. It would also provide an opportunity for questions.
2. Toward the end of the session: The client and consultant can develop a list of actions to take prior to the next session. This list could be based on prior information taught as well as any new readings to be completed. The client could then reflect on the importance of using their tools to help organize and plan for higher-quality training.
3. At the beginning of the next session: The client can keep a monitoring chart that provides feedback about the consistency and volume of mental skills practice. The client can also be asked to reflect on how they feel the training is progressing, what they like, and what they dislike.
4. Monthly: Quizzes can be included on key concepts, both written and verbal, to ensure learned content and skills are being remembered. Questions can be asked in ways that challenge the client not only to remember the key information, but also to clarify ways the information can be used to improve performance and well-being.
5. Quarterly: Review of client monitoring charts to assess mental training improvement as well as how training, preparation, and application of mental training are affecting performance and well-being.

SUGGESTED READINGS

Driscoll, M. (2010). *Web-based training: Creating e-learning experiences*, Chichester: John Wiley.

Neff, R., & Garza, M. (2004). *Roadmap to the zone: Enhancing athletic performance*. Bloomington, IN: AuthorHouse Publishing.

Stodel, E., & Farres, L. (2000). Insights for delivering mental skills training over the web. *Journal of Excellence*, 6, 104–116.

Watson, J., Tenenbaum, G., Lidor, R., & Alfermann, D. (2001). Ethical uses of the internet in sport psychology: A position stand. *International Journal of Sport Psychology*, 32, 207–222.

Weinberg, R., Neff, R., & Jurica, B. (2012). Online mental training: making it available for the masses. *Journal of Sport Psychology in Action*, 3, 182–192.

REFLECTIVE QUESTIONS

1. How important do you feel it is to deliver improvement feedback to your client, and do you feel technology should play an integral role?
2. How do you feel about integrating neurofeedback into mental skills training? What do you like and what are your concerns?
3. Discuss the effectiveness of using a phone versus other technology to provide quality long-distance mental training.
4. How would you effectively implement assessment with distance-based clients?
5. What are some effective ways to deliver mental skills content to your clients using technology (e.g., one-on-one discussion, small-group discussion, lectures, reading, videos)?

REFERENCES

Branstrom R., Duncan L. G., & Moskowitz, J. T. (2011). The association between dispositional mindfulness, psychological well-being, and perceived health in a Swedish population-based sample. *British Journal of Health Psychology*, 16(2), 300–316.

Business Insider (2013, February 7). There will soon be one smartphone for every 5 people in the world. Retrieved from www.businessinsider.com/15-billion-smartphones-in-the-world-22013-2.

Corstorphine, E. (2006). Cognitive-emotional-behavioural therapy for the eating disorders: Working with beliefs about emotions. *European Eating Disorders Research, 14,* 448–461.

Duckworth, A. L., Grant, H., Loew, B., Oettingen, G., & Gollwitzer, P. M. (2011). Self-regulation strategies improve self-discipline in adolescents: Benefits of mental contrasting and implementation intentions. *Educational Psychology: An International Journal of Experimental Educational Psychology, 31*(1), 17–26.

Ellis, A. (2008). *Rational emotive behavior therapy.* In R. J. Corsini & D. Wedding (Eds.), *Current psychotherapies* (8th ed.; pp. 63–106). Belmont, CA: Thomson Brooks/Cole.

Guskey, T. R., & Gates, S. (1986). Synthesis of research on the effects of mastery learning in elementary and secondary classrooms. *Educational Leadership, 43,* 73–80.

Neff, R., & Frey, S. (2013). *Using mobile apps to enhance mental training effectiveness.* Paper presented at the annual conference for Applied Sport Psychology, New Orleans, LA.

Neff, R. S., Weinberg, R., & Jurica, B. (2010). The online mental trainer system: Making quality mental training available to the masses. Paper presented at the annual AASP Conference in Providence, RI.

Neff, R. S., Weinberg, R., & Jurica, B. (2011). Online mental training: Toward the vision of "sport psychology for all." Paper presented at the 2011 AASP Conference in Honolulu, HI.

PsychTests AIM, Inc. (2011, January 2). Emotional intelligence test. Retrieved from http://testyourself.psychtests.com/testid/3038.

Rosen, D. R., Carrier, L. M., & Cheever, N. A. (2013). Facebook and texting made me do it: Media-induced task-switching while studying. *Computers in Human Behavior, 29,* 948–958.

Sung, E., & Mayer, R. E. (2013). Online multimedia learning with mobile devices and desktop computers: An experimental test of Clark's methods-not-media hypothesis. *Computers in Human Behavior, 29,* 639–647.

Weinberg, R. S., & Gould, D. (2011). *Foundations of Sport and Exercise Psychology* (5th ed.). Champaign, IL: Human Kinetics.

Weinberg, R. S., & Williams, J. (2011). Integrating and implementing a psychological skills training program. In J. Williams (Ed.), *Applied sport psychology: Personal growth to peak performance* (pp. 347–377). Palo Alto, CA: Mayfield Press.

Weinberg, R., Neff, R., & Jurica, B. (2012). Online mental training: Making it available for the masses. *Journal of Sport Psychology in Action, 3,* 182–192.

Wilson, K., Gilbert, J., Gilbert, W., & Sailor, S. (2009). College athletic directors' perception of sport psychology consulting. *The Sport Psychologist, 23,* 405–424.

22 The Business of Performance Psychology
A Case Study

Erika Carlson and Robert S. Neff

There are approximately 79 graduate programs in the United States that are preparing students who want to work in the field of applied sport psychology. Once graduated, there are more options than ever for early professionals. Academia, the US military, and university athletic departments are common choices. As a field, it's great that we have a growing number of choices that offer job stability, financial security, and unique experiences to learn and grow as a sport psychology professional. For those adventurous souls who want to ride the entrepreneurial rollercoaster, there is another option: private practice. This option offers its own special risks and rewards. This chapter will highlight the case of "Cindy" as she makes the transition from graduate student to private practice owner and practitioner. While each person's journey into private practice is unique, there are steps that every professional needs to take. Cindy's experience exemplifies these steps and includes both the challenges and rewards of going into business for yourself.

BACKGROUND INFORMATION

This case will highlight Cindy's first year (start-up phase) of practice development and includes a 3–5-year plan to further business growth. Cindy represents many early professionals in the field of sport psychology who have earned a degree (master's or doctorate), have some basic experience, and are eager to start working with clients. Cindy's experience will also highlight some of the tough decisions that young entrepreneurs have to make on the road to being a successful applied sport psychology professional.

DESCRIPTION OF THE CASE

Cindy is a 28-year-old female (unmarried, no kids) who recently earned a master's degree in sport psychology. She is a former soccer player (played two years at a community college and then two years at a Division I program). She knew that she always wanted athletics to be part of her life, but wasn't sure what role in athletics she wanted to pursue. That is, until she took a sport psychology class at her community college. Very quickly, she knew that this was how she wanted to pursue her athletically minded career. A few years later, at the university she attended, Cindy took another sport psychology class. This class was much more theoretical and research oriented. It was interesting, but she was not as captivated as she was during the first class, which was about actually working with athletes. This second class helped her understand that what she really wanted was to do applied work. Therefore, it seemed to make sense to go into private practice. With this in mind, Cindy purposely chose a graduate program focused on applied practice. Upon graduation, Cindy had not only completed all of her coursework but also four internships with different sport and non-sport populations. She was feeling very accomplished, and was ready to "hang her shingle" and start her private practice. Despite all of her coursework and fieldwork experience, Cindy simply didn't know where to begin in terms of starting a business. Many questions came to mind that she didn't have the answers to: How do I pick a business name? What type of legal entity do I need? What is a legal entity? What, if anything, will it cost to get started? After all, it's a service-based business, isn't my cost my education? Where should I set up a shop? In an affluent community where there are many potential clients who can afford my service, but where I can't afford to live? Or, set up in a community that I can afford to live in and build a business there? How much money can I make in private practice? How much money do I *need* to make? The more she thought about it, the more overwhelmed she became. But Cindy was a resourceful problem solver, which is an excellent entrepreneurial trait, and so she began the work of learning how to start her dream business.

It was June, and Cindy had just graduated with her master's degree. She was ready to get to work, but starting a business felt overwhelming. Cindy was lucky to have some close family members who were also business owners. She consulted with them often and they provided her with guidance to put one foot in front of the other. Additionally, she read up on best practices for mental skills training and reviewed every business book and presentation on best practices in consulting that she could get her hands on (Jurica & Neff, 2013; Neff & Jurica, 2014; Neff & Weinberg, 2008). In order to get started, Cindy began by setting her priorities.

Her first priority was getting new clients. This would be the most important and most challenging part of her first year. Building relationships in her community with reputable organizations would help her build a solid reputation. She needed to put a lot of effort into making that happen. Best practices state that 25 percent of her time should be dedicated to building new business (Neff & Weinberg, 2008); however, Cindy felt she would need to put in much more during her first year. Studying these best practices, she learned that she must also create a series of tools to use with her clients. She would need to assess clients (initially and monthly) in a simple and reliable way. In addition, retention of clients would be important. Keeping clients working toward mastery and being able to show measurable improvement would be essential.

THEORETICAL FRAMEWORK/PHILOSOPHY

Like many practitioners with a similar educational path, Cindy primarily uses cognitive behavioral therapy (CBT) as the foundation of her work with athletes. Throughout her graduate school program and fieldwork experience, Cindy learned how to effectively apply skills and techniques to help athletes recognize and restructure their thinking patterns, manage their emotions, and learn skills such as visualization to help prepare, practice, and repeat skills and sequences in their sport. Cindy also uses motivational interviewing to help her clients establish appropriate goal plans, build self-awareness, and increase intrinsic motivation. She will not use psychological testing as she was not trained to use clinical inventories and most tests would be assessing issues outside of her scope of practice. She is confident she can assess her client's mental training needs in a non-formal assessment, just as she did in her fieldwork experiences. Cindy will also be on the look-out for clients who may need to be referred to a licensed clinical psychologist and will be prepared with a referral list of local psychologists.

NEEDS ASSESSMENT

After some deliberation, Cindy decided she would begin her business in the Dallas/Ft. Worth (DFW) area of Texas. It is both affordable and has affluent communities throughout the Metroplex. And, given that she has family there, it also had a built-in support system. Her biggest concern about setting up a private practice here was that there were already a few other sport psychology/mental training practices in the area. Is competition good or bad? Is there enough potential business to go around? Cindy was given advice to complete a SWOT analysis (see Table 22.1). Her research confirmed that the DFW area could easily sustain multiple practices. Cindy was also considering Chicago and Tampa, as each have a comparable cost of living. However, Tampa had a population of 350,000 and Chicago just under three million. Dallas in comparison boasted a population of 6.5 million with low cost of living *and* lots of potential clients. With the additional consideration of family in the area, Dallas made good sense. Thus, Cindy worked out a plan to move to Dallas in August.

INTERVENTION

Prior to her move in August, Cindy spent June and July laying as much ground work as possible for starting her business. The following sections will outline the steps she took to set up her business and prepare herself for applied practice.

Creating a Business Name and Legal Entity

The first step in officially starting her business was creating a name. Cindy wanted the business name to reflect her, but also to allow for possible growth in the future. Using her name only cutoff the possibility of hiring on other consultants in the future. Further, research on branding told her that her name should be in the business name. After a lot of thought she settled on Smith Mind Sports. The business name included her last name and as well as an indication of what her services provide. Cindy completed a fictitious business name search with her state and a domain name search (for her website) and found that her name was available for both. Thus, she registered her business name and purchased the domain name.

The next step was creating a legal entity, that is, determining the type of business ownership she would set up. Sole proprietor? Limited liability corporation? S-corporation? For a review and discussion of the various business types see Carlson and Pfenninger (2014). After much research into the pros (e.g., it's less expensive, fast and easy to set up, provides some tax breaks) and cons (e.g., less tax liability protection, convoluted tax filing, difficult to grow business), Cindy settled on sole proprietorship because it is the simplest and least expensive to set up and she doesn't (yet!) have assets to protect. She determined that it was a good place to begin and she could always change it to a corporation down the road.

Writing a Business Plan and Outlining Business Finances

Next on Cindy's to-do list is writing a business plan. This exercise would take up a significant amount of her next few months. She sought the advice of other business owners to help her

Table 22.1 Cindy's SWOT Analysis

Strengths	Available time to work on the business, enthusiasm Strong network, financial stability Support network, name recognition, diversity of experience
Weaknesses	One-person shop, lack of experience, weak network, unstable financially, no brand recognition (yet!) Unknown number of clients, marketing and networking in different worlds (double effort), limited time working on the business (too much time working in the business) Financial support for many consultants, more overhead, employees to support
Opportunities	Population of 6.5 million, 1 percent = 65,000 (plenty to go around!) Additional opportunity in the corporate world
Threats	Not able to convert potential clients to active clients, business development is too slow Overhead costs, double marketing efforts, limited time Larger-scale business has more resources for marketing and getting ideal consultants on projects

work through her plan. It's a challenging exercise as she has no experience as a business owner and therefore was finding it difficult to plan her business. With the help of colleagues, online resources and templates, Cindy used what she knew about the practice of sport psychology and applied that to the business plan. Creating her plan involved outlining the following: (1) defining the basic concept of the business and how it would operate; (2) outlining the leaders in the business, and their roles and experience; (3) analyzing potential clients, the market, and economic issues affecting the market; (4) defining services and completing a marketing plan; (5) analyzing the competition in the area; (6) developing an operations plan; (7) detailing revenue streams, client numbers, pricing, and expenses; and (8) predicting three to five years of revenue, expenses, and profits.

In the time period from June to August, Cindy continued reading and researching business start-ups. It is common business knowledge that an entrepreneur should have enough money saved to cover at least one year's worth (if not 18 months' worth) of expenses. This helps the entrepreneur to plan for the worst-case scenario. Whether or not to secure a loan is another important consideration. She would have to figure out exactly what she needed for initial costs. How much did she need to start the business? How much did she need to grow the business? Not only would she have to figure out what her expenses were, but also what her revenue would look like. Could she make it? What did she need in order to make it through year one? Would she need another part-time job?

Cindy assessed her year one start-up costs at about $11,000.00. Fresh out of graduate school, Cindy had $14K in savings and school loans totaling $42K. She had been deep in thought about how to best use her savings. Should she live off it while she builds her business, invest it in her business to cover costs, or use it pay off student loans to minimize expenses? Cindy, with the help of a friend who was an accountant, completed a financial statement (see Table 22.2).

Table 22.2 Cindy's Financial Statement (Years 1, 2, and 3)

	Calculation	*Year 1*	*Year 2*	*Year 3*
Revenue Items				
Revenue Stream 1 (Individual Consulting)	Number of clients × fee	$25,000	$30,000	$35,000
Revenue Stream 2 (Team Consulting)	Sum	$30,000	$35,000	$40,000
Revenue Stream 3 (Workshops)	Sum	$10,000	$12,500	$15,000
Revenue Stream 4 (Other)	Sum	$5,000	$7,500	$10,000
Total Income	Sum of revenue streams	$70,000	$85,000	$100,000
Cost of Services				
Assessment Costs	Sum of costs related to assessments given to clients	$2,000	$2,250	$2,500
Product Costs	Sums of costs related to products sold	$1,500	$1,750	$2,000
Consultant Fees/Salary	Either a lump sum salary or a percentage of consulting revenues	$35,000	$40,000	$45,000
Gross Income	Total income − cost of services	$31,500	$41,000	$50,500
Expense Items				
Office Rent	Sum (annual)	$0	$0	$6,000
Phone	Sum (annual)	$1200	$1200	$1200
Organization Dues	Sum (AASP, APA, etc.)	$400	$420	$440
Travel & Entertainment	Sum of business and entertainment travel receipts	$5,000	$7,500	$10,000
Advertising	Sum of invoices	$2,000	$3,000	$4,500
Other	Any other expenses the business incurs	$2,500	$3,000	$3,500
Pre-Tax Net Income	Gross income − all expenses	$20,400	$25,880	$24,860

Cindy decided to use her $14K for living expenses while she got her consulting business off the ground. She would be able to defer her student loan payments for three years, which helped to give her some breathing room on monthly expenses. She would minimize living expenses by having a roommate. The apartment would also serve as the headquarters for Smith Mind Sports (aka her home office). Cindy came to the conclusion that having a virtual office made more financial sense than having a brick-and-mortar office. She had it in her three-year plan to open a traditional office, but for now virtual was the right move. She also decided to get renter's insurance to protect her business-related items from theft or damage. Lastly, once Cindy arrived in Dallas, she opened a bank account for her business.

Operations

One of the biggest unknowns for Cindy was how to operate her practice. She had a lot of work to do in the start-up phase to get ready to "hang her shingle" and take on clients.

Fees. Her next task was to work on fees; Cindy struggled with this piece for a few reasons: (1) she had never charged for her services before so she did not know how to talk to people about her fees and it made her uncomfortable to do so; (2) she did not know how much to charge as a young professional; and (3) she wanted to help a lot of athletes so she hesitated to charge too much, but did not want to be seen as less valuable than the other practitioners in the DFW area. Cindy did thorough research to understand the range of fees other professionals in the area were charging. Again, Cindy had a lot of questions: How much do I charge? How do I package my services? When do I collect payment? What forms of payment can I/ should I take? How can I accommodate different financial needs of my clients? Do I put my prices on my website or will that scare potential clients away?

Cindy decided to package her services in groups of 4, 8, or 12 sessions (for a discussion of various fee models, see Carlson & Pfenninger, 2014). She would offer both a payment program to ease the sticker shock as well as offer an upfront full payment discount to encourage new clients to pay upfront and simplify her accounting. She assessed her competition in the area and decided to price herself on the lower/middle side of her competitors. This was a good compromise to help her earn a fair wage, be in a competitive position with her peers, and earn some solid cash flow with a limited number of clients. Also, her sales training taught her about pre-qualifying clients. That is, to separate out clients who are interested *and* can afford her services. Given that, Cindy decided to clearly post her pricing and packages on her site. This, she thought, would also ease up her conversations about money with clients. They would know what the prices were ahead of time so there should not be any surprises. Additionally, she could point potential clients to her "Services" page on her website so she could be sure they see her pricing prior to coming in for a consultation (sales) meeting.

Client agreements. After deciding upon her fees, the next step required delving into a bit more uncomfortable territory: outlining contract, consent form, and release of information agreements. In her graduate program, Cindy had to review some basic agreements for her internships. She collected each contract and spent an hour with a recommended business attorney to make sure she got this step right. With minimal cost (one hour with the attorney), Cindy was feeling very confident about her agreement forms.

Sales. Cindy needed to build confidence in talking about fees and services and develop a strong value statement to help sell her services. Her research led her to reject the idea of an MBA program (too costly and too much time), so instead she landed on an online sales program. The program provided Cindy with a stronger understanding of sales and helped her to design a structured yet simple sales presentation she could use with her potential clients. After all, regardless of the number of potential clients, she had to be able to convert them to active clients (i.e., get them to pay for her services) in order to sustain a business. This process was *the most* important part of getting cash flow into her new business.

Educational materials. In the period between September and December, Cindy spent time thinking through, reading through, reviewing, and researching all the mental training tools that she used in graduate school. Cindy decided that she would create a client workbook. She followed suggested practices (Weinberg & Gould, 2015) in order to determine what topics to include and create the order of her chapters. Then she outlined her educational pages, worksheets, and supplemental pages. She decided that her workbook would be an ebook. This would cut down on printing and materials and allow for easily making updates.

Marketing

As Cindy worked through her business plan, she created what she hoped to be a solid marketing plan. It would also guide her daily, weekly, and monthly marketing efforts, as well as guide her writing projects, which would be a great way for her to start building her personal "library" of articles and client tools.

Web design/technology. At this point in her young career, Cindy had already given her website some serious thought. In her graduate work, she had already started writing content for her site. She was tempted to take on the work of building the site herself ("How hard could it be?" "I've got time!" "It's too expensive to hire someone"), but after her online business course and talking with colleagues, Cindy came to the decision that the investment of a professional site builder was worth it. A professional site would be her number-one marketing tool; there was no room for sloppiness or poor design. Her research informed her that sites were fairly inexpensive to build ($1,000 upwards) and there were many potential designers that she could find through crowdsourcing to keep prices competitive. Further, she could build as she goes, only paying for what she really needed to get started and as her business grew her site could grow with her.

Another important consideration regarding her web presence was the realization that if people were going to find her, she was going to need to show up high in search engines. However, advanced search engine optimization (SEO) is costly. Although she understood the value of it, Cindy concluded that one of the start-up compromises she would have to make was to forgo paid SEO services. There were no-cost ways to manage SEO, and given her available time she would commit time to enhancing these no-cost options. Cindy worried that her more established competitors would have a big advantage here and she was probably right.

Social media. A final and important marketing consideration was her ability to captain her own social media presence. As a young professional who grew up on social media, the move to a more professional style of social media was doable. She immediately set up her Facebook, Twitter, and LinkedIn accounts and began following, promoting, and linking content. Cindy believed she had an advantage over her competition here, given her age and comfort level with social media.

Marketing plan. In order to effectively market herself and her business, Cindy outlined a marketing plan (see Table 22.3) and monthly marketing checklist (see Table 22.4).

Once cash flow stabilized she would run ads in a local sports magazine. This would be a direct line to her target audience, but would have to wait for now.

Networking

Networking is another "free" resource to maximize and also an incredibly important part of marketing. Cindy needed to research the local youth sports clubs and make a plan on how she would reach out and try to connect with them. With the DFW Metroplex area being as large as it was, there were many clubs. Prioritizing clubs by sport and competitive level seemed like a good way to get started. Since she is a former Division I soccer player, reaching out to soccer clubs would be her top priority. However, Cindy enjoys challenges and has an adventurous attitude and therefore was open to working with a variety of sports.

Table 22.3 Cindy's Marketing Plan

What	When
Club newsletter contribution	January, July, October
Magazine article contributions	Twice per month
Attend sport events (networking)	Once per month
In-house email list blasts	Once per month and special current news
Live Tweets and You Tube "big game" debriefs	When events happen
Ask for introductions from network	Twice per month

Table 22.4 Cindy's Monthly Marketing Checklist

Task	Timing
Post Facebook and Twitter content	At least 4 days/week
Respond to other's posts	At least 3 days/week
Create one video blog	Every other month
Post on my blog	At least 1/month
Contribute to article/blog/interview	Every other month
Send out announcements about posts, videos, articles, etc.	Monthly
Send out mental skills training tip	Monthly
Attend athlete networking event	At least 1/month
Reach out to new connection	Every other month
Reach out to existing connection	Every other week
Continuing education on business and marketing	At least 1/month

Cindy made a goal to dedicate ten hours per week to networking (huge effort, low cost), setting up meetings with coaches, physical therapists, directors of organizations, and board members of local sports clubs. She considered joining the Dallas Chamber of Commerce but decided to set that as a year two goal since there was cost involved. She also looked into Dallas Toastmaster's Clubs. This seemed reasonable as she could join month to month. A few months would give her some dedicated speaking practice, which is an important part of having a mental training business. She hoped it would also allow her to network with others in the club. Her last formal consideration was whether or not to join a local networking group. These groups get together weekly or monthly (depending on the group) and generally only one person per professional specialty is allowed. Fees are low and it's an excellent networking opportunity in her community. Thus, Cindy decided that this was an important part of her marketing plan.

REFLECTION

What Did Cindy Do Well?

Cindy did a good job of researching and organizing the start-up phase of her business. She read and studied business practices both in and out of sport psychology and was clear on what she needed to do (e.g., create materials, network, market, plan financials). She prioritized her tasks (#1 = acquire new clients) and made a financially informed decision about where to live and work. All of these steps increased her chance of success in her start-up phase. Cindy was also smart to do a SWOT analysis of her new area (DFW) so she had a better understanding of herself and her competition. Bottom line, Cindy did well with all of the research, planning, and no-cost business development she could do, given her financial constraints.

What Could Cindy Have Done Better?

Cindy was quite conservative with many of her decisions. If she was willing to tolerate more risk, Cindy could have given more consideration to a business loan to help her through the start-up phase. The loan would allow her to take reasonable steps to grow faster. For example, paid SEO would help get her higher in internet search engines, connecting her with more potential clients and opportunities. A brick-and-mortar office would enhance the perception of her professional image and give her a place to have private in-person meetings, which some clients prefer. Starting her business as a LLC would be ideal and would ensure the legal integrity of her business from the start. Upgrading down the road would be another step she would have to take to help secure her business in the future. Also, Cindy could have invested more into legal support, web design, and professional marketing materials early on, which could help guide her growth and help convert as many leads as possible to active clients.

What Are Cindy's Lessons Learned?

While taking on the responsibility of a loan can feel overwhelming to a young business owner with little to no business experience, the financial support needed to start a business and grow is important to consider. Some folks will have the advantage of having a bigger savings account or family help, but having some financial support allows the business owner to take the steps to increase the likelihood of success. If the practitioner can look at the financial investment as a continuation of the investment they made in their education, that may help it to seem less overwhelming. Ultimately, it takes money to make money.

SUGGESTED READINGS

Carlson, E., & Pfenninger, G. (2014). The business of sport, exercise, and performance psychology in the United States. In G. Cremades & L. S. Tashman (Eds.) *Becoming a sport, exercise, and performance psychology professional: A global perspective* (pp. 160–167). New York, NY: Routledge.

Carlson, E., & Rhodius, A. (2014). Do you need help? Build your support team and alliances. In J. Taylor (Ed.), *Practice development in sport and performance psychology* (pp. 125–140). Morgantown, WV: Fitness Information Technology.

Cheadle, C., Pfenninger, G., & Carlson, E. (2014). Infusing technology in sport, exercise, and performance psychology practice. In G. Cremades & L. S. Tashman (Ed.), *Becoming a sport, exercise, and performance psychology professional: A global perspective* (pp. 160–167). New York, NY: Routledge.

Collins, J., & Porras, J. (2004). *Built to last: Successful habits of visionary companies.* New York, NY: HarperCollins Publishers Inc.

Garland, D. S. (2011). *Smarter, faster, cheaper: Non-boring, fluff-free strategies for marketing and promoting your business.* Hoboken, NJ: John Wiley.

Gladwell, M. (2002). *The tipping point: How little things can make a big difference.* Boston, MA: Little, Brown and Company.

REFLECTIVE QUESTIONS

1. What key numbers in Cindy's SWOT analysis helped her determine that the Dallas/Ft. Worth Metroplex could sustain her business as well as those already in practice?
2. Based on the financial information given in Cindy's case, when does she need to be "cash flow positive" in order to stay in business?
3. Using Cindy's financial statement as a guide, plan out how many individual and team contracts Cindy needs to meet her financial commitments for year one.
4. What steps are most important for Cindy to take to help make her website generate as many leads as possible?

5. What compromises could Cindy make if she wanted to start off with a brick-and-mortar office rather than waiting until year three?
6. Which marketing technique will be most important for Cindy to focus on in year one? Why?

REFERENCES

Carlson, E., & Pfenninger, G. (2014). The business of sport, exercise, and performance psychology in the United States. In G. Cremades & L. S. Tashman (Eds.) *Becoming a sport, exercise, and performance psychology professional: A global perspective* (pp. 160–167). New York, NY: Routledge.

Jurica, B., & Neff, R. S. (2013). Building a private practice: A 21st century guide to equipping sport psychology consultants. Presented at the 2013 AASP Conference in New Orleans, LA. Retrieved from: https://docs.google.com/drawings/d/19vGY_ZpQ81evDWsPmrxOXrClknTh8LWtFKCDVku-WFSw/edit?pli=1.

Neff, R. S., & Jurica, B. (2014). Developing income streams for the full-time sport psychology consultant. Presented at the 2014 AASP Conference in Las Vegas, NV. Retrieved from: https://drive.google.com/file/d/0B0PFnvb6sLnsRkRlT0lKQkc0azA/view?pli=1.

Neff, R. S., & Weinberg, R. S. (2008) Best practice(s): Using the internet to build your applied business. Presented at the 2008 AASP Conference in Louisville, KY.

Weinberg, R. S., & Gould, D. (2015). *Foundations of sport and exercise psychology* (6th ed.). Champaign, IL: Human Kinetics.

23 The Business of Sport Psychology
Using an Online Web-Based Application at an Elite Soccer Academy

Peter Schneider

This chapter outlines my experience in securing an opportunity to provide sport psychology (SP) services to an elite soccer academy. It outlines the approach I took to prepare for this opportunity, the design and delivery of an intervention that combined face-to-face workshops with the use of technology, and ends with a reflection on the work done.

BACKGROUND INFORMATION

After presenting a workshop on using videos to assist athletes with imagery training at the German Association for Applied Sport Psychology to 25 young practitioners, I was approached by one of the participants. We spoke about our current involvement and interests in applied SP, and he mentioned his connections to a classmate currently working at an elite youth soccer academy. My own personal experience in soccer had involved a previous interview with another academy; however, this endeavor was unsuccessful as the club went with a more experienced candidate. Undeterred, I seized the opportunity to find another way into the world of elite soccer and contacted the individual. Through this contact I learned that he would be leaving his current club and that the academy would be searching for a new sport psychology consultant (SPC). He requested my CV and was able to arrange a meeting with the director, where I would be allowed to interview for the SPC position at the club and present my personal theories and approaches in psychological skills training (PST).

Preparing for the Interview

Combining the experience from the previous failed attempt to work with elite soccer players, it was crucial to reflect on a personal theoretical approach before answering any questions in the interview (Henriksen, Diment, & Hansen, 2011; Schneider, 2014). This helped to establish a solid base from which I could give confident and sport-relevant answers. Moreover, it is vital when speaking to soccer coaches and their directors to be able to speak in the vocabulary of the sport (Pain & Harwood, 2004). Having a deep understanding of one's personal theoretical approach helps to translate that theory into applicable topics that will have sport-specific meaning for the potential client. Soccer, in particular, is a sport that has been slow to adapt to the presence of SP and SPCs (Diment, 2014). Traditionally, PST programs have been conducted through the use of workshops and homework exercises, but have not always been successful in producing the desired long-term outcome (Pain & Harwood, 2004). Therefore, it has been suggested that teaching PST through an ecological and integrated approach could be more effective (Beswick, 2010; Diment, 2014). I approached the interview with this basic theoretical underpinning.

The Interview

In order to sell the importance of SP services, a direct line between the needs of the club and the services that could be provided needed to be established. As previously suggested, a soccer-vernacular was chosen when speaking with the director, and details about personal experiences, including those specific to soccer, were exchanged. This helped build a quick sense of rapport and trust, which is critical in the process between an SPC and his/her client (Andersen, 2000). Once the initial line of trust is established, questions about the needs of the club can be steered by the SPC.

The goal of this preliminary needs assessment was to identify broader issues which were important to the club. This was achieved through targeted questions that brought the specific use or purpose of a PST program into clearer light. Although questions can greatly differ depending on the exact scenario, it was important at the youth academy to direct the questions around the development of the player, as well as the culture and philosophy of the club. Some examples include: (1) What are the most important on- and off-field skills players need to learn? (2) How has PST been implemented in the past? Who was responsible? Was it effective? (3) What are the goals for this academy in the future and how does PST play a role in that future?

After hearing the answers to these questions, I was able to connect the PST services that can be offered directly to the needs the director had mentioned. This is in great contrast to my previous interview, where the director and I spoke about my personal skills and knowledge, rather than how I would be of value to the club's specific interests. Therefore, only after paraphrasing and clarifying a general needs assessment for the club, did I begin to lay out a possible plan for an intervention that would provide the U19 and U17 players of this club with an opportunity to learn and apply the psychological skills desired by the director.

During the interview, I mentioned that sales of smartphones have now passed those of computers (Cocotas & Blodget, 2012), and that more and more young people, including those in the aforementioned teams, are using mobile devices to learn, work, and play (Sung & Meyer, 2013). Further, it was imperative to utilize a system within the academy which would allow for a general introduction to what PST is, as well as a method to help better track each of the 40 players in the performance-based teams of the club (Weinberg, Neff, & Jurica, 2012).

DESCRIPTION OF THE CASE

The youth soccer academy is located in Germany and fields teams in the U19 and U17 top youth national leagues (Bundesliga), as well as U16 and U15 teams in their respective top regional leagues. Due to a mixture of personal interest and recommendation from the German Soccer Federation (DFB), there had already been a part-time SPC working in the academy for the past two years. Therefore, the coaches, sport director, and some of the players had previous exposure to an SPC and PST.

Although some time was spent with individual players and coaches of the U15 and U16 teams, this case will focus specifically on the PST intervention carried out with the U17 and U19 teams, or so-called "performance level" teams. Both teams comprised players from two different calendar years, and were a mixture of local players who had come up through the system as well as players recruited from all over the country. All players are required to complete some form of formal high-school education, and the great majority of them plan on playing soccer at some professional level in adulthood. A typical training week has seven practice sessions and one game. With the intense training schedule, players are expected to be highly organized in regard to their schooling and therefore are under high time pressure during the season.

NEEDS ASSESSMENT

The current needs, concerns, and interests of the soccer club were determined through two major methods. The first method involved consistent observation of practices, club-life, as well as day-to-day tasks undertaken by all members of the club. It was often the case that shadowing one coach throughout his or her whole day could reveal a lot about how they choose to plan their sessions, and allowed me to gain a holistic viewpoint. That is to say, I gained more insight than simply to see how a coach "coaches," but also how they speak to players and carry themselves around fellow staff both on and off the pitch. Perhaps another advantage of simple observation was that it allowed me to gain a broad perspective and avoid early conclusions. Once a few behaviors attracted my attention, they could then be targeted in future observations with a more structured approach. Further, the observations were not solely utilized for examining the players or coaches, but also how the support staff were represented and involved.

The second method used in the needs assessment was to have multiple informal interviews with team members and coaches, focusing on building rapport and teasing out possible deficits in performance. It was best to begin informally with coaches and players. Short, quick questions regarding topics other than the main sport helped to build rapport and trust between the SPC and the team members. A gradual shift from off-field topics to performance issues took place as trust was built, and soon enough more concrete questions could come from both the SPC and the players or coaches themselves. It is critical in a team setting to "win" a way into the team and allow the more serious topics to be brought up by the clients. While "patience is a virtue" may be a phrase that is true in everyday life, there is no place it is more true than when working with team athletes.

There were several key issues or themes drawn from the needs assessment at the soccer academy. First, many of the coaches and players had heard of or even worked with an SPC before; however, they were unsure exactly to what extent SP services could help their performance. Moreover, coaches at the U17 level desired to find a way to train and develop important development attributes and skills, such as self-regulation or understanding the importance of quality practice. Second, it was previously a challenge to provide SP education to the majority of the players, and as such only a few players who had shown great interest or had been selected by the staff received SP services. Finally, there was an inadequate structure used to set, evaluate, and monitor goals and improvement of individual players. In response to these issues, a long-term and theory-based intervention would need to be created and carried out.

THEORETICAL FRAMEWORK/PHILOSOPHY

A critical first step in any SP intervention is developing a theory-based framework and philosophy (Schneider, 2014). Andersen (2000) described that although a plethora of strategies and philosophies are both available and effective, it is imperative to determine which of these will be implemented to achieve an eventual behavioral change and thereby improved performance. Two theoretical underpinnings were the core for the present intervention: (1) a cognitive-behavioral approach (Beck, 2011); and (2) a holistic/ecologically based approach (Bateson, 1973; Bronfenbrenner, 1979; Henriksen, Stambulova, & Roessler, 2010). Furthermore, a consideration of McNamara, Button, and Collins' (2010a) Psychological Characteristics of Developing Excellence (PCDEs) was also used to design the intervention. What these approaches postulate, why they were chosen, and how exactly they were applied will be described in the following sections.

Cognitive-Behavioral Approach

The cognitive-behavioral approach is utilized by many SPCs throughout the world (Cremades & Tashman, 2014). At the core of this theory is the presumption that humans are able to change their behavioral actions through the recognition of one's perceptions of past consequences (Beck, 2011). Although simplistic, the idea that humans can illogically and irrationally perceive the causes of past consequences can be no small revelation for some. For example, a player may believe he will perform poorly against a specific opponent because he experienced a poor performance against this particular opponent in the past. He attaches a belief that his poor performance is a result of this past event, thereby causing a perceived loss of control over his current and future actions.

Out of this approach the psychologist Albert Ellis (1962) developed the A–B–C model, where A stands for Activating Event, B for Beliefs, and C for Consequence. Utilization of this approach in the current case consisted of, for example, players being confronted with new knowledge that contains a direct and logical transfer to their past experiences on the field – both in practice and in game situations. Through targeted questioning and discussion with the athletes, players were pushed to draw conclusions about their current beliefs and perceptions of past consequences, and encouraged to apply new mental techniques. The end goal provided them with the perception of control of their own development (i.e., goal-setting) or emotional state (i.e., breath control).

Holistic/Ecologically Based Approach

Vital to understanding a behavior is understanding the context in which that behavior is performed (Gill, 2001). Therefore, no intervention is complete without viewing each individual as a system within their environment (Bateson, 1973). The applied practitioner must recognize that in order to achieve change, the athlete – and specifically the athlete's perceptions or behaviors – cannot be examined as completely separate parts from their environment. This includes both internal factors, such as genetic predispositions, as well as external factors, such as teammates or training conditions.

A broader, more expansive view of the environmental layers that can affect an athlete's cognitions and behavior are demonstrated in Bronfenbrenners's (1979) bioecological model. This model demonstrates four contexts in which a person exists: (1) microsystem – where individuals spend the greatest amount of time, such as their own peer group or team; (2) mesosystem – where separate microsystems interact, which in the sport context might be the mixture of multiple teams in one club; (3) exosystem – influences which do not directly affect individuals, but rather through external interactions, such as fans or other teams in the sport context, may cause indirect consequences; and (4) macrosystem – a country or state, focusing on the greater shared values or cultures of that environment. The cultural importance of soccer in Germany, the particular passion and expectations of fans at the club, as well as the values and beliefs held within the youth teams all make the intervention feasible. Moreover, Henriksen and colleagues (2010) demonstrated how through broader environmental influences positive and long-term behavioral change can be achieved.

PCDEs and Increasing Self-Awareness

When examining youth athletes attempting to achieve success at the adult level, MacNamara and colleagues (2010) uncovered a variety of characteristics that successful athletes have (i.e., PCDEs). They proposed that athletes should have several psychological attributes (i.e., commitment/self-determination, be communicative, an understanding of what it takes to succeed, and self-belief), as well as skills (i.e., goal-setting, focus/distraction control, quality practicing, coping strategies, realistic self-evaluation, and using imagery).

Vital to the concept of PCDEs is that they are not genetic traits, but rather are a mixture of a trainable mindset and skills set. All of the aforementioned attributes described can be built through proper appraisal of hard work and celebrating struggle (Dweck, 2006), which removes focus from outcomes and puts the athlete's concentration onto the process. A major element in changing or improving PCDEs is a person's ability to be self-aware and self-regulate. Zimmermann's (2000) self-regulated learning theory outlined the cyclical way in which new skills and traits are built (i.e., reflection via planning, self-monitoring, and evaluation). Moreover, self-regulatory skills themselves can be learned and are ideal for youth elite athletes looking to achieve performance excellence (Cleary, Platten, & Nelson, 2008; Jonker, Elferink-Gemser, & Visscher, 2011).

INTERVENTION

The combination of these theoretical underpinnings provided the basis and direction for the planned intervention. It was decided that a form of web-based technology, the MentalApp®, would be utilized in conjunction with team workshops in order to: (1) create or increase awareness of current thoughts and behavior in their sport; (2) create a welcoming environment for SP by involving and educating all members of the team, the coaches, and staff; and (3) increase self-regulatory skills. The intervention was completed over a period of six months, involving players and coaches from the U17 and U19 teams as well as the academy's sport director. Initially, all players from both teams were invited to an introductory seminar. The seminar began with a short introduction of myself by the sport director, as well as his personal thoughts on the importance of mental training techniques in the development of soccer players. Then, I took over the seminar and gave a short PowerPoint presentation outlining the purpose and goals of using the MentalApp®. Players were directed to take out their cellphones, to download the application onto their phone, and sign in with a specific access code. The seminar finished with players watching the first video, which describes in detail some of the features of the application, and a short discussion about how the players felt this could benefit them.

Although the director and coaches may have been in positive agreement about the importance of SP skills, the "selling" process to the players had only just begun. Convincing 15- to 18-year-olds to sacrifice and invest some of their time, whether alone or during practice, to learn and apply mental training skills was no easy task. At this early stage, it was important to connect the in-depth needs assessment performed over the past month with the skills and knowledge that could be gained by this intervention. To do this, I cited specific examples from practice or games where players spoke of high anxiety or a loss of focus. This, in combination with the consistent support of the coaches, was the key during the first session in motivating the players to try something new.

MentalApp®

The MentalApp® application provides SP education through short videos and audio clips that are divided into five levels: motivated, calm, confident, focused, and carefree. Each level is then divided into three sections, each describing a different aspect of the SP construct. Furthermore, these sections contain a "learn" section, where the user receives information about the topic, and a "practice" section, where users are provided information with how to apply the previously demonstrated topics. A monitoring chart in the MentalApp® is used both by the coaches and players to keep track of the players' daily and weekly progress. Goals are automatically generated within the application as the athlete completes the levels, but can be edited by the player, coach, or SPC as desired. Additionally, the monitoring chart allows the athlete to leave comments on specific goals, providing possible explanations or further information that can be reviewed later. How the levels were presented during the team workshops and how the monitoring chart was utilized is discussed below.

Level 1: Motivation

Over the next three weekly meetings with the U17 and U19 players, we discussed the three sections of level one. The first major topics included intrinsic motivation, goal-setting, and roadblocks. Intrinsic motivation was discussed with one simple question: "Why?" I wanted to know why these players were here, why they were so motivated to play soccer, and why they would likely be motivated to play professional soccer in the future.

The second topic on motivation revolved around proper goal-setting and building a pathway to an ultimate goal. After learning the principles and types of goals, players were asked to draw up a personal goal for the season and have this goal rated on the SMARTS criteria by a teammate. The next instruction was to work backwards from the season goal to the present day, thereby creating a path to their ultimate goal though performance and process goals. Following this session, the players' current goals were put into the monitoring chart and they were expected to log into the application and check off the daily goals they had set for themselves.

The final topic in motivation revolved around roadblocks for the athletes. Instead of meeting in a classroom, players were put into various competitions during one practice session. These competitions included relay races or small-sided games, and all of them had one thing in common: one team was obviously disadvantaged. Frustrations mounted and players began to complain, first with the coaches and then with each other. We spoke about the roadblocks they had just experienced in these games and the strategies they had used to overcome them. We then connected this experience with the goals we had set, and discussed how there will always be roadblocks, but it is those who utilize coping strategies to deal with them that are successful.

Level 2: Calm

The second level of the program includes information about activation levels and strategies on how to regulate one's emotions. During these sessions, several theories of motivation including Drive Theory, the Yerkes–Dodson Model, and the Individual Zone of Optimal Functioning (IZOF) were introduced. Players were asked to discuss at least two strong performances from the current season and the emotions they attached to these performances. Without going into great detail, we tried to determine which players needed to be calmer, more fired up, or somewhere in the middle to achieve their best performance.

After determining a productive activation level for each player, the teams wrote on a whiteboard known strategies they could use to help regulate their activation. Once they ran out of ideas, I introduced two methods: regulated breathing and progressive muscle relaxation (PMR). To demonstrate the importance of regulated breathing, I brought in a former professional player from the club, who spoke on the importance of controlling one's inhale–exhale ratio. We practiced this ratio, and players were encouraged to practice further at home. In addition, a PMR session led by me was initiated on regeneration days to help players recover from games. A weekly self-regulated PMR session was added to the players' monitoring charts.

Level 3: Confident

In the third level, the main focus of the weekly sessions was learning and applying visualization techniques. I divided imagery's applications into three themes: emotional regulation, learning new techniques and tactics, and building self-efficacy. The first theme was a simple transition from the previous level. We spent at least one session imagining a "dream trip" to a relaxing beach and another one visiting a fiery volcano. The intention was to demonstrate how simply picturing such images can have a physiological effect on their heart rate.

To demonstrate how players can learn new techniques or tactics, I spent time filming certain drills at practice as well as working with the coaches to find specific tactical scenes from recent games. Players were confronted with technical miscues, given instructions from a coach on how to perform the skills correctly, and asked to imagine themselves performing the skill correctly. Tactical imagery was taught during a normal video session, in which players were given a piece of paper with a soccer field on it, and had to draw out where they were on the field in the video.

Building self-efficacy involved asking the players to imagine successful soccer actions during a game and finally walking off the pitch from their next game as winners. Players were asked to not only imagine themselves, but also the stadium, the fans, and the opponent. A goal to use imagery for improving a technique, a tactic, or to build self-efficacy twice a week was set and put into the monitoring chart of the players.

Level 4: Focus

During level four we covered two important mental skills: self-talk and routines. Players were asked to take examples of self-talk from the previous practices and games, or thoughts that occur often during performance. We examined the thoughts in a seminar, determining if their self-talk focuses on the past, present, or future, if it is just a perception or reality, and if it is helping or harming their performance. To demonstrate routines, we went back out onto the soccer pitch, this time using a classic high-pressure situation: the penalty kick. Two teams were created, and a physical-fitness penalty was set by the coach if a player were to miss his penalty. After a first round of shooting, the players were asked about their routines leading up to the shot. Did they have one at all? What kind of thoughts did they notice? How did they think a routine might help them be more automatic? A second round of shooting was performed, and this time each player was allowed to take his time to develop his own routine.

Level 5: Carefree

In the final level, there was one major theme: self-awareness. During these sessions, players were given a chance to write a journal about their performances either during practice or games from the previous week. The focus of the journal was on their emotions, their cognitions, and what strategies they were applying to reach an optimal and consistent psychological level. Through this self-evaluation, players were given room to develop personal strategies and adapt their knowledge to their own individual needs. Our discussions involved an evaluation of the intervention process and what topics were still of interest moving forward.

REFLECTION

The aforementioned intervention is described in its pristine form. That is to say, this is how the intervention was planned and carried out with a good deal of success; however, the limitations and true outcomes should also be presented. To begin on a positive note, it can be said that a pre–post measurement of knowledge and application of mental skills techniques did show at least some improvement in all players. All players of the U17 and U19 teams had knowledge regarding SP constructs and their applications that they did not have before. The greater problem, however, was that only around 25–30 percent of the players were still consistently using the techniques and at certain points almost 50 percent were not completing their goals put forth in the application.

Injuries, Sickness, Call-Ups, and Test Games

The simple fact that players were missing scheduled meetings caused issues with player involvement. There was not a strategy in place to compensate for when players missed sessions, and often when a player fell behind in watching the videos, he also lost motivation to catch-up and simply became an observer rather than a true participant during the following sessions. Providing a partner or offering a make-up session could have helped to alleviate this issue.

Access to Wireless Internet

As simple as it may seem, many of the players did not have access to wireless internet and were therefore unable to stream the videos once they had run out of data on their phones. Although the videos were short, they still can eat up cellular data quickly, especially for teenagers who may have a strict maximum. For a future intervention involving the MentalApp® or other technology, access to quality internet for players should be considered.

Language Barriers

As all videos in the MentalApp® are in English, it was difficult, especially for the U17 players, to understand the concepts presented in the videos. Due to this, much time during sessions was spent re-explaining the concepts in German. Grouping players who speak English better with those who struggle could help, or providing subtitles in the videos might be another solution.

SUGGESTED READINGS

Henriksen, K., Stambulova, N., & Roessler, K. K. (2010). A holistic approach to athletic talent development environments: A successful sailing milieu. *Psychology of Sport and Exercise, 11*, 212–222.

Jonker, L., Elferink-Gemser, M. T., & Visscher, C. (2011). The role of self-regulatory skills in sport and academic performances of elite youth athletes. *Talent Development & Excellence, 3*(2), 263–275.

Weinberg, R., Neff, R., & Jurica, B. (2012). Online mental training: Making it available for the masses. *Journal of Sport Psychology in Action, 3*, 182–192.

REFLECTIVE QUESTIONS

1. How can modern technology be combined with the use of an SPC? Who plays a role in using the technology?
2. What topics should an SPC focus on during an interview with a sports club in order to deliver a positive impression?
3. What strategies should the SPC develop in order to deal with roadblocks during an intervention?
4. How do we create and support an environment to increase self-awareness and self-regulation among athletes and coaches?
5. Why is it important to create self-regulation?

REFERENCES

Andersen, M. (2000). *Doing sport psychology.* Champaign, IL: Human Kinetics.

Bateson, G. (1973). *Steps to an ecology of mind: Collected essays in anthropology, psychiatry, evolution and epistemology.* London: Paladin, Granada.

Beck, J. S. (2011). *Cognitive behavior therapy: Basics and beyond* (2nd ed.). New York, NY: Guilford Press.

Beswick, B. (2010). *Focused for soccer.* Champaign, IL: Human Kinetics.

Bronfenbrenner, U. (1979). *The ecology of human development.* Cambridge, MA: Harvard University Press.

Cleary, T. J., Platten, P., & Nelson, A. (2008). Effectiveness of the self-regulation empowerment program with urban high school students. *Journal of Advanced Academics, 20*, 70–107.

Cocotas, A., & Blodget, H. (2012). The future of mobile. *Business Insider.* Retrieved from: www.businessinsider.com/the-future-of-mobile-deck-2012-3?op=1&IR=T.

Cremades, J. G., & Tashman, L. S. (2014). *Becoming a sport, exercise, and performance professional: A global perspective.* New York, NY: Taylor & Francis.

Diment, G. M. (2014). Mental skills training in soccer: A drill-based approach. *Journal of Sport Psychology in Action, 5*(1), 14–27.

Dweck, C. S. (2006). *Mindset: The new psychology of success.* New York, NY: Random House.

Ellis, A. (1962). *Reason and emotion in psychotherapy.* Secaucus, NJ: Lyle Stewart.

Gill, D. L. (2001). Feminist sport psychology: A guide for our journey. *The Sport Psychologist, 15,* 363–372.

Henriksen, K., Diment, G., & Hansen, J. (2011). Professional philosophy: Inside the delivery of sport psychology service at Team Denmark. *Sport Science Review,* 1–2, 5–21.

Henriksen, K., Stambulova, N., & Roessler, K. K. (2010). Holistic approach to athletic talent development environments: A successful sailing milieu. *Psychology of Sport and Exercise, 11*(3), 212–222.

Jonker, L., Elferink-Gemser, M. T., & Visscher, C. (2011). The role of self-regulatory skills in sport and academic performances of elite youth athletes. *Talent Development & Excellence, 3*(2), 263–275.

MacNamara, Á., Button, A., & Collins, D. (2010). The role of psychological characteristics in facilitating the pathway to elite performance. Part 1: Identifying mental skills and behaviors. *The Sport Psychologist, 24,* 52–73.

Pain, M. A., & Harwood, C. G. (2004). Knowledge and perceptions of sport psychology within English soccer. *Journal of Sport Sciences, 22*: 813–826.

Schneider, P. (2014). Setting up a business in sport and performance psychology: A German perspective. In J. G. Cremades & L. S. Tashman (Eds.), *Becoming a Sport, exercise, and performance psychology professional: A global perspective* (pp. 178–185). New York, NY: Routledge.

Sung, E., & Mayer, R. E. (2013). Online multimedia learning with mobile devices and desktop computers: An experimental test of Clark's methods-not-media hypothesis. *Computers in Human Behavior, 29,* 639–647.

Weinberg, R., Neff, R., & Jurica, B. (2012). Online mental training: Making it available for the masses. *Journal of Sport Psychology in Action, 3*(3), 182–192.

Zimmerman, B. J. (2000). Attaining self-regulation: A social cognitive perspective. In M. Boekaerts, P. R. Pintrich, & M. Zeidner (Eds.), *Handbook of self-regulation* (pp. 13–39). San Diego, CA: Academic Press.

24 Lessons Learned from the Seasoned Practitioner

A Case Study of an Irish Elite Amateur Golfer

Mark J. Campbell and Aidan P. Moran

Golf is a psychologically demanding game for at least three reasons (Moran, 2012). First, it is an untimed sport so golfers have to be prepared to play for as long as it takes (often up to five hours) to complete a round or match. Unfortunately, many club-level and leisure golfers fail to master this challenge and allow themselves to become upset at the apparently slow play of those ahead of them. Naturally, such frustration usually hampers golfers' performance. Second, golf is a demanding sport mentally because players have to take full responsibility for their own performance on the course. Unlike their counterparts in team games, such as soccer or hockey, golfers cannot be substituted if they are playing poorly. Interestingly, some golfers try to evade taking responsibility for their performance by making excuses. For example, they may blame course conditions, their clubs, the weather, and/or the balls they are using. In this regard, an old adage in sport psychology is relevant: "Winners are workers – only *losers* make excuses." Third, the stop–start nature of golf poses a major challenge for players' concentration. Thus, only a fraction of the duration of a game of golf is actually devoted to hitting the ball. Typically, the remainder of the time is spent walking, talking, looking for balls, regretting mistakes, becoming angry or frustrated, and struggling with one's concentration. This disjunction in golf between "playing time" and "thinking time" may explain why Sam Snead, who won a record 82 Professional Golfers' Association (PGA) tournaments, once remarked that *thinking* was the biggest problem in the game. To summarize, golf is demanding mentally because it is an untimed, individual, and discontinuous sport. In view of these issues, golfers are increasingly interested in seeking help and support from psychologists.

Golf in Ireland has a long and proud history (Redmond, 1997). The country has produced many champions, and recent years have seen a surge in the number and quality of amateur and professional golfers. To illustrate, four Irish golfers have captured nine "Major" championships between them in the past eight years. One of these players is the current world number-one player, Rory McIlroy. The Golfing Union of Ireland (GUI), the amateur governing body for men's golf, has a well-established comprehensive coaching and high-performance program in place for young golfers from the ages of 12 and up. This program provides coaching expertise and sport science support and in some instances psychological support. The first author currently occupies the role of team sport psychologist to one of the GUI's provincial teams.

Against this background, the present chapter outlines an ongoing, two-year working relationship with an elite amateur Irish golfer. Psychological consultations, interventions, end of season reviews, and approach to provision are detailed, as well as the theoretical framework from which we draw in the application of psychological principles. Importantly, reflection on the process and provision allows for a detailed lessons learned type of approach, which should be of interest to readers.

BACKGROUND INFORMATION

Carl (pseudonym) is a 34-year-old male elite amateur golfer. He has represented Ireland and his provincial team multiple times, won two major amateur golf championships, and currently competes both nationally and internationally on the amateur circuit. Carl contacted one of the authors initially to work with him for a block of three sessions in the winter of 2012. Stemming from these initial sessions, a professional working relationship was established. This relationship resulted in a collaboration, which has continued to date and has comprised 11 face-to-face meetings and approximately 20 phone/Skype sessions over the course of two years.

At this point, some background information on the practitioners may be helpful. One of the coauthors of this chapter – Aidan Moran (School of Psychology, University College Dublin) – has accumulated over 20 years of applied sport psychology experience in a variety of different settings with some of Ireland's leading athletes and teams (see Moran, 2014). A former official psychologist to the Irish Olympic Squad, he has chaired the Irish Institute of Sport's Professional Quality Assurance Program (PQAP) Committee. The other coauthor – Mark Campbell (Department of Physical Education & Sport Sciences, University of Limerick) – is the founding chair of the Division of Sport, Exercise, and Performance Psychology within the Psychological Society of Ireland, the professional organization for psychologists in this country. He is also a professional member of the Irish Institute of Sport, and in that capacity provided psychological support to Irish Sport Council "carded" athletes. In addition, he has worked with athletes and teams for over ten years and is currently the official psychologist to a number of elite amateur golf teams in Ireland. He is a former professional golfer and has represented Ireland at the amateur international level. Both authors are registered psychologists with the Psychological Society of Ireland.

DESCRIPTION OF THE CASE

Carl made contact with one of the authors because he had gone four years without a win after a breakthrough initial victory in a national major championship. Not surprisingly, at the time of contact, Carl was struggling with his confidence. In his view, he had spent a lot of time in training and practice but had not reaped any tangible rewards for all of his efforts. Additionally, he mentioned a growing inability to concentrate (or, in his words, "focus") for any sustained period of time in practice or in practice rounds. Accordingly, he often felt that he was just "going through the motions" in his golf game. To complicate matters, Carl's other career – his "real job" – was starting to become more and more demanding; at this time, he had a dilemma born of competing interests (i.e., his paid employment versus his sporting career). On the one hand, his job was increasingly successful and rewarding – which gave him great satisfaction. On the other hand, however, his golf game was suffering and he had been deselected from the national panel. Naturally, he was worried that he would not be able to regain his place in the squad. Another issue that concerned Carl was the low age profile of his competitors – with the implication that time was running out for him if he wanted to compete at the highest level in the amateur golf game.

As a result of the issues outlined above, Carl described himself as feeling a bit "like a dinosaur" on the golf teams and provincial panels to which he had belonged. Naturally, he had begun to question his motives for pushing toward selection. However, Carl was desperate to regain his form. He was also unhappy with his current coach and selector practices, and he thought that his age profile was starting to count against him in terms of panel and team selection. Finally, Carl admitted to no longer enjoying the game and the cut-and-thrust of elite-level amateur competition.

THEORETICAL FRAMEWORK/PHILOSOPHY

Effective sport psychology consultation is about increasing awareness and empowering performers (Hemmings & Holder, 2009). This is the primary principle underlying our consultancy work. There are three strands to this approach. First, the intervention model we employ is an athlete-centered model. Second, it is based on the Boulder Science-Practice Model, which crosses several applied domains including clinical psychology (Comas-Diaz, 2006). This model enables psychologists to utilize empirical research to influence their applied practice, while simultaneously allowing their experiences during applied practice to shape their future research questions. So, research can inform best practice and best practice in action can inform future research in the area. Last, the applied practice has a pragmatic approach based upon our experiences in the high-performance environment. These experiences (Olympic Games, National Championships, and advising professional and elite amateur teams) have helped us to understand the complexities of the high-performance environment and the role of organizational culture in sport (see also Wagstaff, Fletcher, & Hanton, 2012), and have also highlighted the needs of athletes/coaches for long-term support.

With an athlete-centered model, the consultant's role is beyond that of psychological skills training and instead focuses on *empowering* clients by equipping them not only with a mental skills toolbox but also with a keen awareness of *how* and *when* to employ these tools. In our view, an effective consultation experience involves progressively increasing client independence and self-reliance (Andersen, 2000; Campbell & Moran, 2014). Theoretically, this process is grounded in research in two key areas – self-regulation (SR) and metacognition (Brick, MacIntyre, & Campbell, 2014, 2015; MacIntyre, Igou, Campbell, Moran, & Matthews, 2014). Put simply, the constructs of SR and metacognition refer to people's knowledge and monitoring of, and ability to exert strategic control over, their own mental processes (Kitsantas & Kavussanu, 2011). To begin with, "*metacognitive knowledge*" involves people's declarative knowledge ("knowing that") and beliefs about how their minds work. In sport, this may involve athletes' belief about their concentration system – such as that it resembles a shower which one can turn on or off as one requires (Moran, 2012). Second, "*metacognitive monitoring*" refers to people's ability to check or reflect on some aspect of their thinking. For example, athletes might check from time to time that their mind is relaxed during a competitive event. Finally, "*metacognitive control*" denotes any strategy that a person uses in attempting to regulate and/or improve his or her skills or performance. For example, athletes might deliberately switch their focus of attention from external factors onto their breathing when they begin to feel tired during a marathon.

In summary, our approach combines a theory-led, evidence-based practice model which draws on practice-based evidence where appropriate. We typically, but not always, employ an integrated model (with coaches and other stakeholders involved), whereby the athletes' *needs* (e.g., for personal growth and development) rather than their performance are at the forefront of the process.

NEEDS ASSESSMENT

The aim of the first three sessions (conducted by one of us, Mark Campbell) was to establish trust with Carl. Building on this trust, I sought to understand the athlete's experience within elite-level golf competition. This understanding was primarily concerned with the athlete's psychological approach to his sport. In addition to a series of interviews with the athlete to establish relevant needs, goals, and knowledge, I used the Test of Performance Strategies (TOPS; Thomas, Murphy, & Hardy, 1999) during the early phases when I worked with the client. Carl completed the TOPS at the beginning and end of a golf season and so had a comparison of his own scores for practice and competition both pre- and post-season and also a comparison to an average elite athlete test score (comparisons based on published results; see Hardy, Roberts, Thomas, & Murphy, 2010). In Figures 24.1 and 24.2, we provide a graphical illustration of these scores and comparisons.

The TOPS profile indicated that Carl had scored relatively poorly on concentration control and also on negative thinking and emotional control. Comments from interviews and observation of golf performances substantiated these findings. Following these early findings, I was keen to examine the training and practice patterns that Carl was currently undertaking.

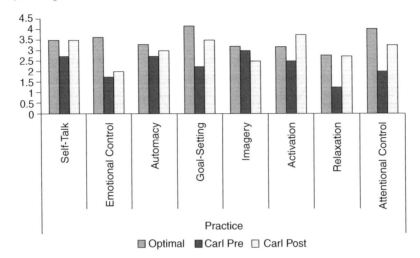

Figure 24.1 Sample TOPS Scores for Practice for Carl Pre- and Post-Season 1

One of my interests as a sport psychologist working with golfers is the efficacy of practice and training. In our experience, many elite golfers' practice patterns are not as effective as they should be and this can hamper their performance in two ways. First, ineffective practice may not provide the golfer with the skills needed to be successful in competition. Second, effective practice should enable the golfer to build confidence, emotional control, and greater self-regulation of their learning and subsequent performance. In Carl's case, he appeared to "mind-lessly" practice by hitting countless balls on a driving range and he reported to me that he would judge a training session solely on the notion of how he was swinging the club during a particular session. Again, it was my impression that Carl was not affording himself any time to monitor his improvement, examine his feedback, and reinforce his learning.

Carl was given feedback regarding the self-rated scores that were lower than the elite average. For practice, the following feedback was given to him:

- **Emotional control.** Something to definitely pay attention to going forward. I think if you can structure your training and practice with good goal-setting throughout, this will lead to better emotional control and satisfaction with how the training goes.

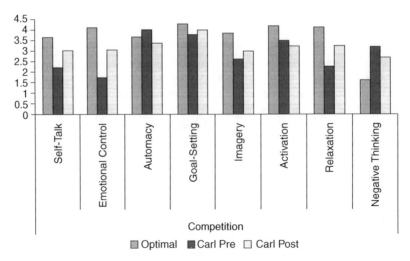

Figure 24.2 Sample TOPS Scores for Competition for Carl Pre- and Post-Season 1

- **Goal-setting.** This is a big area that we can target for improvement and I would encourage you to write down how you think you could set challenges and goals around practice and training. Then we can have a really insightful chat about strategies for you going forward.
- **Imagery.** Depending on what you are trying to do in practice, then you can and should be trying to incorporate more imagery into your pre-shot routine (i.e., see the shot in your mind before you hit it and/or feel the shot and/or hear the shot).
- **Attentional control.** Speaks for itself too. Again, good structure and goals/challenges should alleviate this and get you much more focused and efficient in your practice. Happy to chat but have a think in the meantime and bring some ideas to the conversation.

Carl was also given feedback regarding the self-rated scores that were lower than the elite average for competition. The following feedback was given to him:

- **Self-talk.** This score has lowered from practice, which means that you speak to yourself less in competition. Not sure if this is a good thing as it depends on the content of your self-talk (i.e., whether you encourage yourself or are critical to yourself). Experts' average seems to stay the same or increase slightly. In other words, you are your own best coach and motivator and so should be doing very similar things in practice and competition.
- **Emotional control.** Similar score to practice above. Something to think about working on in the near future. Happy to chat further when you have considered this.
- **Goal-setting.** A big improvement here, but still a little short of the mark. Consider process, performance, as well as outcome goals. Happy to chat further.
- **Imagery.** Use of marginally more imagery in competition. Something to target.
- **Negative thinking.** A little high and probably very related to your emotional control.

Following on from the TOPs assessments and based upon some of the findings, notably Carl's reporting of hindered emotional control in practice (see Figure 24.1) and competition settings (see Figure 24.2), mood profile assessment was initiated (POMS; see Figure 24.3) to monitor and make Carl more aware of his emotional and mood-related states. The mood profiling was undertaken on a more regular basis with Carl and he was encouraged to fill out the mood profile before and after a competitive round. Again, the comparison for Carl was his mood state before and after competition and also to the classic athletic iceberg shape mood profile reported in the literature (see Beedie, Terry, & Lane, 2000, for example).

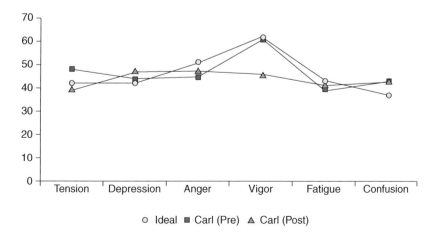

Figure 24.3 Sample Profile of Mood State for Carl Pre- and Post-Competitive Round

The profile was presented to Carl along with the following feedback:

> Your profile looks good, Carl, with the exception of (i) your "vigor" score post round; (ii) your depression score (post round); and (iii) your tension score pre-round. The mood scales are changeable but noticing some of your self-rated moods is an important first step to seeing what areas are working for you and some that may require some work. *You have the ideal "iceberg" shape to your profile pre tee-off* just maybe not scoring high enough on vigor and more lowly on fatigue (but this may be because you filled this out after your round). Again this is a state measure and may be based on your warm-up or finish to your round. Keeping stats and reflecting on three key questions post round may be very helpful with lessening confusion and increasing awareness.

> 1. What worked?
> 2. What didn't work?
> 3. What can I do better?

> Your depression score is slightly too high. Be cautious because a depression score in this range clearly has the potential to impede performance. Research has shown that depressed mood tends to reduce levels of vigor and increase levels of anger, confusion, fatigue, and tension, which are not associated with good performance.

> The following strategies can be very productive in decreasing mood profiles higher than they should be for depression or confusion:

> *   Try to address the cause of your feelings
> *   Put your feelings into perspective to recognize the situation in a broader context
> *   Try to control your thoughts so that they are more positive

INTERVENTION

The aim of the intervention was twofold. First, in line with our philosophy, it was to develop greater meta-cognitive awareness within Carl. Through greater awareness, he could then develop greater self-confidence and have more positive emotional experiences. Second, we wished to equip him with the mental skills he required to improve his cognitions concerning golf performances, specifically so that he could concentrate more effectively and improve his thinking on the golf course by utilizing appropriate types of self-talk.

Through the interviews with Carl, it was apparent that he was very outcome focused and had a very narrow view of what constituted success (e.g., winning an event or making a team). His evaluation of his performances both in practice and competition were narrowly focused on specific results or specific golf swings. From our discussions, it was apparent that he was unsure of alternative ways of gauging success. Additionally, Carl reported getting moody and angry at the slightest dip in form in practice and in competition. He found himself becoming more and more frustrated and angry during and after practice as well as during and after competitions. As a result of some of this information and discussions, one of the intervention sessions revolved around goal-setting and increasing Carl's knowledge of and ability to set appropriate goals so that he could more effectively monitor his performances, his practice, and his confidence levels. Carl was already used to keeping a golf diary after he played competitions. Here he would jot down his statistics for every competitive round. On reviewing this it was found that Carl just noted how many putts he hit per round and how many fairways and greens he hit. I reasoned that this golf diary should be expanded to include more relevant notes and statistics so that Carl could evaluate his performances in a better way. Carl was encouraged to write down information relating to good shots during his round (and also shots that did not work out). The aim of this was to increase the time he spent thinking about the good shots from his round.

Overall, this golf diary was to be a record of a more systematic approach to performance evaluation. For example, he was encouraged to jot down information relating to each practice session as well. Here he could note what he practiced, for how long, and how he felt the session went, in particular what he did well in that session. This more systematic approach helped Carl to monitor his performances and see what aspects were good and what aspects needed improvement. Within this information gathering, he was encouraged to think about his performance routine, what functions it served, and whether he could use it to more effectively concentrate or regulate his emotions. Carl explored his routine (specifically his pre-shot routine) and found that he could adjust it to meet the differing task demands that he encountered during the course of a tournament. This was far more process-oriented than his previous thinking of his performances as a bad round or a good round based solely on a score or a match outcome. This process orientation was complemented and helped by his increased awareness of goal-setting through the interventions which had taken place.

Another early session revolved around the assessment and awareness of mood and emotions. Carl was brought through the mood profiling information and encouraged to see the benefit to this overview on his emotional control or lack thereof. The benefits were outlined and the importance of mood to performance reiterated throughout. Additionally, Carl was able to utilize his expanding knowledge (as the sessions progressed) of the mood/performance relationship and he would regularly, of his own accord, monitor his mood profile by completing the profile assessment pre- and post-round. Again, this approach enabled him to take more control of when and how he performed, but also highlighted to him the important aspect of emotional control, in particular how better performances were usually accompanied by more stable mood. Finally, this greater awareness of mood and emotions enabled Carl to see just how detrimental and cyclical his negative self-talk was becoming for him during performances. Sessions revolved around challenges to stopping or more precisely reorienting negative self-talk into a task-oriented neutral or positive self-talk. This was mostly achieved by getting Carl to notice the content of his self-talk and to reframe the content by trying to answer the simple question of "But what is it that I am actually trying to do now?" The act of answering this question for Carl enabled him to mostly orient himself back into the task at hand, something which he reported to being very beneficial to stopping the cycle of self-talk and changing it to something more relevant.

All of the above intervention details relate to year one of the working relationship. When progressing into year two, much of the same information and interventions were adjusted, reiterated, refined, and so on. The twofold approach remained the approach into year two and beyond. All that changed was Carl's ability to discover and experiment with strategies and solutions himself without in some instances these strategies being discussed prior. The composition of subsequent sessions sometimes entailed listening to his approach and rationale and troubleshooting or providing some evidence for the efficacy or otherwise of what he was trying to achieve. For example, Carl decided that he would like to incorporate mindfulness into his preparations and explored this training and reading on his own. Later sessions then focused on outlining some of the specific reasons as to *how*, *why*, or *when* mindfulness might be beneficial.

REFLECTION

Review of Year One

Based on Carl's early season tournament success and reselection to the national panel, it became increasingly difficult to schedule sessions with each other, and as a result the work between us faltered somewhat when reviewing the year together. Carl identified that he was playing well, enjoying his golf, and did not see the importance of keeping the psychological work up. Upon reflection, Carl mentioned that he was slipping into bad habits "mentally" as the season went on and by the end of season found himself frustrated and exhausted. We resolved to build in more "check-in" type sessions and take greater care when planning a full season together (initially we had planned to work together for three sessions). Carl liked the questionnaires and getting results and mentioned that he would like to have more of this assessment built into the work together for the following year. This also suited our approach as the act of assessing and giving feedback is a powerful tool for learning and increasing the knowledge of the participant. Similar to building a body of evidence, all these assessments and reports were regularly referred back to in order to ascertain progress and subtle differences in Carl's thinking. This approach empowered Carl to take more control and increase his awareness, a central tenet of our theoretical approach to applied work.

Review of Year Two

After the season we reflected on the year that had passed. We were much more satisfied with the scheduling of meetings and Skype check-ins. Carl kept a close eye on his mood himself, reminded me when he wanted to do some assessment or questionnaire, and was able to monitor these and other items (e.g., concentration, sleep quality, mental and physical fatigue) through an app on his phone. Carl reflected that he was increasingly psychologically minded and that he wanted to explore mindfulness more himself in preparation for the upcoming season. The nature of the consultation had changed noticeably as both client and consultant grew into more seasoned roles together. Importantly, Carl reflected that he needed to maintain the psychological work as he performs best when confident and comfortable in his own skin. Importantly, from a consultation point of view, the nature of the work morphed from a supervisor role of helping, organizing, and providing strategies and tools to a more collaborative venture with more of an advisory role of problem solving, knowledge exchange, and small refinements of current strategies.

Future Plans

Now, if we return to the idea of applied sport psychology being fundamentally about empowerment, we can take great solace from Carl's development. He is now playing as well as ever before, has regained his place on the national team, and has played representative golf with distinction in the last 12 months. Furthermore, Carl is able to monitor and account for his improvements and performances in a better way. He is able to articulate and understand many of the issues that impact upon his own performance. Crucially, he is able to develop his own solutions to deal with many of the stressors in the high-performance environment (e.g., match play, stroke play, major tournaments, funding, etc.). He has also become more independent in terms of managing his own performance. While the frequency of our meetings is still somewhat regular (Skype check-in is usually once per month), the nature of them has evolved from the educational role to a reflective consultative process. The process of change described in the case study is far more important than any change in performance outcome even though his performances have improved. Working with this client has been a learning experience as our own approach has evolved. It is now less "skills oriented" than it was some years ago. Rather, it is more reflective in its nature, but still grounded in a theory–practice model. Now athletes have to make more decisions about what supports they require in their quest and thus we have more challenges in how to meet the demands of the athletes. This shift of approach can be described as moving from supervisor to advisor.

SUGGESTED READINGS

Hemmings, B., & Holder, T. (2009) *Applied sport psychology: A case-based approach*. Oxford: Wiley-Blackwell.

Cheadle, C., Pfenninger, G., & Carlson, E. (2014). Infusing technology in sport, exercise, and perform-ance psychology practice. In G. Cremades & L. S. Tashman (Eds.), *Becoming a sport, exercise and per-formance psychology professional: A global perspective* (pp. 160–167). New York, NY: Routledge.

Cotterill, S. T., Sanders, R., & Collins, D. (2010). Developing effective pre-performance routines in golf: Why don't we ask the golfer? *Journal of Applied Sport Psychology, 22*, 51–64. DOI: 10.1080/10413200903403216.

Hanrahan, S., & Anderson, M. (Eds.) (2010). *Routledge handbook of applied sport psychology*. Routledge: London.

Watson, J. C., & Halbrook, M. (2014). Incorporating technology into practice: A service delivery approach. In G. Cremades & L. S. Tashman (Eds.) *Becoming a sport, exercise and performance psychol-ogy professional: A global perspective* (pp. 152–159). New York, NY: Routledge.

REFLECTIVE QUESTIONS

1. Regarding client evaluation of the consultant's effectiveness, how often do you think this should be implemented and what are some challenges versus opportunities?

2. What factors affect the scheduling of meetings with clients? In what ways can a consultant work around long absences due to busy seasons and travel?

3. How often should peer evaluation and mentoring be utilized by a consultant? What value is there to using this approach?

4. When implementing psychological skills programs (PSPs), what works best and for whom? What are some in-season and out-of-season considerations?

5. How and when can the use of tele-consulting be useful? How could we establish if Carl needed any further consultation?

REFERENCES

Andersen, M. B. (2000). Introduction. In M. B. Andersen (Ed.), *Doing sport psychology* (pp. xiii–xvii). Champaign, IL: Human Kinetics.

Beedie, C. J., Terry, P. C., & Lane, A. M. (2000). The profile of mood states and athletic performance: Two meta-analyses. *Journal of Applied Sport Psychology, 12*(1), 49–68. DOI: 10.1080/10413200008404213.

Brick, N., MacIntyre, T., & Campbell, M. (2014). Attentional focus in endurance activity: New paradigms and future directions. *International Review of Sport & Exercise Psychology. 7*, 106–134. DOI: 10.1080/1750984X.2014.885554.

Brick, N., MacIntyre, T., & Campbell, M. (2015). Metacognitive processes in the self-regulation of perform-ance in elite endurance runners. *Psychology of Sport & Exercise* DOI: 10.1016/j.psychsport.2015.02.003.

Campbell, M., & Moran, A. (2014). The practice of applied sport, exercise and performance psychology: Irish and international perspectives. In G. Cremades & L. S. Tashman (Eds.), *Becoming a sport, exercise and performance psychology professional: A global perspective* (pp. 186–192). Hove: Psychology Press.

Comas-Diaz, C. (2006). The present and future of clinical psychology in private practice. *Clinical Psychol-ogy: Science & Practice, 13*, 273–277.

Hardy, L., Roberts, R., Thomas, P. R., & Murphy, S. M. (2010). Test of Performance Strategies (TOPS): Instrument refinement using confirmatory factor analysis. *Psychology of Sport & Exercise, 11*, 27–35. DOI: 10.1016/j.psychsport.2009.04.007.

Hemmings, B., & Holder, T. (2009). *Applied sport psychology: A case-based approach*. Oxford: Wiley-Blackwell.

Kitsantas, A., & Kavussanu, M. (2011). Acquisition of sport knowledge and skill: The role of self-regulatory processes. In B. J. Zimmerman & D. H. Schunk (Eds.), *Handbook of self-regulation of learning and performance* (pp. 217–233). Routledge: London.

MacIntyre, T., Igou, E. R., Campbell, M. J., Moran, A. P., & Matthews, J. (2014). Metacognition and action: A new pathway to understanding social and cognitive aspects of expertise in sport. *Frontiers in Psychology, 5*(1155). DOI: 10.3389/fpsyg.2014.01155.

Moran, A. (2012). *Sport and exercise psychology: A critical introduction* (2nd ed.). London: Routledge.

Moran, A. (2014). Adventures in cognitive sport psychology: From theory to practice. In P. McCarthy & M. Jones (Eds.), *Becoming a sport psychologist* (pp. 96–104). London: Routledge.

Redmond, J. (1997). *The book of Irish golf.* Dublin: Gill & Macmillan.

Thomas, P. R., Murphy S. M., & Hardy, L. (1999). Test of performances strategies: Development and preliminary validation of a comprehensive measure of athletes' psychological skills. *Journal of Sport Sciences, 17,* 697–711.

Wagstaff, C. R. D., Fletcher, D., & Hanton, S. (2012). Positive organizational psychology in sport. *International Review of Sport & Exercise Psychology, 5,* 87–103. DOI: 10.1080/1750984X.2011.634920.

25 "This Isn't What It's Supposed to Be Like!"

"Shifting Sands" and "Unfinished Business" in a Dynamic Sport Performance Context

Tim Holder

The intent of this chapter is to describe the nature of the assessment information gathered and some of the intervention work completed with an Olympic athlete. The intervention work discussed focuses on specific competition preparation (Gould & Maynard, 2009), but also aspects related to overall social support and rehabilitation from injury (Mitchell, 2011). Central to the focus of the chapter is the "shifting sands" over time that are a characteristic of working with many clients over a long period of time. Such dynamic changes that represent the "shifting sands" when working with clients can create substantial challenges as well as clear opportunities for any applied practitioner. This case study identifies the way in which the practitioner was able to refocus his work dynamically in new directions in relation to the client's needs. This often led to "unfinished business" with aspects of the client work that had been planned. This is in rather stark contrast to the manner in which applied practice is represented within many of the texts and academic literature in sport, exercise, and performance psychology professional practice (e.g., Hemmings & Holder, 2009).

BACKGROUND INFORMATION

The client in this case study was a member of a full-time training program in a team sport that was working toward competing at an Olympic Games. The full-time nature of her training meant she was engaged in training activities for six days every week for approximately 45 weeks in the calendar year. The training required for her sport demanded technical precision, physical strength, cardiovascular endurance, flexibility, and substantial mental resilience.

The client had been in training within this sport for over ten years at the time of the case study, and had spent much of her adult life and the latter parts of her youth training and competing with ambition to perform in major championships. The Olympic Games is the pinnacle of sporting performance and the possibility of competing at an Olympics was a significant motivating factor for the client. At the time of the case study, the client had been in full-time training for over three years and had devoted a significant amount of her life to performance in the sport.

Within her training and competition environment she was supported by a team of expert staff. This included full-time coaches, team managers, and specialists from both sports medicine and sports science backgrounds. The sports medicine and sports science support was designed as a multidisciplinary service. As part of this, the client had access to support from physiotherapists, strength and conditioning coaches, nutritionists, physiologists, as well as from a sports psychologist. The sports psychology component of the client's support was delivered in person at her training venue on a consistent basis. The consistency of contact was a feature of the work conducted that many sport psychologists do not have the opportunity to have access to. Such access enabled a thorough understanding of the context and organization of the environment within which she was training and competing (Brown, Gould, & Foster, 2005).

DESCRIPTION OF THE CASE

The case study to be described in this chapter reflects an example of a long-term working relationship with an individual athlete performing in a team sport in the period leading up to and after an Olympic Games. The overall duration of the working relationship was 2.5 years. The case study represents a proportion of the work carried out in collaboration with the client. The elements identified within the case have been chosen in order to reflect the true nature of the work completed and, as such, to identify critical features that speak to the core components influencing practitioner effectiveness (e.g., Sharp & Hodge, 2011).

THEORETICAL FRAMEWORK/PHILOSOPHY

The general approach the author adopts during support work would be termed by many as eclectic or possibly more accurately as holistic (Friesen & Orlick, 2010). The fundamental theoretical framework within which the approach used by the author originates is a cognitive behaviorist perspective (Meichenbaum, 1977). It is also clear that much of the working practices include a significant influence from humanistic, person-centered approaches (Rogers, 1980) to the client work by engaging with them as a person both within and outside of sport. However, it is clear that the fundamental approach to the work the author conducted maintains a driving force and intention for impact (Martindale & Collins, 2005) derived from a cognitive behavioral framework. The additional, more holistic, aspects are applied through the lens of a cognitive behavioral emphasis.

NEEDS ASSESSMENT

The planning that took place in order to deliver service in this particular case study was substantial and ongoing. A significant contributing factor to the quality and quantity of planning that was able to take place is related to the consistent, scheduled contact with the client within her full-time training program. This consistency of contact enabled a thorough understanding of both the client and, most importantly, the client within her performance environment (see Brown et al., 2005). Initial assessment information was collected for the client in an ongoing manner. However, the initial contact with her enabled an interview and observations to be carried out in order to develop rapport and trust (Leach, 2005) and create an interpersonal relationship suitable to maximize the potential impact of any work (Pettipas, Giges, & Danish, 1999).

The results of the consistent contact with the client in her environment led to a constant updating of contextual intelligence (Brown et al., 2005). The importance, within a contextual intelligence framework, of a range of client-relevant information should not be underestimated. It was common practice to arrive at her environment with two things in place. First, contact with other support staff enabled an updating of potentially relevant contextual information to be gleaned and incorporated into the plan for work with the client. Such information ranged from conversations with other support staff about changes that may be of relevance to the client as well as contact with the client herself to update any current information. Second, a clearly identified objective for any contact with the client was put in place. It is clear that this identified objective was relevant and meaningful to her based upon previous work that had been completed. It was crucial that the practitioner understood, and more importantly accepted, that this element of the planning was open and amenable to change. This required that the practitioner planned for uncertainty rather than a level of certainty that such a dynamic context was unlikely to provide. Therefore, there was an acceptance and accommodation for the "shifting sands" that inevitably became part of the challenge and the excitement of working in such a context. The overall principle within the planning for work with the client was that there would always be a plan A, but that identification of the appropriateness of plan A was essential as an applied consideration at all times.

INTERVENTION

Phase 1: Early Indicators of Psychological Needs

During the initial assessment phase with the client, it became clear that one of the challenges from a psychological perspective was in dealing with worry. The short-term and long-term consequences of a worry-biased approach to thinking were discussed and an initial plan was set to help understand and deal with the worrying thoughts.

Initial assessment of the worry experienced by the client indicated a range of sources of worry, some of which were performance related and others which permeated both performance and nonperformance elements of the client's life (e.g., Meehan, Bull, Wood & James, 2004). Once sources had been established, a plan to begin to reconsider the style of thinking she used when addressing sources of worry was created. The main focus of this work was the identification, disputation, and re-formulating of her thinking in those moments. This approach draws upon a range of literature in cognitive psychology that attests to the benefits for emotional functioning of rational thinking patterns (e.g., REBT approaches; Turner & Barker, 2014; Turner, Slater, & Barker, 2014).

"Shifting Sands" Transition 1: Competition Preparation

During the work to develop more effective thinking patterns for the client, a sudden shift in emphasis occurred that required immediate re-prioritization. This shift was initiated as a result of the client reflecting on previous pre-competition experiences and the specific impact of recent competition simulations as part of the training program at this time. The "shifting sands" at this point in time determined that the opportunities available to work with the client needed to be altered, focusing away from broader work related to a range of sources of worry to focusing on specific competition preparation.

Phase 2: Competition Preparation Phase

Through discussion with the client, a significant concern was highlighted in relation to the experience of anxiety in the period immediately preceding performance. The symptom that she identified was an uncontrollable change in her physical state and a resultant change in breathing. Further, a change in breathing was noted by other performers and the client thus felt additional concern that this had a negative effect on other performers around her. Therefore, the client's view about the importance of controlling a perceived uncontrollable change was exacerbated by a knock-on effect to others around her.

When discussing with the client about her experience of physical symptom changes, it became apparent that a period of psycho-education focused on fight-or-flight responses in challenging situations would be a helpful starting point. Having explained this response to the client, her understanding of what was happening in this pre-competition period became clearer when we collaborated to visually represent what was happening in a flow diagram (see Figure 25.1). In addition, to reinforce understanding of the natural bodily response to a challenge, the client was directed to a YouTube link that helped explain further the flight-or-fight response.

This combination of psycho-educational sources assisted the athlete in gaining a greater understanding of the inevitable shift that would occur in her physical state prior to performance. The focus then became her skill in being able to manage such a response in a suitable

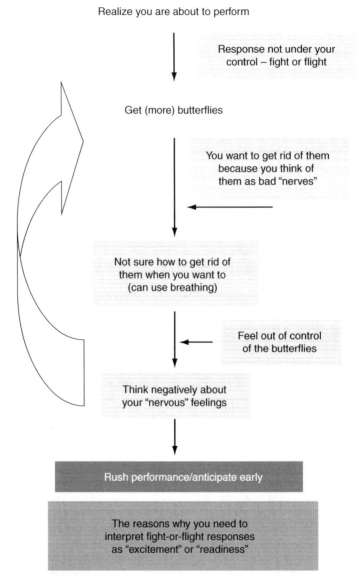

Realize you are about to perform

Response not under your
control – fight or flight

Get (more) butterflies

You want to get rid of them
because you think of
them as bad "nerves"

Not sure how to get rid of
them when you want to
(can use breathing)

Feel out of control
of the butterflies

Think negatively about
your "nervous" feelings

Rush performance/anticipate early

The reasons why you need to
interpret fight-or-flight responses
as "excitement" or "readiness"

Figure 25.1 The "Excitement" Cycle

manner during this period (e.g., Hanton, Wadey, & Mellalieu, 2008). The excitement cycle described in Figure 25.1 identifies a number of possible avenues where intervention could be focused. As the primary indicator of the impact was breathing, the development of a controlled breathing strategy (Edwards & Beale, 2011; Harwood, 1998) was chosen. This complemented the continuing work on the reappraisal aspect of her fight-or-flight response from labeling the experience as nerves to labeling it as excitement and an indicator of performance preparedness. In addition, due to the effect of the psycho-educational component, there was an acknowledgment by the client that experiencing the physical response to a competition situation was to be expected and interpreted as helpful rather than unhelpful (see Hanton et al., 2008). As a result, she could more readily accept the physical changes she experienced and respond to them in a more passive but controlled manner, primarily through the breathing strategy. The breathing strategy utilized was a ratio breathing intervention where she would breathe in for a count of three and out for a count of five.

"Shifting Sands" Transition 2: Injury Rehabilitation

Having returned from competition, the client experienced a significant injury, which meant that she had to prepare for a surgical procedure and a significant period of rehabilitation. This created a significant "shifting sands" moment for the work with the client. The period of time that remained to recover and prepare for the upcoming Olympic Games was considered by the medical support staff to be possible but very challenging. In addition, the success of the surgical procedure was a significant and somewhat unpredictable component of the situation. Within a short period of time the surgical procedure was completed and the client began a period of rehabilitation.

Phase 3: Injury Coping and Recovery

The injury rehabilitation period was optimized through the integration of the work completed by a number of specialist professionals. This included doctors, physiotherapists, strength and conditioning coaches, nutritionists, and the sport psychologist. The key components that were identified with the client for the psychological input was in developing two characteristics: (1) the client's efficacy for performing particular physical movements necessary for training and performance within her sport; and (2) given the tight timeframe to the Olympic Games, a focus on maintaining a patient approach to the recovery process.

In relation to efficacy, Table 25.1 gives an adapted example of an efficacy monitoring form that the client used on a weekly basis to identify her development of physical capability throughout the rehabilitation process. Over time, this form enabled the client to identify with great clarity her improvement in elements of movement that were essential characteristics required by the sporting demands. The client could visually identify a shift over time indicating an increased confidence in her movement capabilities.

The client's desire to return to competition became a potentially dangerous component of her recovery, as to re-injure herself would likely lead to a significant decrease in her chances of performing at the Olympic Games (Ardem, Taylor, Feller, & Webster, 2013). A key focus word for the recovery process became "patience." This concept was reinforced on a regular basis and aligned with the efficacy intervention that indicated the level and pace of progress that was being made. In addition, experiences of other Olympic athletes were searched and the following quote passed onto the athlete as an indicator of the potential change that this

Table 25.1 Self-Efficacy Monitoring Example

Self-efficacy for weight-bearing tasks, December 16
For each of the tasks listed below estimate how confident you feel that you can achieve the task how it is meant to be performed

Task	0%	10%	20%	30%	40%	50%	60%	70%	80%	90%	100%
Bilateral weight bearing on wall											▓
Scapular press-ups on wall											▓
Superwoman single arm single leg										▓	
Superwoman left arm right leg											▓
Superwomen right arm left leg										▓	
Head stand										▓	
Forward roll									▓		
Press-up position leg lifts							▓				
Single leg wall press-ups									▓		
Bear crawls			▓								
Spider crawls				▓							
Handstand		▓									

rehabilitation process could create. The quote not only shows the potential to recover, but also indicates the additional growth that can occur through adversity (Collins & MacNamara, 2012). The following quote from an Olympic medalist about building back up from an injury and a career low was provided to the client:

> I'd been so low so everywhere I looked it was just positive; everywhere I looked it was just better than it was before. I was just climbing that hill, or mountain, whatever you wanna think of it as, and I was just going up and up and up … what pushes you back makes you stronger and that made me so much more confident and so much stronger as an athlete mentally.

"Shifting Sands" Transition 3: Post-Olympic Direction

The final "shifting sands" with the client occurred in the post-Olympic period. The client had successfully recovered from surgery and competed at an Olympic Games. After the Games had occurred, a period of reflection led to a shift in focus once more in the work conducted.

Phase 4: Return to Initial Work

This period brought a significant focus back to elements of work that had been left incomplete earlier in the consulting relationship. The worry and concern that the athlete experienced in this period became the primary focus of the work conducted at this time. At this stage, the client entered into a period of decision making in relation to both sporting and life objectives. This led to considerable challenges for her in identifying the correct avenue and direction for her devotion of energy and time to the sport.

The key work completed with the client revolved around two interconnected factors related to perceived control (e.g., Maynard, 1998). First, the client expressed a range of factors in her life that were causing her concern, only some of which were within her control. An exercise was conducted to consider which aspects were more or less in her control and to identify plans to influence those areas that were within her control. Additionally, the exercise identified that there were many more features within her life as a whole that were within her control and only a small number outside of her control. This assisted in a shift in the other interconnected factor that was her level and intensity of worry. In order to develop this skill of dealing with her concerns and worries, the client returned to the work that had been completed over a year ago, where she had begun to develop the skill of countering her unhelpful thoughts and to develop and restructure more helpful ways of thinking.

Therefore, this final period of work with the client exemplifies the circular, and certainly nonlinear, nature of applied practice. However, it also exemplifies the "shifting sands," creating an opportunity to use previously incomplete work (or "unfinished business") to apply to a new and relevant challenge for the client at that particular point in time (in this case, a focus on broader life development issues in addition to performance-related factors).

REFLECTION

Through the work with this client there are a number of key reflections that warrant consideration for any applied practitioner. The first and most important reflection is about the real nature of applied practice with individual athletes. It is certainly true that the context and availability of contact with the client has a significant impact on the type and style of working practices engaged in by an applied sport psychology practitioner.

In this case, contact with the client was regular, in fact weekly, and was over an extended period of time. As a result of this access to the client, the style in which the work was conducted could be adapted in an optimal manner. By this it is meant that there are differences apparent that contrast with a number of previously cited case-study examples (e.g., Hemmings & Holder, 2009). When reflecting upon other examples of practitioner case studies, it is familiar to see work that seems to seamlessly move through stages of applied practice that indicates a very clear and coherent method. The applied practice observed within such case studies exhibits a pattern of clear assessment information leading to precise intervention strategies, and subsequently evaluation of practice indicating the success of the specific intervention. However, this pattern runs counter to elements contained within the current case.

The challenges and opportunities made prevalent within the context of this case allowed for a focused delivery of service, but one where specific circumstances created necessary changes of direction of the work to fully engage with the client's needs at that particular moment in time. The regular nature of client contact meant that the passage of work conducted with the client was dynamic and in some cases somewhat chaotic compared to the expectations that much of the current literature seems to indicate (e.g., Barker, Evans, Coffee, Slater & McCarthy, 2014; Greenlees, 2009).

Therefore, a significant characteristic from this case suggests that for those in applied practice, or interested in developing into applied practice, the real demands of the role should consider the ever-changing nature of clients' needs and suggest some shift in the emphasis of expectations of how applied practice may evolve. Specifically, it is suggested that to truly adhere to a client-focused approach to working in applied practice, consultants may need to respond more rapidly to client changes of circumstances and be prepared to feel that elements of the applied work are incomplete in relation to previous expectations. This is required in order to champion the necessary emphasis on applied practice flexing to client's needs.

The second key reflection relates to the positive impact on applied practice of working collaboratively with other experts, including coaching staff as well as sports science and medicine practitioners. It is clear that there are numerous examples demonstrating the influence of confidentiality on the possibilities of applied sport psychology practitioners working closely with other experts (Collins, Moore, Mitchell, & Alpress, 1999). However, this case provides another exemplar of where such opportunities to work collaboratively can be a significant advantage in providing effective service delivery and attending optimally to client's needs. For example, within the case the return from injury of the athlete was accelerated by the use of a multidisciplinary approach to the recovery process. Working collaboratively with physiotherapists or strength and conditioning coaches has been identified as providing optimal support (Evans, Hardy, & Fleming, 2000). Within this case, this was particularly evident in the development of efficacy for components of movement required by the client, given her sporting demands. Although this element of the case was particularly beneficial, reflection after the fact revealed that there were further untapped opportunities that could have been optimized through working more closely with doctors, surgeons, and nutritional support.

Therefore, it is clear that when possible applied practitioners should identify and maximize the use of those collaborative opportunities made available for client enhancement through the use of other expert input in a coordinated and planned manner. This, for applied practitioners, requires an understanding and appreciation of the potential contributions that can be made to clients' performance enhancement outside of the scope of sport psychology alone. Thus, trainee practitioners should spend time not only studying the contribution of other experts to sporting performance, but also communicate openly with other available practitioners within the context of work in order to explore possible avenues for collaboration.

Third, the first two reflections allude to a component of applied practice that is evident in both. The component of interest is the importance for effective practice of the applied practitioner's humility. This characteristic is embedded within the acknowledgment of a change in direction due to a dynamic shift in the client's needs as well as in the advantages to be gained from working collaboratively with other experts. Therefore, applied practitioners would benefit from acknowledging and recognizing the important benefits of humility in their own work. This does not mean that sport psychologists cannot feel a sense of significance in relation to client enhancement. However, it does suggest that their effectiveness should always be couched in an understanding that it is only part of the jigsaw of factors that come together to produce optimal performance.

In addition, it is important for practitioners to acknowledge the impact of a dynamic, sometimes chaotic, demand within the applied context. Principally, what is important here is that the dynamic nature of the context and client need is met by a similarly dynamic professional judgment and decision-making process (Martindale & Collins, 2005). In order for this to be the case, it is clear that ongoing evaluation and assessment procedures can enable such dynamism to be integral to applied practitioners' working practices. Therefore, applied practitioners should be wary of making assumptions about the voracity of their assessment information for making effective and optimal decisions within their practice in dynamic, ever-changing client circumstances. Optimal applied practice can be enhanced by a constant sense of uncertainty coupled with an appetite and openness to information in, and outside of, the performance context. Such information can be at the heart of providing a client-focused service delivery that matches the client's needs in an ongoing manner.

The final reflection worthy of consideration, particularly for seasoned practitioners, is the ongoing challenge of relating to clients and maintaining a grasp of ever-expanding modes of communication. These modes of working provide potential opportunities for applied practitioners to enhance their effectiveness and the all-important rapport development with clients. For example, the use of text, email, FaceTime, Skype, Twitter, and other forms of social media can open up potential beneficial avenues of communication and information sharing with clients (Cotterill & Symes, 2014). The author considers that many of these can create a cautious engagement from many applied practitioners due to the dangers associated with security and confidentiality of information shared through many of these forms. However, it is clear that when utilizing some of the technological advances available to practitioners the impact on applied practice can be hugely positive. In the current case under discussion, the use of email, text, Skype, and YouTube clips certainly enhanced the application of psychological principles with the client. Therefore, it is important for applied practitioners to consider the benefits and pitfalls associated with the plethora of communication opportunities available and integrate them into applied practice in an appropriate manner whenever possible.

SUGGESTED READINGS

Brown, C. H., Gould, G., & Foster, S. (2005). A framework for developing contextual intelligence (CI). *The Sport Psychologist*, *19*, 51–62.

Collins, D., Moore, P., Mitchell, D., & Alpress, F. (1999). Role conflict and confidentiality in multidisciplinary athlete support programmes. *British Journal of Sports Medicine*, *33*, 208–211.

Cotterill, S. T., & Symes, R. (2014). Integrating social media and new technologies into your practice as a sport psychology consultant. *Sport and Exercise Psychology Review*, *10*(1), 55–65.

Gould, D., & Maynard, I. (2009). Psychological preparation for the Olympic Games. *Journal of Sports Sciences*, *27*(13), 1393–1408.

REFLECTIVE QUESTIONS

1. How would you optimize the opportunities to work in a multi- or interdisciplinary manner with other practitioners?

2. How would you enable an optimum understanding of the client's situation through a range of assessment and monitoring approaches?
3. Why would humility be important to consider for an applied sport psychology practitioner?
4. How can an applied practitioner deal with the challenge of "shifting sands" in relation to the client's needs?
5. In what way can the "unfinished business" from previous work completed with a client enable a greater effectiveness in future work with a client?

REFERENCES

Ardem, C. L., Taylor, N. F., Feller, J. A., & Webster, K. E. (2013). A systematic review of the psychological factors associated with returning to sport following injury. *British Journal of Sports Medicine, 47,* 1120–1126.

Barker, J. B., Evans, A. L., Coffee, P., Slater, M. J., & McCarthy, P. J. (2014). A dual-phase personal-disclosure mutual sharing intervention and group functioning in elite youth cricket. *The Sport Psychologist, 28,* 186–197.

Brown, C. H., Gould, G., & Foster, S. (2005). A framework for developing contextual intelligence (CI). *The Sport Psychologist, 19,* 51–62.

Collins, D., & MacNamara, A. (2012). The rocky road to the top: why talent needs trauma. *Sports Medicine, 42*(11), 907–914.

Collins, D., Moore, P., Mitchell, D., & Alpress, F. (1999). Role conflict and confidentiality in multidisciplinary athlete support programmes. *British Journal of Sports Medicine, 33,* 208–211.

Cotterill, S. T., & Symes, R. (2014). Integrating social media and new technologies into your practice as a sport psychology consultant. *Sport and Exercise Psychology Review, 10*(1), 55–65.

Edwards, S., & Beale, J. (2011). A report on the evaluation of a breath workshop for stress management by sport psychology students. *African Journal for Physical, Health Education, Recreation and Dance, 17*(3), 517–525.

Evans, L., Hardy, L., & Fleming, S. (2000). Intervention strategies with injured athletes: An action research study. *The Sport Psychologist, 14,* 188–206.

Friesen, A., & Orlick, T. (2010). A qualitative analysis of holistic sport psychology consultants' professional philosophies. *The Sport Psychologist, 24,* 227–244.

Gould, D., & Maynard, I. (2009). Psychological preparation for the Olympic Games. *Journal of Sports Sciences, 27*(13), 1393–1408.

Greenlees, I. (2009). Enhancing confidence in a youth golfer. In B. Hemmings & T. Holder (Eds.), *Applied sport psychology: A case based approach* (pp. 89–105). Chichester: Wiley Blackwell.

Hanton, S., Wadey, R., & Mellalieu, S. D. (2008). Advanced psychological strategies and anxiety responses in sport. *The Sport Psychologist, 22,* 472–490.

Harwood, C. (1998). *Handling pressure.* Leeds: NCF.

Hemmings, B., & Holder, T. (2009). *Applied sport psychology: A case based approach.* Chichester: Wiley Blackwell.

Leach, M. J. (2005). Rapport: A key to treatment success. *Complementary Therapies in Clinical Practice, 11,* 262–265.

Martindale, A., & Collins, D. (2005). Professional judgement and decision making: The role of intention for impact. *The Sport Psychologist, 19*(3), 303–318.

Maynard, I. (1998). *Improving concentration.* Leeds: NCF.

Meehan, H. L., Bull, S. J., Wood, D. M., & James, D. V. B. (2004). The overtraining syndrome: A multicontextual assessment. *The Sport Psychologist, 18*(2), 154–171.

Meichenbaum, D. (1977). *Cognitive-behavior modification: An integrative approach.* New York, NY: Plenham Press.

Mitchell, I. (2011). Social support and psychological responses in sport injury rehabilitation. *Sport and Exercise Psychology Review, 7*(2), 30–44.

Pettipas, A. J., Giges, B., & Danish, S. J. (1999). The sport psychologist–athlete relationship: Implications for training. *The Sport Psychologist, 13,* 344–357.

Rogers, C. (1980). *A way of being.* New York, NY: Houghton Mifflin.

Sharp, L., & Hodge, K. (2011). Sport psychology consulting effectiveness: The sport psychology consultant's perspective. *Journal of Applied Sport Psychology, 23*, 360–376.

Turner, M. J., & Barker, J. B. (2014). Using rational-emotive behavior therapy with athletes. *The Sport Psychologist, 28*, 75–90.

Turner, M. J., Slater, M. J., & Barker, J. B. (2014). Not the end of the world: The effects of rational-emotive behavior therapy on irrational beliefs in elite soccer academy athletes. *Journal of Applied Sport Psychology, 26*, 144–156.

Part II

Training, Supervision, and Mentorship in the Applied Setting

26 The Neophyte Supervisor

Navigating the Swampy Lowlands through Collaborative Approaches to Supervision

Brendan Cropley and Rich Neil

This chapter will present a case study of the supervision of neophyte sport and exercise scientists who are training to work in the field of sport psychology (through the BASES Supervised Experience and Accreditation program). Specifically, the case study will focus on a collaborative approach to supervision that has been instigated through the Cardiff Met Professional Development Group (CMPDG), based in the UK. It is hoped that the case study will offer both experienced and neophyte supervisors insight into the efficacy of collaborative approaches in helping them to navigate the swampy lowlands of professional practice supervision. Thus, the goal of the chapter is to present ideas designed to guide the creation of more operative learning environments that underpin effective supervision.

BACKGROUND INFORMATION

A growing body of literature in the field of sport and exercise psychology (SEP) has been devoted to the examination of the training and development of neophyte practitioners through the process of supervision (e.g., Knowles, Gilbourne, Tomlinson, & Anderson, 2007; Meijen & Manley, 2010; Watson, McAlarnen, & Shannon, 2014). Emerging from this literature has been a general consensus regarding the potential efficacy of the supervisory process in training practitioners to a standard where they are deemed fit and safe to practice autonomously. However, there is also some agreement that research into the mechanisms associated with effective supervision is still in need of attention (Hutter, Oldenhof-Veldman, & Oudejans, 2015). Indeed, while the goals of supervision have been defined by those who govern professional qualifications in the field (e.g., the British Psychological Society [BPS]; the British Association of Sport & Exercise Science [BASES]), the process of supervision and the roles of the supervisor are far less established.

Hutter et al. (2015) outlined that supervision in SEP can serve many different functions from educational (e.g., facilitating the development of the trainee's professional practice skills) to managerial (e.g., quality control of practice). Similarly, others have suggested, among a plethora of additional roles and responsibilities, the importance of the supervisor in fostering reflective practice and self-awareness (Cropley & Neil, 2014), creating opportunities for growth (Watson et al., 2014), ensuring maintenance and promotion of professional ethics (Donaldson-Feilder & Bush, 2009), and supporting trainees to cope with the demands of the profession (Stambulova & Johnson, 2010). To add to these points, striving to achieve such outcomes requires the effective negotiation of the micro-political landscape (e.g., occupational standards) associated with the profession of sport psychology (and sport and exercises science [SES]), and is governed by the supervisor–supervisee relationship (see Silva, Metzler, & Lerner, 2011). Together, these factors make the reality of supervising trainee SEP practitioners somewhat messy and complex. Consequently, for those embarking on tenure as a supervisor, the process can be a daunting prospect.

There are also a number of contextual issues associated with supervising trainee practitioners in the UK that need to be considered, as these help to set the scene for the case study and the potential need for different approaches to supervision. The pathway to accreditation for SES practitioners through BASES involves a program of Supervised Experience (SE). This program formalizes the requirement for trainees to engage in ongoing supervised practice in order to progress toward, and ultimately achieve, the competencies expected for BASES accreditation (for full details, see BASES, 2015). SE candidates have between two and six years to complete the process and, in attempts to demonstrate the development of these competencies, trainees are expected to record all of the activities they undertake during this period (e.g., practice log; supervisor meeting log; reflections-on-practice) as well as gathering a range of accompanying evidence to support their burgeoning knowledge, skills, and experience in their specialist discipline (e.g., sport psychology). Part of the supervisory process, therefore, is to ensure that trainees are given the appropriate support and structure to be able to engage in activities that will help develop the required competencies, as well as overseeing the management of the trainee's portfolio of evidence.

To be accepted onto the SE program, candidates must hold an undergraduate degree and at least be working toward a postgraduate degree in a sport-related subject(s). Supervisees often engage, therefore, in the program outside of full-time education. This creates a number of challenges that shape how the supervisory process can be organized and managed. For example, trainees will often have other jobs while completing the SE program in order to fund their training and development activities, which places significant constraints on the time that they have to engage in supervision and applied practice. Further, trainees have varied levels of understanding of the theory and practice of applied SEP due to the diversity of their educational, sporting, and social backgrounds. While models of supervision (e.g., Integrated Development Model [IDM]; Stoltenberg, McNeill, & Delworth, 1998) are useful guides for informing supervisor behavior and evaluating supervisee development, because of the variety of backgrounds, trainees rarely seem to fit neatly into a specific "stage" when they commence with SE.

Finally, to be permitted to supervise on the BASES SE program, potential supervisors have to be registered by the organization. This requires attendance at a one-day orientation event that outlines the purpose and structure of the program as well as the roles and responsibilities of the supervisor. While elements of "best practice" are also discussed during the event, there is little explicit training and guidance regarding the role, and as such the supervisor is very much expected to "learn on the job."

In light of the preceding discussion, to be better prepared for the complexity inherent within the process of supervision, the *neophyte supervisor* has to develop a clear understanding of: (a) their motivation for supervising; (b) themselves and how mindful they are of their strengths and limitations; (c) their philosophy for supervision; and (d) the internal (e.g., coping mechanisms; role management) and external (e.g., facilities; supervision strategies) resources available (cf. Cropley & Neil, 2014). In addition, it is important to develop the personal and interpersonal skills that are associated with effective pedagogy and mentoring in order to meet both the trainee's and the profession's expectations of the supervisory process (Garvey, Stokes, & Megginson, 2009). These include being open-minded to the possibilities of creating more effective learning environments through the use of innovative and collaborative approaches to supervision.

Collaborative supervision, in different forms, has been used in many disciplines within psychology and have recently emerged as a potentially beneficial process within SEP (e.g., Rhodius & Sugarman, 2014). Such an approach is thought to benefit the supervisee due to the inherent peer interaction, the opportunity for shared reflection, the integration of reciprocal approaches to learning, and the provision of a safe environment for disclosure (Donaldson-Feilder & Bush, 2009). Indeed, the communication behaviors of problem solving, sharing, negotiating, and teamwork are characteristic of collaborative supervision (Sullivan & Glanz,

2000). The approach also allows the supervisor to observe their supervisees in the critical discussion of theory and practice-based problems as well as in mock/role play service delivery scenarios. Further, the reciprocity of collaborative supervision extends to the supervisor themselves, allowing them to be active in their own continual learning, which could be particularly beneficial for those in the early stages of their career (cf. Carrington, 2004).

DESCRIPTION OF THE CASE

As a way of quality controlling the supervisory process, BASES regulations stipulate that supervisors can only supervisee four SE candidates at one time. Within the first two years of becoming registered supervisors, we (authors) had both agreed to supervise the maximum number of candidates each. This was as a result of both the increasing demand for accreditation from those students who had graduated from Cardiff Metropolitan University's applied sport psychology MSc degree, and the paucity of registered supervisors in the local area. It is important to note that, for us, deciding to supervise a particular person is not done based on capacity. Instead, we both instigate a similar selection process whereby both supervisor and supervisee can make an informed choice about the potential suitability of each other based on the supervisee's needs and how compatible we are. This approach follows recent recommendations presented by McCormick and Meijen (2015) that potential trainees should "recognize the importance of selecting a suitable and compatible supervisor" (p. 45). This approach helps to instigate the development of an effective working alliance between supervisor and supervisee and can help to remove some of the barriers to progress that are often found at the beginning of relationships (e.g., supervisee anxiety; lack of empathy).

Following the sentiments of Watson, Zizzi, Etzel, and Lubker (2004), the decision to take on the responsibility to supervise so many candidates at this stage of our careers was not one that we took lightly. While we were clear about our capabilities to manage the workload associated with such a situation, we were also explicit about the challenges we faced to ensure that: (a) individual supervisee needs and expectations were met; (b) we added value to the learning and development of each individual; and (c) we provided the best opportunities for growth for all supervisees.

During this particular "case," the CMPDG consists of two supervisors (authors) and eight supervisees. To demonstrate the diversity of the trainees, all have finished full-time study and are working in different positions both in and outside of sporting organizations. One is a part-time Ph.D. student, and one is a full-time employee at a higher education institution. Finally, three trainees are in their final year of the SE program, three are in the second year, and two are in the first year. Given the aims of the CMPDG, we see such diversity in its members as an opportunity rather than a problem. The group maintains a relatively homogeneous membership, but one that offers a variety of experiences and personalities that supports the reciprocal nature of the group. If supervisees agree with the expectations of membership we are able to overcome the potential power issues between members at different stages of the SE process by allowing each person to explore their own agency and being supported in doing so (see Garvey et al., 2009).

Practically, the group meets formally once per month at Cardiff Metropolitan University and, depending on the nature of the session, meetings are held at different locations on campus (e.g., seminar rooms, sports facilities). The meeting dates are organized in advance for the year to allow the trainees to better manage their external commitments and are usually scheduled for two hours, although this is flexible.

APPROACH/PHILOSOPHY

The CMPDG was constructed as a result of the philosophy for supervision shared by the authors. The development of this philosophy emerged from critically reflecting on our values for supervision in order to better understand why we do what we do as practitioners and super-visors (cf. Cropley & Neil, 2014). First, we value the notion of working *with* the person and not just the professional (or trainee) and are therefore concerned with the holistic development of the supervisee. This is supported by recent beliefs that improving a practitioner's capabilities begins, and is facilitated by, the growth and improvement of that person as a human being (Tod & Bond, 2010). Second, our practice is underpinned by the notion of encouraging supervisees to explore who they are, what they value, and how they can utilize their strengths to help them flourish in the practice environment. This approach helps to protect against the potentially negative effects of transference, where supervisees become overly dependent on the supervisor and potentially start to mimic the supervisor's ideals, behaviors, and emotions (Castillo, 2014). Essentially, we strive to support the supervisee in developing an understand-ing of the self as practitioner. Finally, we believe that learning is most effective when the learner is actively involved in the process. This means that we see our roles as *consultative* rather than that of an *expert educator*; such a perspective requires approaches to supervision that are more guided than dictated. In essence, we agree with Watson et al. (2014) that supervisors should be the "professional guideposts for the professional development of their supervisees" (p. 240).

Taking these values into account, the CMPDG is underpinned by elements of the *phenome-nological* and the *developmental* models (see Van Raalte & Andersen, 2000). From a phenome-nological perspective, our role as supervisors in the CMPDG is not to overtly advise, but rather to create a safe environment in which supervisees can explore themselves, their practice, and the profession of applied sport psychology. From a developmental perspective, we ensure that we understand the supervisee's individual stage of development and needs and as a result attempt to structure various activities within the group to facilitate their progression. Under-standing these needs allows us to make informed decisions about our supervisory roles and therefore make judgments about the level of support or autonomy that might be required. By adopting these principles, the CMPDG inherently offers a form of social support for its members and consequently allows the formation of significantly stronger working alliances between both supervisor and supervisees, as well as between the supervisees themselves. Placing these alliances at the heart of the group's philosophy is thought to better promote supervisees' personal and professional development beyond that of only engaging in individual supervision (cf. Donaldson-Feilder & Bush, 2009).

PREPARATION/PLANNING

In an attempt to deal with the challenges presented so far in this chapter regarding the general, contextual, and situational issues associated with supervision, as relatively neophyte supervisors, we decided to support each others' development by acting as *critical friends* through a process of *peer supervision*. In a similar vein to the processes detailed by Rhodius and Sugarman (2014) and Hemmings (2014), we shared reflection and practice ideas and created challenge and crit-ical thought through a questioning process built on a relationship characterized by honesty, trust, and openness. While this relationship was important for the development and promotion of our supervisory practice, it offered the social support required to cope with demands that we experienced (e.g., multiple roles of practitioner, supervisor, and academic). Further, it allowed us to explore the potential for developing a collaborative approach to supervision based on the principles of *communities of practice*, *reciprocal learning*, and *reflective learning groups*. Subse-quently, we constructed the CMPDG to create a more integrated and formal learning environ-ment for all of our supervisees and as a way of improving the process of supervision by managing the contextual constraints that potentially inhibited the effectiveness and efficiency of our supervisees' development.

In accordance with the suggestions of Donaldson-Feilder and Bush (2009), it was decided to structure the purpose of the CMPDG with a distinct set of aims and member expectations.

These are reviewed every year with the trainee members as a way of monitoring the potential value of the group and to ensure that each new member has some ownership over the group's purpose. The aims, which have remained relatively consistent since its inception, are: (a) to encourage the ongoing development of self-awareness and practice philosophy; (b) to provide a forum for the sharing of practice; (c) to engage members in shared reflective practice; (d) to provide opportunities for supervisees to deliver mock sessions in preparation for service delivery; and (e) to engage members in reciprocal and peer learning. Group members also have to agree to the expectations of membership, which include: adhering to a code of confidentiality; completion of post-meeting learning logs designed to reflect the key insights of learning gleaned from the session; behavior that is considered professional, supportive, and constructively challenging; and taking ownership of the structure, content, and administration of the group's activities. These expectations also extend to the supervisors.

SUPERVISION PROCESS/EXPERIENCE

To achieve the aims of the CMPDG, we adopt a range of strategies and activities that have emerged from both the extant pedagogical and psychological literature, as well as from our own experiences (see Table 26.1).

The principles underpinning the development of, and the supervisor's role in, these activities are taken from the pedagogical values associated with the *zone of proximal development* (ZPD; Vygotsky, 1978). ZPD is defined as "the distance between the actual developmental level of an individual as determined by independent problem solving and the level of potential development as determined through problem solving under adult guidance, or in collaboration with more capable peers" (Vygotsky, 1978, p. 86). Thus, supervisees will develop the competencies required for accreditation more effectively and efficiently if guidance and collaboration with a *more capable other* (supervisor) and peers (other supervisees) is structured in a way to meet the needs of the individual. For example, one of the activities the CMPDG adopts is *case study-based role play*, in which supervisees are presented with a case each week prior to a meeting and asked to prepare to: (a) discuss potential solutions to the scenario; and (b) engage in a role play focusing on the main issues presented in the case. Scenarios within these cases include managing "guilty knowledge" and working with a client whose expectations lie outside the boundaries of the role of the SEP practitioner. These activities allow the supervisee to initially work on their own to conceptualize their personal understanding of the scenario and potential approaches to dealing with the issues before having the opportunity to discuss these initial ideas with other supervisees and then exploring in more depth some of the theoretical and practical implications with the whole group (including supervisors). Indeed, from a Vygotskian perspective the supervisor's role involves mediating the supervisee's learning activity as they share knowledge through social interaction (Dixon-Krauss, 1996). For us as supervisors this process has been equally challenging and rewarding. The activity requires us to act outside of our comfort zones as we have to react to the individual needs of the supervisees and maintain a stance of guiding and supporting their ideas rather than directing supervisees to consider acting in a particular way. Our role as supervisors, therefore, is to operate, where possible, unobtrusively by guiding and *scaffolding* the supervisees' engagement in the activities and the associated learning emanating from the process.

Scaffolding occurs through the use of a number of strategies such as: discussing professional practice issues; directed reading; observation of practice; supervisor disclosure through Q&A; role plays; and collaborative case conceptualization. For example, at the end of the CMPDG meetings, time is always afforded for shared reflection on the content of the meeting. In pairs the supervisees discuss: (a) what was important to them; (b) what they have learned (or will be taking away); (c) what this learning means for them and their practice; and (d) how they will apply their learning. Following the meeting these reflections are recorded by the supervisees

Table 26.1 CMPDG Activities

Activity	Purpose	Application Examples
Case study-based role play	Supervisors are afforded the opportunity to observe trainees in different delivery contexts (e.g., one-to-one; workshops; small-group sessions) and focus on a range of competencies associated with practical service-delivery.	Role plays are generally organized for: (a) intake and rapport building; (b) communication and listening skills; (c) managing congruence between philosophy and practice; and (d) delivering interventions. However, specific cases (e.g., post-tournament team de-brief sessions) are also organized that require the supervisees to plan and engage in case conceptualizations that form the vehicle for post-session reflective practice.
Problem-based learning scenarios	To provide the opportunity for supervisors to present rare and complex situations that the supervisees might experience with their clients in a safe and supportive manner and thus better prepare them for "what if" scenarios.	A scenario is presented to the group who work in sub-groups. Following an allotted time for discussion and problem solving, the groups feedback with the expectation that discussion ensues to encourage supervisees to consider the meaning and justification of their responses. Typical scenarios are associated with professional ethics, guilty knowledge, and gaining entry.
Supervisee workshops	Provides supervisees with the opportunity to practice upcoming sessions with clients. In addition, supervisees have the opportunity to present on an area of sport psychology (e.g., mental toughness) that is pertinent to their work at that particular time.	Supervisees take control of the planning, organization, delivery, and reflective discussion within the session. They direct the duration, location, and activities of the meeting based on their individual needs. Supervisees cover topics from mental skills training sessions to service delivery issues they have experienced.
Online discussions	To encourage more regular and consistent engagement in discussion about the theory and practice of SEP.	CMPDG members (including supervisors) take turns posting a blog onto a private online platform (Google Drive) that concludes with questions and discussion prompts for the other members to comment or respond to. The topics of the blogs can range from procedural issues associated with BASES SE to personal and professional issues related to applied service delivery.
Shared reflective practice	To encourage the development of self-awareness and promotion of practice philosophy. To offer the opportunity to explore experiences in more critical depth and to encourage discussion regarding practice-based issues. Finally, to encourage the proactive engagement in experiential learning.	Shared reflective practice is structured through Driscoll's (1994) model of reflective practice that encourages those reflecting to consider the *what, so what,* and *now what* of the experience. Both supervisors and supervisees split into two smaller groups, with each member having the opportunity to share and reflect on practice-based experiences/issues. Issues and outcomes are shared with the whole group before individuals document the discussion on their issue and (if necessary) add a further layer of individual reflection onto the incident.

and sent to their supervisor for comment. In this way the record acts as a living document that can change and be reviewed to ensure that the supervisee is making the most of the learning that emerges from their engagement in the CMPDG. This approach links to our philosophy for supervision in that we take considerable time and care to structure the group's environment and subsequent supervisee opportunities to maximize their development. Indeed, if we are to achieve the aforementioned aims associated with the development of autonomous practitioners then such an approach to supervision is necessary.

REFLECTION

The CMPDG has provided a real opportunity for engagement in collaborative approaches to supervision and assisted the authors on their journey as neophyte supervisors. Certainly, this approach has been a reciprocal one, and while much of the literature on supervision within SEP has focused upon the perspective of the supervisee's development (e.g., Hutter et al., 2015; Watson et al., 2004), based on our experiences, we agree with Carrington (2004) that greater attention should be given to the potential of the process to foster professional development in the supervisor. As supervisors, the CMPDG has afforded us the opportunity to learn about our own professional practice as well as the fundamentals of supervision that allow the goals of the process to be achieved. Specifically, we have gained a better understanding of how to develop, build, and manage relationships with our supervisees as well as how best to facilitate their relationships with other group members. Additionally, we have become more aware of the potential value we add to each supervisee's professional development and personal growth, which can be a source of anxiety for those beginning their tenure (see Cropley & Neil, 2014). Finally, the group has facilitated the development of fresh ideas for practice and supervision through the challenge that the supervisees create. As a result we have become more innovative in our approaches to supervision that have allowed us to better live our values and beliefs regarding the process of supervision.

Since its inauguration, trainee members of the CMPDG have consistently offered support for the impact that it has had on their learning and development. They have outlined the importance of developing a social network of like-minded people who offer support during what is an intense period of training. Supervisees have also commented on the value of the reciprocal approach to learning and the influence that shared reflection has had on their personal and professional growth. Indeed, the opportunity for shared reflection is relatively unique due to the cultural and ethical issues associated with such practice outside of a formal collaborative environment (e.g., confidentiality issues).

While we have outlined the potential benefits of such a collaborative approach, we have also experienced some challenges that are worthy of consideration. First, there is a natural turnover of group members. As supervisees complete the SE program and become accredited, they leave the group, and as new supervisees are taken on they are emancipated into the group. This has the potential to cause a number of issues in relation to the bond and trust between the group members who need to forge strong peer working alliances in order to feel comfortable before being willing to fully engage with the group's activities. Others have opted for closed group membership when operating similar collaborative peer supervision (e.g., Donaldson-Feilder & Bush, 2009) for these very reasons. However, such a solution is not permissible in the context in which we supervise. It is therefore important to recognize the need to ensure compatibility between supervisor and supervisee and ensure that they are clear about the expectations of the group prior to their engagement. Second, the "hands-off" approach to supervision can cause some discomfort due to the lack of control and perceived impact that the supervisor is having (Silva et al., 2011). When employing strategies such as problem-based learning, for example, it is difficult at times not to step in and offer hints and tips or to model certain behaviors in a way that represents the supervisor's approach. In attempts to overcome this issue, it is important to be clear about your philosophy for supervision and to understand why you value certain approaches to learning. Staying focused on maintaining congruence between philosophy and behavior can then be easier as you can rationalize why certain actions might detract from the learning experience you have created.

We believe that the CMPDG has been a success for a number of reasons. First, the group is relatively small, which allows all members to be fully engaged throughout group activities and protects against passive, social loafing. Second, having two supervisors present allows the group's activities to be managed and structured more effectively as well as providing the opportunity for peer supervision. Third, the range of activities we adopt is diverse and linked directly to the needs of the supervisees and of the SE program. In addition, some of these activities are continuous (i.e., not confined to the formal group meeting), which encourages more consistent engagement in critical discussion regarding the theory and practice of sport psychology. Finally, giving supervisees ownership of the aims of the group and the expectations of its members improves buy-in and thus improves engagement from the very start. In summary, the challenge of supervision within applied SEP is one that is complex and inherently messy. Collaborative approaches to supervision offer an opportunity to navigate these difficulties by embracing peer and reciprocal learning and offering social support to both supervisors and supervisees. It is important, however, to ensure that any collaborative approach undertaken emerges from the philosophy of the supervisor and is structured in a way that facilitates an operative learning environment.

SUGGESTED READINGS

Castillo, S. (2014). Ethical issues in training future practitioners. In J. G. Cremades & L. S. Tashman (Eds.), *Becoming a sport, exercise, and performance psychology professional: A global perspective* (pp. 252–259). New York, NY: Routledge.

Donaldson-Feilder, E., & Bush, Kris. (2009). Achieving effective supervision for coaching psychologists: Exploring a peer supervision/reflective learning group model. *The Coaching Psychologist, 5,* 34–38.

Hutter, V., Oldenhof-Veldman, T., & Oudejans, R. (2015). What trainee sport psychologists want to learn in supervision. *Psychology of Sport and Exercise, 16,* 101–109.

REFLECTIVE QUESTIONS

1. Why is it important to understand philosophy for supervision?
2. What role does reflective practice play for the development of trainee practitioners and neophyte supervisors?
3. How might collaborative learning impact the development of trainee practitioners in sport psychology?
4. What is "scaffolding" and how might it offer an effective approach to supervision?
5. What barriers, for both the supervisor and supervisee, may inhibit the potential benefits of collaborative approaches to supervision?

REFERENCES

British Association of Sport & Exercise Sciences (2015). *BASES supervised experience guidelines.* Retrieved from www.bases.org.uk/Supervised-Experience and www.bases.org.uk/Accreditation

Carrington, G. (2004). Supervision as a reciprocal learning process. *Educational Psychology in Practice, 20,* 31–42.

Castillo, S. (2014). Ethical issues in training future practitioners. In J. G. Cremades & L. S. Tashman (Eds.), *Becoming a sport, exercise, and performance psychology professional: A global perspective* (pp. 252–259). New York, NY: Routledge.

Cropley, B., & Neil, R. (2014). The neophyte supervisor: What did I get myself into? In J. G. Cremades & L. S. Tashman (Eds.), *Becoming a sport, exercise, and performance psychology professional: A global perspective* (pp. 219–227). New York, NY: Routledge.

Dixon-Krauss, L. (1996). *Vygotsky in the classroom. Mediated literacy instruction and assessment.* White Plains, NY: Longman Publishers.

Donaldson-Feilder, E., & Bush, Kris. (2009). Achieving effective supervision for coaching psychologists: Exploring a peer supervision/reflective learning group model. *The Coaching Psychologist, 5,* 34–38.

Driscoll, J. (1994). Reflective practice for practise. *Senior Nurse, 13,* 47–50.

Garvey, R., Stokes, P., & Megginson, D. (2009). *Coaching and mentoring: Theory and practice.* London: Sage.

Hemmings, B. (2014). "It took me 10 years to become an overnight success." In P. McCarthy & M. Jones (Eds.), *Becoming a sport psychologist* (pp. 158–166). Abingdon: Routledge.

Hutter, V., Oldenhof-Veldman, T., & Oudejans, R. (2015). What trainee sport psychologists want to learn in supervision. *Psychology of Sport and Exercise, 16,* 101–109.

Knowles, Z., Gilbourne, D., Tomlinson, V., & Anderson, A. (2007). Reflections on the application of reflective practice for supervision in applied sport psychology. *The Sport Psychologist, 21,* 109–122.

McCormick, A., & Meijen, C. (2015). A lesson learned in time: Advice shared by experienced sport psychologists. *Sport & Exercise Psychology Review, 11,* 43–54.

Meijen, C., & Manley, A. (2010). The supervision process through the eyes of the supervisor. *Sport & Exercise Psychology Review, 6,* 43–46.

Rhodius, A., & Sugarman, K. (2014). Peer consultations with colleagues: The significance of gaining support and avoiding the "lone ranger trap." In J. G. Cremades & L. S. Tashman (Eds.), *Becoming a sport, exercise, and performance psychology professional: A global perspective* (pp. 331–339). New York, NY: Routledge.

Silva, J., Metzler, J., & Lerner, B. (2011). *Training professionals in the practice of sport psychology.* Morgantown, WV: Fitness Information Technology.

Stambulova, N., & Johnson, U. (2010). Novice consultants' experiences: Lessons learned by applied sport psychology students. *Psychology of Sport and Exercise, 11,* 295–303.

Stoltenberg, C., McNeill, B., & Delworth, U. (1998). *IDM supervision: An integrated developmental model for supervising counsellors and therapists.* San Francisco: Jossey-Bass.

Sullivan, S., & Glanz, J. (2000). *Supervision that improves teaching.* Thousand Oaks, CA: Corwin Press.

Tod, D., & Bond, K. (2010). A longitudinal examination of a British neophyte sport psychologist's development. *The Sport Psychologist, 24,* 35–51.

Van Raalte, J., & Andersen, M. B. (2000). Supervision I: From models to doing. In M. B. Andersen (ed.), *Doing sport psychology* (pp. 153–166). Champaign, IL: Human Kinetics.

Vygotsky, L. S. (1978). *Mind in society: The development of higher psychological processes.* Cambridge, MA: Harvard University Press.

Watson, J. C., McAlarnen, M., & Shannon, V. (2014). Facilitating our future: Roles, responsibilities, and the development of the sport, exercise, and performance supervisor. In J. G. Cremades & L. S. Tashman (Eds.), *Becoming a sport, exercise, and performance psychology professional: A global perspective* (pp. 236–242). New York, NY: Routledge.

Watson, J. C., Zizzi, S., Etzel, E., & Lubker, J. (2004). Applied sport psychology supervision: A survey of students and professionals. *The Sport Psychologist, 18,* 415–429.

27 From Mentee to Mentor

A Case Study for the Neophyte Supervisor

Justine Vosloo, Rebecca A. Zakrajsek, and Emma Grindley

Supervision is an important process through which guidance and training regarding applied practice is provided to the trainee/student and Andersen (1994) notes that the term "supervisor" is associated with the person who provides this supervision. However, the Association for Applied Sport Psychology (AASP) transitioned to using the term *mentoring* to describe the supervision that is received toward achieving certified consultant status (AASP, n.d.), but may consider returning to supervision. Thus, the terms supervision and mentoring will both be used to refer to this process of guiding and training sport, exercise, and performance psychology (SEPP) professionals. This chapter will introduce the case of "Chris," a CC-AASP (i.e., certified consultant with the Association for Applied Sport Psychology) neophyte SEPP supervisor and faculty member at a small university. The challenges that this neophyte supervisor encounters are commonplace, and consist of: rapport building, trust and credibility, concern for client welfare, power dynamics, and dual roles, to name just a few. This case study will first provide relevant background information on the mentor and mentee, a description and analysis of the case study will follow, a discussion of a theoretical approach or philosophy will be provided, and steps for preparation will lead into a section for processing and reflecting on the situation.

BACKGROUND INFORMATION

Mentor and Mentee Information

Chris is a Caucasian, heterosexual, male faculty member at a small university. He has been teaching and providing sport psychology services to the athletics department there since completing his doctoral studies in SEPP two years ago. His studies prepared him well for this work, allowing him to learn about SEPP research and practice in the classroom and then apply it to individual and team sessions. His graduate program used a meta-supervision type model that included several faculty and peer mentors, which allowed him to gain guidance and feedback in his professional development. Within this model he became a peer mentor to two fellow students who were consulting with teams and individuals; it is here that he learned some of the basics about supervision and being a mentor (e.g., building rapport, discussing expectations of the process, helping the mentee explore the consulting process and SEPP concepts, allowing the mentee autonomy, and being aware of ethical issues such as transference and countertransference).

Five months ago Chris became a CC-AASP and promptly thereafter was contacted by Tisha. Tisha, an African-American, bisexual female, recently moved back to the area following her master's degree in SEPP. She is excited, and a little nervous, to begin her consulting career and apply all that she has learned during her studies. She aims to gain supervised hours to be able to apply for her CC-AASP status, thus her call to Chris.

Mentee and Client Information

Hattie is a bi-racial, female high-school senior, from a middle class background. Her mom is a first-generation immigrant from Mexico, while her dad is African-American. She has played soccer since age five and has progressed in talent to become one of the school's "stand out" student-athletes that everyone in the school and town knows of. This past year she has attracted significant attention from college scouts and her performance has started to decrease. She is seeking help for her recent struggle to perform under pressure and to manage her anxiety related to "making it" at the college level. Hattie's mom initiated the referral to Tisha as she knew of her graduate training and return to the area. Hattie's coach and team are aware of the referral to Tisha, and are supportive of the consulting relationship. Tisha has been working with Hattie for six weeks. Thus far the consulting sessions with Hattie have focused on what has been going on with training and competition that week, and working through a variety of applied skills such as goal-setting, imagery, breathing, and self-talk.

Mentor and Mentee Relationship

Tisha and Chris first met four weeks ago (two weeks after Tisha started working with Hattie). Within this time they have met three times. Chris has been very excited about mentoring, sharing his passion for SEPP, and helping the mentee. Chris initially had a plan for supervision, but the sessions soon appeared to take the following focus: (1) getting to know Tisha, for example, learning about her background, training during her master's program, career goals, understanding of the SEPP research and consulting frameworks, strengths and weaknesses in communication and interview skills, and the applied techniques she uses; and (2) discussing what Tisha has been doing in sessions and providing feedback on the techniques she has been teaching. Chris found this to be the shape that the sessions naturally fell into as he tried to build rapport with his mentee. However, he also tried to "catch up" with the work she had done with Hattie, feeling some pressure to ensure that she was not "messing up."

After his last mentoring meeting, Chris takes a moment to stop and reflect and becomes aware that he is concerned with how the mentoring is going. He feels that his mentee is not really opening up to him, not sharing all the issues Hattie is facing, and not being aware and/ or sharing all the concerns she is having about the consultation. Chris also feels that Tisha is rushing into interventions, as she is too keen to jump into teaching and being the expert. He senses that there is a nervousness in Tisha, a feeling he recognized in himself as a new consultant in graduate school. Chris has a sense of uneasiness as he thinks about the sessions; it brings up feelings of frustration and worry about Tisha's work and his own abilities about mentoring.

DESCRIPTION OF THE CASE

It is not uncommon for young CC-AASP professionals to find themselves in the position of providing mentoring upon completion of their graduate SEPP program and attainment of CC-AASP status. Neophyte mentors often experience a range of emotions and challenges as they begin their career and enter into their first professional supervisory role. At the same time, mentees early in their consulting experiences who want to earn CC-AASP status also experience a range of emotions and challenges. Consequently, the neophyte mentor and mentee both bring their own thoughts, feelings, and emotions into the mentor–mentee relationship. Unless thoughts, feelings, and emotions are directly discussed, it is not uncommon for the neophyte mentor and mentee to experience a "disconnect" and frustration with the mentoring relationship, much like Chris and Tisha.

Neophyte mentors most likely share many similar feelings and experiences as Chris. As a neophyte mentor, Chris is excited to be practicing, learning, and helping someone new in the field. At the same time he is nervous about getting it "right" and helping Tisha and Hattie, while also enjoying the process himself. His personal feeling of competency is being challenged as the supervision experience started taking on a focus that he did not anticipate. Chris focused on demonstrating his own knowledge about SEPP to the mentee, especially due to his feeling of wanting to establish his role and value as a mentor. The pressure that Chris puts on himself to help the mentee not "mess up" stems from his desire to prove himself as a mentor, which only enhances his frustration and worry about his own abilities.

Chris' desire to prevent mistakes by Tisha may also stem from a concern about Hattie's welfare. As a neophyte SEPP professional, Tisha goes into the supervision relationship eager to prove herself as a consultant. She is aware of the power dynamics within the mentor–mentee relationship and does not want to look like she doesn't know what she is doing. However, the current nature of the supervision meetings and energy within the room may suggest to Tisha that Chris does not fully trust her competency and abilities, which further increase the power dynamics between the mentor and mentee. Consequently, Tisha holds back on the details of the athlete and interventions due to her fear of receiving negative evaluation and feedback. They are both aware of a mild tension and a lack of a steady pace and ease in their meetings, but they have not stopped to process it, thus many of the aspects described above are bubbling right under the surface (subconscious–conscious level). Without some resolution, it is unlikely that the best mentoring is occurring, that either party is enjoying the process, and it could lead to the relationship ending prematurely.

The main concerns in this case study can be understood within the framework proposed by Vosloo, Zakrajsek, and Grindley (2014) for developing the mentor–mentee or supervisor-supervisee relationship. This framework for developing an effective mentor–mentee relationship has three phases: (1) building rapport and establishing a safe environment; (2) providing structure and autonomy; and (3) implementing the transitioning process of the supervisee becoming a supervisor. Within the case study, both Chris and Tisha are eager to be in phase two, providing structure and autonomy. It is common for neophyte supervisors and supervisees to want to move quickly to this phase, given that the focus is on building consulting skills and strategies through developing the supervisee's knowledge and methods of SEPP delivery and reflective practice. However, like the SEPP consultant–athlete relationship (see Petitpas, Giges, & Danish, 1999), it is argued that nurturing a trusting relationship is an essential component in establishing the foundation for an effective supervision experience (Vosloo et al., 2014).

Although Chris made attempts to build rapport with Tisha, several issues that commonly appear in phase one were not addressed (e.g., fear of failure, concern with competency, expectations, mentor and mentee's role in supervision, and the process of supervision). As a result, a trusting relationship and working alliance was not fully developed and a safe environment where the supervisee feels empowered and comfortable to talk openly was not established. Building an effective mentor–mentee relationship is even more important when considering the welfare of the athlete the supervisee is working with. Tisha is not openly discussing what the athlete (Hattie) is experiencing, which suggests her own fear of negative evaluation may be getting in the way of an athlete–centered approach to consulting. As the neophyte supervisor, it is Chris' responsibility to develop the mentor–mentee relationship, and to continue monitoring this relationship throughout the supervision process. Chris can take on a more directive and hierarchical approach up front while nurturing a more collegial supervision relationship as he and Tisha move through phase two.

APPROACH/PHILOSOPHY

Professionals within the SEPP literature have emphasized the importance of supervision training in providing quality supervision and effective service delivery (see Barney, Andersen, & Riggs, 1996; Vosloo et al., 2014). Vosloo, Zakrajsek, Grindley, and Naoi (2010) proposed a mentoring and supervision training model that prepares graduate students with skills to provide supervision. The use of peer mentoring and meta-supervision is a central component of this model. In this case study, Chris' graduate program used a meta-supervision model in which he was exposed to the basics about providing supervision, was a peer mentor, and gained guidance and feedback during his development. This is often not the case with SEPP professionals; Watson, Zizzi, Etzel, and Lubker (2004) found that the vast majority (75.9 percent) of SEPP professionals providing supervision reported little or no supervision training. Chris' experience within a meta-supervision model during his graduate training nurtured an appreciation for the supervision process and seeking supervision when needed. He had also developed several collegial relationships where he could easily contact another SEPP professional to seek feedback and mentorship. As a neophyte supervisor, Chris may benefit from a more consistent meta-supervision experience (e.g., weekly or bi-weekly meetings to discuss his experience and development with the supervision process) and transition into seeking meta-supervision on an as-needed basis as he gains more professional supervisory experiences.

PREPARATION/PLANNING

Since Chris has done some reflection on the relationship with the mentee, additional and guided reflective practice is necessary. Using the six-stage model of reflection (Anderson, Knowles, & Gilbourne, 2004), Chris should reflect on the following questions (modified from Anderson et al., 2004): (1) What happened during these supervision meetings? (2) What was I thinking and feeling during these meetings? (3) What was effective and not effective enough during these meetings? (4) What happened that resulted in this outcome? (5) What else could I have done in these meetings? (6) If a similar situation arose again, what would I do differently? Additionally, it is recommended that Chris share these reflections during meta-supervision with a colleague. This is preferable to self-reflection alone, as Chris may need an outsider to assist him in making an unbiased self-reflection (Watson, Lubker, & Van Raalte, 2011), and the process of sharing reflections with a colleague results in a multiple-stage reflective experience consisting of instant and deferred reflections, thereby deepening the reflective practice (Anderson et al., 2004). Lastly, it may be helpful for Chris to become better versed with the developmental supervision processes (see Andersen & Williams-Rice, 1996; Barney et al., 1996; Tonn & Harmison, 2004).

The neophyte supervisor should also provide Tisha with guidance for self-reflection so she can engage in effective reflective practice. It is suggested that Chris provide Tisha with readings on the topic of reflective practice (see Holt & Strean, 2001; Knowles, Gilbourne, Tomlinson, & Anderson, 2007). Additionally, these readings could have been used during the initial supervision meeting to discuss roles and expectations associated with being the mentor and mentee. For example, Chris could have directly addressed potential roadblocks (e.g., lack of trust, fear of failure, concern with competence) that could have inhibited the development of an effective supervision relationship, and consequently impacted how comfortable Tisha felt disclosing key details with her mentor.

At this point, Chris may need to start over with Tisha, and start with having the conversation mentioned above. It may also be necessary for Chris to establish a supervision contract with Tisha. This document could define mentor and mentee roles, and also define the mentoring relationship. This document would also serve the purpose of "resetting" the relationship and providing a clean start, whereby expectations of openness, trust, empathy, preparation, and reflective practice are clearly defined and agreed upon by both parties. Lastly, since Tisha is a neophyte consultant, she may be struggling with the consulting process because her professional philosophy for consulting is unclear. Chris may encourage a discussion of her approach, and the development of a professional consulting philosophy (see Poczwardowski, Sherman, & Ravizza, 2004 for guidance).

SUPERVISION PROCESS/EXPERIENCE

The dilemma faced by the neophyte supervisor could have been prevented if the mentor took the time to develop a strong level of rapport and mentoring relationship first, before moving into the skill development phase of the mentoring relationship. The best approach at this point would be for the neophyte supervisor to directly address the "uneasiness" present in the relationship, and to process the interpersonal dynamics between him and Tisha. For example, Chris senses that Tisha is holding back information about the details of her individual consultations with Hattie. Chris also feels that Tisha might be too focused on herself during consultations with Hattie, as she appears to be concerned with demonstrating her expertise. This might be a result of Tisha's fear of being criticized by Chris.

Chris is aware of these feelings during sessions, but suppresses them to focus on the session content. This may be due to the fast pace of the session, his uncertainty of how to approach the feelings and issue, and also being aware that his own need to demonstrate his expertise during the supervision meetings with Tisha is also impacting his ability to build a relationship with Tisha. Instead of stopping the session to address these issues as they arise, he continues on somewhat distracted and uneasy.

Chris could use this insight from his own reflective practice and meta-supervision conversations to take responsibility for the elements of the relationship that he is responsible for. Directly discussing his thoughts, feelings, and emotions as a supervisor provides Chris with the opportunity to address the power dynamic, and to help Tisha feel more at ease disclosing her own errors, fears, and concerns with him. It is recommended that Chris ask Tisha for feedback on his actions as a mentor, and to discuss the importance of providing feedback to him as they continue their mentoring relationship. Taking these actions would allow Chris to revisit the important tasks associated with Phase I of the model (i.e., building rapport and establishing a safe environment; Vosloo et al., 2014), and allow for more effective work to be done in Phase II (i.e., structure and building autonomy). Lastly, in each supervision meeting, Chris could purposefully revisit Phase I issues while concurrently addressing Tisha's work with Hattie. For example, Chris may openly revisit both him and Tisha's "need" to demonstrate their expertise and how this might be getting in the way of an athlete-centered approach to consulting and a mentee-centered approach to supervision. At the same time, Chris can be sure to address the SEPP skills Tisha is currently using in her consulting sessions while still monitoring and nurturing a positive relationship and safe environment.

A factor that is not mentioned in this case study but that should be considered is the inherent power dynamics and cultural factors that may be impacting this relationship. Not only is culture influencing the need for multicultural competence development in the mentee, but culture is also impacting the supervision relationship itself (Arthur & Collins, 2010). It is recommended that Chris consider how to address and incorporate the diversity in world-view, personal life experiences, and associations with various cultural groups or identities that may exist between him and Tisha during their mentoring meetings. Arthur and Collins (2010) suggest that doing so could "facilitate a stronger supervisory process" and expand the provision of multiculturally competent SEPP consulting services to clients (p. 271). As a heterosexual, Caucasian male, Chris' experiences and interactions within the training and consulting contexts have been shaped and influenced by the status of privilege he holds (see Butryn, 2002). For example, a client/coach or supervisor may have never questioned or challenged his competency by virtue of holding a "dominant" status in US society. However, Tisha may have encountered many occasions of having her competency and knowledge challenged by others due to her status as a female and racial and sexual minority (see Yambor & Connelly, 1991). These are experiences that Chris has not had or considered. Additionally, Chris should acknowledge to himself that in his role as "supervisor" he has the power to directly impact Tisha's own consulting career. This power exists within his supervisory role, his ability to support or deny her hours toward obtaining CC-AASP, and future recommendations he may make about her work to others. Implicitly, Chris may also view her differently due to her gender, sexual orientation, ethnic affiliation, religion, and spirituality, and lack of awareness of these cultural dynamics may result in increased guardedness, confusion and misunderstandings, and unspoken barriers within the supervisory relationship (Arthur & Collins, 2010).

REFLECTION

Based on the case of Chris the neophyte supervisor and Tisha the neophyte mentee, the following take-home messages for further reflection are suggested:

- Training in the area of supervision/mentoring and cultural factors impacting the supervisory relationship should be incorporated into doctoral programs. In this case study, the neophyte supervisor was previously exposed to supervision models, and received meta-supervision during his graduate training. However, even with this training, challenges were still encountered.
- Both neophyte and experienced supervisors could benefit from incorporating structured reflective practice into their supervision practice, and also seek out the guidance of a mentor with whom they could share their reflective thoughts and concerns. Engaging in continued meta-supervision throughout one's professional career, both as a consultant and supervisor, is strongly encouraged for all SEPP professionals.
- The mentoring process can easily be prematurely and/or too narrowly focused on the skill and technique development component of the mentee's work. As illustrated in this case study, the development of a strong, trusting, and open mentor–mentee relationship is vital for effective supervision. Additionally, this relationship should be frequently revisited, tended to, and protected from potential disruptions. If at any time the interpersonal dynamic between these roles breaks down (and personal emotions and feelings can be a guide/barometer for this), mentors should take it upon themselves to address this disruption and tend to it as soon as possible.
- It is important to note that with time and more experience the mentor will improve in the areas that may currently be of concern and possibly even develop strengths in these areas (e.g., supervision contracts, reflective practice, emotional awareness and insight, and frequent re-evaluation of the mentor–mentee relationship). However, there may be times where this mentor–mentee relationship does not flourish, and in these situations if the steps that are taken do not rectify or improve the relationship, the mentor should consider referring the mentee to another mentor who may be a better "fit" for the mentee.

SUGGESTED READINGS

Barney, S. T., Andersen, M. B., & Riggs, C. A. (1996). Supervision in sport psychology: Some recommendations for practicum training. *Journal of Applied Sport Psychology, 8*, 200–217.

Butryn, T. M. (2002). Critically examining white racial identity and privilege in sport psychology consulting. *The Sport Psychologist, 16*, 316–336.

Donaldson-Fielder, E., & Bush, K. (2009). Achieving effective supervision for coaching psychologists: Exploring a peer supervision/reflective learning group model. *The Coaching Psychologist, 5*, 34–38.

Knowles, Z., Gilbourne, D., Tomlinson, V., & Anderson, A. G. (2007). Reflections on the application of reflective practice for supervision in applied sport psychology. *The Sport Psychologist, 21*, 109–122.

REFLECTIVE QUESTIONS

1. What are the strengths of the mentee and mentor that they bring into the relationship?
2. Identify the main concerns in this case that might prevent the mentor and mentee from having an effective supervision experience. What indicators are present to lead you to your conclusions?

3. Describe what the mentor did well in this case? What did he do to establish a relationship (i.e., build rapport and trust) with the mentee? What could the mentor have done differently to establish a better relationship with the mentee?
4. Identify the steps the mentor and mentee could have taken to change the current situation from occurring. What would have potentially made things worse and what could have been done that could have resulted in a different outcome?
5. What thoughts and feelings would come up for you as the mentee and/or the mentor at the various times (i.e., initial contact asking for a mentoring relationship, first meeting, second meeting, and third meeting)?
6. What have you experienced as a mentor or mentee in a supervisory relationship that worked or did not work for you?
7. Review the three-phase supervision framework and identify which areas you would want to work on as the mentor to increase your competence as a neophyte supervisor. Develop a plan for your self-improvement.

REFERENCES

AASP (Association for Applied Sport Psychology) (n.d.). *Becoming a certified consultant.* Retrieved from www.appliedsportpsych.org/certified-consultants/become-a-certified-consultant.

Andersen, M. B. (1994). Ethical considerations in the supervision of applied sport psychology graduate students. *Journal of Applied Sport Psychology, 6*, 152–167.

Andersen, M. B., & Williams-Rice, B. T. (1996). Supervision in the education and training of sport psychology service providers. *The Sport Psychologist, 10*, 278–290.

Anderson, A. G., Knowles, Z., & Gilbourne, D. (2004). Reflective practice for sport psychologists: Concepts, models, practical implications, and thoughts on dissemination. *The Sport Psychologist, 18*, 188–203.

Arthur, N., & Collins, S. (2010). Culture-infused counseling supervision. In N. Pelling, J. Barletta, & P. Armstrong (Eds.), *Practice of Supervision* (pp. 267–295). Bowen Hills: Australian Academic Press.

Barney, S. T., Andersen, M. B., & Riggs, C. A. (1996). Supervision in sport psychology: Some recommendations for practicum training. *Journal of Applied Sport Psychology, 8*, 200–217.

Butryn, T. M. (2002). Critically examining white racial identity and privilege in sport psychology consulting. *The Sport Psychologist, 16*, 316–336.

Holt, N. L., & Strean, W. B. (2001). Reflecting on initiating sport psychology consultation: A self-narrative of neophyte practice. *The Sport Psychologist, 15*, 188–204.

Knowles, Z., Gilbourne, D., Tomlinson, V., & Anderson, A. G. (2007). Reflections on the application of reflective practice for supervision in applied sport psychology. *The Sport Psychologist, 21*, 109–122.

Petitpas, A. J., Giges, B., & Danish, S. J. (1999). The sport psychologist–athlete relationship: Implications for training. *The Sport Psychologist, 13*, 344–357.

Poczwardowski, A., Sherman, C. P., & Ravizza, K. (2004). Professional philosophy in the sport psychology service delivery: Building on theory and practice. *The Sport Psychologist, 18*, 445–463.

Tonn, E., & Harmison, R. J. (2004). Thrown to the wolves: A student's account of her practicum experience. *The Sport Psychologist, 18*, 324–340.

Vosloo, J., Zakrajsek, R., & Grindley, E. (2014). From mentee to mentor: Considerations for the neophyte supervisor. In G. Cremades & L. Tashman (Eds.), *Becoming a sport, exercise, and performance psychology professional: International perspectives* (pp. 228–235). New York, NY: Routledge.

Vosloo, J., Zakrajsek, R., Grindley, E., & Naoi, A. (2010). Long-term consultation, mentoring and supervision: Ten years, six consultants, three coaches, and one team. Workshop presented at the Association for Applied Sport Psychology, October, Providence, RI.

Watson, J. C., Lubker, J. R., & Van Raalte, J. (2011). Problems in reflective practice: Self-bootstrapping versus therapeutic supervision. In D. Gilbourne & M. B. Andersen (Eds.), *Critical essays in applied sport psychology* (pp. 157–172). Champaign, IL: Human Kinetics.

Watson, J. C., Zizzi, S. J., Etzel, E. F., & Lubker, J. R. (2004). Applied sport psychology supervision: A survey of students and professionals. *The Sport Psychologist, 18*, 415–429.

Yambor, J., & Connelly, D. (1991). Issues confronting female sport psychology consultants working with male student-athletes. *The Sport Psychologist, 5*, 304–312.

28 Helping Ron with Burnout and Career Transition

Martin R. Eubank and David Tod

It was during the first year of my career when Ron plonked himself down in a chair in my office and told me (David) he was tired of swimming. He was thinking he would stop after the forthcoming National Championships. I collaborated with Ron over the following year until he left the institution where I worked to pursue a career as a lawyer. At the time I believed I had been effective because Ron achieved his goals for the Nationals and for his career termination. Since working with Ron, my understanding of psychological service delivery has changed as I have developed. Although I still believe I was effective and acted professionally, my evaluation of the case has broadened. In the first part of the chapter we present the case. In the reflection section we reconsider Ron's story based on our current views of psychological service delivery. Neither interpretation (original or current) can be considered "correct," but each reflects how practitioners' perceptions, beliefs, and assumptions color their interpretations, behaviors, and applied sport psychology work.

BACKGROUND INFORMATION

Ron was an 18-year-old male swimmer making his initial foray into the open ranks. He favored backstroke and had performed well as a junior, having won National titles at different age-group levels. He enjoyed the social currency at school and in his social networks that comes with being a talented sportsman in New Zealand, and had a dream to swim at the Olympics. As part of his plan to become an elite swimmer, he had enrolled in the Certificate in Sport Studies, a program on which I (David) taught and offered applied sport psychology services to the student-athletes.

At that time in New Zealand (the 1990s), there were no requirements for practitioners to be formally supervised. Further, there were no accreditation schemes focused on sport psychology. The situation in New Zealand was similar to many other countries and research from that time hints strongly that practitioners (accredited or otherwise) generally did not engage in supervision (Watson, Zizzi, Etzel, & Lubker, 2004). My experience of supervision was piecemeal. I had a network of individuals, including my master's thesis advisor, a work colleague, a counselor, and a mainstream practitioner from whom I would seek supervision. I also consulted my line manager because, although he was not a psychologist, he did have relevant experience that helped me deal with an ethical issue I faced as I was helping Ron.

Although I did not have a formal supervisor when working with Ron, I rang my master's advisor several times to seek "supervision" regarding the applied work I was undertaking with Ron and others. His approach to "supervising" paralleled his mental skills training, solution-focused style of consulting. He would help me identify specific issues associated with my clients and arrive at practical solutions. In addition, I would seek advice from others, such as the counselors where I worked and my line manager (discussed below).

I was aware that the dual relationship that resulted from me both teaching and working with Ron (and other student athletes) was an ethical issue I needed to address. When I began my job, I understood that part of my role as a teacher was to evaluate the student-athletes' academic performances. When meeting with me as a practitioner, students might have refrained from sharing information with me if they believed doing so could affect their grades. Such a fear may have been compounded by the mandatory requirement that students were to see me twice per year for sport psychology-related assistance (a requirement that was set by the institution administration as part of their application to the New Zealand Qualification's Authority for program approval). In addition, in the first six months of my position I noticed that I was tempted to bend the institution's rules for students such as Ron, with whom I had established a close professional relationship, such as granting assignment extensions for reasons that were typically considered unacceptable excuses.

Prior to accepting the position I was aware that I would engage in dual relationships with students and that there was a mandatory requirement for them to see the sport psychology practitioner. As a fresh-faced graduate, however, I needed a job and there were no other sport psychology teaching or applied positions available in New Zealand at that time. My relationship with Ron occurred during my first few months in the position and his case was one that helped me confront the dual relationship issue. The supervision from my master's advisor and advice from my line manager (as discussed above) was helpful in resolving this issue.

DESCRIPTION OF THE CASE

As Ron and I talked, I recognized threads signaling that he was probably experiencing burnout, according to Cresswell and Eklund's (2006) characteristics (physical and emotional exhaustion, reduced accomplishment and low self-efficacy, and sport devaluation). Ron described feeling run down and "knackered." Upon waking up in the morning he felt tired rather than rested, and he often preferred to stay in bed rather than go to training. He described being lethargic and uninterested in swimming or in attending class. His classes reminded him of swimming and his tiredness. He skipped classes and vegetated in front of daytime TV. Previously he had looked forward to swimming and was happy when he trained well. His training times had been slow and recently a rival had beaten him for the first time. His coach had expressed concern and thought that Ron appeared to be going through the motions rather than training with intensity. Ron believed his recent performances indicated declining ability. Regarding sport devaluation, Ron was questioning his participation in swimming. He asked himself questions such as "Was it worth it?" If he did not represent his country, what would he get out of swimming?

As our collaboration proceeded, we addressed Ron's desire to cease swimming and to plan his retirement. Ron had difficulty accepting his decision, despite thinking it was his best option. Many factors troubling him echoed research on predictors of career termination quality (Park, Lavallee, & Tod, 2013). Ron had a strong athletic identity, one that others (e.g., his coach, parents, and schoolteachers) had reinforced over the years. Ron had linked his worth as a person to his ability to swim. He feared that if he didn't achieve his swimming goals his parents and others would think he was a failure, and he would lose their approval.

PREPARATION/PLANNING

I used Taylor and Schneider's (1992) sport-clinical intake protocol to help frame Ron's case. The protocol shed light on Ron's presenting problem, athletic history, social support, health status, influential life events, and changes (cognitive, emotional, behavioral, and social) prior to his presenting problem. Goal-setting was another tool I used with Ron, to assist in planning and preparation. We identified Ron's major goals and the factors that needed to change for him to achieve his objectives. We then set short-term goals, each with achievement strategies. We drew a diagram recording the goal-setting process on paper, in a hierarchical top-down fashion that resembled a Christmas tree, which Ron could take away. He reported that the diagram was useful because it helped him to break "everything down into specific areas" and increased his confidence that he could manage his stress, illustrating that assessment is a viable intervention.

APPROACH/PHILOSOPHY

In helping Ron, I followed a mental skills training framework informed by a cognitive-behavioral approach. The mental skills training model resonated with the view I held at that time regarding how to help people. For example, I accepted the assumption regarding the interactions among behaviors, thoughts, feelings, and environments. If I could teach Ron how to manage his thoughts and behaviors, then he might be able to reduce his negative emotions, lessen his tiredness, and cope with his environment. As a neophyte practitioner, however, I had a layperson's understanding of the professional helping process: It was about me giving something, such as concrete knowledge or advice, to the client. At heart, I viewed myself as an educational practitioner and I perceived parallels between what I did with athletes one-on-one and how I taught my classes. Many times I found the mental skills training approach effective because clients would ask for strategies and would report finding them helpful.

I also found reading about *behavioral experiments* from cognitive therapy literature helpful with Ron (Beck, 1995). Ron and I would reach some understanding of an issue troubling him. We would explore his thoughts, feelings, behaviors, and coping strategies associated with the issue, along with any influential environmental factors. Then we would identify actions he could undertake to resolve the issue, starting typically with an examination of ways Ron had previously coped with similar circumstances. He would engage in those actions between our sessions before reporting back on the results.

To illustrate, one issue Ron raised was his difficulty in getting mental breaks from swimming. He found that during down-time between classes and away from the water, he would ruminate about his situation. We agreed that trying to avoid thinking about swimming was less helpful than distracting himself by focusing on another topic. Together we shifted through the possible pleasurable activities Ron thought would distract him and absorb his attention, allowing him to take a mental break. We also examined his schedule to identify when such activities could occur. Ron decided he wanted to build model boats. Each boat would normally take him two or three days, because he would take his time to ensure he did a good job. Occasionally, he liked to launch them into a pond near the property where he lived and shoot them with his air rifle. Ron reported the activity achieved its aim, and after spending three or four hours he "felt less wound up."

To help Ron decide what he wished to do after completing the Certificate, he and I engaged in goal-setting to review his current resources, skills, knowledge, and interests, determine what career he wanted, and consider how he would achieve his goals. We arranged for him to have a session with a career counselor, who was an individual with whom I had a professional relationship. Ron believed the time with the counselor had been useful, and one of the options that he was considering was to attend law school. To explore this option, Ron spent time talking with one of his neighbors who was a partner in a law firm. Ron visited his neighbor's office and spent an afternoon in court to see the person operate. We also arranged for Ron to visit a local university's law school to find out if it was possible that he could be accepted. It transpired that he would have a competitive chance of being accepted into the first year of the undergraduate program, based on a combination of his high-school results, successfully passing his Certificate, and writing a strong personal statement revealing why he wanted to become a lawyer. We developed a second goal-setting diagram detailing the short-term goals and achievement strategies that would help Ron get accepted into law school.

SUPERVISION PROCESS/EXPERIENCE

It is unsurprising that the "supervision" I received regarding Ron was ad hoc and less than ideal given my stage of development. Fortunately, in some places around the globe, such as the UK and Australia, educational pathways have developed and come under the auspices of professional bodies legislated to accredit individuals. My master's advisor helped a great deal in terms of adopting a solution-focused approach, particularly around performance and finding ways to help Ron relax. In addition, the counselor at the institution where I worked helped me broaden my understanding of service delivery and pointed me to cognitive therapy, which helped me develop my understanding of behavioral experiments. The counselor also assisted my attempts to help Ron resolve his career transition issues.

My master's advisor and line manager helped me balance my dual role with the students. I established a number of routines to manage my behavior and students' perceptions. I drew on these strategies to ensure that Ron and I were able to have a transparent relationship. I communicated to students on multiple occasions in class that although they were required to see me twice each year, the length and content of those sessions were entirely up to them. Some students, such as Ron, accessed the help I was able to offer; other individuals spent some time talking to me about general topics that may or may not have been related to themselves or sport, and there were people who visited my office long enough for me to sign their training diaries verifying that they had seen me! Sometimes people from the second and third groups would return to see me for sporting or other issues at a later date. To manage a tendency to apply the rules less stringently to those people who were seeing me for sport psychology assistance, I searched for ways to make institutional polices clear to all students from the start of their enrolment, and I would ask myself "How would I act if this person was not seeing me as a practitioner?" I thought this was an issue that needed addressing because, first, I wanted to act in ways that served the clients' best interests, and second, if I applied the institution's rules inconsistently, then I was vulnerable to disciplinary procedures if a student complained. When commenting on the issue, athletes with whom I worked typically responded by saying that they understood the need for me to be fair in the way I worked with all students. Also, I can recall times when I argued for the judicious application of the institution's regulations for students who were not seeing me in my professional capacity. As another strategy, I aimed to give assignment topics, resources, and associated marking criteria to students on the first day of any module I ran. I also worked to ensure the marking criteria were clear so that students could see exactly how I would allocate marks. In addition, I developed the habit of revisiting assignment requirements on a weekly basis in class so that students could not forget them. Indirectly, such strategies encouraged students to come to see me for assistance with their sporting pursuits. Based on my teaching-related behavior, for example, Ron had confidence I could help him because I appeared organized and knowledgeable and he believed I cared about him (and his classmates).

REFLECTION

The supervision I received from my master's advisor at that time was well-suited to my level of professional development and understanding of service delivery. As an inexperienced practitioner working with one of my initial clients, like many neophytes I was focused on ensuring I was competent and demonstrating that I had the skills and knowledge to assist Ron (Tod, Andersen, & Marchant, 2011). Also, my understanding of service delivery focused on an expert problem-solver mindset. Ron had several issues that needed resolving and he had approached me to help him. My master's supervisor helped me work with Ron to identify the solutions to his "problems." Also, in helping Ron develop ways to cope with his circumstances, emotions, and thoughts, I was showing that I was a competent practitioner.

As I have gained experience working with athletes, the solution-focused supervision approach would likely not be as helpful today to either my development as a practitioner or my collaboration with clients (including Ron) as other models, such as relationship-based frameworks. Having built a history of working with and helping athletes, I now have a range of interventions, knowledge, and skills I can draw upon (although I recognize there is value in continually expanding my toolbox and learning new ways of adapting my skillset to new athletes and situations). There is less urgency in needing to demonstrate to myself that I can be effective.

If I were to work with Ron today, then one supervision model that may be more helpful than a solution-focused approach could be a more dynamic model, where greater attention is given to examining the relationships I share with clients and identifying the ways that my own needs, history, and desires influence our interactions and service delivery outcomes (Tod, 2014). For example, like many applied sport psychologists with whom I have talked and studied, early in my career I had a strong "sport psychologist identity." To illustrate, Ron had linked his self-worth as a person with his ability to swim. Similarly, I had linked my self-esteem with my effectiveness as an applied consultant. When I believed I had been effective in helping Ron, I felt good about myself. When, however, I perceived I had made a mistake or Ron did not give me positive feedback, I doubted my ability and felt bad (20 years later I have learned to manage that slightly better). A dynamic approach to supervision would have allowed me to become much more cognizant of my reactions and to appreciate the ways they might have helped or hindered my work with Ron. Also, such an approach would have helped me learn ways to manage my reactions better, and have assisted me in serving Ron's interests first and foremost. For us (David and Martin), there is a lesson to be learned here about supervision that helps the neophyte to reflect not only on the impact of the "solutions" they provide, but also on the relationships they foster with the client and who (in my case), David the Psychologist is and why it's valuable to know. All these things are important to effective practice, and require time and attention in supervision.

Countertransference provides another example of a relationship issue I experienced with Ron, but one I was unaware of at the time because I did not receive dynamic supervision. Countertransference refers to the ways I interacted with Ron that reflected my past real or fantasized relationships (Tod & Andersen, 2012). Again, similar to other practitioners with whom I have talked and studied, I was a "failed" or unsuccessful athlete who had not achieved my sporting dreams. I was captivated by sport psychology knowledge because it helped me understand why I had not attained my sporting desires. A strong motivation I held in helping Ron and other athletes was to ensure they had the sport psychology mentor that I hadn't, but believed would have assisted me greatly in my own sporting pursuits. Similar to my strong "sport psychologist identity" discussed above, a dynamic approach would have allowed me to be aware of the ways my countertransference was influencing service delivery with Ron and provided me with the skills to manage my reactions.

One of the consequences of my strong sport psychologist identity and countertransference was over identification with clients such as Ron. They were "my" athletes and their successes and failures were my successes and failures. I also assumed too much responsibility for service delivery outcomes and did not have an adequate understanding of the various boundaries involved in service delivery. For example, I was unable to differentiate between those service delivery features for which I was and was not responsible (I was responsible for everything!). Another way that over-identification influenced, potentially negatively, the help I offered was that my advice may have been based on what I would have done if I had been in Ron's position rather than viewing Ron's case more "objectively."

I have sometimes wondered how my interactions with Ron may have been different, better, or worse if I had received dynamic supervision rather than the solution-focused advice I had from my master's advisor and network. Given my stage of professional development at the time, I think it may have been detrimental to our collaboration. To me, it seems that a

PST-based, solution-focused model was more suitable for me at that time. First, a solution-focused model allowed me to learn the fundamental elements of effective helping: how to be present with clients; to identify and interpret their issues; and have the skills and interventions to help them achieve their goals and address their challenges. Second, the model resonated with my world-view and how I saw service delivery. It allowed me to act, then, in a somewhat congruent fashion. A supervision model that emphasized an examination of me and my own "stuff," and how that influenced the relationship I had with Ron may have come too early, and distracted me from learning about the service delivery basics needed for me to become a competent, although inexperienced, helper. I'm not sure I was ready for it. For us, there is a further supervision lesson to be learned here. While exploration and self-awareness of the "Psychologist by the Psychologist" has great consequence and meaning, it is a personal and evolving activity that has a time and a place. The skilled supervisor knows when the time and place is right, and also how to use a supervision approach that allows such personal exploration to happen within a "safe space."

As I gained experience I learned: (a) the limitations of relying solely on a PST approach to practice; (b) that a PST approach is not equivalent to adopting a CBT framework; and (c) that the relationship I shared with the client, and how I influenced that, had a tremendous effect on service delivery. My intervention work was, at times, becoming divorced from my emerging and evolving philosophy of practice, and I was in danger of losing my authenticity (Nesti, 2004).

This movement started with Ron. One reason why I delved into mainstream CBT literature (and discovered behavioral experiments) was because the PST interventions I had at the time were not sufficient to help Ron. I needed something else. I was fortunate that the dynamic supervision assistance I received came at a time when I had the ability to appreciate its value. I was also fortunate that the individual took the time to raise these issues, going beyond just critiquing what I did but also challenging me on why I did it that way and how I felt about it. His willingness to do so allowed me to reflect on my philosophy of applied psychology and to identify and learn new ways of working, so I could be consciously congruent about my work and further establish my authenticity as a practitioner.

Throughout our careers, we (Martin and David) have been fortunate to help many wonderful and talented athletes. Ron has stayed in my (David's) memory because working with him exposed me to issues that necessitated consideration of service delivery processes I had not yet experienced at that stage in my professional life, such as the dual relationship and the use of behavioral experiments. It has been worthwhile revisiting and reflecting on his case to compare how my thinking has changed. It is also interesting to conclude that although I might have done some things differently, been more sensitive to certain aspects, and been more confident in myself if I worked with Ron with the knowledge and skills I have today, I am not sure if it would have resulted in drastically different outcomes: He achieved his goals and addressed his issues. For us, that is a great message for inexperienced practitioners who will carry the field forward in the future. Old dogs with new tricks are not necessarily more effective than young dogs with old tricks, as long as those old tricks are the fundamental skills and processes that allow practitioners to help clients gain happiness, find meaning, and live more adaptive lives. In supervision dialogue, we must be committed to look at, but also go beyond, the tricks and tools of the trade and what they achieved for the client, and offer opportunity for the deeper and more personal features of the practitioner and the person behind them to be explored. It is upon this that our congruent philosophy of practice is fundamentally based.

SUGGESTED READINGS

Beck, J. S. (1995). *Cognitive therapy: Basics and beyond*. New York, NY: Guilford Press. This book covers the fundamentals about cognitive therapy.

Richardson, S. O., Andersen, M. B., & Morris, T. (2008). *Overtraining athletes: Personal journeys in sport.* Champaign, IL: Human Kinetics. This book discusses overtraining in athletes.

Park, S., Lavallee, D., & Tod, D. (2013) Athletes' career transition out of sport: A systematic review. *International Review of Sport and Exercise Psychology, 6*, 22–53. This article presents a systematic review of the factors associated with the quality of athlete sport career termination.

REFLECTIVE QUESTIONS

1. Discuss the advantages and disadvantages regarding the strategies that were implemented to manage the dual roles that the practitioner and client shared in this case.
2. What would have been suitable criteria to use to assess the degree to which the practitioner had been effective, safe, and ethical in this case?
3. In what ways do you agree and disagree with the practitioner's belief that the order of the two supervision models experienced was suitable (a solution-focused model followed by a dynamic approach)?
4. If you had been supervising the practitioner when working with Ron, what would have been your goals and methods of approach?
5. If you had been the practitioner in this case study, in what ways would your own history, needs, desires, and behavioral tendencies have influenced service delivery?

REFERENCES

Beck, J. S. (1995). *Cognitive therapy: Basics and beyond.* New York, NY: Guilford Press.

Cresswell, S. L., & Eklund, R. C. (2006). The nature of player burnout in rugby: Key characteristics and attributions. *Journal of Applied Sport Psychology, 18*, 219–239.

Nesti, M. (2004). *Existential psychology and sport: Theory and application.* London: Routledge.

Park, S., Lavallee, D., & Tod, D. (2013) Athletes' career transition out of sport: A systematic review. *International Review of Sport and Exercise Psychology, 6*, 22–53.

Taylor, J., & Schneider, B. A. (1992). The sport-clinical intake protocol: A comprehensive interviewing instrument for applied sport psychology. *Professional Psychology: Research and Practice, 23*, 318–325.

Tod, D. (2014). Daddy and the meaning of service delivery. In P. McCarthy & M. Jones (Eds.), *Becoming a sport psychologist* (pp. 38–45). London: Routledge.

Tod, D., & Andersen, M. B. (2012). Practitioner–client relationships in applied sport psychology. In S. Hanton & S. D. Mellalieu (Eds.), *Professional practice in sport psychology: A review* (pp. 273–306). London: Routledge.

Tod, D., Andersen, M. B., & Marchant, D. B. (2011). Six years up: Applied sport psychologists surviving (and thriving) after graduation. *Journal of Applied Sport Psychology, 23*, 93–109.

Watson, J. C., II, Zizzi, S. J., Etzel, E. F., & Lubker, J. R. (2004). Applied sport psychology supervision: A survey of students and professionals. *The Sport Psychologist, 18*, 415–429.

29 Lessons Learned from a Seasoned Supervisor in Spain

Joaquín Dosil, Santiago Rivera, and Ana Viñolas

When young professionals complete their postgraduate studies they have acquired various skills, but they tend not to feel certain of how to put them into practice. Although their diploma certifies them as experts, closing the books and stepping into the applied field is not an easy transition. They are inexperienced, and if they want to shorten the adaptation time to enter the professional world they often need the guidance that a supervision process provides. Education and training in applied sport and performance psychology (ASPP) aims to facilitate the development and improvement of trainees' skills in order for them to learn how to offer high-quality services and help individuals to become better athletes, and therefore people with improved psychological well-being (Dosil & Rivera, 2014).

According to Hutter, Oldenhof-Veldman, and Oudejans (2014), when beginning sport psychologists get involved in a supervision process, they are interested in learning about two main topics: (1) know-how; and (2) professional development. With regards to knowing how to apply their knowledge and skills, they are concerned with learning about the intake stage (i.e., how to establish the guiding question, assess, interpret, and report the information they gather), the design of a treatment plan (i.e., how to determine goals, plan the intervention, and adapt it to their clients' needs), and the execution of one's goals/plan (i.e., how to implement their various intervention skills, evaluate their work with clients, and determine the appropriate way to terminate the process). Regarding professional development, trainees focus more on themselves rather than on the client's cases. They demand guidance in reflecting on different aspects of their experience (i.e., the actions they have taken, their own development and improvement, how to manage referral and fear of ineffectiveness, and their personal thoughts and emotions), defining their service delivery approach or style (i.e., finding a balance between directive consulting and a client-led approach, how to manage the development of a session, and handling business related issues), and coping with dilemmas (i.e., dealing with the athlete's environment, handling one's motivation, and guarding their personal boundaries). All of these are issues that trainees have to learn how to manage, and it is not uncommon that they often feel anxious and even overwhelmed by the numerous tasks and challenges they will face (Andersen, 2012). Thus, many trainees attempt to gain applied experience with the support of a professional expert who serves them as a supervisor or mentor.

This chapter presents a unique supervision case study that will discuss many of the topics mentioned above in the context of the work carried out by a trainee in Spain with a tennis player over the course of three seasons. It includes and expands upon the experiences of a seasoned supervisor in Spain over years providing supervision, discussing the lessons he has learned, the supervision process approaches he uses to develop trainees, and recommendations for providing effective supervision and training. This can be considered a continuation of "The Seasoned Supervisor: Challenges, Models, and Lessons Learned" (Dosil & Rivera, 2014), which addressed three topics around supervision in ASPP: (1) trainees' challenges; (2) the Applied Learning Programs (ALP) designed to guide the supervision process and experience; and (3) lessons learned as supervisors – all of which will be complemented and discussed in depth in the following case.

BACKGROUND INFORMATION

Supervisor Information

The supervisor (JD) has ten years of applied experience and five as supervisor. He holds a doctoral degree in Psychology, a master's in Sport Psychology, a master's in Counseling and Family Guidance, and a bachelor's degree in Psychology and Educational Psychology. JD is the director of a well-recognized ASPP center in Spain and has worked with a diverse population of individuals in sport (e.g., football (soccer), motorcycle and car racing, track and field, golf, tennis, and basketball), exercise (e.g., on issues such as adherence), and performance (e.g., politicians and businessmen).

Trainee Information

When starting supervision, the trainee (AV) was 23 years old and came from a different region of the country than the one in which she was providing ASPP services. She obtained an undergraduate degree in Psychology and a master's degree in Sport Psychology. Prior to the supervision, she had some professional applied experiences with a local football (soccer) club working with players ranging from 6 to 18 years old, as well as coaches and parents. Additionally, AV was involved with a track and field club where she would deliver workshops to athletes and coaches. Further, as part of her master's studies she did an internship developing a program with the goal of improving communication skills in fitness instructors to increase the clients' adherence to exercise.

Client Information

The client was a female tennis player, 15 years old, and from an upper-class background. She had played tennis since age ten and had become one of the best players in the region. During the season she traveled to several tournaments within Spain and received distance-learning education. Her parents contacted the ASPP center as her performance during competition had started to decline. They had noticed that she was having trouble managing emotions, although her coach mentioned that she was one of the best players during the training sessions.

Supervision Information

The supervisor was one of AV's teachers in her postgraduate studies. This is how she knew about the opportunity offered at the center for sports psychologists wishing to continue their applied learning through a supervision process. When she was close to finishing her graduate studies, AV submitted a formal application and was accepted after her resume was reviewed. The commitment between the supervisor and the trainee was established with a verbal agreement between the parties, and did not include any type of economic profit for either the trainee or the supervisor.

During the first few months, the time devoted to supervision was around six hours per week, and consisted of the trainee participating in various interventions as an observer, with the tennis player's case being the main one. From then on, she was progressively given more autonomy until she became an active member of the team. In the final stages, she was one of the professionals who gave support to junior sport and performance psychologists (SPPs), which was the group of young professionals working at the ASPP center. Concurrently in that time, the trainee complemented her studies with the following courses: MA of Investigation in Physical Activity and Sport Sciences with consequent access to doctoral studies which she was completing at the time of writing this chapter, International Certification in Coaching, International Certification in Sports Coaching, and also participation in several courses for young entrepreneurs. AV explained the main reasons why she was interested in being supervised:

Although I was receiving quality applied training, I felt that I still did not possess the sufficient skills to be able to successfully transition to the professional world. To be able to elicit changes in an athlete or team, it is not only necessary to master specific ASPP techniques, but communication, persuasion, and adaptation skills are also crucial, and they can only be learned with practice. I was also concerned about being able to continue my professional development. In addition, being able to develop quality work, having an appropriate marketing strategy to reach potential customers, as well as being able to design projects and proposals adapted to their needs are basic requirements to find a place in the labor market.

DESCRIPTION OF THE CASE

When the supervision process began, the working team at the ASPP center was composed of the following professionals: the director-supervisor and two SPPs with two and five years of experience, respectively, who had also previously experienced their own process of supervision. In addition, two other psychologists collaborated with the center on several projects; these practitioners also participated in the supervision of the trainee.

Although the chapter focuses mainly on the experience with the tennis player, the following are the various professional areas in which the trainee was involved during her supervision:

- Psychological intervention during training sessions and competition with high-performance athletes of different ages and competition levels in tennis, soccer, soccer refereeing, taekwondo, triathlon, motorcycling, and car racing.
- Executive coaching sessions oriented to enhance skills for effective leadership, communication, personnel management, and emotional control.
- Meetings with clubs/companies to assess their needs, design intervention plans, or reach a financial agreement.
- Company training and project design, including indoor and outdoor training that tried to simulate real working situations (i.e., development of personal and team-building skills through various activities and sports).
- Teaching of professional and personal skills in several ASPP courses to athletes, coaches, policemen, entrepreneurs, and companies.
- Personnel selection of policemen, security guards, or customer service professionals.

APPROACH/PHILOSOPHY

Supervision Model

The supervision was framed within two applied supervision models (i.e., applied learning programs; ALPs) designed to prepare future sport psychologists to work in applied settings after having completed a master's degree (Dosil, 2006, 2008). The first program (Clinical ALP) proposes a learning system that assists in the trainee's progressive incorporation into real cases in which the work is carried out only in the consulting room and follows three different stages: (1) the trainee starts with conceptualizing fictitious cases; (2) the trainee then acts as an observer; and (3) then gradually gains a more relevant role as a practitioner until he/she starts to work "alone" under supervision. Likewise, the second program (Field ALP) consists of applied practice that is backed by a specialist and group of collaborators (practitioners or sport psychologists) who supervise and guarantee the work undertaken by the trainee. It consists of various stages (for more detailed information see Dosil & Rivera, 2014) in which the trainee discusses his/her work carried out in the field during supervision meetings, receives feedback, and plans the next intervention session.

Psychological Approach

The psychological approach that framed the supervision took into account two perspectives: cognitive-behavioral and coaching psychology. The first is a traditional approach in psychology (Whelan, Mahoney & Meyers, 1991), but the second has become more relevant in recent years. Dosil and Viñolas (2014) defined coaching as:

> A technique that can be employed with a person (e.g., athlete or entrepreneur) or group (i.e., working teams) that, by means of goal setting and the formulation of adequate questions (together with other psychological techniques), allows the athlete–coach dyad to establish an action plan and then accomplish it. In coaching, the protagonist is the coach as he/she sets the pace and its content. The process ends when the coach has advanced enough and achieves his/her goals or challenges (personal, athletic or professional).
>
> (p. 345)

The success of every supervision process is dependent on the sense of excellence in the student. It requires the student to perform at his/her best and take full advantage of every learning opportunity during training (Dosil & Rivera, 2014), just as an athlete should do. This is why, in addition to psychological approximation, growth and permanent improvements are considered the pillars of the working philosophy.

PREPARATION/PLANNING

Along with a consideration of the supervision process, the full knowledge of the client's various psychological needs were key aspects taken into account to provide timely and adequate responses (Dosil & Rivera, 2014). Thus, a reasonable time was dedicated to improve observation and assessment skills in the trainee. To achieve this, the supervisor asked the trainee questions that made her reflect on various aspects that could affect her performance (i.e., verbal and nonverbal communication effectiveness, description of the tennis player's routine, how to plan the interviews and define key points, etc.). After the identification of the client's needs, the actions to be taken were discussed and planned, all of which allowed both supervisor and trainee to keep under control variables that could influence the training process and goal achievement (e.g., personal characteristics, resources available, relationships with client and her coach, etc.). This methodology, plus the trainee's proactive attitude, helped her to consistently experience professional development and learning opportunities. Further, JD discussed with AV that achieving an effective psychological intervention as well as a trusting working relationship with one's client requires that she develop a wide range of knowledge about the athlete and her situation and environment (e.g., motivation for continued engagement in the mental training program, social support from parents for maintaining positive attitudes toward setbacks).

SUPERVISION PROCESS/EXPERIENCE

Inexperience generally accompanies a lack of personal and professional competence, and implies various challenges that young professionals will experience (Dosil & Rivera, 2014). These difficulties provide opportunities for the trainee to reflect and serve as a means to learn, develop professionally, and strengthen service delivery skills and approaches. Further, it also provides useful learning opportunities for supervisors in order to better understand how to provide effective supervision to ASPP trainees. Thus, outlined below are the main lessons AV and JD learned throughout her supervision experiences.

Misconceptions About What the Psychologist Does

In order to be hired, young sport psychologists need to clearly know how they will help meet their clients' needs, as well as know how to communicate this to clients. AV considered that

> one of the most important things that I learned was to know how to clearly explain what ASPP can offer to an athlete, coach, team, etc. In this sense, many times it is more important to think about how to sell sport psychology in graphic and communicative means, rather than in the proposal itself.

For example, a proposed project should be written and designed in a simple and clear way, making it visually attractive. The same could be done when editing a video, all of which could communicate what ASPP can offer in an innovative and dynamic way.

Today, the labor market still does not know with clarity what ASPP offers; therefore, for a supervisor one of the key starting points in trainees' professional development is to mentor trainees in translating theory into practice. After learning the theories underlying the psychology of performance, trainees need to develop the competence to communicate their knowledge in a personal and natural way. This is the key to transmitting confidence and establishing a professional relationship with clients. Every person is different and has his/her own communication style; thus, the aim of this aspect of supervision is to emphasize the importance of self-awareness and enhancing one's communication skills. In this particular case with the tennis player, the trainee was initially in an observer role, while the supervisor was the one conducting the psychological training. Through watching JD during the initial meeting with the client and her parents, AV was able to learn the importance of clearly and effectively communicating and "selling" ASPP. For example, she noted how important it was to transmit a professional image to the player and her parents, especially since they came from a wealthy family and could afford a high standard of professional services.

The "Troubleshooter" Image

Psychologists are often still seen as problem solvers, and changing this societal perception is a duty. An integrated working approach that considers psychological skills training from strengths and not only from weaknesses expands the field of work. In this sense, AV explained, "in the ASPP center, we worked from a high performance perspective that goes much further than simply the resolution of athletes' difficult situations." The challenge was to demonstrate the range of services ASPP could offer to clients interested in resolving a specific problem (e.g., building confidence, managing stress, reducing competitive anxiety, etc.). Upon completing an initial intervention process, the clients would have a more accurate idea of what ASPP could offer and would see the benefit of continuing to work with the center throughout the execution of a personalized mental training program.

JD considered that after the first meeting and mental training session, the tennis player experienced the benefits of the work carried out and, in this case, their "troubleshooter" image definitely started to change. For example, once the tennis player started to solve anxiety problems and recovered confidence, she continued working on developing areas in which she was less skilled (e.g., communication skills) and also kept trying to strengthen her psychological skills (e.g., self-motivation). In this way, she included mental training in her daily sport training. Additionally, the technical, tactical, and physical training was taken into account when designing mental training activities, so that the client perceived the training as a complement linked to the skills that she usually practiced (e.g., keeping positive, focused, and able to make proper decisions even though she was feeling angry and frustrated).

Professional Intrusion

Other people "exercise" SPP's functions and the trainee has to know how to face and manage these types of situations (e.g., the client's coach was the person who assumed the psychologist role). In this sense, AV found that "this is one of the main problems found, but the best solution is to learn from the situation, understand why it happens, and develop the skills to find a better solution." Regarding this matter, after years of applied experience, JD took for granted that intrusion is an added difficulty at work and finds it quite normal. Therefore, supervisors should transmit tranquility to the trainee, who often stresses about it, and provide him/her with guidelines on how to approach these types of situations. For example, in this particular case, JD modeled to the trainee how to plan and carry out a meeting with the tennis player's coach in order to explain that the objective of the psychologist was to provide a complement to the coach's and client's work, always fostering the enhancement of other skills through a better mental performance. After having seen JD plan for and conduct such a meeting, AV knew how to face similar situations when she later experienced them during the Field ALP.

Ethical Behavior

It is common that the complexity of situations encountered in professional practice may bring about self-doubts to practitioners. Thus, sharing experiences within the supervision group is an ideal way to avoid making ethical mistakes as both supervisor and trainees discuss and come to clear conclusions. The best time to address ethical delivery of service is during the supervision process (Andersen, 2012); thus, this was a consistent part of AV's training. For example, when the trainee started to carry out working sessions alone with the player, both coach and parents would ask about the session. In supervision she learned how to manage ethical dilemmas such as this. With regards to confidentiality, she learned how to explain this to the parents and discussed that they could always ask the player, who could tell them what she felt comfortable with.

Another ethical dilemma AV experienced occurred when she observed the tennis player training on the tennis court. The client did not perform well and the coach blamed the trainee and asked her not to come again. This was a very uncomfortable situation despite AV trying to keep a low profile and the player indicating that she did not care that AV was observing her training session. This topic was addressed with the supervisor and working team, who normalized the situation and focused on the next actions, including: (a) reinforcing the work carried out in order to enhance the client's engagement with the mental training process; and (b) understanding the coach's behavior, helping him feel secure that his role was not going to be taken over, by giving information about what a psychologist does.

Image of an "Expendable" Professional

If resources are limited, as often happens in sports, the psychologist is not indispensable. Therefore, the ASPP professional must clearly understand his/her role, know how to practice within that role, and offer an added value to clients, demonstrating initiative, and not limiting oneself to merely meeting the initial demand (Dosil & Rivera, 2014). In AV's case, supervision consisted of coaching her to develop skills in proposing and developing interventions oriented toward promoting personal and performance excellence with her clients. This was carried out throughout her participation in several projects in which she could develop assessment skills in order to determine the specific challenge that the client is experiencing, and from there help them to derive an appropriate intervention. The supervisor considered that this was a key element of supervision and aided AV in developing working proposals that would help her become indispensable (e.g., during the intervention development with the tennis player she became another member of the technical team, even establishing a collaborative relationship with the coach). By helping the trainee to grow as a professional and develop her consulting skills, she not only learned how to "put out fires," but also to diversify her range of services, demonstrating to the client that she could benefit from ASPP services even when things are going well. Therefore, in order to become more indispensible, it was necessary for AV to learn how to market ASPP services with not only a preventative approach but also a performance-enhancing one (Rivera, 2015).

Media and Technology

Various forms of media and technology can be used as marketing tools and means of communicating with clients; thus, practitioners must learn how to take advantage of them. In this sense, AV learned how to strategically use social networks and social media to share relevant information with the client, such as videos, songs, or tips, all related to ASPP content that reinforced the intervention work. Additionally, the use of messenger and WhatsApp were essential in maintaining fluent communication when the tennis player traveled. In an implicit way, this also helped to explain the benefits of ASPP.

Essential Competencies in ASPP

The training of ASPP involves developing a number of interpersonal and business development competencies necessary for future professional development, all of which will facilitate the trainee's adaptation to applied practice (e.g., being able to add value to intervention proposals). These are fundamental aspects that are essential for entrepreneurs and business professionals. With regards to developing these competencies in supervision, AV explained that she

> learned communication and leadership skills, how to adapt to clients, as well as other skills such as negotiating during a meeting or selling ASPP products. For example, I negotiated the second year project with the tennis player. All this was very valuable at personal and professional levels, since in many cases these are the same skills that I have to implement during pressure situations with my customers.

In this case, at the start of supervision, AV knew how to apply psychological techniques but did not know when to use them, as this often depended on the situation and the type of sport. Therefore, JD asked her to study the characteristics of the sport (i.e., tennis) and interview people involved in it (i.e., coaches and players) so that she could learn to understand this particular context. This was necessary for AV to develop competence and be able to start working with the tennis player on her own.

REFLECTION

Based on the trainee's and supervisor's experience, six points are highlighted that are important considerations for developing and implementing effective supervision: (1) establishing effective working alliances in supervision; (2) hardships and personal growth; (3) adaptation and flexibility; (4) quest for efficiency; (5) continuous development; and (6) encouraging entrepreneurship.

Establish Effective Working Alliances in Supervision

Fundamental to successful service delivery and supervision is the establishment of trusting and effective working alliances. This is the first step in initiating a satisfactory supervision process for both the trainee and the supervisor, and it is related to the psychological approach outlined above. JD proposed a supervision process centered on AV, aiming to promote reflection rather than only telling her what she should do. In this way, the supervisor must be in charge of conducting the communication process in which mutual expectations are clarified, outlining each individual's level of commitment or the time that they will be able to devote to the supervision work. Economic and other expectations need to be discussed at the outset and can be reflected in a supervision contract. It is better to clear any doubt before beginning the supervisory relationship. In some cases, the supervision process requires the trainee to travel or move to another city, and this has economic, familial, and social costs. These should all be taken into account before beginning supervision.

Hardships and Professional Development

As discussed above, AV experienced many ethical dilemmas that were discussed in supervision. While these experiences were at times uncomfortable and challenging, they contributed to her personal and professional development. In this particular case, it is important to mention that during the first months of supervision the trainee did not receive any economic income from ASPP services, but that AV knew that this could happen when she started to assume more responsibilities. Thus, she knew that compromise and hard work would later turn into economic income. In this sense, AV stated: "I have great memories of that period of time. I made a considerable effort in which step by step I gained responsibilities and experiences." This kind of attitude could be considered an indicator of success in supervision.

Adaptation and Flexibility

Applied practice is dynamic, and being able to adapt is always necessary. Flexibility in responding to unforeseen events allows adjusting to any situation regarding the supervision process (i.e., trainee, method, or working team) and work with clients. High-performance supervisors should be characterized by being a model of these two concepts, both of which help the trainee to focus on opportunities. Neither the supervisor nor the trainee can assume a rigid position on hardships, nor allow for reduced self-motivation or expectations; rather, the supervisor should mentor the trainee on how to obtain the maximum advantage from these types of circumstances. AV found that these attitudes demonstrated by JD helped her feel confident and enjoy the supervision process, while feeling that there were always solutions to each problem.

A work model that sets a line of procedures to be followed is helpful, but these have to be able to be adapted to different variables (e.g., last-minute cancelled appointments, unexpected needs of the coach, impossibility for all team members to be present in supervision meetings, etc.). In the case of AV, it was useful for her to learn to identify the right moment or way to communicate (i.e., phone call or text message) to contact the tennis player, adapting to her availability and mood state. Additionally, she had to find a way to gain the tennis player's trust and confidence, adapting her working style to the client and their various situations, persuading more than imposing. An open-minded attitude for both trainee and supervisor toward learning is always a key point for achieving success in the supervision process.

Quest for Efficiency

This is a key point in the development of effective ASPP interventions and services. Efficiency may be determined by: (1) the fulfillment of the proposed goals (i.e., outcome or task) based on the client's needs; (2) clients' adherence to the psychological skills training (Anderson, Miles, Mahoney, & Robinson, 2002); (3) the trainee's ability to establish good rapport during the first contacts with clients (Sharp & Hodge, 2011); or (4) the trainee's ability to start her own ASPP center with the possibility of being successful. In this sense, AV considered that:

> after ending the supervision period, I am sure that this experience was the best way to become the professional that I am nowadays. In a short period of time, I reached a

personal and professional growth that would have been impossible to attain without the guidance of a supervisor or the support of a working team.

As mentioned before, coping with various situations such as professional intrusion, satisfaction of client's needs (and all the work this entails, such as evaluation, planning, and execution of the intervention), and knowing how to establish a strategy to sell services, are areas that the trainee practitioner had valued in her supervision process. These must be taken into account in this type of experience, where time is limited and much work must be carried out. AV remembered this time as "an exciting moment, which answered my need to know that I was taking the right steps in each moment. It was the best way to focus my motivation on realistic goals, and being productive with an efficient working approach." We must recall that in a high-performance context, the work is not worthwhile if the trainee has a close relationship with the tennis player but she does not achieve results. The client's personal growth is important but needs to be developed along with mental and overall performance.

Continuous Development

This was the philosophical approach that the supervisor and trainee experienced firsthand. The supervisor must promote progressive development of social and personal skills just as he currently does with clients. It is relevant to assume that every opportunity represents a chance to step forward, setting new challenges and acquiring meaningful experiences, as well as enhancing competencies. There is always a chance to do something new, to improve one's method, or design a new mental training activity or task. In this sense, the supervision process should stimulate innovation. AV could have had a correct proposal or one that needed to be enhanced, but the relevant point is that she always kept being creative and proactive on how to train and enhance her own method. Therefore, the supervisor not only stimulated, but trusted and fostered her to participate and propose ideas, even if he was present during a session or meeting. This process also allowed the supervisor to learn new approaches, analyze a situation from a different point of view, and keep growing as an ASPP professional and supervisor.

As mentioned throughout the chapter, some of the most essential skills developed by the trainee in supervision included orientation on how to deal with setbacks, maintaining continuous growth, being integrated into the ASPP practice as another professional (until she opened her own practice), and coming up with strategies to help clients understand what her work was about. It is interesting to consider that many SPPs continue their supervision/consultations throughout their careers as a means of personal development (Baird, 2005), just like the case of our trainee, who has continued being supervised since she started her own business back home. This takes place by collaborating in several projects with the supervisor, now in the frame of a partnership rather than with an explicit supervision purpose. Important to note is that all of this would not have been possible if she had not kept a proactive attitude.

Encouraging Entrepreneurship

We consider this as the greater pending subject for ASPP professionals. When finishing their postgraduate studies they know how to apply psychological techniques and tests, but know little about how to sell their services. As the trainee stated, learning how to design a long-term business strategy not solely oriented to the solution of urgent problems has made a substantial difference in her professional development. In this regard, the most relevant competencies are related to interpersonal skills, strategic thinking, marketing, or the financial aspects of a small business. During the supervision process, all these areas must be taken into account, but in order to be taught, supervisors also need to acquire these kinds of competencies. Thus, learning and achieving excellence is about continuous development for both trainees and seasoned professionals interested in training young psychologists.

SUGGESTED READINGS

Bayne, R., & Horton, I. (2003). *Applied psychology: Current issues and new directions.* London: SAGE.

Carlson, E., & Pfenninger, G. (2014). The business of sport, exercise, and performance psychology in the United States. In J. G. Cremades & L. S. Tashman (Eds.), *Becoming a sport, exercise, and performance psychology professional: A global perspective* (pp. 168–177). New York, NY: Routledge.

Schneider, P. (2014). Setting up a business in sport and performance psychology: A German perspective. In J. G. Cremades & L. S. Tashman, *Becoming a sport, exercise, and performance psychology professional: A global perspective* (pp. 178–185). New York, NY: Routledge.

Van Raalte, J. L., & Brewer, B. W. (Eds.) (2002). *Exploring sport and exercise psychology* (2nd ed.). Washington, DC: American Psychological Association.

REFLECTIVE QUESTIONS

1. Describe the most relevant aspects that you would take into account before starting supervision (as supervisor and as trainee).
2. Analyze the trainees' challenges. Identify which ones imply greater difficulties and propose coping strategies. How would you approach these as a supervisor?
3. How would you help a supervisee design an "elevator speech" (i.e., an efficient and short 30–60-second statement that describes what ASPP is and one's approach)?
4. Design three exercises that you can put into practice to improve your supervisee's interpersonal skills.
5. How would you notice that you are not growing professionally and personally as a supervisor? What would you do to resolve this?

REFERENCES

Andersen, M. B. (2012). Supervision and mindfulness in sport and performance psychology. In S. Murphy (Ed.), *The Oxford handbook of sport and performance psychology* (pp. 725–737). New York, NY: Oxford University Press.

Anderson, A. G., Miles, A., Mahoney, C., & Robinson, P. (2002). Evaluating the effectiveness of applied sport psychology: Making the case for a case study approach. *The Sport Psychologist, 16,* 432–453.

Baird, B. N. (2005). *The internship, practicum and field placement handbook* (4th ed.). Upper Saddle River, NJ: Prentice Hall.

Dosil, J. (2006). Applied sport psychology: A new perspective. In J. Dosil (Ed.), *The sport psychologist's handbook: A guide for sport specific performance enhancement* (pp. 3–18). Chichester: John Wiley.

Dosil, J. (2008). *Psicología del la actividad física y del deporte* (2nd ed.). Madrid: McGraw-Hill.

Dosil, J., & Rivera, S. (2014). The seasoned supervisor: Challenges, models, and lessons learned. In J. G. Cremades & L. S. Tashman (Eds.), *Becoming a sport, exercise, and performance psychology professional: A global perspective* (pp. 243–251). New York, NY: Routledge.

Dosil, J., & Viñolas, A. (2014). Coaching para entrenadores. In M. Roffé & S. Rivera (Eds.), *Entrenamiento mental en el fútbol moderno: Herramientas prácticas* (pp. 342–366). Barcelona: Futbol de Libro.

Hutter, R. I., Oldenhof-Veldman, T., & Oudejans, R. D. (2014). What trainee sport psychologists want to learn in supervision. *Psychology of Sport and Exercise, 16,* 101–109.

Rivera, S. (2015). Psicología positiva en el deporte. In A. García-Naveira & L. Locatelli (Eds.), *Avances en psicología del deporte* (pp. 159–188). Barcelona: Paidotribo.

Sharp, L. A., & Hodge, K. (2011). Sport psychology consulting effectiveness: The sport psychology consultant's perspective. *Journal of Applied Sport Psychology, 23*(3), 360–376.

Whelan, J. P., Mahoney, M. J., & Meyers, A. W. (1991). Performance enhancement in sport: A cognitive behavioral domain. *Behavior Therapy, 22*(3), 307–327.

30 What are My Responsibilities?

A Case Study to Explore Ethical Issues in Supervision of Future Professionals

Sarah L. Castillo

As the field of sport, exercise, and performance psychology (SEPP) grows, the importance of quality training for neophyte practitioners looms particularly large. Given that the number of Certified Consultants within the Association for Applied Sport Psychology (AASP) is now over 500 (Harmison, 2014), the performing public is more likely than ever to encounter a trained professional in the field of performance consulting. Further, certification policy states that "all AASP Certified Consultants are automatically approved to provide mentorship for the required mentored experience" (AASP, 2014, p. 5), although there is no current mandate for training in how to conduct mentorship/supervision. It should be noted that the AASP Fellows approved a change in terminology from "supervision" to "mentorship"; however, the duties required of the senior practitioner and the absence of a mandate for training in supervision did not change (AASP, 2009). Without debating the merits of current policy or terminology, it is clear that a case study devoted to ethical issues in supervision is warranted within this text.

BACKGROUND INFORMATION

The following case describes what may be viewed as a "typical" supervisory situation. Kyle is a graduate student receiving supervision from one of the university's full-time faculty members during the practicum portion of his training. In order to help you derive the largest benefit from this case, it has been arranged in such a way as to provide the perspectives of all stakeholders: (1) the student/trainee; (2) the supervisor/mentor; (3) the clients/athletes; and (4) the university. Although you should put yourself in the role of the supervisor/mentor as you analyze the case of Kyle, it is essential to consider the outside environment and potential pressures placed by other entities. Further, discussions of the supervisor's theoretical orientation, her ultimate decision regarding the student, and the possible ramifications of that decision for the stakeholders, are included.

DESCRIPTION OF THE CASE

The case of Kyle. Kyle was in his fourth year of sport psychology doctoral studies at a small, rural university. With only two sport psychology professors and six graduate students in the program, Kyle had grown quite close to his advisor, who would soon serve as his supervisor/mentor for the required fieldwork experience. Kyle's advisor/supervisor/mentor, Dr. Stephanie Tyler, was almost iconic in the field – widely regarded as one of the finest researchers and practitioners in applied sport psychology. Even before Kyle began his doctoral work with Dr. Tyler, he had read her work, heard her speak, and seen the way other students and professionals reacted to her at conferences with a general reverence. He was equally impressed with her practitioner background, which included several local sports teams, a few individual college athletes, three major league baseball teams, and athletes competing in the Paralympic Games. To say that Kyle was excited about his upcoming opportunity would be an understatement.

Dr. Tyler had worked at the university for over ten years. She had mentored 25 students in their doctoral fieldwork and was well aware of her responsibilities. All 25 of her students had gone on to become AASP certified, so Dr. Tyler was sure she was doing a good job. Something about Kyle gave her pause, however. Kyle did very well in academic classes, but she noticed what she considered "social awkwardness" when she watched him in mock consulting sessions with his classmates. He seemed eager to help, but Dr. Tyler worried that Kyle did not make a strong connection in his consultant role. Kyle spoke and acted in a way consistent with his training in counseling skills (e.g., effective body language, allowing space for the athlete to talk, engaging in appropriate reflection, clarification, questioning, challenging, etc.), but his partners seemed to perceive his actions as contrived. As sessions continued, his classmates became less and less engaged, and Kyle's intervention ideas, which were generally appropriate, fell on deaf ears. Although Dr. Tyler struggled to put a more academic tone to her observations of Kyle's consulting style, the only description she could think of was "forced." He was doing the right things, but his classmates "just didn't believe it." Dr. Tyler had already agreed to act as Kyle's mentor during his fieldwork experience and had no plans to back out. However, secretly she was a bit worried that she might give up her "perfect record" (i.e., all students becoming AASP certified).

Before continuing, please consider Reflective Questions 1, 2, and 3.

After about three months, Kyle was about halfway through his required hours for AASP certification and halfway through the university's fieldwork requirement. However, Dr. Tyler realized she had been justified in her earlier concerns. Kyle was working hard to design appropriate interventions, but his performers simply were not responding. Out of the ten he originally met with, only two had stuck with him to this point. She had personally observed sessions and met with Kyle weekly to discuss his progress, and the sense that performers were uncomfortable working with him came across loud and clear. During her observations, she noticed Kyle's performers leaning away from him, losing focus while he spoke, and fidgeting during the session. Most often, Kyle reported being confused that his rapport with his clients seemed strained: "I'm doing everything I've learned, making sure my comments are appropriate and match the athletes in tone and body language. I don't understand why I'm not making more progress." Dr. Tyler could confirm that Kyle was not doing anything overtly wrong. He was pleasant, encouraging, and appropriate – he just was not connecting. His performers were not suffering any harm at all; they were simply choosing not to continue their sessions with Kyle, and their performances were not improving. Dr. Tyler genuinely liked Kyle and knew how hard he was working to become a good consultant, but she could not shake the uneasiness she had about his potential effectiveness. He was behaving and consulting in an entirely professional manner and still had a couple of athlete-clients left on his roster. On the other hand, he was moving closer and closer to earning the required number of fieldwork hours to complete the experience and apply for AASP certification. She was conflicted about what to do next, and set out to collect some information.

Dr. Tyler took her position seriously, and knew that to help Kyle enhance his effectiveness her approach needed to be informed, respectful, and encouraging. She believed that "triangulation" was just as important to utilize as a supervisor/mentor as it was with her own athlete-clients. She had Kyle's perspective and she had her own observations of Kyle's work. Now she felt she needed to get others' perspectives.

APPROACH/PHILOSOPHY

Dr. Tyler decided to start from scratch. She went back to her guiding philosophy: "Consultant development is the cornerstone of effective practice." During her years as a practitioner, she was able to clarify what she knew, what she did not know, and what she wished she had learned in school. One of the reasons she decided to work in a university setting after so long as a practitioner was to impact the quality of future professionals. She wanted to pass along what she learned out there before someone else made the same mistakes. She could not prepare students for everything, but she could make them think. Then she thought about Kyle. He was smart, dedicated, passionate about the field, and willing to learn. Also useful would be his reverence of her. If Dr. Tyler could address the issue well, she had every expectation that Kyle would hear her, take the issue seriously, and work hard to address it.

Dr. Tyler also looked to her theoretical orientation for guidance. Cognitive behavioral theory (CBT) always resonated with her during her graduate training, and she further cemented her theoretical orientation during her internship. Throughout her career as a practitioner, it was CBT that helped her to focus her intervention decisions. As she looked back at her past supervisees, she realized that her theoretical orientation had made its way into her supervision practices as well. This realization was not entirely surprising, although she had never really thought about it before. She regularly used CBT techniques to develop the behavior of her supervisees, including asking students to complete mental rehearsals of their upcoming sessions with performers, and encouraging them to restructure any self-defeating thoughts that came up after a particularly difficult meeting (for a more extensive review of therapeutic models of supervision, see Andersen, 2002; Watson, Lubker, & Van Raalte, 2011). She was beginning to feel a bit better about things, but still needed to come up with a plan.

Before continuing, please consider Reflective Questions 4 and 5.

PREPARATION/PLANNING

Dr. Tyler's first stop was Dr. Jo-Ann Perry, the Dean of the Kinesiology Department and a personal friend. She asked Dr. Perry to help her troubleshoot the situation. Specifically, she asked Jo-Ann to wear her "Dean" hat, rather than her "friend" hat. Dr. Tyler went over all of the pertinent details, including her uncomfortable feeling about Kyle's "personality for the work." "Part of my job is to be a gatekeeper for the field," Dr. Tyler explained, "and I've never had this feeling before. I don't know if I can support him moving forward." "Wait a minute, Stephanie," said Dr. Perry, "are you telling me that based on a feeling, you are considering denying your support of his fieldwork hours?" She did not let Dr. Tyler respond, but continued,

> Do you have any idea what position that potentially puts the university in? If you deny his hours without longstanding, documented proof of wrongdoing, incompetence, or harm, you open us up to a lawsuit. And you cannot defend that based on a "feeling."

Dr. Tyler had not thought of that, and although she did not have enough legal information to determine whether or not Jo-Ann's concerns were justified, she definitely understood the point: Unless she had more than a feeling, she could not count on Dr. Perry's support if things went forward in this way.

Her next conversation was with the Athletic Director, Jon Kramer. He had always been very generous with Dr. Tyler and the entire sport psychology program – all she had to do was call when she had a new graduate student in fieldwork, and that student had carte blanche to speak with any of the coaches or athletes. Kramer even set aside a private office for the graduate students to use for individual meetings. Although she did not reveal any of her concerns about Kyle, she did ask general questions about how things were going with her supervisees. Kramer had plenty of good things to say, although he mentioned that he had not noticed the usual "spike in perform-ance" that often happens when athletes are initially exposed to mental skills training. Dr. Tyler knew that even if the "spike" Kramer was talking about was all in his head, it was important that he noticed something was different. She thanked him for his time, and let him get back to work. Although Dr. Tyler knew that her best information would come from coaches and athletes that had interacted with Kyle, she did not feel comfortable going forward with those meetings, particu-larly since she did not have any plan in place to handle their potential responses.

Her final call of the day was to a professional colleague with whom she had a strong con-sulting relationship. Dr. Brenda Whitford was a licensed sport psychologist at Universidad Grande in New Mexico. Stephanie and Brenda had been friends and colleagues for 15 years, and Dr. Tyler was sure she would get some good advice. "Brenda," she started, "I have a problem." She explained the whole thing in as much detail as she could, including what she learned in her visits with Perry and Kramer. "Geez, Stephanie," Brenda said "you have some tough decisions on your hands!" The two women talked for about 90 minutes about the legal responsibilities of supervision and mentorship, the importance of gatekeeping, the implications for Kyle's future, and possible solutions. After the conversation, Dr. Tyler felt better about her next steps, although she had a lot of work to do.

Before continuing, please consider Reflective Questions 6 and 7.

SUPERVISION PROCESS/EXPERIENCE

One of the things Dr. Tyler was so grateful for in her own work was the inclusion of a deliber-ate reflective process. Within a few hours after each performance meeting, she sat quietly and considered her work in terms of what happened, what she thought and felt about the session, how she might assess her strengths and areas for improvement, and developed an action plan for the next session with the performer. On more than one occasion, she identified areas for personal and professional growth that had changed the course of her work; yet, until now, she had never thought of including that process for her graduate students. After reading the current literature on how best to implement reflection into her supervision of Kyle, she added both shared and individual reflection work to her current supervision activities (see Knowles, Gilbourne, Tomlinson, & Anderson, 2007; Watson, Lubker, & Van Raalte, 2011). After each consultation, Kyle would go through a directed reflection process very similar to the one Dr. Tyler used in her own work. Kyle would bring those reflections to their weekly supervision meetings, and he and Dr. Tyler would discuss each one in turn.

Further, Dr. Tyler agreed with Dr. Perry that simply describing her feelings about Kyle's ability to connect would not provide a clear opportunity for growth. She needed something more tangible to describe her concerns. So she would asked Kyle to begin videotaping his ses-sions with performers. Although she made it a point to observe his meetings at least once each week, it was important that she and Kyle review the video together, so she could point out instances of "uncomfortable connection." Combined with Kyle's individual reflections, Dr. Tyler hoped that he would begin to recognize when he was not connecting with the performer and learn to re-establish the connection more quickly.

Finally, Dr. Tyler decided to ask Kyle's permission to speak with the performers on his client roster, as well as the athletes that had chosen to stop meeting with him. Although the athletes knew that Dr. Tyler was supervising his work, she did not want to offend Kyle by approaching them without his knowledge. Not only did she realize that their experiences with Kyle were essential to his development, she wanted to make sure that her concerns about him were supported by their feedback.

While Dr. Tyler expected that Kyle would be more than receptive to her new supervision strategies, she wanted to frame her ideas in the context of Kyle's development, rather than as a remediation plan; her presentation, she thought, would be key to implementing these ideas effectively. For their next supervision meeting, Dr. Tyler scheduled a full two hours to allow time for a thorough discussion of her observations and new strategy, along with the opportunity to really give Kyle a chance to talk about his personal observations, areas of comfort or discomfort, and any questions or concerns he might have with the new supervision strategy. When Kyle arrived at Dr. Tyler's office, he looked nervous. Dr. Tyler began

> Kyle, I want you to know that I see how hard you're working, I know how much outside research you're doing to serve your athlete-clients, and I respect the passion you have for making sport, exercise, and performance psychology consulting your career.

Kyle seemed to loosen up a bit and broke into a slight smile. She continued,

> but I haven't been the best supervisor I could have been for you and, as a result, there are a few problems that have cropped up that we haven't yet discussed. I want to spend our time today working together so that both of us can grow into better professionals. Does that sound alright?

Kyle nodded, and Dr. Tyler saw a sense of relief cross his face. Kyle opened up about his concerns over his dwindling client list, his embarrassment to ask for help, and his worry about bothering her with things that he "should know by now." It was the first time in three months that Dr. Tyler felt like she and Kyle could turn things around.

Dr. Tyler introduced each of the three strategies in turn (reflection, analysis of videotaped sessions, and interviews of Kyle's current and former clients), providing clear explanations for what each strategy would provide and how it would help to address the "connection issue." Kyle asked insightful questions and took copious notes and, as Dr. Tyler expected, was more than willing to comply with her new ideas. Dr. Tyler's assessment, combined with her ideas for addressing the issue, helped Kyle to conceptualize things better and reinvest in his work. As the conversation went on, Dr. Tyler noticed him becoming more and more excited. He no longer felt lost; he now had a direction. Dr. Tyler, too, felt much better about Kyle moving forward in his internship, and although she was not entirely sure this would solve the problem, she believed these strategies gave her the best possible way to know for sure. She resolved to be as constructive and honest as possible with Kyle, but also to keep detailed notes and documentation of any future concerns. In this way, should Dr. Tyler feel a need to address the issue more severely (i.e., remove Kyle from his internship), she would have proper justification to present to both Kyle and the university.

Kyle came in for his next supervision meeting more excited than ever, not because he had solved anything, but because he couldn't wait to review things with Dr. Tyler. First, they looked over Kyle's client session reflections. Kyle was incredibly detailed in the objective reviews on what occurred, but provided far less information on his thoughts and feelings during the session. When pressed, Kyle revealed that he really wasn't paying attention to his own emotions and behaviors during meetings with his athlete-clients. He wanted to be entirely focused on them. While Dr. Tyler understood Kyle's rationale, she pointed out that being able to identify his own thoughts, feelings, and behaviors during sessions was an essential part of his development as a consultant. She reasoned, "if you're not willing to pay attention to these things for yourself, it may be affecting your ability to identify and respond appropriately to these things in your clients." Kyle looked as though a weight had been lifted from his shoulders. "Oh my gosh, that makes perfect sense! I can't believe I never thought about it in that way before!" While Dr. Tyler considered this a bit of a breakthrough, she explained to Kyle that emotional awareness and intelligence were not skills that could be learned and effectively practiced overnight; it would take considerable time and effort to improve. They moved on to a video review of one of Kyle's athlete-client meetings. Dr. Tyler stopped the video a number of times to identify instances in which she noticed the "connection problem." Not only was she able to show Kyle specific athlete reactions (e.g., body language, shifts in body position, change in tone/language), but she was also able to point out a few of Kyle's specific behaviors that seemed to engender those responses. In every instance, Kyle reported a total lack of awareness of those behaviors in session, and was able to make the logical connection as to why his clients may have reacted in the ways they did. Finally, Dr. Tyler and Kyle discussed a few of her findings from the interviews she had with Kyle's athlete-clients about their experiences with him. She shared both positive and critical comments, and as she and Kyle talked, it seemed that everything seemed to align: Kyle's lack of awareness of his own emotions and resulting behaviors seemed to be playing a role in the level of comfort in his clients, and his overall effectiveness as a consultant. Things were far from perfect, but both Kyle and Dr. Tyler felt they had identified a specific focus for Kyle's further development.

> Before continuing, please consider Reflective Questions 8 and 9.

REFLECTION

The case of Kyle represents a training issue not widely discussed in the SEPP profession; the *gatekeeping* function of supervision. It is incumbent upon supervisors to determine whether a potential practitioner has what it takes to be an effective consultant, and to safeguard the welfare of potential clients (Lubker & Andersen, 2014). The *hope* is that neophyte practitioners have the "personality for the job" when they make the decision to complete their graduate training. In this way, supervisors are able to focus their gatekeeping responsibilities on competence and appropriate intervention design – the more concrete characteristics of the job.

Unfortunately, as this case demonstrates, supervisor hopes do not always match the situation. In such cases, supervisors have a much more difficult task in front of them – trying to teach something that does not seem teachable (i.e., personality). With Kyle, Dr. Tyler simply wasn't prepared to take on such a task. Although she wanted to make the best decisions possible, she simply waited too long to respond to her initial hesitation with Kyle. Had Dr. Tyler addressed the issue when Kyle was still practicing with his classmates, her solutions could have been developed and implemented much sooner, potentially preserving the relationships between Kyle and his athlete-clients. Further, Dr. Tyler did not have a policy in place for how to handle troubling situations in supervision. Given the number of stakeholders, the legal ramifications of supervisory decisions, and the gatekeeping responsibilities of supervision, appropriate procedures for documentation and remediation must be in place. It is not enough that these things "usually don't happen." It is incumbent upon supervisors to prepare for every eventuality, even though they hope these policies and procedures will not be necessary.

Regardless of her errors, Dr. Tyler did a number of things very well. She determined her intervention strategy with Kyle after a thorough reflection on her supervision philosophy and theoretical orientation. Regardless of the reader's solution in the case of Kyle, the process by which Dr. Tyler arrived at *her* solution is an essential component in effective supervision. In much the same way as the practitioner must have a guiding philosophy with performers and performance interventions, trainee development is best attained when the supervisor operates from a well-thought-out foundation. Next, Dr. Tyler engaged in peer consultation to work through her thoughts and feelings about Kyle prior to acting. Managing her own potential transference and/or countertransference issues added to her objectivity and focus on potential solutions. Third, Dr. Tyler met with stakeholders in Kyle's performance to triangulate her information. The more sources that confirmed her concerns, the more likely it was that she had been noticing a "real" issue. Finally, her approach when confronting Kyle was delicate, supportive, and humble. Her willingness to take responsibility for her role in things and her acknowledgment of Kyle's strengths allowed him to embrace the new strategies, rather than view them as punitive.

Supervision is as difficult as it is essential to the development of future practitioners. The challenges supervisors face may stem from either the gatekeeping or developmental responsibilities associated with the role, and may vary quite a bit within each. Although the case of Kyle depicts only one possible supervision scenario, it is hoped that the case will inspire not only further discussion, but also an investigation of best practices in both the training and development of future SEPP supervisors.

SUGGESTED READINGS

Anderson, A., Miles, A., Robinson, P., & Mahoney, C. (2004). Evaluating the athlete's perception of the sport psychologist's effectiveness: What should we be assessing? *Psychology of Sport and Exercise*, 5: 255–277.

Andersen, M. B. (2002). Sport psychology: Training and supervision. In T. Wilson (Clinical and Applied Psychology Section Editor), *International encyclopedia of the social and behavioral sciences* (pp. 14929–14932). Oxford: Elsevier Science.

Andersen, M. B., Van Raalte, J. L., & Brewer, B. W. (2000). When sport psychology consultants and graduate students are impaired: Ethical and legal issues in graduate training and supervision. *Journal of Applied Sport Psychology*, 12, 134–150.

Andersen, M. B., & Williams-Rice, B. T. (1996). Supervision in the education and training of sport psychology service providers. *The Sport Psychologist*, 10, 278–290.

Knowles, Z., Gilbourne, D., Tomlinson, V., & Anderson, A. (2007). Reflections on the application of reflective practice for supervision in applied sport psychology. *The Sport Psychologist*, 21, 109–122.

Lubker, J., & Andersen, M. B. (2014). Ethical issues in supervision: Client welfare, practitioner development, and professional gatekeeping. In J. C. Watson II & E. F. Etzel (Eds.), *Ethical issues in sport, exercise, and performance psychology* (pp. 151–162). Morgantown, WV: Fitness Information Technology.

Lubker, J. R., Visek, A. J., Geer, J. R., & Watson, J. C. (2008). Characteristics of an effective sport psychology consultant: Perspectives from athletes and consultants. *Journal of Sport Behavior*, 31: 147–165.

Sharp, L., & Hodge, K. (2011). Sport psychology consulting effectiveness: The sport psychology consultant's perspective. *Journal of Applied Sport Psychology*, 23(3), 360–376.

Watson, J. C. II, Lubker, J. R., & Van Raalte, J. (2011). Problems in reflective practice: Self-reflection versus therapeutic supervision. In D. Gilbourne & M. B. Andersen (Eds.), *Critical essays in applied sport psychology* (pp. 157–172). Champaign, IL: Human Kinetics.

REFLECTIVE QUESTIONS

1. What potential ethical challenges might arise during Kyle's mentorship?
2. For each of the challenges you identified for #1, discuss how the athlete-client might be affected if these are not addressed.
3. If Kyle's fieldwork experience had not yet begun, what, if anything, should Dr. Tyler address with Kyle?
4. Given Dr. Tyler's supervision philosophy and theoretical orientation, what might some of her options be for moving forward with Kyle? Are there particular strategies or techniques you think might be effective in addressing these issues?
5. Think about your own philosophy and orientation. How might they guide *your own* interventions as a supervisor?

6. What would be *your* first step in managing the situation with Kyle? Why? Are there ethical considerations that might affect your decision?
7. If you were Dr. Tyler, would you allow Kyle to continue his work with athlete-clients? Why or why not? How would you weigh the responses of the stakeholders (Dr. Tyler, Kyle, Dr. Perry, Mr. Kramer, athlete-clients, etc.) against your professional and legal responsibilities as Kyle's supervisor?
8. What is your opinion of Dr. Tyler's supervision strategy with Kyle? What would you have done differently?
9. Assuming Dr. Tyler's strategy does not help Kyle to resolve the "social awkwardness" with performers, how would *you* move forward?

REFERENCES

Andersen, M. B. (2002). Sport psychology: Training and supervision. In T. Wilson (Clinical and Applied Psychology Section Editor), *International encyclopedia of the social and behavioral sciences* (pp. 14929–14932). Oxford: Elsevier Science.

Andersen, M. B., Van Raalte, J. L., & Brewer, B. W. (2000). When sport psychology consultants and graduate students are impaired: Ethical and legal issues in graduate training and supervision. *Journal of Applied Sport Psychology, 12*, 134–150.

Association for Applied Sport Psychology (2009). Fellows meeting minutes from September 16, 2009, Salt Lake City, UT.

Association for Applied Sport Psychology (2014). Standard Application Form CC-AASP. Retrieved October 23, 2014 from www.appliedsportpsych.org/site/assets/files/1039/cc-aaspstandardapplicationform_2014-04.pdf.

Harmison, R. (2014). Certification review committee update. Presented at the 29th Annual Conference of the Association for Applied Sport Psychology, Las Vegas, NV, October 2014.

Knowles, Z., Gilbourne, D., Tomlinson, V., & Anderson, A. (2007). Reflections on the application of reflective practice for supervision in applied sport psychology. *The Sport Psychologist, 21*, 109–122.

Lubker, J., & Andersen, M. B. (2014). Ethical issues in supervision: Client welfare, practitioner development, and professional gatekeeping. In J. C. Watson II & E. F. Etzel (Eds.), *Ethical issues in sport, exercise, and performance psychology* (pp. 151–162). Morgantown, WV: Fitness Information Technology.

Milne, D., & James, I. (2000). A systematic review of effective cognitive-behavioural supervision. *British Journal of Clinical Psychology, 39*, 111–127.

Watson, J. C. II, Lubker, J. R., & Van Raalte, J. (2011). Problems in reflective practice: Self-reflection versus therapeutic supervision. In D. Gilbourne & M. B. Andersen (Eds.), *Critical essays in applied sport psychology* (pp. 157–172). Champaign, IL: Human Kinetics.

31 Supervising the Millennial

R. I. Vana Hutter and A. P. (Karin) de Bruin

STATLER: We really look like something from the rock age!
WALDORF: No, we look more like something from the Stone Age!

Has it always been that supervisors are confronted with generation gaps? Most probably they have. We are therefore at risk of sounding like a broken record to older supervisors when we wonder how to supervise a next generation. However, isn't it interesting to realize that the generation that is now entering sport psychology practice has probably never heard an actual broken record (Howe & Strauss, 2000)? The generation of the "Millennials" is currently climbing the ranks as young professionals, joining the baby boomers and Generation X-ers in the workplace. As the successors of Generation X they have also been named Generation Y (among many other names), but "Millennials" does more justice to their unique identity. Children born in 1982 were the ones to become the high-school class of the millennial year 2000, hence the name that now applies to the generation (roughly) born between 1982 and 2004.

Howe and Strauss (2000, 2007) described seven core traits of Millennials; they are raised as special, sheltered, but pressured, and are confident, team-oriented, conventional, and achieving. Many of these traits mean good news for the future of sport psychology. As educators and supervisors, it is our task to foster and build on traits that make for good professionals, such as confidence and team-orientation. When supervisors stem from a previous generation than supervisees, a match between the virtues of the generations that are currently supervisors and the virtues of the millennial supervisees is not a given. In this chapter we will discuss supervising Millennials and use a number of stereotypes. We are aware that stereotypes are overly simplistic and reflect only a part of reality. However, for the purpose of framing the supervision case and our experiences, the stereotypes of the Millennials are convenient, and hopefully contribute to a recognizable read. We have tried not to seem like grumpy Muppets Statler and Waldorf, quoted at the start of the chapter. However, the reader should be aware that we (the authors) are members of generation X. We carry the stereotype patch of being latchkey children with high hopes, but pessimistic views of the future. If we, at times, sound like grannies reminiscing that everything used to be better, we are only fitting our own stereotype of cynical GenX-ers; therefore, we request you bear with us in these instances.

One of the (stereotypic) descriptions of Millennials is that they value self-expression over self-control. Moreover, they are said to have high self-esteem and tend to relish responsibility in the workplace. According to the *Telegraph* "this is a selfish, self-regarding generation. 'Let me take a Selfie,' is their catchphrase" (Wallop, 2014). In Dutch this generation is often referred to as "generatie grenzeloos" (e.g., Spangenberg & Lampert, 2009), meaning "generation with no limits or boundaries." This label refers to two sides of Millennials: their ambitious, achieving core attitude, but also the impression that they challenge or overstep limits and boundaries that are self-evident for, and respected by, previous generations. In supervising neophyte sport psychologists, we regularly recognize the stereotype of the Millennial and are challenged by aspects of it. Take, for instance, the supervisee whose client was reluctant of the supervisee visiting her practice. The supervisee went anyway because she felt that observing the client in practice would benefit their work together.[1] Or the supervisee who agreed to "replace" the parents of a young athlete at international tournaments. These examples reflect the stereotypical high self-esteem, strong tendency toward ownership of responsibilities, and the apparent lack of self-control of Millennials. Similar issues challenged us in the case of Nigel (pseudonym) and the cycling team, which we will discuss in more detail in this chapter.

BACKGROUND INFORMATION

Nigel was a student in the post-master program in applied sport psychology (ASP) in the Netherlands. Karin de Bruin (KB) is a supervisor of the program and Vana Hutter (VH) was the program manager at the time Nigel was in the program. To complete the program, trainees conduct at least seven different cases under supervision; the total requirement is a minimum of 70 client contact hours. Cases are supervised in an indirect matter, that is, the supervisor is not present at the client contact. Supervision sessions take place between supervisor and student in separate sessions. For more information on the specific supervision setting and more general supervision challenges within the post-master program, see Hutter (2014).

In our case study, KB has supervised Nigel over a period of a year. During this time, Nigel worked with five cases, three of them were formally supervised by KB. KB and Nigel met nine times for supervision sessions. One of Nigel's cases that KB supervised was a semi-professional team of cyclists. Nigel had previously worked as an assistant-trainer for the same team, a profession he was also qualified for. He was currently working with the team in the role of sport psychologist, as part of his training to become an ASP practitioner. During the casework, the team manager asked Nigel to travel with the team to a training camp abroad. Nigel was (implicitly) expected to both serve as an assistant-trainer and sport psychologist at the training camp. The team manager felt Nigel was a "two-for-one" bargain for the team, and Nigel was happy to be of such great use for them. Moreover, Nigel was expected to share a hotel room with one of the athletes for budgetary reasons. At the time the request of the team manager came, Nigel and KB had not met for supervision for a while.

DESCRIPTION OF THE CASE

KB initiated contact with Nigel three months after their last supervision session. Nigel, as a student in the post-master program, was obliged to keep his supervisor updated on casework, but had failed to do so. KB requested that Nigel inform her on the status of his practical casework. It appeared that Nigel was busy with his second and third case and that everything went, according to his information, smoothly. He didn't feel the need to meet for supervision at this point, but he suggested they meet again in a month's time. KB urged him to make an appointment in the short term and to send her more details about the cases, including the case with the cycling team.

A few stereotypical Millennial challenges may already become apparent. First, we recognize that Millennials want to be (self-)responsible. The need to keep supervisors updated, and to have regular supervision sessions, was not self-evident to Nigel. He is no exception in this respect; VH has frequently overheard supervisees saying that "they don't have an issue or question for supervision" as a reason for not contacting their supervisor regularly. The general high self-esteem noted in Millennials is reflected in the lack of contact with the supervisor and the contention that supervisees "don't need supervision."

Supervisees in the program are required to prepare a supervision sheet, including a supervision question, before meeting with their supervisors (see Hutter, Oldenhof-Veldman, & Oudejans, 2015). The questions Nigel prepared for the supervision session that followed were about the optimal content of the mental training sessions (e.g., how to introduce team-building, what kind of material to use for communication training, how much time to spend on attention skills, etc.). It was only in the supervision meeting itself that it became clear that Nigel was supposed to join the team at their training camp and that he planned to execute the final five sport psychological sessions at the camp. Thus, Nigel came in for supervision wanting to discuss the content of the sport psychology sessions with the team; the supervisor then "stumbled upon" the new information of joining the team, sharing a hotel room, and combining different roles and dual responsibilities, and decided to address the ethical issues involved.

In terms of Millennial issues, Nigel showed high self-esteem in his conviction that he would be successful in separating the roles of assistant-trainer and sport psychologist and circumventing ethical issues of sharing a room with a client. He did not doubt his ability for professional conduct in the complex context he was about to enter. Moreover, the issue of self-control emerged in the case. Nigel did not feel that combining different roles, traveling with a team, and sharing a hotel room was something to reflect on before making decisions about such issues, or to share these aspects of his experience in supervision first. Rather, he jumped to the occasion, anticipating benefits for himself, without contemplating ethical dilemmas or potential downsides of the choice, for either himself or the team.

Placing the Case in Perspective

Nigel's situation is far from unique, although the request to share a room with an athlete may be uncommon, even in the world of sport psychology. As sport psychologists, we work in unusual environments, and these environments come with specific challenges in terms of boundaries, multiple roles, and ethical issues. Multiple roles occur often, and may not pose problems as long as they are incidental and/or the nature of sport psychology services is clearly defined and separated at the onset (Andersen, van Raalte, & Brewer, 2001). However, Andersen et al. also stated that boundaries are inevitably stretched or broken when sport psychologists are entering dual roles. They outline a number of threats to effective service delivery, such as the teams' perception of the sport psychologist as "team buddy," over-identification with the team, and a blurred perspective of the "hat" the sport psychologist is wearing in various situations, leaving both the client and the practitioner confused.

There are clear benefits and clear risks of traveling with teams. Haberl and Peterson (2006) pointed out that traveling with teams maximizes opportunities for effective contact, establishing trust, and accelerating the working relationships. However, they also warned that conversations constantly have to be monitored, and that the close interaction with the team can lead to situations that are uncomfortable for both the sport psychologists and the team.

The different accounts in the literature share a number of conclusions. The atypical environment in which sport psychology operates offers unique possibilities, but also poses specific challenges. Most of these challenges are less-than-ideal situations, but can be overcome. However, to do so requires self-awareness, being quick at problem solving, setting clear and explicit rules of engagement and terms of service delivery, and constant monitoring of ourselves, our ongoing processes, and danger zones. Andersen et al. recommended that sport psychologists "learn to work in nontraditional time segments and locations" (Andersen et al., 2001, p. 17). We agree with this recommendation. However, we also contend that there is a time and place to do so, and feel that for trainees like Nigel it might be too early to enter the complexity of combining roles and to travel with the team as a sport psychologist. The supervisees in our program, such as Nigel, are conducting their first cases as a sport psychologist. We want them to work with cases that provide a powerful and safe learning environment, and that fit well with their current level of competence and confidence. Moreover, in these cases the welfare of the client should not be (extra) jeopardized because the trainee sport psychologist is challenged beyond what can be expected of him or her.

APPROACH/PHILOSOPHY

Generally speaking, KB adopts a process approach in supervision. The supervisee's question is the starting point of every session and through listening, summation, and probing questions the essential issues and its connections gradually become clearer to both the supervisor and the supervisee. If the supervisee's question is about the athlete-client, then the supervisee is challenged and asked to reflect upon the actual meaning of the question: What does it say about the supervisee him/herself? This philosophy requires a basic reflective attitude and a relationship of trust between supervisor and supervisee. Moreover, there has to be a mutual understanding that it has merit for both parties (i.e., supervisor and supervisee) to keep the supervisor informed. These aspects, however, vary depending on the supervisor–supervisee professional relationship. For example, in the case of the supervisee who agreed to "replace" the parents of a young athlete at international tournaments, the supervisee immediately called his supervisor during the weekend to discuss the parents' request and to reflect upon the necessary considerations he had to make around this request. Subsequently, issues such as the risks of combining different roles, traveling with a younger female athlete, and possible implications for their relationship were discussed before making his final decision. The supervisee was challenged to make the appropriate considerations and to put these into specific agreements with the athlete and her parents. The supervisor and supervisee did not agree on the chosen outcome, but both were pleased with the process. On the contrary, Nigel seemed naive to possible ethical issues and possible pitfalls of the situation he was about to enter, and they had to be imposed upon him by KB.

The importance of role clarity of ASP practitioners, respect for personal integrity, and refraining from unnecessary invasion of privacy, are norms and values that are of particular importance to the supervisor, and these were clearly challenged in this case. The supervisor felt that the effectiveness of Nigel's work and the professional image of sport psychology could be compromised if he combined both roles. From the supervisor's perspective, Nigel would fail to meet her personal minimum standards for professional conduct if he chose to travel with the team under the proposed conditions. The supervisee's perspective, on the other hand, was that of being offered a chance that he did not want to miss out on. He regarded the opportunity to travel with the team as a valuable learning experience and good practice as he planned to make combined use of his different qualifications (trainer and ASP practitioner) in future practice. He did not seem to conceive ethical dilemmas with his actions or fully understand the supervisor's issues with them. In fact, he appeared upset and also slightly offended that the supervisor questioned his capacity to separate both roles, challenged him on self-awareness, and urged him to practice self-control in this case.

PREPARATION/PLANNING

KB was not able to anticipate the issue since it only arose during the session. Therefore, KB reacted with a sense of immediacy, feeling that there was only limited time for a process approach in which the supervisee would slowly develop himself toward a far more balanced standpoint. KB and Nigel discussed pros and cons of his decision to join the team at their camp, as well as taking dual roles, and the supervisor explicitly mentioned the ethical code aspects that were at stake here. KB also mentioned that she would ask the educational program management to share their view on executing different roles during the ASP casework.

SUPERVISION PROCESS/EXPERIENCE

Nigel agreed to contact the program manager (VH). VH informed KB and Nigel that she agreed that it was not desirable to combine different roles, and that she preferred that these were not to be executed simultaneously (or immediately following) in cases that were part of the post-master program. Two weeks later the next appointment between Nigel and KB took place. Nigel was well prepared and he discussed his feelings about the last meeting. Although he had gained new insights during the supervision, he was also annoyed that opportunities to develop his practical ASP skills were not addressed. He shared that his self-confidence was negatively affected, while he felt that supervision should instead be focused on increasing his confidence. Furthermore, he stressed that he had not changed his mind about combining the roles and traveling with the team, but did arrange for separate rooms at the training camp. In this meeting KB was also able to discuss her uncomfortable feelings about being kept in the dark for months while Nigel overstepped professional limits. In the end, this mutual sharing of thoughts and feelings increased their understanding of each other and strengthened their working alliance. From that point on, Nigel did inform the supervisor better about the sessions he had with the athletes. In subsequent meetings, KB and Nigel further discussed the combination of roles and possible underlying reasons to do so (e.g., Nigel's desire to fulfill the coach's request and to please him, and the fact that he felt more competent as assistant-trainer than as sport psychologist). They also used role play, which Nigel thoroughly prepared, in order to work out various reactions and actions he would undertake as a sport psychologist and as an assistant-trainer when athletes came to him with problems. They also addressed Nigel's feelings of uncertainty as ASP practitioner, his urge to act flawlessly, and his need for recognition, which he slowly started to identify and discuss in more depth. This process reflects a pattern noted more often in Millennials, which entails a slow process to establish deeply trusting relationships (Rickes, 2010). In his argument, Rickes points out the contrast between this slow process for developing trusting relationships face-to-face with the no-holds-barred approach to openness while engaging in online communications or relationships.

REFLECTION

Reflective practice helps sport psychology practitioners to explore decisions and experiences with the aim of increasing the practitioners' understanding and management of themselves and their practice (Anderson, Knowles, & Gilbourne, 2004). The same holds true for sport psychology supervisors; KB and VH reflected on Nigel's case to come to a deeper understanding of the case itself, the processes in supervision, and the self as supervisors. We adopted a process that can best be compared to Socratic questioning. As a result of our reflective dialogue, a number of "core issues" emerged. Since "it is not the answer that enlightens, but the question" (Eugene Ionesco, *Découvertes*), we will share the themes and questions that emerged in our reflections on the case.

Core Theme I: The Personal Lower Limit of Professional Conduct and "Guilt by Association"

As supervisors we are co-responsible for the supervisees' clients' welfare and have a co-responsibility in gatekeeping to professional practice. Therefore, supervisees will have to meet our minimum limit of professional conduct. In this case, Nigel was pushing the supervisor's limits. In reflecting on this aspect of the case, we discussed the following questions:

- How should we deal with unacceptable behavior of supervisees (i.e., behavior that "trespasses" the ethical and professional standards of the supervisor)? Nigel's plan of action with the team was clearly unacceptable for the supervisor, yet to restrain him appeared very challenging and difficult.
- Perfectionism may be a common trait in sport psychologists and sport psychology supervisors. Moreover, sport psychologists that become supervisors may have "stronger than

average" moral sense, ethical beliefs, and quality of service delivery. Could it be that perfectionistic traits and high professional standards of supervisors raise the lower limit of professional conduct for trainees to undesirable or unattainable high levels? In this case, could it be that KB's own personal high standards for conduct were a bit too strict or firm for Nigel, as a beginner in the field, and she was in fact too harsh on him?

- Unethical, or ineffective, behavior of supervisees can have an impact on the supervisor's professional image. How might fear of "guilt by association" play a role in the supervisor's assessment of the situation? Apart from possible negative outcomes of unethical behavior for Nigel and the team, there may also be negative outcomes for the supervisor, particularly when she's seen as "approving" of Nigel's undesired actions. In other words, how much of KB and VH's actions are led by the responsibility for Nigel and his client, and how much is guided by fear of disrepute of the supervisor and program (perhaps typical for pessimistic Generation-X-ers)?
- Millennial supervisees have the tendency to assume responsibility. Does this tendency conflict with the role of gatekeeper? Is KB capable of assessing Nigel's competence if Nigel does not provide her with regular and complete information on his casework and follows up on supervisory advice?

Core Theme II: Empowering and Restraining Millennials

As supervisors we want to encourage supervisees to become autonomous and nurture their self-confidence. We may well remember our own uncertainties and the lack of confidence in our early career, and the stifling effect it had on us (e.g., Tod, 2007; Tonn & Harmison, 2004). In projecting our own experiences on the supervisees, we may expect that supervisees would need to be encouraged rather than curbed in their actions. From this anticipation, the general high self-esteem of Millennials and subsequent "daring" attitude may come as a surprise. Departing from our own early career experiences, we may not be prepared to confine supervisees, and may lack experience and role models to do so. Add to this the fact that Millennials grew up on praise and confirmation and may not have received a lot of critique or feedback. In the words of Howe and Strauss (2000), they have a sense of specialness and they are wanted, protected, and worthy children. In supervision, this may leave us with a supervisor who is not prepared to restrain the supervisee and a supervisee who is unfamiliar and uncomfortable with being restrained. In reflecting on the matters of empowering and restraining in the case of Nigel, we asked ourselves a number of questions:

- How can we optimally empower Millennials? Quite often supervisees verbally express uncertainties about themselves and their level of competency, but their actions don't always reflect these uncertainties. In the case of Nigel, the insecurities were clearly there and uncovered in more depth later in supervision, but his insecurities were hidden by his actions and overruled by his tendency to be self-responsible.
- How do we tap into the correct cavities in professional self-esteem of Millennials, who are typically high on self-esteem, and may even be overestimating themselves in some areas of competency? Apart from the ethical issues involved, KB felt that Nigel had too much confidence in his ability to deal with the complex situation he was about to enter. When she questioned this ability, Nigel felt belittled, and expressed that his confidence was damaged. How could we have helped Nigel to openly and safely come to a better perspective of the boundaries of his competence? How can we help supervisees, such as Nigel, to honestly monitor, face, and use their professional uncertainties and self-doubt in an effective, formative way?
- Millennials respect authority and want to comply with rules, but their discomfort with change-oriented feedback and accompanying ego-threat can be a true obstacle for learning and the working alliance in supervision. In Nigel's case, the critique of KB hit him quite

hard, and had a clear impact on his ego. He may have "shut down" at the particular supervision session, only to recover from this in the next session when both supervisor and supervisee expressed their feelings about the session. We therefore wondered: How do we restrain Millennials when needed, while keeping the supervision context safe, open, and facilitative of learning?

- In sum, the challenge is: How do we balance empowering the supervisee on one hand, while on the other hand stepping in when they behave inappropriately or lack self-restraint?

Core Theme III: Jumping Through Hoops or Deep Learning?

We guess that each supervisor wonders every now and then whether supervisees actually learn and change in supervision, or that we merely make them jump through hoops while under supervision. If supervisees correct their steps due to intervention by the supervisor, it might be just because they feel they "have to," not because they feel or understand the need to do so. Remember that the Millennial generation has a much stronger tendency to comply with parents, teachers, etc. than, for instance, Gen-X. The questions relating to deep learning in supervision that emerged are therefore perhaps more pressing now than with previous, more rebellious generations:

- How do we separate actions that are corrected because supervisees were told to from instilled values that make them correct their course because they "want to" or at least "understand the need to"? Do we really shape the professional attitudes of supervisees or do we make them go through the right motions as long as we're present and checking? Is this distinction between true learning and socially desired temporary change further complicated when supervisors also act as assessors of the supervisee (as is the case in our post-master program)? And how do we fulfill the role of gatekeeping as a supervisor, when we are unsure how much supervisees are complying with our advice due to control, instead of learning? Nigel knew that KB would assess the case as a whole, and that he would probably not pass the case if he didn't comply with at least parts of her recommendations. This extra (extrinsic) motivation to comply with the supervisor/assessor makes it even harder to determine whether a supervisee adapts his actions due to change of perspective, or as a result of the control of the supervisor. We therefore have no guarantee that the supervision has instilled insight and actual change in Nigel. To act as good gatekeepers, we would ideally be able to predict future behaviors of supervisees with a better assessment of the supervisees' competencies.

Resolving Supervising Dilemmas

To conclude this chapter, we would like to share a number of actions that we have found to be helpful when encountering supervising dilemmas. The first three actions relate to seeking advice from others. Throughout various cases we have sought help and advice from international colleagues with more expertise and experience on the specific matter and on supervision in general. A network of sport psychology experts, and expert supervisors, is indispensable, in our opinion. For simpler issues, or issues where no specific expertise is available, peer consultation of supervisors can be used. In structured peer consultation for supervisors (in our case using the "incident method" protocol) the issue discussed is clarified, placed in a broader context, and advice is gained from peer supervisors. Last, advice, or rather guidance, can be found in supervision of the supervisor, which has been reported in the literature as meta-supervision (Barney & Andersen, 2014). In meta-supervision, supervisors become supervisees and can explore issues encountered in their supervision practice with their supervisor.

Sometimes the issues encountered in supervision call for quite immediate and combined action by the supervisor and the program management. For instance, when the welfare of the trainees' clients is at stake, ethical boundaries are crossed, or when the proper functioning of a trainee cannot be warranted. A good line of communication between supervisors and program management is a prerequisite for intervention in such instances. In our setup, supervisors can signal that gatekeeping may be needed, and the program management acts upon these signals. For example, in some cases additional measures are taken, or additional demands agreed upon with the trainee. For example, trainees can be required to work under extra supervision, or to audio or video record their sessions and discuss them in detail with supervisors. In other cases the trainee has to be put "on hold." A pause in the casework gives the trainee, supervisor, and program management the time to work on deficiencies or problems in the professional practice of the trainee. Although putting trainees "on hold" is always a hard and complex process, our experiences with it are rather positive. Trainees may arrive at the conclusion that the profession, or the demands of the education program, is not for them, and may decide to withdraw from the program. More often, though, the pause is used by the trainee as a break, to recover from the stressful situation they are in, and to grow personally. In these cases we see trainees successfully complete the program after they resume their casework. These cases are very dear to us, and make some of the difficult decisions we have to make concerning supervision and gatekeeping worthwhile.

SUGGESTED READINGS

Andersen, M. B., Van Raalte, J. L., & Brewer, B. W. (2000). When sport psychology consultants and graduate students are impaired: Ethical and legal issues in training and supervision. *Journal of Applied Sport Psychology, 12,* 134–150. DOI: 10.1080/10413200008404219.

Burke, K. L., & Johnson, J. J. (1992). The sport psychologist–coach dual role position: A rebuttal of Ellickson and Brown (1990). *Journal of Applied Sports Psychology, 4,* 51–55.

Ellickson, K. A., & Brown, D. R. (1990). Ethical considerations in dual relationships: The sport psychologist coach. *Journal of Applied Sports Psychology, 2,* 186–190.

Jacobs, S. C., Huprich, S. K., Grus, C. L., Cage, E. A., Elman, N. S., ... Nadine, J. (2011). Trainees with professional competency problems: Preparing trainers for difficult but necessary conversations. *Training and Education in Professional Psychology, 5,* 175–184. DOI: 10.1037/a0024656.

Jones, L., Evans, L., & Mullen, R. (2007). Multiple roles in an applied setting: Trainee sport psychologist, coach and researcher. *The Sport Psychologist, 21,* 210–226.

Kaslow, N. J., Rubin, N. J., Forrest, L., Elman, N. S., Van Horne, B. A., Jacobs, S. C., ... Thorn, B. E. (2007). Recognizing, assessing, and intervening with problems of professional competence. *Professional Psychology: Research and Practice, 38,* 479–492. DOI: 10.1037/0735-7028.38.5.479.

Smith, A., & Koltz, R. L. (2012). Counseling supervision: Where is the manual for working with the Millennial generation? *Professional Issues in Counseling,* Summer. Retrieved from: www.shsu.edu/piic/documents/MillennialGeneration.pdf.

Venne, V. L., & Coleman, D. (2010). Training the Millennial learner through experiential evolutionary scaffolding: Implications for clinical supervision in graduate education programs. *Journal of Genetic Counseling, 19,* 554–569. DOI: 10.1007/s10897-010-9319-8.

REFLECTIVE QUESTIONS

1. What are examples of ways in which Millennials might behave in ASP practice or supervision that illustrate the pros and cons of the stereotypes related to their generation?
2. What are your personal values and beliefs concerning dual roles in sport psychology and clients' privacy?
3. What were the core issues of the supervisor in Nigel's case and how would you have handled them?

4. Reflect on the supervision case described by answering the following questions (derived from the reflective practice cycle of Korthagen):

    a. Describe what the supervisee did and describe what you think the supervisee wanted, felt, and thought?
    b. Describe what the supervisor did and describe what you think the supervisor wanted, felt, and thought?

5. How do you think discrepancies between desires, feelings, and thoughts of supervisee and supervisor affected the supervision and its outcomes?

NOTE

1 We obtained informed consent of the supervisees presented, details have been changed for reasons of anonymity.

REFERENCES

Andersen, M. B., Van Raalte, J. L., & Brewer, B. W. (2001). Sport psychology service delivery: Staying ethical while keeping loose. *Professional Psychology: Research and Practice, 32*(1), 12–18. DOI: 10.1037//0735-7028.32.1.12.
Anderson, A., Knowles, Z., & Gilbourne, D. (2004). Reflective practice for sport psychologists: Concepts, models, practical implications, and thoughts on dissemination. *Sport Psychologist, 18*(2), 188–203.
Barney, S. T., & Andersen, M. B. (2014). Meta-supervision: Training practitioners to help others on their paths. In J. G. Cremades & L. S. Tashman (Eds.), *Becoming a sport, exercise, and performance psychology professional: A global perspective* (pp. 339–346). New York, NY: Routledge.
Haberl, P., & Peterson, K. (2006). Olympic-size ethical dilemmas: Issues and challenges for sport psychology consultants on the road and at the Olympic Games. *Ethics & Behavior, 16*(1), 25–40.
Howe, N., & Strauss, W. (2000). *Millennials rising: The next great generation.* New York, NY: Vintage.
Howe, N., & Strauss, W. (2007). *Millennials go to college* (2nd ed.). Great Falls, VA: LifeCourse Associates.
Hutter, R. I. (V.) (2014). Sport psychology supervision in the Netherlands: Starting from scratch. In J. G. Cremades & L. S. Tashman (Eds.), *Becoming a sport, exercise, and performance psychology professional: A global perspective* (pp. 260–267). New York, NY: Routledge.
Hutter, R. I. (V.), Oldenhof-Veldman, T., & Oudejans, R. R. D. (2015). What trainee sport psychologists want to learn in supervision. *Psychology of Sport & Exercise, 16*, 101–109. DOI: 10.1016/j.psychsport.2014.08.003.
Korthagen, F., & Vasalos, A. (2005). Levels in reflection: core reflection as a means to enhance professional growth. *Teachers and Teaching: Theory and Practice, 11*, 4771. DOI: 10.1080/1354060042000337093.
Owton, H., Bond, K., & Tod, D. (2014). "It's my dream to work with Olympic athletes": Neophyte sport psychologists' expectations and initial experiences regarding service delivery. *Journal of Applied Sport Psychology, 26*(3), 241–255. DOI: 10.1080/10413200.2013.847509.
Rickes, P. C. (2010). Talkin' 'bout my generation. *The New England Journal of Higher Education.* Retrieved from: www.nebhe.org/thejournal/talkin-bout-my-generation/.
Spangenberg, F., & Lampert, M. (2009). *De grenzeloze generatie.* Amsterdam: Nieuw Amsterdam.
Tod, D. (2007). The long and winding road: Professional development in sport psychology. *Sport Psychologist, 21*(1), 94–108.
Tonn, E., & Harmison, R. J. (2004). Thrown to the wolves: A student's account of her practicum experience. *The Sport Psychologist, 18*, 324–340.
Wallop, H. (2014, July 31). Gen Z, Gen Y, baby boomers: A guide to the generations. *Telegraph.* Retrieved from www.telegraph.co.uk/news/features/11002767/Gen-Z-Gen-Y-baby-boomers-a-guide-to-the-generations.html.

32 Applying Approaches and Techniques in Supervision

Taryn Morgan, Angus Mugford, and Christian Smith

Supervision is a key cornerstone in developing the next generation of applied sport psychology professionals. Gaining access to supervision opportunities should be a goal of all students in sport psychology programs. Unfortunately, there are not a plethora of applied experiences available. Students must seek out specific locations or professionals already in the field who are willing to oversee this process. One such opportunity that exists is at IMG Academy in Bradenton, Florida. In this chapter we will focus on the history of the current supervisors, supervision philosophy, and supervision process at IMG Academy, as well as delve into the specific experiences of one student who took advantage of an applied mental conditioning summer internship working with youth athletes from a variety of sports and levels.

BACKGROUND INFORMATION

At IMG Academy, we have trained, supervised, and mentored over 90 students and young professionals over the past 18 years. Specifically, the first and second authors have been supervising for eight and ten years, respectively. Training young practitioners is a task that we definitely do not take lightly; in fact, we take great pride in seeing the progress that open-minded, hard working, and passionate students make when they are fully immersed in daily sessions, feedback, and self-reflection. As Watson, McAlarnen, and Shannon (2014) noted, the supervisor serves as a role model to the supervisee and enters into a relationship that promotes self-reflection, skill and knowledge development, and professional standards for the supervisee. We also know that supervision has its challenges and tends to be a rough rather than smooth ride, because many times this may be the first critical feedback a supervisee has ever had. Indeed, manifesting high-performance psychology means to be coachable and learn, cope with stress, and perform under pressure. It is here where "practicing what you preach" becomes integral to success.

The supervisee we have chosen to focus on for this case study completed his internship during the summer of 2006. He applied via a rigorous process of sending in a resume, cover letter, personal statement, reference letters, and a video of a session. He was working on his master's degree in sport psychology when he applied, had a background as a successful junior and collegiate golfer, and was originally from England. He was selected and joined us for a nine-week internship, where he would be working with youth athletes (ages 8–18) in individual and group (small and large) settings from a variety of sports (baseball, basketball, golf, tennis, and soccer). These athletes were campers who came from all over the world and averaged a 1–5-week stay at the Academy. Sessions with the campers lasted 45–60 minutes in a classroom setting, as well as in the sport setting.

DESCRIPTION OF THE CASE

We realized early on that he was someone who liked to ask questions, as we received emails or phone calls nearly every day from the time he found out he was accepted until the time he joined us on campus. We expect interns to arrive with some nerves, trepidation, and doubt, and this was the case with the current supervisee, as seen by the many questions and initial fears that came across as a lower level of self-confidence. We also noticed quickly that the supervisee had a clear cut "comfort zone." His comfort zone was in golf with smaller groups or individuals. When it came to other sports or larger groups where strong class management skills or crowd control was necessary, the supervisee became nervous and relied on detailed written notes. We also learned that while he was well educated, he sometimes had trouble communicating the concepts to the youth athletes in simple terms. One such instance was when he was teaching tennis players in a group setting and used the term "ruminate" and did not seem to comprehend why they did not all understand the word or concept, and why they would get distracted and not be fully attentive during his session. In his mind, he couldn't fathom students who were not as intent on learning as he had been when he was a student and athlete. Welcome to the real world!

APPROACH/PHILOSOPHY

Strong supervision is one of the major cornerstones in the development of any neophyte sport psychology practitioner. Because the impact a supervisor has on a novice practitioner's skill development and professional behavior is immediate and long-lasting, it is imperative that quality supervision is provided (Watson et al., 2014). In addition, supervision is key to allowing practitioners to hone skills, become more self-aware and learn to better provide services for athlete-clients, and most importantly ensure the welfare of the performer (Van Raalte & Andersen, 2000). Therefore, having a purposeful philosophy and method for training is essential. Although there are many methods of supervision, we are guided by the "Total Consultant" Profile that focuses on six competencies, namely knowledge, relationships, delivery, organization/management, development, and leadership (Mugford, Hesse, & Morgan, 2014).

Overall, we tend to utilize a combined humanistic and cognitive-behavioral framework for psychological skills training (Hill, 2001). The adage that "they don't care what you know until they know you care" is prevalent for us when working with youth athletes because they are definitely not impressed by your degree or your academic knowledge of theories in sport psychology. Instead of credentials, your credibility is what is more important with this kind of young, athletic audience. They want to be engaged and entertained with "sticky" concepts that are easy to understand and that help them deal with the mental challenges of their sport and life.

One well-known model of supervision in the counseling and psychology world is the Integrated Developmental Model (IDM) (Stoltenberg, McNeill, & Delworth, 1998). In the IDM model, growth of the supervisee is based on self and other awareness, motivation, and autonomy. The supervisee progresses through stages of growth for each of these components. In the first stage, the supervisee has limited awareness, high motivation, and low autonomy, which often lead to anxiety as a neophyte practitioner. The second stage is characterized by awareness that is focused on the athlete, high motivation, and a growing autonomy, which can lead to confusion. In stage three, there is a balance of self and other awareness, motivation is stable, and autonomy is more developed, which leads to the neophyte practitioner developing his/her own professional identity.

Silva, Metzler, and Lerner (2007) shared multiple methods for supervision, including self-report, case notes, audiovisual recording, interpersonal process recall, group supervision, live observation, and live supervision. Each of these has their strengths and weaknesses, and supervisors must assess which methods meet the needs of both the supervisor and the supervisee. In the current case, each of the aforementioned techniques was utilized in some manner during the nine-week internship period.

For our IMG Academy supervision philosophy, we have developed a supervisee maturation process that has four major stages. The first stage is *complete observation* by the supervisee. In this stage, the supervisee observes seasoned consultants as they do small- and large-group and individual sessions with athletes in a variety of sports. This stage lasts 1–2 weeks. In comments from the current case's notes, he said,

> While taking in the lecture it became obvious that he (the presenter) was both proficient and well versed when it comes to mental coaching. He made effective use of humor and rhetorical questions, moved around the room (making everyone feel a part of the talk) as well as paused and incorporated real world examples of elite level athletes.

While commenting on observing another presenter, it was noted, "I couldn't get over how simple the message was which he was trying to get across to them."

The second stage is a *getting your feet wet* stage, where the supervisee takes one section of the session and leads it, with the supervisor there to assist for that section and to lead the remainder of the lesson. This stage lasts another 1–2 weeks. The third stage is the *taking the lead role* stage, in which the supervisee does a majority of the session but still has help from the supervisor and has the supervisor as a "safety net." This stage lasts another 1–2 weeks. The fourth stage is the *autonomous* stage, in which the supervisee is now on his/her own to deliver the session, with the supervisor sitting in at first, but then fully on one's own to develop and deliver sessions.

Finally, we have realized that a few specific qualities are found in our most successful interns, due to the nature of the high-demand, fast-paced, ever-changing environment at IMG Academy. These include an unrelenting positive attitude, a passion for the field of sport psychology, and an extremely high work ethic. The game changer characteristic that also emerges is adaptability. One day your session may get cancelled because of rain and the next day you could have over 150 student-athletes sitting in front of you, jammed into a room because the courts are wet. After nine weeks immersed in applied sport psychology, most supervisees can truly say if this is the job for them or not.

PREPARATION/PLANNING

Many would agree that preparation leads to confidence, yet most supervisees do not realize how much preparation it really takes to stand in front of a group of young athletes and deliver a seminar or workshop. As noted in his notes on day two,

> I certainly wasn't prepared for the diversity in age and maturity and feel that presenting to these athletes will certainly be a challenge since I have only ever presented to people my age and older, to people with some preconceived notion of my topic for discussion.

Preparation was a strength of the supervisee, as he would detail every minute of his lecture and practice it over and over before stepping onto the stage. This is a positive characteristic, but also one that makes it a challenge to remain flexible and adaptable in the case of a technology failure, a rowdy group, or a change in plans. Pages of hand-written notes eased some of the tension for the supervisee, but as supervisors we continued to challenge him to rely less on his notes, which caused quite a bit of visible trepidation in the supervisee. It was definitely a challenge for one who used preparation to his advantage as a competitive golfer to grasp the concept that he was not allowed to use notes during his delivery of a sport psychology session.

The supervisor's desire for the practitioner to strike a balance between strong preparation and the ability to adapt to the individual or group was essential, and fit the adage, "teach the student, not the lesson."

SUPERVISION PROCESS/EXPERIENCE

Every day brought a new experience during the internship. In his notes, he would reflect on themes that covered similarities and differences across group sessions for a variety of sports, individual sessions, marketing phone calls, supervisor interactions, sessions in and out of the office, video taping clients in their sport, working with a multicultural population, working in a high-demand environment, and working with other interns who were experiencing the same feelings he was. We have selected a few experiences to highlight as critical incidents from the nine-week experience.

Critical Incident 1: The Comfort Zone – Golf

The supervisee was well aware of his comfort zone, as noted in a report he wrote. He said:

> Given my vast experience with golf and obvious lack of self-confidence regarding what was expected of me, in their wisdom, the IMG Mental Conditioning staff started me off working only with golf clients in order for me to get my feet wet.

During the first presentation, feedback was given to be more aware of the audience. Specifically, this meant to read the audience carefully, and to ask what they understood and use their feedback. Already having "credibility" in the golf world from his experience and knowledge eased many of the fears for the supervisee. The challenge instead was to "dumb down the material when working with eight year olds."

Another large part was going to the golf course and working with athletes as well as filming them playing on the course. The supervisee felt even more in his comfort zone on the golf course and even noted:

> My immediate reaction (to being on the course) was that doing sport psychology out in the sport setting seems far more natural than presenting to a group of athletes in the conference room.

He also added:

> I feel much more at home helping people out in the actual setting compared to the contrived office layout.

In addition, in one-on-one sessions with golfers, you could see the comfort level of the supervisee at its highest. He was quite good at building rapport with the athlete and relating to the challenges they were facing. When reviewing video of himself for these sessions with his supervisors and asking himself what went well, what did he learn and what could be better, the supervisee could easily see how his golf background and knowledge was a strength, but also how he needed to be more comfortable and confident in his presentation style, and not just rely on his golf background as his safety net.

Critical Incident 2: Outside the Comfort Zone – Tennis

Nothing could be scarier to this supervisee than being on stage in front of over 100 tennis players aged 8–18, half of whom do not have English as a first language. This could raise any practitioner's heart rate and perhaps cause a few butterflies in the stomach. One of the favorite moments from the supervisee's sessions with the tennis players was giving him feedback that they probably didn't know what the word "ruminate" meant, which he had used in regards to their self-talk. Further, helping him understand that not every young athlete was going to sit perfectly still and stay 100 percent focused for the entire hour of his session was a focus at this stage of his internship. He learned quickly to apply the "KISS" (Keep it Simple Stupid) principle and gained an understanding that "there is no value to what you know if you are unable to share the knowledge you have acquired with others." Being highly educated, his instinct was to use academic terminology to express the concepts, yet the population he was presenting to struggled to understand these concepts on the same level. Hence, the supervisors challenged him to find the most basic, common, and simple language to convey the message to youth athletes. In video review of his sessions, he saw his nervous habits and lack of initial confidence. By the end of the internship, he also noted a visible difference in his "stage presence" and comfort level in front of the tennis athletes, which allowed him to gain confidence and realize how much he had grown as a practitioner in a short timeframe.

This is also where the supervisee completely realized that understanding your audience is key and that how you present to a group of tennis players may be different to how you present to a group of golfers. Thus, the supervisee felt that it was essential for him to have knowledge of the language and idiosyncratic terms used by athletes in their respective sports. Having an understanding of the basic rules of the sport as well as a bit of knowledge of the who's who and current events in the sport would give him some credibility, without which his job would be harder in terms of gaining buy-in. On the other hand, the supervisor reminded the supervisee and he soon came to realize that sport psychology is a universal language. He noted:

> I realized that sport psychology issues were similar across the board and were not distinct to the sport ... Sport psychology is still sport psychology whether you are talking with a 28 year old, 300 lb. male linebacker or a 16 year old, 100 lb. female figure skater.

Critical Incident 3: Two Baseball Players, No English

One of the more impactful experiences ended up being a co-session with another IMG Academy mental conditioning consultant working with two young baseball players from South America. The supervisee had very limited knowledge of baseball and the supervisor had very limited knowledge of Spanish, so it became a key collaboration to work with the two young boys. A few of the highlights of this experience were simulating baseball routines first in the office then out on the front lawn in front of the building, all the while with the supervisor providing the baseball knowledge and the supervisee providing the translation.

One of the best things about these sessions was that the supervisee had to work together with the other consultant to collaborate and share ideas back and forth, stretching his comfort zone even further. This also helped with one other challenge the supervisee had, which was thinking about what to say next while listening to others; this is something that translation prevented him from doing. As he noted, he had a tendency to "get caught up in my own head when listening to others talk, thinking about what I'm going to say next."

From this, the supervisee learned the value of being "present" and really listening, hearing, and taking in relation to what the athlete was telling him. This allowed him to become a better consultant because he was more focused on the athlete rather than on himself.

Critical Incident 4: Presentation Style

One of the biggest shocks to the supervisee was the huge difference in presenting style from an academic environment to an applied environment. There was no PowerPoint, no academic language, and no big words; the sport psychology concepts were still being taught to young athletes, just in ways they can relate to. Notes written by the supervisee high-lighted this fact, stating,

> The presentation style here at IMG is like no other that I have ever experienced. A typical presentation in school consists of using PowerPoint and talking at people. Here, the emphasis is on interaction using multimedia to support your presentation and the messages you are trying to convey to the audience. The gap between you and the listener is far smaller than when presenting in a university setting in that here it feels like you are almost part of the audience. In higher education everyone has an understanding of the topic you are presenting on but that is not the case here. The typical language and concepts you would use in academia are almost useless in the real world setting or so it seems, an athlete sitting in front of you has no interest in hearing about the intricate differences between the catastrophe theory and the inverted U hypothesis. Instead they need tools, weapons if you like, to utilize in the moments when they get out of their ideal state of being when competing to either psych themselves up or calm themselves down. My father once said to me that one's true education begins once you leave university ... I now see what he means!

In all of this, the supervisee realized that his best strategy was to "allow the lecture to become more of an interaction, a conversation if you will, between the presenter and the audience."

Nine Weeks of Learning

In the nine-week process, the supervisee compiled a list of things that "I know now and cer-tainly wished I knew when I first went in regards to the group sessions." The list included:

1. controlling the environment (seating arrangement, lighting, noise level);
2. using different media to convey your message;
3. considering language and level (avoiding complex language);
4. using personal experience to establish credibility;
5. getting names (learn the names of the athletes);
6. avoiding negating other's opinions;
7. varying the type of questions asked;
8. using applied information and giving them something they can take and use right away;
9. referring to role models;
10. selling the field (to get the buy-in about what you are saying);
11. establishing a presence (set boundaries);
12. using simple messages;
13. understanding that silence is okay, they will answer (learning to be comfortable with a bit of silence);
14. using real-life stories and current events;
15. getting them involved with activities and hands-on learning.

Finally, a key concept that this supervisee, along with every intern at IMG, learned was the true value of "practicing what you preach."

REFLECTION

The supervisee in the current case study realized quite quickly how different the real world of sport psychology consulting was from the academic presentation style. He reflected on much of this in his notes mentioned above and through conversations with his supervisors. From the supervisee's reflections, he was a young clinician who became more confident, stretched his comfort zone, and learned how to adapt to his environment and clients, thereby taking full advantage of his internship experience. From the supervisor's reflections, the supervisee was great to supervise in many ways, yet challenging in others. His work ethic, knowledge, and openness to feedback allowed him to learn quickly and put in the extra effort. But, it was challenging when he was sometimes stuck in his ways and wanting to be too perfect. Therefore, the supervisors continued to challenge him to "unbutton his top button" of his shirt and to not be so stiff, buttoned up, and perfectionistic. As with any supervisee, growth and development is the key to the internship experience and it was easy to see that this supervisee developed into a much better practitioner after being "thrown into the fire" at IMG Academy.

Freeman (1985) highlighted specific guidelines for the delivery of feedback from the supervisor to the supervisee. These guidelines include using feedback that is (1) systematic; (2) timely; (3) clearly understood; and (4) reciprocal. The IMG Academy internship is a very immersive experience whereby the intern experiences a significant amount of mentoring and feedback from various full-time consultants. We feel this can be both a strength and weakness because the intern learns that there are many ways to be successful in the field, but may also be confused by different approaches to the same topic or situation.

Throughout the second through fourth stages mentioned above, the supervisee is encouraged to video-tape their sessions and then watch them after. The supervisee then also watches the videos with his/her supervisor. In addition, the supervisors utilize the "Total Consultant Profile" review sheets (Mugford et al., 2014) and review them in meetings with the supervisee after the sessions. In addition, the supervisor asks the supervisee to think about three questions during a "well–better–learned" reflection process. The three simple questions are: (1) What did you do well? (2) What could you have done better? (3) What did you learn? This was an ongoing process for the current supervisee, and from supervisor reflection seemed to work to continue the daily growth as the supervisee moved from a timid and nervous note-reading student to a confident, composed, and creative consultant.

As with the current supervisee, it is common for neophyte practitioners to experience feelings of failure, doubt, and criticism after many of their initial sessions, especially in stages two and three (Woodcock, Richards, & Mugford, 2008). Indeed, it may feel like a roller coaster of emotions with a range of success and failure experienced early on, walking away from some groups feeling highly successful and others feeling like a complete failure. This is where it becomes imperative for sport psychology professionals to "practice what they preach," when they themselves are the performer in front of a group of athletes. In almost every supervisory relationship we have encountered over the past ten years, there has been the sit-down meeting (many including tears), where the supervision session has been more of a performance psychology consultation. Many challenges are addressed, but some of the most common include where the neophyte professional realizes they are not perfect (realistic perceptions), that they must fail in order to get better (have a growth mindset), mental skills like mental rehearsal and diaphragmatic breathing are valuable tools that help preparation, and they must learn to trust in their abilities. There is also always the discussion on the need to adapt and adjust sessions as needed and to listen to the athletes, rather than taking a cookbook approach to sessions and consulting. Very early on, plan B and C become cornerstones in preparation for consultants.

Supervision in the field of sport psychology provides a gate-keeping role to provide athletes and clients with protection from practitioners who are unprepared to practice (Tod, 2010). Formal supervision should be an integral part of any sport psychology practitioner's process, navigating the journey from novice to experienced professional. Ideally, supervision should continue throughout the life of every consultant's career (Tod, 2007). Unfortunately, there are still concerns over the level and standards of professional development in the field of sport psychology (Tod, 2010). Through effective supervision, neophyte consultants are able to learn, progress, and stretch themselves personally and professionally (Watson et al., 2014). This allows supervisees to grow and gain the self-awareness needed to understand themselves as they impart their knowledge of sport psychology onto others. This is a critical stage of progress for the supervisee to gain confidence, but is also critical for supervisors to ensure quality in the field of sport psychology for generations to come. This is why we both enjoy the role as supervisors, but also take it very seriously.

SUGGESTED READINGS

Anderson, M. B. (2000). *Doing sport psychology*. Champaign, IL: Human Kinetics.

Anderson, M. B. (2005). *Sport psychology in practice*. Champaign, IL: Human Kinetics.

Cremades, G., & Tashman, L. (Eds.) (2015). *Becoming a sport, exercise, and performance psychology professional: A global perspective*. New York, NY: Routledge.

Dungy, T. (2010). *The mentor leader*. Carol Stream, IL: Tyndale House Publishers, Inc.

Falender, C. A., & Shafranske, E. P. (2004). *Clinical supervision: A competency-based approach*. Washington, DC: American Psychological Association.

Halliwell, W., Orlick, T., Ravizza, K., & Rotella, B. (2003). *Consultant's guide to excellence*. Chelsea: Zone of Excellence Publishing.

Hanrahan, J., & Andersen, M. B. (Eds.) (2010). *Routledge handbook of applied sport psychology*. New York, NY: Routledge.

Hill, K. L. (2001). *Frameworks for sport psychologists: Enhancing sport performance*. Kluwer Academic Publishers.

Hunt, S. T. (2012). *Common sense talent management*. Chichester John Wiley.

Maxwell, J. (2010). *Everyone communicates, few connect*. Nashville, TN: Thomas Nelson.

Silva, J. M., Metzler, J. N., & Lerner, B. (2007). *Training professionals in the practice of sport psychology*. Morgantown, WV: Fitness Information Technology.

Stolovitch, H. D., & Keeps, E. J. (2002). *Telling ain't training*. Alexandria, VA: ASTD Press.

Zachary, L. J. (2012). *The mentor's guide*. Chichester: John Wiley.

Zachary, L. J. (2005). *Creating a mentoring culture*. Chichester: John Wiley.

REFLECTIVE QUESTIONS

1. Why is it important to have a structured method of supervision when working as a supervisor in sport psychology?
2. How are the four stages of progression that an IMG Academy supervisee experiences in a nine-week period critical to the development of an applied sport psychology practitioner?
3. How would you go about incorporating the 15 key concepts that the current supervisee wished he had known at the beginning and utilize them to develop your sessions?
4. Discuss why it is important for a new consultant to be open to feedback from supervisors.
5. Why is "knowing your audience" such an important component to effective delivery of sport psychology messages?

REFERENCES

Freeman, E. (1985). The importance of feedback in clinical supervision: Implications for direct practice. *The Clinical Supervisor, 3*, 5–26.

Hill, K. L. (2001). *Frameworks for sport psychologists: Enhancing sport performance*. Berlin: Kluwer Academic Publishers.

Mugford, A., Hesse, D., & Morgan, T. (2014). Developing the "total" consultant: Nurturing the art & science. In G. Cremades & L. Taschman (Eds.), *Becoming a sport, exercise, and performance psychology professional: International perspectives – Approaches and techniques in supervision* (pp. 268–275). New York, NY: Routledge.

Silva, J. M., Metzler, J. N., & Lerner, B. (2007). *Training professionals in the practice of sport psychology.* Morgantown, WV: Fitness Information Technology.

Stoltenberg, C. D., McNeill, B. W., & Delworth, U. (1998). *IDM Supervision: An integrated development model for supervising counselors and therapists.* San Francisco, CA: Jossey-Bass.

Tod, D. (2007). The long and winding road: Professional development in sport psychology. *The Sport Psychologist, 21,* 94–108.

Tod, D. (2010). Training and professional development in applied sport psychology. In S. J. Hanrahan & M. B. Andersen (Eds.), *Routledge handbook of applied sport psychology* (pp. 21–29). New York, NY: Routledge.

Van Raalte, J., & Andersen, M. (2000). Supervision I: From models to doing. In M. Andersen (Ed.), *Doing sport psychology* (pp. 153–165). Champaign, IL: Human Kinetics.

Watson, J. C., McAlarnen, M. M., & Shannon, V. R. (2014). Facilitating our future: Roles, responsibilities, and the development of the sport, exercise, and performance supervisor. In G. Cremades & L. Taschman (Eds.), *Becoming a Sport, exercise, and performance psychology professional: International perspectives – Approaches and techniques in supervision* (pp. 236–242). New York, NY: Routledge.

Woodcock, C., Richards, H., & Mugford, A. (2008). Quality counts: Critical features for neophyte professional development. *The Sport Psychologist, 22*(4), 1–17.

33 Student's Supervised Practice on Helping an Elite Swedish Golfer

Application of the Halmstad Applied Sport Psychology Supervision Model

Natalia Stambulova, Urban Johnson, and Lukas Linnér

The focus of this chapter is a case study with an elite Swedish golfer, conducted by a student-consultant (the third author) during his first year in the applied sport psychology (ASP) advanced-level course at Halmstad University (Sweden) under the supervision of the first two authors. Positioning the case as a central part of the chapter we surround it by outlining the specific context of ASP education and supervision as well as with reflections of both the supervisee and supervisors on the process and outcomes of this case study.

BACKGROUND INFORMATION

The Course and Supervision Approach

The case study described in this chapter exemplifies supervised practice of a student-consultant during the course "How to work in ASP" at Halmstad University. In our previous publication (Stambulova, Johnson, & Linnér, 2014) we introduced the course and a particular approach we have developed in ASP supervision, which we termed the Halmstad Supervision Model (HSM). The HSM consists of: (1) *preconditions* addressing students' and supervisors' backgrounds, as well as contextual and organizational issues that influenced development of the HSM; (2) *underlying frameworks* and *goals* for ASP supervision; (3) *philosophy* representing values and principles, theoretical orientations, and ASP areas addressed in supervision; (4) *process*, including forms, methods, and content, as well as the climate and ethics of supervision; and (5) *outcomes*, with students' feedback and achievements. We positioned the HSM as a "local model" that takes into account the Swedish culture, sport system, and local institutional contexts (e.g., limited possibilities to hire external supervisors that led to the course leaders having dual roles in terms of teaching and supervising).

The Supervisee and Supervisors

At the time of the case study, the student-consultant (Lukas) had already graduated from the sport science program at Halmstad University, and received his bachelor and European master's degrees in sport and exercise psychology. His own athletic background was in golf and therefore he understood a lot of nuances of golf to competently communicate with the elite golfer-client. Being a student, Lukas demonstrated almost an equal interest to sport psychology research and applied work, and he was motivated to make "a transition from theory to practice" in his first ASP intervention.

The supervisors of Lukas' case study were two professors and leaders of the ASP course who also had worked together for more than a decade on creating the content of the course and the HSM. The first author was Lukas' main supervisor, and the second author was his co-supervisor for the case study. The fact that we both knew Lukas before the course (during his bachelor and master's studies) facilitated our working relationships.

DESCRIPTION OF THE CASE

Description of the Client, "Billy"

Client as a person. Billy was a 25-year-old man from Sweden that related most aspects of himself and his life to the game of golf. When asked to sum up himself in five words, apart from what related to golf, Billy said: *analytical, anxious/worried* about how other people perceived him, *persistent* (i.e., he liked to complete things and did not give up easily), *open-minded* (i.e., he did not judge people straight away, and considered himself to be a generally social person, but not when in new groups), and wanting *to be in control.* The consultant's impression of Billy was a person who was ambitious, determined, educated, honest, and open in sharing his thoughts. Through statements like: "I don't want to be in anyone's way" or "I have the feeling they are better than me," the impression was also that Billy had low self-confidence.

Billy explained that he "didn't want to be just one in the crowd" and "wanted to be remembered and make his mark." Social evaluation and recognition seemed important to him. This feature of Billy was well visible in a homework assignment in which he described his role models (famous singers) and in following discussions where he shared a wish to incarnate their characteristics into his personality and being. Meanwhile, the impression was that he already was some of what he wanted to become (e.g., charismatic, brave, went his own way), which highlighted the issue of Billy's somewhat inaccurate self-perception.

Client as an athlete. Billy had played golf since he was six years old. When he turned 14 he made it a goal to attend a national golf high school, a goal he reached. Many of the students at the golf high school played for the Swedish junior national team, but not Billy. Like many times in his life, he was one step behind, almost but yet not making it. For Billy this was fuel to prove them wrong! After high school, Billy decided to stay in Sweden and not go to college in the United States as everyone else did, even though he could and significant others believed he should. At the time of the intervention, Billy played golf at the highest level in Sweden and was within the qualifying process of the European Tour. When Billy played, he sometimes struggled with cognitive anxiety provoked by future-oriented thoughts disturbing his ability to focus on the present moment.

Client's social roles and environment. Billy lived, worked, and trained at different locations several hours apart. He estimated that he was away from home 50 percent of the time, which also meant he sometimes was away from his girlfriend and dog for several days. Billy had most of his relatives close to where he lived, but his parents lived three hours away and his sister lived abroad. Billy worked part-time as a fitness coach and was part of an elite development team to receive financial support; however, he did not utilize the team's coaches, which most golfers did. Instead, Billy had a coach who had followed him since he was 11 years old. Five years earlier, this coach had moved two hours away, but Billy still met him about four times per year. During the previous year their relationship took a turn for the worse. The coach had prioritized someone else, which Billy found annoying and problematic.

Billy was in a steady relationship with his girlfriend. He did not have a lot of friends, but this was fine with him, as he mentioned: "I'd rather have fewer friends that are close than many superficial ones." Billy's friends, his social roles, and his environment all related to golf, including his girlfriend, whom he had met in high school when they were both enrolled.

Client's situation before the intervention. Billy's situation before the intervention revolved around establishing himself as a professional golfer and making a living out of playing golf. Billy's improvement had gradually, year by year, turned upwards, and during the end of the previous season he had made it into the second qualifying stage (out of three) of the European Tour, a level of competition he had never been at before. Training and competing in golf took most of Billy's time, and also stressed him the most. Golf was a big part of his identity and this was something he wanted to find a better balance in (e.g., when golf performance was poor, Billy still wanted to feel good about himself).

Client's perceived future. Billy wanted to become a professional golfer playing on the big scenes. He saw himself playing on the European Tour full-time within four years and committing to the game professionally for another 20 years. After the 20-year plan, he considered his active career to be finished, and his plans became less detailed (e.g., possibly continue within golf in some role, but not competing). He was also planning to move in with his girlfriend and thought they could have children within six years.

Goals and Preliminary Plan for the Intervention

Based on the analysis of the information collected, four *working issues* or *goals* for the intervention were set: (1) to deal with future-oriented thoughts during play (later – the cognitive anxiety issue); (2) to work with Billy's confidence (i.e., confidence issue); (3) to help solve the coach situation (i.e., coach issue); and (4) to stimulate Billy to self-explore other aspects of the self apart from what related to golf (i.e., self-exploration issue). Prioritizing the working issues was based on the analysis of the client's sport and life situation. During the initial phase of the intervention, Billy was within the qualifying process of the European Tour and his main goal at the time was to perform well during the qualifying stages. Therefore, it was not wise to work on all the issues in parallel. The client and consultant decided that up until the second qualifying stage, *the cognitive anxiety issue* should be in focus, and after the second qualifying stage and evaluation of the situation, new issues could be addressed. It was believed that then working with *the confidence issue* was the proper way of progressing because it could aid both his performance and potentially his self-exploration. In regards to *the coach issue*, the plan was to advise Billy to deal with this during the off-season, so that if the situation turned problematic there was time to help Billy through such a transition. *The self-exploration issue* was more a part of Lukas' than the client's agenda, and therefore it received the most peripheral position compared to the other working issues.

APPROACH/PHILOSOPHY

To guide the ASP supervision process, we use primarily the scientist-practitioner model (Jarvis, 1999; Lane & Corrie, 2006), lifelong learning (Vygotsky, 1983), and career development (Savickas, 2002; Super, 1957) frameworks which complement each other in addressing supervisees' professional, educational, career, and personal development. Preparing students for ASP work in the Swedish sociocultural/sport context, providing feedback on students' practical work, and stimulating their professional reflexivity were set as major "instrumental" supervision goals. These were complemented by meta-goals of introducing ASP professional culture and encouraging the development of the students' professional philosophies and individual styles of consulting. To reach these goals, several forms of supervision (e.g., individual, group, cross, peer) and relevant methods (e.g., instruction, group discussions, analysis of ASP video, recorded role plays, filming and analyzing a real session with the client) were used. In addition, a set of "scaffolding tools" (e.g., guidelines on how to structure the first and a regular meeting with the client, collect information about the client and structure the description of the case, structure progress notes, and plan for the assessment – see more in Stambulova et al., 2014) was introduced to the students as their "bottom line" to facilitate their critical thinking and create approaches that best match their clients. Discussions and assignments stimulating students' reflexivity in regards to the ASP field, diversity of approaches consultants might use, professional philosophy, and style of consulting are considered as a "red thread" (i.e., a major theme) of the course and the supervision process.

By *philosophy* in the HSM we mean principles and values that are currently accepted in ASP professional culture, both internationally and in Sweden. For example, client-centered approach, theory-driven practice, holistic developmental perspective, ethical work, positive psychology, and humanistic perspectives (see more in Stambulova & Johnson, 2010) are all included in our ASP course as underlying criteria for a high-quality ASP intervention. For example, foci on basic ethical norms, ways of collecting and analyzing the client's information, principles of prioritizing working issues, encouraging the supervisees to find theoretical frameworks and relevant research facilitating their intervention planning, and individualized assessment of the intervention have been traditional topics both in classes and supervision meetings. One of our highlights is encouraging supervisees to see their professional repertoire as broader than working solely on performance issues and to take *a whole-person approach*; that is, considering athletes as developing individuals doing sport and having other life issues (e.g., studies, work, friends, and family).

Many of the aforementioned principles and values are visible in the case study and reflections on the supervision process described below. For example, although performance issues prevailed in the content of the intervention, the description of the case was done in a manner that allows seeing the client as a whole person and not only as a golf performer. When the working issues were identified, discussed with the client, and prioritized based on the analysis of the client's situation, several theoretical frameworks and applied tools were implemented; assessment of the intervention was planned to fit the criteria of relevance to the client and the case (i.e., individualized) with pre-, during-, and after-intervention measurements. The client-centered approach was also obvious when the student-consultant made changes in the initial plan to follow the changes in the client's situation and agenda.

PREPARATION/PLANNING

The students in our ASP course are self-responsible for finding clients to work with for about six months throughout the one-year course. At the beginning of the course we (the teacher-supervisors) usually introduce a set of recommendations on how to search for a client (e.g., "think about yourself and who can be a good client for you, especially in the first intervention") and provide scaffolding tools (see more in Stambulova et al., 2014) on how to create an intervention plan, including how to collect the client's information, analyze it, decide on the working issues, and prioritize them. We also address communication issues (e.g., how supervisees are expected to introduce and position themselves within the intervention process) and discuss a consultant–client cooperation agreement, including ethical principles that guide the supervised practice (e.g., right to withdraw at any time, confidentiality, limitations, conduct, and working alliance). Usually, ethical issues and consultant–client agreements are also discussed in students' peer group meetings, facilitating their understanding of the bottom line of ethical service delivery. The students are recommended to introduce ethical issues to their clients during the very first meeting, but to sign the ethical agreement a bit later when the issues to work with are clarified and approved by the client.

As to the particular case described in this chapter, Lukas was acquainted with his client during a previous golf research project, and they bonded through mutual experiences of professional golf. The idea of starting a working relationship was later introduced in relation to Lukas taking the ASP course. To understand the psychological portrait of the client, three meetings and one observation of a competition including meeting most of the client's social network (i.e., girlfriend, coaches, friends) were conducted, together with homework assignments (e.g., what the client wanted to work on, what he had tried before, and characteristics of his role models). The collected information served as the basis for a working plan (i.e., describing the case, goals, relevant theoretical frameworks, preliminary content and weekly plan for the intervention, and assessment). The supervisors provided their feedback on the working plan and it was also presented in the class and critically reviewed by peers.

SUPERVISION PROCESS/EXPERIENCE

Having a set of the working issues outlined, Lukas felt confident to start working on them in the order they were prioritized. But in reality the intervention went differently, and after working on *the cognitive anxiety issue* Lukas had to refocus to *the coach issue*, which got high priority according to the client. The coach issue also took much more time than was expected. Therefore, *the confidence issue* was addressed more briefly than planned, and *the self-exploration issue* was left almost untouched.

For a novice consultant, making changes to the working plan can be stressful. Lukas later reflected (Linnér, 2012) that by learning from related literature, the supervisors' experiences, and exchanges in the peer group he was prepared to be flexible in following changes in the client's situation. Below, Lukas' intervention experiences are shared and complemented by comments from the supervisors' perspectives.

The Intervention

The cognitive anxiety issue. The first working issue was (as planned) Billy's cognitive anxiety. Being analytic and having thoughts of the future during play was feeding Billy's worry and negatively affecting his performance. A self-talk workshop was conducted based on the model of psychological preparation for peak performance (Hardy, Jones, & Gould, 1996) and Hardy, Oliver, and Tod's (2009) framework of self-talk and performance. The self-talk–performance relationship was discussed, followed by how one can work with self-talk. Billy was then taught how to reconstruct thoughts using a thought-stopping technique. Progressing from the session, Billy identified situations during practice where the technique was useful, practiced it until the second qualifying stage of the European Tour, and used it in competition with some success (see assessments below).

From the supervisors' perspective, dealing with this working issue Lukas was well prepared by several classes on performance enhancement mental training and a role play exercise where he taught one mental exercise to a fictitious client (other student) and received critical feedback on his (self-invented) exercise and performance as a consultant from supervisors and peers. Additionally, Lukas knew the concept of self-talk from his previous research projects. Therefore, as supervisors we could give him space to be autonomous in this work and to gain confidence in his ability.

The coach issue. Billy played the second qualifying stage of the European Tour, finishing within a respectful position, but unfortunately did not qualify for the final stage. The week after, while talking with him on the phone it became apparent that the coach situation had taken a turn for the worse and that Billy's analytical self was wearing him down. Billy was given a task to analyze the pros and cons of staying with his current coach versus transitioning to a potential new coach that was within his network. The client was also instructed to determine the three most important aspects he wanted in a coach. The rationale was to utilize his ability to analyze accompanied with writing it down on paper. After doing so, Billy felt less anxious and more in control. Keeping in mind the possibility of Billy's transition to a new coach, discussions were planned on the concepts outlined by the athletic career transition model (Stambulova, 2003). The situation did, however, rapidly turn into a crisis-transition (i.e., Billy could not cope with the situation). The mobilization model of counseling athletes in crisis-transitions (Stambulova, 2011) was incorporated into the theoretical disposition to guide the work (i.e., articulate the problem, analyze resources and barriers, encourage a strategic decision, formulate new goals, establish an action plan). In follow-up meetings, Billy decided on an action plan that included ending the working relationship with the old coach and starting a relationship with a new coach. Role playing was also incorporated into meetings with Billy, using assertiveness training (Yukelson, 2006) to promote a strategy to deal with and structure the "relationship-ending" conversation with the old coach. The assertiveness "manuscript" for the conversation was transcribed and Billy continued to practice this at home for several weeks. Through the assertiveness training, Billy showed remarkable progress and he was determined to deal with the situation. However, the transition was prolonged when the old coach cancelled several meetings initiated by Billy. In the end, Billy moved on and the relationship-ending conversation took place several months later, with a shared belief (according to Billy) that this was for the best for both Billy and the coach.

From the supervisors' perspective, the coach issue appeared more difficult for Lukas to deal with and he needed more help, especially when the client showed some crisis symptoms (e.g., emotional discomfort, inability to make a decision); the mobilization model of counseling in crisis-transitions was used. At the same time, there were several good own insights into his work (e.g., pros and cons list engaging the client's analytical ability, assertiveness "manuscript" for the conversation with the coach). Further, the role play incorporated in this part of the intervention was according to Lukas inspired by his own experiences with role plays in the course.

The confidence issue. As mentioned above, the confidence issue was put aside when the coach situation became more relevant. In addition, the coach situation took much of the off-season time and energy from Billy. Therefore, when the coach situation was considered to be under control, the pre-season training had already started, and Billy was clear with his interest in performance-oriented intervention strategies. During the pre-season, after changing his coach, Billy made some changes in his technique. When changing technique it is vital to trust the new swing. Therefore, Billy was given a routine drill where the essence of making a decision, and then trusting it while executing the shot, was practiced. The point was to adapt the intervention to the new situation (i.e., aiding in the change of his swing technique), but at the same time focusing the work in a way that could be used as a foundation for the continuation of the proposed intervention (i.e., confidence). Meetings were then carried out discussing confidence (Vealey & Vernau, 2010), expectations, demands, and the relationship between confidence and anxiety. These meetings were perceived as a turning point, changing Billy's perception of what confidence was and how it could be built. An imagery strategy was then introduced and Billy's imagery ability was assessed using the sport imagery evaluation exercise (Vealey & Greenleaf, 2006). Based on the assessment, Billy then trained his imagery ability and identified situations wherein he felt less confident. The intervention was then planned to continue by providing scripts of situations wherein he could imagine feeling more confident, using role models to promote how-they-would-do-it thinking, and then having Billy imagining doing such things. Because of the time constraints, this work was not completed, but the client received enough information to continue on his own.

From the supervisors' perspective, after coping with the difficult coach issue, Lukas felt it was easy to come back to performance-oriented work, and he was able to relate the confidence issue to both previous issues (i.e., anxiety and changing a coach). In this (final) part of the intervention he was more autonomous again, and his own experiences as a former professional golfer facilitated his performance-oriented work with the client.

The self-exploration issue. As it is obvious from the case description, Billy organized his life as revolving mainly around golf, and he planned to continue his golf career for the next two decades. But there is never a guarantee that the client can follow the plan since some unplanned events (e.g., career-ending injury) might change it. Having in mind the whole-person approach and athletic retirement research findings (e.g., Park, Lavallee, & Tod, 2013), Billy was introduced to potential difficulties upon retirement if not prepared for it in advance. But the client did not feel really committed to dealing with this issue, and it was left as a recommendation for his further consideration.

From the supervisors' perspective, we encouraged Lukas to follow the client's agenda, but at the same time to carefully introduce the whole-person approach in order to make the client better prepared for the possibility of involuntary termination as an active golfer. We know Lukas made a good effort in promoting the self-exploration issue, but Billy stayed with his opinion that it was too early for him to think about termination. On the positive side, we can mention that Lukas directed the client's attention to, and educated him on, the issue.

Assessment

An individual assessment profile in relation to the working issues was developed, outlining: when (e.g., before, during, after); what (e.g., confidence); how (e.g., 0–5/10/100, pie chart or a validated instrument); and why (e.g., baseline, monitoring). Considering how the intervention unfolded, assessments were rearranged and simplified. Single-subject questions (0–10/100), a monitoring diary (e.g., routine, imagery), and self-made instruments (e.g., self-perception) were used. Several aspects were assessed initially (e.g., confidence, imagery ability, self-perception), but due to how the intervention ended (see next section) these aspects were never followed-up. With regards to handling cognitive anxiety, the intervention generated minor, but according to the client meaningful, changes. With regards to the coach situation, Billy went from thinking the situation was terrible to handle (12 out of 10), to feeling in control after the assertiveness training (7 out of 10), and later on felt that the meeting with the coach was not something that was worrying him (2 out of 10).

Termination of the Intervention

When the six months intervention time had passed (and the supervised practice was over), Billy was in his pre-season and had started to work on the confidence through imagery part of the intervention. After 16 sessions, a concluding meeting was held where Billy provided his comments on the intervention and working relationship. Overall, he believed that it had been meaningful, fun, and easy to relate to because it had all been based on things or people (i.e., role models) he liked. Billy also stated that he had learned that he was braver and more charismatic than what he had thought before (i.e., change in self-perception). Billy was positive toward a continued collaboration, but in the end withdrew from interest.

REFLECTION

The Supervisee's Reflections on the Supervised Practice

Looking back at this supervised practice experience and being a novice consultant, I was very motivated to help the client, trying to find "all the problems" and working to fix them. But in reality, and as I learned, working with people, or for that matter changing psychological aspects in people, takes time. In the beginning I felt somewhat scattered in trying to understand the client's psychological portrait and what the working issues really were. My way to manage this was to put everything else aside, and just submerge myself in all the information I had collected about the client, and relate it to relevant theories. What I came up with I then discussed with my supervisors. From these discussions I learned how to better connect different parts of the information to the overall situation of the client and find the problems behind the client's symptoms, and this helped me formulate and prioritize the working issues for the intervention.

One of the most interesting situations I experienced during the intervention was one phone call with the client (part of the coach situation). This was my first "counseling" experience and coming out of it I grew a lot in my role as a consultant. Billy was upset and opened up to me in a way he had not done before. The conversation therefore developed in a direction that I did not expect. Even so, I managed to turn him around, get him more positive and constructively focused on the situation (i.e., partly the coach situation, but also missing the final qualifying stage of the European Tour). This conversation was a turning point for me as a consultant, as much as it was a turning point for Billy in his situation.

Coming out of this supervised practice, I did not feel as though I was the same person, which should be understood as something positive. Through the course and the interactions with the client, peers, and specifically the supervisors whom encouraged reflexivity, I matured a lot and became much more self-aware. In our previous publication (Stambulova et al., 2014)

I reflected that supervisors should take a look in the (scientific) mirror and assess what they automatically bring to the process. This holds true for consultants as well. Through the intervention and supervised practice I understood that it was much less about the client than what I had thought before, it was much more about myself, and what I brought to the process.

One more thing that grew important to me, and that I have incorporated as part of my philosophy, is to feel that I am myself and that I am not trying to be or act as someone I am not. For me, this is how I feel I gain the trust of a client and build a relationship. One example was when Billy and I played table tennis. This was a good situation to build rapport. Doing this seemingly harmless and not so sport psychology consulting activity was, however, a great way for me to get Billy to loosen up and to get to know him even better. For example, I observed that when Billy missed or hit a poor shot, he had automatic reactions that I guessed were similar to the ones he faced when playing golf. So, through play and by simply being ourselves I got valuable information about my client and how to help him with his performance, and also had a good time.

To summarize the overall supervised practice experience, I would say that the supervisors encouraged in-depth analysis and reflexivity as well as provided practical tools, structure, and good advice. The supervision provided a sound basis for the intervention work with the client along with support for my personal and professional development, and for that I would like to express my deepest gratitude to both supervisors.

The Supervisors' Reflections

During the supervised practice experience, Lukas went through a transition from understanding sport psychology as a science to understanding it also as an art in terms of how to relate the knowledge he had before the intervention (and learned during it) to the concrete client and his situation and needs. During the course, Lukas reflected on his theoretical perspective and professional philosophy, and in the end formulated his thoughts in a final report about the intervention (Linnér, 2012). Being involved in supervising Lukas both in research and applied work, we can reflect that there was a difference between the two supervision processes. In the research supervision, his project was in the center of our attention more than his personality, whereas it was vice versa in the ASP supervision, where his stronger and weaker points and his individual style of consulting were no less important than discussion of the client. Lukas (at the time of that case study) looked more mature than many other students, presenting himself in a professional manner and trying to be autonomous. He was analytical and reflective, attentive to detail, but also could keep in mind the whole person and the situation. He had good communication skills and knowledge of the sport that helped him to establish a working alliance with his client. During analysis of a filmed session with the client, it appeared that Lukas needed to be more attentive to the client's body language and respond to the client's reactions in order to maintain meaningful dialogues; the work on developing his consulting style followed. Lukas was ambitious and confident and ready to learn more from others and from his own experiences. As he later reflected in his final report:

> when going into this course I believed I was going to manage the task [the intervention] quite well, that being a consultant was something for me. I still [in the end of the course] believe this, but what I have learned is that I need to learn even more and that I need to be more humble towards the future and its challenges, and that is good.
>
> (Linnér, 2012, p. 11)

At the end of the course, we always have talks with the students about their future plans and discuss "how they fit to the profession and how the profession fits them." Such a career talk with Lukas revealed that he liked the applied work, but saw a future in research. After graduation, Lukas was appointed a teaching position at our university and after three years of teaching and administrative work (as head of the sport science program) he started his PhD education, keeping his applied practice as a part-time private business.

SUGGESTED READINGS

Stambulova, N., & Johnson, U. (2010). Novice consultants' experiences: Lessons learned by applied sport psychology students. *Psychology of Sport and Exercise 11*(4), 295–303.
Stambulova, N., Johnson, U., & Linnér, L. (2014). Insights from Sweden: Halmstad Applied Sport Psychology Supervision model. In L. Tashman and G. Cremades (Eds.), *Becoming a sport, exercise, and performance psychology professional: International perspectives* (pp. 276–284). New York, NY: Routledge.

REFLECTIVE QUESTIONS

1. What is your perception of strong features of the HSM?
2. What do you see as limitations in applying the HSM?
3. How do you think supervisors should balance controlling supervisees and giving them space to be autonomous?
4. What might you consider as advantages of working with athlete-clients from the holistic developmental perspective?
5. Read again the description of the client, Billy. What directions of future work with this client do you see?

REFERENCES

Hardy, L., Jones, G., & Gould, D. (1996). *Understanding psychological preparation for sport: Theory and practice of elite performers.* New York, NY: John Wiley.
Hardy, J., Oliver, E., & Tod, E. (2009). A framework for the study and application of self-talk within sport. In S. D. Mellalieu & S. Hanton (Eds.), *Advances in applied sport psychology: A review* (pp. 37–74). New York, NY: Routledge.
Jarvis, P. (1999). *The practitioner-researcher: Developing theory from practice.* San Francisco, CA: Jossey-Bass.
Lane, D. A., & Corrie, S. (2006). *The modern scientist-practitioner: A guide to practice in psychology.* London: Routledge.
Linnér, L. (2012). *Golf … golf … golf: A Swedish elite golf player with high athletic identity and low confidence striving to improve performance.* Intervention report (official exam paper). School of Social and Health Sciences, Halmstad University, Sweden.
Park, S., Lavallee, D., & Tod, D. (2013). Athletes' career transition out of sport: A systematic review. *International Review of Sport and Exercise Psychology, 6,* 22–53.
Savickas, M. L. (2002). Career construction: A developmental theory of vocational behaviour. In D. Brown & Associates (Eds.), *Career choice and development* (4th ed.; pp. 149–205). San-Francisco, CA: Jossey-Bass.
Stambulova, N. (2003). Symptoms of a crisis-transition: A grounded theory study. In N. Hassmén (Ed.), *SIPF Yearbook 2003* (pp. 97–109). Örebro: Örebro University Press.
Stambulova, N. (2011). The mobilization model of counseling athletes in crisis-transitions: An educational intervention tool. *Journal of Sport Psychology in Action, 2,* 156–170.
Stambulova, N., & Johnson, U. (2010). Novice consultants' experiences: Lessons learned by applied sport psychology students. *Psychology of Sport and Exercise 11*(4), 295–303.
Stambulova, N., Johnson, U., & Linnér, L. (2014). Insights from Sweden: Halmstad Applied Sport Psychology Supervision model. In L. Tashman and G. Cremades (Eds.), *Becoming a sport, exercise, and performance psychology professional: International perspectives* (pp. 276–284). New York, NY: Routledge.
Super, D. E. (1957). *The psychology of careers.* New York, NY: Harper & Row.
Vealey, R. S., & Greenleaf, C. A. (2006). Seeing is believing: Understanding and using imagery in sport. In J. M. Williams (Ed.), *Applied sport psychology: Personal growth to peak performance* (5th ed.; pp. 306–348). London: McGraw-Hill.

Vealey, R. S., & Vernau, D. (2010). Confidence. In S. J. Hanrahan & M. B. Andersen (Eds.), *Routledge handbook of applied sport psychology* (pp. 518–527). New York, NY: Routledge.

Vygotsky, L. S. (1983). Istoriya razvitiya vysshih psihicheskih funkcii [History of the development of higher mental functions]. In A. V. Zaporozhets (Ed.), *L. S. Vygotsky, Complete works*. Vol. 3 (pp. 5–328). Moscow: Pedagogika.

Yukelson, D. P. (2006). Communicating effectively. In J. M. Williams (Ed.), *Applied sport psychology: Personal growth to peak performance* (5th ed.; pp. 174–191). London: McGraw-Hill.

34 The Provision of Optimal Performance Training for a US Swimming Club Team Utilizing Supervision and Peer Mentoring

Robyn Braun, Amanda Myhrberg, Melissa Thompson, and Jodi Yambor

Peer mentoring is a process through which a more experienced individual encourages and assists a less experienced individual in developing his or her potential within a shared area of interest. The resulting relationship is a reciprocal one in that all individuals in the partnership have an opportunity for growth and development. Peer mentoring can be complementary to the traditional supervisor–supervisee relationship. The purpose of this chapter is to provide an example of how peer mentoring was used in a psychological skills training program within a US competitive swimming setting.

Sport, exercise, and performance psychology (SEPP) trainees often find that peer mentors are more approachable and easier to relate to due to their commonalities with each other, therefore creating a safe learning environment. Supervisors are often perceived as authority figures and this may discourage the mentee from seeking help and guidance (Ender & Kay, 2001). Furthermore, the structure of the program allows for maximum engagement of the mentee at all levels within limited placement opportunities. However, peer mentoring also has its shortcomings. Unsuitable pairings between the mentor and mentee is one of the common problems that can affect the performance of the partnership. The supervisor plays an important role in developing the foundation for this type of program. The following illustrates the implementation of a peer mentoring program within a multi-year academic setting for SEPP graduate students.

BACKGROUND INFORMATION

The Area Tallahassee Aquatic Club (ATAC) is a US competitive swimming program. There are approximately 250 year-round participants, with an additional 150 swimmers who participate only in the summer. The swimmers range in age from 5 to 21 years. ATAC trains daily, in the 50 meter by 25 yard pool, at the Trousdell Aquatic Center in Tallahassee, Florida. The team is composed of three major groups: senior (15–21 years of age), pre-senior (11–14 years of age), and age group (5–10 years of age). ATAC is a high-level program that consistently sends swimmers to Junior and Senior Nationals, as well as the World Championship and Olympic Trials.

The head coach of ATAC programs is Terry Maul, who has over 40 years of coaching experience and is an American Swim Coaches Association Level 5 coach. Additionally, Coach Maul is the spouse of the applied supervisor and has a master's degree in sport psychology. The head pre-senior coach is Eddie Von Hertsenberg and the head age group coach is Gerry Norris. Coach Maul was extremely receptive to the graduate students working with his team; he discussed it with his assistants and they were excited about the opportunity that would be offered to their swimmers.

DESCRIPTION OF THE CASE

A holistic approach was utilized in the development of sport psychology services for the three different competitive swimming groups at ATAC. According to Visek, Harris, and Blom (2009), physical, cognitive, emotional, and social developmental differences need to be considered when working with athletes. Therefore, Piaget's concrete operational and formal operational cognitive stages were taken into account when working with the various groups (Piaget, 1954, 1969). A peer mentoring consulting team provided the sport psychology services. This was the first time this particular consulting team had worked with the ATAC program. However, some of the swimmers in the senior and pre-senior groups had prior exposure to sport psychology. Additionally, only the primary consultant had a swimming background. Therefore, all members of the consulting team needed to become acclimated to this particular team and sport.

APPROACH/PHILOSOPHY

The Multi-Level Peer Mentoring Consultant Team

The primary mission of the peer mentoring consulting team is to provide interested students with exposure to applied sport psychology settings while allowing more experienced consultants to have opportunities to mentor their peers. The peer mentoring program matches mentors and mentees who are roughly equal in age and have the power to provide task and psychosocial support (Terrion & Leonard, 2007). The consulting team consists of a primary consultant, a secondary consultant, and a shadow. Each role serves a purpose not only to aid in the development of the athletes' mental skills training, but also to help develop leadership skills within the consulting team. It is important to note that an internship supervisor manages the peer mentoring team, aiding in the consulting team's educational development in applied SEPP.

As the team leader or mentor, the primary consultant has several responsibilities within the peer mentoring consulting team. This individual acts as the liaison to the athletic coaching staff and athletes to gain information about the team and schedule meetings with the team. Primary consultants are also responsible for communicating and scheduling times with the other consulting team members. He/she should have face-to-face meetings with the consulting team once per week to review the consultation process from the previous week, discuss and plan the upcoming session with the team, and discuss the roles and expectations of each member. In addition to providing team consultation, the primary consultant may offer individual consulting sessions. Furthermore, he/she is responsible for communicating and reporting back to the supervisor.

The secondary consultants' chief duty is to provide support to the primary consultant. Secondary consultants exhibit this support in the form of being a sounding board for session ideas, conducting sessions if the primary is not able to attend, and providing individual consulting sessions. The secondary should take an active role within the consulting team by sharing observations and asking questions about the consulting process.

Finally, the shadow functions as the member of the team with the least amount of consulting experience or the least experience with that sport. Shadows are responsible for contributing to the weekly meeting through offering ideas for session activities, reporting observations after team sessions, and asking questions about the consulting process to help broaden his/her knowledge base. Similar to how roles evolve on sport teams, the extent of involvement of a shadow will depend on the consulting team's needs/wants, and the desires and qualifications of the shadow.

Before the season begins, it is important to establish firm roles within the peer mentoring consulting team. A lack of role clarity or role acceptance can cause tension within the consulting team, thus it is important to define roles before the consulting team meets with any athletes or coaches (Bray, Beauchamp, Eys, & Carron, 2005). Typically, the primary consultant is the most experienced person on the consulting team. Therefore, in order to be considered a primary consultant, the student must have progressed through the mentorship program and have successfully completed the graduate courses of Introduction to Sport Psychology, Applied Sport Psychology, and Introduction to Counseling or Group Counseling. Only the internship supervisor has the authority to promote a student to the role of primary consultant. The secondary consultant is a student who has previously been a shadow, has successfully completed the Introduction to Sport Psychology course, and is currently enrolled in the Applied Sport Psychology course. The shadow is typically a first-year student who has not yet been familiarized with the consulting process. Again, it is important to reiterate the significance of defining the roles of each member of the consulting team in order for the team to understand his/her responsibilities.

Eight Steps to Consultation Adaptation

Murphy and Murphy (as cited in Murphy, 1995) developed an eight-step model of sport psychology consultation based on cognitive behavioral therapy (CBT; Figure 34.1). The first step is the consultation orientation, which involves determining whether consultation is desirable and possible. This first step also includes the development of an agreement outlining the parameters of the consultation. The second step is sport familiarization, ensuring that the consultant is familiar with the athlete's sport so that effective communication is possible. During this step, key sport-specific factors impacting the athlete's performance should be identified. Step three is the evaluation and assessment stage. It is at this point that relevant information is obtained in order to ascertain the key mental skills for the sport, reasons for performance blocks, and potential intervention targets. Step four is goal identification. In this step, the consultant identifies in specific terms the nature of the mental–performance relationship and suggests specific interventions based on the analysis of step three data to improve the athlete's coping skills. The evaluation and assessment process, as well as goal identification, initiates the group and individual interventions, which constitute steps five and six, respectively. Step five, group intervention, follows an educational approach, where psychological skills are explained, taught, and then applied to the athletic setting. The consultant should be systematic in developing a rationale for the importance of mental skills and demonstrating how these can assist in developing sport skills. Step six pertains to individual intervention. It is at this point that the development and practice of psychological skills training takes place with individual athletes or teams. Athletes will often discuss personal issues at this stage. It is important to know your own limitations as a referral for issues outside one's competency may be necessary. Subsequent to team and/or individual intervention, step seven involves conducting an outcome assessment used to evaluate whether the goals outlined in step four have been met. Lastly, step eight reassesses the goals, and if necessary modifies the plan(s).

The cognitive-behavioral approach presented above offers the advantages of being based on both educational and coping skills. This approach is consistently used in the peer mentoring team's work with athletic teams. The key to a successful intervention is having a coherent outlook (Perna, Ogilvie, & Murphy, 1995). Thus, following the eight-step model of sport psychology consulting allows all members of the peer mentoring team to have a conceptual understanding of the consulting process. Moreover, all consultants know what should be accomplished during each phase.

PREPARATION/PLANNING

Prior to beginning sport psychology consulting with the ATAC teams, the consulting team met with the head coach and the various swimmers from each group to discuss the goals and objectives for the season. As a whole, the head coach stated that it was important for all groups to focus on staying positive throughout the entire year. It is easy for athletes to develop a negative attitude

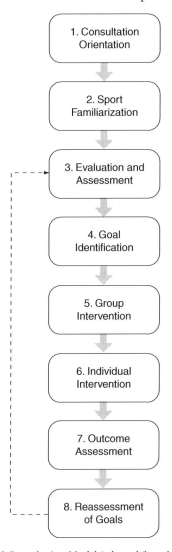

Figure 34.1 The Cognitive-Behavioral Consultation Model (adapted from Murphy, 1995)

while training at high intensity levels. Furthermore, the swimmers also confirmed that maintaining a positive attitude was extremely important to improve their performance overall. The swimmers expressed that the sport psychology services could help them both as a team and individually.

In addition to the meeting with the coach and swimmers, the consulting team observed several practices. The team observed practices for all three groups to understand the different demands and coaching styles. The primary consultant helped explain the different swimming terminology to the secondary consultant and the shadow. Furthermore, the secondary consult-ant and shadow researched the sport of swimming on their own to gain more information.

Once the consulting team had a basic understanding of the needs and wants of the groups, the consulting team began preparing the sessions. Prior to meeting, the primary consultant instructed the secondary consultant and shadow to think of ideas to correspond with the theme of positive thinking for the season. During the initial consulting team meeting, the primary explained the expectations and roles of each member. The primary consultant was the leader of the group; however, it was expected that all members contribute to the planning and consulting sessions. The primary felt it was important that everyone be involved in all aspects of the consulting process.

For example, the topic of one session dealt with how attitudes (positive or negative) can affect the swimmer and other teammates. During the consulting team meeting, the members discussed the different activities they thought would best demonstrate this concept. After discussing all the ideas, the consulting team as a whole decided on the activity. In this example, the swim team would be split into two teams to compete to build the tallest Jenga tower. Each swimmer was given an index card with a name and adjective on it – for instance, motivator Marissa (i.e., keep the team motivated to win) or Fighting Frank (i.e., get into fights with your team). Then the swimmer must act out what the card says to do without sharing what the card says while playing the game of Jenga. One group had all negative index cards and the other had all positive index cards. The teams played two additional rounds: (1) the teams switched from being positive to negative and vice versa; and (2) all swimmers were given positive cards except for one person, who had a negative card.

Once the activity was decided, an outline of the session was made to determine which consultant would lead each part of the session. Each session began with a quick recap of the previous session and it was generally led by the shadow. In the example above, since the secondary came up with the activity, he/she was in charge of the directions and running the activity. In general, the person who created the activity provided the directions to the team. The primary was in charge of debriefing the activity, and discussing applications to swimming and to life. The shadow was also in charge of delivering the hook for the next session. The hook was a simple sentence that would tease the group about the topic for the following week. For example, one hook was "How well do you know your best friend?"

SUPERVISION PROCESS/EXPERIENCE

Group Consultation Process and Self-Evaluation

As stated before, the consulting team would meet once each week to plan and evaluate sessions for the ATAC swimming groups. These planning meetings allowed the team to evaluate the progress of the swimming group sessions. Typically, the primary would lead the discussion by asking what went well during the previous session and what they could have done better. This line of questioning allowed the team to gage their performance.

When the consulting team evaluated the Jenga activity, several important points were discussed. The consulting team concluded that what went well included: (1) the activity was fun and interactive for the swimmers; (2) directions were given in a clear and concise manner; and (3) the swimming groups were able to have meaningful conversations about how this activity applied to both sport and life. The consulting team also discussed what could have gone better during the session, including: (1) the shadow did not seem included and got lost on what to do while the swimmers were completing the activity; and (2) some of the younger swimmers had a difficult time acting out their "character." Based on the session self-evaluation, the consulting team encouraged the shadow to take a more active role. The primary reassured the shadow that if she got lost someone would help her out. It was discussed that we can talk all day about the consulting process, but talking and doing are two very different things. Thus, the shadow was encouraged to step out of her comfort zone and interact more with the swimmers during the session.

Supervision Process

The internship supervisor, though not officially a part of the consulting team, plays the most important role in the development of the applied sport psychology consultants. The supervisor is responsible for assigning and developing consulting teams. Weekly meetings were held for multiple consulting teams with the supervisor. These weekly meetings were used to allow consulting teams to discuss the progress of their teams, share and refine ideas, and to bring up relevant consulting questions. Additionally, the supervisor would bring case studies to be discussed by the group in order to assess how the students might handle a situation. The consulting team was also required to meet with the supervisor individually at least four times each semester. The individual meetings were used to present observation notes, discuss the consulting team's performance, and (when available) to present video of the consulting team in action. Additionally, if an internal conflict arose between team members, the supervisor would intervene and assist in finding a resolution. Time between the weekly meetings and the individual consulting team meetings allowed the consulting team the opportunity for internal reflections.

REFLECTION

The structure of the consulting team allows for peer mentoring on a consistent basis during all phases of the delivery of sport psychology services. This structure allows the peer consultants to provide each other with feedback. Based on the authors' experiences with peer mentoring and feedback, the following reflections were made: (1) an identification of what makes a successful peer mentoring program; (2) the importance of developing self-awareness; and (3) having the opportunity to develop one's personal consulting style.

What Makes a Successful Peer Mentoring Program?

There are four key ingredients that promote the success of a peer mentoring program: (1) trust, (2) confidence, (3) support, and (4) appreciation (Tietze, 2012). To provide the most successful environment for mental skills training with the athlete clients, the structure of the consultant team must foster each of these constructs.

First, mutual *trust* is a vital component to any relationship. The consulting team members must trust each other to prepare properly for the planning sessions, for the delivery of sport psychology services, and to speak openly without competition. Each team member should feel their peers are equally as committed to the quality of work. Since trust is a key component in peer mentorship, the group cannot be affected by interpersonal conflicts. If an interpersonal conflict arises, it should be addressed immediately. The supervisor may need to intervene to help mediate the situation. Second, each team member must have *confidence* in his/her knowledge and abilities, though not overconfidence. Furthermore, team members must have confidence in the peer relationship. For example, all team members should feel confident that everyone will act in appropriate and ethical ways. Third, it is necessary to *support* each other. For instance, if one team member goes completely "blank" while describing an activity, another team member should be ready to assist. The consulting team environment should be a supportive one and not a competitive one. Lastly, *appreciation* for one another promotes openness. It is important that team members be able to openly share ideas without fear of being criticized or worrying about another member "stealing" his/her idea. Group members should be open to discuss problems, weaknesses, and difficulties.

In order to develop and maintain these four key components, it is necessary that each team member has a clearly defined role on the consulting team. When team members are unclear about their roles and responsibilities, even the best team can find themselves off track or having conflicts (Gratton & Erickson, 2007). Similar to sport teams, consulting team effectiveness can be improved by role clarity and role acceptance. When the roles of individual team members are clearly defined and understood, collaboration will improve (Gratton & Erickson, 2007). Moreover, if a task requires creativity (i.e., designing a new activity for a mental skill), the members are more likely to invest time and energy in collaboration. As the consultant team develops, the roles may begin to shift. Therefore, it is also important to create a plan to review the roles and progress of the consulting team. For instance, as the secondary consultant and shadow gain more confidence, they will be given more responsibilities. Of course, in high-functioning peer mentor teams, the primary consultant would assist in developing confidence in the other consulting team members.

Self-Awareness

Self-awareness is another important aspect that will enhance the peer mentoring process. Each team member should continually develop his/her self-awareness. Being self-aware allows the consultant to understand his/her strengths and weaknesses, become cognizant of his/her limitations, and fully accept themselves (Srebalus & Brown, 2001). For all consulting team members, it is important to be conscious of one's own limitations and to understand that not all team members have the same limitations. Consider the example provided in this chapter. Most shadows do not have a consulting background and/or have not taken a counseling or applied sport psychology course. Therefore, it is ill-advised for shadows to conduct individual sessions with athletes. For the team to function well, the shadow must be aware of this limitation in his/her training. Furthermore, it is extremely important to be aware of one's own biases and experiences and how these may influence consulting. Any unresolved issues may interfere with the client–consultant relationship (Srebalus & Brown, 2001).

Developing One's Personal Consulting Style

When considering the case above that utilizes a peer mentoring program, it is important for each consultant to have the opportunity to develop his/her consulting style. It is easy for the secondary or shadow to mimic the style of the primary consultant or the supervisor. For example, the shadow may have an introvert personality while the primary may have an extravert personality. Therefore, it is essential that each consultant teach and act in a manner that is true to their own personality. Each member should develop a consulting style that is reflective of his/her own personality, the training and feedback received, and his/her level of experience (Mohanna, Cottrell, Wall, & Chambers, 2011). Using continued reflection, feedback, and evaluation of one's consulting style will help the consultant become more aware of his/her natural style. Furthermore, all consultants should continue to adapt their consulting style to match the various personalities of the athletes receiving services and put the athletes' needs first.

Overall, peer mentoring can help promote personal and professional development (Luna & Cullen, 1998). Peer mentors are usually more approachable and easier to relate to due to their commonalities with each other. This allows for increased risk-taking in a safer learning environment. A peer mentor is in a position to understand exactly what the less experienced student is facing because they have recently been through similar experiences. Utilizing a peer mentoring program enhances practitioner development, allows for maximum participation of students at all levels, and fosters professional relationships.

SUGGESTED READINGS

Birrer, D., & Morgan, G. (2010). Psychological skills training as a way to enhance an athlete's performance in high-intensity sports. *Scandinavian Journal of Medicine & Science in Sports, 20*(s2), 78–87.

Borders, L. D. (2012). Dyadic, triadic, and group models of peer supervision/consultation: What are their components, and is there evidence for effectiveness? *Clinical Psychologist, 16*(2), 59–71.

Cumming, J., & Hall, C. (2002). Deliberate imagery practice: The development of imagery skills in competitive athletes. *Journal of Sports Sciences, 20*(2), 137–145.

Mullen, P. H. (2003). *Gold in the water: The true story of ordinary men and their extraordinary dream of Olympic gold.* New York, NY: St. Martin's Griffin.

Newman, D. S., Nebbergall, A. J., & Salmon, D. (2013). Structured peer group supervision for novice consultants: Procedures, pitfalls, and potential. *Journal of Educational & Psychological Consultation, 23*(3), 200–216.

USA Swimming. (2014). Mental training strategies. Retrieved from: http://usaswimming.org/DesktopDefault.aspx?TabId=1555&Alias=Rainbow&Lang=en.

Zakrajsek, R. A., & Zizzi, S. J. (2007). Factors influencing track and swimming coaches' intentions to use sport psychology services. *Athletic Insight: The Online Journal of Sport Psychology, 9*(2), 1–21.

REFLECTIVE QUESTIONS

1. What steps would you take as a secondary or shadow if you disagreed with the primary?
2. As a primary, how would you encourage all team members (i.e., secondary and shadow) to contribute to the planning session?
3. Describe ways you would work as a consulting team to incorporate creativity in consulting with an athletic team?
4. How might you divide the responsibilities of planning and session delivery between the primary, secondary, and shadow?
5. As a primary, how could you encourage and/or mentor the secondary and shadow to branch outside of his/her comfort zone?
6. What changes could you make to the structure of the peer mentor design that might also be effective?

REFERENCES

Bray, S., Beauchamp, M., Eys, M., & Carron, A. (2005). Does the need for role clarity moderate the relationship between role ambiguity and athlete satisfaction. *Journal of Applied Sport Psychology, 17*, 306–318.

Ender, S. C., & Kay, K. (2001). Peer leader programs: A rational and review of the literature. In S. L. Hamid (Ed.), *Peer leadership: A primer on program essentials* (monograph no. 32, pp. 1–11). Columbia: University of South Carolina, National Resource Center for the First-Year Experience and Students in Transition.

Gratton, L., & Erickson, T. J. (2007). Eight ways to build collaborative teams. *Harvard Business Review, 85*(11), 100–109.

Luna, G., & Cullen, D. (1998). Do graduate students need mentoring? *College Student Journal, 32*, 322–331.

Mohanna, K., Cottrell, E., Wall, D., & Chambers, R. (2011). Developing your teaching style and techniques. In R. Jones & F. Jenkins (Eds.), *Key tools and techniques in management and leadership of allied health professions* (pp. 119–128). London: Radcliffe Publishing.

Murphy, S. M. (Ed.). (1995). *Sport psychology interventions.* Champaign, IL: Human Kinetics.

Perna, F., Ogilvie, B., & Murphy, A. (1995). Consultation with sport organizations: A cognitive-behavioral model. In S. M. Murphy (Ed.). *Sport psychology interventions* (pp. 241–246). Champaign, IL: Human Kinetics.

Piaget, J. (1954). *The construction of reality in the child.* New York, NY: Basic Books.

Piaget, J. (1969). *Science of education and the psychology of the child.* New York, NY: Viking.

Srebalus, D. J., & Brown, D. (2001). *A guide to helping professions.* Needham, MA: Allyn & Bacon.

Terrion, J., & Leonard, D. (2007). A taxonomy of the characteristics of student peer mentors in higher education: Findings from a literature review. *Mentoring & Tutoring: Partnership in Learning, 15*(2), 149–164. DOI: 10.1080/13611260601086311.

Tietze, K. O. (2012). Conditions for peer group supervision within the group setting. Retrieved from: www.peer-supervision.com/Ebene2/voraus.html.

Visek, A. J., Harris, B. S., & Blom, L. C. (2009). Doing sport psychology: A youth sport consulting model for practitioners. *Sport Psychologist, 23*(2), 271–291.

35 Looking for Guidance and Support Among Colleagues

Peer Supervision and Mentoring in ENYSSP

Michala Bednáriková, Peter Schneider, and Grzegorz Więcław

The European Network of Young Sport Psychologists (ENYSSP) provides its members several ways of obtaining continuous professional development. One of the opportunities available is a peer consultation session (PCS), which is ENYSSP's approach toward delivering peer supervision and mentoring. In this chapter, the reader can learn when, how, and in what way ENYSSP provides its members with an opportunity to learn from each other through the PCS.

BACKGROUND INFORMATION

Supervision is perceived as a tool for development among many helping professions (Carrol, 2007; 2008; Hawkins & Shohet, 2006). Thus, it should be an integral part of the education and practice of sport, exercise, and performance psychology (SEPP) professionals as it is especially important for continuous professional and personal development (Andersen & William-Rice, 1996). Similarly, as Gallacher (1997) suggests, we perceive supervision and mentoring to be developmental processes "that share foundations and whose purposes, elements, and competencies overlap" (p. 192). Although we agree that there are several differences between those processes, throughout this chapter we will use both terms as synonyms.

Peer supervision and mentoring are emerging as alternative and/or complementary methods to a traditional supervision and mentoring approach. Hawkins and Shohet (2006) prompt that peer supervision has many advantages, but one needs to be aware of its limitations compared to traditional supervision. We will provide readers with our own experiences in regards to the advantages and limitations of peer supervision at the end of this chapter.

There are many supervision models, which vary in their specific goals, theoretical basis, type of leadership, members' roles, and/or steps in procedure (Borders, 2012). Theoretical orientation can be derived from different approaches toward behavioral change, such as cognitive-behavioral, phenomenological, and psychodynamic models (Van Raalte & Andersen, 2000). Even though there are many specific goals that can differentiate among supervision models, all supervision models have one goal in common, which is to increase the competence of the practitioner (Van Raalte & Andersen, 2000). For example, Borders (2012) emphasized the importance of several goals, including: (1) improving skills; (2) providing mutual support and affirmation; (3) learning from practitioners from different theoretical traditions; (4) giving focused and objective feedback; (5) encouraging self-monitoring and self-growth; and (6) contributing to role development, job satisfaction, and reducing burnout. For each practitioner, it is crucial to define his or her own learning needs and goals, and to choose a model accordingly (Borders, 2012).

As such, supervision models have several formats that need to be considered when one is looking for supervision – dyadic, triadic, and group (Borders, 2012). All can be used in traditional supervision and in peer supervision. In our case, ENYSSP have chosen a group format for the PCS. There are several reasons why practitioners choose this format for receiving their supervision, such as economy of time, money, or expertise. In addition, Hawkins and Shohet (2006) noted it is ideal if group supervision comes from choice rather than from having no other available option. In group supervision it is the feedback, reflections, and input from peers which provide added value compared to the other formats. The group format provides input from peers with various educational backgrounds and experiences that are reflective of the cultural diversity of its members.

When, how, and in what ways ENYSSP provides its members with an opportunity to learn from each other through a PCS is described below. Based on the example of a novice SEPP consultant, the chapter authors depict peer supervision and mentoring practiced at ENYSSP as a valuable part of professional development both formally, as set up through a network-type organization, as well as informally among colleagues.

DESCRIPTION OF THE CASE

This section presents the case of a novice SEPP practitioner (for the purposes of this text, we will call her Tina), who has recently graduated from an international sport psychology master's program abroad. Following her graduation she decided to return to her home country and establish her own sport psychology practice. One of her external challenges was that sport psychology in her country was a new, unexplored area. Athletes, coaches, and organizations have approached it with a variety of responses, including suspicion and caution, but rarely with enthusiasm.

As a result of this environment, another barrier for her was the lack of an established professional pathway for sport psychology practitioners, and only a handful of other active consultants. In the first two years of practice she made many connections, completed a few contracts, and continued to popularize sport psychology in the local market. She found that people involved in sport and exercise business were becoming more and more open to welcoming sport psychology both as a field of expertise and practice. Being well educated at top universities specializing in psychology and sport sciences, she felt she had enough of a theoretical background to discuss cases of individual and collective clients. What she missed during her education was a glimpse into the practical side of what she was doing; thus, she needed to network with other practitioners who were perhaps more knowledgeable and could offer their insights and advice.

Being a young, relatively inexperienced, and growth-oriented consultant, she was looking for formal supervision to enrich her own professional development. She could not find anyone to fit the profile of a highly educated and practically minded consultant who preferably spoke her native language, lived nearby, and was willing to formally supervise her face to face. She had a meaningful formal supervision experience during her practicum at the university, but lacked the hands-on insights. She was not always able to find a common language with her supervisor and often they spent time on theoretical debates instead of figuring out how to solve the case at hand. In addition, she had belonged to ENYSSP for the past two years and attended two of their annual workshops. She liked the emerging idea of online PCS meetings and decided to join them, first as an observer and then as an active participant who was discussing cases and had her cases discussed.

Thus, through the eyes of Tina, this chapter provides the reader with an applied example of how peer supervision and mentoring can supplement, or in some cases substitute for, a traditional model of supervision. It shows the story of a young practitioner in search of guidance, support, and knowledge exchange, who decided to go to other young SEPP practitioners who were willing to share their experiences and ways of thinking. Through structured discussions over real cases that other young practitioners were dealing with in different parts of Europe, the PCS at ENYSSP provided her and many other young consultants with a unique and important opportunity for support, guidance, and growth.

APPROACH/PHILOSOPHY

ENYSSP is a network that provides its members with several approaches to obtaining continuous professional development. One of these is the PCS, which is ENYSSP's approach toward delivering peer supervision and mentoring. We will describe the theoretical background of the process, its general and specific goals, and the organization of a PCS itself.

Philosophy

Developing a working and well-structured philosophy is a vital part of success in the SEPP field (Henriksen, Diment, & Hansen, 2011; Schneider, 2014). Before the first PCS was ever held, its creators came together to research and construct a theoretically sound approach for peer-to-peer feedback and mentorship. The founders decided to establish the main theoretical approach based on Vygotsky's work. Vygotsky (1962) stated that humans learn through their interaction and communication with others. Moreover, the use of discussion with peers and mentors is the main driving force behind a gained understanding of a topic or idea (Vygotsky, 1978). Second, the effectiveness of communication in a small group as a learning tool was established. Small groups are able to engage in purpose-driven targeted discussion that allows for the application of knowledge (McKeachie, 1994). In fact, the "wisdom of crowds" (i.e., the ideas of many brought into a single discussion) has even been referred to as an integral part of million-dollar decision making in the world's most popular sport, soccer (Kuper & Szymanski, 2014).

Goals

While the purpose of the ENYSSP PCS is the development of the practitioners themselves, the central and end goal is to ensure the welfare of the athlete or performer (Van Raalte & Anderson, 2000). This is accomplished through the process of improving the sport psychology delivery services of ENYSSP PCS participants, the great majority of whom are at the beginning of their SEPP careers. Furthermore, ensuring that the welfare of the client is taken into account first holds a high moral and ethical standard; these standards are shared by many SEPP organizations around the world, such as the Association for Applied Sport Psychology (AASP) and the European Federation of Sport Psychology (FEPSAC) (Stambulova, Johnson, & Linnér, 2014).

In addition to the central goal of a high ethical standard, the ENYSSP PCS seeks, as suggested by Van Raalte and Anderson (1993), to improve inter-/intra-personal skills, tackle organizational issues, and offer new and innovative techniques for the participants. With greater numbers of students in the field of applied sport psychology and few supervisors (Yambor & Thompson, 2014), the ENYSSP PCS provides a platform where peers can experience and practice feedback sessions. Furthermore, peer mentorship, as opposed to traditional supervision, is preferred by young practitioners due to its accessibility, open atmosphere, and greater relatedness between participants (Yambor & Thompson, 2014).

Approach

With enough theoretical support to show the effectiveness of small-group learning, the PCS creators searched for theoretical underpinnings in regards to the structure and agenda of each meeting. For example, Nilson (1998) stated that it is imperative to give small groups detailed and purpose-filled roles and directions at the start of the session. Therefore, all active participants are divided into three specific roles at each PCS: (1) process leader (PL); case submitter (CS); and peer consultant(s) (PC).

To be able to skip the introduction of the process at each single PCS, the organizers decided to implement one additional role – the role of observer. This role is optional, passive, and dedicated for those who have no or limited experience with PCS procedures. The learning outcome of the observer is to become familiar with the procedure to be able to actively participate in the future. To become an active participant in a PCS one needs to have participated in the observer role for three sessions.

With roles established, concrete steps and a strict structure was developed in preparation for each PCS meeting:

1. PCS organizers determine and publish a time, date, and place for the next meeting.
2. The PCS organizers choose a PL for the next PCS.
3. The PL publishes a deadline to submit cases from all participants.
4. Once collected, the PL sends all submitted cases to each participant for voting. The participants rank the cases they wish to discuss from first choice to last, and send this information privately to the PL.
5. The participant whose case is given the most votes is named the CS.

The step-by-step preparation for a participant and the process of a PCS will be presented in the following section.

PREPARATION/PLANNING

Preparation for a PCS is an integral part of the process and supports the effectiveness of the flow of the session itself. We will start with discussing how the SEPP consultant decides to use PCS, how to prepare a case for submission, and what learning potential the consultant can utilize for development. All of these will be explained with the example of our young practitioner, Tina.

The preparation for PCS has several phases and each of these phases can be a learning experience. In the first phase, Tina has to choose a case, for which she would like to get feedback and further suggestions on how to proceed. As a practitioner may experience, one may have too many options on how to proceed, or none. This is reflective of a situation commonly experienced by a PCS participant. For a novice practitioner, it also can be a new area of intervention with which one does not have practical experience yet, or sometimes a new sport with which he/she has not worked before. To summarize, there are a variety of situations and cases that can be considered for PCS submission. There is only one recommended limitation for submitted cases – it should be an open case where suggestions coming from the PCS can be taken into account for future interventions.

Once Tina decides on the case for submission, she needs to write a short summary of the case and its current status. She includes information such as with what "issue" the client initially looked for a sport psychologist, background of the client, how the issue is demonstrated, what are its effects, what coping strategies was the athlete using, interventions that were delivered so far, and how the client has responded. At the end, Tina states the main question for which she seeks an answer.

While it is not the primary goal of the PCS, in this phase of preparation, Tina reflects upon her client and the work done with him/her thus far. Reflective practice is suggested as a tool for professional and personal development (Anderson, Knowles, & Gilbourne, 2004; Cropley, Miles, Hanton, & Niven, 2007). Reflection itself, especially in its written form, can bring new insights into the case, but more importantly as mentioned by Cropley et al. (2007), it improves self-awareness and increases knowledge that is critically important for delivery of quality service.

The second phase of preparation begins after all cases are submitted. The PL then sends the cases to participants for voting. As a participant, Tina has to read through all the cases and choose which cases she finds most interesting and useful for discussing during the PCS. This is usually done based on several interests, such as similarity to the cases one has, experience with similar situations which could be shared, or out of curiosity on the submitted case. In this phase, Tina can learn from the experience of others, and more importantly acquire knowledge from a variety of cases.

After voting, one case is chosen and the last phase of preparation begins. If this is Tina's case, then she has no other preparation to do. If this is one of her peers' cases, then she takes the role of PC. For Tina, being a PC means to look deeper into the case, reflect on the case, prepare a set of clarification questions, understand the theoretical framework, and make the first formulations to answer the case submitters' main questions. This preparation phase is voluntary; one can choose their level of participation and still be valuable to the PCS itself. Despite it being voluntary, it is recommended that one invest the time and utilize it as an opportunity for learning and development. By answering the question "what would I do in this situation?" and thinking it through, one can gain and/or refresh theoretical knowledge and act as if it was one's own case to solve. We believe that the above-mentioned learning experiences increase the value of the PCS and it is upon the participants' decision to which degree they decide to use it.

SUPERVISION PROCESS/EXPERIENCE

After the preparation phase, the PCS begins and has six distinct phases (ENYSSP, n.d.): (1) gathering information by asking questions of the CS; (2) analyzing the situation; (3) suggesting solutions; (4) reactions from the CS; (5) evaluation; and (6) closure. The entire process is planned to last approximately an hour and can be efficient and structured if well led. As previously discussed, during the PCS there are four different roles one can be involved with (i.e., PL, PC, CS – supervisee or an observer). The PCS can have a different effect on Tina's learning depending on the role she takes. The roles are in rotation as the case is selected by voting. There are also different moderators, and supervisors are not always the same. The moderator overlooks the entire process, keeps track of time, and makes sure everything runs according to the procedure (ENYSSP, n.d.). The moderator, however, does not take an active part in the discussion of the case and may not provide the supervisee with any ideas for a solution. There are few individuals at ENYSSP with enough experience to moderate the PCS. Tina, the young SEPP practitioner discussed in this case, has yet to lead a session.

The peer supervisors are active members of the PCS, who take turns to question the supervisee, discuss a point, or provide her with guidance and support. The number of supervisors varies from meeting to meeting, but typically ranges between four and eight. Then, there is a supervisee whose case is being discussed. Most of the time, she listens to what peer supervisors discuss; at the beginning she responds to questions and elaborates on the case and, at the end, she gets a chance to summarize the meeting and propose solutions. As mentioned in the previous section, there might also be observers who are inexperienced PCS participants, unfamiliar at that point with the procedure.

Supervision experience from the point of view of a supervisee is unique, because one's case is being shared with other practitioners who are there to help deepen the understanding of the case and provide possible solutions. Obviously, Tina likes to have her case picked for discussion because it gives her an opportunity to see the issue she is dealing with from a different perspective. Of course, it is preferable to have a case discussed with several consultants so one is able to learn from different perspectives. However, when Tina has a case to discuss and it does not get picked for the PCS, she knows she can always turn to her personal peer supervisor for guidance during their weekly online meeting (an additional opportunity for gaining peer supervision beyond the PCS that Tina began with a peer PCS member). Being a supervisee is a meaningful learning experience. It is a process that is solution-oriented and often reveals one's convictions as well.

In accordance with the idea of learning through interaction with peers (Vygotsky, 1962; 1978), being a peer supervisor is equally meaningful. One gets to know about cases other practitioners are dealing with. Discussing these cases helps to relate to one's own professional approach and methodology. Additionally, when Tina is in the role of peer supervisor, she is automatically placed in a think-tank type of experience where she is requested to think about what she would do in a similar situation. At the same time, in her role as PC (just like the supervisee), she has to listen to other perspectives and views from other supervisors. Most importantly, in both roles (i.e., supervisee and PC) Tina gets a sense of support and guidance from her peers and colleagues, which is invaluable, particularly at the beginning of her SEPP career.

In summary, ENYSSP welcomes all its members to take an active part in the online PCS process and thus, as an organization, encourages young SEPP practitioners to seek peer supervision and mentoring on top of their formal supervision experiences, especially when there is a lack of such possibility. Although some peers may not be as experienced and knowledgeable as older colleagues, they are typically better able to relate to the cases discussed at the PCS, and perhaps have more time and commitment to serve in this role.

REFLECTION

Advantages and limitations of the PCS process will be discussed in the following paragraphs, as well as what one can learn when participating in the process of a formal peer supervision experience like the ENYSSP PCS.

Advantages

Multiple advantages for the young practitioner can be identified when participating in the ENYSSP PCS. These include the accessibility of feedback and peers, exposure to new/heterogeneous techniques, theories, and cultures, as well as a judgment-free environment, which is of great importance for a novice practitioner. The combination of these three advantages allows for personal and professional growth, as each session strengthens the trust and stretches the minds of those participating. We will look at each one of these advantages in more detail.

Accessibility of peers. It has been proven over half a century ago that people learn through communication in small groups (Vygotsky, 1962), and the ENYSSP PCS provides small groups of peers to practice this communication. Through a highly organized and concentrated discussion, participants give and receive constant feedback about their thoughts and beliefs regarding SEPP. The online format of the ENYSSP PCS allows members in remote locations or those looking for different theoretical approaches to meet easily and effectively.

Exposure to new techniques, theories, and cultures. Participants in the ENYSSP PCS are exposed to both male and female practitioners from different geographical locations in Europe. Mixing these practitioners in a single session presents each participant with different theoretical approaches and complex cultural influences. As the world of sport becomes increasingly culturally diverse, the ability to recognize cultural differences enhances a practitioner's capacity to emphasize and eventually improve cross-cultural consultations.

A judgment-free environment. A growth mindset and a love of failure should be promoted by sport psychologists in order to encourage the development of one's skills (Dweck, 2006). However, some young practitioners lack confidence when speaking to highly experienced supervisors. Due to the relatively young age of the PCS participants, the judgment-free zone is highly appreciated by those starting off in the field. It allows them to make open suggestions, no matter how strange they may seem at first, without fear of being perceived as incompetent. Further, they are provided with the support needed to learn how to improve their style and craft.

Limitations

There are, of course, limitations that do apply to the ENYSSP PCS. One of these limitations is the limited experience among the participants. There is unfortunately no substitute for a practitioner with over 20 years of experience, or a consultant who has consistently worked with elite athletes. However, even due to this lack of experience, many students and young practitioners find that the ENYSSP PCS peer supervision and mentorship are equal or even more effective than those supervised by expert participants (Tod, 2007; Watson, Clement, Blom, & Grindley, 2009).

A second limitation is the lack of personal human contact. This means that the PL keeps each participant restricted to one question or complete thought before the next participants may reply. While this allows for good structure, it also causes some information to possibly remain untapped and answers to be incomplete.

The last and third limitation is that the PCS focuses mainly on the case itself and does not discuss other important issues, such as the process of service delivery and relationship issues such as transference and countertransference. Although it is not stated that these cannot be brought up, the rigid structure of the PCS procedures, and the online and group meeting format minimize the flexibility and opportunity to discuss other related service delivery issues.

Final Reflections

Thanks to the online PCS meetings Tina has met colleagues who have helped her to tackle specific professional dilemmas. Having more perspectives about the case ultimately results in a deeper exploration of the issue at hand. As an example, we can use one of Tina's cases in which she was requested to improve the concentration of a young athlete. Tina could focus purely on this request, which came from the athlete, her parents, and also from the athlete's coach. Despite this, she decided to discuss it with peers and as a result of this process realized that what looks like a lack of concentration during practice might be a symptom of fatigue as well.

In fact, she has established an ongoing collaboration with another young SEPP practitioner, also a member of ENYSSP and an active participant at PCS, and they have peer-supervised each other weekly for over a year now. This exchange has brought her even more valuable experiences and a chance to get involved in regular peer supervision to meet her needs. Clearly, both formal and informal peer supervision have enriched her professional practice, varied her approach and methods, as well as provided her with an ongoing chance for peer support in order to keep a high standard of professional practice.

There are several directions one needs to take into account when searching for development opportunities. Peer supervision and mentoring as provided by the ENYSSP PCS is one of the alternatives. It may not feed all the needs the practitioner has, but as our own experience has proved to us, it can feed many of them. As a result, if one participates in traditional supervision at the same time as participating in ENYSSP and the PCS, the topics one discusses and gets supervisory feedback on can help the neophyte practitioner to grow from some of the "basic issues" one has at the beginning of a SEPP career.

SUGGESTED READINGS

ENYSSP. (n.d.). European network of young specialists in sport psychology. Retrieved from http://enyssp.org.

Benshoff, J. M. (1992). *Peer consultation for professional counselors.* Ann Arbor, MI: ERIC/CASS.

Cross, A. (2011). Self- and peer assessment: The case of peer supervision in counselling psychology. [Electronic version] *Investigations in University Teaching and Learning, 7,* 73–81.

Hein, S., & Lawson G. (2008). Triadic supervision and its impact on the role of the supervisor: A qualitative examination of supervisors' perspectives. *Counselor Education & Supervision, 48,* 16–31.

Titkov, A., Bednáriková, M., & Mortensen, J. R. (2014). Peer mentoring and peer supervision: Nordic experiences. In J. G. Cremades & L. S. Tashman (Ed.), *Becoming a sport, exercise, and performance psychology professional: A global perspective* (pp. 293–299). New York, NY: Routledge.

Wylleman, P., Harwood, C., Elbe, A.-M., Reints, A., & de Caluwé, D. (2009). A perspective on education and professional development in applied sport psychology. *Psychology of Sport and Exercise, 10,* 435–446.

REFLECTIVE QUESTIONS

1. When would you consider peer supervision as a source of professional support and/or guidance?
2. How does attending a PCS provide advantages for your development as a practitioner?
3. How would you fill the development gaps that the PCS does not fill?
4. Given the description above of ENYSSPs PCS, how would you develop and implement your own PCS?
5. What characteristics should cases have that are submitted for consideration for a PCS?

REFERENCES

Andersen, M. B., & Williams-Rice, B. T. (1996). Supervision in the education and training of sport psychology service providers. *The Sport Psychologist, 10,* 278–290.

Anderson, A. G., Knowles, Z., & Gilbourne, D. (2004). Reflective practice for sport psychologists: Concepts, models, practical implications, and thoughts on dissemination. *The Sport Psychologist, 18,* 188–203.

Borders, L. D. (2012). Dyadic, triadic, and group models of peer supervision/consultation: What are their components and is there evidence of their effectiveness? [Electronic version] *Clinical Psychologist, 16*(2), 59–71.

Carrol, M. (2007). One more time: What is supervision?. *Psychotherapy in Australia, 13,* 34–40.

Carrol, M. (2008). Supervision and transformational learning. *Psychotherapy in Australia, 14,* 12–19.

Cropley, B., Miles, A., Hanton, S., & Niven, A. (2007). Improving the delivery of applied sport psychology support through reflective practice. *The Sport Psychologist, 21,* 475–494.

Dweck, C. S. (2006). *Mindset: The new psychology of success.* New York, NY: Random House.

ENYSSP. (n.d.). ENYSSP. Retrieved from http://enyssp.org/members/pcs/procedure.

Gallacher, K. K. (1997). Supervision, mentoring, and coaching: Methods for supporting personnel development. In P. J. Winton, J. A. McCollum, & C. Catlett (Ed.), *Reforming personnel preparation in early intervention: Issues, models, and practical strategies* (pp. 191–214). Baltimore: Paul H. Brookers Publishing.

Hawkins, P., & Shohet, R. (2006). *Supervision in the helping professions.* Glasgow: McGraw-Hill.

Henriksen, K., Diment, G., & Hansen, J. (2011). Professional philosophy: Inside the delivery of sport psychology service at Team Denmark. *Sport Science Review, 1–2,* 5–21.

Kuper, S., & Szymanski, S. (2014). *Soccernomics.* New York, NY: Nation Books.

McKeachie, W. (1994). *Teaching tips* (9th ed.). Lexington, MA: D.C. Heath.

Nilson, L. B. (1998). *Teaching at its best: A research-based resource for college instructors.* (1st ed.) Bolton, MA: Anker Publishing Company.

Schneider, P. (2014). Setting up a business in sport and performance psychology: A German perspective. In J. G. Cremades & L. S. Tashman (Eds.) *Becoming a sport, exercise, and performance psychology professional: A global perspective* (pp. 178–185). New York, NY: Routledge.

Stambulova, N., Johnson, U., & Linnér, L. (2014). Insights from Sweden: Halmstad Applied Sport Psychology Supervision model. In J. G. Cremades & L. S. Tashman (Eds.), *Becoming a sport, exercise, and performance psychology professional: A global perspective* (pp. 276–284). New York, NY: Routledge.

Tod, D. (2007). The long and winding road: Professional development in sport psychology. *The Sport Psychologist, 21,* 94–108.

Van Raalte, J. L., & Andersen, M. B. (1993). Special problems in sport psychology: Supervising the trainee. In S. Serpa, J. Alves, V. Ferreira, & A. Paula-Brito (Eds.), *Proceedings: VIII World Congress of Sport Psychology* (pp. 773–776). Lisbon: International Society of Sport Psychology.

Van Raalte, J. L., & Andersen, M. B. (2000). Supervision I: From models to doing. In M. B. Andersen (Ed.), *Doing sport psychology* (pp. 153–165). Champaign, IL: Human Kinetics.

Vygotsky, L. S. (1962). *Thought and language*. Cambridge, MA: MIT Press.

Vygotsky, L. S. (1978). *Mind in society*. Cambridge, MA: Harvard University Press.

Watson, J. C., Clement, D., Blom, L. C., & Grindley, E. (2009). Mentoring: Processes and perceptions of sport and exercise psychology graduate students. *Journal of Applied Sport Psychology, 21*, 231–246.

Yambor, J., & Thompson, M. (2014). A supervision model utilizing peer mentoring and consultation teams in the provision of applied sport psychology services. In J. G. Cremades & L. S. Tashman (Eds.) *Becoming a sport, exercise, and performance psychology professional: A global perspective* (pp. 285–292). New York, NY: Routledge.

36 Multicultural Supervision

Experiences in an International Master's Program

Janaina Fogaça and Sae-Mi Lee

Supervision is a process of overseeing professionals to ensure their practice promotes clients' well-being and the trainee develops as a competent and ethical practitioner (Van Raalte & Andersen, 2000). Moreover, given we are all cultural beings, every encounter should be considered a multicultural one (Hanrahan, 2011), including those in supervision. Best practices of supervision indicate that multicultural awareness should always be present (Ellis et al., 2014). In addition, Miville, Rosa, and Constantine (2005) suggested that a supervisor's multicultural competence is crucial for the supervisee's multicultural learning. For example, supervisors could share their own cultural experiences, values, and biases with their supervisees to facilitate multicultural learning through the process of supervision (Miville et al., 2005). Further, Miville et al. proposed that the supervisory working alliance is essential for multicultural supervision, which requires an agreement on supervisory goals, supervisory tasks, and role clarity. Although research on multicultural supervision has been growing, literature on what multicultural supervision actually looks like and how multicultural considerations should be integrated in supervision is still limited. In addition, due to limited illustrations of multicultural supervision in sport and exercise psychology (SEP), it is unclear whether research suggestions from counseling and psychology are appropriate and applicable for SEP supervision.

Therefore, the purpose of this chapter is to present a case of supervision in applied sport psychology, which occurred in an observably multicultural environment. The authors describe and critically analyze the factors underlying the case and demonstrate the complexities of multicultural supervision. Moreover, we offer reflective questions and suggestions to encourage readers to view supervision through a cultural lens. By reading this chapter the reader will be able to answer how culture affects supervision, why critical reflections (Knowles & Gilbourne, 2010) are important, the benefits and drawbacks of various supervision styles, and how one might integrate this knowledge and awareness into one's own practice.

BACKGROUND INFORMATION

The applied supervised experience was part of the mandatory practicum experience of the European Masters Programme in Sport and Exercise Psychology (EMSEP). The practicum consisted of 15 European Credit Transfer and Accumulation System, which are equivalent to a total of 410 hours including preparation, applied work, and evaluation. Students were responsible for finding and negotiating their own practicum placements.

The practicum work discussed in this chapter was carried out with an amateur volleyball team that participated in a regional league in Finland. The team consisted of 11 players between 18 and 25 years old and one head coach. They practiced twice each week. Their championship began in October and finished in March. However, my (first author) practicum was only during the fall semester, which included their pre-season and the first half of the championship.

Preparation for the practicum included mental skills delivery workshops and practicum seminars. During the semester of practicum, biweekly group supervision meetings were held and individual supervision was available upon request. In addition, students were required to maintain a log of work hours and write SOAP (subjective–objective–assessment–plan) notes of each team observation and the services provided. However, the supervisor did not review these notes until the end of the practicum period. At the end of the practicum, we were required to give a final presentation about our practicum, interventions, and evaluations, and submit a portfolio including our reflective notes, logs, and practicum-related material.

It is important to note here that I (the first author) was a Brazilian studying in Finland, working with a Finnish volleyball team. Additionally, my supervisor was Spanish and my peers in EMSEP were from all over the world. This mixture rendered a complex cultural interaction during the supervision process, which will be discussed throughout the case.

DESCRIPTION OF THE CASE

The work with the volleyball team consisted of group interventions throughout the fall semester. Because they were an amateur team with limited extra time to dedicate to volleyball beyond their professional responsibilities, they had limited time and space for interventions. The limited time and my easy entry to the team due to my volleyball experience and relationship with the coach motivated me to develop sport psychology interventions that were mostly integrated into their practices. Additionally, during the pre-season, I used team and individual goal-setting in brief team sessions at the beginning of the practice. I gave constant feedback on their goal-related results during the season, based on statistics of their performance created by myself.

During the season I also developed, with the coach, practices where the coach could challenge the athletes to increase their psychological readiness. For example, instead of serving while standing still in the back of the court, a common service drill, the serving practice was integrated in the latter half of their warm up, after they ran sprints, making it more challenging to refocus before serving and more similar physiologically to a game situation. We also integrated communication strategies in passing drills. The athletes were letting many balls fall between them because they were not calling who would be in charge of the ball. To intervene, the coach and I first introduced a rule where athletes had to talk every time they would touch the ball. This helped them get used to being vocal and playing at the same time. Subsequently, we talked about decision making and gave them the choice of when to talk, using feedback as a way of reinforcing their behavior. I also used team-building activities before the start of the season. Finally, we developed fast-paced practices that were more challenging for the athletes in terms of being focused and prepared, which seemed to be a needed improvement for their performance. These interventions were paired with short psycho-educational team sessions on focus and pre-performance routines as well, which were delivered at the beginning of practices.

APPROACH/PHILOSOPHY

Because I came from a clinical psychology background and was used to focusing on the relationships and theoretical understanding of clients, this was my initial expectation. I expected my supervisor to address the theoretical underpinnings of various sport psychology approaches. However, I found that the classes and seminars were primarily focused on mental skills training techniques rather than theories. Although this was unfamiliar at first, the exposure to a primarily technique-based approach motivated me to improve my delivery of these popular technique-oriented sport psychology interventions (e.g., goal setting, imagery). I was particularly interested in goal setting, which became a central part of my intervention plan. Moreover, my previous supervision experience in clinical psychology included intense supervision through both on-site individual and group supervision (with an on-site supervisor) and group supervision at the university (with a university supervisor). Thus, I expected close and frequent supervision during my sport psychology practicum as well.

Another important part of my approach to practicum was the use of reflections, which were required in the form of reflective notes. The reflections included content of sessions or observations of the team, a space for comments, and my planning of future sessions, which guided my subsequent services. Looking back, I was primarily engaged in technical and practical reflections rather than critical reflections (Knowles & Gilbourne, 2010), which will be discussed further in the reflection section of the chapter. This focus does not mean that there was not any critical thinking involved in my practice or that technical reflections are inferior; rather, we are noting that critical reflections were not intentionally facilitated through supervision.

PREPARATION/PLANNING

Although a practicum was not required until our third semester, we started preparing for it early on during our first year in the master's program. We were offered mental skills training workshops conducted by experienced sport psychology professionals and we held practice sessions with classmates during seminars. These were extremely beneficial in exposing ourselves to sport psychology interventions and refining our delivery. Our supervisor also suggested readings that could help in intervention planning (e.g., Andersen, 2000). In addition, throughout our first year, we held discussions on issues surrounding the practicum: how to present ourselves to clients; professional ethics; intervention planning; and program delivery.

SUPERVISION PROCESS/EXPERIENCE

As mentioned above, my supervision was primarily through group supervision because direct individual supervision was only offered on an ad-hoc basis. Moreover, we were encouraged to use personal reflections for self-awareness and self-evaluation, which were reviewed once the practicum was complete. Group supervision with peers from extremely diverse backgrounds was an interesting, and often challenging, process for several reasons. First, students were at different stages of the practicum, so a large portion of the time was spent discussing practicum placement concerns. Second, when we did discuss cases during group supervision, the discussions were confusing because students had very different conceptualizations and philosophies of what best practices should look like. It was even difficult to understand peers' point of views at times because I was unsure of what context and world-view they were operating from, not to mention the challenges of thinking about how I would apply these different perspectives to the specific Finnish team I was working with.

In retrospect, encountering such complexity was a unique and rewarding experience; nonetheless, it was extremely confusing at the time. My peer group came from four different continents and held quite different views on issues such as performance, well-being, and the role of a sport psychology consultant. For example, some students thought that the sport psychology consultant should be tough and directive; others thought that a consultant should give space and freedom for the clients to decide for themselves. Some would argue that self-determination theory made absolute sense, while others would suggest that extrinsic motivation can be more powerful in some cultures than intrinsic motivation. Thinking back, these disagreements could be great material for deep cultural discussions and critical reflections about sport psychology. However, during my practicum I felt that we mostly disagreed and, because we largely operated from a positivistic framework believing there is one truth that is applicable to everything, many times we did not expand on our views but stuck with them. Without structured discussions or purposeful dialogue on cultural influences, I often felt frustrated during group supervision. Although I can understand some of my peers' viewpoints much better today than I could then, and feel extremely appreciative of the intense cultural experience, I feel that I may have learned valuable lessons during this period if I understood the method behind the madness. Supervision could have been intentional and transparent in encouraging students to be open-minded and accepting of the fact that there could be numerous answers and truths to the same question. I would have found our discussions more effective had I not been constantly worried about coming to a final correct conclusion in our discussions.

As direct individual supervision was not a practicum requirement, I only sought out individual supervision once during my practicum. It was after I observed that the players were making the simple but frequent mistake of letting the ball drop because no one was calling the play. Although I initially attributed this to a lack of communication, I was not confident on how I should intervene in this case because I was aware that Finns are typically quieter. I was unsure if the Finnish way of solving this issue would be to talk more, as Brazilians would do, or if they had another solution that was more congruent with their culture and communication styles. Therefore, after a class with my supervisor, I asked her if we could schedule an individual supervision session to discuss this question. However, rather than scheduling a separate individual supervision session, my supervisor managed the case by asking focused questions on the spot. She asked me what was going on and asked me what I thought was the best intervention based on my conceptualization of the case. I explained to her that I thought it would be useful for the team to improve communication, especially if it is informative and not evaluative. I thought it should not be too uncomfortable for the team to address this issue and that I could not think of any other solution. She expressed that this approach seemed appropriate, based on my case conceptualization, and that I should move forward with my plan, but that I should be sensitive and mindful of their reactions. We discussed the case for five minutes and did not have a formal meeting to address it further.

Although the various modes of training and supervision were all valuable experiences, in my specific case I believe that my previous experience in applied sport psychology was pivotal to my practicum experience. My personal volleyball background came into play, first, when I had to secure a practicum placement. Finding my own practicum placement with minimal to no help was a completely new experience; I soon came to realize that networking was an important asset in applied practice in Finland and, perhaps, in other countries where sport psychology may not yet be well established (Lee, Titkov, & Mortensen, 2014). Because I previously played volleyball in town, I had contacts in the area that could help me find a team to work with. My networking sources and previous experience with sport psychology interventions with volleyball teams was fundamental to my quick adaptation to the independent supervision style and compensated partly for the lack of formal direct individual supervision. I already had training on how to observe teams, what to look for during these observations, and how to plan interventions based on these observations. This previous consulting experience fostered my confidence in being able to proceed with my practicum independently and helped me feel less lost than some of my classmates, who needed more individual supervision and more time for discussions during group seminars.

Despite the relative ease of entry, I still felt unsupported because I felt as if my supervisor did not care about my success. At the time, it was frustrating to experience such an independent supervision style because I felt like the entire responsibility for quality service was mine and mine alone. This feeling continued throughout my practicum, especially after my individual supervision encounter. In my view, I felt rushed and overlooked since I only had time to discuss a specific case conceptualization issue without an overall discussion about my practicum. Although today, through more critical reflections, I believe there were more cultural motives and contexts related to this supervision style, which will be discussed further in the reflection section below, at the time I could not understand these factors and often felt confused and alone.

Lastly, the evaluation portion of the practicum was also quite lax. My self-evaluation was facilitated by the reflections that I wrote, but I had close to no feedback from outside the team during my practicum. Nonetheless, the practicum experience was very satisfying and rewarding overall, despite the limited amount of direct individual supervision time. I felt that I grew as a consultant who could be independent and competent in unknown territory. However, I believe I could have developed more with closer supervision, as it would have been more consistent with my expectations, cultural background, and learning style. Maybe with the assistance of someone with an outsider perspective, I could have reflected better about how different personal factors affected my observations, interpretations, and interventions as well. For example, in retrospect, my own previous experience as a volleyball athlete, my previous knowledge of the coach (i.e., the client), and my approach to delivery of mental skills influenced how I integrated mental skills into physical practice and my use of feedback on athletes' goal-setting. This personal development occurred as I continued my educational journey rather than during my practicum via the supervision process.

REFLECTION

Many aspects of this supervision case deserve further reflection. Even though my internationally diverse supervision experience is one that most people will not easily encounter, there are lessons learned that one can transfer to all supervision processes, even to seemingly homogeneous supervision environments in which many sport psychology professionals may be familiar. This section reflects on various aspects of multicultural supervision, including the use of reflection in supervision, the hegemonic practices of SEP, and the importance of adopting a cultural lens.

Reflective Practice and Supervision

As mentioned above, I regularly took reflective notes and found them to be extremely helpful in planning and evaluating my services. Although I did not realize it at the time, I was engaging in reflective practice, which has various advantages. It can help the practitioner deal with internal tensions, become aware of potential issues, become self-evaluative, and increase overall service effectiveness (Anderson, Knowles, & Gilbourne, 2004). Recently, the British Association of Sport and Exercise Sciences started requiring supervisees to provide evidence of competence in reflective practice (Knowles & Gilbourne, 2010).

Various types of reflections facilitate personal and professional development: technical, practical, and critical reflections (Knowles & Gilbourne, 2010). Knowles and Gilbourne (2010) explain technical reflections as the description and evaluation of one's practice, while practical reflections add an element of exploring meaning beyond the technical analysis of the intervention process. Critical reflections, however, include a critical engagement with attention to the broader social structure (e.g., power dynamics in relationships) instead of solely focusing on the individual consultation (Knowles & Gilbourne, 2010). Critical reflections could include thoughts such as the cultural influences in using goal-setting or how interventions based on a performance discourse could be harmful or beneficial.

In retrospect, I realize my reflections were mostly technical in nature. For example, on the day that we did a team-building activity, I described the activity and debriefing process, commented on the athletes' reactions and feedback, and reflected on how I could improve my plans for the championship that was coming up the following weekend. This type of reflection can be useful in assessing the client's response to different interventions to adjust and improve its effectiveness (Knowles & Gilbourne, 2010). In my specific case, it was the most helpful tool for my practice, given that I did not receive regular direct individual supervision. The group supervision sessions were helpful at times, but were not always individualized and timely enough to help me plan and modify my interventions.

Although I did not consider them at the time, deeper reflections about contextual meaning or social structures involved in my practice could have been extremely valuable for my development as a consultant. I was in a country with a different culture to mine, which affected my interactions with my clients, my colleagues, and my supervisor. Therefore, critical reflections about the case, such as the reflections we are employing in this chapter, could have helped me become aware of and adapt to the new environment and feel more confident while being immersed in the independent Finnish culture. Considering the challenges and complexities of multicultural supervision, we believe all types of reflections can and should be an integral part of supervision.

Despite how valuable reflective practice was to my professional development during and after this practicum case, Watson, Lubker, and Van Raalte (2011) caution practitioners not to use self-reflection as a substitute for formal supervision. Without someone regularly questioning the supervisee's approach or evaluating supervisees as a gatekeeper to the field, reflective practice can "get us somewhere, but probably not as far as we need to go in order to become self-aware and truly reflective practitioners" (Watson et al., 2011, p. 166). Rather than using either reflective practice or supervision, Watson et al. (2011) suggest integrating both to ensure quality SEP training and services.

Hegemonic Practices of Sport and Exercise Psychology

Although supervision has two purposes – case management and professional development (Van Raalte & Andersen, 2000) – my supervision was primarily concerned with case management. Supervision was mainly rooted in skill acquisition and sharing of cases without further probing into the theoretical underpinnings of such approaches and techniques. There may be several reasons for this. One influencing factor may be the dominant tendencies of SEP as a field. Researchers have critiqued SEP as being restrictively focused on performance enhancement and the application of CBT-based mental skill techniques (Ingham, Blissmer, & Davidson, 1999). Ingham et al. (1999) argued that "the UK and the U.S. had tended to neglect the person and had failed to address the dynamics of the personality as they articulate with social structures and cultures" (p. 237). Moreover, they pointed out that "applied sport psychology has embraced a technicist discourse that is a functional, performance-enhancing, tinkering-with-the-self discourse rather than an understanding-of-the-self discourse" (p. 240). Such an approach may be reflected in how some sport psychology consultants describe their work as primarily concerned with performance issues and not personal issues, as if one could separate the two.

This focus may have influenced the supervision approach as well. As practitioners neglect understanding and addressing the holistic person, a parallel process may be occurring in supervision as well, where supervisors focus on case management and techniques rather than the supervisee's holistic development. Moreover, this may have led not only to the skill-oriented supervision style, but also the lack of formal individual supervision. If there were more of a focus on the person in sport psychology practice, there may have been more of a focus on the person in supervision. When engaging in multicultural supervision in applied sport psychology, it may be important to critically engage in the purpose of one's practice and who and what benefits from the dominant hegemonic practices of SEP.

Cultural Differences in Supervision: Who Has the Knowledge?

Both clinical and sport psychology professionals have suggested guidelines for best practices in supervision. Ellis et al. (2014) listed supervisor requirements such as proper credentials and expertise, a minimum of one hour of direct individual supervision per week, investment in supervisees' development and well-being, and sensitivity to power dynamics and boundaries. Barney, Andersen, and Riggs (1996) proposed both individual and group supervision as essential, in addition to establishing a good supervisory relationship. Overall, these guidelines seem to suggest the importance of the supervisor as the expert and gatekeeper of the field.

When looking into this chapter's case, however, it is clear that not all of these factors were present in supervision. Clearly, a more independent approach was adopted and less emphasis was given to direct guidance. Although this may seem excessively independent, this approach is consistent with the Finnish higher education teaching style, which frequently follows a progressive inquiry process that emphasizes autonomy and self-regulation of learning (Pirinen, 2009). This approach takes advantage of diversity and builds a "creative chaos" environment rather than a structured, controlled institutional process in order to provide freedom to foster knowledge development (Pirinen, 2009). In fact, the Finnish students seemed quite comfortable with this supervision and learning style. Some of my Finnish peers even wondered why I was so unconfident and needy for wanting more direct supervision time.

Moreover, this autonomous teaching and supervision style is consistent with researchers' efforts to counter hegemonic SEP practices. Scholars argue that there is no one correct approach to applied sport psychology because knowledge is socially constructed and is always situated (Ryba, Schinke, & Tenenbaum, 2010). Anderson et al. (2004) also argued that the positivistic framework is limited in real-world situations where contexts are diverse and complex. This was clearly demonstrated in my case: a Brazilian working with a Finnish team, being supervised by a Spanish professor, and discussing practicum issues with classmates from all over the world. Our situation involved so many perspectives and elements that the supervisor-as-the-expert approach would be inefficient, if not impossible. As frustrating as it was, there was no one answer or best approach; there were only attempts to learn and be cognizant of possible differences. Therefore, even though the independent and indirect approach to supervision offered in Finland does not adhere to the suggested best practices of supervision in clinical and sport psychology, it was consistent with the Finnish education system. Moreover, in our opinion it was more realistic and appropriate for the program's multicultural environment. The lack of critical reflections about the motives for the use of autonomous practices and answer-less discussions was more questionable than the lack of direction in supervision per se.

One factor that could have aided my adaptation would have been a stronger and more transparent supervisor–supervisee alliance, in which my supervisor was aware of cultural dynamics and clearly explained the context of the education system and the supervision style. Moreover, it should be that students learn the value of adopting a cultural lens and open-mindedness through supervision. Previous biases and cultural influences were not discussed in individual or group supervision. Besides, a more active facilitation of the discussions we had in group supervision could have fostered better learning and less confusion throughout the supervision process. We can see from this case that one cannot assume that adopting cultural lenses will occur naturally, even in observably multicultural environments. Given this fact, it is important to infer that cultural awareness and competence will not naturally develop in a seemingly homogeneous environment either. Thus, purposeful discussion and integration of multicultural components are vital to all supervision processes.

SUGGESTED READINGS

Abbott, G., Gilbert, K., & Rosinski, P. (2013). Cross-cultural working in coaching and mentoring. In: J. Passmore, D. B. Peterson, & T. Freire (Eds.), *The Wiley-Blackwell handbook of the psychology of coaching and mentoring* (1st ed.; pp. 483–500). Oxford: Wiley-Blackwell.

Falender, C. A., Shafranske, E. P., & Faicov, C. J. (Eds.). (2014). *Multiculturalism and diversity in clinical supervision: A competency-based approach.* Washington, DC: American Psychological Association.

Inman, A. G., & Ladany, N. (2014). Multicultural competencies in psychotherapy supervision. In: F. T. L. Leong (Ed.), *APA handbook of multicultural psychology: Vol. 2 applications and training* (pp. 643–658). Washington, DC: American Psychological Association.

REFLECTIVE QUESTIONS

1.   Why does supervision need to be viewed through a cultural lens?
2.   What are the cultural backgrounds of all involved parties in this case? How did it affect the supervision process?
3.   How did reflective practice help and/or hurt supervision in this case?
4.   How did the dominant practices of applied sport psychology influence this supervision experience?
5.   What could supervisors do to facilitate multicultural group supervision?

REFERENCES

Andersen, M. B. (2000). *Doing sport psychology.* Champaign, IL: Human Kinetics.

Anderson, A. G., Knowles, Z., & Gilbourne, D. (2004). Reflective practice for sport psychologists: Concepts, models, practical implications, and thoughts on dissemination. *The Sport Psychologist, 18,* 188–203.

Barney, S. T., Andersen, M. B., & Riggs, C. A. (1996). Supervision in sport psychology: Some recommendations for practicum training. *Journal of Applied Sport Psychology, 8*(2), 200–217.

Ellis, M. V., Berger, L., Hanus, A. E., Ayala, E. E., Swords, B. A., & Siembor M. (2014). Inadequate and harmful clinical supervision: Testing a revised framework and assessing occurrence. *The Counseling Psychologist, 42*(4), 434–472.

Hanrahan, S. J. (2011). Sport psychology services are multicultural encounters: Differences as strengths in therapeutic relationships. In D. Gilbourne & M. B. Andersen (Eds.), *Critical essays in applied sport psychology* (pp. 145–156). Champaign, IL: Human Kinetics.

Ingham, A. G., Blissmer, B. J., & Davidson, K. W. (1999). The expendable prolympic self: Going beyond the boundaries of sociology psychology of sport. *Sociology of Sport Journal, 16,* 236–268.

Knowles, Z., & Gilbourne, D. (2010). Aspiration, inspiration and illustration: Initiating debate on reflective practice writing. *The Sport Psychologist, 24,* 504–520.

Lee, S., Titkov, A., & Mortensen, J. R. (2014). Nordic supervisee experiences in applied sport psychology. In J. G. Cremades & L. S. Tashman (Eds.), *Becoming a sport, exercise, and performance psychology professional: A global perspective* (pp. 300–307). New York, NY: Routledge.

Miville, M. L., Rosa, D., & Constantine, M. G. (2005). Building multicultural competence in clinical supervision. In M. G. Constantine & D. W. Sue (Eds.), *Strategies for building multicultural competence in mental health and educational settings* (pp. 192–211). Chichester: John Wiley.

Pirinen, R. (2009). Actualization of learning by developing (LbD): An analysis. *International Journal of Emerging Technologies in Learning, 4,* Special Issue 3: ICL, 46–58.

Ryba, T. V., Schinke, R. J., & Tenenbaum, G. (2010). *The cultural turn in sport psychology.* Morgantown, WV: Fitness Information Technology.

Van Raalte, J. L., & Andersen, M. B. (2000). Supervision I: From models to doing. In M. B. Andersen (Ed.), *Doing sport psychology* (pp. 153–165). Champaign, IL: Human Kinetics.

Watson, J. C., Lubker, J. R., & Raalte, J. V. (2011). Problems in reflective practice: Self-bootstrapping versus therapeutic supervision. In: D. Gilbourne & M. Andersen (Eds.), *Critical essays in applied sport psychology* (pp. 157–176). Champaign, IL: Human Kinetics.

37 Global Practice and Training in Applied Sport Psychology
Probationary Team Psychologist

Hin Yue Li

Psychologists in clinical and counseling settings traditionally stress one-on-one consultation (Clay, 2012). It gives the public an image of psychologists as introverted and intellectual. While such an image is one of many elements that attracted me to pursue this profession, it is not necessarily an accurate portrayal of sport psychologists, who spend a lot of time with both individual athletes and teams. In a team setting, it is not uncommon that a psychologist may have to work and interact with more than 20 clients (i.e., athletes) at the same time for long hours, not to mention providing on-field support. It can definitely challenge a psychologist-trainee to get out of his/her comfort zone and be professional and productive. Thus, in this chapter, I describe and reflect on my experience as a probationary sport psychologist working with a young team.

BACKGROUND INFORMATION

To become qualified as a psychologist in Australia, one needs to graduate from an accredited program, which normally provides a sufficient amount of theoretical training, research opportunity, internship/practicum experience, and professional supervision (Li & Jiang, 2014). When I did my doctoral program, I had completed no less than 1,500 hours of practicum. It consisted of both general population and sport opportunities. For example, one of the most interesting experiences during the practicum was the period when I worked with the under-18 regional men's field hockey team. I worked with them for about three to four months in total as preparation for the upcoming annual national tournament. Directly after finishing my work with the under-18 team, I was assigned to work with the under-15 team for a similar length of time, also for the national tournament for that age group. These two experiences were the first time I worked with hockey and team sports in general. The national men's field hockey team, nicknamed the Kookaburras, have been at the top tier of international hockey for decades (i.e., have placed in the top four in the Olympic Games since 1980) and is one of the most popular sports in Australia. At the time I started my practicum, they had just won the Olympic gold medal.

I was the first sport psychologist they worked with or who was officially introduced to them. The head coach of all the hockey teams in this province was completing his Doctor of Philosophy in coaching and sport psychology. He was very familiar with sport psychology and thus, at that time, took action and brought sport psychology services into both junior teams. I was fortunately assigned to fill this spot.

The head coach and I had two very interesting meetings before the series of practicums started. During these two meetings, we met to outline my involvement with the teams. One issue that came up was his suggestion that a referral system be used for clinical issues. I insisted that I, as a probationary psychologist, could offer my professional help. However, upon further discussion with my supervisor, I agreed that my services to the team would be performance-oriented and if there was anything clearly out of my expertise I would refer out.

After those two initial meetings, I mainly communicated with the team coaches, players, and the team manager. The under-18 team coach (referred to in this case as Coach J) was a very experienced hockey coach. He had been coaching this team for a number of years. He did not seem to have an authoritative coaching style and wanted to create an anxiety-free atmosphere in training. He was a very nice person with an "Aussie" care-free style and good relationships with the players.

DESCRIPTION OF THE CASE

I met the team during the first day of training. I first met with the team manager, who then introduced me to Coach J and the assistant coach. They told me about the combination of the players they had selected. All 20 players came from 11 district clubs, whereas eight players were teammates from the same club. In other words, almost half of the players could easily form a sub-group within the team or had done so even before the formation of this under-18 team, while the rest did not know each other beforehand, and could feel scattered and isolated. Furthermore, some players had played for the regional team for a number of years. Some even had competed together previously on the under-15 team. There was also a very small number of newly selected players. Considering all this interpersonal information, group dynamics and communication were some of the key issues the coaches and I agreed to address during the team formation stage.

The training period started in May. They trained three days per week for 1.5 hours. In addition, some players still had to handle some schoolwork, activities, and responsibilities for their local club training. Thus, they could be quite stretched in terms of time management. Coaches suggested having a session addressing this issue, whereas I also recommended another session for general relaxation. Coach J mentioned that he would like to see his team competing with a strong spirit, which included good communication and confidence. According to his years of experience, he strongly believed that confidence played a vital part in this competition, particularly when all regional teams were so close in quality. He specifically pinpointed that overtime in competition and penalty shots were anxiety-provoking situations. Players' confidence, as individuals and as a team, was the key to outperforming their opponents.

During the meeting with the head coach, held a month before the start of training, he had mentioned "focus" as an important facet of the mental training for the teams. The head coach stressed that good and professional players should be able to minimize their mistakes during the game, particularly not making similar mistakes twice. Further, young players should learn to reflect and self-correct during the game, otherwise their opponents would know their weaknesses.

APPROACH/PHILOSOPHY

Based on my graduate training, particularly at the time when I delivered services to the hockey team, psychological skills training (PST) and cognitive and behavioral therapies (McArdle & Moore, 2012) were the key sources guiding my intervention. After the series of meetings with coaches, my role was to bring in specific sport psychology skills and knowledge to the team. I was instructed to organize weekly workshops on topics, including concentration, relaxation, pre-competition routines, time management, and self-awareness. In other words, I was employing a sophist (Corlett, 1996) or "practitioner-led" (Keegan, 2010) approach, which focuses on skill development and instruction-based interaction. As previously mentioned, according to the head coaches' request, a PST model was the most suitable for the group work and lecture (Aoyagi & Poczwardowski, 2011). In addition, a PST model was appropriate because it emphasizes skill development rather than "fixing" athletes' mental problems (Dosil, Cremades, & Rivera, 2014). Consistent with Dosil and his colleagues' review, my work with the teams included the following psychological skills: goal-setting, relaxation, concentration, imagery, self-talk, and team communication. I did not implement biofeedback training, partly because of the team and field setting.

With regards to the supervision I received during this practicum experience, it gave me an important support and platform for reflection. My supervisor taught me about the psychological skills utilized in the intervention with the team, helped me to design the sessions, and gave me feedback to develop my own ideas. More importantly, by employing a psychodynamic approach, my supervisor guided me to explore my relationship with him and my relationship with the coaches and athletes.

PREPARATION/PLANNING

I received a team information handbook covering contact details of all supporting staff, training times, player etiquette, uniform information, tournament details, and information for parents. Apart from the team coaches and manager, a number of names in the list of support staff drew my attention. Several team member roles were outlined, including captain, vice-captain, sheep dog, and a number of train-on members. I thought I should actively interact with the two captains, as they might be able to help me fit into the team. Also, I was very interested in the role of sheep dog, which was designed for the youngest first-year player. He was supposed to keep track of his teammates and make sure the whole team arrived at the field or any particular areas where they should be according to the coaching plan.

A final area that caught my interest was the large section in the information packet concerning players' parents. They had set up a communication channel for the parents to show support to the players without affecting the training and coaching. Since my name was not included in the supporting staff, I prepared a letter to send to all the parents. I briefly introduced some of the topics I was going to cover and my contact information. Taking my supervisor's advice, I did not explicitly address the issue of confidentiality in the letter, but I did have a mutual understanding about protecting players' confidentiality within my professional boundary with all coaches.

Apart from planning the team workshops, one thing was very important as an ongoing preparation for my service: "hanging out." As Andersen (2000) stated, "hanging out" is part of the entering and preparatory process into service delivery. Incoming sport psychologists are supposed to get themselves to become part of the scene and by being there help the athletes feel comfortable with their presence. Trying to fit into the team was an essential process of rapport-building across various philosophical frameworks. To me, "hanging out" meant taking the rapport-building process a step forward by choosing to take off my psychologist hat and simply try to be present at the field. I helped pick up the water bottles and balls during training, and thanks to the coaches I joined in penalty games. As a total stranger coming from a foreign country, the "hanging out" process provided an extra challenge for my social skills. For the sake of rapport-building and later intervention, I was willing to step outside my comfort zone and stick with it.

All group meetings were held in the dressing room right after training. My first one with the team was about time management, titled "If you fail to plan, you plan to fail." Following my step-by-step preparation, I first took the opportunity to introduce myself to the team. I told the team that I was new to hockey and made fun of my own English accent. I always believe in making good use of self-disclosure to build rapport (Andersen, 2000). I then started off with sharing how I use my diary. In 30 minutes, this workshop covered the concepts of prioritization, scheduling, and goal-setting.

The second workshop was about concentration, titled "Pay Attention." Attention selectivity and shifting were explained. Referring to the head coach's concern, the concept of re-focusing was the key message for the athletes. The players were quiet until someone started to share his experience in penalty shots. Coach J then joined in the discussion and even set up the topic of the week afterwards, "Concentration and Confidence in Penalty Shots." When it came to penalty shots, players were very active in sharing. One player stated: "The whole game stops. Everyone is looking at you. That's the pressure." Another one shared: "I was very nervous and awkward. I just tried to hit the ball real hard." It led the group to look for a "solution." The captain and a player shared their pre-shot routine or mental rehearsal, which involved a series of visualizations. These two examples of using visualization of a perfect shot gave me a great opportunity to introduce the concepts of positive self-talk, relaxation, imagery, and pre-shot routine to the group. The latter two areas particularly drew their attention and built up momentum for workshop topics in the next two weeks. I also invited the goalkeepers to share their experiences, so as to give the players another perspective to look into the issue. The workshop ended with an actual penalty shooting game at the pitch, as Coach J suggested.

The workshops of the following weeks covered the topics of pre-competition routine, relaxation, and visualization. When we discussed routines, we shared stories about famous NFL, Rugby, and Australian football players' routines. The players enjoyed such discussions and started to talk about their "habit" before competitions. For example, one player ate almost the same type of food for lunch every game day. As expected, routines for both macro and micro sporting events were covered (Lidor, Hackfort, & Schack, 2014). Music, imagery, and warm-up exercise turned out to be the common elements for routines in macro events, such as half an hour before competitions. When I offered to make them an album with music, relaxation, and an imagery script, they requested to add "Eye of the Tiger" from the Hollywood movie *Rocky*. Imagery and positive self-talk were discussed the most when it came to micro events, like a penalty shot. Later, the coach and two athletes mentioned their dreams. They shared how vividly they could remember their dream and even felt pain or exhaustion after waking up from a dream with physical exercise. While I tried not to dwell on the areas of dream analysis, it did give me an opportunity to reinforce vividness and controllability as the key elements for imagery (Vealey & Greenleaf, 2001). Athletes were asked to formulate their pre-performance routine in a worksheet at the end.

The last workshop I conducted with the team was about team strength and communication. I started off asking athletes to think of an animal or any living creature that could represent the team. They, however, found it difficult. I then turned to ask how they would describe the teammate sitting next to them. Such questions did not go well with them, so I switched the focus to communication. I let them participate in an exercise called "Hog Calls." It required them to mix and form groups with eyes or mouth closed. They were engaged and enjoyed the games. I debriefed with them about the importance (i.e., willingness) and effectiveness (i.e., common language) of communication. By identifying the role of leaders and format of effective communication, I wanted to further facilitate the team development from storming to norming stages (Tuckman, 1965). Later, Coach J conducted an extra session with them. He let them brainstorm the key or strength of the team by encouraging the senior players to take the lead. They all agreed with the importance of positive atmosphere or, as they put it, "camaraderie" among themselves. They were encouraged to respect and support each other particularly in adverse situations. This extra session went very well and further mixed the players regardless of their seniority, background, and social groups.

SUPERVISION PROCESS/EXPERIENCE

I learned a great deal from this placement, not only from the actual experience, but also from the supervision I received. Weekly supervision helped me to reflect on my work and better prepare me for the upcoming sessions. My supervisor would comment on my workshop plan and conduct role play scenarios with me. For example, before making the relaxation CD, my supervisor invited another schoolmate to role play with me. We simulated the situation in which I taught progressive muscle relaxation for the first time. My supervisor and schoolmate commented that I just read through the script without any personal interaction. This experience provided valuable lessons that helped me when recording relaxation CDs for different players.

Supervision also built my confidence and clarified some blind spots. For example, when delivering the workshops, I always wanted to ask the questions I had planned. I also expected to get the feedback or answer I wanted from those questions. Instead of trying to explore stories from players, I was more focused on the mental skills I wanted to implement. In supervision, I realized that I had been viewing my plan for a workshop like a script for a presentation. I felt more secure if I had a script to follow. Supervision helped me to understand my own insecurity and anxiety whenever things turned to possible uncertainty.

Another important lesson learned in supervision related to the lack of individual consultation experience during the practicum. As mentioned before, during normal training periods I would be "hanging out" on the pitch. Together with all those workshops, I did have the opportunity to interact with the players, but I was not requested for any individual consultation throughout the placement. It was quite different from my expectations. There were a couple of times that players came to me and shared their experiences or stories, including their interactions with the coaching staff, injury, or history of this regional team. I was very interested in the exchange, in that none of them turned out to be official consultations. Supervision helped me to look at this issue, together with my expectation of providing intervention, through the lens of professional identity. I could not deny that I wanted to provide performance-related and even clinical services on an individual basis to feel like I was a competent "psychologist." I treated "hanging out" purely as preparation to pave the way for my desired intervention. It indeed echoed my resistance against referral requests during the meetings with the head coach. When I interacted with players, I might have jumped to giving answers (i.e., solution mode) instead of following the players' interest of sharing. I was fixated with "how am I doing?" rather than considering "what does my client actually need?"

In supervision I also learned about the nature of the athlete–coach relationship. I had ongoing communication with Coach J regarding the arrangement of the workshops every week. I asked many questions and learned from him. I was interested in how and why he would interact with the players. He demanded from the team members, but he was not harsh. He always tried to share his experiences as a way to motivate young players. Based on my textbook knowledge, I thought that a positive and encouraging style was good for the players, until a senior player expressed to me that he would like to see more discipline and seriousness in the team. On that occasion, I showed my empathy for his coaching expectations and encouraged him to set training goals. I discussed this conversation during supervision and such sharing made me realize, as a probationary psychologist, that there may not be a golden rule of coaching and there is a possible discrepancy of expectations between coaches and athletes.

Apart from reviewing my actual service, my supervisor guided me to reflect on the transference elements in supervision. I seemed to treat my supervisor as a boss and parent figure. On one hand, there were occasions when I expressed worry over being judged by him. On the other hand, I expected he would protect me when facing challenges, such as potential criticism. It made me aware of how I tend to relate to people, and authority figures such as coaches in particular. In addition, I was introduced to the concept and practice of mindfulness (Gardner & Moore, 2007). Although I could not further bring it to the hockey team at that time, due to inexperience, I have started to explore the concept and gradually apply it to my personal life and professional practice (see also Si, Zhang, Su, Zhang, Jiang, & Li, 2014).

REFLECTION

With regards to the consulting experience, one main area of reflection was the limitation of only providing weekly workshops to the team. These meetings occurred at the end of training sessions, thus when the workshop finished the athletes would not stay around, but were picked up by their parents. It limited the opportunity to engage in any private conversation for exploring personal or follow-up issues. It would have been more beneficial to the team if the workshops were held prior to or in the middle of training sessions. At least, I would have been able to follow-up with the players during the second half of the training, my "hanging out" time.

Referring to my need to do individual work to fulfill my professional identity, I have had further reflection recently. As Hadfield (2014) described after his years of work with the New Zealand world champion rugby team, his main foci had always been the ongoing communication with coaches and group work with the team. He tried hard to remain "in the background and pitching in and helping out wherever I could around the team" (p. 227). Bringing this focus to my current work with team sports, I try particularly hard to join as many team meetings as I can so as to immerse myself in the team before trying to deliver any "intervention." To help me feel more comfortable during the "hanging out" period, I have now learned to first communicate with coaches and see if there is any specific duty I can do on the pitch; in addition, I carry a video camera and record the training. It helps me to learn the sport and gives me topics to discuss with players when the opportunity arises.

Overall, this practicum allowed me to work with a challenging team with various players and coaches. It broadened my scope in sport psychology, sharpened my understanding of psychological skills training, and, more importantly, helped me to redefine my concept of "psychology service" as well as my role as a sport psychologist.

SUGGESTED READINGS

Andersen, M. B. (Ed.). (2000). *Doing sport psychology*. Champaign, IL: Human Kinetics.
Andersen, M. B. (Ed.). (2005). *Sport psychology in practice*. Champaign, IL: Human Kinetics.
Bronson, P., & Merryman, A. (2013). *Top dog: The science of winning and losing*. New York, NY: Random House.
Epstein, M. (1995). *Thoughts without thinker: Psychotherapy from a Buddhist perspective*. New York, NY: Basic Books.
Hadfield, D. (2014). Rugby in New Zealand. In P. C. Terry, L. W. Zhang, Y. H. Kim, T. Morris, & S. Hanrahan (Eds.), *Secrets of Asian sport psychology* (pp. 223–245). Retrieved from http://peter-terry.wix.com/books.
Gardner, F. L., & Moore, Z. E. (2007). *The psychology of enhancing human performance: The mindfulness–acceptance–commitment (MAC) approach*. New York, NY: Springer.
Jackson, P., & Delehanty, H. (2013). *Eleven rings: The soul of success*. New York: Penguin.

REFLECTIVE QUESTIONS

1. When working with a team, who is the client?
2. What is one's role as a (probationary) sport psychologist in a well-established team?
3. What is the role of art and science in sport psychology consultation?
4. What is and is not an expectation in supervision?
5. How would transference and countertransference influence the supervisor–supervisee relationship and interaction?

REFERENCES

Andersen, M. B. (2000). Beginnings: Intakes and the initiation of relationships. In M. B. Andersen (Ed.), *Doing sport psychology* (pp. 3–16). Champaign, IL: Human Kinetics.

Aoyagi, M. W., & Poczwardowski, A. (2011). Models of sport psychology practice and delivery: A review. In S. D. Mellalieu & S. Hanton (Eds.), *Professional practice issues in sport psychology: Critical reviews* (pp. 5–30). London: Routledge.

Clay, R. A. (2012). Beyond psychotherapy: To meet the vast unmet demand for services, psychologists are seeking alternatives to traditional one-on-one therapy. *Monitor on Psychology, 43*(1), 46–50.

Corlett, J. (1996). Sophistry, Socrates, and sport psychology. *The Sport Psychologist, 10*, 84–94.

Dosil, J., Cremades, J. G., & Rivera, S. (2014). Psychological skills training and programs. In A. G. Papaioannou & D. Hackfort (Eds.), *Routledge companion to sport and exercise psychology: Global perspectives and fundamental concepts* (pp. 327–342). London: Routledge.

Gardner, F. L., & Moore, Z. E. (2007). *The psychology of enhancing human performance: The mindfulness–acceptance–commitment (MAC) approach.* New York, NY: Springer.

Hadfield, D. (2014). Rugby in New Zealand. In P. C. Terry, L. W. Zhang, Y. H. Kim, T. Morris, & S. Hanrahan (Eds.), *Secrets of Asian sport psychology* (pp. 223–245). Retrieved from http://peterterry.wix.com/books.

Kegan, R. J. (2010). Teaching consulting philosophies to neophyte sport psychologists: Does it help, and how can we do it? *Journal of Sport Psychology in Action, 1*, 42–52.

Li, H. Y., & Jiang, X. B. (2014). Looking through the supervisees' eyes: Australia and China. In J. G. Cremades & L. S. Tashman (Eds.), *Becoming a sport, exercise, and performance psychology professional: A global perspective* (pp. 308–314). New York, NY: Routledge.

Lidor, R., Hacfor, D., & Schack, T. (2014). Performance routines in sport: Meaning and practice. In A. G. Papaioannou & D. Hackfort (Eds.), *Routledge companion to sport and exercise psychology: Global perspectives and fundamental concepts* (pp. 480–494). London: Routledge.

McArdle, S., & Moore, P. (2012). Applying evidence-based principles from CBT to sport psychology. *Sport Psychologist, 26*(2), 299–310.

Si, G. Y., Zhang, G. J., Su, N., Zhang, C. Q., Jiang, X. B., & Li, H. Y. (2014). *Athletes' mindfulness training manual.* Beijing: Beijing University Press. (In Chinese).

Tuckman, B. W. (1965). Developmental sequence in small groups. *Psychological Bulletin, 63*(6), 384–399.

Vealey, R. S., & Greenleaf, C. A. (2001). Seeing is believing: Understanding and using imagery in sport. In J. M. Williams (Ed.), *Applied sport psychology* (4th ed.; pp. 247–283). Palo Alto, CA: Mayfield.

38 Who's Supervising the Supervisor?

A Case Study of Meta-Supervision

Alison Rhodius and Mathew M. Park

Stated in its simplest form, meta-supervision is "supervision of supervision" (Barney & Andersen, 2014, p. 341). This is an important, but often overlooked, element of training in sport psychology practice. This chapter covers a case study that involves the work of a supervisee, her supervisor, and his meta-supervisor. The focus of the chapter is on helping meta-supervisors understand their role and explore ways they can facilitate competent supervision in sport psychology.

BACKGROUND INFORMATION

It seems pertinent to give a little background on the authors' supervision training prior to background on the meta-supervision case study. By doing so, it will highlight a little of the different types of training that are involved in applied sport psychology work. The first author (AR) is chair of the Master's (MA) Sport Psychology Program at John F. Kennedy University (JFKU), and her formal applied training involved doing supervised experience (applied work) for British Association of Sport and Exercise Sciences (BASES) accreditation, where the focus was on performance enhancement/non-clinical work. She had no formal training in being a supervisor during this work, however (which is common in a non-clinical sport psychology track), as she left the UK before receiving the workshop training that BASES now offers supervisors listed on the BASES Supervisor Register (www.bases.org.uk/Supervised-Experience-FAQ) and that the British Psychological Society (BPS) now offers (Tod, Eubank, & Andersen, 2014). Since becoming a faculty member at a US institution and also becoming a certified consultant by the Association for Applied Sport Psychology (CC-AASP), she regularly supervises MA interns and post-master's and doctoral trainees. This supervision in turn involves informally learning from a meta-supervisor and her peers on a regular basis.

The second author (MP) has expertise in performance enhancement training (MA in Sport Psychology), clinical work (PsyD), and formal supervision training as part of his doctoral and post-doctoral work. He is a CC-AASP and is now the meta-supervisor in the Sport Psychology Master's Program at JFKU.

Below are brief descriptions of the main characters involved in this case study and a short narrative of the case.

Meta-Supervisor (at JFKU we call this role the Fieldwork Coordinator)

Liz is a 32-year-old Caucasian female who has a master's in Sport Psychology and a PsyD in Clinical Psychology. She has been supervising for two years and has also been a CC-AASP for two years. Liz is now a Core Faculty member in a graduate sport psychology program.

Supervisor

Max is a 34-year-old Korean-American male who has been supervising for three years. He has a master's in Sport Psychology with no clinical training. He is currently an adjunct faculty member in a graduate sport psychology program and has his own private practice in sport psychology. He was trained in the United States and has been a CC-AASP for the past three years.

Supervisee/Intern

Amanda is a 25-year-old Caucasian female currently earning a master's Sport Psychology degree. She played on a four-year university golf team and studied Kinesiology. She came to California from the Mid-West.

Client

Carlos is a 15-year-old Latino-American male who is an elite junior golfer (scratch golfer; has a 0 handicap). He comes from a low socio-economic status (SES) family and his parents are first-generation immigrants, born in Mexico and Spanish-speaking only.

DESCRIPTION OF THE CASE

Amanda (intern) has been blending the lines of her role as a sport psychology intern. She really likes her client, Carlos (client), and has a soft spot for him. She continues to discuss how much she feels sorry for him and how unfair his life is because of his "overbearing" parents. Carlos has an opportunity to play golf in college on a scholarship, but his parents are struggling financially and are forcing Carlos to help with the family business after high school, thus missing out on the opportunity to pursue his dreams of playing college golf. Carlos is torn and his golf performance has been impacted. As Amanda is trying to help support Carlos, there has been an increased sexual attraction toward each other and Amanda says she is unaware of this.

She cares for him and feels sorry for him. She is helping Carlos more than just as a mental skills coach and is often feeding him lunch and providing transport for him. Max (supervisor) is trying to increase Amanda's awareness of her sexual attraction toward Carlos, pointing out some of her unprofessional behaviors. However, when Max talks to Amanda about her boundaries, she tries to defend herself by saying she's "just feeling sorry for him" and that this is her way of building rapport. Max is getting increasingly frustrated with Amanda and the situation because he is unable to talk about this issue with Amanda without her getting defensive and guarded.

APPROACH/PHILOSOPHY

The meta-supervision discussed in this chapter is part of the new JFKU sport psychology supervision model. This model has been developed from our experiences of supervising interns and supervisors over the past 25 years, and a consideration of some relevant literature in the field (e.g., Bernard, 1997; Hart, 1982; Stoltenberg, 1981; Teitelbaum, 1990).

Meta-supervision can be a complex process and something that many supervisors may not have had any formal training in (Barney, Andersen, & Riggs, 1996). Our model was created to provide a framework for the meta-supervisor and to help facilitate the supervision process. This model begins with an assessment of the supervisor's background in supervisory roles and an understanding of one's working model of supervision. Ten main questions are asked and discussed with new supervisors to begin this assessment:

1. What does supervision mean to you?
2. If you have had prior experience in supervision, can you describe your supervision style?
3. What are some of your strengths as a supervisor?
4. What has been one of the most challenging experiences of supervision? How did you overcome this challenge?
5. If you have not had any prior experience in supervision, what do you imagine to be one of the most challenging aspects of supervising, and how do you imagine handling that situation?
6. Can you recall a supervisor you had during your own training that had a positive impact on you? What is it about their style that resonated with you?
7. How have you developed competencies for working with individual and cultural diversity? And how would you impart those skills to your supervisees?
8. How do you identify your own biases and assumptions in your work?
9. What are some of your personal goals for this supervisory experience?
10. How will you know when you have achieved these goals?

Gaining an understanding of a supervisor's theoretical approach, style, and beliefs of supervision can help facilitate the meta-supervisor's work with the supervisor.

Barney et al. (1996) reported the lack of formal training in supervision within the sport psychology field and, more recently, Castillo (2014) stated how regrettable it is that supervision (and mentoring) practices are not discussed more. Many current supervisors may not know of any models of supervision or techniques used in the supervision process. To address this need, a *Sport Psychology Supervisor's Training Manual* was created at JFKU to help supervisors gain a more in-depth understanding of the supervision process. This training manual consists of an overview of existing models used in sport psychology supervision, guidelines on how to supervise, expectation of supervisors, and a qualitative account of previous responses to various assessment questions in the JFKU sport psychology supervision model. Some of the models mentioned in sport psychology literature are referenced in the JFKU *Sport Psychology Supervisor's Training Manual.* These models are Hart's (1982) three-stage model of developmental supervision, Stoltenberg's (1981) integrated developmental model, Teitelbaum's (1990) supertransference, and Bernard's (1997) discrimination model. When supervision is discussed in sport psychology, these are the models that are most often referenced and cited in the literature.

The JFKU sport psychology supervision model references existing models of supervision because it can help facilitate the process of developing one's own working model of supervision (Silva, Metzler, & Lerner, 2007). Hill (2001) stated that "theoretical models suggest questions, explanations, and predictions for the phenomena they describe" (p. viii); thus, discussing models of supervision not only helps provide a framework for the supervisors to follow, but also helps them to reflect on their work. Not all theories or models are created equal, and some are more useful and easier to apply than others. But they are still fundamental building blocks which we can use to "find guidelines and patterns" (Gill & Williams, 2008, p. 29).

The model we have developed highly encourages meta-supervisors and supervisors to work from their "craft knowledge" (McFee, 1993): (1) knowledge gained from life experiences (e.g., as human beings, athletes, coaches, parents, teachers, etc.); and (2) knowledge from situations where they have to learn in the moment and use their intuition (see Gladwell, 2005). It is recognized that knowledge developed through "craft" experiences (McFee, 1993) are important in the development of various skills (Schön, 1983). When Egan (1998) referred to the idea of wisdom, he gave an example of someone who may be "brilliant academically but incompetent in social interaction" (p. 20). He stated that wisdom forms the basis for practical intelligence or common sense. Egan (1998) suggested "knowing 'how' rather than merely knowing is critical in helping others" (p. 20). The importance of demonstrating the knowledge of knowing "how" in meta-supervision helps to model for supervisors what this process will look like with their supervisees. In addition, Hemmings and Holder (2009) have argued that applied knowledge from the experiences of practitioners is extremely valuable in order to shape theory, research, and practice in the future. No field of psychology has developed methods and theories that hold true for all populations, so we must use them solely as guidelines (Gill & Williams, 2008).

PREPARATION/PLANNING

In preparing someone to be a meta-supervisor, it is assumed that they have some supervisory experience already. In addition, their own background would ideally involve some training in supervision, but unfortunately this does not exist in many sport psychology programs. Assuming that the meta-supervisor has had some training and experience in supervising various levels of supervisees, it would be important to make sure they have regular contact with the supervisors under their care, and have regular opportunities to observe the supervisors in action (an important element in addressing the supervisors' transference and countertransference).

Additionally, meta-supervisors may use reflective practice to address aspects such as their own strengths and challenges that they have experienced. It may also be beneficial for the meta-supervisor to review the ten assessment questions themselves and focus on reflective practices. Reflective practice (RP) can be defined as "an intentional process that enhances self-awareness and understanding through thinking about applicable 'events'" (Rhodius & Huntley, 2014, p. 91). In this case the "event" is supervising trainees. RP is an excellent tool for being an effective supervisor and meta-supervisor that, in turn, can be used with trainees as part of their development and learning process (Rhodius & Huntley, 2014). We would encourage meta-supervisors to help supervisors use RP in their initial phases of learning how to be a supervisor as well as continually throughout the process. Perhaps the meta-supervisor can meet with the supervisor once per month to facilitate the meta-supervision process and discuss what they think and feel about their own supervision work (i.e., their highlights, challenges, what they have learned about themselves as a supervisor and what changes they need to make, if any, going forward). This process is borrowed from a model by Gibbs (1988) that is cited often in the literature (e.g., Knowles, Gilbourne, Cropley, & Dugdill, 2014).

In addition to reflective practice, meta-supervisors are encouraged to continue working on personal and professional growth by attending conferences (e.g., AASP), participating in supervision training and forums, reading updated literature on theoretical approaches and techniques in sport psychology, taking continuing education classes on supervision, networking with other meta-supervisors and sport psychology colleagues, invigilating oral exams, and teaching in sport psychology graduate school programs. If a meta-supervisor's primary training comes from clinical or counseling psychology, it is also imperative for the meta-supervisor to understand the ethical and professional considerations unique to the field of sport psychology.

SUPERVISION PROCESS/EXPERIENCE

The following vignette shows an example in which Max (supervisor) is getting frustrated with Amanda (intern) as he tells the story to Liz (meta-supervisor).

MAX: I am really frustrated with working with Amanda right now. I am struggling to facilitate the process because she doesn't seem like she wants to take any of my suggestions. I need a little bit of help in what to do.

LIZ: What have you tried?

MAX: I have tried to gently ask her about her feelings toward Carlos. I have asked her why she wants to help him so much, but she seems to be putting up barriers to me now. Part of me wonders if she sees her unethical behaviors and doesn't want to admit it.

LIZ: I hear you are frustrated and feel as if barriers have been put up. What do these barriers look like to you?

MAX: I just feel like she is undermining my authority and she is being disrespectful because she is not taking any of my suggestions.

LIZ: So you don't feel respected in your role as her supervisor. What does respect look like to you?

MAX: Well, technically I am overseeing her work and she needs to listen to my suggestions. Respect is when she understands and acknowledges that I have more experience than she does and she should at least take my suggestions and implement them immediately.

LIZ: So I'm hearing that respect to you is when she acknowledges that you are coming from a place of experience and authority and should take your suggestions and implement them.

MAX: Yes – then I don't think I would feel as stuck and frustrated as I have been with her.

LIZ: It sounds like respect is something very important to you. Do you think respect is also something that might be important to Amanda?

MAX: What do you mean?

LIZ: Well, do you think Amanda would also like to feel respected in her work?

MAX: Yeah, I suppose so. But how does that change anything about how inappropriate her behaviors have been with Carlos?

LIZ: Well let's explore something real quick. What do you think respect would look like to her?

MAX: I don't know, maybe she wants me to trust her more?

LIZ: Trust? Would you mind sharing more?

MAX: Well, she tells me to trust her because she knows she will never act on intimate feelings toward any of her clients. But I'm afraid she might unless I do something about it. You see, I had a friend during my graduate training and he had feelings toward one of his clients. I told him to be careful about his feelings toward his client, but he didn't listen to me and they ended up sleeping together during a retreat. The aftermath was awful. He and his supervisor got into so much trouble and I want to avoid that from ever happening again.

LIZ: I'm sorry to hear that about your friend. It makes sense to me why you would have such strong feelings toward wanting to help Amanda. However, do you think your level of trust with Amanda has been impacted by your previous experience with this graduate school friend?

MAX: Hmm … I don't know.

LIZ: Is there anything Amanda has done that has broken your trust?

MAX: Well, not really. She always seems to be honest and frank with me during our supervision. She always shows up on time and seems to take supervision seriously. However, I am not comfortable with her giving rides and feeding Carlos because I feel like it will lead to something inappropriate.

LIZ: Have you discussed with Amanda why you feel like giving rides and feeding Carlos can be problematic?

MAX: I have not talked about it directly, but I did express concern about the issue.

LIZ: Well, if you don't mind, can I suggest some approaches that may help lower some of the barriers you've felt recently with Amanda. Does that sound okay?

MAX: Yeah, that sounds good.

LIZ: The first thing I would take notice of is your own personal feelings especially toward this subject matter of sexual intimacy with clients. Explore what comes up for you when you think about this topic. The more you can sit with your own discomfort and become comfortable with the uncomfortable, the more direct you may be able to be in your supervision with Amanda. Sometimes, simply naming the issue (or the elephant in the room) can solve a lot of miscommunication and it can foster a safe environment of exploration. You are right, sex with clients is not okay and we want to be vigilant so that we can avoid that at all cost. However, sexual attraction and feelings are normal and sometimes inevitable. It's important to discuss this in supervision as honestly as possible so that feelings can be explored, and awareness can be increased both for the supervisor and for the supervisee. Developing an effective game-plan through previewing can help give supervisees guidance on what to do. Normalizing that having feelings (without action) are okay, can help foster a safer environment for supervisees to explore their true feelings and thoughts in supervision. This can help build more trust in the supervisory relationship.

REFLECTION

This short vignette highlights the elements of multicultural awareness, countertransference, shared responsibility, and reflective practice, which are key elements in the JFKU sport psychology supervision model. As a Korean-American male, Max may have felt that his authority was undermined when he was in a position of power and Amanda did not respond the way he felt she should have responded (i.e., obediently). Respect may have looked differently to Max than it did to Amanda. Amanda may have thought she was extremely respectful by showing up on time, taking her work with Max seriously, and challenging some of his thoughts to show that she really cared about this work and this client. Because of cultural differences, Max and Amanda may have felt differently as to what respect looks and feels like. It was apparent to the meta-supervisor that Max was experiencing countertransference, especially in regards to the topic of sex with clients. Max's lack of trust with his friend from graduate school seemed to be projected onto Amanda and it was important for the meta-supervisor to bring awareness of Max's previous experiences and explore how it impacted his current work with Amanda.

Shared responsibility is also important to note from this example. With Amanda being in her last internship, Max may find himself playing more the role of a consultant to Amanda during his supervision with her, in order to help equip Amanda on being more independent and on her own (instead of coaching and micromanaging her every move). Lastly, RP was introduced when the meta-supervisor asked Max to explore his own feelings around the topic of sex with clients. The meta-supervisor had asked Max to reflect on his feelings, even if they brought him discomfort. As described above, RP is an essential tool for developing awareness and learning from experiences and can be utilized by trainees, supervisors, and meta-supervisors in various scenarios. The short vignette provided above offered several examples of a rich exchange in a meta-supervision process.

Meta-supervision is a key component of good training for practitioners because of the direct impact a supervisor has on the trainee, but is a topic that has been mainly overlooked for a long time. Supervising the supervisors seems an obvious aspect of training, but is something that many people do not even realize is not happening on a consistent basis. We would recommend that supervisors receive adequate training that follows some ground rules established by a professional organization such as AASP.

In addition, we contend that continuing education credits (or continuing professional development – CPD) on the topic of supervision should be not only available, but a mandatory part of re-certification or re-accreditation to be a supervisor. The dialogue on supervision in this field has been started, but there is a great deal more to discuss and to put in place for the benefit of our up-and-coming trainees and for the field's credibility. Continuing the dialogue on the topic of supervision as a whole will inevitably lead to further discussion and training (and monitoring) processes around the bigger topic of meta-supervision, because it cannot continue to be a "wild west" of supervisors when the future of our applied field depends on how the practitioners are supervised. The meta-supervisor is key in this training of supervisors (when there are a group of supervisors working for an institution), in addition to the training that individuals should obtain during their own studies (their master's or doctoral training), and from professional organizations (e.g., AASP, BASES, BPS, etc.).

SUGGESTED READINGS

Barney, S. T., & Andersen, M. B. (2014). Meta-supervision: Training practitioners to help others on their paths. In J. G. Cremades & L. S. Tashman (Eds.) *Becoming a sport, exercise, and performance psychology professional: A global perspective* (pp. 339–346). New York, NY: Routledge.

Silva III, J. M., Metzler, J. N., & Lerner, B. (2011). *Training professionals in the practice of sport psychology*. Morgantown, WV: Fitness Information Technology.

Van Raalte, J. L., & Andersen, M. B. (2000). Supervision I: From models to doing. In M. B. Andersen (Ed.), *Doing sport psychology* (pp. 153–165). Champaign, IL: Human Kinetics.

REFLECTIVE QUESTIONS

1. When reading about the supervisor (Max), what were your initial thoughts on the way he reacted to the intern (Amanda)?
2. How would you address your own assumptions and biases as the meta-supervisor (Liz) before talking with the supervisor (Max)?
3. What did the meta-supervisor (Liz) do well?
4. What could Liz have done better?
5. What are three takeaways from this chapter that you can use or apply to help your work as a meta-supervisor?

REFERENCES

Barney, S. T., & Andersen, M. B. (2014). Meta-supervision: Training practitioners to help others on their paths. In J. G. Cremades & L. S. Tashman (Eds.) *Becoming a sport, exercise, and performance psychology professional: A global perspective* (pp. 339–346). New York, NY: Routledge.

Barney, S. T., Andersen, M. B., & Riggs, C. A. (1996). Supervision in sport psychology: Some recommendations for practicum training. *Journal of Applied Sport Psychology, 8*(2), 200–217.

Bernard, J. M. (1997). The discrimination model. In C. E. Watkins, Jr. (Ed.), *Handbook of psychotherapy supervision* (pp. 311–327). New York, NY: John Wiley.

Castillo, S. (2014). Ethical issues in training future practitioners. In L. S. Tashman & G. Cremades (Eds.), *Becoming a performance psychologist: International perspectives on service delivery and supervision* (pp. 252–259). New York, NY: Routledge.

Egan, G. (1998). *The skilled helper: A problem-management approach to helping* (6th ed.). Pacific Grove, CA: Brooks/Cole.

Gibbs, G. (1988). *Learning by doing: A guide to teaching and learning methods*. Oxford: Oxford Brookes University Further Education Unit.

Gill, D. L., & Williams, L. (2008). *Psychological dynamics of sport and exercise*. Champaign, IL: Human Kinetics.

Gladwell, M. (2005). *Blink*. New York, NY: Little, Brown and Company.

Hart, G. M. (1982). *The process of clinical supervision*. Baltimore, MD: University Park Press.

Hemmings, B., & Holder, T. (2009). *Applied sport psychology: A case-based approach*. Chichester: Wiley-Blackwell.

Hill, K. (2001). *Frameworks for sport psychologists*. Human Kinetics: Champaign, IL.

Knowles, Z., Gilbourne, D., Cropley, B., & Dugdill, L. (Eds.) (2014). *Reflective practice in the sport and exercise sciences: Contemporary issues.* New York, NY: Routledge.

McFee, G. (1993). Reflections on the nature of action-research. *Cambridge Journal of Education, 23*(2), 173–183.

Rhodius, A., & Huntley, E. (2014). Facilitating reflective practice in graduate trainees and early career practitioners. In Z. Knowles, D. Gilbourne, B. Cropley, & L. Dugdill (Eds.), *Reflective practice in the sport and exercise sciences: Contemporary issues* (pp. 91–100). New York, NY: Routledge.

Schön, D. A. (1983). *The reflective practitioner.* London: Temple-Francis.

Silva, J. M., Metzler, J. N., & Lerner, B. (2007). *Training professionals in the practice of sport psychology.* Morgantown, WV: Fitness Information Technology.

Stoltenberg, C. (1981). Approaching supervision from a developmental perspective: The counselor complexity model. *Journal of Counseling Psychology, 28*, 59–65.

Teitelbaum, S. H. (1990). Supertransference: The role of the supervisor's blind spots. *Psychoanalytic Psychology, 7*(2), 243–258. DOI: 10.1037/hoo79155.

Tod, D., Eubank, M. R., & Andersen, M. B. (2014). International perspectives: Training and supervision in the United Kingdom and Australia. In L. S. Tashman & G. Cremades (Eds.), *Becoming a performance psychologist: International perspectives on service delivery and supervision* (pp. 324–330). New York, NY: Routledge.

39 Mindfully Dynamic Meta-Supervision
The Case of AW and M

Mark B. Andersen, Steve T. Barney, and Andrew K. Waterson

In applied sport, exercise, and performance psychology (SEPP), discussions of meta-supervision (i.e., the supervision of supervision, the training of practitioners to become competent supervisors) are at least 20 years old and go back to the first published account of a meta-supervision program (Barney, Andersen, & Riggs, 1996). Even though 20 years have passed since, the topic of meta-supervision is still relatively rare in the literature, often being a small part of some other research or discussion article. For example, Watson, Zizzi, Etzel, and Lubker (2004) mentioned a meta-supervision issue when they reported that 47 percent of the membership of the Association for Applied Sport Psychology (AASP) had not received any training in supervision. Recently, however, the topic of meta-supervision has begun to emerge, albeit in a small way. There have been calls for more training in supervision processes, along with suggestions for new supervision training models (e.g., Vosloo, Zakrajsek, & Grindley, 2014). Currently, there is a growing literature on peer supervision in our field, but a review of that topic is beyond the scope of this case study (see Chapters 34 and 35 in this volume for examples). Barney and Andersen (2014a) have explicitly addressed the current status and the future of SEPP meta-supervision. These same authors have incorporated mindfulness into a core feature of meta-supervision: the dynamics within the supervisor–supervisee relationship (Barney & Andersen, 2014b).

BACKGROUND INFORMATION

The Meta-Supervision Relationship

As is often the case in therapeutic work with clients, the quality of the collaborative relationship can be a key factor in the success of supervision and meta-supervision. Rogerian, or human-centered, approaches to counseling, supervision, and meta-supervision may serve as good models for fostering adaptive spaces where growth and development can be optimized. Within this framework, meta-supervisors operate under the assumption that supervisors in training have the capacity to resolve issues and problems but may benefit from an environment where they can be open to experiences and fully engaged with the process. The meta-supervisor acts as a guide and support and is attuned to the developmental needs of the supervisor in training. The humanistic approach to meta-supervision is non-judgmental and inherently nurturing, but not passive and without form. Issues are dealt with openly and transparently in the present moment; awareness leads to knowledge, which gives power to change. To be effective, the meta-supervisor must become attuned to the needs, insecurities, and strengths of the supervisor in training, and the supervisor in training becomes attuned to the motives and non-directive style of the meta-supervisor. Both parties learn to become more adept at conjoint mindfulness or attunement (Siegel, 2012).

A relatively new field of study, interpersonal neurobiology, has emerged as an explanatory platform for abstract constructs such as attunement, awareness, relationship, and other ideas relevant to human-centered theory. Having a neurobiological foundation helps people from myriad disciplines become more human centered, perhaps without even knowing that they are. Resources such as Siegel (2012) help demystify interpersonal neurobiology and make the research accessible to a wide variety of practitioners.

The Goals of Meta-Supervision

Meta-supervision, or supervision of supervisors-in-training, is designed to enhance the quality and efficacy of the supervisory process. Supervision can be a difficult, complex process that is essential in helping budding SEPP professionals learn the craft. As stated above, there is a paucity of training models for neophyte supervisors. We hope, by sharing a case and other insights we have learned through the years, to provide a relationship-centered and neurobiological foundation for ongoing improvement in this area.

DESCRIPTION OF THE CASE

We would like to emphasize that there is not "a case" in this chapter, but rather a tale involving (at least) three people directly, and many more people indirectly (often as internal representations of significant others) who have influenced the interactions of the three main characters. There has been no attempt to disguise the meta-supervisor (Mark [M], the first author) or the meta-supervisee (Andrew [AW], the third author). The story of their relationship has already been told in the autoethnographic part of AW's doctoral dissertation (Waterson, 2015), which is in the public domain. AW and M are happy to be identified in this chapter. AW's supervisee-client, however, has been disguised.

The Meta-Supervisee: Registered Psychologist and Doctoral Student

AW came to our master of applied psychology program (sport and exercise psychology emphasis) already registered (licensed) as a psychologist in Australia. He had completed four years of psychology education plus two years of full-time supervised practice to gain registration. My (M's) first encounter with AW was at his interview during the selection process for entrance into the program in late 2010. I recall a well-dressed, good-looking young man who seemed to be doing an adequate job of compensating for the anxiety that interviews of this sort usually provoke. I also recall thinking that there was an impish quality that was occasionally sneaking through his impression management efforts. Already being a registered psychologist set AW apart from most of the candidates that year, but there was something almost defensive about already achieving registration. At one point in the interview, I asked him about some of his strengths as a psychologist, and here is that exchange as AW (2015) reported it in his autoethnography:

> When I interviewed for my doctorate program I told M that my greatest strength as a practitioner was my ability to engage clients. M looked at me puzzled and asked, "If you can do that, why do you want to come back to university?" I came back in search of the psychologist tool kit, the interventions, theories, and therapies that would make me feel like a *real* psychologist. I came back because I felt like a fraud. After completing four years of training, exploring all manner of therapies and theories, I have realised that everyone has their baggage and feeling fraudulent is normal. I had too much paint covering me in the form of anxieties, walled-off emotions, past traumas, and automatic unexamined patterns of behaving and feeling.

(pp. 130–131)

At the time of the interview, AW could not have formulated the above understanding because he was remarkably well armored and surprisingly un-self-reflective. I recall an early exchange AW and I had about emotions, and he stated something like "I can get really angry sometimes." I asked if he had ever explored the roots of his anger, and he responded: "I don't really feel like I need to; I like my anger." AW did not seem terribly interested in himself, almost blasé, but I suspected his indifference was a type of defense to avoid going to places of despair. He would get there finally, but it would take him a good deal of time.

Neophyte mindful practitioner. In our applied master program with a sport and exercise psychology emphasis, those students who make excellent progress academically and in contributions to class discussions in their first year of the program may apply for our professional doctorate of applied psychology. This upgrade involves an additional year of coursework, 500 more hours of practicum, and a doubling in size of the thesis/dissertation.

In AW's first year of the program, I had presented a seminar on some basic principles of mindfulness, and when he came to me to discuss his (then) master thesis research, he was interested in doing something about mindfulness interventions with golfers. That sounded okay to me, and he agreed (somewhat reluctantly) to take the eight-week mindfulness-based stress-reduction course that Kabat-Zinn (1982) had established in the late 1970s. I suggested to AW that if he were to use mindfulness with golf clients or research participants, then he probably needed to establish his own mindful practice, and if he upgraded to a doctoral degree then here was a path to doubling the size of his thesis/dissertation. He could write an autoethnographic study of himself going through the process of becoming a mindful practitioner to accompany his case study in mindfulness for a golfer. He then agreed to something he was not prepared to do (at that time). As he wrote: "My resistance to self-disclosure has made writing autoethnography incredibly challenging. My supervisor warned me that if I wasn't happy to get naked for my autoethnography, then I at least needed to get down to my 'jockey shorts'" (Waterson, 2015, p. 73). AW ran away from that challenge for over 18 months, but came back and completed his dissertation and is on his way to becoming an exemplary mindful practitioner.

The meta-supervisee's client. We will call him Fred. He is about 15 years older than AW, but he initially followed a similar educational path as AW. He completed his four years of psychology education and was in the process of completing his last year of the master of applied psychology in the same program AW had begun three years previously before upgrading to a doctoral degree. AW had been registered as a psychologist long enough to qualify as a registered supervisor of other psychologists, and supervising Fred fit neatly into AW's doctoral-level practicum demands. He could count his time with Fred as part of his total 1,500 hours for his doctoral degree. When Fred was seeing AW for supervision he had placements with an under-18 boys' field hockey team and also a rugby team. AW supervised only his work with the field hockey team.

Fred was extremely keen to become a sport psychologist. The motivations to become a practitioner were, for Fred, complex, multi-layered, muddied, and at times internally inconsistent. In other words, Fred was just like most other students entering the profession. One need that set Fred out a bit more than many other students was a nearly desperate desire to be loved and appreciated for the *gifts* he could bring to athletes and coaches. Fred also had a long history of working as a case manager in public sector organizations. He had a strong orientation to a "here's-your-problem-and-here's-how-to-fix-it" mode of operation. Fred also had a fairly robust sense of entitlement, which may have been compensation for his doubts about his worthiness of being loved. I hoped that Fred and AW would learn a lot from each other, but I knew there were going to be conflicts.

The Meta-Supervisor

My (M's) formal tertiary education in psychology began 45 years ago at the University of California, and after all this time with bachelor, master, and doctoral degrees in psychology, a year-long psychology internship in a prison, two years of formal training in psychodynamic psychotherapy, decades of mindfulness and other meditative practices (off and on; I am nothing if not inconsistent), study in neuropsychotherapy, working with performing artists and athletes from juniors to Olympians, and writing numerous articles and book chapters on supervision, I still feel like a fraud sometimes. But over the years I have gotten better at being okay with feeling fraudulent and incompetent. More easily than in my early career, I can notice when such harsh judgments rise and hook me into doubt and anxiety, and then watch them fall and fade away. My internal critic sets such unpleasant traps for me, and I can usually recognize (sometimes later rather than sooner) that they are, like many other judgments I make, *empty*, or at least of dubious reality.

My multiple roles with AW. It is probably more the rule than the exception that academics teaching and supervising students in professional psychology degree programs end up in multiple roles with students in training. In this case, I was AW's seminar leader/ instructor for four different classes, his principal doctoral dissertation advisor, his practicum placement supervisor for almost 500 hours of his applied work in the field, his program coordinator, and finally, his meta-supervisor. Those are a lot of hats to wear, and the roles (and hats) can get a little blurry at times and even begin to look like other hats that should not be donned. For example, in our psychodynamic supervision of AW's practica, occasionally the conversations would drift and begin to sound like psychotherapy. Such blurring and drifting are inevitable, but can be managed by mindful attention to the paths being taken. When sliding from supervision to psychotherapy, we would both often stop and acknowledge that we were on a path that AW should take with his psychotherapist and that we needed to take the material that had come up and look at it from the perspective of how it might influence his work with his clients, and not examine the sources or ontogenetic history behind AW's concerns (material to explore in therapy). AW and I used the metaphor of hats for the different roles we had with each other, and sometimes AW would open a meeting with, "I need you to put on your program coordinator hat right now because I have to talk about some issues and problems with some other instructors." It takes a certain amount of vigilance to keep multiple roles in check, but I think AW and I did a fairly good job of compartmentalizing (or "hatting") our interactions.

APPROACH/PHILOSOPHY

A Three-Pronged Approach

There are myriad approaches to supervision and meta-supervision. Each contains nuances and subtleties that differentiate it from others, but there are some consistencies as well. As we described above, the quality of the supervisory relationship is central in moving the work forward. A second key concept foundational to effective supervision and meta-supervision might be termed *awareness*. Being aware of subtle and more obvious characteristics and patterns of behavior that interfere with the supervisory process brings about the ability to make course corrections and move the work forward. Although Rogerian and human-centered approaches enhance one's level of awareness, the means tend to be relatively non-directive. We have found a three-pronged approach to be helpful in directly navigating the sometimes treacherous paths toward awareness or enlightened supervision. Drawing from psychodynamic perspectives, Buddhist philosophy, and recent developments in interpersonal neurobiology can be helpful in this regard. Each contains tools and processes designed to increase awareness and refine the attunement between individuals.

Psychodynamic Supervision

Psychodynamic supervision emphasizes those largely pre- and unconscious drives, motives, and conflicts that ebb and flow in interpersonal relationships. This type of supervision may take a supervisor-in-training-centered theme where the meta-supervisor guides the supervisor-in-training toward a better understanding of the dynamic contents and processes of the supervisory experience. Psychodynamic meta-supervision can also take on a supervisory matrix-centered theme in which the relationship dynamics between the meta-supervisor and supervisor in training are at the core. Regardless of the theme, working to identify those transferences, countertransferences, ego-defense mechanisms, and affective reactions that influence the nature and quality of supervision is central to psychodynamic meta-supervision. Using traditional dynamic techniques such as free association, reflection, interpretation, and so forth augment the supervisor-in-training's level of awareness. As supervisors-in-training become more consciously aware of these dynamic factors, they can bring them to the forefront and work them through.

Buddhist Philosophy

Buddhist approaches provide a contemplative framework for meta-supervisors to present, listen to, and advise supervisors-in-training in a compassionate, nonjudgmental fashion (Rabin & Walker, 1987). Various strategies may be employed to quiet distractions and be present with the circumstances at hand. Meditation, chanting, controlled breathing, and other mindfulness-building exercises may be adjunct activities outside meta-supervision sessions. Inherent in Buddhist ideology is the belief that life and worthwhile pursuits are processes rather than accomplishments. One is continually becoming a competent and adept meta-supervisor or supervisor-in-training, necessitating the presence of a guide or advisor throughout the lifespan. Just as Buddha was a great teacher, the meta-supervisor becomes a mentor and a guide for the supervisor-in-training to gain (relative) professional enlightenment and insight, not through lectures or direct instruction, but through paths of self-discovery and insight. One of the goals of the Eightfold Path of the Fourth Noble Truth of Buddhism is for the individual to attain (at least occasionally) a state of egolessness or *no-self*. In more Western terms, the extent to which meta-supervisees can drop their egos, the more likely they will connect deeply with supervisees (and clients) and realize the fundamental condition of universal inter-relatedness. Another path to realizing relatedness is the growing field of interpersonal neurobiology.

Interpersonal Neurobiology (and Talking about Brains)

Over the past decade, attention has been turning to neurobiological approaches to counseling and therapy (e.g., Rossouw, 2014). Understanding the social brain can also be helpful in the supervisory process. Contrary to what some practitioners may believe, useful analogies and insights can be gleaned from basic levels of brain knowledge. For example, Siegel (2012) recommends using a model of the brain fashioned from the human hand as a simple tool for understanding neurobiological processes. With the palm facing one's face, folding the thumb across the palm and then bringing the fingers down over the thumb completes the model. In this position, the wrist represents the flow of sensory information from the spinal cord; the thumb becomes the primitive limbic structures; the palm of the hand is the collection of nuclei that receive information from the body, and the fingers are the neo-cortex, the thinking, reasoning, and social portion of the brain. Being present and attuned in relationships depends on input from mirror neurons (Iacoboni, 2008) and other frontal and prefrontal circuits.

Having a simple conceptual hand model might help supervisors-in-training understand underlying neurological operations in social settings. As long as the fingers are wrapped around the thumb, the prefrontal cortex exerts regulatory control over the primal defensive impulses of the limbic system (fight, flee, freeze). Reason overrides reactions, and brain centers for higher cognition and interpersonal empathy (Iacoboni, 2008) flourish. In those moments where prefrontal regulation is limited, limbic structures can exert their alarmist influence without restraint. Social circuits shut down; interpersonal presence and awareness diminishes;

resonance between people fades, and the supervisory process may grind to a halt. Something as simple as the behavioral and visual cues of mindfully wrapping the fingers around the thumb can serve as a signal for meta-supervisees to activate cortical structures in service of down-regulating limbic system reactivity. The epiphenomena (i.e., mental states as products of brain activity) of interpersonal presence, attunement, and resonance with others (e.g., supervisees) are dependent on the integration and communication of the different levels of the brain. When information flows freely up and down the levels of the brain, then the possibilities of connecting with others increases. When there are blockages and limbic responses dominate, then we may move toward avoidance, protection, and withdrawal. Such basic knowledge of brain functions can help meta-supervisees recognize when they are moving away from, rather than toward, the supervisees in their care.

PREPARATION/PLANNING

AW took four years to complete his three-year doctoral degree. Such stretching of time to complete is common in many professional degrees in Australia because such degrees are usually jam-packed with time-consuming requirements. Most students also need to work to support themselves during training. AW did not enter meta-supervision until his fourth year, and I (M) think of his first three years as preparation (coursework, practica, dissertation) for his initial foray into supervision training. His third year, however, was probably the most significant, in terms of preparation for psychodynamic and Buddhist philosophical meta-supervision, in that he completed advanced doctoral-level coursework in supervision (e.g., Andersen, 2012), psychoanalysis and Buddhism (e.g., Epstein, 1995), mindfulness (e.g., Siegel, 2012), and the neuroscience of psychotherapy (e.g., Cozolino, 2010).

The Meta-Supervision Intake

The intake for meta-supervision with AW looked and sounded much like supervision intakes my colleagues and I have described before (e.g., Andersen, 2012). Similar to beginning other supervision relationships, our meta-supervision intake began with me asking AW, "Well, what would you like to accomplish in our meta-supervision relationship?" From the get-go, meta-supervision is meta-supervisee centered, but in this case, because I already knew of AW's growing interest in psychodynamic modes of operation, I colored my first question with a focus on our professional and interpersonal relationship. AW discussed a professional tension that he wanted help with as a supervisor. In his autoethnography (Waterson, 2015) he wrote:

> In supervision I discovered that I have two different psychologist personas: the "nice" psychologist and the "good" psychologist. The nice psychologist is a problem solver. The nice psychologist sees his brothers in his clients and wants to fix their problems. He is an eight-year-old who would rather be teased ... than have either of his brothers feel shame. The nice psychologist has compassion for others and is protective, and although this is a positive trait for building strong therapeutic relationships, it can also be a problem. The nice psychologist tries so hard to protect others that he can rob clients of the opportunity to build their own resilience and coping skills. The benefit of being the nice psychologist is that helping my clients avoid painful emotions also reduces my guilt. Countless times as a psychologist I have felt tremendously guilty that I haven't had to manage the challenging circumstances that others have faced. When I feel like I am *fixing* as a psychologist, I can allay my guilt. Unfortunately, this fixing is not always beneficial for my clients. The "good" (or maybe *good enough*) psychologist is a work in progress. When I am practicing as the good psychologist, I continue to provide empathy and genuine concern for my clients. I am still the nice psychologist, but I am measured.

I notice my counter-transferences about wanting to save my brothers, and I regulate my need to reduce my own guilt. As a good psychologist I let the client sit in all the awful feelings, and I make this choice for the good of the client.

(p. 78)

This tension between the good and the nice psychologist morphed into a different kind of problem in AW's supervision of him. The nice supervisor would let some of Fred's questionable choices and behaviors slide and not confront Fred, which led to frustrations and anger aimed at both Fred and himself. AW and I agreed to work on helping him manage his two personas better for the ultimate benefit of Fred as a psychologist and for the health, safety, and well-being of Fred's athlete clients. We also agreed to a dynamic examination of his relationship (e.g., countertransferences) with Fred and all its frustrations, disappointments, conflicts, Ah Ha! moments, progress, pride, and shame. We also agreed to dip into the dynamics of our relationship with our transferences and countertransferences to each other. I use the word *dip* here because AW was still somewhat anxious about exploring our intra- and interpersonal spaces within meta-supervision, and to manage his anxieties about such deeply personal excavations we needed to take things slowly. In AW's (Waterson, 2015) early words (when we first started regular supervision) about not going too deeply, we would engage in "psychodynamic [meta] supervision for dummies" (p. 114). And, of course, all of our supervision processes would occur within an ever-present atmosphere of mindfulness and neurobiological awareness.

Agreement on Ground Rules and Creating the Nonjudgmental Space

A central ground rule of psychodynamic psychotherapy, supervision, and meta-supervision is that the clients, supervisees, or meta-supervisees make every effort to say whatever pops into their hearts, or heads, or somatically in their bodies, regardless of how silly, embarrassing, shameful, apparently unrelated, or irrelevant those emerging feelings or thoughts seem. The effort is to try not to censor, because whatever arises in the course of treatment or supervision probably has something to say of importance. But we all censor; no one ever reveals everything that is happening. The agreement, in the last recorded words of the Buddha, is to "do your best."

The other major ground rule, or understanding, is that the environment where meta-supervision takes place is a nonjudgmental space. AW knew that ideally our work together would be a place of nonjudgment, care, authenticity, compassion, and love, but ideals are just that, *ideals*, which will not ever be fully reached. Judgment will come marching in, defenestrating our mindful awareness, activating defensive limbic brain structures, and hooking us into unhappiness. We agreed that when harsh judgments raised their hydra-like heads we would attempt to sit back and watch them writhe and hiss and squirm so we could better understand their sources and realize their hurtful but ultimately insubstantial and empty reality.

SUPERVISION PROCESS/EXPERIENCE

Sharing Our Experiences: The Story of AW and M

Just before embarking on his new role as a supervisor, AW (Waterson, 2014) wrote, in a reflective piece as part of his coursework in supervision and mindfulness, the following:

As I approach a new phase in my career, becoming a supervisor, I am feeling more confident than I have in previous transitional phases. When I began seeing clients I experienced the normal, but anxiety provoking, need to be a perfect psychologist. Similarly, when I arrived back at university I experienced anxiety around my ability to demonstrate to my new classmates that I am a competent psychologist. As I prepare to work with my first supervisees … I don't feel the same pressure to be perfect. I am confident in my ability to help guide new psychologists through their initial experiences with clients. During my time as a neophyte supervisor I expect that I will make mistakes, and that I won't have all the answers for my supervisee. The realization that others are less critical of me than I am of myself has developed through my own practice of mindfulness. It is through mindfulness that I have realized that I expect to be perfect in many aspects of my life, and that my default state is to ruminate about mistakes that I have made. When I begin supervising a student I will feel incompetent, out of my depth, and like a fraud. The difference now is that I am confident that I can sit with this feeling. I know that I can feel incompetent and be a good supervisor at the same time.

(pp. 6–7)

AW seemed to be sitting in a salubrious and (mostly) nonjudgmental space to begin his first forays into helping student psychologists upon their new, and often anxiety provoking, paths.

The Messiness of Intersecting Histories and Multiple Roles

And here is where it all starts to get really messy. Before supervising Fred, AW had completed a one-year placement with the same boys' hockey team that Fred was now servicing. AW had done excellent work with the team, establishing solid working relationships with both the coaches and the boys. AW, of course, had strong personal investments with the team and the work he had done. Passing the baton to Fred carried with it both positive and problematic elements. On the positive side, AW had an intimate understanding of the team's dynamics and the personalities involved, so he could help Fred navigate through the complex psychosocial environment. On the problematic side, AW's investments might get in the way of helping Fred find his own path rather than subtly being pushed to continue in AW's footsteps. The messiness continues in that I was Fred's course coordinator, and I was also his past and current instructor with knowledge of his contributions to classroom discussions and his performances in role plays. At the same time AW was supervising Fred's placement with the hockey team, I was also Fred's supervisor for his work with rugby. This situation meant that I was not a naive and disinterested party when it came to Fred's work. My prejudices and biases (and judgments) about Fred would need to be held in check (sometimes not successfully) so that my experiences would not pollute AW's interactions with Fred and his meta-supervision with me. As mentioned earlier, intersecting roles and histories are unavoidable in the tertiary education of psychologists, but the intersecting (and colliding) worlds of Fred, AW, and me were some of the most convoluted I had ever encountered.

There's Something about Fred

Almost immediately, AW ran into some frustrations with Fred. For example, in their first formal supervision session after the initial intake, Fred was ten minutes late to his appointment with AW, and he hadn't called ahead of time to let AW know he was running behind. The apology for being late seemed, to AW, to be perfunctory and not quite sincere. In meta-supervision, AW said that he mentioned to Fred that it was "okay." But it wasn't okay. AW told me that he became activated and angry with what he perceived to be Fred's unprofessionalism. I am sure AW was recalling what I had said a few times in his classes about tardiness. My harsh spiel goes something like this: "To be late to an appointment (or to class) is both narcissistic and rude. It communicates to the other that, 'My time is more important than your time.' It is unprofessional in the highest degree." I give students the example:

If you had an appointment with the head coach of an Olympic team, you would never be late. That professional appointment is not any different than the appointments you have to attend class or supervision sessions. Punctuality and preparedness for meetings speak to your level of professionalism. Please make sure they speak well.

This pattern of Fred doing (or not doing) something that activated AW, and AW suppressing his anger in supervision and not responding to Fred to help him realize what was happening, would emerge again and again. In meta-supervision, AW and I talked about his hesitancy to confront Fred, his suppressed anger, and how it all might be connected to the tension between his "nice" psychologist (now supervisor) and his "good" psychologist. The most dramatic example of Fred reporting something in supervision and AW flying into a suppressed rage occurred around session six or seven. Fred talked about going on a weekend training camp, an hour or so away from the usual practice venue. In the evening, after the activities of the day, and after the boys had gone to bed, the coaches invited Fred to go out drinking with them. Fred reported that he had stayed out drinking until 1:00 am with the coaches. He thought it had been a great experience and that he felt it had helped connect him with the coaches. He also added that he thought it was okay because he could "hold his liquor." Inside, on hearing this story, AW was going ballistic, but what he came up with in response to Fred's story was: "You might want to rethink going out drinking with the coaches until so late." Fred's response was, "Okay, but I didn't get drunk, and it seemed like a way to become part of the team." For AW, he was hooked into anger and amygdala activation; his mindful attunement had gone walkabout, and the Buddha of Compassion was taking sick leave. On various metaphorical and neurobiological levels, AW had exited the room, and the safe, nonjudgmental, interpersonal space had gone cold.

AW left it at that, but when he arrived for meta-supervision, he was incensed and ready to beat Fred severely about the head and shoulders, and also to beat himself up for not confronting his supervisee. When AW related this story to me, I responded with,

> Okay, you seem quite activated right now. Let's look at that response. Is this about Fred's behavior, or is there more involved here? I certainly agree that staying out late and drinking with coaches is seriously problematic on several levels, but let's see if there is more.

AW was getting better at self-reflection, and after a pause he said,

> I think it is also about me in that the team is my baby, and I don't want someone else coming in and messing up all the good things I did. So I am pissed off that Fred is trampling on MY stuff, and then I think the coaches and players are eventually going to think "Andrew sure let us down with this new guy," and so I have disappointed them.

If we had had an fMRI of AW then, his right prefrontal cortex would have lit up the screen. I said: "That's good! Well, not good that you feel this way, but good that you can see that your responses are all wrapped in your history with the team and with Fred." I added: "Is there anyone else you are disappointing?" This question is designed to get at current feelings and their connections with past histories of shame circuits being activated. AW hung his head and said, "Yeah, of course. It's you. I think you will think I am a shit supervisor, and I let you down. I know that's stupid, but there it is."

Here, AW and I are moving to the heart of psychodynamic meta-supervision, and that is the relationship between him and me. His countertransferential rage at Fred, and transferential shame at disappointing me are fueling his discombobulated state. My countertransference to AW kicks in big time as the soothing protective big brother, and I move into comforting him and also bringing him mindfully back to the present reality of meta-supervision because he has been hooked into amygdala activation that could use some cortical (using language and re-storying his experience) downregulation. I begin with a story about AW and me, and I modeled curiosity.

> Isn't it fascinating. You have all the evidence in the world from over three years of working together with me that whatever you bring to our interactions that I will refrain from judgment, that I will be interested in anything shameful you have to say, and that I will make every effort to hold your stuff in loving care, and yet here we are stuck with disappointing someone who is really hard to disappoint. I think you are actually disappointing someone else, because it is almost certainly not me. It is like someone else has walked into the room unannounced and unrecognized, but still wagging his (or her) finger at you. I am not sure who that transferential object is and what happened with him or her, and that exploration is probably for your therapy, but let's try to mindfully come back into the room, right here, right now, and see that there are only the two of us here, and see if we can let the shame know that he has been noticed, and it is time for him to fade.

My big-brother (or big-daddy) countertransferential responses to clients, students, supervisees, and meta-supervisees pop up all the time, and my actions to comfort and soothe are sometimes premature, and I need to keep reminding myself that soothing others' anxieties is also soothing mine and when "fixing" my distress in the presence of their distress I am jumping the gun, and what I really should be doing is mindfully sitting with their and my discomforts. It's the way we *caretaker selves* are built.

In AW's next supervision session with Fred, he became directive right at the beginning and told Fred the story of his anger and activation about drinking with the coaches and how he should have told Fred what was happening for him. Fred initially was taken aback and could not see the harm in going out with the coaches, and that his decision to do so was a rational choice in service of building better relationships. Fred's defensiveness activated AW all over again, and then he laid down the law. He said something like:

> Here it is Fred. This is what is going to happen. If you get invited out for drinks with the coaches, go ahead and go, but you are going to order one beer, nurse it for 30 or so minutes, and then you are going to leave.

AW went on to explain all the pitfalls of staying out late and drinking with the people one is serving. In the end, Fred actually *got* what the problems were.

AW would become activated over things Fred did and said many times during supervision. AW was getting frustrated that he kept falling into the unmindful and uncompassionate trap of anger. Once developed and refined through experience, neural pathways primed for defensive patterns of behavior (fight, flee, or freeze) become easily triggered, and AW's anger reactivity had an extensive history of long-term potentiation.

I supervised Fred for his rugby placement, and I could easily empathize with AW. One day in meta-supervision AW said: "I did it again; I got angry with Fred and just wanted to smack him." I think I surprised AW when I responded with: "Yeah, I supervise his rugby placement, and there are days when I just want to smack him too." A meta-supervisor modeling that the supervisee's actions also hook him and that he regresses to petulant anger can help meta-supervisees feel not so alone in their frustrations with themselves and their supervisees. We all get caught up at times by regressive and countertransferential amygdala activations. The Buddha of Compassion leaves the room, and the seven-year-old child in us wants to start yelling or throwing things. Over time, AW became much kinder to his seven-year-old child when he appeared in the room. All in all, AW and Fred learned heaps from each other even though a lot of that learning was painful.

One way to help counteract many of our activations (e.g., anger, shame, embarrassment) that crop up in supervision and meta-supervision is to invite the Buddha of Compassion back into the room and ask what he would be thinking and feeling right now. In contrast to AW (and me) getting angry at Fred, the Buddha of Compassion would ask such questions as: "I wonder what happened to Fred, and who wounded him so much, that he desperately needs to be loved and accepted and valued?" and "I wonder what I can do to soothe the hurt child who was probably told his contributions were not worthy?" Curiosity, compassion, and love: it's a hard combination to beat.

Not Quite Termination

AW finished his supervision with Fred and his meta-supervision with me, but he and I were not really through yet. There was still the issue of completing his doctoral dissertation, some small parts of which you have read in this chapter. He has competed his dissertation, and our relationship keeps evolving. Right now, we are colleagues working together to get some publications from his thesis, and he is off on a big adventure working with Olympic teams in New Zealand.

As for Fred, I have one last story to tell. In our last supervision for his rugby work we were going over his experiences and what he had learned. Near the end of the meeting he said:

> I have something I want to tell you that happened a couple days ago. I think I had an epiphany. I had just left a dinner with some of the other students, and several were complaining that they did not know enough to go out in the world and be sport psychologists. They were complaining that the program didn't teach us enough. I got caught up in all the bitching, and was thinking, "Yeah, I didn't get all I needed. I need more practice in doing relaxation. I really don't know how to do imagery well yet. My motivational interviewing skills are crap," and so forth. And then it struck me as I was walking across a street that all that doesn't really matter so much. I have loads of time to learn more stuff. What really matters is that I have finally learned that the most important thing is to form loving, compassionate, and caring relationships with those athletes and coaches I work with, and the rest will eventually take care of itself. I just had to tell you that.

I was so touched at that point that I was a bit overwhelmed. I think I said: "Fred, that is wonderful." In the end, Fred had learned probably the biggest lesson of all, and he wanted to please his big daddy with his epiphanic story. He did just that. Fred is now well on his way.

REFLECTION

The types of yarns we have spun here are plentiful in the practice of applied SEPP. The opportunities to reap their full benefits often come from being mindful and open to those lessons hidden between subtext and dynamic processes. Having a background in psychodynamic supervision, Buddhist practices of mindfulness and acceptance, and interpersonal neurobiology can help meta-supervisees and meta-supervisors establish a safe, nonjudgmental, holding space filled with loving kindness where defensive transferences and countertransferences are readily recognized, and where physiological reactions are downshifted so authentic relationships can flourish, and work with clients (athletes, performers, supervisees) can progress.

As for the future of meta-supervision, we are both hopeful and pessimistic. There is a long history of paying limited attention to supervision in SEPP, but the previous book (i.e., Cremades & Tashman, 2014) to which this volume is a companion went a long way to bringing supervision to a needed visible position in the field. Meta-supervision, however, still seems like *a bridge too far*. We hope that, for the future development of SEPP, meta-supervision will eventually become a bridge that most professionals willingly and enthusiastically cross.

SUGGESTED READINGS

Andersen, M. B., Van Raalte, J. L., & Brewer, B. W. (2000). When applied sport psychology graduate students are impaired: Ethical and legal issues in supervision. *Journal of Applied Sport Psychology, 12,* 134–149. DOI: 10.1080/10413200008404219.

Lubker, J., & Andersen, M. B. (2014). Ethical issues in supervision: Client welfare, practitioner development, and professional gatekeeping. In J. C. Watson II & E. F. Etzel (Eds.), *Ethical issues in sport, exercise, and performance psychology* (pp. 151–162). Morgantown, WV: Fitness Information Technology.

Van Raalte, J. L., & Andersen, M. B. (2000). Supervision I: From models to doing. In M. B. Andersen (Ed.), *Doing sport psychology* (pp. 153–165). Champaign, IL: Human Kinetics.

REFLECTIVE QUESTIONS

1. If you were just starting to be trained in supervision of sport, exercise, and performance psychologists, what would you want in a meta-supervisor? For example, what sort of theoretical orientation would work for you? What sort of interpersonal attributes would you hope for in a meta-supervisor? Would you want instruction and guidance or something else, such as challenge and debate? Describe your ideal meta-supervisor.

2. Please fantasize that it is now ten years after your first training in supervision, and you have supervised many SEPP students and practitioners. You now wish to gain more knowledge about supervision. In this future fantasy scenario please respond to Question 1 from a position of a seasoned supervisor seeking advanced meta-supervision.

3. Resistance is a common feature of therapy, supervision, and meta-supervision. Resistance can come in many forms, such as resistance to learning, resistance to becoming vulnerable, resistance to powerful others, or resistance to self-examination. In what ways in your training as a sport, exercise, or performance psychologist have you been resistant? What are the origins of those resistances? If you have overcome your resistances, how did you do that?

4. Transference and countertransference are nearly universal phenomena, and they occur in both supervision and meta-supervision, and of course in psychotherapy and SEPP practice. What were some of your most profound transferences and countertransferences (both positive and negative) in your work with athletes and performers and in your supervision of your own or others' work? What are the sources of those transferences and countertransferences?

5. In counseling and clinical psychology, the subjects of supervision and meta-supervision are huge territories of inquiry, research, and debate. In the SEPP literature, maps of research and inquiry into supervision and meta-supervision are small countries, figuratively about the size of Monaco. Given that supervision is a core feature of training, why do you think attention has been so limited?

REFERENCES

Andersen, M. B. (2012). Supervision and mindfulness in sport and performance psychology. In S. M. Murphy (Ed.), *The Oxford handbook of sport and performance psychology* (pp. 725–737). New York, NY: Oxford University Press.

Barney, S. T., & Andersen, M. B. (2014a). Meta-supervision: Training practitioners to help others on their paths. In J. G. Cremades & L. S. Tashman (Eds.), *Becoming a sport, exercise, and performance psychology professional: A global perspective* (pp. 339–346). New York, NY: Routledge.

Barney, S. T., & Andersen, M. B. (2014b). Mindful supervision in sport and performance psychology: Building the quality of the supervisor–supervisee relationship. In Z. Knowles, D. Gilbourne, B. Copley, & L. Dugdill (Eds.), *Reflective practice in sport and exercise sciences: Contemporary issues* (pp. 147–159). London, England: Routledge.

Barney, S. T., Andersen, M. B., & Riggs, C. A. (1996). Supervision in sport psychology: Some recommendations for practicum training. *Journal of Applied Sport Psychology, 8*, 200–217. DOI: 10.1080/10413209608406477.

Cozolino, L. (2010). *The neuroscience of psychotherapy: Healing the social brain* (2nd ed.). New York, NY: Norton.

Cremades, J. G., & Tashman, L. S. (Eds.). (2014). *Becoming a sport, exercise, and performance psychology professional: A global perspective*. New York, NY: Routledge.

Epstein, M. (1995). *Thoughts without a thinker: Psychotherapy from a Buddhist perspective*. New York, NY: Basic Books.

Iacoboni, M. (2008). *Mirroring people*. New York, NY: Farrar, Straus, & Giroux.

Kabat-Zinn, J. (1982). An out-patient program in behavioral medicine for chronic pain patients based on the practice of mindfulness meditation: Theoretical considerations and preliminary results. *General Hospital Psychiatry, 4*, 33–47. DOI: 10.1016/0163-8343(82)90026-3.

Rabin, B., & Walker, R. (1987). A contemplative approach to clinical supervision. *Contemplative Psychotherapy, 4*, 135–149.

Roussow, P. J. (Ed.). (2014). *Neuropsychotherapy: Theoretical underpinnings and clinical applications*. Brisbane, QLD, Australia: Mediros.

Siegel, D. J. (2012). *The pocket guide to interpersonal neurobiology: An integrative handbook of the mind*. New York, NY: Norton.

Vosloo, J., Zakrajsek, R., & Grindley, E. (2014). From mentee to mentor: Considerations for the neophyte supervisor. In J. G. Cremades & L. S. Tashman (Eds.), *Becoming a sport, exercise, and performance psychology professional: A global perspective* (pp. 228–235). New York, NY: Routledge.

Waterson, A. K. (2014). Self-reflection: Supervision training & the neuroscience of psychotherapy. Unpublished manuscript available from the third author.

Waterson, A. K. (2015). Mindfulness, practitioner development, and golf: An autoethnography and a case study (unpublished doctoral dissertation). Victoria University, Melbourne, Australia. Retrieved from www.vu.edu.au/library.

Watson II, J. C., Zizzi, S. J., Etzel, E. F., & Lubker, J. R. (2004). Applied sport psychology supervision: A survey of students and professionals. *The Sport Psychologist, 18*, 415–429.

40 Incorporating Technology in Supervision

Using Interpersonal Process Recall to Enhance Reflective Practice

Lauren S. Tashman and J. Gualberto Cremades

Supervision provides an essential function in the professional development of sport, exercise, and performance psychology (SEPP) trainees in the applied setting (Vosloo, Zakrajsek, & Grindley, 2014). Andersen, Van Raalte, and Brewer (2000) stated:

> impaired sport psychology consultants, that is professionals and graduate students whose behavior, inadequate training, personal situations, or psychopathology are having a negative influence on the delivery of services, have the potential to do harm to the athlete-clients, damage their own professional standing, and bring disrepute to the field.
>
> (p. 134)

The supervisor has many roles and responsibilities in this process, including overseeing the experiential learning of the trainee (i.e., application of applied practice skills in real-world scenarios), evaluating the professional practice skills of the trainee and his/her suitability for the profession, assuring the trainee is engaging in ethical practice and meeting standards of competency, facilitating the trainee's professional development, and arguably most importantly, ensuring that the trainee is providing safe, effective services to his/her clients (Milne & James, 2000). Thus, ensuring that SEPP trainees receive effective supervision is essential not only for their own benefit, but also to protect their clients as well as the field.

There are many approaches, frameworks, and techniques that can be used in supervision. Further, advances in technology can provide a means for optimizing SEPP training and professional development (Tashman & Cremades, 2014). Incorporating technology into supervision must be done mindfully as it is not the technology that enhances the education and training, but rather how it is utilized that determines its effectiveness (Garrison & Akyol, 2009). Few examples exist for how to incorporate technology into supervision (e.g., Pitt et al., 2015; Van Raalte, Petitpas, Andersen, & Rizzo, 2016). Therefore, the aim of this chapter is to provide an additional example of incorporating technology into SEPP supervision and training.

BACKGROUND INFORMATION

Interpersonal process recall (IPR; Kagan, 1965) is a process-focused self-discovery learning technique used to access in-the-moment experiences of interpersonal interactions (Cashwell, 1994; Larsen, Flesaker, & Stege, 2008). It enables the exploration of particular moments rather than the elicitation of broad based generalizations (Larsen et al., 2008). The process entails reviewing a video recording of a particular experience or performance in order to illuminate one's internal processes (e.g., thoughts, feelings, behaviors, sensations) at the time of that experience. The video is paused at various points either by the individual whose performance was recorded or the IPR session facilitator in order to reflect on particular moments. If the facilitator initiates the reflection, he/she utilizes a prompt (e.g., what were you thinking at the time?, how did that make you feel?, what did you want him/her to tell you? what did you think he/she was feeling about you? anything going on there?) to elicit exploration of what was experienced in that moment refraining from commenting, providing feedback, asking leading questions, or asking why something was experienced. IPR can be used with individuals as well as in group settings (Kagan, 1965).

In order to effectively facilitate an IPR, Larsen et al. (2008) recommended being patient upon utilizing a recall prompt, allowing the individual some time to "engage in the complex task of remembering, reflecting, and ultimately articulating their thoughts" (p. 25). In addition, they provided several recommendations for framing IPR questions and conducting effective IPR sessions: (1) phrase questions in past tense to encourage clients to refrain from focusing on how they feel now while watching the video; (2) deemphasize content and focus more on process; (3) frame questions concisely and succinctly while maintaining a flexible conversational style; (4) outline potential questions in advance; (5) attend to nonverbal behavior during the IPR; (6) prepare oneself to work with heightened emotion and facilitate exploration of inner processes; (7) prepare oneself to focus on the individual rather than oneself (i.e., personal opinions and reactions); (8) understand that while both more and less reflective clients can benefit from IPR, this may impact the IPR experience; and (9) provide a debrief or wrap up at the end of the IPR (Larsen et al., 2008).

IPR is a method that can be used in sport by coaches, SEPP practitioners, and physical education instructors to provide a different approach to video feedback in which the athlete/client takes more of an active role and the coach/practitioner/teacher takes more of a passive role, rather than vice versa (e.g., Jambor & Weekes, 1995). Additionally, it can be used as a tool in supervision and training, allowing the trainee to direct the review and reflection on their service delivery experiences while the supervisor or a peer mentor facilitates and prompts that reflection. In a discussion on the use of IPR in counselor training, Cashwell (1994) proposed that this procedure helps trainees become more aware of the dynamics of the relationship between the counselor and the client. As a result of their stage of professional development, neophyte practitioners tend to be more focused on themselves (i.e., their own thought processes, how to proceed next, etc.) during sessions with clients. Therefore, as a result of their limited active listening skills, they may miss important verbal or nonverbal cues from the client and/or may not have enough time to process everything that occurs during a session. Thus, IPR allows the trainee practitioners to re-experience the session, reflecting on their experiences, approaches, and blind spots, as well as the potential experiences and thoughts of the client during the session. It helps trainees slow down the experience of the session, giving them the time needed to reflect on and articulate the varied aspects of their experiences during a client session (Larsen et al., 2008).

When including IPR in supervision, Cashwell (1994) proposed several additional recommendations; for example: (1) clearly emphasize the purpose and process of the recall session to the trainee; (2) create a non-threatening environment; (3) attend to nonverbal aspects of the trainee throughout the IPR session; and (4) facilitate the self-exploration of the trainee by only using relevant open-ended questions and recall leads, avoiding teaching, advising, or commenting about what the trainee did or could do differently during the recall session. In addition, it is important to bring the focus back to the experience at the time of the session when a trainee starts focusing on critiques, more broad generalizations, or memories of other stories related to the session (Larsen et al., 2008).

Clearly, the aim of conducting an IPR is to encourage reflection on one's experiences. It has been argued that reflective practice is an essential component of SEPP training and practice, enabling individuals to not only evaluate their ability to apply their knowledge, but also to enhance one's understanding of other influential aspects of service delivery, such as self-awareness, self-management, interpersonal skills, and professional practice skills (e.g., Anderson, Knowles, & Gilbourne, 2004; Cropley, Hanton, Miles, & Niven, 2010). As Anderson et al.

(2004) paraphrased, "in order to use the self as an effective instrument in practice, it is necessary to know, understand, and accept the self" (p. 189). Combining the use of IPR with additional methods of reflective practice can increase the depth and breadth of reflection (for reviews on various reflection frameworks see, for example, Anderson et al., 2004; Cropley, Miles, Hanton, & Anderson, 2007; Tashman & Cremades, 2016).

DESCRIPTION OF THE CASE

The case study in this chapter describes an assignment that a group of six second-year master's students participated in during the first of two practicum courses they were required to complete as part of their degree program. The purpose of this first practicum course was to provide the neophyte practitioners with initial service delivery experiences while receiving both supervision and peer mentoring. The class met once per week for three hours for 16 weeks, discussing various service delivery-related readings in the first hour and allowing for group supervision during the last two hours of the meeting. Both individual and direct supervision opportunities were available outside of class meetings.

APPROACH/PHILOSOPHY

The approach taken in the case study outlined in this chapter was grounded in several supervision models. First, Hart's (1982) developmental model indicates that supervisees progress through three stages during supervision. At first, the focus is on skill development, then personal growth, and finally integration of their applied practice skills and personal development. Second, Stoltenberg's (1981) developmental model of supervision outlines three levels of practitioner development that should be taken into consideration. In the first level, trainees have limited experience, and thus tend to be highly motivated yet at the same time experience high anxiety, lack confidence, fear being evaluated, and are highly self-focused. Ronnestad and Skovholt (1993) stated that an early neophyte trainee

> naturally lacks the competency to perform professionally and is generally painfully aware of it, even though much energy is invested in concealing it. The student is eagerly looking for ways to narrow the gap, to be able to perform well, and to do this as quickly as possible. There is an urgency and often an intensity in the quest to master the demands of meeting clients and interacting in a professional way.
>
> (pp. 396–397)

In the second level of Stoltenberg's (1981) developmental model, trainees typically experience fluctuating confidence and motivation, vacillate between autonomy and dependence, often resulting in resistance, and allow their moods and perceptions of competence to be affected by their perceived success with clients. In the third level, trainees are generally more stable and secure in their confidence and motivation, have begun to develop a sense of their theoretical framework and philosophy of practice, and exhibit the ability to effectively utilize themselves as a tool in the intervention process.

A third model utilized in the training method outlined in this chapter was a person-centered approach to supervision (Lambers, 2000). In this approach, just as in person-centered applied practice, it is assumed that the trainee has the capability to effectively develop himself/herself and the supervisor functions as a collaborator in this process rather than an expert. Finally, peer mentoring and supervision were also utilized. There are several models of peer supervision generally organized into three categories: (1) dyadic, in which peers take turns in consultation and/or supervision roles; (2) triadic, in which one supervisor works with two supervisees; and (3) group, in which a group of peers and/or supervisor participate in supervision together (for a review see Borders, 2012). Watson, Clement, Blom, and Grindley (2009) found that SEPP graduate students perceived many benefits of peer mentoring, including its informal nature in comparison to professional mentoring, the openness of the relationship, the ability of the peers to relate on a similar level, the ability to get other students' perspectives, and its influence in the building of social connections.

PREPARATION/PLANNING

In the second semester of the students' first year in the program, the students completed a performance enhancement course in which they: (1) learned about and practiced psychological skills training (e.g., working with clients on confidence, anxiety, goal-setting, imagery); (2) gained a foundation of knowledge related to applied SEPP professional practice (e.g., understanding and beginning to develop active listening and attending skills, providing services to individuals versus groups, conducting needs assessments and designing goal-driven, evidence-based interventions); (3) began reading about and engaging in reflective practice; and (4) observed second-year master's students and CC-AASP practitioners in their applied SEPP work. Some of the course activities and assignments they completed in preparation for their practicum experiences included, for example: case analyses, a reflective paper on potential challenging clients, an observation of a performance, development of imagery scripts and motivational videos, a reflective paper on their lessons learned in observing applied SEPP practice, and a case study assignment in which they designed and implemented a psychological skills training intervention for a classmate.

An additional preparatory assignment involved conducting an IPR with their case study client. To complete this task, students were first given several readings prior to coming to class so that they had an initial understanding of the purpose and process of an IPR session. In class, the IPR procedure was discussed and demonstrated. For example, one student volunteered to be videoed doing various soccer drills. Then, in the classroom, the professor conducted an IPR session with that student and subsequently allowed all the students to ask questions and practice using IPR prompts. To complete the assignment they submitted a video of the IPR session with their client as well as a reflection paper on their skills and experience with the procedure. The professor then provided feedback on their IPR skills (e.g., covering things such as their ability to describe the purpose and process of an IPR to the client, their use of recall prompts, their ability to stick to the prompts and not add any commentary, opinions, etc. during the IPR, their choice of points in the video to pause and ask the client to reflect, use of active listening skills, demonstration of attending skills, and their facilitation of a wrap-up at the end of the IPR).

SUPERVISION PROCESS/EXPERIENCE

The purpose of the IPR assignment outlined in Table 40.1 was to encourage the neophyte SEPP trainees to engage in several stages of reflection (both self- and other-directed) on their service delivery skills and abilities. This was the first time this multi-staged IPR process was used in the practicum course. The assignment was done twice throughout the practicum (i.e., first halfway through and second toward the end) in order to allow the supervisor to provide both a formative and summative evaluation of the trainees' service delivery skills. Each time, the process was completed as outlined in Table 40.1.

Table 40.1 Multi-Staged IPR Supervision Process

	Task	Description
1	Client Session	Each trainee video-taped a session with one of his/her clients.
2	Peer-Mentored IPR	Each trainee had a session with a peer mentor from the class who conducted an IPR on his/her client session, helping the trainee to reflect on his/her service delivery skills, approach, etc. (Note: students took turns in the role of peer mentor conducting an IPR versus SEPP practitioner participating in an IPR.)
3	Reflection	Each trainee wrote a reflective paper analyzing lessons learned during the IPR about oneself and one's service delivery skills.
4	Group Supervision	The supervisor facilitated a group supervision session in which segments from trainee client videos were reviewed while one's peers and supervisor encouraged the student to elicit feedback and reflect further.
5	Supervisor Feedback	The supervisor reviewed each trainee's client video and read each reflection paper, providing feedback on their SEPP skills, insights related to effective applied practice, and encouraging more in-depth reflection.
6	Individual Supervision	The supervisor had individual supervision meetings with each student, discussing lessons learned and the IPR experience. Both the supervisor and trainee explore in depth each one of the lessons learned. The supervisor is now allowed to discuss his/her feedback and interpretation of events and responses.

REFLECTION

This was the first time this process was utilized during the supervision provided in the practicum. Consequently, there were several considerations and modifications apparent that could improve the use of this procedure. The following reflections should be considered in order to optimize the use of IPR in supervision:

- *Consideration and clarification of an appropriate client session.* Given the unique nature of SEPP applied practice, student trainees in the practicum course were engaged in varying types of service delivery experiences (e.g., working with individuals versus groups, varying types and levels of clients, in-office versus outside-of-office client meetings, etc.). Given the unique nature of SEPP applied practice, use of the IPR technique was appropriate for all of the trainees' experiences. However, more communication and collaboration with the trainees regarding the purpose and process of the assignment would have made the process smoother.
- *Clarity of purpose and goals.* As mentioned above, the supervisor reflected that it would have been helpful to ensure that the purpose of utilizing this approach in supervision was effectively discussed prior to the assignment and that goals were clarified for the trainees. Consideration of both the supervisees' and supervisor's parts regarding the goals for the IPR might aid in optimizing the use of this technique (e.g., What skills does the supervisor want the supervisee to self-reflect on? Are there particular challenges that the supervisee is experiencing that he/she would like feedback from the supervisor on?).
- *Assure that trainees review sessions in a timely manner.* As stated earlier in the chapter, the purpose of IPR is to help trainees reflect on their in-the-moment experiences with clients. Thus, the IPR needs to be conducted in a timely manner (i.e., within 48 hours) so that trainees can vividly and accurately remember what they were experiencing at the time (Tashman & Cremades, 2014).
- *Supervisor instruction regarding preparation of videos for IPR.* Given the purpose and process of this technique, IPRs can be very time consuming. According to Larsen et al. (2008), a 50-minute client session can result in a two- to three-hour IPR. Thus, due to time constraints and mental fatigue, Cashwell (1994) suggested that videos be reviewed

prior to the IPR as it may not be possible to review an entire client session. Therefore, supervisors need to consider supervision goals and provide guidance on this aspect of the process. For example, trainees can be required to review an entire session with the advanced knowledge that this may require a lengthy period of time; trainees can preview their videos prior to the IPR selecting particular parts of the video to use; or supervisors can preview the videos, selecting particular sections. In making this decision, it is important to consider the benefits and drawbacks of supervisors or trainees preselecting sections of videos. For example, this may result in a biased approach to the IPR session in which trainees can intentionally or unintentionally avoid selecting particular aspects of their sessions, and/or the potential trainees' reflections can be limited if an entire session is not reviewed.

- *Assure working and effective technology.* This is an important consideration initially for videoing client sessions, considering factors such as camera placement, working audio, video equipment is on and recording, and individuals can be clearly seen throughout the entire session. Additionally, this is an important consideration for the IPR sessions, bearing in mind factors such as limiting distractions (e.g., if students are using their laptops to review videos, making sure they have turned off any chat or email features, the IPR sessions are being conducted in appropriate locations), protection of confidentiality of clients, and preparation of technology (e.g., playback of videos is functioning properly).

- *Focus on both process and content.* Supervision is generally focused on content (i.e., what the trainee is doing or not doing with clients and why). However, the aim of IPR is to focus on process, affording trainees the opportunity to reflect on what they were experiencing at various points throughout the session with the client. It is recommended that IPR utilized in SEPP supervision and training focus on both process and content in order to result in the greatest professional development gains for trainees. Thus, both supervisors and trainees need to remember to consider both elements when conducting and debriefing IPR sessions.

- *Provide support and encouragement to trainees.* As mentioned in the previous point, supervision tends to be more focused on trainees' service delivery skills. As such, trainees are more familiar and comfortable with focusing on content (Larsen et al., 2008). Consequently, it is important for the supervisor to support trainees with their openness and willingness to be vulnerable in order to consider and discuss the process aspects of their service delivery experiences. In addition, this is an important discussion to have with trainees prior to the peer-conducted IPR sessions to ensure that peer mentors facilitate this type of environment as well.

- *Effective instruction and practice on IPR technique.* In order for the IPR assignment to be most influential in helping trainees to reflect on and evaluate their service delivery skills, thereby enabling quality professional development, it is important for supervisors to provide effective instruction and multiple opportunities for practice of the IPR technique. For example, provide readings and resources on the technique, demonstrate and model the IPR procedure, and have trainees role play the process.

- *Assignment of peer mentors.* As can naturally happen in any group, bonds and friendships get formed by trainees in group supervision. While this has many advantages (e.g., the facilitation of relationships conducive to deeper reflection and greater professional development), it can also have various disadvantages (e.g., limited cohesion among the whole group, trainees always working with the same peers). Therefore, it is recommended that the supervisor assigns peer mentors for the IPR in order to encourage the entire group of trainees to form a more cohesive bond with each other, enabling them to learn from a variety of perspectives.

- *Pre-selection of segments to review during group supervision.* As was discussed above, the IPR process can be time consuming. While there were two hours set aside each class meeting for supervision, this was not enough time to review complete client sessions for all trainees. In this particular case, the first time this assignment was conducted during the practicum, it was only possible to review the first few minutes of each trainee's client session. Thus, in order to allow for a more comprehensive and varied exploration of the trainees' experiences, they were instructed to pre-select segments of their client sessions for the next IPR. This resulted in the trainees coming into the supervision meeting prepared to review particular aspects of their experiences with clients (e.g., challenges they were having, questions they had, and/or aspects of their approach that they wanted feedback or guidance on). Consideration of how much instruction supervisors should provide to trainees regarding how to select segments of the videos should be based on several factors, such as the particular group of supervisees, their stage(s) of professional development, and the goals of supervision.

- *Supervisor-led IPR.* Prior to individually meeting with the trainees and providing them with written feedback after watching their videos, supervisors could conduct an IPR session with each one of the trainees. This enables an additional layer of reflection, allowing the supervisor to further encourage trainees to examine content- and process-related aspects of their client sessions.

- *Optimizing peer feedback during group supervision.* Along with a lack of familiarity and comfort in focusing on process elements of service delivery, the graduate trainees were also challenged with knowing how to effectively give and receive feedback and constructive criticism to their peers. Thus, the supervisor found it was necessary to provide a great deal of guidance and modeling in this area, particularly given the developmental level of these supervisees (Borders, 2012). According to Tietze (2012), trust, confidence, support, and appreciation are essential components of effective peer supervision. Therefore, approaching the group as though they were a team and incorporating various task and social cohesion activities proved useful to enhancing group supervision meetings.

- *Utilize a structured reflection framework.* It is recommended that a structured reflection framework be provided for both the written reflection paper (e.g., Anderson et al., 2004), as well as to aid students in preparing for group supervision meetings (e.g., Hutter, Oldenhof-Veldman, & Oudejans, 2014).

- *Modify timing of reflection.* In this particular case, student trainees were asked to complete their written reflections after the IPR session, prior to the group supervision meeting. However, during the group supervision meeting many other aspects of their experiences and service delivery processes in general were discussed. Thus, having trainees complete the written reflection after the group supervision meeting, or allowing students to add an additional entry to the reflection post-meeting, may have some additional benefits to helping students learn from the experience.

- *Consider including the client.* Larsen et al. (2008) proposed that including both trainee and client in the IPR session may provide additional insight and points of reflection for trainees, providing them with insight into the client's perspective. Thus, if possible, it is recommended that some IPR sessions with trainees include the client. This may be particularly beneficial to trainees in the first and second developmental stages.

In summary, IPR can be a very useful tool to incorporate into supervision and training in SEPP. It affords trainee practitioners the opportunity to reflect on their own thoughts/feelings during sessions, the challenges they experience, their behaviors and approaches, and the experiences of the client, as well as helps them learn how to build more effective client–practitioner relationships (Cashwell, 1994). Further, it enables the supervisor to more effectively facilitate professional development and uphold standards of applied practice by directly observing trainees' professional practice skills, avoiding an over-reliance on simply discussing cases (Townsend, Iannetta, & Preeston, 2002).

SUGGESTED READINGS

Barney, S. T., Andersen, M. B., & Riggs, C. A. (1996). Supervision in sport psychology: some recommendations for practicum training. *Journal of Applied Sport Psychology, 8,* 200–217.

Griffith, B. A., & Frieden, G. (2000). Counselor preparation: facilitating reflective thinking in counselor education. *Counselor Education and Supervision, 40,* 82–93.

Kagan, N. I., & Burke, J. B. (1976). *Influencing human interaction using interpersonal process recall: A student manual.* Houston, TX: University of Houston.

Kagan, N. I., & Kagan, H. (1991). Interpersonal process recall. In P. W. Dowrick (Ed.), *Practical guide to using video in the behavioral sciences* (pp. 221–230). Oxford: John Wiley.

Tashman, L. S., & Cremades, J. G. (2013). *Performance Enhancement Training Tool (PETT)* [Software]. Retrieved from http://peinnovate.com.

Tashman, L. S., & Tenenbaum, G. (2013). Sport psychology service delivery training: The value of an interactive, case-based approach to practitioner development. *Journal of Sport Psychology in Action, 4,* 71–85.

Yambor, J., & Thompson, M. (2014). A supervision model utilizing peer mentoring and consultation teams in the provision of applied sport psychology services. In J. G. Cremades & L. S. Tashman (Eds.), *Becoming a sport, exercise, and performance psychology professional: A global perspective* (pp. 285–292). New York, NY: Routledge.

REFLECTIVE QUESTIONS

1. Given the outlined purpose and process of IPR, what advantages and disadvantages are there for using this technique in supervision?
2. What advantages and disadvantages could there be in having a peer mentor conduct the IPR session with the trainee practitioner?
3. How might you alternatively have incorporated IPR into the supervision process/experience?
4. What alternative approaches to reflection could have been utilized in this case study assignment?
5. Given your reading of the chapter and case, how could you integrate the use of IPR and reflection into your supervision processes?

REFERENCES

Andersen, M. B., Van Raalte, J. L., & Brewer, B. W. (2000). When sport psychology consultants and graduate students are impaired: Ethical and legal issues in training and supervision. *Journal of Applied Sport Psychology, 12,* 134–150.

Anderson, A. G., Knowles, Z., & Gilbourne, D. (2004). Reflective practice for sport psychologists: concepts, models, practical implications, and thoughts on dissemination. *The Sport Psychologist, 18,* 188–203.

Borders, L. D. (2012). Dyadic, triadic, and group models of peer supervision/consultation: what are their components, and is there evidence of their effectiveness? *Clinical Psychologist, 16,* 59–71.

Cashwell, C. S. (1994). Interpersonal process recall. *ERIC Digest.*

Cropley, B., Hanton, S., Miles, A., & Niven, A. (2010). Exploring the relationship between effective and reflective practice in applied sport psychology. *The Sport Psychologist, 24,* 521–541.

Cropley, B., Miles, A., Hanton, S., & Anderson, A. (2007). Improving the delivery of applied sport psychology support through reflective practice. *The Sport Psychologist, 21,* 475–494.

Garrison, D. R., & Akyol, Z. (2009). Role of instructional technology in the transformation of higher education. *Journal of Computing in Higher Education, 21,* 19–30.

Hart, G. M. (1982). *The process of clinical supervision.* University Park, PA: University Park Press.

Hutter, R. I. V., Oldenhof-Veldman, T., & Oudejans, R. R. D. (2014). What trainee sport psychologists want to learn in supervision. *Psychology of Sport and Exercise.* DOI: 10.1016/j.psychsport.2014.08.003.

Jambor, E., & Weekes, E. M. (1995). Videotape feedback: make it more effective. *Journal of Physical Education, Recreation & Dance, 66,* 48–50.

Kagan, N. I. (1965). *IPR-interpersonal process recall: Stimulated recall by videotape. Exploring studies of counseling and teaching.* East Lansing, MI: Bureau of Educational Research.

Lambers, E. (2000). Supervision in person-centered therapy: Facilitating congruence. In E. Mearns & B. Thorne (Eds.), *Person-centered therapy today: New frontiers in theory and practice* (pp. 196–211). London: Sage.

Larsen, D., Flesaker, K., & Stege, R. (2008). Qualitative interviewing using interpersonal process recall: Investigating internal experiences during professional–client conversations. *International Journal of Qualitative Methods, 7*(1), 18–37.

Milne, D., & James, I. (2000). A systematic review of effective cognitive-behavioural supervision. *British Journal of Clinical Psychology, 39*, 111–127.

Pitt, T., Lindsay, P., Thomas, O., Bawden, M., Goodwill, S., & Hanton, S. (2015). A perspective on consultancy teams and technology in applied sport psychology. *Psychology of Sport and Exercise, 16*, 36–44.

Ronnestad, M. H., & Skovholt, T. M. (1993). Supervision of beginning and advanced graduate students of counseling and psychotherapy. *Journal of Counseling & Development, 71*, 396–405.

Stoltenberg, C. D. (1981). Approaching supervision from a developmental perspective: The counselor complexity model. *Journal of Counseling Psychology, 28*, 59–65.

Tashman, L. S., & Cremades, J. G. (2014). The wave of the future: Integrating technology into service delivery training. In J. G. Cremades & L. S. Tashman (Eds.), *Becoming a sport, exercise, and performance psychology professional: A global perspective* (pp. 347–353). New York, NY: Routledge.

Tashman, L. S., & Cremades, J. G. (2016). The need for case analysis and reflection in sport, exercise, and performance psychology. In J. G. Cremades & L. S. Tashman (Eds.), *Global practices and training in applied sport, exercise, and performance psychology: A case study approach.* New York, NY: Routledge.

Tietze, K. O. (2012). Conditions for peer group supervision within the group setting. Retrieved on August 15, 2015 from www.peer-supervision.com/Ebene2/voraus.html.

Townsend, M., Iannetta, L., & Preeston, M. H. (2002). Clinical supervision in practice: A survey of UK cognitive behavioural psychotherapists accredited by the BABCP. *Behavioural and Cognitive Psychotherapy, 30*, 485–500.

Van Raalte, J. L., Petitpas, A. J., Andersen, M. B., & Rizzo, J. (2016). Using technology in supervision and training. In J. G. Cremades & L. S. Tashman (Eds.), *Global practices and training in applied sport, exercise, and performance psychology: A case study approach.* New York, NY: Routledge.

Vosloo, J., Zakrajsek, R., & Grindley, E. (2014). From mentee to mentor: Considerations for the neophyte supervisor. In J. G. Cremades & L. S. Tashman (Eds.), *Becoming a sport, exercise, and performance psychology professional: A global perspective* (pp. 228–235). New York, NY: Routledge.

Watson, J. C., Clement, D., Blom, L. C., & Grindley, E. (2009). Mentoring: Processes and perceptions of sport and exercise psychology graduate students. *Journal of Applied Sport Psychology, 21*, 231–246.

41 Using Technology in Supervision and Training

Judy L. Van Raalte, Albert J. Petitpas, Mark B. Andersen, and Julia Rizzo

Although supervision is a key component of applied work in many fields, discussion of supervision in applied sport psychology did not begin until the mid-1990s (Andersen, Van Raalte, & Brewer, 1994; 2000; Watson, Zizzi, Etzel, & Lubker, 2004). In 2014, Cremades and Tashman published the edited book *Becoming a Sport, Exercise, and Performance Psychology Professional: A Global Perspective*, which included 16 chapters representing practitioners from four continents dealing directly with supervision of applied sport, exercise, and performance psychology. Over the course of two decades, the topic of supervision has grown from rare mention in the sport psychology literature to a solid stream of inquiry and discussion.

One aspect of supervision that has received little attention even in recent years is the role of technology in supervision and training. The focus of this chapter is on the use of technology in the supervision and training of applied sport psychology practitioners. We begin with a definition of supervision and a discussion of various technologies that can be used to enhance and facilitate supervision and training. Next, a case study is presented, which is followed by a discussion of the philosophical approach used and planning and preparation needed. The chapter concludes with suggested readings and review questions.

Applied sport psychology supervision is a relatively long-term interpersonal relationship that facilitates trainee self-knowledge and understanding of their strengths, weaknesses, and needs via a supervisor's supportive feedback and communication. The purpose of supervision is to ensure the care of athlete-clients. A secondary, but important purpose is the development of competent, knowledgeable, ethical practitioners (Van Raalte & Andersen, 2000).

BACKGROUND INFORMATION

The technology used in supervision includes tools such as one-way mirrors, video, online discussions, communication technologies, record-keeping software, and online survey software that can facilitate self-awareness and enhance the opportunity for people to learn from each other. These technologies allow trainees to view others working with athlete-clients, to review their own work independently and in conjunction with colleagues and supervisors, and to keep records of their work. Using technology in this manner can help trainees to identify blind spots, evaluate themselves, consider interpersonal dynamics between their athlete-clients and themselves, and lead to discussions of interpersonal dynamics between trainees and supervisors. Furthermore, technology can enhance vicarious learning related to service delivery and supervision as trainees consider the work of other practitioners.

One-way Mirrors

One-way mirrors are partially transparent and partially reflective. When one side of the mirror is brightly lit and the other side is dark, the lit side appears to be a mirror but viewing is possible through the glass from the darkened side. One-way mirrors enable sport psychology trainees to practice their service delivery in a private room while being observed by peers or a supervisor. If peers are present, they benefit from the observation of real-time sport psychology service delivery by a practitioner of a similar level of competence, a type of model that has been shown to be effective in enhancing learning (McCullagh et al., 2014). Process comments from the supervisor and group discussion during the sessions by peers in the adjoining room ensure that trainee peers learn from the experience.

After the session is complete, trainees can share their impressions of the encounter. The opportunity for trainees to assess their own work enhances self-awareness and learning. For training sessions that involve peers serving as clients, it is also possible for the "client" to provide feedback to the trainee consultant about the sport psychology experience. It is valuable for such feedback to focus on strengths as well as weaknesses. For example, "What kinds of things did the sport psychology trainee do to build rapport?" and "What got in the way of building rapport?" Comments from the client such as "I liked the way you didn't say much so I could tell the whole problem and get it off my chest" or "You didn't really let me finish what I wanted to say" or "It seemed to me like you were interested, and I felt comfortable talking to you" help trainees understand the dynamics of sport psychology service delivery. Sport psychology trainees can also benefit from feedback about the session from peers and supervisor observing. Peers offering such feedback gain practice in making constructive comments in an effective manner. The supervisor can also offer feedback and facilitate the development of observation, analysis, and constructive commentary skills among the group.

Digital Video Review

Video review of entire sessions or particular moments within sessions can help to validate and reinforce trainees' learning experiences. Such reviews allow trainees to observe themselves and their clients' verbal and nonverbal behaviors. For example, a trainee can watch how the client's body posture changes in response to questions or comments from the trainee. Many trainees have a tendency to be self-critical, which can lead to improvement, but may also negate strengths and sap confidence. A "good, better, how?" analysis of video sessions can be effective. The trainee starts by identifying what went well in the session. This initial analysis is followed by what could have been better, which is immediately followed by a discussion of how improvement could be accomplished. Video review that is shared with a supervisor, who provides supportive feedback, can help trainees gain confidence in their abilities and enhance the likelihood that they will build upon their strengths. Problematic trainee behaviors or skills that need improving can sometimes be understood more easily when seen on video. The goal of using video review technology is to help individuals identify the advantages and disadvantages of their personal service delivery style.

Before digitally recording any sessions, athlete-clients must be informed about the process of recording and about how the digital information will be used. In accordance with informed consent guidelines, athletes have to be given the right to decline being recorded without any repercussions. Trainees may want to keep the video footage of their sport psychology sessions and review it over time to learn more about their applied skills and approaches and also to see how their personal style evolves. Trainees are obligated to ensure the security of these recorded sessions. If security cannot be maintained, then erasing the digital video content is the action that must be taken.

Online Discussions

Online discussions can be held using a variety of online classroom management systems (e.g., Blackboard, Moodle). Whatever approaches are selected, it is essential those online environments are confidential and that trainees be alert to confidentiality issues and aware of online posting guidelines that ensure proper language and respect for others. Some topics may not be suitable for online discussion.

Required weekly postings about applied work such as "What applied work have you done this week?" and "What are your thoughts and feelings about this work?" and "Provide at least one question for the group to discuss with regard to applied sport psychology work" can allow sport psychology supervisors to understand and remain updated on trainee field-work experiences and questions. Further, such postings provide the supervisor with information about where there is unfinished business with regard to trainee applied work. For example, based upon online postings, the supervisor can see when trainees do not fully understand or are not comfortable using a particular technique. The supervisor might also note if a trainee has developed a reliance on one or two specific techniques at the cost of further development.

Trainees gain further experience by providing feedback to each other in online forums. Commenting on online posts of their peers enables trainees to practice providing and receiving feedback about applied work. By carefully considering the experiences of peers at similar skill levels, trainees can gain a rich understanding of the breadth of sport psychology service delivery. Such postings can be enhanced by discussions of both the original posts and the comments made about the postings. By considering the content of the online postings and comments about the postings, the supervisor and trainees can identify areas that require more attention, live feedback, or practice, and opportunities to address such issues can be provided.

Skype, FaceTime, and Related Communication Technologies

Skype, FaceTime, and related communication technologies are generally free or low-cost, and allow supervisors to both hear and see the nonverbal expressions of trainees when factors related to time or distance prevent being physically present with each other in supervision. Technology that allows people to listen with both their ears and their eyes tends to be more effective than written or audio-only communication methods (van Wassenhove, Grant, & Peoppel, 2004). One shortcoming of these communication technologies is that their confidentiality cannot be ensured. It is important for all involved to be aware of confidentiality issues when discussing applied work online.

Communication technologies may also be useful for holding supervision meetings when distance or scheduling preclude meeting in person. Such technology allows for observation of nonverbal and verbal communications that may convey important supervision information. In addition to ensuring quality service delivery, supervision meetings provide an opportunity for continued relationship building between the trainee and supervisor.

Record Keeping

As part of their ethical obligations, sport psychology trainees and supervisors should keep records of their applied work and supervision sessions (American Psychological Association, 2002; 2010). Technology can facilitate the keeping of such records via spreadsheets, text documents, and commercial practice management systems. Such technology should be secure, password protected, and backed up. Models of helpful and user-friendly formats can easily be provided and shared by supervisors. Record-keeping technology is efficient and effective, but is subject to problems related to security, confidentiality, and technology failure.

Evaluation Via Online Survey Software

In an effective supervisory relationship, supervisors provide feedback to trainees, and trainees also have the opportunity to provide feedback to supervisors about their supervisory skills and the supervision relationship. Evaluation discussions can be held in person but may be enhanced by the use of technology such as online survey software (e.g., Google Forms, Qualtrics, SurveyMonkey). Surveys that are regularly used on an annual or more frequent basis can provide the opportunity to highlight key issues in supervision and to track changes over time.

DESCRIPTION OF THE CASE

Multiple forms of technology can be used to enhance the supervision and training of sport psychology practitioners. The following case description demonstrates the use of technology in a graduate-level course for applied sport psychology trainees. This course is designed to provide practice experiences working with peer-clients who present with sport-related issues. The course is held in the college's counseling training facilities that feature adjacent practice and observation rooms with built-in audio- and video-recording capabilities and a one-way mirror. The focus of this case is on how the supervisor uses technology to enhance the learning experiences of sport psychology trainees.

In this example, the sport psychology trainee subscribes to a service delivery approach in which she strives to build a supportive relationship with her client to assist the client in maximizing his potential as a ski jumper. She adheres to the belief that the client is the expert on himself and that her role is to create a supportive environment in which the client feels confident enough to leave past failures behind him and shift his focus to finding possible solutions (Petitpas, 2000). The client–graduate student interaction takes place in the training lab with the course supervisor and six fellow graduate student trainees observing.

The trainee begins the session by greeting the client with the question "How can I help you?" The supervisor comments to the classmates who are observing the interaction that the trainee's question may have inadvertently positioned her as the expert. The client's response of "I'm not sure" and his movement from sitting up to sitting back in his chair may be signs that he is waiting for the trainee to take the lead. The class members benefit from observing both the verbal and the nonverbal communications of the client and trainee in-vivo.

Later in the session, the client makes the statement: "I'm just so frustrated. I know I can do it, but I just screw up every time I get close to moving up." The supervisor asks the students who are observing to write down what they would have attended to in the client's statement. The supervisor also points out that the trainee's reply – "How are you coping with the frustration?" – has the advantage of shifting the client's focus from the past to the present.

When the session is over, the trainee and client return to the observation room and discuss the session. The trainee immediately begins speaking about her shortcomings and what she has done poorly. The supervisor reminds her to use a "good, better, how?" approach, which leads her to begin by considering and sharing what went well during the session before moving to what could have been better. "Good, better, how?" feedback pertaining to the trainee is also garnered from the client. During this debriefing, classmates contribute to the conversation, identifying additional strengths the trainee demonstrated. They also can share what they might have attended to after the client said "I'm just so frustrated. I know I can do it but I screw up every time I get close to moving up."

A parallel process in sport psychology service delivery and supervision may become apparent as the trainee discusses difficulties in the session and responds to feedback from the class and supervisor. For example, a trainee who focuses on resistance with the client in the sport psychology relationship may exhibit resistance in the supervision relationship. Such a trainee may be frustrated that their athlete-client will not share more feelings, while at the same time express to the supervisor that an approach the supervisor or a classmate proposes will not be helpful. A process-oriented supervisor may choose to focus on the parallel processes to increase trainee self-awareness. That is, to highlight the trainee's responses to feedback and consider how they might be similar to those the athlete-client experienced. Creating a supportive environment for trainee self-disclosures and discussions sets the stage for all the trainees to explore the advantages and disadvantages of different models and approaches to service. Receiving feedback immediately following a session can be particularly powerful.

Trainees can benefit from viewing and critiquing their videos, examining their underlying thoughts and feelings that occurred during the session, perhaps using an interpersonal process recall approach (Kagan & Kagan, 1997). That is, trainees can control video playback and supervisors and fellow trainees can serve as inquirers, helping trainees to investigate their thoughts, feelings, and conceptualizations regarding the interaction. Writing a paper that includes consideration of the session, comments of the supervisor and class, and a review of the session video can help the trainee consolidate learning.

Online discussions about challenges and lessons learned from participating in, viewing, and discussing these sessions allows trainees to share their experiences with each other and their supervisor. Trainees and the supervisor can learn from and comment on the postings. These experiences allow them to continue to build relationships and develop skills outside of the classroom setting.

These examples illustrate some of the benefits that can be gained from the use of technology in enhancing the learning experiences of trainees in the classroom. In particular, one-way mirrors in classroom settings and the use of video allow sport psychology trainees to become aware of blind spots they may have in their communication styles or self-presentation, to value the importance of nonverbal communications, and to obtain others' feedback on the advantages and disadvantages of their developing interpersonal styles with clients.

APPROACH/PHILOSOPHY

The philosophical approach to supervision and training described in this case is consistent with educational and developmental approaches that focus on understanding of the self and environment (e.g., Stoltenberg, 1981; Stoltenberg & Delworth, 1987). These approaches help individuals to identify and build upon their strengths, to hone decision-making skills, and to use adaptive strategies. This approach is tailored to work with athletes and is consistent with the Littlefoot model (Petitpas, 2000). With regard to consulting and supervision, the quality of relationships consistently correlates positively with positive outcomes (Petitpas & Tinsley, 2014).

A benefit of this philosophical approach is that it creates a safe environment for athlete-clients and also promotes trainee growth. Trainees are safe to share success, to make mistakes, and to ask questions. Strengths are built upon, and errors are not hidden, but rather they are considered, addressed, and used as valuable teaching moments.

PREPARATION/PLANNING

To be effective when using technology in supervision, supervisors and sport psychology trainees must prepare and plan for applied work. Some of the preparation is academic, becoming familiar with relevant theory, sport psychology intervention tools, interviewing and counseling skills and techniques, and ethical and technical issues related to incorporating technology into the supervision process. Some of this preparation is practical. Practice sessions with peers in a classroom setting can familiarize trainees with the logistics involved in starting and ending sessions and in managing record-keeping tasks. Giving and receiving supervision in a *safe* classroom environment can also serve as a foundation for applied work with athlete-clients and can help support ongoing growth and feedback as encounters with client-athletes and classroom work occur simultaneously. Some of the preparation for service delivery is psychological, a willingness to take risks and learn new things from both supervisor and trainee peers. Supervisors must also have the motivation to assume responsibility for trainee work and athlete-client wellbeing. Finally, some of the preparation involves attention to concrete aspects of the process, such as adequate rooms for sessions (e.g., training labs with one-way mirrors and video), working video equipment that supervisors and trainees understand how to operate, and secure online systems for group discussions.

Trainees and supervisors may also choose to use session evaluation forms. Session evaluation is a collaborative process in which trainees share their experiences of the session with the supervisor based on previously agreed goals or objectives. A sample session evaluation form might include trainee experiences of the relationship, supervisor style, and overall feelings associated with the supervision session (Duncan, Miller, Wampold, & Hubble, 2010). Trainees might also use similar evaluation forms in their work with athlete-clients.

SUPERVISION PROCESS/EXPERIENCE

Barney, Andersen, and Riggs (1996) proposed a systematic training model for supervisors and programs in sport psychology to help prepare trainees to become competent supervisors. The program includes coursework on theories and models of supervision, supervision practica, and having senior supervisors oversee neophyte supervisors' work (meta-supervision – the supervision of supervision; Barney & Andersen, 2014). In sport psychology settings, supervisors and trainees both have responsibilities in the supervisory relationship (Lubker & Andersen, 2014). Competent supervisors are knowledgeable, skilled, and have credentials related to supervision (Ellis et al., 2014). They facilitate an effective supervisory relationship, invest in trainee welfare and development, maintain trainee confidentiality (as appropriate), pay attention to the power differential (and boundaries) between trainee and supervisor, observe, review, and monitor trainees' consulting, attend to diversity issues, and provide fair, respectful, honest, formal feedback. Such supervisors continue to develop and evaluate their supervision skills, support the development of self-awareness, and facilitate and model the integration of theoretical approaches with applied work. Such supervisors serve as ethical and responsible role models who facilitate trainee development.

Trainees also have responsibilities in the supervision relationship. Trainees are expected to be ethical and knowledgeable and to learn and grow during the supervision process. With regard to development, trainees should be open-minded, responsible, and honest, with a focus on client welfare. Above all, trainees need to be willing to engage in self-reflection on their own strengths and weakness and how their psychosocial ontogenetic histories of developmental successes, setbacks, and traumas may influence, for good or ill, their interactions with clients. Supervision is a type of *assisted* self-reflection, and there are various types of technology that can be incorporated into supervision to aid such reflective processes and to meet challenging and important supervision goals for both supervisors and trainees.

Using technology in supervision involves in-person supervision meetings as well as a host of other activities such as live observation through one-way mirrors, discussions of recorded sessions, analyses of cases and situations presented online, and exploring trainee questions about processes and techniques. This type of supervision requires extra time and involvement from trainees and supervisors, but results in trainees who have learning opportunities above and beyond what they would experience if they were working without technology and the collaboration of classmates. Used in this manner, technology does not supersede high-quality relationships, but rather adds to and enriches the supervision process.

REFLECTION

Supervision involves an ongoing interpersonal relationship between the supervisor and trainee, with the goals of ensuring the well-being of athlete-clients and helping trainees develop the requisite skills, understanding, and self-knowledge necessary for applied sport psychology work. The supervision process, in a supportive environment, grows and matures with honest communication, close contact, and feedback to address strengths and weaknesses. The use of technology can enrich supervision experiences for trainees and supervisors.

One-way mirrors allow trainees to observe others' sport psychology sessions in real time and imagine what they would say or do in a similar situation. Being observed while providing sport psychology services adds pressure, but also provides trainees with opportunities to receive immediate and supportive feedback, which can enhance learning. Sessions that are recorded on video can be reviewed several times and allow trainees to observe themselves. The value of such repetition is clear, but the risks to confidentiality for clients are significant if care is not taken to secure video material. Online discussions allow trainees to provide and receive supervision/feedback from peers and to share issues that might seem too trivial to bring up in live supervision (or that have been overlooked for other reasons).

The costs of using technology in supervision are the extra time and expense needed for equipment and training and the additional risks to confidentiality that accrue through the creation of video and other online materials. Some might see the use of technology as a replacement for human interaction. This chapter highlights how technology can be used to enrich (and not supplant) the relationships among supervisors, trainees, and athlete-clients.

SUGGESTED READINGS

Andersen, M. B. (Ed.). (2000). *Doing sport psychology*. Champaign, IL: Human Kinetics.
Andersen, M. B. (Ed.). (2005). *Sport psychology in practice*. Champaign, IL: Human Kinetics.
Van Raalte, J. L., & Brewer, B. W. (Eds.). (2014). *Exploring sport and exercise psychology* (3rd ed.). Washington, DC: American Psychological Association.

REFLECTIVE QUESTIONS

1. Describe how you might implement technology into your individual and group sport psychology supervision. What are the costs and benefits of the approach you describe?
2. Describe some of the ethical considerations related to technology in supervision and how you might handle them.
3. What other forms of technology might be useful for sport psychology supervision and why?
4. How might technology in supervision enhance learning for students and practitioners from diverse backgrounds (e.g., non-native English speakers, people with disabilities)?
5. Under what circumstances might one choose to forgo the use of technology in supervision? Explain why one might make such a choice.

REFERENCES

American Psychological Association. (2002). Ethical principles of psychologists and code of conduct. *American Psychologist, 57,* 1060–1073. DOI: 10.1037/0003-066X.57.12.1060.
American Psychological Association. (2010). Amendments to the 2001 "Ethical principles of psychologists and code of conduct." *American Psychologist, 65,* 493. DOI: 10.1037/a0020168.
Andersen, M. B., Van Raalte, J. L., & Brewer, B. W. (1994). Assessing the skills of sport psychology supervisors. *The Sport Psychologist, 8,* 238–247.
Andersen, M. B., Van Raalte, J. L., & Brewer, B. W. (2000). When applied sport psychology graduate students are impaired: Ethical and legal issues in supervision. *Journal of Applied Sport Psychology, 12,* 134–149. DOI: 10.1080/10413200008404219.

Barney, S. T., & Andersen, M. B. (2014). Meta-supervision: Training practitioners to help others on their paths. In J. G. Cremades & L. S. Tashman (Eds.), *Becoming a sport, exercise, and performance psychology professional: A global perspective* (pp. 339–346). New York, NY: Routledge.

Barney, S. T., Andersen, M. B., & Riggs, C. R. (1996). Supervision training in sport psychology: A graduate practicum. *Journal of Applied Sport Psychology*, 8, 200–217.

Duncan, B. L., Miller, S. D., Wampold, B. E., & Hubble, M. A. (Eds.). (2010). *The heart and soul of change: Delivering what works in therapy* (2nd ed.) Washington, DC: APA Press.

Ellis, M. V., Berger, L., Hanus, A., Ayala, E. E., Swords, B. A., & Siembor, M. (2014). Inadequate and harmful clinical supervision: Testing a revised framework and assessing occurrence. *The Counseling Psychologist*, 42, 434–472. DOI: 10.1177/001100013508656.

Kagan, H., & Kagan, N. (1997). Interpersonal process recall: Influencing human interaction. In C. E. Watkins, Jr. (Ed.), *Handbook of psychotherapy supervision* (pp. 296–309). New York, NY: John Wiley.

Lubker, J., & Andersen, M. B. (2014). Ethical issues in supervision: Client welfare, practitioner development, and professional gatekeeping. In J. C. Watson II & E. F. Etzel (Eds.), *Ethical issues in sport, exercise, and performance psychology* (pp. 151–162). Morgantown, WV: Fitness Information Technology.

McCullagh, P., Ste-Marie, D., & Law, B. (2014). Modeling: Is what you see, what you get? In J. L. Van Raalte & B. W. Brewer (Eds.), *Exploring sport and exercise psychology* (3rd ed.; pp. 139–162). Washington, DC: American Psychological Association.

Petitpas, A. J. (2000). Managing stress on and off the field: The Littlefoot approach to learned resourcefulness. In M. B. Andersen (Ed.), *Doing sport psychology* (pp. 33–43). Champaign, IL: Human Kinetics.

Petitpas, A. J., & Tinsley, T. M. (2014). Counseling interventions in applied sport psychology. In J. L. Van Raalte & B. W. Brewer (Eds.), *Exploring sport and exercise psychology* (3rd ed.; pp. 241–259). Washington, DC: American Psychological Association.

Stoltenberg, C. (1981). Approaching supervision from a developmental perspective: The counselor complexity model. *Journal of Counseling Psychology*, 28, 59–65. DOI: 10.1037/0022-0167.28.1.59.

Stoltenberg, C., & Delworth, U. (1987). *Supervising counselors and therapists: A developmental approach.* San Francisco, CA: Jossey-Bass.

Van Raalte, J. L., & Andersen, M. B. (2000). Supervision I: From models to doing. In M. B. Andersen (Ed.), *Doing sport psychology* (pp. 153–165). Champaign, IL: Human Kinetics.

van Wassenhove, V., Grant, K. W., & Poeppel, D. (2004). Visual speech speeds up neural processing of auditory speech. *Proceedings of the National Academy of Sciences of the United States of America, 102*, 1181–1186. DOI: 10.1073/pnas.0408949102.

Watson II, J. C., Zizzi, S. J., Etzel, E. F., & Lubker, J. R. (2004). Applied sport psychology supervision: A survey of students and professionals. *The Sport Psychologist, 18*, 415–429.

Conclusion

42 Incorporating Case Analysis into the Practice and Training in Sport, Exercise, and Performance Psychology Practitioners

J. Gualberto Cremades and Lauren S. Tashman

As mentioned in the first chapter of this book, there is no formula for applied sport, exercise, and performance psychology (SEPP) practice. There is no equation to be solved; practice requires the ability to artfully apply research and theory from SEPP and other related fields (e.g., counseling, psychology, sport sciences). Further, neophyte practitioners are faced with learning how to effectively translate the knowledge they have gained throughout their education into an understanding of how to put that knowledge to use in applied SEPP practice. Moreover, students and young practitioners not only need to develop professional practice knowledge and experience; learning how to effectively navigate the myriad ethical considerations and potential challenges is also essential (e.g., Moore, 2003).

As has been presented throughout the chapters in this book, the use of case analysis can be an effective means of accumulating professional practice knowledge. Further, it provides an opportunity to practice applying one's knowledge in real-world scenarios. Therefore, in this final chapter of the book, we cover the "why" and "how" of incorporating case analysis into SEPP practice and training.

WHY CASE ANALYSIS: DEVELOPING KNOWLEDGE AND SKILL IN COMPLEX, DYNAMIC DOMAINS

Various researchers have proposed that learners progress through stages or phases as they become more experienced or expert in a given domain. For example, Fitts and Posner (1967) outlined three phases of learning: (1) cognitive, (2) associative, and (3) autonomous. A few years later, Rumelhart and Norman (1978) outlined three modes of learning: (1) accretion, (2) restructuring, and (3) tuning. Additionally, Dreyfus and Dreyfus (1986) outlined five stages through which learners progress, highlighting the qualitative shifts that occur throughout the process of learning: (1) novice, (2) advanced beginner, (3) competent, (4) proficient, and (5) expert. Regardless of the particular model, at first learners are simply accumulating facts and information, then progress to learning how to apply the facts and information they have learned, and ultimately advance to learning in what situations and at what times to utilize their knowledge (West, Farmer, & Wolf, 1991). Therefore, as learners gain new knowledge and have the opportunity to work with and apply their knowledge, their ability to use it becomes more effective.

Developing the ability to effectively apply and utilize one's knowledge occurs as the result of engagement in deliberate practice activities specifically aimed at improving one's knowledge and skill (Ericsson, 1998; Ericsson, Krampe, & Tesch-Römer, 1993). Thus, it is not the quantity of time spent learning that is most important, but rather the quality of the learning and practice that allows one to develop expertise. Specifically, quality learning necessitates resources, motivation, and effort (Ericsson et al., 1993). Hence, targeted, intentional repetition of performance and continuous opportunities to practice applying one's knowledge are an essential element of effective deliberate practice (Guest, Regehr, & Tiberius, 2001).

In dynamic and complex domains, there is no one formula for applying one's knowledge across situations. Therefore, a key element of deliberate practice is situational awareness, which must be developed in order to make sense of the situation one is in and effectively determine how to apply one's knowledge to suit that particular situation. This entails developing the ability to rapidly and effectively perceive and attend to relevant information, integrate that information with one's knowledge and construct meaning from it, and anticipate and make predictions about the future impact of that information (Endsley, 1995). Thus, in complex problem-solving situations, more experience and expertise enhances one's ability to effectually utilize situational awareness in order to effectively and more fluidly selectively attend to the available information and apply one's knowledge. In contrast, individuals with little to no experience lack the knowledge and skill to determine what to pay attention to in a given situation and how to make sense of the information available to them. Their working memory becomes overloaded as they attempt to consciously process all the information and determine what approach to take and how to apply their knowledge. Therefore, the development of situational awareness is essential. This remains an important skill in dynamic contexts despite one's level of expertise. Even experts need to continue to hone their situational awareness skills as they must resist complete automaticity to avoid misinterpreting or failing to notice important information due to a bias from their previously accumulated knowledge and experience (Ericsson, 1998).

Consequently, in complex domains, such as SEPP service delivery, a practitioner must be able to flexibly and adaptively apply his/her knowledge as each situation brings some novelty in comparison to past situations (Schwartz, Bransford, & Sears, 2005). Thus, developing what Hatano and Inagaki (1986) referred to as adaptive expertise rather than routine expertise should be an important focus of training in SEPP. According to Hatano and Inagaki (1986), routine experts consistently produce the same superior, exceptional, and automatic performance (e.g., a chef who masters how to make a few particular dishes and proceeds to make them over and over again), whereas adaptive experts derive innovative, flexible, and creative ways to exhibit superior performance (e.g., a chef who continuously produces new menus and makes new superior dishes). In SEPP practice, routine expertise then would be the practitioner who masters a particular procedure for goal-setting and uses that for all of his/her clients, whereas a practitioner who has developed adaptive expertise would take into consideration his/her particular clients and their situations/environments in order to innovatively develop and apply a goal-setting procedure most effective for each of them.

Adaptive experts are better at thinking and acting flexibly, handling uncertainty, and understanding new or atypical situations (Fazey, Fazey, & Fazey, 2005). The adaptive expert can recognize when highly practiced and mastered procedures are not sufficient and need to be modified or adapted, whereas a routine expert would simply apply an already mastered procedure (Gott, Hall, Pokorny, Dibble, & Glaser, 1992). In dynamic contexts where factors and variables change within and across situations, and new and atypical situations are frequently encountered, adaptive expertise is essential. According to Bransford, Brown, and Cocking (2000), adaptive experts are able to perform flexibly and innovatively because they continue to refine their knowledge and skills based upon what they learn from each experience they encounter. Thus, not only can neophyte practitioners benefit from case analysis in order to develop adaptive expertise, but professional practitioners can also benefit in order to continue to refine their adaptive expertise.

In summary, with regards to SEPP training and supervision, there are many benefits to incorporating case analysis. First, during the early phases of learning, a student or neophyte practitioner is focused on gaining foundational knowledge, amassing factual information such as concepts, theories, definitions, and research. As they progress through the phases, learning becomes more focused on how, when, and why to use the information and knowledge they have accumulated. Thus, case analysis provides a means of practicing applying one's knowledge in real-world situations. It supports the process of developing procedural and conditional knowledge and professional practice skills by helping students and neophyte practitioners hone their ability to apply the concepts, theories, definitions, and research they have learned. For example, a novice student will have learned about self-determination theory, but will be challenged with knowing how to explain it to a client as well as how to apply it in different situations. By utilizing case analysis, the student can practice how to describe this theory and its implications as well as learn when, why, and how it applies to particular individual or group client scenarios.

Second, a benefit of case analysis is that it can enhance deliberate practice in SEPP education and training by intentionally aiming toward the improvement of the neophyte practitioner's consulting skills and abilities. As discussed in the next section, there are many ways that case analysis can be designed and thus, it can enhance the intentional nature of one's learning as well as provide more quality means of engaging in practice. In the classroom setting, case analysis can offer a more interactive approach to practicing how to apply one's knowledge and, in supervised practice, it can increase the number of structured opportunities to engage in that practice (as opposed to solely relying on what may be limited clients and experiences during training).

Third, case analysis can enhance the development of situational awareness. This skill focuses on learning how to prime one's selective attention as well as improve one's ability to know what to do with the information one has attended to. Neophyte students or practitioners with elementary active listening skills, when meeting with or observing a client for example, will likely have a difficult time deciding what to pay attention to and not know what to do with that information. Thus, case analysis affords the neophytes additional opportunities to practice these skills and refine their situational awareness, essentially enhancing their ability to navigate a variety of professional practice situations and cases.

Therefore, a final benefit of incorporating case analysis into SEPP education and training is its usefulness for developing adaptive expertise. As discussed above, SEPP professional practice is a complex and dynamic endeavor for which many factors and variables need to be taken into consideration in order to determine how to effectively apply one's knowledge in a given situation. Case analysis provides the opportunity to practice applying one's knowledge across varying situations and, thus, can help students and neophyte practitioners develop the ability to not only master applied practice skills but, more importantly, do so creatively and innovatively in a way that best suits each particular client and situation. An important note here is that case analysis can be beneficial to any level of learner or practitioner since situational awareness and adaptive expertise must consistently and continually be deliberately practiced. Thus, more advanced practitioners and experts can also benefit from case analysis since the learning process in the SEPP field never ends.

INCORPORATING CASE ANALYSIS: LEARNING HOW TO EFFECTIVELY APPLY KNOWLEDGE IN THE REAL WORLD

There are many different ways to incorporate case analysis into the classroom and training in SEPP. One must be mindful of choosing the right time and approach to doing so based on the information discussed above in order to result in effective outcomes. We provide below some example considerations and strategies for utilizing case analysis:

1. **Case development**: A first consideration regards the nature of the case to be analyzed. Will it be a real-world example (e.g., a professional athlete or team), a scenario developed by the professor or supervisor (e.g., a hypothetical case or a real-world example from his/ her own or a colleague's professional practice), or a case derived by the student/trainee (e.g., a hypothetical situation or a real-world example from his/her own professional prac-

tice)? One important consideration here is the level (i.e., amount of knowledge and/or experience) of the student/trainee. Namely, learning tasks should reflect the knowledge base and experience level of the individual(s), with more guidance being provided to those with less experience (Kalyuga, Ayres, Chandler, & Sweller, 2003).

2. **Analysis/question development**: A second consideration is the determination of how the case will be analyzed (i.e., what questions will be used to analyze the case and derive a "solution" to the scenario). The analysis should be designed in a way that challenges the individual, encourages the use of resources, gives the individual some ownership over the process, reflects an authentic task, is consistent with the complexity of the context of the case, and has a clear, intentional purpose (Savery & Duffy, 1996). Again, the level of the individual(s) (i.e., their knowledge, skill, and experience) should be considered when deriving the purpose and analysis of the case study.

3. **Worked examples**: As is provided in the chapters in this book, worked examples in which the scenarios as well as the "solutions" to the scenarios are provided (e.g., Atkinson, Derry, Renkl, & Wortham, 2000) can be an effective means of incorporating case analysis, particularly for more novice, lower-level learners with limited practical experience. However, this method can also be useful for more experienced practitioners in order to help them expand their range of approaches and encourage continued adaptive expertise. When using this approach, encouraging additional discussion, analysis, and reflection are essential. Further, an important consideration here is the experience level of the individual providing the worked example. On the one hand, providing an example from a "model" similar in experience level to the individual can be beneficial, however, a more expert "model" may also be effective in order to advance one's knowledge (Tashman & Tenenbaum, 2013).

4. **Think, pair, share**: This is an active learning method in which individuals first analyze a case on their own, then discuss in pairs, and finally share their case analysis with the whole group. Thus, this approach may be particularly useful in classroom or group supervision settings. It is advantageous in that it requires each individual to first work through the case individually before getting insight into the thoughts and approaches of others. Further, it capitalizes on several influential learning theories: (a) constructivism (i.e., learning is self-constructed by actively creating and testing one's knowledge and theories; Piaget, 1983); (b) social constructivism (i.e., learning is collaboratively constructed with culture and social context being important considerations; Vygotsky, 1978); and (c) constructionism (i.e., learning is constructed most effectively when one's knowledge and skill are shared publicly; Harel & Papert, 1991).

5. **Jigsaw**: This is another active learning method in which individuals are first put into small groups. Each group is responsible for discussing and analyzing one element of the case. Then new groups are formed consisting of one person from each original group. In this second group, the "experts" for each segment of the case from the first groupings share their information with the new group. The task of the second group is to compile all the information about the case in order to create a full picture and analysis of the complete case. This approach capitalizes on the use of collaboration where individuals have the opportunity to test their own understandings, examine the understandings of others, and develop and test new ideas and understandings (Savery & Duffy, 1996). A modification on this strategy could be to assign each first group a different case to be analyzed. Thus, an additional benefit of both this and the think, pair, share approaches are that they can allow for multiple cases to be analyzed.

6. **Role play**: Utilizing this active learning approach, individuals can be tasked with acting out their proposed "solutions" to the cases. This approach adds to the complexity of the activity by not only requiring that the student/trainee critically think about the case, but also actively demonstrate their ability to apply their knowledge and skill. In order to develop the skills and abilities associated with higher-level learning and cognitive processes such as analysis, application, synthesis, evaluation, and creation (Bloom, 1976), individuals

must be provided with opportunities to actively engage and practice with their knowledge rather than just listen (Bonwell & Eison, 1991).

7. **Incorporating technology**: Technology can also be incorporated – for example, by using an online learning community. We have co-developed such a community whereby students and practitioners around the globe can interact and analyze each other's cases. This learning system, the Performance Enhancement Training Tool (PETT; peinnovate.com; Tashman & Cremades, 2014), was created as there was an evident need for a means of practicing applying one's knowledge, engaging in collaborative learning, as well as having the opportunity to continue one's professional development within the applied SEPP community.

8. **Reflection**: Regardless of the approach used for the case analysis, reflective practice should be implemented and encouraged in order to support the development of knowledge, independence, and self-regulation of the student/trainee (Savery & Duffy, 1996). There are many ways that this can be incorporated. For example, active learning strategies such as listing pros and cons of the approach used in the case, writing a one-minute reflective paper about the case, or brainstorming alternative approaches to handling the case could be implemented. Additionally, reflective frameworks such as those mentioned in Chapter 1 or others can be implemented, such as analyzing what was done well, what could have been done better/different, and what was learned (Mugford, Hesse, & Morgan, 2014), or analyzing what the various individuals in the scenario (e.g., clients, practitioners, other stakeholders, etc.) wanted, did, thought, and felt, as well as the congruence and discrepancies among these for each individual (Korthagen & Vasalos, 2005).

CONCLUSION

We began our previous book (Cremades & Tashman, 2014) by suggesting a need for a culture of competencies in SEPP (Cremades, Tashman, & Quartiroli, 2014). Given the complex, dynamic nature of applied SEPP practice, competencies should not be viewed as a culminating set of skills. Rather, they should be established in order to provide a foundation for SEPP education and training, outlining the pathway for developing the knowledge and skills that need to be mastered. Upon mastery of this foundation, practitioners consequently need to deliberately practice applying their knowledge and honing their skills in order to advance through the stages of learning, optimize their situational awareness, and develop adaptive expertise.

Utilizing case analysis capitalizes on the benefits of discovery learning (Bruner, 1961) in which individuals need to garner past knowledge and experience in order to discover new knowledge, understandings, relationships, and approaches. Therefore, utilizing problem-based, situated learning takes learning out of the classroom into the real-world, placing it in a meaningful context requiring active engagement and processing (e.g., Williams, 1992; Woolfolk, 2008). As we have discussed throughout this chapter, case analysis provides a means for neophyte and more experienced practitioners to develop their competencies and build upon that foundation.

REFERENCES

Atkinson, R. K., Derry, S. J., Renkl, A., & Wortham, D. (2000). Learning from examples: Instructional principles from the worked examples research. *Review of Educational Research, 70*, 181–214.

Bloom, B. S. (1976). *Human characteristics and school learning.* New York, NY: McGraw-Hill.

Bonwell, C. C., & Eison, J. A. (1991). *Active learning: Creating excitement in the classroom.* ASHE-ERIC

Higher Education Report No. 1. Washington, DC: The George Washington University, School of Education and Human Development.

Bransford, J. D., Brown, A. L., & Cocking, R. R. (2000). *How people learn: Brain, mind, experience, and school*. Washington, DC: National Academy Press.

Bruner, J. S. (1961). The art of discovery. *Harvard Educational Review, 31*, 21–32.

Cremades, J. G., & Tashman, L. S. (2014). *Becoming a sport, exercise, and performance psychology professional: A global perspective*. New York, NY: Routledge.

Cremades, J. G., Tashman, L. S., & Quartiroli, A. (2014). Initial considerations: Developing the pathway to become a sport, exercise, and performance psychology professional. In J. G. Cremades & L. S. Tashman (Eds.), *Becoming a sport, exercise, and performance psychology professional: A global perspective* (pp. 3–11). New York, NY: Routledge.

Dreyfus, H. L., & Dreyfus, S. E. (1986). *Mind over machine: The power of human intuition and expertise in the era of the computer*. New York, NY: The Free Press.

Endsley, M. R. (1995). Toward a theory of situation awareness in dynamic systems. *Human Factors, 37*, 32–64.

Ericsson, K. A. (1998). The scientific study of expert levels of performance: General implications for optimal learning and creativity. *High Ability Studies, 9*, 75–100.

Ericsson, K. A., Krampe, R. Th., & Tesch-Römer, C. (1993). The role of deliberate practice in the acquisition of expert performance. *Psychological Review, 100*, 363–406.

Fazey, J., Fazey, J. A., & Fazey, D. M. A. (2005). Learning more effectively from expertise. *Ecology and Society, 10*, 4 [online].

Fitts, P., & Posner, M. I. (1967). *Human performance*. Belmont, CA: Brooks/Cole.

Gott, S., Hall, P., Pokorny, A., Dibble, E., & Glaser, R. (1992). A naturalistic study of transfer: Adaptive expertise in technical domains. In D. Detterman & R. Sternberg (Eds.), *Transfer on trial: Intelligence, cognition, and instruction* (pp. 258–288). Norwood, NJ: Ablex.

Guest, C. B., Regehr, G., & Tiberius, R. G. (2001). The life long challenge of expertise. *Medical Education, 35*, 78–81.

Harel, I. E., & Papert, S. E. (1991). *Constructionism*. Westport, CT: Ablex.

Hatano, G., & Inagaki, K. (1986). Two courses of expertise. In H. A. H. Stevenson & K. Hakuta (Eds.), *Child development and education in Japan* (pp. 262–272). New York, NY: Freeman.

Kalyuga, S., Ayres, P., Chandler, P., & Sweller, J. (2003). The expertise reversal effect. *Educational Psychologist, 38*, 23–31.

Korthagen, F., & Vasalos, A. (2005). Levels in reflection: Core reflection as a means to enhance professional growth. *Teachers and Teaching: Theory and Practice, 11*, 47–71.

Moore, Z. E. (2003). Ethical dilemmas in sport psychology: Discussion and recommendations for practice. *Professional Psychology: Research and Practice, 34*, 601–610.

Mugford, A., Hesse, D., & Morgan, T. (2014). Developing the "total" consultant: Nurturing the art and science. In J. G. Cremades & L. S. Tashman (Eds.), *Becoming a sport, exercise, and performance psychology professional: A global perspective* (pp. 268–275). New York, NY: Routledge.

Piaget, J. (1983). Piaget's theory. In P. Mussen (Ed.), *Handbook of child psychology* (3rd ed.; Vol. 1, pp. 703–732). New York, NY: Wiley.

Rumelhart, D. E., & Norman, D. A. (1978). Accretion, tuning, and restructuring: Three modes of learning. In J. W. Cotton & R. L. Klatzky (Eds.), *Semantic factors in cognition* (pp. 37–53). Hillsdale, NJ: Lawrence Erlbaum Associates.

Savery, J. R., & Duffy, T. M. (1996). Problem based learning: An instructional model and its constructivist framework. In B. G. Wilson (Ed.), *Constructivist learning environments: Case studies in instructional design* (pp. 135–148). Englewood Cliffs, NJ: Educational Technology Publications, Inc.

Schwartz, D. L., Bransford, J. D., & Sears, D. (2005). Efficiency and innovation in transfer. In J. Mestre (Eds.), *Transfer of learning from a modern multidisciplinary perspective* (pp. 1–51). Charlotte, NC: Information Age Publishing Inc.

Tashman, L. S., & Cremades, J. G. (2014). The wave of the future: Integrating technology into service delivery training. In J. G. Cremades & L. S. Tashman (Eds.), *Becoming a sport, exercise, and performance psychology professional: A global perspective* (pp. 347–353). New York, NY: Routledge.

Tashman, L. S., & Tenenbaum, G. (2013). Sport psychology service delivery training: the value of an interactive, case-based approach to practitioner development. *Journal of Sport Psychology in Action, 4*, 71–85.

Vygotsky, L. S. (1978). *Mind in society: The development of higher mental processes.* Cambridge, MA: Harvard University Press.

West, C. K., Farmer, J. A., & Wolf, P. M. (1991). *Instructional design: Implications for cognitive science.* Upper Saddle River, NJ: Prentice Hall.

Williams, S. M. (1992). Putting case-based instruction into context: Examples from legal and medical education. *The Journal of the Learning Sciences, 2,* 367–427.

Woolfolk, A. (2008). *Educational psychology: Active learning edition* (10th ed.). Boston, MA: Pearson Education, Inc.

Appendix
Answers to Reflective Questions

CHAPTER 2

1. **What should consultants consider in order to effectively prepare for working with a team?**
    During a session with a team you have the opportunity to educate them on various mental skills, allow them to self-reflect, help them build self-awareness, and ultimately aid them in strengthening their mental toughness. Although the typical session only lasts 50 minutes, there is an abundance of provisional measures that must be carried out in order to provide effective services to the team. These methods consist of, but are not limited to, reviewing research, interviewing multiple informants, and making observations. Research allows you to sustain adequate and up-to-date knowledge on the field which leads to the use of current evidence-based approaches to applicably benefit the team. It is also important to understand the sport and the sport's culture; this can be done by speaking with coaches, athletic trainers, or even by doing your own research (i.e., books, websites, peer-reviewed articles). Interviewing multiple informants (i.e., coach, athletic trainers, physical trainers) can also assist in an effective session. This allows you to obtain more information on the team from different professional perspectives and roles. Just like a puzzle, the more information you have the more successful you will be at determining an effective approach. Finally, observation is a critical method in effectively strengthening the team's mental skills. Although interviewing the athletes about their physical game is beneficial, going out and observing allows you to see the team's strengths and weaknesses through a sport psychology lens. This method also allows the opportunity to strengthen rapport with the team. Being at practices and competitions can send a message that you care about their wellness and you want to help them.

2. **How can you build your confidence as a first-time consultant?**
    Naturally, as a first time consultant, you will want to over-prepare. However, it's important to know that a majority of the time a session will not go exactly as planned. What is more important is having a strong understanding of the material you want to bring in session and remembering to trust what you know. You do not have to cover every possible point. Instead, know the key points that you want to discuss during the session; this will allow for flexibility. In preparing for the sessions with the team in the case study, we wrote down bullet points on the general information that we wanted to cover in each session as well as our main goals (i.e., what we wanted the athletes to get out of each session). It is also important to keep in mind that, like any sport, experience/practice will help build confidence. Unfortunately, as a first-time consultant you do not have much experience to contribute to your confidence. Because we didn't have prior experience to use to build our confidence, we used self-talk and effective preparation to enhance our confidence. More specifically, we used self-talk as a way to put our focus where it needed to be and keep our confidence high (i.e., presenting skills, knowledge on the topic, thinking on our toes) as opposed to lowering our confidence and focusing on the things we didn't feel confident about (i.e., answering questions athletes had and facilitating conversation). Each new experience is an opportunity to grow. You will have great days and days that aren't so great; each one is as important as the last. Learn from these experiences. Perceiving these new experiences as challenges rather than as threats is a fundamental aspect to building confidence as a consultant and your growth in the field (Dweck, 2006). We found it beneficial to keep a self-reflective journal in which we would jot down areas within each session where improvement was needed, but just as important, areas that we felt went well. It is also important

to find a way to be as naturally you as possible; by doing so you will be performing at your best because it is genuine and automatic. Being your natural self while incorporating the lessons in sport psychology will not only help you perform optimally and confidently, but also create lasting impressions on those who you work with.

3. **What should one consider in order to determine the best style/approach to use as a sport psychology consultant?**
    It is important to know that one size does not fit all. There are many different factors that contribute to the formation of your teaching style/approach. Gaining an understanding of the nature/culture of the sport/team as well as effective approaches to the lessons you will be teaching is crucial. You want to make sure you get the message across in the best way possible. In order to do so, you need to know who you are working with, what you are working toward, and your client's most effective learning style. In some cases, finding the best teaching approach is a trial-and-error process and can vary from session to session. By incorporating different teaching styles (instructor, thinker, explorer, guide – see Barbazette, 2008) as well as various learning styles – visual (images, videos, modeling), tactile/kinesthetic (hands on learning), auditory (discussion, lecture) – in a single session, you will be more likely to provide the optimal learning environment for those with whom you work.

    For the consultants in this chapter, our approach at the beginning was more instructor-focused, with the use of a PowerPoint for a visual learning style. Although at the time this seemed like a good approach, it was evident in the first session that the athletes were bored and not paying attention to the information as intently as we had hoped. In this situation it did not matter how visually appealing the PowerPoint presentation looked, but rather the athletes were not processing the information in an effective way. Therefore, we changed our approach to a more hands-on method (i.e., activities related to the topic of the sessions) and took more of a facilitator role (i.e., facilitating the discussion in the group and allowing the athletes to do most of the talking). This approach worked well for the culture of the team and allowed the athletes to learn and apply the various mental skills directly to their sport.

4. **What are the pros and cons to working with multiple consultants in the field?**
    There are many influential aspects to working with other consultants in the field, as well as some areas that can make things a little more challenging. On the one hand, in many cases, two heads are better than one. Different individuals bring more experience and ideas to the table, which can facilitate higher-quality lessons, understanding of different areas of expertise, and personal experiences such as taking part in different sports, cultures, etc. By adding individuals to work alongside you, the ideas flow, lesson plans and fun activities can arise, and teamwork can take a lot of pressure off each individual taking part in the consulting. Another very useful benefit from incorporating multiple consultants is building upon each other's strengths as well as areas needing improvement. While working with a team, each consultant can integrate each other's strengths and enhance the overall effectiveness of each lesson.

    On the other hand, the potential cons of working with others could be the difficulty of working together when the consultants have varying theoretical approaches or philosophies, competencies, and/or personalities. It may become difficult to adapt to working alongside someone else especially when you have ample experience in the field. Certain styles may work better for one individual than the other and these could potentially clash if there is a lack in communication, commitment, and work ethic among the consultants. Just like any environment, learning to work together as effectively as possible as well as making sure communication is effective will take pressure off of each consultant, facilitate the learning process for both the clients and consultants, and establish a cohesive unit. Overall, there are tradeoffs, but with the proper work ethic and communication, team consulting can be a very effective tool in your work.

5. **What are some of the ethical considerations when working with a client or team of similar age?**
    Being close in age with the tennis team made it difficult at times to wear the sport psychology hat. For this reason, it was extremely important to be mindful and continue to keep a professional relationship with the team. It was essential to remember that the athletes were not our friends but our clients; it was okay to joke around and have fun with the team, but boundaries were necessary and an understanding of these boundaries was crucial.

    A great deal of time had been spent with the team on and off the court. This time helped to facilitate a strong understanding of who each individual athlete was both as an athlete and person. It was natural for us to care about the athletes and want them to do well in all their competitions. However, it was also extremely important to keep in mind that we were not fans but rather resources for the athletes. It can become difficult to fully grasp this concept at the onset of one's consulting experience, but with time this realization will occur. Another instance that took place on a regular basis was running into clients while on campus. This did not seem like something that would be difficult to deal with, but at times it became slightly uncomfortable. As the consultant, it is common to want to greet the athletes that you work with as they pass by, but confidentiality is very important and doing so may result in sacrificing that confidentiality. It may be best to leave the choice with your client and allow them to greet you or take notice of you. This will avoid the breach of confidentiality and leave the ball in their court (no pun intended). Another way of handling this would be to discuss this ahead of time with the client, particularly in your first session. As long as the client is comfortable and their confidentiality remains intact, you approached the situation successfully.

CHAPTER 3

1. **How would you approach working with a client who is losing his confidence?**
    Confidence is a strong belief in one's own abilities related to positive thoughts and feelings. A confident athlete feels like he/she can perform well. Psychological skills training can boost it very well, but an athlete has to understand how his/her mind works. Therefore, it may be useful to explain to the athlete what happens to him once he/she does not feel confident. In most cases (based on my experience with clients), a lack of confidence is due to negative thoughts. They are usually linked either to past mistakes or potential failure. In both cases, these thoughts disrupt concentration as the athlete does not focus on what he/she is doing. In addition, fear of failure may cause physical discomfort such as nausea, shaking, extreme sweating, etc. During that, the athlete cannot perform his/her usual motor skills and will start doubting himself/herself. Negative emotions may also affect breathing, which becomes shallow and thus physical symptoms become stronger. Playing sports at that time is very difficult as one does not feel well. Joy from playing is gone and negative emotions become stronger. Once the athlete understands this process, he/she can move on and start working on making changes.
    Psychological skills training can then take place. I usually start with concentration and engage in discussion with clients about what they focus on during training and competition. After that we talk about things that disturb them and find ways to refocus whenever needed. Self-talk is also a crucial topic. Athletes need to be aware of their own thoughts in order to change them and take advantage. Thus, we usually spend at least an hour talking about specific situations during which athletes tend to think negatively. Together we reframe these thoughts and in addition visualize what the change is going to feel like in real situations. Other psychological skills follow, including goal-setting and relaxation. When athletes know what they want to accomplish and work on it daily, the goals are suddenly not so far away. The same applies to knowing how to relax and feel well in the moment, as they may transfer it to competition and have a nice physical experience during their performance. Last, we usually talk about the athlete's strengths and things that they have achieved already. It is a nice way to evoke positive emotions, dedication, and determination for further practice and boost one's confidence level.

2. **Based on what criteria would you set up a mental training plan for a new athlete who has approached you?**
    It is always important to consider several things such as the client's age, competition level, previous experience with mental training, and time of the year (whether the athlete is in season or not). Working with kids is obviously different than working with adults. Language that is being used must be more simple, as well as the materials provided to them. Professional athletes are usually more aware of what's happening with them before, during, and after competition (but not always!) and thus working with them is usually focused on bigger details than with athletes at lower levels. When working with athletes who already have an experience with mental training, it is crucial to find out whether their experience has been positive or negative. It is also important to find out what psychological skills they already use and how it works for them. Finally, it is best to start working with athletes during their off-season and teach them the basics before their competitive season starts. However, if that is not the case, we must adjust by starting slowly and finding a way that works best for the individual you are working with.

3. **How would you conduct and utilize the performance profiling approach?**
    I usually start by asking my clients whether they have an idea of what characteristics every great athlete in their sport must have. It slowly turns into a little brainstorming session as clients get more into it. Throughout the whole process of performance profiling, it is important to remind clients what they are responding to. For example, you may say: "Remember, you shall be thinking of how important this characteristic is for a great player on a scale from 1 (not important at all) to 10 (very important)" or "Remember, you are evaluating yourself at this time! How good are you at this particular skill on a scale from 1 (not good at all) to 10 (very good)?" At the end of the process, remind your client why you did the whole thing and tell them that based on all the information you collected you will prepare an individual mental training plan for them. They will be interested in knowing more and look forward to the next session.

4. **How would you approach your first meeting with an athlete?**
    It is always important to create a relationship with your client. Therefore, I usually start my work with every individual by doing a little "interview." We discuss where he/she comes from (family), what he/she does besides playing sports (school or work), and what sport he/she plays. It is important to follow the athlete's body language to find out whether he/she is ready to open up and honestly respond to any type of difficult questions that may evoke discomfort and negative emotions. If you are being sincere and act in a friendly manner, it usually does not take a long time to build the relationship with clients. Once you have good eye contact with the client and you see that he/she trusts you, you can go ahead and ask questions such as what issues he/she has before, during, and after his/her performance. You can also ask about feelings, thoughts, and fears, but make sure that the athlete's discomfort is not too great during the first session!

5. **How would you engage other individuals directly affecting your client into communicating or even working with you in order to help the client?**
    Working with coaches, parents, trainers, and others who may affect your athlete is very important. If your client is okay with this, it is usually not that hard to chat with these people and find out how they influence the athlete. It is important to try to get them "on the same boat" – explain to them that you are trying to make their work easier by helping the athlete to find their "mental reserves." Talking to coaches is a great way to learn more about athletes. This information is crucial because it helps to get a more complete picture of the athlete. Talking to parents is essential when working with kids because parents are usually those who affect them the most, and thus also may cause lots of blocks and issues their children may have. Some parents are too pushy and that often causes stress for their children. As a reaction to that they are not able to control their emotions during their game and end up underperforming. Their parents do not understand that, but also do not realize that they are the ones causing it. Being honest with these parents and helping them to understand and realize that they may be the source of the issue is critical! It sometimes happens that you lose your clients because of that (parents do not want to hear negatives), but if they really care about the well-being of their children, they accept it and will even work on changing themselves as well. That is the best reward for your hard work!

CHAPTER 4

1. **How should a practitioner's approach differ when working with an elite athlete versus an athlete at a lower level? Why?**
    My first point of emphasis is the one thing that remains the same, which is the content or the message. A Spanish teacher once told me that there is more than one way to get to the Port of Spain, the capital of Trinidad and Tobago. In my opinion, this is essentially the case in terms of working with both elite and non-elite athletes. For instance, in terms of creating a comfortable environment for an elite athlete, I would be a bit informal when building rapport. When dealing with a youth athlete, in most cases I would be careful not to be too informal while still fostering a comfortable environment.

    The elite athletes I have worked with in Trinidad and Tobago and the Caribbean region have been mostly in an individual capacity. The ideal environment for these sessions was very informal. In most cases, sessions were held at a training facility, pool, and other open areas.

Non-elite athletes would generally be part of a group session or meet one-on-one in a more formal setting. This group would generally prefer more interactive sessions where they can have fun while learning. Because these athletes are at a lower level, sometimes the importance of mental toughness is unknown to them. Illustrating some success stories from elite athletes has worked well as a buy-in for this group. These illustrations would generally be along the lines of mental skills that have been successfully used by an elite athlete.

2. **How should you approach working with an athlete that has lost his or her motivation after an injury?**
    The first thing I would point out is the fact that injuries happen and there are a lot of renowned athletes who came back from being injured. It is also important to emphasize the things that they are feeling physically, emotionally, and psychologically are to be expected and are natural. Many athletes believe that post-injury they are weaker than they were before.

    Past experiences have caused me to use a particular approach in dealing with reduced motivation among athletes who have been injured. This process consists of two phases.

    Phase I: Understanding the Importance of Physical Therapy
    As a former athlete who has been injured, I understand the importance of physical therapy. Have I always done what my athletic trainer or physiotherapist requested of me? No. This approach obviously was not the best. It is my role to help athletes recognize that physical therapy not only helps make them physically stronger, but also mentally stronger as well. I lead the discussion by asking if they have ever done these types of exercises on the injured area and they have generally said no. Essentially, I then explain that post-injury physical rehabilitation can actually contribute to improving strength, performance, and motivation.

    Phase II: Restarting Full Training
    Athletes sometimes find it hard to go slow and take their time. Although they have the all-clear to begin training, it is important to be realistic. At this stage, the practitioner should remind the athlete that he or she has not trained for a particular period so it is to be expected that fitness level and performance will be lowered. What I have seen in the past is that athletes assume that their level of performance has dropped because of the injury. This then negatively affects their motivation. Understanding that this is a natural developmental phase in terms of their recovery can aid in increasing their motivation.

3. **What do you do when an athlete is interested in seeing you for individual sessions but the coach is against it?**
    This would depend on the dynamics of the situation, because it is important for the practitioner to have a good relationship with the coach as well. Once the athlete in question is an adult, I would leave it up to him or her to decide if they would like to see me despite their coach's disapproval. It's essential for athletes to maintain a positive ongoing relationship with their coach, as this is paramount. If our sessions could compromise the relationship he or she has with the coach I would advise against it. A second option would be to not make the coach aware of the sessions.

    When working with junior athletes I generally liaise with the parents since they are the ones that schedule sessions with me. If the athlete wants to see me and the parent agrees then I would conduct the session. My role in both scenarios initially would simply be to offer suggestions.

4. **How can you help an athlete increase his or her level of confidence?**
    In terms of approach, there are two main things I attempt to highlight in helping an athlete build his or her confidence. Specifically, there are some things that they can control and others they have no direct control over.

    Things they can control are extremely important. I believe that this is where most of their attention should be if they want to increase their level of confidence. The list includes the little and sometimes automatic things done especially when they perform their best: training, preparation, strategy, technique, skill, strengths, mental toughness, game plan – the list goes on.

    Things they cannot control are sometimes very distracting and can impede performance. I tend to bring to light the fact that although their attention should be on the things they can control, they ought to be aware of the things that they have no control over as well. Always understand that the former needs most of their attention and energy. The latter deals with opponents' preparation or actions, weather, facilities, officials, and spectators, to name a few.

5. **How would you approach working with an elite athlete who no longer wants to train?**
First, the reason why he or she no longer wants to train must be known. This decision is ultimately up to the athlete. Nevertheless, I would also want the athlete to remember why he or she started playing the sport in the first place and whether or not the ultimate goal in the sport has been achieved. It would be important to mention that some athletes experience a great deal of stress both in training and outside the training environment. This can cause athletes to lose their motivation to participate in the sport, resulting in a loss of passion. In addition, training can sometimes feel like a chore or simply work that just has to be done. This is important because athletes want to know that they are being understood and heard. The athlete would be encouraged to think back or even write down the real reasons for his or her continued participation over the years. Some possible outcomes could be them remembering the fun they had or the fact that they still want to win a particular championship.

6. **What may be one of the biggest hurdles faced by athletes after an injury?**
The lack of motivation faced by athletes after an injury is the biggest challenge in my opinion. Athletes who are accustomed to performing at a high level can find it extremely difficult to lessen this workload, as required post-injury. Additionally, they would have had specific objectives to achieve both in training and competition. The lessened workload can sometimes seem as if training is not helping them get to where they need to be. This is where the lack of motivation comes in. The small steps on the road to recovering can sometimes seem overwhelming. In making matters worse, an athlete can decide to deviate from the slow and steady plan and take matters into his or her own hands. An example of this is an athlete thinking that he or she can do more than what was recommended by the athletic trainer or physiotherapist. When doing too much too soon they can potentially re-injure themselves and this means going back to the beginning. Other potential hurdles could be, for example, lack of confidence and fear of re-injury. It is recommended to consult the literature and research on the psychology of sport injury.

7. **How could the approach utilized in this case study be tailored to work with athletes within a team environment?**
My suggestion for a team environment is to ensure that the message is the same in terms of content. Because it is a group, interaction is key to ensuring that the team is engaged. What has worked well for my practice is having some fun activities at the start and relating them to the topic or theme of the session. Some people in Trinidad and Tobago say that prevention is better than the cure. In a group setting, I would suggest a proactive approach that educates the team about injury, overcoming it, and some of the experiences of injured athletes. For instance, it has been stated that motivation is one of the biggest hurdles faced by athletes after injury. A proactive approach would be to make the team aware of this, outlining what they should expect and discussing concrete steps they can take to improve their level of motivation.

CHAPTER 5

1. **How might an SPC work with an athlete who is referred by a coach?**
The most important issue of sport psychology service is to develop appropriate strategies for helping an athlete deal with his/her problems and enhance athletic performance. First, communication with a relevant coach and observations of practice and competition are recommended to get further information on the client. Second, proper psychological measures, including psychological skills, coping strategies, motivation, self-confidence, and mental toughness, can be used to evaluate an athlete's mental status. Third, based on the results of the inventory evaluation, a follow-up interview can be conducted to identify the psychological issues of the client. Following these procedures, the SPC is able to collect substantial information to more objectively assess the demands of the client and figure out appropriate education programs and interventions.

2. **What are your considerations for choosing an appropriate measure to evaluate an athlete's psychological characteristics?**
When beginning a new consultation with an athlete, valid assessment of psychological skills is a critical tool to provide an SPC with useful information about the athlete's characteristics. The data gained from an assessment of psychological skills can offer the direction for further face-to-face interviews and the development of effective sport psychology interventions. Therefore, it is

important that the assessment measures used by the SPC are instruments guaranteed to offer psychometric validity and conceptual basis, and suitable to an athlete's developmental stage. When working with high-performance athletes, sport-specific questionnaires are recommended because these tests are more likely to identify specific target behaviors that occur in particular situations of individual athletes. For this reason, traditional psychological tests may be of little practical value in examining target behaviors in the process of sport psychology service. Besides, it is important to not only inform the athletes, coaches, and parents about the purposes of psychological assessment, but also necessary that the SPC explain how the data will be utilized and with whom the data will be shared.

3. **What kind of theoretical framework would you use when working with an athlete similar to the one described in this chapter?**
   A cognitive-behavioral approach is recommended when an SPC works with a young athlete similar to our case. In our work, we recognized the young boxer's personal demands such as stress management, motivation, and self-confidence enhancement; therefore, this holistic approach could help the client restructure negative thinking and recognize the value of daily training. To address the effectiveness of sport psychology service, we reinforced several mental skills (e.g., self-talk, arousal regulation, relaxation, concentration, goal-setting, communication) and modified these techniques to be sport-specifically tailored for the athlete, and taught her to practice them from the field of training to competition. We believed that the application of this cognitive-behavioral process would afford the athlete an opportunity to use these mental skills practically and determine whether they matched her developmental needs. From the outset, we also explained to her that success in sport was her dream and responsibility, and we aimed to support her to achieve her goals.

4. **What kind of psychological skills would you utilize to enhance an athlete's mental toughness?**
   Mental toughness refers to a set of positive attitudes, thoughts, and behaviors even in the face of adversity, pain, and self-doubt. When athletes are able to deal with challenges, setbacks, and physical pain, they can make every effort during training and when competing. The characteristics of a mentally tough athlete include strong self-belief, motivation, concentration, and coping ability with stress. Therefore, mental toughness training is suggested to cover mental skills such as self-confidence build-up, goal-setting, focus and refocus training, as well as arousal regulation and stress management.

5. **What challenges might an SPC face when the athlete is a busy traveler? How could the SPC and athlete deal with these challenges?**
   Sport psychology services for an international athlete may be postponed as the athlete frequently travels abroad to participate in competition and training. However, to promote the continued implementation of mental skills during a road game, ongoing contact is helpful for consistent commitment of learned mental skills. By using modern technology, the SPC can keep contact with the client when he/she is away from home. The SPC has to change some of his/her traditional delivery methods to keep effective communication with athletes who travel away or abroad. For example, while the athlete travels away and feels reluctant to contact the SPC by telephone, electronic media (e.g., LINE app and email) offer easy access to keep communicating with the SPC. It is noticeable that the SPC must understand the ethical standards of providing internet services, such as confidentiality, data transmission, and data storage, in order to maintain good quality sport psychology consultation.

CHAPTER 6

1. **If you were the psychologist in this case study, how would you approach managing the various confidentiality issues related to working with Lucy?**
   A key focus in effectively managing the various challenges to confidentiality that arose was to ensure that discussions regarding what was/was not to be shared, how it would be shared, and with whom, were regular ongoing discussions with Lucy. It was vital within the initial session to not only clearly outline the instances where confidentiality would be breached (i.e., duty of care), but also to highlight the differences between the various servicing approaches that would be involved in her injury rehabilitation program (i.e., individual psychology sessions, combined somatic/psychology sessions, progress review meetings with

artistic staff). To assist in the continuity of care and alignment with the various individual health professionals' treatment programs, it was vital to ensure the agreed upon levels of information that would be shared were confirmed with Lucy ahead of time and were also regularly reviewed. Additionally, ongoing education and advocacy regarding the ethical guidelines and considerations for the management of health and personal information was provided to all artistic staff.

2. **Who is "the client" in this case study? Is there more than one? If so, which client takes priority – ethically or legally?**
   From an ethical standpoint, the primary client in this case study is Lucy. While the psychologist is employed by the dance training institution to deliver services to its students, the health and well-being of the student is the highest ethical priority as the direct recipient of psychological services. However, legally, the psychologist is responsible to her employer (i.e., the dance training institution) for delivering psychological services. So in this instance, the psychologist has two "clients" – an individual and an organization.

3. **What type of case management and treatment approach(es) could be applied in this situation?**
   In this case study, the biopsychosocial approach to injury management was utilized, which is an individual-centered model that considers both the person, their health challenge(s) (i.e., injury), and their social context. The approach to case management and treatment included a focus upon: early intervention; future injury/re-injury prevention; an individually tailored rehabilitation program; active engagement within the training environment; increasing activity and return to full-time training load; regular reviews of progress; and evidence-based decisions made in collaboration with all stakeholders (i.e., student/dancer, health team, and artistic staff).

4. **What ethical considerations are additionally required when dealing with a client who is a minor? As the psychologist, how would you manage these considerations?**
   Given Lucy was only 15 years of age (where a minor is defined as under the age of 18), consideration regarding the boundaries of confidentiality was required in relation to any liaison and/or discussion with her parents. Furthermore, Lucy's intellectual capability to understand and provide informed consent needed to be determined to ensure that she was fully aware of the parameters under which psychological services and the management of her health and personal information within the dance training context would operate. This became particularly important given that Lucy lived independently with another similar-aged student, located interstate and away from her parents.

5. **What is the primary outcome that needs to be achieved?**

   a. **For Lucy?**
      The primary desired outcome for Lucy involved balancing the active support of her recovery from injury so that she could return to full functionality within her dance training, minimizing any negative psychological impacts of the progress/lack of progress in her injury rehabilitation. Complications during Lucy's treatment period included her reported and observed struggle regarding whether she wished to continue to pursue a professional career in dance (i.e., remain at the dance training institution or return home).

   b. **For Lucy's parents?**
      The primary desired outcome for Lucy's parents centered upon their care and concern for her overall health and well-being, not just about her injury. In this case study, Lucy's parents were supportive of whatever decision she made regarding whether she continued with her dance training or returned home. However, this level of support is not always evident and in many other cases parents have been observed to place undue pressure upon students to continue with their training and career focus despite poor progress in injury rehabilitation.

   c. **For the health team?**
      The primary desired outcome for the health team was for Lucy to successfully complete her rehabilitation to a pre-injury and/or pain-free functioning level, thus enabling her to fully participate in the standard full-time dance training activities. However, this would not be at the expense of her overall health and well-being, and regular reviews as part of the ongoing rehabilitation process would assist in determining any required shifts in desired outcomes.

d. For the artistic teaching team?

The primary desired outcome for the artistic teaching team was for Lucy to fully recover from her injuries (i.e., be fit for purpose) and return to a full-time load as soon as possible, so as to keep up with the demands of all the required dance training activities.

e. For the training institution?

The primary desired outcome for the training institution was to have all their dance students performing at their best both physically and psychologically, which would assist with the further development of their dance skills and abilities in line with the course requirements.

f. Are any of these at odds with each other? If so, how could they be managed?

On a surface level, the primary outcome appeared to vary/be at odds across a range of these stakeholder groups. However, this was managed by the psychologist through regular reflection regarding "Who is the client?" as well as by ensuring that Lucy's needs in terms of her overall health and well-being were discussed and recognized to be the highest priority.

CHAPTER 7

1. **Explain the role of parents and spectators in the socialization process of young athletes.**

   Various authors such as Arnold (1999) have highlighted the importance of sports to provide particularly rich contexts for personal growth. On one hand, there is a shared belief that sport contributes to the moral development of young athletes, because the foundations of sport reflect concern for fairness and well-being. On the other hand, it is argued that sportspersonship is worsening in youth sports due to parents', spectators', and coaches' emphasis on winning at all cost and overemphasis on success, as it happens in professional sport. So, parents and spectators are significant adults that act as role models, like coaches, teachers, teammates, and professional athletes, and could transmit different values to young athletes.

2. **What kind of values are transmitted through sport?**

   Lee, Whitehead, and Balchin (2000) using the Youth Sports Values Questionnaire (YSVQ) identified the value priorities among 500 male and female participants aged between 12 and 16 years. In their study, the most important values were enjoyment, personal achievement, sportsmanship, and contract maintenance; least important was winning. However, the review of empirical studies carried out by Shields and Bredemeier (2007) conclude that different kinds of values are transmitted through sport depending on the age of the participants, the type of sport, and other contextual features such as the parents', spectators', and sports institutions' value system.

3. **What are the strengths and limitations of Barcelona's Campaign to promote parents' sportspersonship in youth sport?**

   The two main strengths of the campaign are that: (1) it was based on the assessment of players' needs for fair play and sportspersonship in youth sport. In this sport context the main problems associated with sporting competitions were related not with on-field situations, but rather occurred off the field. For this reason the Barcelona Sports Council requested the development of a campaign on the psychological aspects of spectators' positive participation in sport. (2) It was spread across a variety of different formats with a shared message always included in all the materials.

   The main limitation was that the campaign attempted to influence spectators' behaviors, but the ones that behave in an appropriate way did not receive any positive reinforcement. If we want to modify parents/spectators behaviors in youth sport, we need to praise them for the positive and supportive behaviors they exhibit toward players, coaches, and referees, and not for the verbalizations that reflect a win-at-all-costs attitude. In our study of the assessment of the effects of the campaign, referees of football and basketball games received only 4 percent of encouragement and 68 percent of criticism, reflecting that some parents place too much emphasis on winning. In this sense, we have to assume that the elements of the campaign were insufficient by themselves to change the spectators' behaviors toward referees.

4. **Explain the most inadequate spectators' behaviors that were observed in basketball and soccer games and what effects could produce these behaviors in children.**

   The campaign was assessed through the direct observation of the behaviors of parents during youth football and basketball games (i.e., ages 9–10 years old). Behaviors were grouped into three dimensions: (1) encouragement; (2) instruction; and (3) punishment. The distribution of behaviors was different depending on the target of the communication. On the one hand, players received mostly encouragement from their parents (68 percent), a moderate quantity of technical instruction (27 percent), and only 5 percent of punishment. On the other hand, referees received only 4 percent of encouragement, a similar amount of instructions as players (28 percent), but mostly criticisms (68 percent). According to the aforementioned results, we could conclude that the most inadequate spectators' behaviors were criticism toward the referees and technical instruction to the players. These behaviors are usually imitated by players and could produce an attitude of winning at all costs.

5. **What does the "Juga verd" (play green) campaign add to previous values campaigns and which psychological principles are the basis for this campaign?**

The goal of the campaign was to praise the spectators' positive behaviors toward players, coaches, and referees, and give extra scores based on spectator behaviors which are taken into account in the outcome of the match. This campaign gives a maximum score of ten points, with part of the final score depending on the competitive score of the game, but also taking into consideration coaches' views of the behaviors of the opposing team coaches and players, a parent's view of the spectators' behavior, the spectators' view of the opposing team behavior, and the referee's view of the spectators, coaches, and any remarkable fair-play behavior of the athletes. The campaign, from a cognitive-behavioral perspective, assumes that if we want to change the values in youth sport, we have to change the contingencies of the sport context as well, especially the ones related to parents and spectators, such as rewarding parents for their supportive behavior toward referees and applauding the players' fair-play behaviors toward their opponents.

CHAPTER 8

1. **What were the similarities and differences between these two athletes?**

Similarities. Both athletes were female, and of a similar age. Both had recently made the transition to living away from home, and were living on-site at a talent-development academy. Both athletes had defensive playing positions, meaning mistakes were often punished by the team conceding a point, and thus mistakes were to be avoided wherever possible. The academy had the clear goal of developing players to become international standard. As such, both athletes had experienced a transition from being one of the best players in their team to having a lot to work on, and being a long way short of "expectations." Feedback from the coaching staff at the academy had given both players a number of areas to improve. Both athletes were experiencing problems with injuries and fitness. As a result of the above, both athletes were experiencing difficulties with their confidence and self-esteem, exacerbated by evidence of classic maladaptive thought habits such as perfectionism, all-or-nothing thinking, and catastrophizing. Both athletes seemed motivated to seek support and attend one-to-one meetings.

Differences. Belle appeared to be genuinely seeking performance improvements, in accordance with the feedback received from coaches. As such, Belle committed to the various tasks and exercises, and experienced clear progress as a consequence. On reflection, it appeared Lynn may not have been ready to focus on performance issues – instead needing to spend some time coping with the emotional experiences of moving away from home, receiving substantial constructive (or negative) feedback, and the recent knee injury. Ostensibly, Lynn needed to "feel better" before she could progress to "playing better." As such, Lynn did not adhere to tasks that were explicitly designed to improve either performance or confidence, or both. Notably, Lynn's performance profile and goals appeared to be highly "self-handicapping" – focusing only on "improvables," never strengths, and setting goals in areas where she could not train until her knee rehab was complete. Perhaps under the surface, Belle appeared happy to take responsibility for solving the problems she faced, whereas Lynn responded as though it was unfair and unjust that she should face such challenges.

2. **What signs and symptoms are presented in this case study that could have been used to inform the selection of a philosophy and consulting style:**

a. **For Belle**

Belle presented with a clear performance focus, and we frequently focused on performance issues. As such, adopting aims that focused on performance seemed highly appropriate.

Belle appeared to be comfortable with the "commodities" approach to both mental and physical skills: i.e., "you do not currently have (enough of) this skill, but with practice you can gain it and it will enhance your performance." This is arguably the core assumption of Mental Skills Training, and it also reflects quite a strong implicit belief that a person's capability can be developed (i.e., incremental beliefs of "growth mindset" – cf. Dweck, 1999). As such, the "hard-science" or certaintist philosophy, that what can be shown to work for others must also work for Belle – was also a good fit. Both the aims and philosophy are complementary to a "practitioner-led" consulting style – i.e., "I am the expert as I know the research and theory." Sure enough, even though this style was adopted unconsciously as a function of previous experiences, it was a good fit for Belle. Her responsiveness and adherence, as well as the relatively quick experiencing of benefits, could be taken as indicators that the adopted style was a good fit for Belle.

b. For Lynn

Lynn found herself in a performance-focused environment, and the psychological support was assumed to adopt "performance" as the main aim. However, on reflection, aims focusing on welfare and negotiating a challenging life-transition would appear much more suitable. Lynn was less comfortable talking about performance, and appeared to imitate the comments of coaches in her performance profile – an extrinsic and superficial approach, rather than reflecting on what was of intrinsic interest to her. Of course, at 20 years of age we should not expect all athletes to be able to accurately articulate their emotions and intrinsic interests – but the psychologist should arguably have understood this and not taken "absence of evidence as evidence of absence" (e.g., if she didn't talk much about emotions, that doesn't necessarily mean they are irrelevant"). There were signs in Lynn's non-adherence to the support offered that she did not believe, deep down, it would help, and this might imply implicit beliefs that ability is relatively fixed, and unresponsive to practice (entity beliefs of "fixed mindset" – cf. Dweck, 1999). This would also begin to explain the more unpleasant experience of receiving constructive feedback, as compared to Belle, because such comments become a summative label, not a temporary description. Such a deep-seated belief would likely both undermine any attempt to pursue improvements (i.e., goals, self-talk) or critical self-reflection (i.e., performance profile). Articulating, examining, and challenging such beliefs would likely require the adoption of a highly individualistic philosophy – such as "construalism" – because the beliefs are so deep-seated as to seem "part of who she is" and "just natural." In this situation, arguments based on "research suggests" or "other people seem to benefit" are almost irrelevant to the client. Aims focusing on welfare and uncovering an athlete's emotional life, alongside construalist (or "soft-science") assumptions would be a good complement for a "client-led" consulting style, and on reviewing the case there are several instances where adopting a "practitioner-led" prescriptive approach appears to have been ineffective. Perhaps the most telling indicator that a "client-led" style might have been more effective was the apparent rapport and "ease" of sessions when the focus was not on performance. One of our most comfortable and friendly conversations was the final (unplanned) meeting after Lynn had decided to leave the academy.

3. **What might be the pros and cons of being able to adopt different theoretical and philosophical frameworks with different athletes?**
This case study presents an argument that being able to adopt different aims, philosophies, and styles allows a SEPP practitioner to meet the needs of a wider range of clients, and thus be more successful more often. However, there are several drawbacks. First, there is a significant burden of training involved, to become conversant with different approaches and able to implement different styles. Second, to date, much of the literature in this area is diffuse (across many different books/articles), disparate (i.e., not easily compared or reconciled), and inaccessible (i.e., language and concepts). This chapter and others like it seek to reduce this problem by offering single, coherent, and accessible frameworks that at least offer an entry point into a complex topic. Third, even when the relevant concepts are grasped in principal, there remains a significant challenge of incorporating them into practice. Typically, practitioners appear to develop from "hard-science" and "practitioner-led" approaches to recognize and adopt "soft-science" and "client-led" approaches (e.g., Tod & Bond, 2010). However, at present this development appears to occur "organically" with no clear intention or common framework to understand why such changes occur. A common outcome is for

practitioners to claim an "eclectic" style: haphazardly deploying attributes from different approaches on a trial-and-error basis (i.e., pragmatism). Failure to provide a coherent style may lead to a disjointed client experience, such that apparent lynchpin assumptions can be abandoned and while most clients will not be able to explain why this "feels weird," consider the following. SEPP: "This training should work for everyone (hard-science)." Client: "I did what you said and it didn't work." SEPP: "Oh well, everyone is different (soft science)." Finally, even when a SEPP practitioner can adopt different styles, there is a considerable effort involved in learning to evaluate which style or philosophy is most likely to suit each client, and then adjust accordingly. Unfortunately, very few clients will be able to clearly articulate their preferred philosophical assumptions or consulting style, although many (not all) will be able to clearly identify their preferred aims. Hence, the responsibility arguably does fall to the SEPP to get this right. The arguments presented here are that being able to understand, recognize, and adapt to different philosophical and theoretical "needs" enables the practitioner to help a wider range of clients, more reliably. Further, as was the case in this case study, being able to recognize when one's assumptions are not suiting the client may even allow for "error correction" before the relationship is terminated or deemed unsuccessful.

4. **What were the warning signs that Lynn's needs and expectations were not well suited to the assumptions being used, and what could have been done about it?**

    * The performance profile that fixated only on improvables and refused to acknowledge areas of relative strength.
    * The setting of goals in areas that were not suitable to be pursued until the injury rehab was complete.
    * The apparent non-compliance with injury rehab.
    * The non-compliance with clearly explained and explicitly agreed psychological strategies to support confidence and performance.

    Each of the above arguably represented a level of "self-handicapping," where choices and decisions only served to undermine progress and preserve the status quo. This is likely unconscious and not deliberate, but these should have been clear warning signs that my assumptions and approach were not working for Lynn.

    * Adopting the exact language of the coach feedback and not integrating these comments into a more personal evaluation may reflect an extrinsic or superficial approach that served to "hide" the underlying issues.
    * Appearing more chatty and friendly when not focusing on performance issues. In retrospect this should have been a clear indicator that pursuing performance was not ideal – but remember the academy only existed to create future international-level players.

5. **How could you incorporate an awareness of philosophy and theoretical frameworks into your own practice?**
    This is probably the most difficult question of all. The common framework and vocabulary offered here may help to organize reflections and supervision on the matter – that is the intention of this chapter. Further, philosophical and theoretical considerations may be deliberately incorporated into the planning of support, as well as one's post-session notes and reflective practice. At present, these issues are often overlooked in notes and reflective logs. It may also be possible to include explicit cues and checkpoints within one's support – for example, the end of the intake or need analysis phases – where philosophy can be explicitly reviewed and evaluated. Of course, in any moments where clients appear to be unhappy, non-compliant, or simply confused, that may be a good trigger to review the assumptions made so far, and consider making changes. Reflecting on (1) the accuracy of assumptions; and/or (2) their appropriateness for each client; as well as (3) the consistency over time and between levels (aims, ontology, style) are all promising places to begin incorporating these issues into one's practice. Further still, it may be possible to review one's capability in enacting different approaches, as well as comfort levels when doing so. Finally, of course, one option is to choose and stick to a preferred coherent "system." Know that style well, sell it, accurately deliver it proficiently, but don't deliver it to clients that won't benefit from it. Ostensibly, a small-but-satisfied client list is better than a very big client base with very varied opinions on how good the service was.

CHAPTER 9

1.   **What difference would it make to you as an SPC to formulate and work from a coherent professional philosophy (if this is not already the case)?**
     It is very easy as an SPC to fall in love with specific exercises and to adopt a tool-based approach. This may work fine in some cases, but our experience is that when interventions fail or athletes do not progress in their psychological development, it will often be due to inconsistencies in the consultant's approach. A professional philosophy provides an overall framework for the sport psychology work of an individual consultant or a team of consultants. The idea is that optimal sport psychological interventions must be based on a coherent service delivery model that integrates the entire efforts of the consultant's work (Poczwardowski et al., 2004), from basic beliefs and values over intervention theories to specific services and methods. Developing and formulating a professional philosophy stimulates a practitioner to ask very important questions related to the very foundations of his or her work. Questions could include: To what extent must coaches, parents, teammates, and other parts of the environment be involved in an intervention for it to be successful? To what extent do athletes need to thrive and find meaning to perform to their potential? Can a high-performance mindset be developed in the athletes prior to major championships or must the consultant follow the athletes to high-pressure competitions? What does it really mean to be mentally strong and what effects are we striving for? Does a sport psychologist have a responsibility to optimize sporting environments or only athletes? What theories do I wish to work from? Answering such questions provides a basis to deliver very focused and values-based interventions and to be able to make solid decisions under high pressure.
     In a team of SPCs, formulating a professional philosophy has further advantages. In some cases a sport federation for some reason has to replace one consultant with another, an athlete may move from a talent group to a senior national team, or an individual athlete may work with one consultant even though a different consultant is most often traveling with the team to competitions. In such cases a shared professional philosophy provides consistency and focus to the intervention.

2.   **How would you use the ACT perspective versus more traditional cognitive interventions to work with an athlete/team on performance anxiety?**
     A lot has been said about the ways in which interventions from an ACT perspective differ from more traditional cognitive interventions, ranging from "it's a completely new paradigm" to "there is not much difference really." The two approaches are both *cognitive* and thus agree that thinking and emotions have an important impact on behavior and on performance. To us, a major difference relates to how you deal with negative thoughts and emotions. More traditional (second wave) cognitive approaches will work to *change the content of thoughts and emotions*. Examples hereof are strategies to control your inner dialogue, focus on positives, and deliberately entering your ideal performance state. ACT or third-wave cognitive approaches aim to change an athlete's *relation to thoughts and emotions*. Examples hereof are strategies to accept and be willing to have negative thoughts and emotions, and to engage in the sport task rather than in the task of combating or controlling such emotions.
     In sport we find this distinction to be very important. We experience that a number of myths are quite rooted in elite sport, such as: mentally tough athletes are always calm and never afraid; strong athletes always hit their "zone" when it really counts; a strong mindset equals positive thinking; and many more. These are all statements that contradict our experience when working with elite athletes. We believe that introducing third-wave perspectives will alleviate some of the pressure that comes from these myths and provide more room for athletes to be who they are. We also see our definition of mental strength (see above) as a means to this end.

3.   **How would you, through a focus on team and personal values, assist athletes in handling high-stress situations and adversity during and between matches?**
     In competitions as well as in daily life, athletes are often put in demanding or anxiety-provoking situations and dilemmas. In these cases, the athletes experience turmoil of emotion and are likely to be pushed around by their feelings. No one wants to experience doubt, uncertainty, or anxiety, and according to ACT our automatic response will be to engage in actions that alleviate unpleasant thoughts and feelings but not necessarily bring the athletes closer to their desired ends.
     To assist athletes in handling high stress and adversity, we advocate values clarification as an effective tool. If an athlete's values are unclear, he or she will more easily be pushed around by automatic thoughts and feelings. But clear values cannot stand alone as a strategy to handle stressful situations. We need to teach athletes to register their tendency to engage in reactive behaviors

to alleviate unpleasant feelings. We need to build their willingness to accept such feelings. And we need to help them to a clear formulation of the values they want to live their athletic career by. This will come together as an antidote to reactive behavior and allow athletes to more often engage in values-consistent behavior, even in the face of high-pressure situations and adversity.

4. **What are particularly relevant issues for you as an SPC to consider when preparing athletes for a championship during which expectations, media attention, and pressure are expected to exceed anything the athletes experienced before (e.g., at the Olympics)?**
Sport psychology preparation of athletes to competitions often involves noting their common and distracting thoughts and emotions and teaching the athletes to handle these. The Olympics is different in many ways but most importantly in terms of the importance attributed to the event. When athletes prepare for a high-pressure event such as the Olympics, particularly for the first time, it is very hard to predict how they will think, feel, and react. It is likely they will experience thoughts and emotions that differ from all previous experiences in content, frequency, duration, and intensity. For this reason, our experience is that it is likely a futile effort to teach athletes to handle specific thoughts and feelings that are expected to arise. Rather, it makes better sense to teach them metacognitive strategies to deal with what comes up in a flexible, accepting, and values-connected way. Our experience is that when athletes experience unexpected emotions they unfortunately tend to try to ignore them or hope they will go away. This also means that it is very advantageous for the sport psychologist to have a close dialogue with the athletes on a daily basis, which essentially requires that the consultant travels with the team or athletes to the event.

5. **How can an SPC prepare for delivering service in high-pressure contexts, for example through colleague support systems and clarification of his or her own values?**
During a championship, much like the athletes, the consultant is likely to experience demanding or anxiety-provoking situations and dilemmas. Examples hereof are responding to requests from the media, balancing client confidentiality with the coaches' legitimate need to know what is going on with the athletes, and being told in confidentiality about athlete behavior that is unethical or likely to minimize medal potential. Such situations often demand a quick response and the consultant is likely to experience turmoil of emotion. Mindfulness training and values clarifications are important tools to help the consultant deal with these emotions, but our experience is also that a collegiate support setup is very helpful.

CHAPTER 10

1. **How can an SP work toward reducing or managing the barriers that exist in seeking sport psychology support?**
An aim is to find a balance between being seen as an integral part of the coaching team, valued and accepted by academy staff, while maintaining an independence to provide confidence in the confidentiality of services. It is important to reflect on how your own behaviors as an SP may be contributing to any lack of engagement to ensure that you are not hidden in the background and make every effort to communicate with players outside of scheduled sessions (e.g., over lunch or after training). We have found it beneficial to promote a positive view of psychology toward optimum performance and well-being rather than to deal solely with player problems. With consent, working and communicating visibly with players considered to possess positive psychological characteristics (e.g., team captain) can have an instant impact on perceptions of who should and could work on psychological aspects of performance.

2. **What key skills can the SP develop in coaches to enable them to positively affect team belief?**
We encourage coaches to be aware of how their verbal and non-verbal communication influences individual and team belief during training and on match days. This involves providing role clarity and setting goals with the player in training that highlight progression and mastery of skills, and in matches setting objectives that relate to key work that the player has achieved in training. Team talks prior to matches provide an opportunity for coaches to highlight past successes and acknowledge effort and progression as well as to reiterate simple messages and tactical instructions that suggest a readiness and preparedness to perform. The challenge for coaches during games is to acknowledge positive player intentions and effort in relation to these objectives rather than outcomes and to ensure that their body language is consistent with their verbal feedback. We have found this nonverbal communication plays a fundamental role in players' perceptions of how performance is being evaluated during matches.

3. **What skills could an SP focus on to positively affect momentum during a game?**
   Players have highlighted a number of cues that influence their perceptions of momentum before and during games that include positive body language when walking out onto the pitch, motivational self-talk in the team huddle before the game, and supportive teammate and coach responses to individual errors. We encourage players to take control of momentum through their preparation and responses to game situations and identify key individuals within the team to police these reactions and support the player appropriately when needed. We have developed routines prior to games that enable players to draw on relevant social support and during games to meet the possible threats to momentum – for example, conceding a goal. In these situations, identified players are responsible for ensuring that communication and body language remain positive and that the team is projecting to their opponents a confidence in their ability to overcome the setback and face the next challenge to ensure that momentum remains in the balance and within their control.

4. **What strategies can the SP develop with individual players to help maintain belief post-match after a team loss?**
   The foundation for the work in this area is achieved in training and prior to matches when setting multiple measures of success beyond outcomes such as scoring a goal as a striker, keeping a clean sheet as a goalkeeper or winning the match. With the young footballer it is important to emphasize that they are in a developmental phase and as such goals should relate to self-referenced improvement and increased confidence in executing new skills developed in training. With this mindset, all playing opportunities can be viewed as research into how the player is going to achieve their ultimate objectives and, as such, failure can only result from not learning anything from the playing experience. To assist emotion regulation we encourage players to send a text or email a report after training and matches that evaluates performance in relation to the previously set objectives. This includes three things that they felt they achieved, three areas in which they felt they could have performed better, then highlighting any strategies that they are going to take forward into the next performance, and then finally how this information will help structure their training and objectives in the coming week. We agree with the player that after this correspondence the text relating to how they could have performed better is deleted and represents closure of that performance to discourage unnecessary rumination.

5. **What are the key messages that an SP could disseminate to parents to shape a young player's perception of achievement and success in training?**
   Beliefs about what it takes to be a successful footballer and what constitutes success and achievement are influenced by parent interactions with players. We work with parents to help them assess how their beliefs about the professional football environment (e.g., "only one in a million make it as a professional," "to be a success you have to make sacrifices," "you can't show any weaknesses if you want to be selected to play") influence their behaviors and thought patterns and consequently how these positively impact their son or daughter. We encourage parents to challenge maladaptive beliefs by providing alternative evidence that can help shape a more helpful perspective. For example, in response to the belief that "you can't show any weaknesses if you want to be selected to play" we may discuss players in the team or on the world stage that have experienced performance slumps but maintained their place in the squad. The intention here is not to change parent beliefs, but to weaken the strength that they have in them. Such a shift (in this example) can help reduce risks associated with overtraining and encourage player interaction with the SP for mental skill development. Players will often look to parents during games for encouragement or approval and, so, as with coaches, it is important that parents are aware of how their expectations prior to and body language during matches communicates how they determine success and achievement.

CHAPTER 11

1. **When conducting a baseline assessment, what information would you provide and what information might you withhold from the client at this stage and why?**
   When providing a client with an intervention, in particular an intervention that may alter the results of a biofeedback or neurofeedback modality, such as respiration rate, heart rate, galvanic response, and electrical activity of the brain, it is important to avoid providing the client with any information which may change the first baseline assessment. Consider the timing of the intervention and education phase, and be consistent. Even closing the eyes can impact upon the results from the modalities.

2. **When introducing breathing techniques to an athlete for the first time, how long should you spend in the practice phase and why?**

When introducing a new breathing technique to a client, consider one minute (or less) training blocks initially to prevent the side-effects of incorrect breathing. It is important to note that breathing incorrectly, in particular over-breathing for more than one minute, can cause cutaneous and peripheral blood circulation to be reduced, and can have other undesirable physiological symptoms, such as tingling in the fingers and lips, and reduced sensory perception, balance, dizziness, and vision. When introducing a new breathing technique, for example PLB, you should be aware of the above symptoms and inform the athlete that if they feel dizzy at any point they should stop the new breathing technique. When you are confident the athlete has mastered the correct technique, consider increasing or decreasing the time accordingly. You should be aware of the following factors when introducing a breathing technique to an athlete: (1) taking five or six breaths incorrectly can alter your blood's pH level and thus alters your blood's capacity to deliver oxygen throughout the body; (2) breathing incorrectly for three minutes is enough to decrease the amount of oxygen to the brain and heart by 30 percent; and (3) correct and timely use of the breathing strategy should be predominantly athlete-led (with some consultant guidance) when introduced nearer to or in performance. Inappropriate use of diaphragmatic breathing techniques, including PLB, can bring about both wanted and unwanted changes. Unwanted changes may facilitate too much relaxation in the body, or feelings of tiredness. Athletes must be informed about both the benefits and consequences.

3. **What changes might you expect to see from pre-baseline to the practice phase that you may also see in the intervention phase?**

If performed correctly and depending on the individual, you may typically see a reduction in respiration rate from the pre-baseline phase when compared to the intervention phases. You would also expect to see some change, in particular a reduction in respiration rate during the practice phase. Do not worry if you start to see gradual changes and a reduction in respiration rates during practice (phase 2). The main take-home message here is that you do not inform the client about the exact nature of the technique before phase one.

4. **What are artifacts in biofeedback, and what steps would you take to prevent the risk of artifacts?**

Most of the latest mobile biofeedback equipment contains active noise cancellation technology. Historically, artifacts could occur through movement of cables or other external sources; however, the latest technology contains carbon-coated cables to minimize this. In active settings and as part of good practice, ensure you firmly attach the cable to the client to avoid cable movement. Certain clothing can cause static; always ask the client to wear a cotton-based top when attaching a biofeedback modality and ensure you switch off mobile phones.

5. **What are biofeedback modalities? What modality might you use for a client you have been working with, and why?**

Biofeedback is a process of monitoring physiological responses, such as muscle tension (using surface EMG), psychophysiological arousal (using galvanic skin response), heart rate, respiration rate, body temperature, and electrical activity of the brain (using EEG) – known as neurofeedback.

CHAPTER 12

1. **What other psychology principles/concepts/models/frameworks could be applicable in this particular case?**

It is important to acknowledge that every client case will be unique with regard to circumstances, resources available (e.g., time, budget), as well as the needs presented by the client in question. A number of psychological principles could be applied to cases with equal validity, but often come from opposing theoretical frameworks; thus, it is inevitable that only a few models can be drawn from when designing the interventions for each case. There are a number of additional psychology principles that would have been, and were, suitable for our particular case. While we may not have made direct reference to these additional principles within our case presentation, they did influence the work we conducted with this particular client.

For example, cognitive behavior therapy (CBT) provides a useful framework for sport psychology interventions. CBT is a form of psychotherapy that assists clients with understanding how their thoughts and feelings play a fundamental role in influencing their resultant behavior. One particular aim of CBT is to help clients understand that while we cannot control every aspect of our lives, we can control how we interpret and deal with the components of our unique environments. Additionally, accompanying principles that we reinforced throughout our intervention were the importance of process orientation and intrinsic motivation. Emphasizing how and where athletes should channel their attention and what nature of motivation they should strive to embody is very important for excellence in sport. Process-oriented athletes and/or practitioners understand and value the concept that results and outcomes are inevitable by-products of a process developed within a particular organizational climate or environment. While outcome orientation involves athletes fixating more heavily on the end product and/or the results of performance, process-oriented athletes lean more toward valuing and prioritizing a continuous investment in the smaller steps involved in creating a desired outcome. While it may seem obvious that process orientation is the intended approach, we believe that a healthy combination of the two is beneficial. Clients should always have a profound idea and vision of what they ultimately strive to achieve (e.g., outcome orientation), and thereby always have these ultimate goals set in place; however, it is more important to focus consistently on each small step required to achieve these goals and let the results take care of themselves. The above concept links well with intrinsic (i.e., task) and extrinsic (i.e., ego) forms of motivation. Practitioners must assist athletes in understanding the differences between these motivational orientations, and further assist athletes and teams in identifying their own makeup within these two components. Finally, it is also useful to draw on goal achievement theory as well as the methods behind developing transformational leadership when striving to create the best psychological high-performance environment for athletes.

2. **What were some of the limitations of this case? How did, or could, we have handled these limitations?**
It is inevitable that within any case there will be limitations to the intervention and it is valuable to consider a few of our limitations in order to establish how to improve the structures and approaches for future clients. One particular limitation that we experienced was difficulty establishing complete buy-in to the sport psychology intervention by all players. The majority of the group responded positively to our efforts, but there was a handful of players that had limited interest. This resistance proved to be challenging for us. As a team sport, rugby requires a collective effort for success; if some players are implementing certain processes established as a group while others have no interest in complying, then the potential success will always be limited. Coupled with this is the stigma often associated with consulting a psychologist, as well as the misperception and lack of knowledge around how sport psychologists can assist performance and athlete development. One way to overcome this for future cases is to negotiate buy-in from all players on a one-on-one basis at the beginning of the season, or preferably in the off- or pre-season period. Through this medium we can unpack each player's individual views and opinions of sport psychology, open up channels for them to clarify any misunderstandings and concerns, outline to each player the intended process and how important they are to the success of the envisioned interventions, and promote the value of participation and buy-in becoming a core element of the team norms. Therefore, for future cases such as this one it is vital that respect, credibility, and trust are established right from the start and maintained throughout the season.

Another difficulty that will inevitably be faced by practitioners is the "quick fix" mentality. At times, clients expect sport psychology practitioners to come in and conduct quick interventions providing immediate results. It is the practitioner's choice to decide on how they want to approach these kinds of cases. From our perspective, we follow a series of processes when dealing with clients involving cyclical steps, such as thorough assessment, intervention design, intervention implementation, intervention feedback and adjustment, and overall reflection. In our opinion, the nature of our work needs to be holistic and organic and this requires patience, time, and a commitment to change. These "quick fix" mentalities can affect the quality of work presented and can influence the sustainability of the intervention implemented.

3. **What could we do differently in the future in this type of case?**
A large portion of our intervention process involved group sessions. Although we did consult players one-on-one in an informal manner, it would have been beneficial to the overall process, given we had the budget and the timeframe, to have invested more focus into individual development by means of formal one-on-one sessions. These could have been scheduled before or after practices and with two practice slots each week we could have "serviced" a healthy number

of athletes each week. Furthermore, there was limited integration of mental skills training into on-field training sessions. For future involvement it will be useful to consider creative ways of developing certain mental skills such as confidence, focus, communication, and motivation during training sessions. With limited time in training, it may be unrealistic to try to separate physical training from mental training and, therefore, an amalgamated approach where athletes can develop in both areas simultaneously would be beneficial. Finally, while we did take part in the pre-season testing, by means of one-on-one consultations as expressed in our chapter, for future cases we would certainly want a more in-depth assessment process which we can reflect back on and utilize in additional one-on-one sessions throughout the season.

4. **What factors could have been damaging to our intended approach? What could we have done differently to take these into consideration when designing and implementing our intervention?**

    Two additional difficulties we experienced that could have damaged our intended approach were the limited willingness by the coaching staff to maintain structures once implemented and the limited impact and reach we had on teams below the first-team setup. While we did invest some time in coaches' sessions, designed for upskilling purposes which proved valuable, we could have spent more time meeting both formally and informally with coaching staff. This would have highlighted the purpose and rationale behind additional structures we had built with players and how they could assist in ensuring sustainability of these models.

    In addition to this, we were involved primarily with the first-team setup. Rugby is a contact sport where injuries are inevitable and where the success of a club depends largely on the depth and quality of its player base. With this in mind, it is natural for players to regularly move up and down between teams due to injury and performance status. It would have been beneficial to have extended our structures and influence to lower teams not only to ensure wider knowledge of how the systems work, but also to extend to the other teams the benefit and value that we believed our intervention was providing. This would have helped improve the player quality throughout the club.

    There are a number of elements we could do differently in the future in order to take these factors into consideration and limit their negative effects. Having a coaching staff that does not buy into one's approach as a sport psychologist is always a possibility. It is crucial that prior to integrating oneself into the program, one must obtain trust and respect from the coaching staff. It is important that the practitioner present an envisioned plan of action and establish how the coaching staff views his/her potential input. The coaching staff need to reinforce the methods and suggestions rather than questioning them or opposing them. The success of these kinds of interventions depends largely on the maintenance of the structures set by the coaching staff. They ultimately need to see and appreciate the value of what the practitioner is creating in the environment.

    Coupled with establishing this trust and buy-in by the coaches, there is a need to ensure there is flexibility for the services the practitioner is likely to be offering. Coaching staff are often set in their ways of doing things and are often threatened by change. The practitioner needs a flexible environment with flexible systems and structures. If one's approach is going to be questioned and opposed at every level of a sporting organization, then one will experience inevitable difficulties and challenges. Furthermore, it is necessary to establish good rapport and trust with key stakeholders (i.e., all coaching staff throughout all teams, committee members and even sponsors and partners) in the organization. From our experience, we know that there will often be inadequate knowledge of and experience with the politics of sport club setups and that, at times, practitioners may be faced with structures that do not allow for a holistic approach.

    Additionally, with Stuart (the first author) being involved as one of the practitioners (coaches) and as one of the players, we could have developed a more creative role for his involvement. Being positioned as a player and as a "coach" presents an exciting avenue to making significant differences in a team setup. A person in this position has a big influence over how the interventions are implemented and also has direct access to how the team responds to the different methods developed.

5. **What psychological advice can we give coaches when considering developing high-performance environments for athletes?**

    Throughout our approach and reflection we have heavily promoted the concept of creating the correct psychological environment and climate for athletes. While there are a vast number of sources for opinions and suggestions regarding the creation of such environments, which should all be considered, there are a couple of viewpoints that we would like to present. One particular concept is that the player has to be prioritized at all times. In modern-day sporting setups, the priority is often ensuring results of an overall team, sometimes at all costs, where there is subsequently limited personal focus and attention. Dealing with athletes is a complicated venture considering that coaches are extensively managing athletes with different personalities and characters, talents, personal visions and goals, as well as types and levels of motivation. Successful performance excellence requires the ability to unlock the personal potential of each athlete involved. Successful performance climates therefore hinge on being able to speak, in part, to each athlete's circumstances. Therefore, by prioritizing the players, the coach empowers them and gives them the opportunity to develop responsibility, accountability, autonomy, and transformational leadership. Thus, coaches should set up efficient and honest communication channels, allow the players to make mistakes, build confidence, prioritize a focus on strengths, chunk processes together, constantly evaluate, and always ensure confidentiality.

CHAPTER 13

1. **How do emotion and anxiety regulation play a role in helping an athlete to regulate his/her arousal?**
    Emotion and anxiety regulation play a central role in helping an athlete to regulate his/her arousal. This is because arousal is based on both psychological (cognitive and emotional) and physiological components. According to Hanin's Zone of Optimal Functioning Model, athletes perform their best when they are in their optimal emotional zone. As long as athletes are in their positive emotional zone, they will perform optimally. In order to regulate one's arousal level, it is important to consider that learning to relax is essential: excessive muscle tension is triggered by mental input, which is generated by worry and anxiety prior to performance. The most popular techniques for arousal regulation are: (a) somatic techniques such as autogenic training, progressive relaxation, and biofeedback; and (b) cognitive techniques such as self-talk, meditation, and imagery.

2. **How would you design a psychological competition plan for an athlete in preparation for a competition?**
    The objective of the psychological competition plan (PCP) is to mentally and physically prepare an athlete for optimal performance. The PCP establishes a general action plan that covers the various situations in which an athlete's perception is important. This perception guides the athlete to create the best competitive emotional and motivational state, which allows for effective handling of distractions and unexpected situations. The PCP is rationally developed and it is not the same as superstitious rituals, which are based on irrational beliefs and sport myths.
    In order to design a PCP it is important consider the following aspects: (1) Create a script about the moments that each athlete considers as the most important, including warm-up. Athlete cooperation is essential and one must consider the specifics of the particular sport. (2) Analyze what kind of mental content is most often used by the athlete while competing (e.g., thoughts, emotional feelings, or images). A form that is most effective must be chosen for the particular performer and the specific situation. One can design training simulation with high physical and psychological demands to analyze the adaptive response to adversity. (3) Learn to direct attentional focus to the key elements of athletic performance. (4) Establish a refocus plan based on self-awareness when optimal focus is lost so that the athlete can refocus back onto relevant cues.

3. **Think of a fear an athlete might have related to his/her performance. Describe how you would use systematic desensitization to help him/her overcome that fear.**
    The purpose of systematic desensitization (SD) is to teach the athlete to do something that is incompatible with the anxiety the athlete feels in a specific situation. The athlete can imagine various situations that are related to the specific situation while his/her muscles are relaxed. The basic steps of the SD process include the following. (1) Establish an anxiety hierarchy related to those competition situations involved in and leading up to the target situation ranked in order from the least disturbing to the most disturbing. (2) Learn a relaxation technique; in sports, one of the techniques used is muscle relaxation. (3) Conduct training in SD. The athlete should start relaxed and imagine a scene that represents the weakest item on the hierarchy while maintaining the relaxed state. This process must continue and the anxiety cues are gradually decreased until the athlete can face their fears without experiencing anxiety.

4. **What things do you need to consider in order to effectively implement psychological skills training for athletes with disabilities?**

Generally, few changes are needed in the context of psychological skills training with athletes with intellectual, sensorial, or physical disabilities. However, it is important to consider that adaptations related to communication issues might be necessary and there are some slight adaptations to mental skills training that one should take into account that could be beneficial (Hanrahan, 2015). These include: (1) adapt a relaxation technique that will be used (i.e., athletes with cerebral palsy with high levels of spasticity can skip the tension phase of progressive muscle relaxation); (2) imagery must be performed for viewing and feeling the body itself in competition (i.e., for a wheelchair basketball player, the chair is part of himself); (3) in the case of cerebral palsy, one can often observe problems in being able to understand the athletes. Nevertheless, as with any other athlete, sport performance enhancement with disabled athletes should strive to attend to the particular characteristics of this population (e.g., muscle spasms, accessibility to stadium).

5. **How would you design and implement cognitive strategies, such as rational emotive therapy, when working with athletes with disabilities to improve their coping strategies?**

RET is an example of a cognitive strategy that allows practitioners to explain how specific strategies can be improved when facing a situation in which the athlete responds with fear and anxiety. The foundation for intervention involves identifying thoughts that are related to the antecedent (e.g., poor throw), as well as the unexpected consequences that might induce the anxiety or fear (e.g., substitution, upset audience). The issue is neither in the antecedent nor in the consequence. The main work with RET must be accomplished by identifying inadequate thoughts (e.g., "nobody will love me if I fail") and teaching the athlete to transform these debilitating thoughts to more facilitative ones (e.g., "I will throw it as I do in practice. I have done it many times and I know how to do it"). Once the athlete trains his/her thinking patterns to be more optimal, he/she will be able to face a competitive situation in a more adaptive manner.

CHAPTER 14

1. **How can you use the social ecological model to inform your needs assessment approach?**

The multiple levels of this model helps us think a bit outside the psychosocial determinants of exercise behavior. Typically, we dwell on readiness to change, self-efficacy, knowledge, and other personal characteristics. The social ecological model forces us to consider the individual's micro-environment, including peers, work colleagues, and family, as well as the physical environments. The access (or lack thereof) they have to specific behavioral settings can make a difference in building momentum to change. I always want to know if they can walk safely from home, if they have access to equipment at home, and some additional details about access to settings near work or in the local community.

2. **What are the major challenges that Eleanor is facing in sustaining a healthy lifestyle?**

As sport and exercise psychology professionals, sometimes we over-estimate the value of their attitude or short-term progress. In this case, Eleanor – though still quite young – faces many physical challenges to a healthy lifestyle. Any participant who is obese and is choosing to exercise will encounter some discomfort engaging in what is classified as mild or moderate exercise. Additionally, for a person with a BMI of 42, there are years of eating habits to address. These patterns can be hard for adults to change, especially if the environmental barriers are high.

3. **What dysfunctional thoughts might be challenged in this case?**

There are several worth addressing, especially if you have training in rational emotive therapy. You may find these themes in many clients, just like themes may repeat themselves if you do a lot of work with athletes from one sport climate. Eleanor believed strongly that "all of my family must support this or it just won't work." Well, it would certainly be easier if they did, but the all-or-nothing nature of this thought makes it dysfunctional. If she holds onto this idea, and actually expects (or demands) her family to change, it will be just another excuse for her why she can't succeed. How about some version of "I should be so much better at healthy eating"? You can have some fun with this line of thinking (i.e., the "shoulds," depending on your relationship with the client). In a court of law, their behavior would be self-evident. She has a BMI of 42 – would a jury say "she is good at eating healthy" or "she is not good at eating healthy"?! When these thoughts are not managed, many clients in this program get to the overwhelming thought "I'll be like this forever – I can't change."

4. **What are the benefits of taking a motivational interviewing approach to health perform-ance consultations?**
    The neutral, autonomy-supportive stance recommended in motivational interviewing has been helpful in my work as much as any theory. This approach, which helps clients resolve their own ambivalence to change, and empowers them to choose the direction and pace of change, works well matched with your own theory of choice. Many benefits emerge as you adopt this approach. Clients are forced to do most of the work in the session, and they feel less judged by consultants. Obese clients are often used to being judged as lazy or less worthy than others, so if you can create a place of mutual respect, then learning can happen. Many of these clients are highly successful lawyers, teachers, cooks, moms, and dads, but they just haven't figured out how to be an active person who eats well.

5. **What are some ethical considerations in this case?**
    The first issue is competence, which is obviously at the core of practice. To be effective at apply-ing your skills in this area, supervised or mentored experience is recommended as you adapt to the new setting. This transition is especially important for new consultants and those used to working primarily in sport settings. Additionally, there is a growing literature of evidence-based interventions (using motivational interviewing or other approaches), so it can be helpful to find some reading and web-based resources to support your work. Another issue within this type of collaborative consultation that we face is the sharing of protected health information. Since the work involves other professionals in other settings not in our local area, we rely on email, phone, and a web-based database to manage the care of a client. Some of these forms of com-munication are secure, others are not. Consultants are encouraged to pursue training in the HIPAA law (in the United States) or to understand the regulations in their region of practice. The final issue worth mentioning is client respect and dignity. Though many clients have a history of poorly managed health behaviors including sedentary lifestyles and overeating, they often have a high level of skill and competence in other areas of their lives. Each client deserves respect and nonjudgment. These clients can benefit greatly from our services, and this work can offer great rewards for the consultant.

CHAPTER 15

1. **Who are the key stakeholders in this intervention? Why is this an important consideration?**
    The school principal, teachers, parents, and the children themselves are the key stakeholders. A whole-school approach is more likely to succeed in changing students' physical activity behav-iors according to the social ecological model. Therefore, building a climate where all teachers and students work together to develop the knowledge, skills, and attitudes toward health-enhancing physical activity is necessary.

2. **What are some key psychological correlates for physical activity in children? Why is this an important consideration when designing an intervention?**
    Aligned to the social ecological model, correlates (factors associated with behavior) and deter-minants (factors with a causal relationship) can generally be classified into five groups. The five groups and examples of these in children and young people include demographic and biological variables (e.g., sex, age, socio-economic status); psychological, cognitive, and emotional vari-ables (e.g., depression, perceived ability, exercise self-efficacy); behavioral attributes and skills (e.g., previous physical activity, recent past behavior, and sedentary time); social and cultural variables (e.g., parental encouragement, peer support); and physical environment variables (e.g., access to facilities, living within a highly walkable environment).

3. **What is the difference between modifiable and non-modifiable correlates of physical activity? Why should modifiable correlates be targets for intervention?**
    A distinction can be made between modifiable and non-modifiable (e.g., age, gender, genetics and, to an extent, social class) correlates and determinants of behavior. Those that can be modi-fied or controlled are the ones we need to understand and prioritize in the design of evidence-based interventions (Sallis, Owen, & Fotheringham, 2000). Modifiable correlates may include individual factors (e.g., motivation toward physical activity or perceived competence in motor skills), or environmental factors such as social influence (e.g., social climate created by adult leaders) and the physical environment (e.g., access to leisure and sports facilities, transport infrastructure within one's locality). Understanding the correlates of physical activity for

children will allow the intervention designer to approach the behavior they are trying to change more holistically, ensuring that their intervention has a greater chance of success. For example, amongst the non-modifiable correlates (e.g., age or sex), the intervention designer will recommend activities known to appeal to their target age or sex. Among the modifiable correlates, within the psychological category (e.g., a child's exercise self-efficacy) the intervention designer, knowing that self-efficacy is highly correlated to physical activity for children, will include strategies to enhance self-efficacy in their intervention design. Within the environmental category (e.g., the physical environment), the presence of accessible sport and leisure facilities is a known correlate of physical activity for children, and more specifically the presence of safe adults within these facilities. Even though the intervention designer may not be able to influence the number of physical activity facilities available locally, their intervention material will direct their target group to existing quality facilities with well-supervised programs in order to encourage the target group to make use of this key influencer of behavior.

4. **Outline an example of how the Youth Physical Activity Promotion Model could be used to promote physical activity in a youth population.**
   In the YPAP model, reinforcing factors influence a child's physical activity behavior directly and indirectly. The direct effect is when teachers actively help a child, for example by teaching the child skills during their physical education lesson. The indirect effect is seen when significant others influence the child's evaluation of the activity, their ability, and their perception of whether the opportunity is worth it (through the predisposing factors). Teachers, parents, and peers working together and combining their efforts to encourage active participation developed the reinforcing factors in this intervention program.

   The enabling factors include variables that allow youth to be physically active and are predominantly biological or from the physical environment. The enabling factors are those that permit a child to be active; these are classified as biological or from the physical environment. A child's fitness level, skill level, or percentage body fat are biological factors that influence activity. In addition, the physical environment the child is exposed to, the presence or absence of parks, equipment, and structured exercise or sport programs are also known to influence physical activity. Both direct and indirect effects of enabling factors are noted in this model. Essentially, YPAP suggests that youth who have positive self-perceptions (am I able?) and feel that participating has valued benefits (is it worth it?) are more likely to regularly participate in physical activity.

5. **How can modeling be used as an effective intervention strategy for increasing teacher confidence when teaching a new subject?**
   Full modeling (66 lessons), partial modeling (45 lessons), or team teaching occurred as part of this intervention. Modeling the lessons worked for a number of reasons. It produced individually tailored practical experiences that teachers could see, copy, try out, and alter in a safe environment. These concrete examples of how to deliver the lessons in the school context, taking into consideration the school's limitations (e.g., in terms of facilities and challenges as well as learning new content to teach). This provided teachers with increased confidence in their ability to teach, allowing them to learn vicariously through the facilitator or in practice themselves once ready.

   The modeling of the lessons by the facilitator also provided teachers with the opportunity to observe, question, and develop pedagogical content knowledge. Through observation of the facilitator (an expert in physical education pedagogy), teachers were exposed to teaching strategies tailored to their own class. This served to enhance their self-efficacy, and their outcome expectations for a safe and fun class for their students. Consequently, as teachers moved from knowing what to teach (content knowledge) to knowing how to teach (pedagogical content knowledge), the likelihood of them altering their behavior and actually teaching O&AA increased over the duration of the intervention. Thus, modeling was a necessary and effective strategy to enhance the likelihood of teachers moving from the safety of a structured class environment to an outdoor space with unlimited boundaries and a potential lack of structure.

CHAPTER 16

1. **What was the greatest takeaway you learned from the chapter? Describe how you can immediately begin applying this takeaway to your consulting work.**
   A key takeaway from the chapter was the discussion of the application of cognitive skill development (CSD) to the field of performance psychology. Often performers have to remember a great

deal of information in order to perform successfully. Thus, information about CSD could be used in the following ways: (1) helping the performers learn information more quickly and with greater accuracy; (2) talking with coaches about the best way to present the information so the performers grasp information and feedback quickly, especially during performance; (3) assessing performers with a learning styles inventory and attention style survey to identify how each performer learns and attends to information best in order to then modify memorization methods for each performer; (4) creating a composite of how the team learns and attends to information best so the coach can adjust (if he/she wants to) how he/she presents information or teaches skills; and (5) identifying the general cognitive skills that underlie a particular performance domain in order to determine how those skills are best trained. Combining research-based drills with sport-specific applications would help ensure these cognitive skills are transferred to the performance context.

2. **What were some of the challenges the author faced when initiating work within this environment? What challenges do you face when working with your clients? What is a new approach you could try to overcome one of the greatest challenges you face?**
    The author was initially an "outsider" in this community due to her lack of military/combat experience. She had to speak about managing stress to a population who had previously experienced some of the greatest stressors present in today's world. She also faced the stigma present in the military with regards to getting help, especially when it dealt with the brain or psychology. In the sport context, readers may face similar stigmas with athletes in regards to the stigma associated with receiving help managing stress or the word psychology. The individuals with whom one works are also often misinformed about the field of sport and performance psychology. They tend to think it is for problem athletes versus those who want to get better. In order to overcome this, readers could try changing some of the terminology they use to reflect their language, perhaps making some of our performance psychology jargon more palatable and concrete. For example, instead of saying "mind," use the word "brain" and reinforce the effectiveness and concreteness of the techniques by having the clients use biofeedback. This may help show them the effects they cannot see otherwise.

3. **What is your consulting model and/or philosophy? Describe how you would apply your model and/or philosophy with this population.**
    The first, and arguably most important, aspect to keep in mind is that developing a consulting model and philosophy is an evolving process. Therefore, practitioners should expect the two to change and actively look for ways in which one's model and philosophy can change. Not only is the growth imperative for one's practice, but it also provides practitioners with a reflective tool. While the model and philosophy should adapt with one's professional and personal growth, it may also adapt to the environment in which the practitioner works. For example, with the model presented in this chapter, I place strong emphasis in my current military contracting position on rapid skill acquisition and cognitive skill development. However, when I work within the sporting context the performance psychology component is brought to the forefront.

    My consulting philosophy has changed as I have personally and professionally grown and experienced success, obstacles, and failures. For example, when I was starting out my career in performance psychology, I did not think of it as long-term, as I do now. I was not factoring in the athlete's career longevity as much as I believe I should have into my daily performance training sessions and advice. While I urge practitioners to remain adaptable, it is also important to realize what elements should remain stable over time. For example, some of my core beliefs are: (1) the performer is my first priority; (2) truly listen no matter what; and (3) everyone and everything is my best teacher. These have not experienced much change as they are based on my personal values and belief structure.

    Other helpful recommendations when developing and evolving one's consulting model and philosophy include: (1) write/sketch it out and keep a working copy of the document; (2) edit the model and philosophy when the ideas come to mind, saving multiple copies as the most updated version may not always be the one preferred; (3) talk to other practitioners about their consulting approaches; (4) invite respected practitioners with different perspectives to provide their feedback on the model and philosophy; (5) listen to their feedback and integrate it based on fit; (6) integrate knowledge from business leadership, coaching, and other professional areas that can inform the model and philosophy from a different angle; (7) update one's model based on continued learning from current research and practical application; (8) identify and integrate the top 3–5 personal values and core beliefs within the philosophy; and (9) stay true to oneself during this process.

4. **What other concepts or techniques would you have considered integrating within the interventions?**

    I would have integrated more pattern-recognition drills and techniques to enhance the development of pattern recognition in more novice soldiers. In addition, I would have spent more time working with coaches/instructors to design their current training to enhance situational awareness. Further, aside from the development of observation skills (i.e., perception), I would have spent more time working with other stakeholders to facilitate the person's knowledge of what the cues mean (i.e., comprehension) and ability to anticipate subsequent events more accurately (i.e., projection). Theoretically, this would in turn enhance pattern recognition.

5. **What components of CSD did the author highlight in this chapter? How would you go about developing these or other cognitive skills with your population?**

    The primary cognitive skills discussed that underlie performance were observation skills, working memory enhancement, and short- and long-term memory. Following are several examples of how to apply CSD with various sport populations. For example, with football I would work on applying some of the short- and long-term memory techniques to help the athletes remember the playbook. Once the players developed a working foundation of the playbook, I would integrate recall drills within conditioning sessions because this is the state in which they have to remember the plays, rather than just learning them in a resting state. Similarly, with a baseball pitcher, I would do some working memory and short-term memory drills to enhance his ability to track pitches thrown and the outcome of thrown pitches with the batters. With a hitter or infielder, I would provide visual processing speed training integrating strobe-type glasses and other modalities in order to increase the amount of visual information the brain processes in a given amount of time. This could help the batter recognize pitches quicker and with greater accuracy, and allow infielders to react more accurately to the trajectory of the ball.

CHAPTER 17

1. **How did the models implemented help the psychologist understand the problem in its full context?**

    Models are always very important; they are the frameworks that will help the psychologist to maintain control over the direction of the work with the client; they are the guidelines. In this case it was important to use an educational approach to coach John in new performance skills, but also to use a clinical psychology framework to help him overcome fear and loneliness.

2. **How do cultural differences impact performance? How might a psychologist need to take into consideration cultural differences when working with performers?**

    In the case of a very high level of performance, cultural differences are extremely important. Each acrobatic discipline and each country brings its own values, and non-conformity to them can easily create conflict if there is no discussion. A psychologist or performance psychologist must know these differences and be ready to ask questions of the performers about it in order to be respectful. The performance psychologist should also promote open discussion during his/her meetings.

3. **If you were the psychologist in this case, how would you assess/analyze John's fear of performance?**

    It could be interesting to use formal tools like psychological testing, but because this was a daily work, discussions would bring as much. Also, it is appropriate to use self-evaluation because it forces the artist to be self-conscious, to put a constructive regard on himself and be able to repeat the process many times.

4. **How would you implement the fear–trust–responsibility continuum into working with John?**

    The advantage of working with the same performers for 20 weeks is that it is a work in progress. Training eight hours per day helps one to learn a lot about oneself and having the opportunity to share that with colleagues is probably the most powerful tool. Discussions over so many weeks support commitment and respect in various contexts, like artistic classes, languages classes, acrobatic training, and also free time. It has to be done in a very simple, small-steps manner: talk, act, talk again, adjust, and act again.

5.   **What are the benefits to the client of working in an interdisciplinary team of specialists?**
Being able to work with specialists who see events and people according to their own backgrounds helps a lot to cover the "in-between" parts of events. That part is frequently a source of mistakes because nobody pays enough attention to it.

CHAPTER 18

1.   **What strategies might a consultant use to overcome resistance toward mental training when these services have been regarded through an athlete's lens as a sign of personal weakness?**
Mental training is not always a widely accepted service to athletes across nationalities and ethnicities. Some athletes originate from countries where these services are regarded as a sign of personal weakness, and more specifically, mental weakness and insecurity. Within some cultures, it is already known that machismo is a central part of self-presentation (see Kontos & Arguello, 2005 for an example). Added to this complexity, the current case study is situated within the sport of boxing, where male athletes tend to present themselves as mentally tough and rugged. Many of these athletes are also from inner-city areas. To overcome this form of resistance when it is encountered, it is often useful to engage the athletes in conversational interviews where a deeper understanding of his/her origins might be garnered. During these conversations, questions about how mental training is regarded could be asked. These questions might relate to the athlete's perspective, his/her broader familial perspective, and in addition, the personal coach's perspective of these services. From the conversational interviews, the consultant and athlete can open up a space to discuss the nature of mental training skills and how these might be best aligned with the cultural and personal vantage of the athlete. Follow-up with resistant athletes necessitate ongoing discussions, as receptiveness to mental training work tends to be earned a little at a time. With the aforementioned athlete, it has taken three years to gain complete buy-in, even with a significant major games gold medal supporting the dyad's collaboration. Hence, patience and mindfulness regarding how to proceed in the journey toward the inclusion of mental training support is a necessity. The receptiveness might progress, regress, and progress once more until, ultimately, there is complete commitment.

2.   **What strategies can be used to better frame stress in an immigrant athlete, when stress is experienced as embarrassing?**
The case study reveals an athlete who has been challenged by stress overload for much of his national team career. The athlete became nervous approximately 48 hours before his first fight and then would remain over-aroused throughout the tournament. The athlete by his usual nature is a kind and caring person, and in fact the sort of team member who creates synergy within a traveling national team. However, 48 hours before a fight he would become progressively agitated, and in the final 24 hours before a fight he would stop talking, eating, and sleeping. Moreover, he would not open his hotel room door so the coaching and sport science staff could not support him while he was under emotional and psychological strain. Upon discussion, after a major tournament in which the athlete suffered a panic attack in the warm-up area and barely made it to the ring for his fight (a close loss he could have won), he sat with the national team coaches and mental training consultant and they discussed what had transpired. Though the staff suggested that the athlete had suffered a panic attack, the athlete was adamant that this was not the case. He felt that he had eaten a meal that upset his stomach, and what unfolded in the changing room was only the result of stomach upset. Nearly one year later, when the athlete and mental training consultant began to work together in earnest, the athlete recognized that his previous experience was a panic attack. It took a full year for him to verbalize this to anyone. The athlete viewed the panic attack as his own emotional fragility. Over the course of two years of discussions, the athlete now speaks openly about his nerves, and when he begins to feel nervous, he and the mental training consultant go out for walks. These walks include discussions about nerves, but more importantly, the act of asking for support in itself seems to reassure the athlete. This athlete has been undefeated internationally for over 12 months, traveling the world. Moreover, he is now a settled athlete who encourages his teammates to be open about their feelings as opposed to suppressing these to the point of panic and performance decline. Hence, the opportunity to support such athletes might not be in the form of a selected mental training skill, reattribution training, or decatastrophizing (see Schinke, Peterson, & Couture, 2004). Rather, a more basic and less clinical approach might work

equally well in such cases, where a conversation is less formal in format and also in context, through an evening walk. These discussions could serve to diffuse stress, and with them the athlete could touch on his fears and concerns, situating these in discussions where he/she can dictate the amount and moments where disclosure works for the client.

3. **What strategies might be used to overcome a coach's negative label of an athlete?**
The case above and the previous two questions and answers have revealed a focus on the athlete's work with a mental training consultant. However, mental training consultants do not always accompany national teams to international tournaments. In the case above, the athlete and coach were engaged in a pattern in which the athlete's performance became unpredictable. The coach eventually regarded the athlete as a talented athlete that could not be counted on. The athlete was aware of this perception, as athletes are usually very attuned to their training and tournament environments. When I began to work with the athlete, even throughout the aforementioned major games where the athlete won his gold medal, the coach was uncertain whether stress overload would resurface at some point in the tournament. This caused the coach to also become stressed in advance of each successive fight where he worked with the athlete. Much of the discussion over the course of the major games event and for several months after necessitated a reframing of the athlete's previous pattern to one that could be predictable and overcome through a positive approach. The coach needed to revisit how he worked with the athlete, how he spoke to the athlete in front of his teammates, and also how he saw the athlete's previous challenges. Eventually there was recognition that the athlete's on-site mental preparation and warm-up were the root of the previous anxiety pattern, and that their reconfiguration would contribute to the outcome of ongoing excellence. When working with athletes labeled as having a certain mental challenge, once the challenge is being overcome with the athlete, those in the environment, especially the coaching staff, need to become reflective in how they view and describe the athlete among themselves and to peer athletes. This reflective process requires a certain amount of vigilance on the part of the coaching staff and mental training consultant to monitor, and also a receptiveness on the part of the coaching staff to work in the best interest of each athlete.

4. **What aspects of the boxer's identity contributed to his pre-competition anxiety?**
Over the course of recent years there has been an emergence within the broader trajectory of cultural sport psychology referred to as intersectionality of identity. There has been a special section in the psychology of sport and exercise (see Schinke & McGannon, 2015) devoted to this emerging area. The argument is now being put forth that each athlete brings multiple identities into training and competition. These identities might include gender, sexual orientation, race, ethnicity, educational background, family of origin, nationality, and many other possible social locations. The revealing or masking of these identities is thought to either contribute or deter from performance. When identities are not acceptable from the vantage of one's nationality and the sport's subculture, the athlete is then expected to subvert this part of him/herself. Also, athletes' identities are arguably fluid, with certain social locations fitting better in certain circumstances, such as with peer athletes, and certain identities matching better when working with coaches. As well, certain identities might be viewed within the subculture as belonging more in the training environment or the competition environment. In the case of the boxer discussed above, his stress load was exacerbated by the fact that personal vulnerability is not a typical part of being a male and a boxer, two social locations. Furthermore, this boxer viewed mental training work as outside of the norm in his country of origin. With three identities working against the opportunity to collaborate with the athlete and reveal his vulnerability, the athlete engaged in an open discussion with the mental training consultant about his personal conflict in this new/alien resource and how the resource might erode these identities. Hence, the work that the dyad needed to undertake was to explore how these services could align with various identities, such as being a formidable tournament performer and as a veteran athlete on the team, who could be emotionally strong enough to reach out and attempt mental training. Upon achieving early success in the tournament, the boxer then opened up a third possible identity that replaced his reputation as anxious with a more mindful and emotionally ready performer.

5. **How might the case study above be framed as part of a critical acculturation process?**
The boxer discussed in this case study seems to have embarked on a fluid process of acculturation. Within the earliest sport psychology literature, including our own, acculturation has been regarded as something that an athlete achieves, as she/he overcomes a cultural transition.

Within our most recent scholarship (e.g., Schinke & McGannon, 2014) we have discovered that acculturation is an process that an athlete undergoes through a career, with moments of resolution and moments of frustration. Referring to the case study above, the athlete was initially resistant to mental training as such work was regarded as a sign of weakness on his part. Then, during the aforementioned major game, the athlete bought into the process of sport psychology services, likely because his peers were also using this resource in their competition preparation before each bout. After he earned his gold medal, the athlete then reverted back to several months of resistance, where he lost touch with the consultant, and the consultant's interpretation is that the services were not being used because once more having these in place was a sign of weakness on the part of the athlete. More recently, the athlete has re-engaged with the services. What we wish to point out is that the acculturation process includes times of resistance, times of synergy, and once more, times of resistance. The athlete and those who work with him must navigate this fluidity in order to effectively support the athlete and ensure he receives positive social support throughout his amateur career.

6. **When working with an immigrant athlete, why is recognizing one's own identity an important aspect of the acculturation process?**
Acculturation may be most effective when it is a shared process, with all individuals embracing, encouraging, and including the varying cultural norms and practices that exist in that sporting context. This is in contrast to simply adopting the predominant cultural norms and practices. This shared process includes having a welcoming environment for all athletes, coaches, and team personnel – this can be accomplished through learning one another's native languages, celebrating national festivities, and sharing meals with traditional cultural dishes. Another important aspect of the shared acculturation process includes recognizing and revealing one another's identities. By recognizing, and then sharing, your own personal biases along with your cultural beliefs, norms and practices, you can open up lines of communication with your athletes, who may then also feel more comfortable opening up and expressing themselves. The athlete will then feel more supported and accepted for who they are, leading to less psychological distress and better performance.

CHAPTER 19

1. **How would you use Lerner and Lerner's Five Cs model to design an intervention to positively influence youth development?**
Lerner et al. (2005) suggested that positive youth development requires healthy development in competence (i.e., positive view of one's action in domain-specific areas including social, academic, cognitive, and vocational), confidence (i.e., an internal sense of overall positive self-worth and self-efficacy), connection (i.e., positive bonds with people and institutions), character (i.e., respect for societal and cultural rules), and caring (i.e., a sense of empathy for others). These components of positive youth development could be addressed as follows within an intervention program.
    Competence: Provide opportunities to obtain and display competence in various areas (e.g., through the completion of worksheets or homework, participation in various activities and games). It is important that games not be exclusionary (e.g., games that involve losers sitting out – everyone should be able to participate for the duration of the activity). Find opportunities to catch people doing well (i.e., give positive feedback related to participation and achievement in various activities).
    Confidence: Again, provide positive feedback where appropriate (be sincere). Within Life-Matters, confidence is directly addressed through a worksheet that contains 18 different methods of enhancing self-confidence. Confidence is also a part of trust activities that involve trusting others as well as oneself.
    Connection: Continually change who works with whom, instead of allowing participants to form cliques that by their very nature make other people feel excluded. Include group activities that involve "getting to know you" activities, trust (as mentioned above), and group problem solving.
    Character: Include debriefs and discussions regarding rules (both stated and unstated). Have participants reflect on how they might want to be remembered.
    Caring: Discuss what others can do to make other people feel better about themselves. Consider including activities whereby participants experience what it might be like to have various disabilities (e.g., blindfolded or only being able to use one arm). Have participants reflect on the real loves in their lives, what lifts them and gives them joy.

2. **Discuss the similarities and differences of race and ethnicity. How would these influence your intervention development?**
Race is related to biological factors and ethnicity is related to sociological factors. Race cannot be changed; it is a result of genetics and is not influenced by location or learned behaviors. Ethnicity is the learned cultural behaviors that are usually typical of specific regions of the world. It is important to realize that there are multiple ethnicities within a single race of people. One should never make assumptions about ethnicity based on race. If running an intervention program for a group of people from the same race, recognize that it is likely that they represent different ethnicities within that race, meaning that norms, values, and behaviors will likely differ within the group.

3. **Name and describe three factors that you might need to keep in mind if you were to deliver a pre-existing mental skills training program from your country in a country with different values, norms, and beliefs.**
   a. Language. Even if the same general language is spoken, there will be differences in terminology and nuances. Do not assume that words, phrases, sentences, or handouts are interpreted in the same way.
   b. Motives/goals. What I think is important may not be what they think is important. Try to avoid making assumptions. Recognize that what I think and the way I think is not the only way of doing so, and that other ways are not inherently better or worse – just different.
   c. Etiquette. Ways of greeting, interacting with others, and making decisions may differ. Instead of barging in and doing things the way I normally do at home, take time to observe others. If possible, find someone who is familiar with the culture who is willing to describe and discuss how things tend to be done in the country I am visiting.

4. **What are three things in your life that you take for granted that may not be readily available in other parts of the world?**
Hanrahan: Running water, the ability to go to sleep with a feeling of safety, easy access to plentiful amounts of healthy food.
Tshube: Access to clean water, electricity, and a home to live.

5. **What are two biases you may have that could potentially get in the way of effectively working individually with an athlete from a different culture?**
Hanrahan: I value autonomy, education, and competence. I get frustrated when I come across people who don't have these same values. I may want them to be excited about the opportunity to learn, to be able to improve their skills and lives, and to take responsibility for themselves. They, however, may be content to live the lives they are currently living, with no desire to learn or improve skills. I don't perform my best as a teacher or a psychologist when I am frustrated or when I try to instill my values in others, disregarding theirs.
Tshube: I grew up in Botswana in a very conservative culture that emphasized community values. Parents worked collectively to raise their kids under common values shared by the community. Elders were and still are (at least in remote villages) responsible for passing knowledge from one generation to another. Elders emphasize community life and communalism as a living principle of which the basic ideology is a community identity. The aim of every elder/educator in the village is to produce and present an individual as a community culture-bearer and culture is a community property. Individual identity is not emphasized at the expense of community identity. Potential biases and possible contrasts include holding athletes of a different culture to the same expectation. I am working on it.

CHAPTER 20

1. **What are the major challenges Phil is facing? How would you prioritize those concerns?**
The primary performance-related challenges facing Phil include: performance anxiety and over-arousal, lack of confidence, negative self-talk and frustration, isolation from teammates, focus and attentional issues, and the potential of academic performance consequences. However, there were additional clinical issues that need to be ruled out (i.e., depression). Whereas it is generally thought to be best practice to address the most severe clinical issue first (Hersen & Thomas, 2007), Dr. Jones assessed Phil's concerns and developed a therapeutic plan that she believed to be most beneficial to Phil.

Although addressing Phil's isolation from teammates seemed like an important place to start, this isolation was believed to be stemming from other concerns, such as lack of confidence, embarrassment, or anger and frustration. Dr. Jones believed that by increasing Phil's confidence and decreasing his frustration, there may be improvements in Phil's interactions with his teammates, leading to increases in social support and mood. Additionally, because Phil sought Dr. Jones' consult for his athletic performance problems, she decided that his negative self-talk, over-arousal, and performance anxiety associated with fielding and hitting were the most appropriate starting point for her intervention. Despite starting with performance concerns, Dr. Jones remained vigilant in other areas, especially those associated with Phil's decreased social contact, academic-related concerns, and depressive symptoms.

2. **What client/team factors should be considered when deciding whether a client/team is a good candidate for the specific types of technologies listed in the case study? Consultant factors?**

    Several things are worth considering when choosing to incorporate technology into sport, exercise, and performance psychology consulting. For one, the consultant should be aware of the client/team's history of technology use. Without fully understanding the reason for its use, how the technology works, and the potential benefits related to its use, clients may be unwilling to use technology to its potential. Further, some clients may not be comfortable or knowledgeable about the use of technology and may be unwilling to use it for these reasons.

    The consultant should also be aware of the client's access to technology. If Phil does not have a smartphone with the capability of utilizing performance-enhancing apps, discussing their use in session will be of little use. If Phil travels extensively and does not have access to Dr. Jones' biofeedback equipment, it will not assist him in continuing to improve performance. If that were the case, Dr. Jones would need to take great care to transition Phil from using biofeedback technology in the office to monitoring himself in the field.

    Moreover, the consultant should consider how the client/team has used similar technologies in other situations. For example, has Phil used video-conferencing to check in with friends or family while he travels? If so, has he liked it, has he experienced problems with it, how comfortable is he with its use, and does he understand the limitations associated with its use? The consultant should ask how familiar the client is with the uses and limitations of technology. For instance, although Phil may regularly text his friends and family, making him familiar with the logistics of texting as a means of communication, is he aware of its privacy limitations? Has he considered what might happen if he lost his phone or who might be tracking his messages? Although these may seem like benign issues in relation to sport, exercise, and performance psychology, he may not wish for others to know the specifics of his consultation, in the event that his texts were somehow made public. It is important to remember that information uploaded to the internet may never fully be erased, so information Phil shares with his consultant now, as part of his intervention, could be retrieved years later.

    Clients with limited history and knowledge about technology in consultation will likely require a slower pace, using technology in limited capacities at first, then advancing to more intricate technological interventions as they become more familiar with the uses and limitations of the technology. Further, the consultant will need to take the education phase of consultation seriously with regard to technology to ensure that the client/team receives the greatest benefit with the least potential for harm.

    Even if Dr. Jones were to determine that Phil is a good candidate for the use of technology in consultation, she is bound by her own competence in the area. That is, she should ask herself several questions: What is her history of use of technology in consultation? What access does she have to the various types of technology she intends to use in consultation? What uses/limitations has she found for using technology in consultation? Can she troubleshoot problems that may occur? Is she trained to use the technology appropriately? Is the specific technology a valid treatment option? Although sport, exercise, and performance psychology, in many cases, is a collaborative endeavor, failure of the consultant to demonstrate competence with the use of technology during consultation is a breach of ethics and it may carry very real consequences for the athlete. Consequently, the consultant looking to incorporate technology into her/his work should consider her/his competence with *each* type of technology considered and pursue necessary training as needed.

3. **How might your approach to using technology in consultation change if Phil were a youth athlete on a travel team? A high school athlete with no interest in playing in college? In an adult recreational league?**

If Phil were younger and a minor, the use of technology could change a great deal. To start with, depending on age, the client may or may not have a smartphone. Further, any technology that the client was asked to download to his/her phone would need to be approved by the parents, and should be thoroughly vetted by the consultant. It would also be much less likely that communication via social media or texting would take place directly with the child. Such communications would either go through the parent or have the parent's permission to occur. Further, age is an important factor in the willingness and comfort level of most individuals with regard to their use of technology, and while the child may be very comfortable with the use of technology, the parents or guardians of the child may not be.

Adult recreational clients present different benefits and challenges to using technology in consultations. Adult clients are more likely than high school or youth clients to have time restraints that limit their availability for in-person sessions, and potentially for performance enhancement in general. Whereas lack of time may increase the client's desire to utilize technology as it can be accessed at the client's leisure, lack of time and awareness of technology could limit the client's likelihood of exploring new technology or feeling comfortable with technological use. Lack of comfort could manifest in the minimal use of technology, but also in concerns related to confidentiality and the potential of private information being accessed by third parties, or a lack of willingness to use the technology to its fullest potential and benefit.

4. **What are the ethical/legal concerns of using technology in sport, exercise, and performance psychology consultations? When is technology not appropriate for utilization? How might you, as the consultant, navigate those concerns?**

This is a very large question that would require a great deal of text to answer. For this reason, the authors encourage readers to seek out additional readings on this topic (e.g., Watson, Schinke & Sampson, 2013). However, in brief summary, the primary ethical and legal concerns related to using technology for consultations include: insurance and cross-boundary certification/licensure, intake information, informed consent, confidentiality, appropriate use of services, competency, record-keeping, and personal presence on the internet. Many of these concerns can be successfully addressed and navigated through effective communication between client and consultant at the onset of service delivery and throughout the process. However, concerns related to insurance, certification/licensure, and record-keeping should be extensively researched and continually evaluated for best practice and legal implications. The consultant should also seek peer or mentor consultation when confronted with situations that elicit unease or uncertainty.

Unease or uncertainty can manifest in many ways. Technology is not appropriate for consultation services when either the consultant or the client are not comfortable or ready for services to be provided using technology, or when the presenting concern requires more direct observation and/or focused treatment than is possible via technology. Treatment goals and objectives should be assessed intermittently to evaluate their appropriateness for technology intervention. When new technology is implemented or considered, the consultant and client should discuss the advantages and disadvantages of the technology, as well as the client's interest and expectations for using the technology.

5. **What disadvantages might each of the types of technology used in this case present in a real-world situation?**

Throughout the case, many of the technology interventions (e.g., session reminders, text messages, apps) could be accessed and utilized on Phil's computer or mobile device. Despite cellular phones developing into hand-held computers, there are still concerns about their reliability. When traveling, unreliable cell coverage could limit Phil's use of video-conferencing/FaceTime, texting, or accessing applications that require internet service.

There may also be concerns about the lack of privacy and/or confidentiality related to some forms of technology. Many applications on smartphones, tablets, and computers back up information to the Cloud. While the Cloud is generally considered to be helpful for storage and access, information stored on the Cloud has the potential of being lost or hacked.

Finally, although technology may provide the client with frequent reminders to engage in mental training and provides a comprehensive destination for tracking progress, it is only as useful as the client and consultant make it. That is, the client may receive reminders about logging his self-talk, journaling about a recent practice, or completing a survey to track progress, but if he does not actually enter the information into the application, it will do him little good. In that sense, technology may provide a false security blanket. Along the same lines, the client still must put in the work to train mentally. Using a guided meditation application can be useful, but if he hits play and then spends his time ruminating on negative self-talk and judging himself for previous mistakes instead of practicing meditation, he is not likely to benefit fully. Technology is a great adjunctive therapeutic method, but just as one hour of consultation cannot replace a week's worth of "homework," technology is useless without deliberately practicing the skills it supports.

CHAPTER 21

1. **How important do you feel it is to deliver improvement feedback to your client, and do you feel technology should play an integral role?**
    It's critical for the client to be receiving feedback about all aspects of training. This includes fitness, technical, mental, and performance feedback. At every stage of the athlete development process, the athlete, coaches, parents, and SPC need to know what's working well and what needs improvement. Without feedback, it becomes a process of trial and error, which is usually very inefficient. Specific to mental feedback, when the athlete can see multiple indications that the mental training being done is paying off, it's much more likely that confidence and motivation will be high and the work will continue. As was stated in the chapter, mental skills need to be practiced consistently so they become habit. If the athlete doesn't know progress is happening because it can occur gradually at times, then chances are effort will cease. This is where technology can play a significant role. It can gather the data, store it, and even graph it automatically so all participants of the athlete–coach–parent triad can see it.

2. **How do you feel about integrating neurofeedback into mental skills training? What do you like and what are your concerns?**
    Neurofeedback holds such great promise. In the past, limitations of sensors required gel to be applied for there to be a good connection with the scalp. Few athletes were willing to go through that process. In addition, the cost of the hardware was very high and the quality of the software was very low! However, now that dry sensor technology is proving reliable and the software and pricing have improved, SPCs will be able to use this form of feedback with more of their clients. One concern is that SPCs end up spending too much time gathering neural feedback and too little time teaching the cognitive skills necessary to control the brainwaves. There is also a need to better establish a connection between specific brainwave patterns and performance.

3. **Discuss the effectiveness of using a phone versus other technology to provide quality long-distance mental training.**
    Because of the convenience of smartphones, it's clearly the ideal device to make the central point of long-distance mental training. In addition, teens tend not to want to use computers and prefer to do almost everything via their phone. When one of the most difficult parts of working with teens is getting them to follow through, SPCs need to use the technology teens prefer. SPCs can conduct video-conference calls, deliver video or text content, and track their clients' progress, all from a smartphone.

4. **How would you effectively implement assessment with distance-based clients?**
    Specific to performance enhancement and not counseling, there are several possible ways to effectively assess the needs of distance-based clients. Example methods include: (1) online athlete, coach, and/or parent interviews of past performance; (2) completion of self-report or guided checklists of common performance issues (i.e., choking, frustration, slumps, etc.); (3) use of valid and reliable assessment tools designed to measure specific psychological skills or sport psychology-related constructs (i.e., mental toughness, pre-performance anxiety, confidence, etc.); (4) journal writing about ideal or troubled past performance; and (5) performance observation through TV, video, or recorded past performances.

5. **What are some effective ways to deliver mental skills content to your clients using technology (e.g., one-on-one discussion, small-group discussion, lectures, reading, videos)?**
    Example ideas for delivering mental skills content using technology include: (1) online video conferencing (i.e., Skype, GoToMeeting, etc.); (2) ebooks and reports; (3) websites; (4) mobile

apps; (5) DVDs; (6) video recordings; and (7) audio recordings. However, depending on the age and maturity of the client, not all of these methods may be "effective." One test of educational effectiveness is whether information transfer and retention have occurred. It's not enough that the client simply understands the material – there must be retention as well as the ability to use or apply it to enhance performance or well-being. Further, technology can enable coaches and parents to oversee the learning process and increase the chances of mastery occurring. As such, websites and apps that track client usage are greatly preferred over simply conducting online meetings or emailing digital content.

CHAPTER 22

1. **What key numbers in Cindy's SWOT analysis helped her determine that the Dallas/Ft. Worth Metroplex could sustain her business as well as those already in practice?**
    The Dallas/Ft. Worth Metroplex has a huge population and a very reasonable cost of living, comparable to Chicago or Tampa. But the enormous population of Dallas makes for favorable math (so many potential clients!) and increases the odds of sustaining a business. Because there are already other practices, it's reasonable to assume many people in the area have been exposed to the concept of mental training. Exposure (knowing what it is and how it can help) is a key factor in those who seek mental training services.

2. **Based on the financial information given in Cindy's case, when does she need to be "cash flow positive" in order to stay in business?**
    If Cindy meets her revenue goals for year one ($70K), she will be comfortable. She will have $35K of income to support herself (she can do this in Dallas); she will have money to pay taxes ($6K), all expenses paid ($11K), plus start-up fees ($11K). If Cindy makes $50K, she will have to adjust by lowering expenses to $8K. The minimum Cindy can make in year one in order to stay in business (without a loan) is $45K. Cindy's $14K savings will run out by the end of May, so she must be cash flow positive by June in order to stay in business.

3. **Using Cindy's financial statement as a guide, plan out how many individual and team contracts Cindy needs to meet her financial commitments for year one.**

    Individual Clients: Packages:

4 sessions = $480 × 10 new clients	= $4,800.00
8 sessions = $920 × 8 new clients	= $7,360.00
12 sessions = $1320 × 10 new clients	= $13,200.00
TOTAL =	$25,360.00

    Team Contracts:

    1 – Fall (July–November) contract with a competitive soccer club providing parent education, team mental training, and coach education.

    $10,000.00

    1 – Winter (October–March) contract with a competitive basketball club providing parent education, team mental training, and coach education.

    $10,000.00

    1 – Spring/Summer (February–August) contract with a softball or baseball travel club providing parent education, mental training, and coach education.

    $10,000.00

    TOTAL = $30,000.00

    Workshops:

    The goal is to secure two speaking events each month of year one. If Cindy can charge $1,500.00 for each paid gig, she will need to secure seven of them. Obviously, if she charges less she will need more paid gigs. The rest of the speaking engagements will be excellent ways to build her business, get in front of parents and athletes and feed them into her individual program. Plus, she will have to network in order to set up the workshops.

    TOTAL: $1500 × 7 = $10,500.00

Returning Clients (Renewals)
Discounted rates on packages for those who continue.
4 renewal sessions $440.00 × 3 renewals = $1,320.00
6 renewal sessions $600.00 × 3 renewals = $1,800.00
8 renewal sessions $720.00 × 3 renewals = $2,160.00

TOTAL = $5,280.00

4. **What steps are most important for Cindy to take to help make her website generate as many leads as possible?**
To generate as many leads as possible, Cindy will have to commit to the following actions:

- create a professional website and set up no-cost SEO (i.e., search engine optimization);
- set up her social media presence and actively engage (e.g., Facebook, Twitter, LinkedIn);
- book two speaking engagements each month;
- collect contact information from all attendees and begin monthly emails;
- blog weekly and post on her website;
- network with other business owners, club coaches, and board members of sport clubs in her community.

5. **What compromises could Cindy make if she wanted to start off with a brick-and-mortar office rather than waiting until year three?**
If Cindy wanted to start off with a traditional office, she would need to secure a loan. The loan would allow her to invest in an office, furniture, décor, and additional advertising for her business. It will also generate additional financial commitments and put the pressure on to make money and keep up with the payments. The advantage of having the office is that her business would appear more professional, she would have the option of meeting prospective clients and active clients in person, and she could try to find office space in an athletic business (physical therapy, athletic training), which would help with her networking and access to athletes.

6. **Which marketing technique will be most important for Cindy to focus on in year one? Why?**
Cindy's number-one marketing technique should be networking. Building relationships with coaches, clubs, and organizations is imperative to generate enough leads to get new clients in the door. Because she's the new kid on the block, people will need to get to know her and feel comfortable recommending her to their athletes, coaches, organizations, etc. Building a *large* network fast is the key to early business development. She should start with people she already knows and has credibility with – former soccer players or coaches, coaching directors, meeting parents of her families' kids. Anyone and everyone she can connect with. This also fits well with the start-up phase because networking is low-cost, but takes a lot of time.

CHAPTER 23

1. **How can modern technology be combined with the use of an SPC? Who plays a role in using the technology?**
There are currently many smartphone applications as well as online organizers and planners available to coaches, athletes, and SPCs. If used appropriately this technology can help to create a more fluid exchange of information between the client and the SPC. Moreover, technology has allowed sport psychology (SP) services to become more accessible to a greater amount of people, often at a lower cost. The first step is to choose the appropriate technology in relation to the needs, goals, and resources of the client. While many neurofeedback and biofeedback programs might seem helpful, not every club or individual can afford or even desire to work with such equipment.

Once the appropriate application has been chosen, it is the responsibility of the SPC to become an expert with this tool before attempting to use it in application with clients. Just as SPCs advise athletes to practice mental techniques before using them in competition, so should an SPC understand how the application could be of use to his/her client. This includes predicting possible roadblocks and preparing for them accordingly. Perhaps most important is that the technology cannot completely replace an SPC, but if used in a complementary manner, can greatly improve the effectiveness of SP services.

It is recommended that coaches, athletes, and the SPC all play a role in using the technology. This could mean that the SPC needs to educate the coaches on how to best utilize the application for their particular needs. Athletes are likely to respond well to the idea of using the application if their coach also supports this effort. Use this as a motivational force and help the athlete understand how a fluid exchange of information often increases their chances at success on the field of play.

2. **What topics should an SPC focus on during an interview with a sports club in order to deliver a positive impression?**
A major focus of the interview should be the needs and current philosophy of the club. The SPC should do his or her best to make the interview more about the client than his/her own abilities and skill set. In general, those interviewing the SPC may have little to minimum education and practical experience with SP, meaning that speaking about the theoretical underpinnings of SP might impress at the beginning of the interview, but leave a lack of connection between the SPC and client.

Listening to the current goals and directions of the club can give the SPC the ammunition necessary to land the position. Mentioning a practical application that directly reflects the needs of the club helps to build quick rapport and allows the SPC to demonstrate their knowledge and competence. Finally, staying away from too much sport-specific knowledge is also recommended. This helps to avoid venturing too far out of one's competencies and coming across as disingenuous.

3. **What strategies should the SPC develop in order to deal with roadblocks during an intervention?**
Due to the greater numbers of athletes, it is wise to develop a type of "buddy-system" between players. This is because with a greater number of players there is also a greater chance that players will be missing at sessions due to a variety of reasons (i.e., sickness, injury, called up to another team). Have each player find a partner who is learning the same material, and if one of them misses a session, they are responsible for their buddy to catch up.

Have a concrete but flexible plan. Dates, times, places, and session leaders should all be set ahead of time. This schedule needs to be communicated and available to all coaches and staff at the club. The more concrete the schedule, the more likely the coaches are able to plan around it. Nevertheless, provide "open days" which can be used specifically to make up for lost days on which a seminar had to be canceled. This helps to ensure structure and understanding for the unknown events that occur during a full season.

4. **How do we create and support an environment to increase self-awareness and self-regulation among athletes and coaches?**
There is no simple answer to creating and maintaining a successful talent development environment, but increasing self-awareness and self-regulation can be improved if the norms of the club demand that they be so. This demand comes from two main actions: (1) creating a place for these abilities to grow; and (2) training coaches and staff to reinforce actions related to self-awareness and self-regulation.

Self-awareness comes from consistent feedback from the environment combined with time for self-reflection. By providing consistent feedback related to one's strengths, weaknesses, and current goals, the club helps to shape a player's awareness. The player should be given proper time, space, and exercises to reflect on how this external feedback agrees with his own beliefs.

Self-regulation is highly intertwined with self-awareness. The coaches, staff, and teammates must demand from each other that a certain standard of regulation is kept. This includes health aspects (e.g., sleep, diet), physical aspects (e.g., skills, endurance), and psychological aspects (e.g., communication, emotional regulation). It is the process of self-regulation itself that needs to be positively reinforced rather than the results that come from the actions. Managers and coaches need to stress that dedication and hard work on the daily details, rather than short-term developmental spurts or successes, are what create a champion.

5. **Why is it important to create self-regulation?**
The skill of self-regulation is vital for all athletes wishing to compete at the elite and/or professional level. Although there will be many people along the way that help athletes to reach their goals (i.e., coaches, trainers), at the end of the day it is the athletes who bear the full responsibility of success or failure. Therefore, elite environments should demand a great deal of independence and self-reliance from their athletes so as to build proper goal-orientation and a healthy obsession with constant improvement. Not every athlete will win a medal at the Olympics, but self-regulation can be applied in all aspects of life, inside and/or outside of sport.

CHAPTER 24

1. **Regarding client evaluation of the consultant's effectiveness, how often do you think this should be implemented and what are some challenges versus opportunities?**

   Everyone needs feedback on how they are doing from time to time and practitioner psychologists are no different. Evaluation works best the longer the relationship has been ongoing, but there exists some critical times for carrying out these evaluations. The first important time is after an initial set period of work together, be it three, five, or ten sessions. Typically, a goal or multiple goals would have been set for these sessions and a timely evaluation after this period of time can enable the further development of the work together. The next important time would be at the end of a season/year working together. An evaluation of the consultant's effectiveness around this time can enable an effective transition into the next phase of work together (pre-season and season planning). Finally, after the end of a relationship an evaluation should always be carried out. This can be an illuminating evaluation as the client may be more honest and more forthcoming in their feedback, safe in the knowledge that the relationship has come to an end. The challenges for the consultant can be to hear critical feedback about themselves and how they interact with clients, and the opportunity for the consultant then is to utilize this feedback to augment their own performances with future clients.

2. **What factors affect the scheduling of meetings with clients? In what ways can a consultant work around long absences due to busy seasons and travel?**

   There are myriad factors that can interfere with meeting schedules with clients, particularly those who are elite or full-time professional athletes, where there are often long competitive seasons and a lot of travel involved. Working around these issues can be a challenge. Several strategies, however, can be particularly effective in dealing with this. First, technology can bridge the distances that prevent conventional face-to-face consultations (for more on technology see Question 5). Software such as Skype and FaceTime, for example, can help clients and consultants connect and meaningfully liaise with one another from remote sites and geographically challenging locations. Second, good planning with the client can ameliorate later difficulties (due to absences and busy seasons) if sessions have been planned well in advance and an agreed schedule of work and sessions have been laid out with an upcoming busy season in mind. Finally, text messaging, checking-in, and email can enable a continual top-up to work that may have been carried out weeks and months previously. Small, short reminders can be effective and serve to keep the rapport and connection with the client going through long absences.

3. **How often should peer evaluation and mentoring be utilized by a consultant? What value is there to using this approach?**

   Peer evaluation and mentoring should be utilized as often as possible. The value of this approach is the creation and maintenance of a community of practice. Learning and developing excellence is essentially social in nature and having like-minded peers to problem-solve and learn from is a key part of developing consulting effectiveness.

4. **When implementing psychological skills programs (PSPs), what works best and for whom? What are some in-season and out-of-season considerations?**

   The debate about how best to deliver and integrate psychological skills remains an ever-present one in applied sport psychology. There is so much variability in implementing PSPs that a key question relates to an understanding of the context. Key considerations can be:

   1. age of the athlete;
   2. timing in relation to other coaching and the timing of the client's season;
   3. a detailed understanding of the athlete's needs when developing PSPs.

   Some key recommendations to consider are:

   1. Psychological skills are best developed alongside physical and technical skills.
   2. Psychological skills need to be evaluated and developed over time.
   3. The psychological demands of the particular sport both in training and in season/competition differ and vary. Implementing an array of psychological skills and strategies to target these differing psychological demands at different time points is critical.

5. **How and when can the use of tele-consulting be useful? How could we establish if Carl needed any further consultation?**

   The expanding role of technology in the provision of psychological consultations using tele-communication technologies presents unique challenges and opportunities. The potential benefits for clients (i.e., elite athletes) who have geographical and time management challenges due to the nature and demands of their sports are huge. As with all technologies, two issues are worthy of consideration before embarking on the tele-consulting route:

   1. the psychologist's knowledge of and competence in the use of the telecommunication technologies being utilized; and
   2. the need to ensure the client has a full understanding of the increased risks to loss of security and confidentiality when using telecommunication technologies.

   For more information and guidelines around the delivery of tele-consulting please see the following link to the American Psychological Association's guidelines:

   www.apapracticecentral.org/ce/guidelines/telepsychology-guidelines.pdf

   Finally, on the issue of how we could establish whether Carl needed any further consultation, we would have to assess his needs around the consultations so far in a very similar fashion to how we would go about assessing the needs of clients following face-to-face conventional consultations.

CHAPTER 25

1. **How would you optimize the opportunities to work in a multi- or interdisciplinary manner with other practitioners?**

   This can be a significant challenge for many practitioners for whom the majority of their training and experience may have been working in isolation directly with performers or coaches. The ability to challenge the way in which you, as a practitioner, can be effective by collaborating is a key task for developing practitioners to take on. The extent of this challenge can be heightened by the range of potential practitioners that could be part of collaborative service delivery. For example, working with medical staff can bring different challenges than working with strength and conditioning experts. This can occur due to the breadth of working practices adopted by different support services, including issues such as confidentiality. Developing effective communication channels to other support practitioners is key. Maximizing opportunities to understand their roles and develop approaches to sharing information and working more collaboratively is essential. This may necessitate working at different times and in different venues.

2. **How would you enable an optimum understanding of the client's situation through a range of assessment and monitoring approaches?**

   There are a number of key aspects to consider in accessing a thorough and rigorous understanding of the client's needs. Key to this is respecting the contribution that understanding the performer's environment can make to the identification of the client's needs and the subsequent organization of how service delivery can be executed. The impact that key personnel (e.g., coaches) can exert on the performer, and the overall cultural impacts of their situation (e.g., approaches to training and competition preparation) need to be established early on in the contact with the client. This suggests that there are potentially damaging limitations to the assumptions of accuracy through interview assessment procedures alone. Therefore, observation should be utilized as a core method for collecting assessment information about the client in their performance and training contexts. Without this, applied practitioners can be over-reliant on second-hand or biased information coming from interviews.

3. **Why would humility be important to consider for an applied sport psychology practitioner?**

   The overall philosophy of applied practice is a key component for all practitioners to develop over time. The foundations of an overarching philosophy are the values and beliefs that practitioners bring to their work. All practitioners should consider the contribution that humility can play in applied contexts. The behaviors associated with humility lie at the heart of client–practitioner relationship quality and influence the working alliance through an openness to alternative solutions and a preference to seek client-relevant solutions rather than practitioners considering themselves to be the conduit through which all solutions must be sought. The need to maintain a humble approach can enhance working relationships. It is important to develop a questioning approach and place emphasis on truly seeing the client through his/her own experiences. This can develop rapport and trust and establish an effective overall working alliance.

4. **How can an applied practitioner deal with the challenge of "shifting sands" in relation to the client's needs?**

    The reality of working in an applied practice situation has, as explored within this chapter, a number of potential frustrations inherent within it. Not least among these is the need to be adaptable and flexible if the true, current needs of the client are to be addressed. This accepts the dynamic nature of the relationship to be central to the effectiveness of the working practices. This provides a frustration to the applied practitioner who may be committed to a particular line of work with the client at a specific point in time that cannot be completed (or come to fruition) because it is no longer the primary need of the client. An openness to change (and a humble attitude) along with an acceptance of the prioritization of working with the client's needs lead to a requirement to develop dynamic working practices. The use of professional judgment and decision-making (PJDM) approaches can monitor and develop speedy responses to changing circumstances.

5. **In what way can the "unfinished business" from previous work completed with a client enable a greater effectiveness in future work with a client?**

    One of the potential benefits of working with clients in a long-term relationship is that there is an opportunity to address current needs of the client by drawing upon the skills and techniques utilized in previous work. This helps to draw upon the client's expertise in a different manner than beginning something completely new (which may be necessary at times), potentially enhancing the efficiency of the working relationship, and optimizing the speed at which client progress can be made. If previous work is left incomplete (as is often in reality the case), it can still be greatly beneficial to the client's current needs. If the work completed has been focused on understanding (psycho-education) and the development of skills, then these can be picked up again later more rapidly and integrated into working practices in a dynamic manner.

CHAPTER 26

1. **Why is it important to understand philosophy for supervision?**

    A philosophy for supervision is constructed from a set of principles, values, beliefs, and prejudices that guide an individual's practice. As a result, a philosophy for supervision will fundamentally impact on the way in which a supervisor constructs the environment in which supervision will take place (e.g., how relationships are developed and managed, how power is viewed and shared) and thus how the supervisor works with their supervisee(s). What we do as supervisors is unavoidably linked to these values and beliefs about the role and the pedagogical principles that underpin the climate for learning created with a supervisory arrangement. Consequently, gaining an understanding of these principles and shaping them into a philosophy for supervision improves our understanding of our own practice and allows the identification of those aspects that either facilitate or hinder the pursuit of the goals of supervision in SEP. Indeed, a well-conceived philosophy provides the foundation upon which supervisors and supervisees can learn in a consistent and coherent manner without becoming too situation specific or too reactive. For example, those individuals who do not understand their philosophy are less likely to be aware of the reasons *why they do what they do*, which might hinder their effectiveness when faced with new contexts, scenarios, or challenges within the process of supervision.

2. **What role does reflective practice play in the development of trainee practitioners and neophyte supervisors?**

    Reflective practice is a process that allows us to transform our experiences into learning and use that learning to inform and improve our future actions. Without reflective practice it is likely that we will simply accumulate a number of hours of "doing" rather than accumulate the learning required to improve the effectiveness of our practice. In addition, reflective practice allows us to gain a better understanding of ourselves and the principles that underpin our behaviors. As a result, it orients us to consider how we might make better use of our strengths and improve those aspects that limit our practice in attempts to engage in both supervision and professional practice more successfully. Through reflective practice we are able to generate a better understanding of our "knowledge-in-action" (the accrual and interplay of different forms of knowledge [e.g., theoretical, personal, situational] that allows us to actually "do" SEP) and the shortcomings of this knowledge in relation to dealing with the practice-based issues we face on a day-to-day basis. As a result of these points, reflective practice is a fundamental aspect of professional SEP practice and should therefore not be seen as something that is an "add-on" to what we do. For the neophyte supervisor, reflective practice allows the exploration of values and beliefs in order to better understand and establish a philosophy and associated supervisory behaviors/actions that are congruent with each other. It also offers us the opportunity to really question *what we do* and *why we do it* to challenge normative behaviors and thus develop our practice in a way that is innovative and context-specific. Consequently, supervisors have a professional responsibility to engage in reflective practice in attempts to ensure that they are offering supervisees the best possible "service." Finally, reflective practice can offer the neophyte supervisor an appropriate coping mechanism by facilitating the supervisor's exploration and "sense-making" of the dilemmas that they are faced with during the early stages of their tenure.

3. **How might collaborative learning impact the development of trainee practitioners in sport psychology?**

Collaborative approaches to supervision are designed to: (a) encourage the ongoing development of self-awareness and practice philosophy of the supervisee; (b) provide a forum for the sharing of practice; (c) engage members in shared reflective practice; (d) provide opportunities for supervisees to deliver mock sessions in preparation for service delivery; and (e) engage members in reciprocal and peer-learning. It is thought that such opportunities are likely to enhance and facilitate quicker learning and development than a more traditional didactic supervisory arrangement alone. Specifically, a collaborative approach is thought to benefit the supervisee due to the inherent peer interaction and shared reflection, and the provision of a safe environment for disclosure. Indeed, the communication behaviors of problem solving, sharing, negotiating, and teamwork are characteristic of collaborative supervision. Further, the approach allows the supervisor to observe their supervisees in the critical discussion of theory and practice-based problems, as well as in mock/role play service delivery scenarios. Finally, the approach offers an informed way of empowering supervisees to take responsibility for their own learning, as well as that of their peers. In doing this, supervisees start to develop the problem solving, critical thinking, communication, and listening skills that are widely associated with effective applied SEP practice.

4. **What is "scaffolding" and how might it offer an effective approach to supervision?**

The term *scaffolding* is a pedagogical principle concerning the role of the educator, or in this case the supervisor. It has been associated with the idea of *orchestration* as a way of supporting learners in a way that meets their individual learning needs by incrementally improving a learner's (e.g., supervisee) ability to build on prior knowledge. Essentially, this involves making ongoing assessments of supervisees' current knowledge and understanding of theory and practice and, where they are faced with a particular issue that is beyond their current capacity, offering the structure and support to help guide the supervisee to develop new knowledge and appropriate solutions. This may involve the use of specific tasks (e.g., role play, case conceptualization) that involve supervisor assistance in the first instance, but once the supervisee, with the benefit of scaffolding, masters the task (or develops appropriate knowledge and understanding), the scaffolding can then be removed and the supervisee should be encouraged to gain responsibility for their own growth. This approach serves to help develop supervisees into self-regulated learners where the supervisor plays both an active (questioning and guiding) and passive (supporting) role in the progression of the trainee toward professional status. Scaffolding also allows the supervisee to exercise their own agency within the learning process and thus explore more purposively who they are (and who they want to be) as professional practitioners. This occurs by giving the supervisee a "voice" in the approach they take to developing the competencies associated with accreditation and/or certification.

5. **What barriers, for both the supervisor and supervisee, may inhibit the potential benefits of collaborative approaches to supervision?**

Collaborative approaches to supervision are built upon the willingness of the supervisor to: (a) share the power; (b) engage in self-disclosure; (c) share responsibility in the decision-making process; and (d) encourage individual engagement and group interaction (equality). They are also reliant on the supervisee being: (a) honest; (b) open to the possibility of new ideas; (c) willing to accept responsibility for their own learning and that of others; and (d) able to communicate and contribute to the collaborative process. Without these fundamental aspects, the success of collaborative supervision is likely to be effected. While the ideas of equality and sharing ideas in a problem-solving process can be appealing, the ideal and the reality are sometimes far apart. Not all supervisees, for example, are willing to share equally in a symmetrical collaborative decision-making process or offer examples of their own applied practice for fear of reprisal and criticism within the group. Instead, some are more comfortable in maintaining their social position within the group by remaining relatively "unknown." In attempts to overcome this issue, identifying it and exploring it with the group on a regular basis can help to alleviate the strain that such thinking brings. The supervisor has to also consider how to innovatively encourage engagement in the collaborative process and be willing to be an active part of the group in order to remove such social tension.

Another significant barrier is associated with the ability, and motivation, of the supervisor to facilitate such a group. Individuals have their own learning needs and preferences, which require considerable skill to support while navigating opportunities for collaboration. While the collaboration helps to undoubtedly enhance supervisees' learning through peer engagement, it is important not to overlook individual needs and to ensure that each group member is able to develop their own identity, style, and approach to applied practice that might be very different from others within the group. Finally, associated with this is the potential barrier of time. It takes considerable effort to organize, facilitate, and review a collaborative supervisory process, especially in the follow-up to meetings to discuss with individuals the application of their learning. Such barriers need to be considered prior to organizing supervision in this way in attempts to proactively deal with any issues that may occur and to ensure that a collaborative process is right for both the supervisor and the supervisees.

CHAPTER 27

1. **What are the strengths of the mentee and mentor that they bring into the relationship?**
   Mentee: The mentee's SEPP education, decision to seek out supervision, and overall passion, excitement, and nervousness.

   Mentor: The mentor's SEPP education, years of practice, and experience and training with mentoring are all strengths. Additionally, the mentor's passion for SEPP, excitement to supervise, conceptualization of the supervision plan, awareness of his/her emotions, and time taken to reflect on what the mentee is saying about the supervision process and relationship.

   Discussion points:

   - Both come into the relationship by their own choice and each brings SEPP knowledge and excitement about the actual consultation work. What could it be like if one party was not excited about the relationship or coming into it as a "have to" rather than "want to"?
   - Even with excitement, training in supervision, and having a plan, issues can still arise. What plans have you made that you had to revisit or adjust once you started the work? For example: lesson plans, sport psychology consultations.
   - The mentor's self-awareness and self-reflection time are crucial to enhancing the quality of the supervision and building the supervision relationship. In this case it was his taking the time to listen to his emotions, frustration, and worry, which led him to further reflect. What emotions may arise if you were the mentor or mentee in this case? What do your emotions lead you to do?

2. **Identify the main concerns in this case that might prevent the mentor and mentee from having an effective supervision experience. What indicators are present to lead you to your conclusions?**
   Fear of appearing less than competent: Both mentor and mentee come in with some nervousness. Both parties want to show that they are competent and do not want to mess up. This is okay if these thoughts and feelings are shared and processed. In fact, sharing this can build rapport and trust. However, when our ego gets in the way, and time and energy are spent on working to not show weakness and being fearful of being found out, then it sets up barriers to really do the work that needs to be done in supervision.

Communication: Not taking the time to be clear about what the mentor is experiencing and expecting from the mentee.

Cultural competence: Becoming more aware of any possible cultural factors that may impact the supervision relationship (e.g., gender, race, privilege).

3. **Describe what the mentor did well in this case? What did he do to establish a relationship (i.e., build rapport and trust) with the mentee? What could the mentor have done differently to establish a better relationship with the mentee?**
   For this question, you should make a list for the three questions, such as:
   - Items for what the mentor did well may include: enthusiasm, caring about how the mentee was conducting her work and wanting to do the best for her, making an initial supervision plan, self-reflection, willingness to stop and decide on what to do next.
   - Items for establishing a relationship may include: getting to know her background, training, career plans, strengths and weaknesses, as well as what she was doing in sessions.
   - Items for what the mentor could have done differently include: clarity up front about roles and expectations, and discussion of concerns and issues that could impact the supervision relationship (e.g., cultural factors, power dynamics, fear of failure, etc.).

4. **Identify the steps the mentor and mentee could have taken to change the current situation from occurring. What would have potentially made things worse and what could have been done that could have resulted in a different outcome?**
   Discussion of this question could be based around things that could have occurred before and during the sessions, as well as other communications (e.g., phone, email, written material/mail). Such items may include how expectations of each other are set, how and when communication will occur, the timetable for periodic reviews of the mentor–mentee relationship, and may also include discussion of contracts or agreements for the supervision process. Examples of factors that could have made the situation worse include: ignoring the concerns in the supervision relationship, failure to discuss each party's concerns adequately, the mentor using their power and authority to diminish or control the situation, or the student discontinuing the supervision relationship.

5. **What thoughts and feelings would come up for you as the mentee and/or the mentor at the various times (i.e., initial contact asking for a mentoring relationship, first meeting, second meeting, and third meeting)?**
   Individuals could generate a list for both the role as mentee and mentor to not only help prepare for the mentor role but to remember what it can be like as the mentee. Discussion here would be based around specific emotional reactions to the situation and power relationships. Emotions such as excitement, nervousness, and anger and what each of those mean and the thought process behind them, could be discussed (e.g., nervousness, which comes from not knowing what will happen in the meeting, wondering if we will get along, being unsure of how much more the other person knows than me, and what that means). In general, there will be some emotions related to uncertainty and fear that would then lead into relaxation and trust. Discussion could then evolve around what to do with each of those to foster the best supervisory relationship.

6. **What have you experienced as a mentor or mentee in a supervisory relationship that worked or did not work for you?**
   For this question it is suggested that individuals generate two lists (one as mentor and the other as mentee) based on their personal experience. Included here could also be elements/factors that have worked in other supervisory or power relationships (e.g., work, school, family), and factors that impacted the relationship that are not commonly addressed (e.g., cultural differences or failure to acknowledge the impact of cultural competency). All these factors can be brought together in a group session and discussed. Further discussion could include how you as a mentor bring into the relationship those things that have been identified as things that work and how you avoid those not working items. A conversation around what to do when those "not working" elements manifest, or when things that you think are working turn out to be not working for your supervisee, could follow.

7. **Review the three-phase supervision framework and identify which areas you would want to work on as the mentor to increase your competence as a neophyte supervisor. Develop a plan for your self-improvement.**

One approach to this question would be to draw the three phases and add personal comments and notes to each phase that may include personal strengths, weaknesses, and practical plans for enhancement. These documents could then be discussed in dyads or small groups to garner further personal insight, advice, and support. In turn, this encourages the skills of personal reflection, making action plans, and working with mentorship/consulting with peers about personal growth.

CHAPTER 28

1. **Discuss the advantages and disadvantages regarding the strategies that were implemented to manage the dual roles that the practitioner and client shared in this case.**
   The reader should consider the advantages associated with the solution-focused approach adopted in supervision, whereby there was an immediate safe space to (1) allow the practitioner to discuss specific instances of where their dual role with the client may have created an ethical challenge or other conflict of interest; and (2) provide a mechanism for proactive and practical solutions to help the practitioner manage his own and students' perceptions of his behavior. This included empowering the student clients to drive the length and content of their consultancy sessions, and applying academic rules and assessment information consistently and fairly to students who were and were not "clients." The reader should also consider the extent to which the solution-focused approach may have facilitated transparency in the client–practitioner relationship at the expense of its quality and ease of development. Evaluate whether there is a risk of the practitioner overcompensating for fear of "special treatment" or some form of academic reprisal.

2. **What would have been suitable criteria to use to assess the degree to which the practitioner had been effective, safe, and ethical in this case?**
   The reader should consider the importance and methods of evaluating the effectiveness of sport psychology practice, and identify those used here. This includes, for example: (1) client feedback on what was useful about the intervention and why, and what form of impact it had created; (2) client feedback leading to intervention change; (3) client engagement in, and adherence to, the intervention strategies; (4) the willingness and extent of practitioner engagement in the supervision process; and (5) client trust and confidence based on effective practitioner skills (being organized and knowledgeable) and personal qualities centered around care and authenticity. The reader should consider the value of these methods, and whether others might be used. Ethical principles relating to the respect and responsibility shown to the client in the approach taken and interventions used should be considered, including the reflections of the practitioner when evaluating the degrees of congruence between his own developing beliefs about practice and what was actually done.

3. **In what ways do you agree and disagree with the practitioner's belief that the order of the two supervision models experienced was suitable (a solution-focused model followed by a dynamic approach)?**
   Readers should consider their own professional development in answering this question, and reflect on the reasons put forward by the practitioner as to why the order was appropriate. Based on the case, this includes the importance of the goodness of fit between the supervision model and the level of professional development and understanding of service delivery of the trainee. The chapter describes a phased supervision approach, where the emphasis is initially placed on learning the fundamental elements of effective helping, followed by a model that emphasized the practitioner as the delivery tool, but only when they are ready to understand this aspect of competent service delivery. The reader should also reflect on the important quality of a skilled/good supervisor to know when the time and place is right for this to happen, and how such personal exploration should be facilitated.

4. **If you had been supervising the practitioner when working with Ron, what would have been your goals and methods of approach?**
   This is a personal answer that should be generated by the reader. To facilitate this, the readers are encouraged to reflect on the case and how their own background, training, and perceptions, beliefs, and assumptions about their emerging or established model of supervision would inform their dialogue with the trainee. Readers should consider how they might have gone

about this supervision similarly or differently to those supporting the trainee in the chapter, and why this would be the case.

5. **If you had been the practitioner in this case study, in what ways would your own history, needs, desires, and behavioral tendencies have influenced service delivery?**

This is a personal answer that should be generated by the reader. To facilitate this, readers are encouraged to reflect on the case and how their own background, training, and perceptions, beliefs, and assumptions about their emerging or established model of professional practice would inform their service delivery. Readers should consider how they might have gone about this work similarly or differently, and reflect on how interpretations of, and behaviors toward applied sport psychology work are colored and shaped by their own professional development and thinking.

CHAPTER 29

1. **Describe the most relevant aspects that you would take into account before starting supervision (as supervisor and as trainee).**

As a supervisor:

- Getting to know the trainee's characteristics in various aspects, such as: education, professional experience, motivation, learning, and economic expectations.
- Holding a meeting in which the foundations of the supervision process are established, including, for example: workplace functioning, goal-setting, standards and methodology, compromises, clarifying everyone's role.
- Establishing a relationship of trust with the trainee.

As a trainee:

- Having a great attitude, being motivated to learn, striving to always have an open mind, being fearless, and searching to be creative.
- Following the guidelines and activities suggested by the supervisor as closely as possible, taking in constructive criticism and being proactive.
- Establishing and maintaining a relationship with the supervisor based on trust.

2. **Analyze the trainees' challenges. Identify which ones imply greater difficulties and propose coping strategies. How would you approach these as a supervisor?**

It is important to deeply understand the way in which they affect the trainee's development as a future SPP. Then, analyze which ones are more complex depending on the trainee's particular case in order to be able to support him/her in the most specific manner following the guidelines presented in the chapter. The following include greater difficulties experienced by trainees, particularly early on in supervision:

- How to explain what ASPP is: The trainee knows the theory but does not feel confident when he/she needs to explain it to the clients. In this situation, the supervisor has to teach the trainee how to: (a) enhance communication skills (i.e., listening, asking questions, speaking naturally, synchronizing verbal and nonverbal communication, etc.); (b) if possible, analyze the client's needs and plan a communication strategy; and (c) during the conversation adapt it to the current situation. This will help the trainee feel more self-confident.
- Professional intrusion: When coaches have not previously worked with SPPs they feel that we are stepping into their working area. In this case, the supervision process needs to help the trainee understand that this attitude is normal and that he/she should focus on giving a proper explanation of what ASPP entails, as well as establishing a working alliance with the coach. This helps the coaches feel that they keep the control of their player's training process.
- Ethical behavior: Relationships with clients or other stakeholders imply a power game and trainees often do not feel confident enough to say no. For example, as discussed in the chapter, coaches, parents, or managers may want to know confidential information about the athletes, and once again, one of the keys is to enhance communication skills and answer properly and politely.

3. **How would you help a supervisee design an "elevator speech" (i.e., an efficient and short 30–60-second statement that describes what ASPP is and one's approach)?**
   It is important to take advantage of the opportunities to make a good impression and sell the work that could be carried out in the area of ASPP. In this sense, it is interesting for the trainee to consider the design of an elevator speech. This has the aim of enhancing his/her marketing strategy through a summarized explanation of the main services that could interest a potential client. In order to design it, the following aspects should be taken into account:

   - Content development defining the key items that could impact the speech targeting a client's interest.
   - Development of a script based on the following ideas: (a) introduce the solution to a problem (client's need); (b) communicate with assertiveness; and (c) be able to do all of this in less than a minute.
   - Practice the elevator speech.
   - Practice how to answer different questions with different levels of complexity.

4. **Design three exercises that you can put into practice to improve your supervisee's interpersonal skills.**
   When a new athlete requests ASPP services, ask the trainee to carry out any of the following tasks:

   - Prepare a plan for an initial interview.
   - Be in charge of a certain part of the initial interview.
   - Research the characteristics of the sport, their main features, terminology, rules, etc.
   - Prepare an activity to assess, intervene, or train any psychological skill.

5. **How would you notice that you are not growing professionally and personally as a supervisor? What would you do to resolve this?**
   Performing as a supervisor also involves a range of skills in order to help the trainee's development, and to objectively assess the degree of his/her progress is necessary to determine how the seasoned professional is performing. In this sense, if you find that you are not growing as a supervisor, it is important to:

   - analyze the various factors involved in your performance (e.g., motivation, skills, time availability, characteristics of the relationship with the trainee);
   - set growth goals as well as indicators of achievement for you and the trainee.

   Search for supervisory models from different professional areas to enhance your approach to supervision.

CHAPTER 30

1. **What potential ethical challenges might arise during Kyle's mentorship?**
   Recall that supervision involves two main responsibilities: (1) protection of the welfare of current and future clients (professional "gatekeeping"); and (2) trainee development. Each of these responsibilities comes with its own set of ethical challenges, many of which can be seen in the case of Kyle. A few possible challenges are mentioned below:

   a. As with the majority of supervision occurring during the course of graduate training, Dr. Tyler is acting as not only Kyle's supervisor, but also his academic program director, professor, and evaluator. These multiple relationships have the potential to cloud Dr. Tyler's judgment in any number of ways, as well as Kyle's ability to manage the feedback he gets from Dr. Tyler (e.g., is her feedback delivered as part of her role as supervisor, professor, or program director).
   b. Certainly, although the case of Kyle does not overtly address the issue, the elements of transference and countertransference have the potential to influence decision making by both Dr. Tyler and Kyle. Whether Kyle places Dr. Tyler in the role of a past influential person in his life (i.e., parent) or Dr. Tyler interacts with Kyle in the role of "older sibling" and tries to "fix" the problem rather than provide guidance, Kyle's professional development and growth is stifled.
   c. Given how little we know about Kyle early in the case study, "trainee impairment" may be a concern. The presence of a clinical issue that may be hindering Kyle's ability to connect with his classmates and future clientele is clearly an important ethical concern for Dr. Tyler.

d. Dr. Tyler's concern with her "perfect record" (i.e., all graduates becoming AASP certified) has the potential to cloud her judgment with Kyle, causing her to either overlook Kyle's difficulties and mistakes or become overly critical of them when, in fact, they may be routine developmental challenges for neophyte consultants.

2. **For each of the challenges you identified for #1, discuss how the athlete-client might be affected if these are not addressed.**

In any and all ethical considerations, the athlete-client must be of the utmost concern. In each of the ethical considerations mentioned in Question 1, albeit to varying degrees, Kyle's current and future clients could suffer harm ranging from the disappointment of trusting a consultant with their performance potential only to feel disconnected, to having their performance hindered by ill-conceived or ill-advised intervention strategies, to becoming unwittingly involved in a psychological issue for which Kyle needs professional assistance.

3. **If Kyle's fieldwork experience had not yet begun, what, if anything, should Dr. Tyler address with Kyle?**

Dr. Tyler should immediately address her concerns about "connection" with Kyle, regardless of whether or not she is able to attach concrete terminology to her feelings. The longer the issue goes without discussion or remediation, the more athlete-clients are potentially affected. It might be worth designing a detailed supervision plan in advance so that Kyle has as much time as possible to address the issue in a supervised setting.

4. **Given Dr. Tyler's supervision philosophy and theoretical orientation, what might some of her options be for moving forward with Kyle? Are there particular strategies or techniques you think might be effective in addressing these issues?**

Supervision using a cognitive-behavioral model generally entails training the supervisee in the techniques he will be using with his athlete-clients. It is Dr. Tyler's responsibility to identify both productive and unproductive behaviors and provide appropriate training, reinforcement, and guidance in order for Kyle to appropriately re-structure these cognitions and behaviors. Miles and James (2000) categorized specific supervision techniques as "enactive" (e.g., role plays, live supervision), "symbolic" (e.g., discussions, written exercises, case presentations), or "iconic" (e.g., live or video modeling.) Any or all of these would be appropriate when operating from a cognitive behavioral supervision orientation.

5. **Think about your own philosophy and orientation. How might they guide *your own* interventions as a supervisor?**

As discussed above, supervisors' theoretical orientations generally guide their supervision practices. Those supervisors holding a cognitive-behavioral orientation will likely incorporate role plays, discussions, and/or video into their supervision practices. On the other hand, those that subscribe to a more humanistic orientation may seem far less directive, with supervisors endeavoring to create a safe teaching and learning environment while promoting trainee responsibility and self-actualization. Finally, supervisors who practice with a psychoanalytic orientation may focus on an investigation of possible transference and countertransference, helping trainees manage any resistance to true self-awareness, or the recognition and challenge of unconscious thoughts and actions.

6. **What would be *your* first step in managing the situation with Kyle? Why? Are there ethical considerations that might affect your decision?**

In general, the best and most ethically sound first step would be to speak directly with Kyle about any concerns. Confronting the issue immediately, before it has the potential to affect client well-being, reduces the ethical quandary.

7. **If you were Dr. Tyler, would you allow Kyle to continue his work with athlete-clients? Why or why not? How would you weigh the responses of the stakeholders (Dr. Tyler, Kyle, Dr. Perry, Mr. Kramer, athlete-clients, etc.) against your professional and legal responsibilities as Kyle's supervisor?**

Before responding to this question, review the positions and associated responsibilities of each stakeholder. Then, project yourself into your career a bit. Will you be a licensed psychologist? Will you be AASP certified? Both? Although you should address the question from the perspective of a university faculty member, your professional licenses and certifications will provide another layer of ethical and legal responsibility to consider.

8. **What is your opinion of Dr. Tyler's supervision strategy with Kyle? What would you have done differently?**

    Although Dr. Tyler did quite a few things correctly in terms of assessing the situation and designing a strategy to address the issues in Kyle's internship according to her professional philosophy and theoretical orientation, she did them quite a bit later than she could have. By the time Dr. Tyler acted, Kyle was already six months into his internship, and the majority of his athlete-clients had already had a negative experience, causing them to leave the consulting relationship. In addition, although this particular situation may not be commonplace in supervision (i.e., the trainee having a personality and style not conducive to making connections with athlete-clients), it would have benefited Dr. Tyler to have policies, paperwork, and solutions in place ahead of time. This would have allowed a much shorter response time and an easier navigation through these difficult issues. Finally, although it is not commonplace for SEPP graduate training programs to require students to participate in personal therapy (Andersen, Van Raalte, & Brewer, 2000), Dr. Tyler might have considered this option for Kyle given the links between low emotional intelligence and mental health. Although Dr. Tyler is not a licensed psychologist, a referral for Kyle to visit a competent professional may provide additional information one way or the other.

9. **Assuming Dr. Tyler's strategy does not help Kyle to resolve the "social awkwardness" with performers, how would *you* move forward?**

    A number of concerns must be balanced when determining what to do next, including the protection of current and future clients, the responsibility to address Kyle's development, and the legal issues arising from your final decision. If you remove Kyle from his internship, it may affect his ability to complete the requirements for graduation. If you allow Kyle to complete his fieldwork, he may alienate the remaining athlete-clients on his roster. In a private practice setting, Dr. Tyler could elect to no longer supervise Kyle, or decline to sign-off on the supervision hours required for AASP certification; however, in an academic setting there are potential legal ramifications for the university, including the lack of a policy in place to address such issues and the lack of long-term documentation of Dr. Tyler's concerns and remediation attempts.

CHAPTER 31

1. **What are examples of ways in which Millennials might behave in ASP practice or supervision that illustrate the pros and cons of the stereotypes related to their generation?**

    Stereotypical characteristics attributed to Millennials are: high self-esteem, a strong tendency toward ownership of responsibilities, the apparent lack of self-control, and a need to comply. Examples of accompanying behaviors illustrating these characteristics are: choosing to become the sport psychologist of high performers and expert athletes/athletic teams despite the lack of experience in the psychological guidance of clients (see, for example, Owton, Bond, & Tod, 2014); limited engagement in supervision, and only actively seeking supervision when the supervisee is experiencing some overt doubts or troubles; difficulties in limiting oneself when it comes to the use of social media, for example becoming Facebook friends, communicating through Twitter with clients, and use of other social media without hesitation or reflection; and more general behaviors directed in a friend-like manner with the client and/or the mandating party (e.g., the sports organization, technical manager) (related to what Andersen, Van Raalte, & Brewer, 2011 call becoming the "team buddy").

2. **What are your personal values and beliefs concerning dual roles in sport psychology and clients' privacy?**

    Multiple roles often occur in the sport context. Although the question should be answered by the readers themselves, we (the authors) believe that dual responsibilities require high levels of self-awareness, constant self-monitoring, and experience. We agree with Andersen et al. (2001) that taking dual responsibilities should be incidental, clearly defined, and separated at the onset. The choice to combine roles should be made consciously and carefully. In the decision to enter multiple roles, practitioners should, in our opinion, take into account all sides of the equation (i.e., the benefits of combining roles, the benefits of keeping them strictly separated/preventing multiple roles, the risks of combining roles, and the risks of declining multiple roles). These types of decisions require a specifically strong reflection on who benefits from potentially combining roles, the practitioner or the client(s).

Another specific aspect of sport psychology service delivery is concerned with athletes' privacy. In the sport context, especially when working on-site, the privacy of athletes is easily compromised, and a natural respect for privacy is not always a given in sports. KB is co-author of the code of conduct of the Dutch Association for Sport Psychology, which prescribes that sport psychologists respect people's right to privacy and confidentiality. A guideline that we try to instill in trainee sport psychologists is not to invade more into the privacy of athlete clients than strictly necessary. However, we are aware that "staying ethical, while keeping loose" (Andersen et al., 2001) is a balancing act in terms of refraining from unnecessary invasion into the personal life of athletes.

3. **What were the core issues of the supervisor in Nigel's case and how would you have handled them?**

Core issues were displaying unethical behavior, trespassing the minimum threshold of professional conduct, and lack of transparency and self-reflection. There are many different ways of handling these issues. The professional decision making for supervisors in these types of situations is complex. While thinking on their feet (remember that the issues only surfaced within the session) the supervisor has to reflect on her own role in the process, seek a balance between the educational needs of Nigel and the welfare of his clients, take the explicit and implicit demands of the program into account, and try to maintain a safe supervisory environment for Nigel. Different outcomes of this professional decision-making process are possible, ranging from a very firm approach on one end (forbidding Nigel to continue his casework, and officially notifying the program of problematic behavior) to a laissez-faire approach on the other end (letting Nigel have his way, and waiting to see how this plays out in practice). For each position on this range there are pros and cons for the supervisor, Nigel, Nigel's clients, and the supervisory relationship. In reflecting on the situation, both KB and VH now feel that they, ideally, would have taken a clearer stance in this situation. A better collaboration between the program management and supervisor would have ideally led to a short pause in the case, to allow KB time with Nigel for a process approach toward his decision making and professional conduct.

4. **Reflect on the supervision case described by answering the following questions (derived from the reflective practice cycle of Korthagen):**

a. **Describe what the supervisee did and describe what you think the supervisee wanted, felt, and thought?**
b. **Describe what the supervisor did and describe what you think the supervisor wanted, felt, and thought?**

This question offers you the opportunity to reflect in a structured way to come to a better personal understanding of the case. The questions are derived from Korthagen's ALACT model (e.g., Korthagen & Vasalos, 2005). Korthagen and Vasalos criticize other reflection models, such as Kolb's cyclic model, for being too rational or cognitive in nature. In supervision (and in applied sport psychology service delivery in general), less rational sources also guide behavior. By answering the questions regarding what each actor in the situation wants, does, thinks, and feels, we can reach a higher awareness of these less rational factors. Moreover, looking at congruence and discrepancy between the needs, actions, thoughts, and feelings of both parties one can contribute to both a deeper reflection on the case and the development of ideas for alternative courses of action. We suggest that readers search for congruence and discrepancy on two different levels. First, have a look at the needs, actions, thoughts, and feelings of KB and Nigel. Are they congruent within each person? For example, Nigel's need for recognition and support of the supervisor do not seem to align with his actions. The thoughts expressed by KB regarding concern for role confusion or conflict are not necessarily congruent with her feelings of fear for professional disrepute as a supervisor.

Second, we can have a look at congruence and discrepancy between the needs, actions, thoughts, and feelings of Nigel on one hand and KB on the other (see also Question 5). What kind of feelings and needs in this situation do they have in common? For instance, both KB and Nigel seem to have a high sense of care for the team and the desire that Nigel delivers good services to the team. In what ways do their needs, actions, thoughts, and feelings differ or perhaps even clash? KB, for example, expresses that she wants to stay updated about the case, while Nigel seems to want independence and responsibility.

5. **How do you think discrepancies between desires, feelings, and thoughts of supervisee and supervisor affected the supervision and its outcomes?**
In this case there seemed to be large attitudinal differences between Nigel and KB. Nigel felt that the supervision should be aimed at serving his needs, while KB felt that she was (held) responsible for both the client's welfare as well as shaping Nigel's professional attitude and ethical awareness. These discrepancies may have had a strong impact on the communication and rapport between KB and Nigel. Both actors were working toward different ends in this situation, which probably broke up the cooperation that supervision ideally constitutes, and left them both unhappy with the outcome at first. Both may have experienced that the other did not understand or attend to their needs; therefore, the tone of communication may have become more agitated or (passive) aggressive, and thus, less optimal. Additionally, both may have experienced that their needs, boundaries, role, competence, etc. were ignored or over-looked. The thoughts and feelings occurring with this sense of not being "seen" by the other may have further hindered the communication, as well as the connection between KB and Nigel. With time, reflection, and preparation for the next session, both were able to (at least partly) overcome these discrepancies, and understand the other's perspective as well. This has probably helped them to restore the supervision relationship to some extent.

CHAPTER 32

1. **Why is it important to have a structured method of supervision when working as a supervisor in sport psychology?**
A structured model of supervision guides the supervision process and ensures that supervisors follow a step-by-step process rather than taking a haphazard approach to supervision. This protects the supervisee and ensures that they receive quality in-depth supervision, rather than happenstance supervision. In addition, the model of supervision allows for the development of practitioners and also provides safety to clients who may work with the supervisee in the future, thereby helping to ensure the welfare of the performer. The impact of supervision is both on the supervisee but also the people who work with them in the future; therefore, quality supervision allows for quality consulting in the future.

2. **How are the four stages of profession that an IMG Academy supervisee experiences in a nine-week period critical to the development of an applied sport psychology practitioner?**
The four stages of development (complete observation, getting your feet wet, taking the lead role, autonomous) allow for a slow but steady immersion into consulting and presenting. These stages are critical because in each stage, continual growth occurs and builds on the foundation built in the supervisee's school experience. Therefore, each stage increases the supervisee's knowledge, comfort level, confidence, and presentation skills. The stages also help the supervisee follow the "process," just like we encourage our athletes to do on the way to their goals.

3. **How would you go about incorporating the 15 key concepts that the current supervisee wished he had known at the beginning and utilize them to develop your sessions?**
The best way to go about incorporating the 15 key concepts the current supervisee highlighted would be to focus on one at a time and to think about how each one fits into the situation that you find yourself in. Asking questions of supervisors, observing others who are doing presentations, preparing for anything that may and will happen, and allowing yourself to get out of your comfort zone will also aid in incorporating these concepts. You could even formulate a checklist as you are designing your sessions to see if you have thought about the key concepts and how to incorporate them into the session that you will be presenting.

4. **Discuss why it is important for a new consultant to be open to feedback from supervisors.**
It is imperative that new consultants realize that they do not know it all and see feedback as a gift. Supervisors want to make a supervisee better, therefore the more the supervisee embraces a growth mindset and sees the feedback as a way to improve and not as if they are failing, the sooner they will become an improved consultant. Many interns who come to IMG Academy have been very successful in everything they have ever done, so hearing that they are not "getting an A" during their presentations can be very daunting to hear and sometimes difficult and emotional to accept. But, the supervisee will not get any better if they have a fixed mindset and are closed minded when they are given feedback. This is also where the supervisee has a

great opportunity to practice what they preach and utilize the skills they are teaching others to help themselves.

5. **Why is "knowing your audience" such an important component to effective delivery of sport psychology messages?**

This concept relates back to the important concept of "they don't care what you know until they know you care." It also relates to preparation and knowing who you are teaching. If you are talking to a group of 18-year-olds like they are ten-year-olds, you will not connect. In the same vein, if you are talking to a group of ten-year-olds and using complicated words and theories, they will quickly lose interest. In addition, if you are talking to a group of tennis players and do not understand what "love" means, it may be hard to get your message across or to have any credibility. Therefore, knowing your audience allows you to match the message to the audience, to connect with the audience, and to feel more confident as you are presenting your material.

CHAPTER 33

1. **What is your perception of strong features of the HSM?**

As the authors of the model, we see three major strengths of the HSM. First, it is grounded in general ASP supervision principles and frameworks but designed as a local model (i.e., rooted in the socio-cultural, sport system, and local institutional contexts). This also means that other scholars who develop their supervision models might learn from us but are expected to adapt our ideas to their respective contexts and local conditions. Second, the HSM is theoretically based, and the background theories (i.e., the scientist-practitioner model, the lifelong learning conceptualization, and career development model) complement each other in addressing the supervisees' professional, educational, career, and also personal development. This means that supervisees are considered not only as students, but also as young professionals who learn how to work in the real world and develop their professional philosophy, repertoire, and style of consulting to proceed on a more autonomous basis after the course. Third, the HSM model covers the supervision process as a whole (pre-conditions, goals, philosophy, forms, methods and scaffolding tools, ethics and climate, etc.) stimulating reflections of both supervisees and supervisors about various aspects of the supervised ASP practice.

2. **What do you see as limitations in applying the HSM?**

As with any framework, the HSM can't cover all the situations in supervisees' work and supervision process, and therefore its limitations should be recognized and ways to compensate for them created. The first limitation we work on is the dual role issue (i.e., teachers and supervisors are the same people) that requires careful positioning of both students/supervisees and teachers/supervisors in the classes and supervision meetings. The dual role issue also limits professional feedback to supervisees, and to compensate for a lack of supervision resources we use cross-supervision, peer supervision, and guest teachers with a possibility for the students to discuss their cases with the guests. Recently, two more supervisors have been recruited from the graduates of the course who already gained more education and practical experiences. The second limitation is time constraints. One six-month intervention is not much time to make the supervisees autonomous, and we also don't have educational time resources to go to the places where the supervisees work to observe and advise them on-site. This limitation is partly compensated by filming assignments (i.e., the student's filming of one real session) with further analysis by the supervisee and the main supervisor. To continue, educational orientation of the course is sometimes in contradiction to students' wishes to incorporate the techniques (e.g., cognitive behavioral therapy) they are briefly introduced to during the course, but are not trained enough to use. As a solution we recommend interested students to continue their professional education in the other ASP course available in Sweden that focuses specifically on cognitive behavioral therapy in working with athlete-clients.

3. **How do you think supervisors should balance controlling supervisees and giving them space to be autonomous?**

ASP supervisors have a responsibility for ethical and competent work of their supervisees to ensure effectiveness of interventions and – even more important – clients' safety and welfare. Therefore, an important controlling function is obvious and within the HSM it is executed through the supervisees' written and oral reports, the aforementioned filming assignment, and supervisors' relevant feedback. To give space to be autonomous is also important because only in this way can the supervisees develop the necessary confidence to continue to work in the real world. Obviously, these two aspects should be well balanced. In the supervisors' experiences, a dynamic throughout the educational year has been observed. Usually the supervisees need more help and support at the very beginning of their planning and conducting an intervention, and they tend to be more autonomous in the second half of the supervised work. But this general tendency has variations depending on the supervisee's personal qualities, learning abilities, and competencies. Some students are more mature and competent than others, and with them more autonomy can be permitted throughout the intervention, with the controlling function executed in a more discreet manner.

4. **What might you consider as advantages of working with athlete-clients from the holistic developmental perspective?**
    In ASP interventions an athlete is often conceptualized as an athletic performer, and therefore interventions are mainly focused on performance enhancement with only quick fixes in terms of other issues in the client's life. Conceptualizing an athlete as a whole person and relevant holistic understanding of athletes' development are beneficial for sport psychology practitioners in several ways. These are: (1) encouraging a holistic view of the clients' personal, social, athletic, and non-athletic characteristics; (2) considering and bridging the client's past, present, and future; and (3) allowing strategic thinking in terms of preparing the clients for forthcoming challenges/transitions. Working from the holistic developmental perspective might not only enrich the consultant's professional repertoire, but also add to their clientele. This perspective is also beneficial for athlete-clients, helping them to increase their self and career awareness, as well as to perceive their sport as part of life and not vice versa.

5. **Read again the description of the client, Billy. What directions of future work with this client do you see?**
    Keeping in mind that the client is a professional golfer with high performance ambitions, we would first recommend to continue working with *performance issues* including various *self-regulation skills*, and also facilitating his refocusing from his "analytical mode" (e.g., reflecting before and after practices, competitions) to "performance mode" (e.g., in which he needs to trust his body and his competencies). In parallel, the second issue might be facilitating his *transition to the new coach*. We would recommend encouraging the client to formulate lessons learned (good and less good experiences) with the previous coach, to learn more about the new coach's personal and professional qualities and based on these build the relationship with the new coach. Third, *the self-exploration issue* might be brought in focus using career planning and stimulating the client's interests in activities other than golf (e.g., studies) to broaden his social and support network and to keep him on the safe side in the case of forced golf career termination. Fourth, because an injury is one of the most widespread reasons for forced career termination, we also recommend working with the client on an *individualized recovery and injury prevention program* to make him less vulnerable in terms of injuries, burnout, and premature career termination.

CHAPTER 34

1. **What steps would you take as a secondary or shadow if you disagreed with the primary?**
    The best defense is an offense! In constructing peer mentoring experiences, disagreements are bound to arise. Therefore, it's important to have a process in place for grievances from the beginning. As a secondary or shadow, the least confrontational approach when a disagreement comes up is to ask questions to better understand the situation. Sometimes as a secondary or shadow you might not have all the information and rather than jump to conclusions it is best to ask questions to get a better understanding of the situation. If with further explanation there are still disagreements, there are two courses of action: (1) come up with an alternative that everyone can agree on; or (2) request mediation from the supervisor. An important guiding rule, however, is to avoid disagreement in front of the sport team or athletes.

2. **As a primary, how would you encourage all team members (i.e., secondary and shadow) to contribute to the planning session?**
    Planning sessions are designed to plan for future sessions with the athletic team. As a primary,

in order to encourage contribution all team members need to know in advance what type of sessions they should be planning for. If team members have time to prepare it will be a more constructive meeting. Another approach would be to ask each team member to bring an activity to the planning session. Even though the primary is the more experienced team member, sometimes he/she might not have the best idea for the session with the athletic team. It is important to keep an open mind, and if you have to provide constructive criticism for a shadow or secondary, explain your position and feedback clearly.

3. Describe ways you would work as a consulting team to incorporate creativity in consulting with an athletic team?

Sport psychology consulting is part science, part art. The art or creative side is best harnessed when you give people the freedom to make mistakes. When you allow each person on the team to go for ideas and new activities, but reassure them that there is a safety net, there are more opportunities to be creative. It may be useful to create a list of variables in a consulting session (e.g., location, topic, session lead, type of activity, etc.) and attempt to modify at least one element in each consulting session.

4. How might you divide the responsibilities of planning and session delivery between the primary, secondary, and shadow?

As a consultant you can only learn so much by observing; at some point you have to put your feet to the fire. At first, dividing planning and session delivery would first go to people's strengths and where they are comfortable. As the season goes on, each team member should attempt a portion of the session that would push them out of their comfort zone in an effort to grow as consultants. A critically important element of the peer mentor design is the post-delivery reflection. A post-delivery reflection meeting is generally led by the primary consultant. This meeting allows members to reflect on their own performance as well as to provide feedback to the other team members. Furthermore, the primary consultant is responsible for communicating with the supervisor and scheduling supervision meetings. Additionally, if a session was video-recorded the consulting team can reflect on the session with the guidance of the supervisor.

5. As a primary, how could you encourage and/or mentor the secondary and shadow to branch outside of his/her comfort zone?

It depends on the shadow or secondary. Some are very eager and you might have to pull in the reins a bit; others are shy and unsure of their abilities. There are several methods that might work for a secondary or shadow to get them out of their comfort zone: (1) have them practice during planning sessions; (2) reassure them that as the primary you will help them if they get stuck or unsure; and (3) try to take small steps, do not just have them run the whole meeting by themselves – rather, have them take ownership of a part of the session.

6. What changes could you make to the structure of the peer mentor design that might also be effective?

One thing that could be changed is set-up within the consulting team. With some teams, it is difficult enough to have two people give a session, but having three people talk during one session can sometimes be confusing for the consultants and the athletes. It might be beneficial for the shadow to only come to planning sessions and only go to athlete sessions when they have completed the required coursework to become a secondary consultant.

Another adaptation for smaller programs might be that all individuals involved in primary service delivery meet for peer mentoring sessions. Multiple organizational structures could exist for this approach, including dyads or small groups for mentoring. Student consultants could video or record the delivery of a session or have a peer attend the session just to observe. Then, students could discuss strengths and weaknesses of the session. Regardless of the structure, the supervisor has an incredibly important role in the organization and supervision of the experience.

CHAPTER 35

1. When would you consider peer supervision as a source of professional support and/or guidance?

The most common reason for looking for peer supervision is limited/no availability of senior supervisors. In such an instance it can partially replace supervision. However, one needs to take into consideration that peers who are novice professionals have limited experiences and therefore the need for traditional supervision will remain in place.

In ENYSSP's case we recommend presenting cases when the consultant does not have a supervisor, has a supervisor who has time limitations, and/or if the consultant would like to hear a "second opinion." Peer supervision can be supportive when the consultant needs support in a difficult situation professionally, would like to brainstorm about the case, and would like to hear suggestions about some possible ways for how to bring the case forward. This can result from several reasons, such as new area of intervention or a new type of sport with which one has limited experience.

2. **How does attending a PCS provide advantages for your development as a practitioner?**
    Whether you are in the role of case provider, peer advisor, or session moderator, the PCS helps you see the cases from a wider perspective. The heterogeneity of the group results in broader ideas for moving the case forward. The clear structure of the PCS also helps participants to think in a more structured way. Brainstorming brings out-of-the-box thinking which might result in very simple but effective intervention ideas. The PCS broadens one's point of view – both theoretically and practically. It offers a chance to meet with fellow professionals all over the world (if organized online) and to keep in touch with them. Further, it helps define one's professional philosophy and approach to practicing SEPP.

3. **How would you fill the development gaps that the PCS does not fill?**
    The main limitation for novice professionals when using peer supervision within a group of other novice professionals is that there is a limited experience of those peers. Therefore, their guidance might be more theory- than practice-based. One way to reduce this limitation is to use an eclectic group of peers instead of one-to-one peer supervision. We consider the PCS as one – but not the only – way to develop professionally and find support. We strongly recommend looking for a senior supervisor who suits one's needs. Outside of supervision, one shall deepen their knowledge by reading books and research articles and by attending an extra course or study programs.

4. **Given the description above of ENYSSPs PCS, how would you develop and implement your own PCS?**
    The structure as used now by ENYSSP is tested by time and experience; however, it is rather a recommendation than an obligation for another PCS. Professionals shall start by creating a peer group as a first step. From our experience, the more heterogeneous the group is, the more advantages it will bring to its members. Heterogeneity can come from professional background, experience, but also from interculturality, as in the case of the ENYSSP PCS.

    ENYSSP provides regular PCS on an online basis due to the distance constraints of its members. However, it can be a face-to-face set up if the group members are living in the same location. If the group consists of one nation (e.g., Germany), the need for procedure translation into its native language arises. Last but not least, as with any development, the group needs to meet regularly; in the case of ENYSSP, a PCS takes place every six weeks.

5. **What characteristics should cases have that are submitted for consideration for a PCS?**
    There are some attributes that we may consider as basic qualifiers for case submission. First, the case should still be open, which means that the proposed solutions have a chance to be tested. Second, it is recommended to submit cases in which one has already delivered several interventions/meetings. This results in deeper knowledge about the client and his/her environment, so the peer group can bring more suitable solutions. If these conditions are fulfilled, then a practitioner should choose such a case in which he/she has doubts about how to proceed, would like to dive deeper, toward the core of the issue, or feels the need to step back from the case and hear different perspectives.

CHAPTER 36

1. **Why does supervision need to be viewed through a cultural lens?**
    We are all cultural beings with diverse backgrounds, world-views, and social practices (Hanrahan, 2011); thus, every encounter is a multicultural one, including those in supervision. It is clear from this case that one's cultural background influences one's approach to and practice of applied sport psychology. Cultural influences extended beyond differences in behavioral practices to differences in conceptualizations of constructs as well. Without multicultural considerations, there is a danger of ethnocentric approaches and attitudes. Moreover, best practices in

supervision indicate the importance of awareness of multicultural factors because these can affect both the supervisor–supervisee alliance and the supervisee–client relationship, as well as the effectiveness of services.

2. What are the cultural backgrounds of all involved parties in this case? How did it affect the supervision process?

The supervisee was a Brazilian student who was familiar with a directive and close supervision style. The supervisor was a Spanish professor who was familiar with the Finnish style of supervision, which is based on independent learning. The peer group supervision included students from various parts of the world who had very different understandings of concepts such as performance, well-being, and the role of a sport psychology consultant. The clients were Finnish, which added another level of complexity.

The supervisee's background affected her expectations for supervision, which caused discomfort and confusion during the supervision process. For example, she expected regular comments on her services from the supervisor, but the supervisor only addressed questions or offered feedback if the student asked directly. Even then, limited time was dedicated to individual supervision. Developing a stronger supervisory alliance with the supervisor at the beginning, learning about each other, understanding contexts, and clarifying expectations could have helped decrease frustrations and confusion. However, this may not have been consistent with the autonomous Finnish supervision style. This illustrates the importance of communication and awareness when engaging in multicultural supervision.

3. How did reflective practice help and/or hurt supervision in this case?

The reflections used in this case were technical in the sense that they focused on what the supervisee had done, whether it went well, and how to improve future interventions. Reflective practice contributed to the supervisee's accountability, since it obliged her to reflect on her choices for interventions, what she was observing in sessions and practices, and what was truly helpful for the team. Therefore, the reflections aided the effectiveness of her work and partially compensated for the lack of direct individual supervision.

On the other hand, different types of reflections, such as critical reflections about personal meaning, environmental influences, and social contexts of supervision and practice, could have been useful and appropriate, especially considering the multicultural environment. For example, critical reflections could have helped the supervisee understand Finnish culture and the disagreements she encountered during group supervision. This could have helped supervisees adapt to the supervision style rather than feeling like one was receiving improper supervision because it was different from what one expected.

Finally, it is important to note that the reflections were partly used by the supervisee as a substitute for supervision. Because she felt low support from her supervision, she focused on the reflection as a source of assessment of her work and accountability. However, reflective practice does not substitute supervision (Watson et al., 2011), and both supervision and reflective practice should be integrated into one's practice of sport and exercise psychology (SEP).

4. How did the dominant practices of applied sport psychology influence this supervision experience?

There may be several reasons for why this real-life supervision case was inconsistent with suggestions from the literature on best practices of supervision. First, the supervision in this case may have simply been reflective of the dominant tendencies of the SEP field. Ingham, Blissmer, and Davidson (1999) argued that SEP as a field has been limitedly focused on applying techniques based on cognitive behavioral theories (CBT). Although this is a valid, theory-based approach, critiques of CBT have argued that the focus on techniques leads to a limited focus on understanding the person as a whole. It also adopts an individualistic approach, which may be insufficient in fully understanding human behavior. This is problematic as it leads to a fragmented view of the person solely as a performer, as if this identity is separate from the person (Ingham et al., 1999). Nevertheless, as this has been the focus of the field, a parallel process of focusing on content and technique more than personal and professional development may have been happening in supervision as well.

Furthermore, the multicultural environment may have been ill-suited for traditional forms of supervision. In a homogeneous environment a more structured and consistent top-down approach where the supervisor has the knowledge and transfers it to the supervisee may be appropriate. However, in this case where everyone has different philosophies and cultural identities, it was not only unnatural, but also inevitable that supervision was less directive and more open, chaotic, and creative.

5. **What could supervisors do to facilitate multicultural group supervision?**

    Before engaging in multicultural group supervision, it seems important to clarify members' expectations and preparation for the process. It was clear that individuals' backgrounds affected the group experience in this case. It could have been useful to develop and strengthen the supervisory alliance beforehand to learn about one another's backgrounds and styles. If the supervisees had clear and accurate expectations about multicultural group supervision, including the role of the supervisor, supervisee, and the group supervision purpose and process, group supervision could be more effective and meaningful for everyone. In addition, the individual needs of the supervisees could be better understood and addressed.

    When initiating group supervision, it seems important to be reflexive in discussing everybody's cultural backgrounds and how it affects one's work in SEP. According to Miville et al. (2005), this discussion could be initiated by the supervisor through modeling. The supervisor could share their own cultural experiences, values, and biases with supervisees, which could help the supervisees in being more mindful of their own values and biases and more appreciative of others' viewpoints. It was demonstrated in this case that reflexivity does not always occur naturally, even when group members experienced substantial cultural differences; therefore, it seems important to be purposeful when facilitating such discussions. These discussions should be designed to help supervisees detach from their own point of view, understand and appreciate others' viewpoints, and recognize that, in real life, especially when applying a cultural lens, there may be multiple solutions to the same problem.

    Finally, using critical reflections could be beneficial and necessary for multicultural group supervision. Encouraging and facilitating critical reflections on both individual and group levels could aid the supervisees in reflecting more critically about the group supervision process, their own biases, as well as their practicum experiences. A critical reflection could also contribute to deeper reflections and learning of peers' experiences and viewpoints, making the group discussions more fruitful.

CHAPTER 37

1. **When working with a team, who is the client?**

    Athletes are the main clients and the target of services. Coaches are both co-workers and clients. For planning and even actual work (i.e., workshop), sport psychologists can work together with the coach to design a best-fit model, workshop, or presentation for the players. Although coaches rarely bring up their own issues to sport psychologists, they are the ones observing and judging sport psychologists' services because those psychological services provided to the athletes directly affect the coaches' work. Referring to junior athletes, athletes' parents can also be a significant contact person, whereas they may not necessarily be the direct clients.

2. **What is one's role as a (probationary) sport psychologist in a well-established team?**

    Drawing from Andersen's (2000) and Hadfield's (2014) comments, sport psychologists should try hard to "immerse" themselves in the team and keep constant communication with the coaches. Sport psychologists can work on mental skills, team development, and more importantly team culture, but it will be much more effective if athletes take the initiative. Sport psychologists can help coaches to observe the team and athlete leaders, so as to find the right timing to intervene or make suggestions.

3. **What is the role of art and science in sport psychology consultation?**

    Whereas sport psychologists should be knowledgeable and competent enough to deliver mental skills training and meet the athletes' needs, it is unwise to see yourself as someone who can give solutions to all athletes' "mental problems." It is recommended to interact or communicate with athletes as a "normal" person and get to know them. It is not the point to label them as someone with "mental problems" seeking help.

4. **What is and is not an expectation in supervision?**

    I expected my supervisor would give me advice on my planning and help me evaluate the work I have done. Also, I unconsciously wanted to impress my supervisor. After all, my supervisor is also my professor in the graduate program. Whereas the supervision did meet my expectation, my supervisor also helped me to reflect on my own identity as a psychologist and how I relate to certain people, such as an authority figure.

5. **How would transference and countertransference influence the supervisor–supervisee relationship and interaction?**

Although transference and countertransference are concepts developed in psychoanalytic therapy, such phenomenon can definitely exist in the working relationships between psychologists and athletes, and the supervisor–supervisee relationship (Van Raalte & Andersen, 2000). Following-up on the previous question, the way I wanted to impress my supervisor and expected a "model answer" from my supervisor is a typical transference phenomenon replicating how I tend to interact with those I regard as authority figures, including my father and, particularly, mentors, teachers, and bosses. My supervisor did share his possible countertransference with me (i.e., want to take care of me emotionally) and we spent time reflecting on such issues. The related power difference within the supervision was also explored. I was reminded how to work around such issues and maintain the equal status relationship with my clients, even with the differences in age and position (see also Baird, 2001).

CHAPTER 38

1. **When reading about the supervisor (Max), what were your initial thoughts on the way he reacted to the intern (Amanda)?**

When reflecting on Max's reaction to the intern, it is important to keep in mind multiculturalism, and how different situations can look across different cultures. In this case study example, respect was highlighted; this is an aspect of applied work that should be considered from a multicultural perspective. It is also important to be aware of your own emotional reaction to the case and to ask yourself what these emotions are, and where these emotions are coming from. You may side with Max or Amanda, but pause for a second and ask yourself what is it about their story that you resonate with. Is there anything about Max or Amanda's stories that reminds you of anything in your life? Be thoughtful and check out your assumptions through the use of RP. You can perform RP on your own or with a colleague to increase your awareness of how you think, feel, and behave in various situations with a range of populations.

2. **How would you address your own assumptions and biases as the meta-supervisor (Liz) before talking with the supervisor (Max)?**

Exploring one's own assumptions and biases is a difficult and challenging task. However, it is imperative that we do this work as a meta-supervisor so that we can be self-reflective, honest, and multiculturally competent in our work. We live in a diverse world working in a diverse field. It may be helpful to first practice immersing oneself in ethnographic situations that cause discomfort; for example, working with a particular population that you have little to no experience with is often useful as part of training. Using RP and processing your thoughts and feelings during these experiences is important so the "uncomfortable" feelings don't become barriers to success.

3. **What did the meta-supervisor (Liz) do well?**

To address this question, think about what resonated with you when reading the vignette, then ask yourself "why?" Exploring why you resonate with something can often lead to you examining core beliefs and values hidden beneath the behaviors we see. Learning, adapting, and modeling ways of meta-supervision can help us increase our own awareness of how and why we do what we do in our work as meta-supervisors.

4. **What could Liz have done better?**

When answering this question, use an imagery exercise and think about putting yourself in Liz's shoes and assess the situation through her eyes. Try to imagine sitting in Liz's seat, seeing through Liz's eyes, and hearing through Liz's ears. When you can connect with the emotional experience of the situation, while also thinking rationally, you may be able to understand more clearly both the emotional and rational thoughts of the situation to give you the best depiction of how you may have handled the case.

5. **What are three takeaways from this chapter that you can use or apply to help your work as a meta-supervisor?**

This question is asking for you to apply what you have read into your work as a meta-supervisor or supervisor.

CHAPTER 39

1. **If you were just starting to be trained in supervision of sport, exercise, and performance psychologists, what would you want in a meta-supervisor? For example, what sort of theoretical orientation would work for you? What sort of interpersonal attributes would you hope for in a meta-supervisor? Would you want instruction and guidance or something else, such as challenge and debate? Describe your ideal meta-supervisor.**
    At the point of entering into the area of meta-supervision, students or neophyte practitioners would (usually) already have considerable experience in having their own work with clients supervised. They are not beginners, but moving into meta-supervision might feel like starting supervision all over again. Similar to early supervision experiences, the power and knowledge differential between meta-supervisor and meta-supervisee is often substantial, and this imbalance can work in both positive and negative ways. For example, the meta-supervisor's knowledge may be viewed as a comfortable and safe haven where the meta-supervisee knows that the meta-supervisor's experience will help guide, comfort, explain, instruct, and support the meta-supervisee's navigation through the sometimes turbulent waters of supervision. Other meta-supervisees may perceive the knowledge and power differences as threatening, and they may feel they will eventually be found out as incompetent frauds. These perceived intimidations often mirror the meta-supervisee's early experiences in supervision. In responding to this question, you might want to reflect back on your early supervision experiences, what went well, what went not so well, when you learned the most, when you felt some level of despair at your perceived competence, and so forth, and then take what you learned in early supervision and maybe apply those experiences to your fantasized beginning meta-supervision training.

2. **Please fantasize that it is now ten years after your first training in supervision, and you have supervised many SEPP students and practitioners. You now wish to gain more knowledge about supervision. In this future fantasy scenario, please respond to Question 1 from a position of a seasoned supervisor seeking advanced meta-supervision.**
    This fantasy question may be difficult to answer, especially for students who are in the beginning phases of supervision and do not have a lot of experience (e.g., may have had only one supervisor so far). For readers who have had several years of supervising sport, exercise, and performance psychologists, there are several different ways to approach these questions. One might start with a "where-am-I?" type of question in reference to one's knowledge and experiences in the models or frameworks one uses in supervision. Do you sit comfortably with a model of supervision that resonates with you? Do you wish to further consolidate your use and understanding of that model at the next level of meta-supervision? Or, at this fantasized point in your career do you want to expand your repertoire to include other models? Consolidation of knowledge and expansion of repertoires are both equally valid ways to approach advanced meta-supervision. Whatever path you choose in this fantasy, please reflect on why this path was chosen along with the conscious (and reflect on the potential subconscious) reasons for your choice.

3. **Resistance is a common feature of therapy, supervision, and meta-supervision. Resistance can come in many forms, such as resistance to learning, resistance to becoming vulnerable, resistance to powerful others, or resistance to self-examination. In what ways in your training as a sport, exercise, or performance psychologist have you been resistant? What are the origins of those resistances? If you have overcome your resistances, how did you do that?**
    There is a major problem in responding to these questions, and that is that a lot of resistance in therapy and supervision is most often unconscious. To ask you to reflect on what may be largely unconscious material is both an unfair and an extremely difficult task to accomplish on one's own (we usually need some guides to help us explore the subterranean world of the unconscious), but insights can be gleaned from thoughtful reflection. For these questions, please look back on your time in supervision and recall when your resistances actually became conscious or when they were pointed out by a supervisor, or even by a fellow student early in your training. Think about what happened to you when your resistances became known (e.g., shame, guilt, surprise, fascination, confusion, denial). After your initial emotional and cognitive responses to recognizing your resistances, then what happened? Maybe reflect on how discovering and overcoming those resistances changed you cognitively, emotionally, and behaviorally. Another problem with these questions is that exploring the sources of your resistances would usually be a topic for your psychotherapy, and not your supervision. Discovering and acknowledging your resistances in supervision and figuring out ways to walk around them so that you can better

serve your clients fits in the realm of supervision practice. Excavating the sources of those resistances lies more in the landscape of psychotherapy.

4. **Transference and countertransference are nearly universal phenomena, and they occur in both supervision and meta-supervision, and of course in psychotherapy and SEPP practice. What were some of your most profound transferences and countertransferences (both positive and negative) in your work with athletes and performers and in your supervision of your own or others' work? What are the sources of those transferences and countertransferences?**

    As in Question 3, there are some difficulties in thoroughly answering these questions because a great deal of countertransference and transference operates at unconscious levels. To move toward examining the sources of your positive countertransferences with your clients, you might reflect back on those athletes or performers with whom you really enjoyed working and with whom you felt a strong personal connection. Did those connections feel like other bonds you have had with some people in your past? For your negative countertransferences, maybe recall those clients you didn't connect with, or who bored you, or with whom you became angry or frustrated, and then see if you can find similar feelings to significant others in your past. This same sort of examination can be done for your positive and negative transferences to your supervisors (e.g., those supervisors you loved and thought were brilliant, those supervisors who intimidated you and made you feel anxious). Transferences and countertransferences are sometimes not one-to-one phenomena connected to experiences with real people in your life. For example, a positive transference to a supervisor can be based on childhood fantasies of the good mother you wish you had had. These phenomena are also not age- or gender-bound (e.g., working with a near same-age male supervisor can be experienced as similar to those feelings you had when you were with a beloved grandmother when you were a child).

5. **In counseling and clinical psychology, the subjects of supervision and meta-supervision are huge territories of inquiry, research, and debate. In the SEPP literature, maps of research and inquiry into supervision and meta-supervision are small countries, figuratively about the size of Monaco. Given that supervision is a core feature of training, why do you think attention has been so limited?**

    One historical, and maybe superficial, reason supervision and meta-supervision have received limited attention in SEPP is that the field did not grow up in university psychology departments. Rather, this field had its origins in the 1960s and 1970s in what then were called departments of physical education (PE), later morphing in the 1980s and 1990s into exercise science departments. So, the practitioner training traditions of relatively long-term and intensive supervision of practica, placements, and internships for counseling and clinical psychology graduate students may have been missing. That speculation, however, does not seem to hold a lot of water and appears leaky when one considers that in the professional training in PE departments there was/is a long tradition of student-teaching placements that involve a substantial amount of supervision. Also, in coach education within those same PE departments, student coaches undergo many hours of mentoring (essentially supervision by another name) with senior coaches. The interesting question is why didn't these long-established supervision traditions in coaching and PE translate over to SEPP from the beginning? We don't know, and we really don't have any solid answers for this question, but rather, we have more questions. One of those questions for speculation centers on the core business of supervision (and meta-supervision): reflecting on practice and becoming a critical and self-reflective practitioner. Over the last 20 years there have been sporadic calls for SEPP students and practitioners to engage in supervision and self-reflective processes, but only in the last few years has the *volume* of those calls been turned up a notch or two. For us, it appears there has been a type of collective resistance to supervision, which seems odd given that supervision is, arguably, one of the most important experiences in the development of SEPP practitioners. The question is: why has SEPP as a field, until recently, been somewhat un-self-reflective?

CHAPTER 40

1. **Given the outlined purpose and process of IPR, what advantages and disadvantages are there for using this technique in supervision?**

    Some advantages include allowing trainees to: become more self-aware of their own internal processes during client sessions; take more of an active role in their professional development; explore process as well as content aspects of their service delivery experiences; gain more accurate access to their experiences via the use of video recall; have the opportunity to explore and develop their interpersonal relationship skills; and engage in multiple layers of reflection.

Some disadvantages include: the time-consuming nature of IPR; need for adequate training in facilitating an IPR; and challenges in ensuring effective peer mentorship.

2. **What advantages and disadvantages could there be in having a peer mentor conduct the IPR session with the trainee practitioner?**
    Some advantages include: the informal nature of peer mentoring in comparison to supervision by a professional; the tendency for increased openness; the ability of the peers to relate on a similar level; the ability to get other students' perspectives; and the ability of peer mentorship to foster increased social connectedness.

    Some disadvantages include: the need for peers to be adequately trained in IPR; the tendency of peers to form groups and stick to patterns in working with each other; and the limited role of the supervisor in facilitating reflection on one's SEPP service delivery experiences.

3. **How might you alternatively have incorporated IPR into the supervision process/ experience?**
    Some alternative approaches to incorporating IPR into supervision include: having the trainees conduct an IPR with a client; the supervisor conducting the IPR with the trainee; doing an IPR of a role-played client session; including the client in the IPR session; having specific goals for the use of the IPR (e.g., to reflect on a particular type of client experience, the use of a particular approach to service delivery, etc.); and conducting an IPR of a supervision session to help trainees reflect on lessons learned in supervision.

4. **What alternative approaches to reflection could have been utilized in this case study assignment?**
    Some alternative approaches that could have been utilized include: providing trainees with a structured framework for their written reflections; including a reflection as part of the debrief at the end of the IPR; providing trainees with a structured framework to prepare for the group supervision component of the IPR; and recording the group IPR session to then conduct a follow-up IPR on the group IPR session.

5. **Given your reading of the chapter and case, how could you integrate the use of IPR and reflection into your supervision processes?**
    As discussed throughout the chapter and the previous questions, there are many ways to incorporate IPR into one's supervision processes. It is important for supervisors to be mindful about including this process, considering various factors such as the developmental phase of the trainees, time available for supervision, goals of supervision, methods for optimizing the reflective practice component of the process, the importance of providing effective training on the IPR process, ensuring effective use of technology, and facilitating the appropriate environment during the IPR session as well as providing support and cohesiveness among the peer mentors.

CHAPTER 41

1. **Describe how you might implement technology into your individual and group sport psychology supervision. What are the costs and benefits of the approach you describe?**
    In going about answering this question, you might want to ask yourself a more basic question of: "Would you use any of the technologies mentioned in this chapter in individual and group supervision?" If yes, which ones and why? If not, then why would you not like to employ the technologies? This question gets at your own biases for (or against) the use of technologies in supervision. Where do you think those biases come from? There are obvious logistical costs and benefits to using technologies in supervision, but biases reflect your personal views on how technologies may benefit supervisees (and you as the supervisor) and also how some technologies may help diminish the supervision experience.

2. **Describe some of the ethical considerations related to technology in supervision and how you might handle them.**
    The appropriate ethical guidelines should be consulted when developing and implementing

technology into supervision. Core ethical principles that should be considered are informed consent, confidentiality, and accessibility. In the event that the supervisee audio- or video-records sessions for supervision, the client should be informed of the purpose and have the right to not be recorded, without penalty. Additionally, information regarding the destruction of the audio and video tapes should be provided to the client as it pertains to confidentiality. The use of a one-way mirror for training purposes also poses a question of confidentiality because other supervisees are often observing, increasing the number of individuals who share confidential information. Appropriate measures must be taken to ensure confidentiality of the client and supervision process. The purpose of using technology in supervision is to enhance the training for supervisees and the level of care for clients, which makes accessibility of technology an important ethical consideration.

3. **What other forms of technology might be useful for sport psychology supervision and why?**

Sport psychology supervisors may want to incorporate movie software into supervision. Movie software can be used by supervisees to add voice commentary on supervision to case presentations. Supervisors might also encourage supervisees to try applied sport psychology apps that could be recommended to athlete-clients as a way to develop their understanding of sport psychology techniques and possibilities. As noted below, such technology can enrich supervision by adding to case presentations and self-awareness with regard to sport psychology. It is important to consider, however, that technologies in supervision may act to marginalize some students who are not familiar with such software and apps and/or do not have convenient access to the technology.

4. **How might technology in supervision enhance learning for students and practitioners from diverse backgrounds (e.g., non-native English speakers, people with disabilities)?**

There are advantages for using technologies in supervision, particularly for people from diverse backgrounds. For example, in cases where language might be an issue (e.g., non-native speakers, people whose disabilities make language production slow) technologies can give supervisees more time to produce language (online forum, blogging). It is important to consider, however, that technologies in supervision may also act to further marginalize students and practitioners from diverse backgrounds and those with limited economic and infrastructure resources (e.g., you can Skype [video chat] with full video with some supervisees, but others have limited downloads or slow dial-up feeds and can only use audio).

5. **Under what circumstances might one choose to forgo the use of technology in supervision? Explain why one might make such a choice.**

There are several reasons why one may not use technology in supervision. Due to the ever-changing nature of technology, individuals may lack knowledge regarding the benefits and implementation of technology. It is our hope that this chapter has provided information about the value of technology in supervision. Another reason one may forgo the use of technology is to preserve confidentiality of the client and to maintain ethical standards. The reliability of technology must also be considered before implementation, which may result in supervisors and supervisees deciding to not use technology in certain situations. Additionally, the cost of technology may prevent some and deter others from using it in supervision.

Index

Taylor & Francis eBooks

Helping you to choose the right eBooks for your Library

Add Routledge titles to your library's digital collection today. Taylor and Francis ebooks contains over 50,000 titles in the Humanities, Social Sciences, Behavioural Sciences, Built Environment and Law.

Choose from a range of subject packages or create your own!

Benefits for you

» Free MARC records
» COUNTER-compliant usage statistics
» Flexible purchase and pricing options
» All titles DRM-free.

Benefits for your user

» Off-site, anytime access via Athens or referring URL
» Print or copy pages or chapters
» Full content search
» Bookmark, highlight and annotate text
» Access to thousands of pages of quality research at the click of a button.

REQUEST YOUR **FREE** INSTITUTIONAL TRIAL TODAY

Free Trials Available
We offer free trials to qualifying academic, corporate and government customers.

eCollections – Choose from over 30 subject eCollections, including:

Archaeology	Language Learning
Architecture	Law
Asian Studies	Literature
Business & Management	Media & Communication
Classical Studies	Middle East Studies
Construction	Music
Creative & Media Arts	Philosophy
Criminology & Criminal Justice	Planning
Economics	Politics
Education	Psychology & Mental Health
Energy	Religion
Engineering	Security
English Language & Linguistics	Social Work
Environment & Sustainability	Sociology
Geography	Sport
Health Studies	Theatre & Performance
History	Tourism, Hospitality & Events

For more information, pricing enquiries or to order a free trial, please contact your local sales team:
www.tandfebooks.com/page/sales